Silent Cinema

The Vampire (Robert G. Vignola, 1913). Gelatin silver print. Source: George Eastman Museum.

Silent Cinema

A Guide to Study, Research and Curatorship

Third Edition

Paolo Cherchi Usai

THE BRITISH FILM INSTITUTE
Bloomsbury Publishing Plc
50 Bedford Square, London, WC1B 3DP, UK
1385 Broadway, New York, NY 10018, USA

BLOOMSBURY is a trademark of Bloomsbury Publishing Plc

First published in Great Britain 2019 by Bloomsbury on behalf of the British Film Institute
21 Stephen Street, London W1T 1LN
www.bfi.org.uk

The BFI is the lead organisation for film in the UK and the distributor of Lottery funds
for film. Our mission is to ensure that film is central to our cultural life, in particular by
supporting and nurturing the next generation of filmmakers and audiences. We serve a
public role which covers the cultural, creative and economic aspects of film in the UK.

Cover design: Louise Dugdale
Cover image: *King Lear* (William V. Ranous, Vitagraph, US, 1909). Decomposed fragment of
a 35mm nitrate positive (George Eastman Museum – Davide Turconi/Josef Joye Collection)

A catalogue record for this book is available from the British Library.

Library of Congress Cataloging-in-Publication Data
Names: Cherchi Usai, Paolo, author. | British Film Institute, issuing body.
Title: Silent cinema : a guide to study, research and exhibition / Paolo Cherchi Usai.
Description: Third edition. | London, UK ; New York, NY : Bloomsbury on behalf of the
British Film Institute, 2019. | Includes bibliographical references and index.
Identifiers: LCCN 2018029480 (print) | LCCN 2018033397 (ebook) | ISBN 9781911239147
(ePDF) | ISBN 9781911239130 (ePub) | ISBN 9781844575299 | ISBN 9781844575299
(hb :alk. paper) | ISBN 9781844575282(pb :qalk. paper) | ISBN 9781911239147 (ePDF) |
ISBN 9781911239130 (ebook)
Subjects: LCSH: Silent films–History and criticism.
Classification: LCC PN1995.75 (ebook) | LCC PN1995.75 .C4613 2019 (print) |
DDC 791.4309–dc23
LC record available at https://lccn.loc.gov/2018029480

ISBN: HB: 978-1-8445-7529-9
           PB: 978-1-8445-7528-2
           ePDF: 978-1-9112-3914-7
           eBook: 978-1-9112-3913-0

Typeset by Integra Software Services Pvt. Ltd.
Printed and bound in India

To find out more about our authors and books visit www.bloomsbury.com and sign up for
our newsletters.

IN MEMORY OF
ANGELO RAJA HUMOUDA (1937–1994),
A PALESTINIAN REFUGEE IN ITALY,
FOUNDER OF THE CINETECA D.W. GRIFFITH,
A POLITICAL ACTIVIST
FOR THE UNITED STATES OF EUROPE.

MY FIRST TEACHER OF FILM HISTORY.

Contents

List of Illustrations

Charts

Diagrams

Plates

Preface to the Third Edition

There is a good chance that most readers of this book are 'born digital'. The first films they saw on a large screen were probably made and exhibited in a medium of little or no resemblance to the one used in motion picture theatres during the twentieth century. Many of these actual or potential lovers of cinema never held in their hands a strip of positive film, let alone a negative. To a large extent, this guide to the study of silent cinema has been expressly written for them. When its first edition appeared in 1991, I had just begun to be familiar with a relatively young scholarly discipline. The list of unanswered questions I was compiling for my own reference was already quite long, and it kept growing at an exponential rate. I was very inexperienced, too, but so enthralled about the topic that I decided to give my book a suitably alluring title, *Burning Passions: An Introduction to the Study of Silent Cinema*.

By the time a revised and expanded edition of the manual appeared in 2000 under the more conventional but slightly misleading title *Silent Cinema. An Introduction*, what once was a remote frontier in academic film studies had turned into a blossoming research field. Back in 1987, a multinational bibliography on early cinema edited by Emmanuelle Toulet and further enlarged by Elena Dagrada listed 181 scholarly books and articles published between 1949 and 1978, an average of six works per year; from 1979 to 1994, their number soared to 1,313, corresponding to seven new studies produced each month. The trend was echoed by the rediscovery of the first thirty years of cinema in collecting institutions. Fewer than two thousand silent feature films were known to survive in 1962; fifteen years later, the figure had already risen to almost six thousand titles.

Satisfying as it may have been, this harvest of prints and information was nothing compared to the avalanche of silent films and related documents that came back to light in the following decades. More than fifty thousand features and shorts produced from 1894 to 1929 are currently extant, and the rediscovery process is far from over. In 1999, one could keep track of what was being written on the history of silent cinema in at least three or four languages; this is now a distant mirage, so many are the monographs, essays, and doctoral dissertations that are pouring from scholarly research undertaken in all continents. Getting to know them all has become a formidable goal. Another sign of the changing times is the further subdivision of the 'silent cinema' period into narrower chronological segments.

There is an international association for the study of early cinema, Domitor, whose declared agenda rarely ventures beyond films made after 1915; some members of the group are convinced that film production in the years 1894–1900 will keep them busy for a lifetime. Faced with this cornucopia of expertise, learning the basics of how to study silent cinema can be a daunting task without some preliminary guidance. Today's students have one great advantage over their predecessors, in that so many more silent films are accessible for viewing than ever before, but the embarrassment of riches comes at the cost of not necessarily knowing what to look for, other than the usual suspects: Chaplin, *Metropolis*, Méliès, the cinematic pantheon codified by textbooks and popular encyclopedias or websites.

I have no desire nor the inclination to suggest which silent films should be seen first, as I believe that a normative approach would inevitably kill at the outset any curiosity or pleasure to explore the amazing visions offered by cinema in its formative years. What this new incarnation of the book attempts to do instead is to stimulate an interest in how these visions were created, who were the people who made and enjoyed them, where did they manufacture and share them with others, what were the machines used to achieve their projects, and why were these visions embedded in long, fragile, and often flammable rolls of perforated celluloid. I had originally conceived this work as an expression of my dual belief that there is no better way to engage with an unknown culture than blending with it, and that it is important to do so in that culture's own terms. I did my best to remain faithful to these principles in the pages that follow. For this very reason, writings from the silent film era represent a significant portion of the bibliography. As in previous editions, textual and audiovisual resources – listed at the end of the volume with page references for each section – are provided in lieu of what would have otherwise loaded the text with a massive set of endnotes.

This guide is structured into three intertwined strands: a summary of concepts (what silent cinema was during its commercial life); a research tool (how it can be studied and preserved); a theoretical discussion (why it matters as an expression of culture). After a 'digital' prologue, the first part of the book (a preliminary orientation, organized by topic) describes how films were made, exhibited, and seen during the silent era; the second half – addressed to those who are interested in delving further into the subject – explains why they look so different today, and what sense can be made of the discrepancies. The moment when silent cinema ceased to be a form of mass entertainment and turned into an object of recollection and rediscovery (it happened around 1929, when silent films were still being shown in many countries on a regular basis) is the watershed connecting one episode to the next. Like separate reels of one and the same projection print, all of its segments belong to a single narrative journey, and should be viewed as a continuum. Their unifying theme is the ongoing transformation of cinema over time. Its origin, emergence, flourishing, and precipitous demise; its destruction, survival, copying, reassembly, and eventual migration into other types of visual experience (back to the 'digital' frame story) are all expressions of highly complex, mutable, often contradictory approaches to history.

Preserving film is perhaps the most tangible proof of our ambiguous relationship with the notion of posterity as applied to the motion picture. My goal in this respect is to make it more transparent by showing that silent cinema was primarily a performing art – with or without live music – and that it is still possible to admire it as such, regardless of its material or immaterial reincarnation as cultural heritage. Listening to Bach's cantatas in recorded form never prevented music lovers from doing the same in a concert hall, when feasible. There is nothing wrong with silent cinema duplicates, either, insofar as they encourage the freedom to choose between the migration and the performance.

The emphasis on the chemistry, mechanics, showmanship, and material evidence of the film, both as a source of history and as an object of empirical analysis, is my way of tackling the question of viewers' rights in strategic terms. The appearance of this volume coincides with the near extinction of analogue film formats, an event announced for many years already. The extinction, however, has not yet occurred. At the time of this writing, various types of photochemical stock are still being produced, albeit in very small quantities. There are filmmakers who are using it. There are places where it is exhibited. If this continues to happen, explaining how cinema was initially crafted may contribute to its renaissance. Conversely, if (or when) the end comes, there may be some value in offering an introductory account of early film technology and presentation, either as an archaeological trace or – more optimistically – as the blueprint for potential rebirth. Other art forms have been resurrected this way, centuries after their demise. There is no reason why cinema should be excluded from this possibility. Either way, I find this message in a bottle worth delivering.

Revising a book on a periodical basis can be a tedious, often unrewarding chore. I had done so twice already with this one, and I was determined that it should not happen again. Faced with the unappealing prospect of yet another instalment, I found the perfect excuse for rewriting the text almost in its entirety, in the realization that so much has changed in what we know about silent cinema since the latest edition of this volume went to press almost twenty years ago. Having more silent films to watch is a wonderful thing, as long as it is not taken for granted that we are also seeing them better than before. To illustrate my point I have chosen Georges Méliès' canonical masterwork *A Trip to the Moon* to accompany the reader in the itinerary from the dawn of silent cinema through its fleeting heyday, its precipitous demise and near extinction, its revival in film museums, specialist and mainstream festivals, academic studies, the creation of new silent films

with vintage equipment (such as the Wisconsin Biograph 35mm shorts, made in 1999 with a 1907 camera) and commercial or amateur digital formats. 'Archival cinema' and 'new silent cinema' are now film genres in their own right, fertile grounds for experiments by artists who borrowed, reassembled, and reshaped images from silent films to create alternative views of our world.

Describing this entire trajectory on a worldwide scale in a single volume required a draconian selection from the mass of evidence at our disposal, both in film scholarship and in film preservation. Aware as I am of my own limitations in being able to keep up with the burgeoning literature on the subject, I feel fortunate for the very generous help from friends and colleagues of various nationalities who were kind enough to show me in translated form the main contents of books and essays written in languages I do not know; their names and institutions are listed separately in this volume. I take, of course, full responsibility for all the errors and omissions I may have incurred; my apologies are directed in particular to specialists in specific areas of silent cinema, as they will find here only a very tiny part of what they have uncovered in the course of their studies. For the sake of synthesis, I also had to take many shortcuts by greatly simplifying concepts that I know would have deserved much longer explanations. Sacrificing detail to clarity is, I think, an acceptable price to pay in a book for committed beginners.

A book lives for as long as it fosters constructive debate. I am keen to be part of it, and to learn from other participants. Please send your suggestions, proposed amendments, and opinions to p.cherchiusai@gmail.com.

Rochester, New York, March 2019

Acknowledgements

Over the years, students of the L. Jeffrey Selznick School of Film Preservation (both in the certificate course and in the Master of Arts programme held in partnership with the University of Rochester) have reviewed early drafts of the book, and offered their guidance on making the text more accessible and consistent with their needs in learning how to study silent cinema and the methods used to ensure its permanent accessibility. This volume is primarily intended as a tribute to their commitment and enthusiasm in this field. One of the Selznick School's most gifted alumni, Cynthia Rowell, brought her editorial insight to disentangle countless details and improve the book's readability. With extraordinary patience and enthusiasm, Peter Bagrov, Donald Crafton, Jacques Malthête, Laurent Mannoni, and Jean-Jacques Meusy have assisted me in checking, amending, and clarifying the factual information gathered for this book. With equal generosity, Richard Abel brought my attention to several texts for inclusion in the bibliographic section.

At the Richard and Ronay Menschel Library of the George Eastman Museum – one of the best collections of books and periodicals on early cinema and photography in the late nineteenth and early twentieth century – Ken Fox and Deborah Mohr gave me the privilege of unlimited access to the Rare Books stacks. Todd Gustavson, Curator of the museum's outstanding Technology Collection, helped me in figuring out the mechanisms inside some of its most rare machines. In the museum's Moving Image Department and in other areas of the institution, my colleagues Kyle A. Alvut, Nick Brandreth, Jared Case, Elizabeth Chiang, Spencer Christiano, James Harte, Darryl G. Jones, Nancy Kauffman, Anthony L'Abbate, Zach Long, Sophia Lorent, Jurij Meden, Gordon Nelson, Mark Osterman, Jesse Peers, Deborah Stoiber, Jeffrey L. Stoiber, Edward E. Stratmann, Patrick Tiernan, Ben Tucker, and Caroline Yeager shared their curatorial and technical expertise in answer to countless questions and requests.

In their respective areas of knowledge, many scholars, curators, librarians, and technicians from all over the world have shared their expertise and answered countless questions – either in person or in writing – on virtually every topic covered by the book. I would like to thank in particular Vito Adriaensens, Antti Alanen, Janice E. Allen, Gyöngyi Balogh, John Belton, Bo Berglund, Joanne Bernardi, Aldo Bernardini, Agnès Bertola, Camille Blot-Wellens, David Bordwell, Teresa Borges, Stephen Bottomore, Geoff Brown, Mario Calderale, Laura Carrillo Caminal, Philip C. Carli, Suresh Chabria, Ian Christie, David Cleveland, Guido Convents, Malcolm Cook, Roland Cosandey, Andrea Cuarterolo, Daniela Currò, Patricia De Filippi, Béatrice De Pastre, Virchand Dharamsey, Christophe Dupin, Bryony Dixon, Aleksandar Erdeljanović, Almudena Escobar López, Antoni Espadas Castillo, Dino Everett, David Farris, Sergei Filippov, Roland Fischer-Briand, Mark Fitz-Gerald, Tone Føreland, David Francis, André Gaudreault, Jane C. Ginsburg, Marcin Giżycki, Andrea Glawogger, Nancy

Goldman, Karola Gramann, Charles 'Buckey' Grimm, Tom Gunning, Øivind Hanche, Lara Hetzel, Alexander Horwath, Xuelei Huang, Kae Ishihara, Livio Jacob, Pavla Jánásková, Sigurjón Jóhannsson, Sergei K. Kapterev, Wolfgang Klaue, Daria Khitrova, Sebestyén Kodolányi, Martin Koerber, Ines Kolbe, Richard Koszarski, Antonia Kovacheva, Anna Kovalova, Edith Kramer, Isabel Krek, Juraj Kukoč, Márton Kurutz, Meg Labrum, Stephen C. Leggett, Alfonso López Yepes, Tobias Lynge Herler, Patrick Loughney, Yevgeni Margolit, Ron Magliozzi, Mike Mashon, Jill Matthews, Tina Meloni Stacchini, Carlo Montanaro, Fabrice Montebello, Charles Musser, Tara Najd Ahmadi, Sungji Oh, Hidenori Okada, Hisashi Okajima, Jan Olsson, Eva Orbanz, Manuela Padoan, Oscar Pallme, Julie Papaionannou, Piera Patat, Louis Pelletier, Rutger Penne, Michał Pieńkowski, Florence Poulin, Valérie Pozner, Bujor Ripeanu, David Robinson, Grzegorz Rogowski, Elif Rongen-Kaynakçi, Regina Schlagnitweit, Heide Schlüpmann, Eric Schwartz, Jean-Claude Seguin, Robert L. Shanebrook, Werner Sudendorf, Catherine A. Surowiec, Erlendur Sveinsson, Ashley Swinnerton, Hans-Jürgen Syberberg, Kristin Thompson, Georgina Torello, Katie Trainor, Yuri Tsivian, Casper Tybjerg, Soeluh van den Berg, János Varga, Timothy Wagner, Jay Weissberg, Jon Wengström, George Willeman, Elżbieta Wysocka, Howard Yang, and Joshua Yumibe.

Translations of excerpts from articles and documents were kindly provided by Viktorija Eksta and Daria Khitrova (Russian), David Farris (Urdu), Tullan Holmqvist (Danish), Erin Palombi (German), and Shota Tsai Ogawa (Japanese).

Brief sections of this book are adapted from some of my previous publications: 'The Color of Nitrate: Some Factual Observations on Tinting and Toning Manuals for Silent Films' *Image* vol. 34 nos. 1–2 (Spring-Summer 1991), pp. 29–38; 'A Charter of Curatorial Values', *Journal of the National Film and Sound Archive* [Canberra] vol. 1 no. 1 (Spring 2006), pp. 1–10; 'The Davide Turconi Collection of Nitrate Film Frames (1897–1944)' (Joshua Yumibe, co-author), *Journal of Film Preservation* no. 85 (October 2011), pp. 46–9; 'Early Films in the Age of Content; or, "Cinema of Attractions" Pursued by Digital Means', in André Gaudreault, Nicolas Dulac, and Santiago Hidalgo (eds.), *A Companion to Early Cinema* (Oxford and Malden, MA: Wiley-Blackwell, 2012), pp. 527–49; 'The Archival Film Festival as a "Special Event": A Framework for Analysis', in Alex Marlow-Mann (ed.), *Film Festival Yearbook 5: Archival Film Festivals* (St Andrews, Scotland: St Andrews Film Studies, 2013), pp. 21–40; 'The Conservation of Moving Images', *Studies in Conservation* vol. 55 no. 4 (2010), pp. 250–7, partially reproduced as 'The Digital Future of Pre-Digital Film Collections', *Journal of Film Preservation* no. 88 (April 2013), pp. 9–15; and the Foreword to Carol O'Sullivan and Jean-François Cornu (eds.), *The Translation of Films, 1900–1950* (Oxford: Oxford University Press/The British Academy, 2019), pp. xvii–xix.

About the Author

Paolo Cherchi Usai is Senior Curator of the Moving Image Department at the George Eastman Museum in Rochester, New York, and Adjunct Professor of Film at the University of Rochester. He is co-founder of the Pordenone Silent Film Festival, of the L. Jeffrey Selznick School of Film Preservation, and of Domitor, International Association for the Study of Early Cinema. Among his books are *The Griffith Project* (BFI, 1997–2008), *Film Curatorship: Archives, Museums, and the Digital Marketplace* (Austrian Filmmuseum, 2008), co-authored with David Francis, Alexander Horwath, and Michael Loebenstein, and *La storia del cinema in 1000 parole* (Il Castoro, 2012). He established in 2015 the Nitrate Picture Show, the world's first Festival of Film Conservation. A resident curator of the Telluride Film Festival, he directed the silent feature films *Passio* (2007), based on his book *The Death of Cinema* (BFI, 2001), with music by Arvo Pärt, and *Picture* (2015), from an original score by the Alloy Orchestra.

Note

Film titles are given in their original language, followed by the English release title (if known), the name of the director or production company, and the year of first release. Archival titles of unidentified films, and literal translations of films not released in English language, appear between square brackets.

Introduction

Fig. 1 Multi-rack magic lantern with film projector. Eduard Liesegang oHG, Germany, *c.* 1900. Source: F. Paul Liesegang, Handbuch der praktischen Kinematographie. Leipzig: Edition Liesegang's Verlag, 1908, p. 233.

From 1889 onwards, people around the world were involved as cinematographers, artists, scientists, technicians, entrepreneurs, and audiences in the manufacture, creation, and exhibition of motion pictures seen through a strip of celluloid, either on machines for individual viewing or on a large screen. Born in France and the United States at about the same time, this invention quickly caught the curiosity of the public, soon becoming a phenomenon of vast cultural and economic proportions. Moving images were not revolutionary per se: they had been made and experienced for a very long time in the form of shadows cast against hard surfaces or sheets of woven fabric, then by the use of optical devices aimed at producing an illusion of movement. Wayang, a theatrical performance where puppets or human dancers created dynamic silhouettes between a light source and a screen, was imported no later than the first century AD to South-East Asia from either China (yĭng xì), or India, or both areas of the continent. The magic lantern, born in the seventeenth century, is the first known technique for projecting still or animated images in a dark room, through a painted sheet of glass and a lens; remote precursors of this device came from Turkey, Iran, and Central Asia. Many other systems followed, all endowed with the same power of evoking visions of real or imaginary worlds.

The technology devised in the 1890s took a further, decisive step in yet another direction. Its artificial dreams were brought to light by a semi-automatic or automatic machine, activated by a crank that was similar to those employed in some manually operated musical instruments. The resulting effect was a spectacle of unprecedented realism, complexity, and emotional appeal. This novelty was largely indebted to the invention of photography in the early nineteenth century, but two other innovations made it look different from all its ancestors: first, a semi-transparent and flexible strip containing a great number of sequential images; second, a mechanism designed to move the image carrier between a light source and a lens at regular intervals. These inventions were merged around 1894–5 into a single entity, variously referred to with terms such as 'animated views' or 'motion pictures'. Some linguistic groups found the words inadequate to describe this kind of visual experience: in Urdu, for instance, the preference was for 'shabistan', whose literal translation is 'kingdom of the shadows'. After some discussion, Louis and Auguste Lumière decided to call their equipment 'Cinématographe'; the name, and the product associated with it,

became so popular that an abbreviated version of the word became identified with the medium as a whole, despite the stubborn resistance of Lumière's competitors in the English-speaking world.

A byproduct of the Industrial Revolution, cinema was initially promoted as an optical marvel. In later years, this claim was updated through the attempts to find elements of specificity in the new mode of expression. Inevitable as it was, the independence war against the other arts – stage theatre in particular – was a collective exercise in wishful thinking. The only specific feature of cinema was that it functioned as a cultural digest of its time, the point of convergence for many other forms of expression. Pantomime, circus, variety shows, *tableaux vivants*, literature, academic paintings, photographs, magic lantern slides, postcards, advertising, travel lectures, caricature, journalism, science, fashion, and the applied arts, not to mention music, were all part of cinema's genetic code. It was also called 'photodrama' and 'photoplay', among many other designations, not at all 'silent cinema', although the word 'silence' was sometimes mentioned as a point of distinction. Aesthetic concerns of a higher profile were frequently debated, but this occurred almost exclusively among the intellectual élites of the period. When 'sound on film' entered the scene, it wasn't a complete surprise, either. Music had been heard countless times in motion picture theatres, either live or through phonograph players and other mechanical instruments; spoken words, too, as well as noises deliberately made for the screen. The true revolution was, again, of mimetic nature. Recorded soundtracks took cinema another step closer to the so-called 'real' world; its fictional representation was 'all talking, all singing', as it was promoted worldwide in the late 1920s, not unlike the songs and the speeches that had been heard in theatres for the past two decades, only more accurately so. Television was also on the horizon: the first recorded transmission of an image in motion dates from 1926.

In purely empirical terms, it is arbitrary to divide the history of cinema into a 'silent' and a 'sound' era. The first silent feature film from Iran, the comedy *Abi va Rabi* ([Abi and Rabi], Ovanes Ohanian, 1930), was released when 'talkies' had already spread across North America and Western Europe; many other silent films were produced well into the 1940s in the Soviet Union and in Asia, as testified by the Chinese feature *Mitu de gaoyang* ([Lost Lambs] or [Lost Children], Cai Chusheng, 1936) and by Semyon Timoshenko's comedy *Nebesnyi tikhokhod* ([Slow Flyer], 1946), released as a silent in 1947. Films with no soundtrack continued to be made throughout the rest of the twentieth century, and they still are to this day, but they are 'silent' only in a heavily mediated sense of the term. The 'specificity' of cinema's first thirty years was in fact almost identical to that of a magic lantern show, another performing art involving optics (the image carrier), mechanics (the projection apparatus), one or more technicians in attendance, one or more artists or lecturers in the proximity of a screen, and an architectural space where 'animated views' were presented to audiences. Other pieces of equipment such as gramophone players or automated sound devices were also employed on many occasions, but the nature of the spectacle was essentially the same, as it demanded a coordinated effort to make machines and people work in perfect synchrony for the entire duration of the programme. When optical sound was applied to the film stock, cinema did not cease to be a performance; it only changed its instrumentation.

The first objective of this book is to describe and explain – in necessarily broad terms – how silent cinema came into being and found its expression through a sequence of activities and events that included the manufacture of cellulose stock with a photographic emulsion, the operation of machines for recording and exhibiting moving images, the production of dramatic or non-fictional works expressly made or adapted for the screen, and their collective experience in theatrical or domestic settings (space constraints have assigned all too brief roles here to animation, industrial, ethnographic, amateur, scientific, avant-garde, and educational filmmaking, but they are all integral to the narration). This process incessantly evolved in various communities and industries around the world, taking the form of many different creative methods, technologies, financial schemes, and social values, too diverse and too complex to be expounded within the boundaries of a single introductory volume. In the name of brevity, generalities are given here priority over details about national contexts; on the other hand, no single formula on broader subjects like human rights, religion, gender, race, politics, ethnicity, welfare, and other social issues can be pigeonholed into a non-existent silent film era of identical shape in all continents and countries at all times (for example, cruelty to animals and pollution were rarely denounced in motion picture shows of the early twentieth century; one of the few surviving films on these topics, a documentary short made in the United States around 1923 – *Be Kind to Dumb Animals* – is not a flattering promotion of the cause). These and other themes will be encountered as small signposts throughout the text, brief reminders of how yesterday's world looked.

Silent cinema was one of the first global manifestations of modernity. The story told in the following pages is therefore international in its scope; France, the United States, and Great Britain are its main protagonists, because these countries were of crucial importance in raising and developing the technology, the industry, and the aesthetics of cinema. Italy, Germany, Denmark, Sweden, Russia, and the Soviet Union also were major players in Europe, as were Japan, China, India, Australia, and New Zealand in the Asian continent and in the Pacific. South America was a significant marketplace for film distribution from abroad; much remains to be discovered about early film exhibition in the Middle East and Africa, the almost exclusive expression of colonial powers.

The vast majority of surviving silent films are held by private and public collecting institutions around the world; because of this, a substantial portion of this book is dedicated to what these institutions do, and how they can contribute to a better knowledge of silent cinema. The words 'archive' and 'museum' will often be used interchangeably, but they refer to very different ways of looking at cultural artefacts. Film museums and archives should not be confused with film libraries: by and large, archives are concerned with cinema as a document of history, with the archivist providing the conceptual and practical tools for the on-site consultation of the objects – generally by appointment – in specially equipped rooms; libraries are focused on the users, who should feel free to browse the collections at any time with little or no supervision, except where warranted by the rarity and fragility of the items. Most museums have dedicated areas for scholarly research as well (also by appointment), but they take a more selective approach to the acquisition and exhibition of film collections. These activities are primarily driven by curators, who are responsible for choosing what to acquire and show to the public, in accordance with specific collection policies. The digital marketplace has somehow blurred these distinctions, but their essence remains valid to this day. There are no such things as 'archival books', or 'archival paintings': the very concept of 'archival cinema' must also be questioned, as it implicitly dictates a content-driven approach to film culture.

Rather than following a strictly chronological or geographical order, the chapters of this volume are structured in a narrative sequence where history is initially read backwards, from the present to the invention of cinema. The book opens with a brief survey of the consumption of

silent films as digital facsimiles: their analysis is followed by an outline of their material, technological, and cultural provenance, which represents one of the core objectives of this work. The actual story begins in Chapter 2 with a flashback to the late 1890s, when flexible strips of cellulose were chosen as the preferred carriers of consecutive photographic images. Colour film, and the optical or chemical processes used to expand its chromatic range, is the subject of Chapter 3; Chapter 4 examines the apparatus – cameras, lights, processing equipment, projectors – used to make and exhibit motion pictures. Chapter 5 presents the individuals who operated these machines and saw them in action; Chapter 6 explores the physical spaces where these activities took place. Chapter 7 is an overview of the films produced and exhibited in the silent era. Their principal themes and genres are only briefly mentioned in relation to the cultural, financial, legal, and material factors influencing the creation and reception of the works, in their countries of origin and elsewhere.

How these works were actually presented in motion picture houses is the subject of Chapter 8, where the main aspects of a typical show are sketched out, from the audience's arrival in the theatre to the unfolding of the cinematic performance and its intermissions. Chapter 9 is dedicated to the live, recorded, or automated sounds produced while the projection was taking place. After the film has been exhibited for the last time as a commercial product, the second half of its material biography begins to unfold. Its salient phases are explained in Chapter 10, from the deliberate or accidental destruction of film prints to their rescue by individuals and institutions committed to prolonging their useful life and to learning more about their past adventures. The results of this detective work, as illustrated in Chapter 11, constitute the body of evidence drawn upon in scholarly works about silent cinema. To secure the permanent availability of salvaged films for present and future generations, museum and archive curators oversee the duplication of these vulnerable objects; Chapter 12 describes the basic methods adopted in this process. The cumulative damages and alterations suffered by film prints, and the remedies applied with analogue and digital techniques for the sake of their preservation, are assessed in Chapter 13. The last two chapters are devoted to the practice and theory of curatorial work: Chapter 14 provides advice on how to handle, observe, and study original and duplicate copies of silent films; Chapter 15 is a discussion of the main principles and questions pertaining to the collection, preservation, and public exhibition of silent cinema as a cultural phenomenon.

Many of these principles can be profitably applied to the study of cinematic works in general: for many decades after the end of the so-called 'silent era', films continued to be made, distributed, and exhibited in essentially the same way as they had been for much of the first three decades of the twentieth century, the only difference being that live performers in the vicinity of the screen were an ancillary option rather than a requirement. Nevertheless, silent cinema occupies a very special place in the history of the visual arts. In symbolic terms, it is an intermediate milestone between Plato's cave (moving images made and exhibited without machines) and digital technology, where human labour is reduced to a minimum in the image capturing process, and virtually to nil in the course of theatrical exhibition, once the equipment has been programmed and calibrated. Georges Méliès' ambition to make cinema through 'artificially arranged scenes' (as he called them in his memoirs) has become a common occurrence in the early twenty-first century; it is only fitting to evoke his name as

our mentor in the voyage we are about to undertake in the following pages, from post-digital cinema to 'pre-cinema' (otherwise called 'early popular visual culture') and back. Arbitrary as it is, like all subdivisions of historic time into discrete periods, 'silent cinema' is a useful term of reference as the beginning of a trajectory leading from one kind of artificiality to another.

Silent cinema was a tiny seismic episode in the geology of visual arts, but had long-term repercussions of much greater magnitude than at the time of its emergence at the end of the nineteenth century. This can be best appreciated by simply considering how Méliès' primordial 'animated views' have morphed into such pervasive features of our everyday lives that a large portion of humanity seems to be taking their existence for granted. Nevertheless, we can and should be able to live without moving image technology. For a brief period of time, cinema didn't even need electricity in order to exist. Motion pictures were projected with other kinds of light sources, only slightly more sophisticated than those available in 1946 to the Bedouin shepherds who discovered seven scrolls of precious manuscripts in a cave along the cliffs of the Dead Sea. In all their humble beauty and inherent transience, silent films are the parchment scrolls of cinema; looking at them, directly or through suitable duplicates, may help our understanding of one of the greatest mysteries of the human mind, aptly summarized by experimental filmmaker and writer Stefan Themerson in an evocative phrase: 'the urge to create visions'. The 'artificially arranged scenes' described here did not see the light only by virtue of celluloid strips, or machines, or screens, or people, but because of their unique coexistence in an organic whole. In this book, we will call these collective visions 'cinematic events'.

Chapter 1

Pixels

Fig. 2 Enlarged view of 1,000 pixels in a frame of *Le Voyage dans la lune* (Georges Méliès, 1902) from a digital copy in 2K resolution. Source: Private collection.

Le Voyage dans la lune (*A Trip to the Moon*, 1902) is one of the most celebrated works produced in the silent film era. Its director, Georges Méliès, proudly considered it the crowning achievement of his career. The film was reproduced in all the major formats and media devised since the invention of cinema, so numerous that it is impossible to tell how many copies are in existence around the world. A large number of them were made with the same techniques used by Méliès in the early 1900s. Many were destroyed over the course of the years. The more we go back in time, the fewer extant copies we find of this cinematic milestone: at least twenty-five film archives, museums, and private collections have 35mm or 16mm duplicates of this title, but only one print created under the filmmaker's direct supervision is known to survive. On the other hand, *A Trip to the Moon* is everywhere, readily accessible from as many pieces of digital equipment as those in use across the globe. The quantitative gap between the single remaining print manufactured in 1902 and the billions of virtual replicas available today is too wide to be ignored. This numerical curve can be turned into a story. It is the moral tale of why silent cinema is both ubiquitous and endangered, a commodity and a treasure, depending on how we look at it.

Most viewers of the twenty-first century have encountered *A Trip to the Moon* for the first time on a small digital screen. They are probably aware that it was originally shown on a much larger one, but generally assume that all the people who viewed it had the same kind of experience: the mad scientist, the rocket in the moon's eye, the selenite monsters, the expedition's triumph after a perilous adventure at the bottom of the sea. It is also taken for granted that moving images produced at the time of Méliès were of uneven quality because that is how cinema was back then, a technology so primitive that, for instance, human movement could only be reproduced at a faster speed than in reality. As we discover that more than one version of *A Trip to the Moon* can be seen in digital form, however, the notion that a silent film is always one and the same is brought into question.

Some reproductions of Méliès' film are better than their siblings. One is in colour, another in black and white. This image was cropped, that one wasn't. There are different title cards at the beginning of the film, depending on which version is being viewed. Images are sharper here than they are there. This version runs a bit slower than the other one. There are at least two possible explanations for such discrepancies: either the reproductions were made with different techniques, possibly at a higher or lower resolution, or we have been looking at different things, with no other connection to each other than a title, a storyline, and a sequence of events captured by one or more cameras. A single strip of negative was used for *A Trip to the Moon*, but there are other films by Méliès where the same shot appears to have been taken with two lenses at slightly different angles, depending on the copy we are looking at.

It is perfectly normal not to pay any attention to these incongruities, because we don't have to. When searching for *A Trip to the Moon* on the Internet in our leisure time, it is enough to choose one of the colour versions, obeying a natural impulse towards chromatic realism, but for all we know the film may have been originally shown only in black and white, then somehow colourized at a later time. It is only when we start formulating such conjectures that the small rectangle in front of us becomes a window to another era, to a visual culture that existed not so long ago and yet seems so incredibly remote. We are looking at the facsimile of a silent film. We may decide to find out more about it, in which case the replica suddenly becomes a potential vestige of something else. *A Trip to the Moon* had been shown in many projection rooms, to many collective audiences around the world. The screenings may have been accompanied by music. The images may have looked sharper. The film may have made a different, maybe stronger, impression on its public in 1902; that may still be the case today, if some of these conditions could be met or at least approximated. This intellectual leap of faith is very easy to achieve with other forms of artistic expression; less so with silent cinema.

Facsimiles

The vast majority of us have seen a famous painting for the first time in the form of a photograph, then maybe in its original incarnation on a visit to a museum. We may have listened to the recording of a great symphony, and liked it so much that we couldn't wait to hear it again in a live concert, if at all possible. A documentary on the Alhambra palace in Granada may have been so intriguing that we decided to make Spain our next holiday destination. This kind of impulse is rarely felt with cinema, for two good reasons: first, because it is commonly believed that – contrary to the above examples – a film has no 'original' to speak of, therefore there is no intrinsic difference between our digital Méliès and its theatrical avatar, other than the size or the sharpness of the picture, with the possible extra gratification of watching it in the company of a large crowd. The other reason is that most people feel no particular need to see *A Trip to the Moon* – or, for that matter, any film – on the big screen in order to fully appreciate it. In addition to this, digital reproductions enable us to study the film in much greater detail by stopping, slowing down, and enlarging portions of the image at will; we can select, reassemble, and replay individual shots or entire sequences in order to better examine their structure; we can readjust the chromatic balance, or even see the film in black and white if we so prefer.

The second part of this line of argument is not only perfectly valid, but also entirely consistent with how people have studied painting, music, and architecture since reproduction techniques were employed in their respective areas of interest. For many generations, photographs and sound recordings have enriched the lives of millions of women, men, and children who would otherwise never have been able to visit a museum or a concert hall. Art history and music are taught and learned at the highest academic levels in the most remote areas of the planet, and no one would question the revolutionary effect of new technologies in the education sector. These tools have also been very beneficial to the study of cinema; this is especially true in the case of silent films, because of their negligible value as commercial products (except for a small minority of 'greatest hits').

Had it not been for digital resources, the first three decades of film history would have remained the playground for a tiny minority of scholars and hardcore cinephiles. Access to archival collections in digital formats has been no less important for film archives and museums, whose preservation work had previously received scant attention outside specialized festivals and academic conferences. Last but not least, films of the early period are now inspiring or being recycled for the creation of entirely new works. Silent cinema is reconnected with the present, bridging what once looked like an insurmountable gap between the spectators and their own visual history.

The main motivation for not venturing beyond the digital experience of silent cinema – the alleged lack of a theatrical 'aura' in motion pictures – is more problematic. Much as it is hailed as a powerful form of aesthetic expression, cinema has always been perceived as an art of reproduction; its legitimacy as a cultural phenomenon was therefore hampered by the very nature of the technology that made it possible in the first place. The fact that cinema is also an industry further reinforced the prejudice that accompanied its irresistible growth over much of the twentieth century. The importance of this variable, however, should not be overestimated. Music, architecture, theatre, and all the other fine arts, not to mention literature, are industries as well; their productions are normally the results of projects that are commissioned, marketed, and paid for by their respective clients. There may be a difference in the size of the financial investments required for their creation, but no art form is qualitatively ranked in quantitative terms: great novels and great songs can be distributed in huge numbers, and make large amounts of money. Attending a concert, a stage play, an opera, or a gallery exhibition is one thing; a film is apparently something else. The 'aura' just isn't there.

Marketplace

Production companies and exhibitors have relentlessly tried to make cinema more 'special' than before through novel attractions for their audiences, from giant screens to three-dimensional pictures. Film archives and museums had to take a different route, eventually securing a profitable niche in the 'digital restoration' business. Private collectors were quick to follow suit. A new version of *A Trip to the Moon* (Lobster Films, 2011) was premiered at the Festival de Cannes, with all the hype and controversy surrounding the exorbitant price tag (estimated at 450,000 euros or half a million US dollars – about 30 euros or 33 US dollars for each of the film's 13,375 frames) attached to the digital remake of Méliès' fourteen-minute blockbuster; with much less fanfare, the alleged first 'colour film' created by British pioneer Edward Raymond Turner in 1902 through an additive trichrome system found its way to the front webpage of BBC News on 12 September 2012. By then, silent cinema had fully entered the realm of mainstream media. The ripple effect of film history's migration to digital would soon be felt around 'canonical' films, the Promised Land where collecting institutions, funding agencies, and commercial entities sealed an ambiguous and yet compelling alliance.

Film archives and museums had fought for many decades to save and project their priceless and endangered collections, mostly with chronically limited resources. They were also racing against time because of the gradual decay of chemically unstable prints, but everyone knew all too well that they couldn't possibly preserve everything. Then, in the midst of the so-called 'digital revolution' (2000–10) and the concurrent decline of film as the preferred medium for public exhibition, these institutions began to translate films into pixels. For a brief period of time, they continued to use motion picture stock for long-term conservation (film negatives) and presentation (film positives) while taking full advantage of the manifold possibilities offered by the new technology: removing scratches and dust from the images, making them steadier, compensating for colour fading or partial loss of the film's photographic emulsion. As soon as it became clear that the very survival of film stock manufacturing was under threat, digital took the lead in archival work once and for all. Consciously or not, museums and archives made a virtue out of necessity by slowing down – or discontinuing altogether – their plans for film preservation on film, and by embracing digital, with the blessing of the industry, the acquiescence of curators, and the enthusiasm of public opinion. Film reels belonged to 'dusty shelves', a debasing figure of speech about all things antiquarian; digital was slick, spotlessly clean, and did not occupy so much space.

What 'digital' means here is of little consequence: the magic letter referring to pixel resolution, 'K', became a benchmark of quality and, indirectly, of cultural clout. The measuring sticks of a high-quality 'restoration' were designated 2K, 4K, 6K, and so on, the numbers being often used with a certain degree of liberality: a film may have been announced as a '4K transfer', but then screened at a lower resolution. The adoption of digital was accompanied by an implicit but unequivocal partition of archival film collections into two broad categories: on the one hand, the films already preserved in analogue form, but of very limited public appeal; on the other, popular films that may or may not have been fully 'restored', but were ripe for digital treatment. The selection process that derived from this hierarchy of commercial and promotional values is dictating which silent films we are allowed to see in digital formats on the big screen, and which ones must be confined to low-resolution replicas, or to those museums, archives, and festivals where silent films can still be exhibited in their original media. There are still a number of important titles that have not been preserved at all; they are more at risk than the others, because collecting institutions may decide not to go beyond a digital transfer from the original film elements.

The short-term financial advantages of this approach come at a heavy price to the public, and to the ethics of film preservation. Silent films that had been previously restored by photochemical means are repackaged as 'digital restoration' projects, thus bending terminology to marketplace-driven rhetoric. There is, in some cases, a compelling argument for resuming work on a title that has been restored before, as occurred when an almost complete 16mm print of Fritz Lang's *Metropolis* (1927) held by a film archive in Argentina revealed over twenty minutes of footage never found on other copies. Once completed, the new version was deservedly greeted by applause from the public and media commentators. Praising the achievement in reconstructing the film's original narrative structure would have been enough. The language used to do so, unfortunately, took its toll on film preservation's customary lexicon.

In mid-2011, the San Francisco Silent Film Festival announced the American premiere of the expanded *Metropolis* under the heading 'restored digital print', a manifest contradiction in terms. There is no such thing as a 'digital print' of a film, and the digital file in itself certainly wasn't 'restored', but this was not the point. What mattered was the juxtaposition of concepts: it is a 'restored' film, not one of the many other versions already in circulation; it is 'digital' – that is, a state-of-the-art presentation; it is also a 'print', meaning that it comes from an artefact, the kind of objects museums and archives are meant to collect. Combined in this and other ways, the three words – a hybrid of technical jargon and corporate hype – are believed to validate what would otherwise be

ignored. 'Film preservation' is in itself insufficient: the process must be given a distinctive brand in order to be taken seriously.

Aura

The roots of this semantic battle have obvious psychological connotations. From the point of view of their users, motion pictures had no particular value as artworks; but the same could be said of countless objects (pottery, tapestries, devotional paintings) now on display in public and private collections worldwide. The presumed difference between cinema and other types of aesthetic expression relied upon two basic assumptions: first, that film was progressively altered by the very act of its presentation by means of a machine; second, that the creative work it embodied was the serial product of a matrix, and that additional copies could therefore be created upon demand, thus making it unnecessary to take special precautions about any individual print.

The intrinsic flaw in these seemingly plain statements lies not in the inferences they were drawn upon, but in their steadfast reliance on technological variables. All human-made objects deteriorate in time, whether by prolonged usage – a book, a wooden table, a piece of jewelry – or through exposure to their environment. The only difference is in the rate of decay: millennia for ceramics (if they are not broken), centuries for paintings and frescoes, decades for an unprotected daguerreotype. Etchings, albumen photographic prints, and Babylonian seals were also struck from matrices; their survival or disappearance does not affect the value attributed to copies before their acquisition by a collecting institution.

The closest equivalents to motion picture film in this respect are magic lantern slides and phonograph discs. Like film, they were produced in multiple copies; like film, every viewing experience or listening event involved a degradation of the carrier; like film, they cannot be experienced without an apparatus – which is where any useful comparison between moving images and most of the other arts is bound to fall apart. Magic lantern specialists have debated whether or not it is preferable or even advisable to show original glass slides as opposed to their digital reproductions. The option of playing (on special occasions) original phonograph discs instead of replicas of their sound recordings is occasionally debated in institutions where these materials are collected and preserved, but no technology for analogue preservation on a mass scale is currently available. The field of moving image conservation is taking yet another approach, influenced by at least two important factors. The first view – by far the most common – is that cinema in general is regarded primarily as a form of mass entertainment, the product of an industry providing audiovisual 'content' to consumers worldwide. This leads to the opinion that those who look at moving images are fundamentally indifferent to – or unaware of – the technology adopted for their exhibition, thus providing a rationale for preserving films on whatever media are available at the lowest possible cost.

The second presumption – encouraged in the academic world by reductive interpretations of Walter Benjamin's often-quoted essay *Das Kunstwerk im Zeitalter seiner technischen Reproduzierbarkeit* (*The Work of Art in the Age of Mechanical Reproduction*, 1936) – is that the lack of an 'aura' of uniqueness in projection prints determines their inferior value as artefacts, thereby justifying the replacement of a damaged print with an allegedly identical replica as a normal occurrence in the life of a motion picture work (an excellent analysis of the issue is contained in Miriam Bratu Hansen's last book, *Cinema and Experience* [2012]). The consequences

of this attitude to the conservation of cinema as an integral part of the cultural heritage have been profound. The physical deterioration of film was a given not only in the commercial circuit, but also for archives and museums, to the point that the making of a so-called preservation element – for instance, a duplicate or 'intermediate' negative – was implicitly regarded as a sufficient response to the gradual wear and tear of the projection copy: when a print became unusable, another one would be struck from the matrix. Most of the damage to film copies was caused by human errors in projection, equipment maintenance, film handling and shipping, but because prints were deemed to be ephemeral by default, there was little or no real commitment to establishing stricter rules for their most appropriate treatment in a curatorial context. So far, the few attempts made to implement procedures and protocols derived from standard museum practice in the other arts and in repositories of rare books have been, by and large, unsuccessful.

Migrations

The advent of digital technology has brought a further twist to this story by fostering the illusion that the problem no longer existed, in that converting photographic images into digital files would bypass the 'integrity' conundrum altogether. This, too, was a misconception, as digital files can corrupt like film stock, only more abruptly so. What changed was, of course, the 'object' of decay: digital data, files, and folders, instead of a celluloid or plastic roll coated with photographic emulsion. The theory went as follows: all motion pictures are reproductions; audiences have no particular interest in how they are exhibited, as long as they look gorgeous on the screen; digital carriers do not degrade over time as film prints do. Therefore, there is no real incentive in pursuing the goal to preserve cinema in its original media and formats. That being the case, it is not only admissible but also desirable to preserve film history in a medium that best satisfies the needs of the consumer. What 'digital' can or cannot achieve is a technicality; deciding what its objectives should or should not be is a prerogative of the user. Born as an adjective and raised as a noun, 'digital' has grown into a verb, an all-encompassing shorthand for each of the following definitions:

Digital restoration is the overall set of technical and curatorial procedures aimed at making the moving image appear (by means of digital image manipulation or processing) as close as possible to what it presumably was at the time of its original release, or according to the intentions of its maker. The tools available to film preservation professionals in the digital domain have enabled them to achieve what would have seemed impossible with traditional photographic chemical methods: colour, contrast, and image stability can be greatly improved (more faithfully to the original or, problematically, even beyond) with techniques previously unimaginable in a film laboratory. A responsible use of these resources can successfully complement the 'analogue' restoration process, whose modus operandi is unique and distinct from its digital counterpart.

Digitization is the process of converting analogue photographic material into digital files for the purposes of public access. This is the great promise of digital technology: in theory, hundreds of thousands of films originally made and distributed on cellulose and plastic carriers can be made accessible to a much wider audience in a variety of formats. Digitization does not equal digital restoration, in the sense that 'analogue' moving images are turned into digital files, regardless of their original condition. A 'digitized' moving image is not necessarily 'restored'.

Digital preservation entails a technological infrastructure capable of making the 'digitized' and 'digitally restored' moving image permanently available for viewing. By wide consensus in the industry and among collecting institutions, there is no such infrastructure at the present time, in the sense that there is no known technique for ensuring that the restored or digitized moving images will remain intact for an indefinite future. The two main obstacles facing moving image archivists and curators are the need to migrate the digital files periodically, and the rapid obsolescence of the equipment used for storing them. In its aptly titled report *The Digital Dilemma* (2007), the Science and Technology Council of the Academy of Motion Picture Arts and Sciences issued a stark warning in this regard: 'by current practice and definition, digital storage is short-term', with the effect of potentially allowing 'the historical phenomenon of technological obsolescence to repeat itself' and to make digital repositories 'tied either to continuously increasing costs – or worse – the failure to save important assets' (pp. 1, 56).

The three concepts – digital restoration, digitization, digital preservation – are frequently merged in the commercial and advertising sectors into the term 'remastering', in the presumption that consumers will become more aware of the improvements achieved in the course of the digital duplication process. The word 'remastering' was originally used for audio recordings to describe the process of improving sound quality; in film, the term is most often applied to the transfer of image and sound from a photochemical film to digital. The problem with all this terminology is that the distinctions it suggests are too subtle (or too muddled) to be understood or appreciated by a non-specialized audience and by the funding bodies of collecting institutions. For both constituencies, 'digitization' means everything: conservation (safeguarding for ever), restoration (making vintage films look new), immediate and unlimited access (here, immediately, at any time).

The confusion is compounded by that fact that there is no consensus on the very definition of preservation, restoration, and conservation among moving image specialists (as further explained in Chapter 13). One of the reasons for this is the concurrence of two separate intentions in a single action. At a purely theoretical level, the act of digital migration is meant to accomplish at the same time the goals of protecting *and* enabling the widest dissemination of the 'content' in a form as pristine as when it was originally made. This reductionist approach fails to account for the inherently ephemeral nature of the digital formats, their vulnerability to data corruption, and the impossibility of exercising a full intellectual control over an almost infinite body of works in constant, exponential growth.

Ethics

'Digitizing' everything, 'restoring' the most important works, and keeping all photochemical prints in climate-controlled warehouses is the threefold strategy that has emerged in film archives and museums at the dawn of the twenty-first century. It is a flawed, contradictory, and dangerous route, but it is better than having no strategy at all. When it comes to digital copies of analogue elements, however, another dilemma comes to the surface. Its formulation involves, again, the question of whether or not it is advisable to keep all the films in the same manner, and if so, what are the most economical ways to achieve this. Assuming that 'everything' (whatever that means in the digital domain) can actually be protected, there is no easy answer to the question on what kind of conceptual framework will enable archives and museums to distinguish themselves from the many other 'content providers' proliferating in

the digital sphere. It may well be that the solution adopted by *force majeure* for silent film collections (that is, selecting the most representative or outstanding works on the basis of a curatorial judgement) will eventually have to be applied – with the required amendments – to their digital counterparts as well.

No matter what the specific policies are in each institution, it would be useful for all parties involved – funding agencies, curators, and their audiences – to have a common view of the philosophical grounds upon which film collections are maintained. First and foremost, there should be clarity on the reasons why they should be preserved at all: there are equally legitimate arguments for protecting them just because they are the best and most stable extant materials, or because their survival represents the historical traces of a past technology to be studied by future generations. A silent film in 35mm format may just be a convenient source for duplication onto other media, but it could also be the carrier of a distinct cinematic identity, impossible to equate with a visual experience conveyed by other means. A shared understanding should be reached on whether this uniqueness is worth protecting as an aesthetic principle, or as part of a business strategy, or as a matter of nostalgia. Future audiences may care for the revival of a 35mm projection as a curatorial performance, as an archaeological trace, or as an object of curiosity similar, say, to the prototype of a steam engine or to the tools used for a fourteenth-century woodcut. Any of these approaches has its own legitimacy, as long as they are expressed as unequivocally as possible, with a solid, persuasive rationale.

It also makes sense to say publicly and unambiguously whether moving images are being preserved for their 'content', or for the overall cultural environment they represent. In the former case, the way in which these images are kept and made accessible is irrelevant, and there is no need to keep a film on motion picture stock for reasons other than its proven longevity under adequate storage conditions. In the latter, curators must accept the responsibility to ensure that the audiences of future generations will be able to experience silent cinema in the same way it was seen at the time of its creation. It is important to add that such concern is not contingent upon the media and formats to be preserved. A collecting institution specializing in moving images should be as committed to the presentation of a 35mm print on a Kinetoscope made in 1893 as to showing how moving image files were seen on a digital device manufactured in 2018. Neither apparatus will be commercially available in 3018, but this is not a good enough reason to disregard the importance of exhibiting them long after the technologies they represent are defunct.

In addition to this, moving image repositories have not always been effective in explaining how they want to be identified. The terms 'film archive' and 'film museum' are often used as synonyms; this confusion has the effect of weakening these institutions from a political perspective by implicitly ratifying the notion that neither formula is appealing enough to their audiences. For several years (1999–2004), the National Film and Sound Archive of Australia was called ScreenSound Australia, in the presumption that the new name would attract a greater degree of public attention. Two respected European institutions, the Cinémathèque Royale de Belgique/Koninglijk Filmarchief and the Nederlands Filmmuseum in Amsterdam, were renamed, respectively, Cinematek (2009) and Eye Film Instituut Nederland, home to the Eye Filmmuseum (2010). Effective as they may be from a marketing perspective, these denominations are the symptoms of a changing relationship between the venues and their patrons. Depending on how the institutions

call themselves, the public determines whether or not they are fashionable enough to be visited.

By remodelling traditional terms such as 'cinematheque' or by erasing them altogether, collecting institutions dedicated to the moving image are not necessarily betraying their statutory mission, but they are distancing themselves from what they perceive as its most unattractive connotations: 'museum' is a place to go for paintings and sculptures, not for cinema. Even when abiding to convention, terminology varies in relation to different linguistic contexts. In Spanish, 'filmoteca' and 'cinemateca' are basically equivalent, but the second term is used mainly in South America; in Russian, 'kinoarkhiv' is more common than 'filmoteka', but none of these words appears in the official title of the two major moving image collecting institutions in the Russian Federation; in German, the distinction between 'kinemathek' and 'filmarchiv' reflects the dichotomy in the English-speaking community; similarly, French language emphasizes the predominance of exhibition (in 'cinémathèque') as opposed to conservation (in 'archives du film'; 'musée du cinéma' tends to be employed for the display of objects such as machines, costumes, posters, and other memorabilia). The rise and subsequent adoption of digital carriers for motion pictures has further obfuscated this already convoluted dictionary, introducing the neutral but uninviting label 'moving image archive'.

Placebo

In another telling contradiction, film curators have consistently argued for the distinctive nature of the moving image as opposed to other forms of aesthetic and cultural expression, and tried at the same time to assert their professional role by presenting themselves as worthy of acceptance in the art conservation world, without being able or willing to take the full consequences of their ambitions. Not surprisingly, neither the 'fine arts' nor the 'arts and crafts' communities have really treated their cinematic equivalents as their peers, if only occasionally, and for the sheer convenience of hosting audiovisual works in gallery installations (a sad conundrum of film curatorship is that many artists of the late twentieth century reinvented their cinematic work in electronic or digital form for the sake of being admitted to museum galleries; in other words, a mode of expression had to adapt itself to the exhibition space rather than vice versa).

The effects of this mutual uneasiness in the field of film conservation are paradoxical to say the least. Fine arts museums routinely show digital copies (often in video monitors) of early twentieth-century films related to famous painters and photographers, and do the same to provide ancillary evidence on a given painting style or movement, but they also acquire (frequently for large sums of money) digital-born works that they regard as unique, even though their permanence will be dependent upon the ongoing migration of the data on other carriers, a duty they happily delegate to digital information technicians. Conversely, moving image archivists and curators are keen to flirt with museum practice without truly engaging with it beyond some perfunctory statements of intent. The more this placebo treatment is endorsed by film curators, the more digital technology gives them an excuse to circumvent the conservation issue without having engaged with it at all: a digital file doesn't get scratched, therefore there is no longer a need to be concerned about it as an object, which amounts to an outright abdication of responsibility.

There is something ironic in this unconscious and yet pervasive attitude towards the film artefact: the more it loses its status of 'material' (or, worse, it is treated as an expensive liability because of the effort needed to keep it in a refrigerated vault), the more wholeheartedly it is legitimized as a cultural resource. On the one hand, academic literature in film preservation prides itself on repeatedly using the term 'ethics', and has grown accustomed to quoting the works of eminent art historians of the past, such as Cesare Brandi or Alois Riegl, as their sources of inspiration; on the other, cinema is virtually absent from specialist publications on the conservation of the cultural heritage. Conversely, film curators have seldom demonstrated a genuine interest in hosting research from experts in other domains within their conferences and periodicals.

This mutual indifference was never justifiable on the grounds of intellectual integrity – even at a time when cinema was a second-class citizen in academic curricula – and it is no longer sustainable on pragmatic grounds, given the increasing cross-pollination between the arts. Film curators and preservation experts can no longer afford to discount what is happening in other disciplines; this is also true, of course, the other way round. Both have failed to explain to their colleagues – let alone to non-specialists – why they share the same concerns. Time has long been ripe for reversing the trend and opening the doors to a rigorous, constructive, and non-antagonistic dialogue between the parties. Whether the parties are willing and able to do so is another matter.

So far, the debate on the theatrical revival of silent cinema in digital form has revolved on the issue of fidelity to film in purely visual terms, with special emphasis on ease of access and image 'definition' or 'resolution', the latter describing how many pixels can be reproduced on a digital display apparatus (a syndrome exposed by David Bordwell in his book *Pandora's Digital Box: Films, Files, and the Future of Movies* [2012]). The very meaning of the term 'pixel' depends upon the context in which it is used; common language identifies it as a unit of measurement, the smallest component of the digital image. There is no univocal shape for a pixel, as its graphic representation could theoretically be a square, a rectangle, or a circle. The greater the number or density of the pixels arranged in a spatially uniform grid, the greater the digital image's resolution.

Content

In everyday parlance, a greater number of pixels translate as an image of better quality, which may be appropriate for a digital-born picture.

Photochemical works produced during the silent film era and through most of the twentieth century, however, are made of clusters of silver salts randomly suspended in a gelatin solution (Fig. 3). Their shape is irregular, too; they are not arranged in an orderly fashion, and can be counted only very approximately. Small as they are, the silver salts of a film emulsion are solid, three-dimensional objects (Fig. 4); in a digital copy, pixels are data expressed in iconic form. Therefore, computing the number of pixels in the reproduction of a

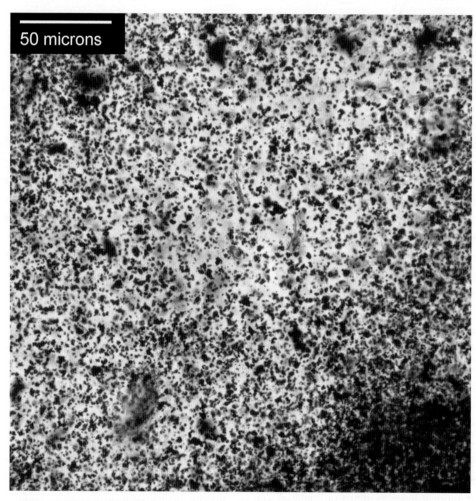

50 microns

Fig. 3 The film emulsion at the microscope: *Le Voyage dans la lune* (Georges Méliès, 1902). Frame enlargement from a 35mm nitrate positive. Source: Private collection.

Fig. 4 Microscope view of silver salts in a photographic emulsion (*Highlights and Shadows*, James Sibley Watson Jr, 1938). Frame enlargement from a 35mm nitrate positive. Source: George Eastman Museum.

1915 film is like comparing apples and oranges, as the calculation only tells us how many geometric figures of identical shape were used to translate the analogue image into a regular grid (Fig. 2). The tenth-generation photochemical duplicate of such a film still looks ugly when digitally shown at a 6K resolution.

A silent film shown in a theatre as a digital file also confronts the viewer with a challenge that was specific to cinema in its first thirty years, when projection speed could vary considerably according to the time and place of its screening. Digital projection is designed for the exhibition of new productions, at a rate of 24 or more frames per second. In the home entertainment business, there are systems that allow the display rate to be slowed down; so far, this is not possible in a

theatrical context: the frame rate can be changed in the transfer from film to digital, as will be explained in Chapter 13; the results of this adaptive process are often disappointing.

Over the years, much effort was put into obtaining a more accurate digital reproduction of the chiaroscuro and chromatic balance that is typical of many nitrate film prints; major steps forward in this direction have been made since the early twenty-first century. To the curators' dismay, some specialists in digital transfers are inclined to make unilateral decisions in the opposite direction. In the aesthetics of the digital-born image, sharpness and contrast are ruled by the taste of contemporary audiences, who generally have a strong predilection for sharpness over texture. In the absence of a film curator who is familiar with the way a film looked in its original medium, and is able to compare the digital files with their sources, digital replicas are shiny but lifeless mimicries of what the film was at the time of its existence as a photographic object. The glacial look of these digital silent films is compounded by their implacable steadiness, which was certainly not the case when a film was run through the sprockets of a film projector. There is software designed to alleviate this embalming effect; the reluctance to correct it is due to the fear that an audience accustomed to a rock-steady image will perceive it as a flaw.

When all these alterations are combined, the digital reproduction of a silent film becomes the immaculate but sterile interpretation of what it was: it is still called 'cinema', but it has been reduced to 'content'. At the dawn of the electronic image and of its digital successor, film curators and manufacturers of motion picture stock made the fatal mistake of engaging in a competitive discussion on how the new medium compared with the old. The terms of reference were, at first, how many lines appeared on the screen, then how many pixels were contained in one frame of 35mm film: in 2000, this number was believed to be about twenty million; two years later, the estimate was between four and fourteen million; in 2012, the figure rose to forty million. In doing so, advocates of film played the kind of numbers game that the digital industry was confident it would win sooner or later, with the further advantage of a promised 'lossless' migration of data for an indefinite future (some visual information is lost in the duplication process by photochemical means from one generation to the next). The fact that a photographic frame has no pixels was irrelevant: by the time the numbers matched, the game was over.

Instead of pursuing a hopeless analogue battle by digital rules, it would have been best to state the obvious: 'film' and 'digital' are just unlike from each other, not better or worse, in a twofold sense.

The images are different in themselves, as one is produced by transparency (grains of salt on a perforated plastic strip, obstructing the light from reaching its projection surface), the other without (beams or points of unobstructed light projected or generated on a screen); one appears intermittently, the other constantly, affecting human vision either according to a rhythmic pattern (the regular alternation of light and darkness), or as a continuous flow. Neither of these explanations would have changed the course of technological history, but it would have been good for film critics, scholars, and curators to at least make the point. If they didn't, it is because they were uninterested in doing so, were unable to explain their views, or didn't know how to make themselves heard. Had they done so soon enough, the proclaimed status of film as an art form would have been substantiated by a fairly simple distinction between cinema, the electronic image (now called 'video' in the art gallery world), and the digital realm. It would have been equally easy to draw a comparison with other forms of visual expression: a tree can be painted in watercolour, in oil, as a fresco, and so forth. It could be photographed as a daguerreotype, in an albumen print, or in a gelatin silver process. A tree is a tree, but each pigment, carrier, or technique transmits a different impression of it.

Performance

The past cannot be rewritten, let alone with conditionals. For the time being, it is still possible to safeguard and cultivate a quintessential feature of film exhibition: a live performance involving (a) the previous activation of a photographic process for capturing consecutive images; (b) its eventual manifestation as an object; (c) its presentation through a mechanical apparatus, implemented and controlled by individuals as part of the show. These factors are pertinent to the entire history of the medium, but silent cinema offers an additional constituent: (d) the live enactment of music, noises, or spoken words in front of a collective audience during projection. Cinema is more than the embodiment of a creative work called 'the film'; the object that carries it is a necessary but not sufficient requirement for its existence. Silent cinema comes to life when all its elements are brought together in a distinctive type of architectural space (the projection room), all at the same time (the show), with a specific type of machine (the film projector), and in the presence of artists, lecturers, or other operators.

The first requisite – the making of motion pictures by means of a photographic camera – belongs to the history of cinema, and cannot be modified. The second survives in the form of fragile but resilient artefacts, the film elements preserved in archives and museums after their long, unforgiving odyssey in theatres and warehouses across the world. The third variable needs preservation, too: it is represented by all the equipment and human expertise needed to install the projection machines, keep them in good order, and make them function. The fourth ingredient of a silent film event is the knowledge and talent of the people who contribute with their own sounds to the achievement of the motion picture show. Silent cinema is the synthesis of all these components. Take one away, and it becomes something else: content, nostalgia, archaeology at best.

Silent cinema has become the guinea pig of a scientific project where computer imaging has entered the realm of biology. On 30 March 2016, a representative of the Technicolor Company in Los Angeles presented *A Trip to the Moon* in the form of DNA samples assembled by a team of scientists at Harvard University. The photo shown on p. 20 (Fig. 5) shows Jean Bolot, Vice-President of Research and Innovation at Technicolor, holding a small glass tube containing about one million copies of Méliès' 1902 film. In its essence, the procedure for storing and retrieving the genetic code of a motion picture film is relatively straightforward: in the encoding phase, a digital rendition of the film (a sequence of 0s and 1s) is translated into another long sequence of four nucleotides, A (Adenine), C (Cytosine), T (Thymine), and G (Guanine) in two strands coiled around each other. The ACTG string is converted into artificial DNA, an identical sequence of nucleotides; the synthesis is obtained with commercially available equipment. At this point, the film's DNA can be stored indefinitely. It is retrieved with a sequencing apparatus, a dishwasher-size machine that spins and sorts the four DNA sequences. Once brought back to the correct order, the ACTG strands are finally decoded into 0s and 1s through the backwards application of the first step (as a result of another experiment, storage of moving images in living bacteria was demonstrated on 12 July 2017 by the Harvard Medical School). In the following pages, we will undertake another experiment of reverse engineering by travelling back in time to the early twentieth century: a period when people were using much simpler but no less astounding machines to create, exhibit, and share their complex visions of the world.

RULE 1

Cinema is a theatrical performance.
A film, its carrier, the machines, and the people
involved in the motion picture show
contribute to the creation of a live event.

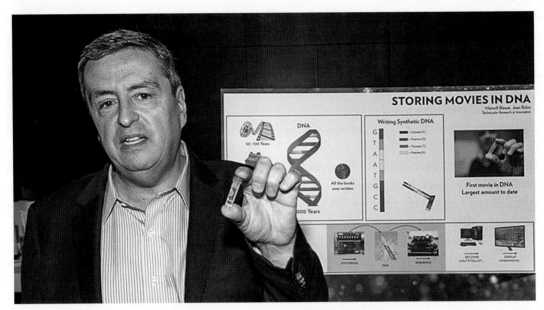

Fig. 5 Technicolor scientist Jean Bolot shows a glass tube containing the DNA synthesis of *A Trip to the Moon* (Georges Méliès, 1902). Los Angeles, 30 March 2016. Source: John Sciulli/Getty Images for Technicolor.

Chapter 2

Celluloid

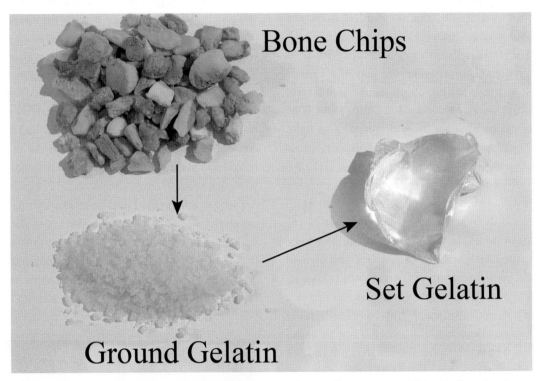

Fig. 6 The manufacture of purified gelatin for motion picture film. Source: Photo courtesy of Robert L. Shanebrook.

The cinematic event was born as an application of photography to the visual representation of movement. Its embodiment is a long ribbon of transparent flexible material (the film 'base', generally made in cellulose of various kinds during the silent era), wound into one or more rolls. Its average thickness is between 0.11 and 0.16mm for nitrate stock. It is covered on one side with a very thin semi-transparent layer of gelatin – crushed animal bones, the same that are used in some foods, only in a much purified form – blended with millions of irregular pieces of silver bromide, commonly referred to as 'silver salts', invisible to the naked eye but easy to detect with a microscope (Figs. 3 and 4). The grains are randomly suspended in the gelatin, and extremely sensitive to light. This compound is the photographic emulsion. It has a creamy colour (with a very slight blue tint) when unexposed. The importance of gelatin and silver in the history of cinema is illustrated by the fact that the Eastman Kodak Company of Rochester, New York – the world's largest manufacturer of motion picture stock – controlled a significant percentage of the world's silver mines, and used specific animal breeds and herds to make the purest gelatin for photographic emulsions (Fig. 6). In this sense, cinema was fundamentally at odds with environmental concerns and animal rights.

Several brief exposures of consecutive areas in the emulsion through the lens of a camera allow the creation of an equal number of virtual images impressed on this surface by the grains of silver bromide reacting to light. At this stage, however, the chemical reaction occurring on the emulsion remains invisible. In order to obtain a real image, the emulsion must be subject to a further treatment. With the aid of chemical agents, all the areas of the emulsion where the silver bromide had been exposed to light in the camera are transformed into very fine grains of silver metal. Like its silver bromide counterpart, these grains are very irregular in shape (their profile is more uniform in modern film stock). They have also turned black: the more intense the light coming from the lens and the longer the chemical agents are applied, the darker the silver metal grains become. Conversely, all the areas of the emulsion surface covered by silver bromide that were not exposed to light have remained unaffected by the process. This silver bromide, unchanged from its original state, is then removed from the emulsion through another chemical reaction. Having been taken away, the substance in which they were suspended has become completely clear.

In a strip of motion picture film, the gelatin is laid over a nitrate, acetate, or polyester base. In a piece of exposed film held up against a light source, all the white areas of the filmed image appear as black; the parts corresponding to the dark areas are clear. In those where only a modest amount of light has come through the lens, fewer particles of silver bromide have turned into black silver metal; because of their lower density, those sections of the image will appear as grey. The motion picture stock that derives from this process is called 'negative' because the image's tonal values are reversed: white is black, black is white (if the film stock is seen through a white light). This object is not yet a film, but it makes it possible to strike a large number of individual film prints ('positives'), almost identical to each other (Fig. 7a–b). In its essence, the method used to create a projection print is identical to the one followed in photography, with the only difference being that a semi-transparent matrix – the negative – is used to generate an image on a semi-transparent carrier instead of a piece of paper.

The film negative is put in contact with, or in close proximity to, another strip of sensitized film stock. A stream of light passes through the negative and exposes parts of the emulsion in the film underneath.

Fig. 7a–b Two consecutive frames from a 35mm camera negative and their resulting images on a 35mm projection print. Unidentified film, Germany, c. 1928. Source: Private collection.

The dark parts of the negative do not allow the light to pass through, therefore leaving the corresponding areas of silver bromide in the emulsion below unaffected. By the same token, the transparent areas of the negative (that is, those without silver metal) let the light pass through, and change the silver bromide of the positive stock into silver metal, which becomes black by the application of the very same chemical process that was used for the negative film. The areas that were black on the negative are now clear; those that were transparent are now black. The cinematic image has begun to exist. It is now time to describe the plastic base upon which it can be seen.

Film

Film history is often perceived as an inevitable path bringing cause to effect, but it is worth remembering that the sequence of events was not at all linear. To begin with, the English neuter name 'film' – adopted in many languages to indicate both the motion picture stock and the creative work derived from it – could be either male (in French and Russian) or female (*la película* in Spanish), and was subject to gender change in Italian form: in the first decade of the twentieth century, it was a 'she' (*la film*) before turning to the current masculine form (*il film*); it is hermaphrodite in Slovenian (*film* is male, unless it is an animation work, *risanka*). Its material genesis was also adventurous. One of the greatest precursors of cinema, French scientist Étienne-Jules Marey, explored the nature of movement through the medium of film as early as 1889 with 90mm and 60mm non-perforated stock; around 1899, he moved to the 35mm format, also without perforations. There were attempts to produce photographic images for motion picture carriers other than film, well after the invention of cinema: the Kammatograph (Leonard Ulrich Kamm, Great Britain, 1898–1900), for instance, used a glass disc with about 350 to 550 frames arranged in a spiral (Fig. 8 and Fig. 9); a similar technique was later applied to Charles Urban's Spirograph with a flexible disc (Fig. 10 and Fig. 11) and to Gianni Bettini's glass plates (1912), projecting 576 images arranged in thirty-six parallel rows.

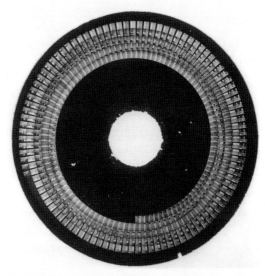

Fig. 8 Kammatograph, 1898–1900. Unidentified scene [*Street View*]. Glass plate (30.5cm diameter) with *c.* 550 frames, 8.4 × 6mm each. Source: George Eastman Museum.

Fig. 9 Kammatograph, 1898–1900. Unidentified scene [*Street View*], detail. Source: George Eastman Museum.

Fig. 12 Théoscope viewer and loop with photographic cards. Théophile-Eugène Lacroix, Paris, 1900. Source: Cinémathèque française. Photo by Stéphane Dabrowski.

Fig. 10 Charles Urban, Spirograph, 1923. *Oregon Lumber Flume*, Urban Spirograph catalogue no. 109. Flexible disc on Eastman diacetate film (26.7cm diameter) with c. 1,200 frames, 5.6 × 4.1mm. Source: George Eastman Museum.

Fig. 11 Charles Urban, Spirograph, 1923. *Oregon Lumber Flume*, detail. Source: George Eastman Museum.

An impression of continuous movement is also given by the Mutoscope (patented in 1894 by Herman Casler) through several hundred photographs on cards attached to the axis of a cylinder (Plate 10). The paper 'roll' was run – for about one minute – like a flipbook in coin-operated machines for individual viewing through a peephole with a magnifying glass. The same effect was achieved

on a smaller scale by Léon Gaumont's Kinora (1900–10; it was previously called Kinora Casler-Lumière, based on Casler's original patent), and by another French device, the Théoscope (1900), produced by Théophile-Eugène Lacroix (Fig. 12).

Most of these devices are regarded as footnotes in the chronicle of moving image technology. Still, their creators were animated by the same flair for innovation that triggered the more successful efforts in devising a practical tool for exhibiting photographic images in sequence. The earliest film stock distributed on a commercial basis (1889) was the result of a research project conducted by Henry M. Reichenbach on behalf of George Eastman. The origins of celluloid are a matter of dispute: in different ways, Alexander Parkes (1855), the brothers John Wesley and Isaiah Smith Hyatt (1865), Hannibal Goodwin (1888), and Reichenbach himself, all contributed to the invention of motion picture film. Around 1890, a French-born Scottish inventor, William Kennedy Laurie Dickson, was using the newly developed carrier in his experiments for Thomas A. Edison. He eventually chose the 35mm format for the Kinetoscope (Fig. 13), another coin-operated automatic device (driven by an electric motor) that allowed one spectator at a time to view 50-foot (15-metre) strips of film with a running time of about twenty seconds (at 40 frames per second; some sources mention slower or higher

Fig. 13 Edison Kinetoscope, 1894–1900, with open lateral panel to show the film path in the viewing equipment. Source: George Eastman Museum.

speeds). After its first public appearance in 1893, the Kinetoscope achieved such popularity that 35mm film became the format of choice for motion picture making and exhibiting on other machines.

George Eastman established the Eastman Kodak Company in 1892 ('Kodak' was the name of his 1888 patent for a still camera). Kodak's early method of manufacturing film had improved upon previous attempts by John Carbutt (Philadelphia) and the Celluloid Company in Newark, New Jersey, but problems with the chemistry of the process were still so daunting that Eastman virtually stopped making motion picture film stock for almost three years, from late 1892 to mid-1895, just about six months before Auguste and Louis Lumière's inaugural screening to a paying audience in Paris on 28 December 1895 (the legendary event at the Grand Café on Boulevard des Capucines was not the first in the

history of cinema: Gray and Otway Latham began their Eidoloscope showings in New York on 20 May of the same year). Not knowing where else to find film stock, Dickson began acquiring it from a Boston-based competitor of Kodak, Thomas Henry Blair, in April 1893. The Lumière brothers had also bought cellulose stock for their experiments from the European branch of Blair Camera in London, then from Victor Planchon, and eventually set up their own manufacturing plant in Lyon.

They did so partly because Eastman was showing no particular desire to enter the film business. He was busy promoting Kodak's photographic products for the amateur market, and shared Edison's and Lumière's belief that there was no future for cinema. Eastman was startled by the dramatic surge in demand for film stock after December 1895, and was unprepared to deal with it. It was only after he bought the Blair Camera Company and its technology for making longer strips of 35mm stock (1899) that Kodak established its leadership in the film market worldwide. The triumph of cinema as a form of mass entertainment in the first three decades of the twentieth century is connected to Eastman's belated takeover of a product he had initially snubbed.

At one of the international conferences of film entrepreneurs held in Paris during 1909 (the first was attended by Eastman himself in February of that year), it was formally agreed that 35mm should be the universal format for theatrical motion pictures. It is rather strange for such statement to be made so belatedly, since no film producer or exhibitor would have argued otherwise at that point. Georges Dureau, the only reporter (from the weekly *Ciné-Journal*) who was allowed to attend part of the proceedings and a gala dinner held by Eastman on 4 February (Fig. 14a–b), did not fail to notice this oddity.

Fig. 14a–b Souvenir menu (4 February 1909) for the closing reception of the International Convention of Film Producers in Paris, with autographs by the participants. See also Fig. 93. Source: George Eastman Museum.

Emulsion

At the end of the silent film era, more than three hundred tons of silver were acquired every year by Eastman Kodak to be dissolved in nitric acid and transformed into silver bromide. The concentrated solution was heated to the point of evaporation, then cooled, leaving a thick milky crust of flat, plate-like crystals. To ensure their purity, the solid residue was repeatedly dissolved in distilled water and re-crystallized. From this point, all operations were conducted either in total darkness or in varying degrees of subdued red or green light, according to the type of emulsion required. Once combined with potassium bromide, highly purified gelatin, and

distilled water, the crystals were evenly distributed within the photographic emulsion. The resulting substance is highly sensitive to humidity: because of the gelatin, it expands when immersed in a developing or colouring bath, and it shrinks when drying.

In its primordial form, a photographic film emulsion was sensitive only to blue and violet light, in addition to invisible ultraviolet radiations; hence its commonly used names, 'plain' or 'blue sensitive' film stock. With the inclusion of very small amounts of certain pigments, the emulsion was 'dye sensitized' in order to react to green and yellow light (some formulas also contained an iodide that gave the emulsion a yellowish appearance). Initially called isochromatic, film emulsions of this kind were soon renamed orthochromatic. This was the black and white film stock generally used in cinema until the mid-1920s; it could capture all of the above colour radiations but was insensitive to red, which would therefore appear on the screen as black. Filmmakers had to carefully monitor colour balance for costumes, sets, and the performers' makeup; in the early era, backgrounds for interior shots were painted in various shades of grey.

In spite of these and other shortcomings (clouds against a blue sky were mostly invisible), orthochromatic motion picture film stock remained in use until the early 1940s, mainly for special effects, and for the cyan colour separation in the three-strip Technicolor process, from the early 1930s. A single type of emulsion was employed for both positive and negative films until about 1897; at that time, manufacturers began producing positive stock specifically made for brighter and more contrasted projection prints (Lumière's catalogues listed two negative and two positive stocks). Only two kinds of 35mm orthochromatic film were available from Eastman Kodak as of 1915, a positive and a negative. The latter was generically promoted as 'motion-picture negative film'; from 1917, it was given the more formal title of Motion-Picture Negative Film Par Speed 1201, when the company started to differentiate its offerings to a fast-growing clientele. Positive film stock was less sensitive than the negative, as it could be exposed for a longer period of time during printing. Pathé inaugurated its own production plant for film negatives in 1912, followed in 1913 by another one for positive stock. At that time, a German-based company, AGFA (Aktiengesellschaft für Anilinfabrikation), had a yearly output of 30 million metres (100 million feet) of positive film.

In the previous decade, around 1903, Eastman Kodak had introduced a new kind of photographic emulsion, sensitive to almost the entire spectrum of visible radiation (hence its name, 'panchromatic'); it was obtained through the addition of another set of dyes into the mixture of silver bromide and gelatin binder. Kodak's first commercial application of panchromatic film occurred only in 1912, a commission from the French company Gaumont for an experimental technique of colour cinematography (Chronochrome, described further in Chapter 3). Panchromatic film had an unpromising start in the film industry. Laboratories were unwilling to process it, as this would have required modifications to the infrastructure already in place for film developing rooms. A few sections of *Queen of the Sea* (John G. Adolfi, 1918) were shot on a panchromatic negative: the stock was very expensive, and had to be used within two months from manufacture before expiring. Once the problem was solved and the price gradually decreased, film producers in the United States adopted the new product on a larger scale.

The Headless Horseman (Ned Van Buren, 1922) is the first feature-length film entirely shot on a Kodak panchromatic negative, produced from 1923 on an industrial scale (AGFA had started

doing so in 1917). Five years later, the newly named Kodak 1203 panchromatic film stock was the standard for all major film production companies. Its lower sensitivity demanded powerful light sources on the set, prompting innovation in the technology of interior lighting, but that was a relatively modest price to pay in exchange for panchromatic film's ability to reproduce a much wider range of intermediate shades of grey. Projection prints continued to be made on orthochromatic stock throughout the silent period, with some adjustments to the emulsion speed.

Over the years, some European companies (such as Pathé in France, AGFA in Germany, Gevaert in Belgium, and – to a minor extent – Atrax in Italy) established their place alongside Kodak as suppliers of motion picture film stock. A few of them were represented in the North American market, notably a Dupont-Pathé consortium with its manufacturing plant in Parlin, New Jersey, opened in 1925. AGFA's 'Extrarapid' negative was presented in 1922, followed in 1924 by the company's first intermediate and 'reversal' stocks ('reversal' film is a negative transformed into a projection print through a two-step chemical process). By 1930, Eastman Kodak had produced forty-five different kinds of photographic emulsion for nitrate stock, twenty-seven for diacetate. A main character in silent film history (hero and villain at the same time) and its antagonist (more virtuous in some respects, but not without its flaws) are now introduced.

Base

At the end of the nineteenth century, the preferred carrier for motion picture film was cellulose nitrate; it remained so until February 1951, when it was gradually superseded by cellulose triacetate (films on a flammable base were used until the late 1950s in the Soviet Union and a few other countries). Sulphur and sodium nitrate – soon to be transformed into acid compounds – were the two raw chemicals used for the manufacture of nitrate base. The other main ingredient, cotton waste or flax, was broken into small pieces and given a powerful blast of heated air to remove all moisture. Sulphuric acid and nitric acid were mixed with the cotton, making it soluble in the other substances to be added; the excess acid was extracted in perforated baskets. After repeated washing and drying, the snowy substance had become pyroxylin (partially nitrated cellulose), a product similar to guncotton but not as explosive.

Cellulose nitrate is naturally prone to decay, and can easily be affected by the chemical agents used in film developing; to avoid both, the substance went through a chemical stabilization process before being mixed with camphor (for the plasticizing of nitrocellulose) and various solvents like acetone, benzole, alcohol, sulphuric and acetic ether, methyl alcohol, and amyl acetate. The relative stability of nitrate film stock depended upon the accuracy with which pyroxylin was stabilized; this may explain why two nitrate positive films kept for a long time at the same temperature and humidity may decompose at different rates. Shrinking of the film base, on the other hand, was unavoidable, as cellulose nitrate is permeable to water (thus making the stock expand when humid, and contract when dry): the shrinkage rate of a positive film could reach 1.25 per cent just six months after manufacture.

The cellulose compound was poured into large rotating barrels; within hours, the mixture became a thick, pale yellow, viscous liquid referred to as 'dope'. Once transferred to cylindrical tanks (Fig. 15), the syrup-like substance was converted into sheets of appropriate thickness through three different methods: from 1889 to early 1899, by pouring it over a single piece of polished glass laid on a table measuring 200 feet, or 60 metres (Fig. 16); from April 1899, by performing the same

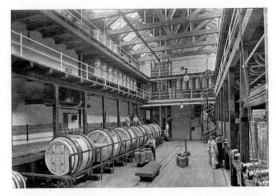

Fig. 15 Mixing barrels for celluloid. Eastman Kodak Company, Rochester, New York, c. 1912. Source: Frederick Arthur Ambrose Talbot, Moving Pictures. How they are made and worked. London: Heinemann, 1912; Philadelphia: J.B. Lippincott Co., 1914, p. 54.

operation on a continuous metallic belt, or by squeezing the dope through a revolving drum, also with a perfectly smooth surface. Manufacturing plants were obsessive about cleanliness in all working areas: dust has always been one of the worst enemies of film stock. Temperature and humidity levels were carefully monitored and kept constant to achieve uniformity in the response of the final product to environmental conditions and mechanical stress while the film was used in shooting, developing, and projection.

Fig. 16 Cellulose base and emulsion coating table. Eastman Kodak Company, Rochester, New York, c. 1890. Gelatin silver print. Source: George Eastman Museum.

After drying under jets of highly purified warm air to evaporate the solvents, the fine transparent base was covered with a layer of photographic emulsion. A chemical binder, probably made of methyl alcohol, water and gelatin, or camphor and fusel oil (amyl alcohol), glued the two together (this extremely thin layer, also known as 'undercoat' or 'subbing', had been previously applied to one side of the base). Once the two layers were firmly secured to each other through drying by contact with the surface of a large heated drum, the final product was sliced into several strips of the desired width, the emulsion being recognizable as the matte or opaque side of the film (with few exceptions, the base always looks shinier when held against a diagonal light source). Kodak introduced in 1903 an extra layer of very faintly coloured anti-halation gelatin to prevent the film from curling and forming a haze on the photographic images; the colouring agent had the effect of absorbing most of the parasitic light interference. The curling of film was provoked by the fact that the film emulsion is extremely sensitive to variations in humidity, and far more subject to shrinkage than the cellulose base to which it is attached (the difference in shrinkage rates for film base and emulsion is a major cause of mechanical damage to negatives and projection prints).

Industry practitioners were well aware of the dangers inherent in the use of film stock made on such a flammable material, and almost immediately looked for suitable alternatives. Cellulose diacetate stock, also known as 'safety film' like all other successors of nitrate, was manufactured from the first decade of the twentieth century (Arthur Eichengrün and Theodore Becker had developed the material in 1903); Eastman Kodak delivered a first batch of 35mm safety film in May 1908 to Charles Pathé, who was profoundly dissatisfied by its performance. Cellulose nitrate

was sufficiently strong and flexible to withstand repeated use; it could be easily slit and perforated; it did not absorb and expel too much moisture. Conversely, early diacetate stock was not as transparent as nitrate; being less flexible than its flammable equivalent, it could easily break. Cameramen and projectionists also complained about diacetate stock's significant curling and shrinkage. Dangerous as it was, nitrate film offered them a much better performance during shooting and screening.

Positive film on a 'non-flam' diacetate base (it was not immune from burning, but it did so very slowly) fared better in the amateur market, for screenings in hospitals and schools, and in other special projects (Gaumont's Chronochrome, 1912). Further research on acetate chemistry resulted in modest but encouraging progress in the late 1920s: projection prints of Abel Gance's *Napoléon* (1927) were struck on 35mm film with a diacetate base manufactured by Pathé. The company's founder remained cautious: 'everybody knows', he said, 'that safety film is one and a half times more expensive to the manufacturer than nitrate cellulose' (*Cinéa-Ciné pour tous*, no. 79, 15 February 1927, p. [3]). Nitrate film was made with readily available and inexpensive solvents such as wood alcohol and small amounts of camphor and fusel oil. Pathé's scepticism was assuaged only when better and cheaper solvents entered the market.

Ozaphane, a French patent for motion picture stock on extremely thin (0.04mm) cellophane film, was introduced at about the same time. French and German companies made it available in various formats (16mm, 17.5mm, 22mm; also in 24mm and 35mm during the early sound era), with or without perforations (Fig. 17). An entire feature-length film could be stored in one or two reels: 3,000 metres (almost 10,000 feet, or ten reels) of Ozaphane film had a total weight of

Fig. 17 Unidentified film (Germany, c. 1928). Ozaphane 17.5mm positive with five rectangular perforations on the frame line. The original sample is tinted pink. Source: Cinémathèque française.

Formats

The choice of 35mm (some early films are actually on 34.8mm stock) as the standard gauge for the commercial exhibition of motion pictures was a matter of convenience: Edison and his staff were using strips of unperforated 70mm film provided by the Eastman Kodak Company, and thought that cutting it in half would produce an image that was good enough to be seen through a magnifying glass in a properly fitted device for individual viewing through a peephole (the Kinetoscope). It later turned out that enlarging it many thousand times on a big screen was also good enough for a collective audience, and all major producers were in agreement about this. Early 70mm film projection was a sight to behold (in photochemical terms, picture detail is directly proportional to the area of the sensitized emulsion exposed to the lens of a camera), but entailed the use of a much greater quantity of material for the same running time; films of this size would also be more difficult to handle if edited together into longer rolls. This did not prevent the American Mutoscope & Biograph Company from marketing its 68mm films for the vaudeville circuit from 1896 to the early 1900s. The negatives were perforated in the camera (one round hole on each side of the image) at the time of shooting; projection prints had no perforations at all (Plate 9). Their aspect ratio (the proportion between an image's width and height) was about 1:1.37, not too different from a 35mm frame but far more impressive if projected on a large screen.

When the April 1909 Paris conference of film producers and manufacturers belatedly ratified the consensus on 35mm film as the standard film format, its conquest of the world market was already a fait accompli. In previous years, many inventors and entrepreneurs had promoted various kinds of film gauges, most of them short-lived.

7 kilos (15 pounds), as opposed to 20 kilos (44 pounds) of conventional celluloid. Ozaphane's photographic images were chemically embedded in the non-flammable base; unfortunately, picture quality could not compare with that of nitrate or diacetate film, which is why Ozaphane was never used as a theatrical format on a large scale. Its commercial life ended in the early 1930s.

The largest of all (Plate 21), with a single frame along the width of the film stock, was Lumière's 75mm (1899), but its frame size (60mm wide and 45mm high, with an aspect ratio of 1:1.33) was slightly smaller than Biograph's. Two years earlier, the American Veriscope Company had made a 63mm film with five perforations on each side (aspect ratio 1:1.75) to document a boxing match, *Corbett vs Fitzsimmons – Heavyweight Boxing Match* (1897; Plate 3).

Other formats were suggested by John A. and Edward P. Prestwich (Great Britain, 1897, 60mm, with four perforations on both margins of the frame); Georges Demenÿ (France, 1896, also 60mm; see Plate 2), in films that differed from the rest in their uneven relationship between frames and perforations (fifteen every four frames); Auguste Baron (France, 1899, 50mm, one round perforation per frame; see Plate 14). The system devised by Max and Emil Skladanowsky (Bioscop, Germany, 1895, 55mm, Plate 20) is special in more than one respect. It required the alternate projection of frames from two separate strips of film (Fig. 18); each of them had three round perforations reinforced with metal studs, two of them matching the frame line (a later design had four smaller round perforations, with no metal protection). Their shows must have been rather noisy events.

The rise of amateur and non-theatrical markets triggered a search for the most practical application of smaller formats. Among the first was the Chrono de poche (15mm, with a single perforation on the frame line, Plate 15), marketed in France by Gaumont in 1900, together with a portable spring-wound camera, the first of its kind. The Warwick Trading Company in Great Britain introduced in 1902 a 17.5mm film (also with a single perforation) for the Biokam, a camera that could print and project film, like Lumière's Cinématographe. Heinrich Ernemann joined the competition between 1903 and 1908

Fig. 18 Max Skladanowsky, Germany, 1895. Dual projector for coupled 55mm film strips (see Plate 20), as shown in an undated photograph. Note the profile of the single-blade shutter. Gelatin silver print. Source: George Eastman Museum.

(Ernemann-Kino, Plate 6), followed by Pathé and others over the next two decades. It was only with Pathé's 28mm non-flammable film, however, that a non-standard format became truly profitable. Its frame size was only slightly smaller than the 35mm format. The unusual but user-friendly design of Pathé-Kok's 28mm equipment (1912) became popular in the rural areas of Europe and North America: the compact hand-cranked mechanism not only fed the film through the projector's lens, but also generated power for the light source. A peculiar feature of European 28mm film, printed on diacetate stock from 35mm nitrate negatives, is its asymmetric perforation system: three holes per frame on one side, one at the opposite margin (Plate 12). Prints made for the North American market from 1917 (Pathéscope) have three perforations on each side.

Eastman Kodak's response to Pathé-Kok was the release of yet another format that would soon become the darling of amateur and independent filmmakers. The first commercial version of 16mm stock, Kodascope, was a 'reversal' film; negatives and positives soon followed, in addition to a rental library of considerable size (Plate 13). With very few exceptions, all 16mm elements were struck on a non-flammable base. Pathé responded in 1922 with an even smaller gauge, 9.5mm (Pathé-Baby), distributed in metal cartridges ready for use, an instant commercial triumph. It was a tiny masterpiece of ingenuity: title cards were printed in four or fewer frames, with a notch on the margins that slowed down the projection speed to allow the texts to be read (Plate 17). With its rich catalogue of non-fiction, shorts, and abridged versions of feature films from nitrate negatives, Pathé-Baby managed to contain Kodak's supremacy in the market without being able to subvert it. The lukewarm response to Pathé-Rural (Plate 22), a 17.5mm gauge launched by Pathé in 1926, brought a temporary end to the corporate struggle for the non-theatrical market.

Other firms came up with further ideas, competing with each other in resourcefulness and eccentricity. In 1910, an Italian entrepreneur patented a 35mm film stock where each frame was divided to accommodate two separate images (Plate 18); Edison's 22mm safety film (Home Kinetoscope, 1912–16) had three parallel strips of frames just over 5mm wide, each of them separated by a line of perforations (Plate 5); in Germany, Oskar Messter's Kino-Salon or 'Salon-Kinemesster' (1908, Plate 7) squeezed four rows of frames and two perforation lines in a 35mm safety film of just 2 metres in length (6.5 feet). Its running time was equivalent to 32 metres (105 feet) of standard format. The largest motion picture film stock ever made on celluloid during the early twentieth century was called Oko (Kazimierz Prószyński, Poland, 1913), consisting of a 120mm strip divided into rows of fifteen frames each. The silent film era also witnessed a number of experiments in three-dimensional cinema – mostly on standard 35mm film – to be viewed with anaglyph glasses (Plate 50).

None of these inventions ever achieved wide sales; most of them hardly went beyond the prototype stage. The images recorded on these 'orphans' of technology (other examples are shown in Plates 4, 8, 11, and 16) are often unique. They are also the most difficult to see: the machines needed to project them are extremely rare, and it is expensive to transfer them onto modern carriers.

Frames

A significant percentage – if not the majority – of the objects produced by humankind for everyday life are rectangular: doors, windows, roofs, the perimeter of the room where you may be sitting now, and the bed you sleep in, all seem to reflect our desire to inhabit an orderly world. Rectangles are found everywhere, from a sheet of paper to the surface of a table, a book, a painting on the wall. A rectangle was the object of the quest of the 'golden section' in ancient Greece. A strip of film is a rectangle, too, albeit elongated to the extreme. Magic lantern artists and practitioners didn't see things that way, given that most of their projected images were in the form of circles and squares. In the Edison laboratory, Dickson initially followed

Fig. 19 [*Newark Athlete*] (W.K.L. Dickson and William Heise, 1891). 19mm nitrate positive for horizontal display, with round frame and a single row of film perforations. Source: Library of Congress.

this tradition, which is why some of his earliest films have frames that look like medallions (Fig. 19). A simple consideration soon persuaded him that he was proceeding in the wrong direction. A magic lantern slide is a piece of glass containing one or more images; the slide itself has indeed square corners, but its projected image could be enclosed in a circumference, with a pleasing effect for the audience. Cellulose film did not encourage such niceties: as a portion of the object had to be sacrificed to perforation, wasting additional space in such a costly material didn't make sense. The entire surface of the film stock was covered by sensitized emulsion; there was no reason not to exploit it to the maximum.

The next best option was a square frame, identical to what had been used in magic lantern shows. This initially looked like a better alternative, as no projectable surface would be lost, other than the perforated edges of the film stock. It would also have been a safe choice, considering that viewers had been used for many decades to square pictures projected on the screen. A simple unit of measurement – 1 inch (about 25 millimetres), the width of a man's thumb – determined the sizes of the top and bottom length of the frame. In theory, the image could also

have been photographed alongside the edges of the film stock, rather than across its length, but it wouldn't have been much wider, and projectors would have had to run the film horizontally rather than vertically (that possibility was contemplated as well).

A decisive argument in favour of the vertical design of film and its related equipment was, again, the economy of scale: a hundred square images would occupy a hundred inches; in a rectangular image with a height of three-quarters of an inch (19 millimetres), the same number of frames would fit in a shorter film, at a lower cost per foot. Horizontal paintings, prints, and drawings – not to mention photographs – of rectangular shape were the norm almost everywhere, and it seemed natural that film should follow the same rule. In this sense, silent cinema is the result of a creative mediation between quantity (the amount of film stock to be deployed for the longest possible running time), quality (the accuracy in photographic reproduction), and tradition (the preferred shape of images for display).

In 1896, two French pioneers – Henri Joly and Ernest Normandin – remained loyal to the legacy of the square frame (Fig. 20), but nobody

Fig. 20 *Place de la République à Paris* (Henri Joly, 1896). 35mm nitrate positive with five perforations on each side. Frame size, 21–23mm (h), 23–24.8mm (w); aspect ratio, 1:1.02 to 1:1.08. Source: Filmoteca Española. Photo courtesy of Irela Núñez del Pozo.

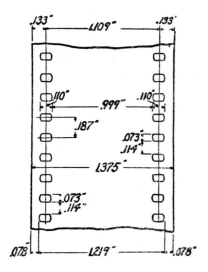

Fig. 21 The 'standard' dimensions (in inches) of 35mm motion picture film in the mid-1910s. Source: Standards Adopted by the Society of Motion Picture Engineers. Washington, DC: The Society, 1917, n.p..

followed their example. All other film producers and manufacturers already knew that each frame of a 35mm positive film was to be about 24mm wide and 18mm high (Fig. 21), with 54 frames per metre (16 frames per foot). The 1:1.33 aspect ratio was maintained until the advent of optical sound (the aspect ratio of silent films reissued with variable density soundtracks is approximately 1:1.16, almost a square: see Fig. 198b). The only known anamorphic system of the silent era is Henri Chrétien's Hypergonar (1927), used in a short film by Claude Autant-Lara, *Construire un feu* (made in the winter of 1928–9 and premiered on 5 December 1930).

The illusion of an expanded field of vision was occasionally achieved by mechanically altering the frame's aspect ratio, or by increasing the size of the projected image (Magnascope, 1926) with special lenses. The rest is experimental cinema: in Italy, Filoteo Alberini's 70mm wide-angle films (Fig. 22 and Plate 11) made in 1911; in France, Raoul Grimoin-Sanson's Cinéorama, a failed attempt to surround the audience of the 1900 Universal Exhibition with ten projectors arranged at 360 degrees; and the memorable triptych sequences of Abel Gance's *Napoléon*, involving three adjacent images projected simultaneously from three 35mm projectors to form a widescreen image with a 1:3.99 aspect ratio, the broadest rectangle ever seen in silent cinema.

Fig. 22 Unidentified 70mm film ([*Street Scene, Rome*], Filoteo Alberini, 1911). Positive image from the 70mm nitrate negative reproduced in Plate 11. Source: George Eastman Museum.

Perforations

Motion picture film wasn't always endowed with perforations. Some early manufacturers thought they could do without them; once the film base was covered with photographic emulsion and delivered to the clients in a pristine roll, filmmakers and production companies were free to decide how many holes, if any, were needed to make it work with the camera and projection equipment at their disposal (see, for instance, Plate 19). Eastman Kodak motion picture stock was initially sold without perforations (perforated stock was offered from 1902 on an optional basis). The American Mutoscope & Biograph Company produced a series of films in a large unperforated format, and they looked magnificent (Plate 9). Like other films of this kind, they were moved across the machines with rollers or grips, tightly holding the edges of the print and transporting it to the next position. Film entrepreneurs changed their mind when they realized that the slightest variation in the thickness of the film stock, or a small imperfection or wear of the rollers, was enough to make the movement slippery and compromise the steady appearance of the images on the screen.

Clutching the celluloid strip at its margins also resulted in a gradual abrasion of the emulsion; viewers would soon be looking at a picture that may have been sharp at its centre, but was increasingly covered with a rain of scratches at its sides. Thus began the search for a painful but inevitable compromise, a territorial dispute about the areas of the film stock that should be awarded to the image or sacrificed for the sake of its sharpness, stability, and durability. The technological history of cinema is a long debate between two reluctant allies – perforations and frames. They both wanted more land in which to dwell, but they needed each other (a third party, the optical soundtrack, would join

the match in the early 1930s, stealing part of the frame area).

Punching holes at the margins of the celluloid strip allowed a transport mechanism to move it, one frame at a time and at regular intervals, in front of the camera and the projection lens; it was only a matter of establishing the most appropriate shape and size for these holes. Triangles had been briefly considered, and then summarily dismissed. Square holes were the next candidates, but rectangles eventually won the contest: the profile of film perforations – four of them (each 2.5 by 1.7mm) on both sides of the frame – was established in the early 1890s by the personnel of Edison's laboratory. Their first commercial application was implemented with Edison's Kinetoscope between April 1894 and 1900. By the early 1900s, the Kinetoscope was a thing of the past. The Edison perforations, however, not merely survived but thrived, staying with film throughout the twentieth century and beyond.

Such longevity is a testimony to the brilliant response by W.K.L. Dickson to the dual challenge of constantly advancing the film through the camera and viewing device, and ensuring that the recorded photographs would be seen as a uniform sequence of still pictures in quick succession. Dickson did not achieve this overnight, as shown, for instance, in a film fragment with perforations only at the lower edge of the print (Fig. 19); it took some time for him to realize that it was best to apply them on both sides, so that the tension derived by the transport of the film stock through the mechanisms would not create a distortion of the celluloid strip and, consequently, of the sensitized or exposed emulsion.

The system chosen by Auguste and Louis Lumière for their Cinématographe films was even simpler, consisting of a single circular perforation every 20 millimetres on each side of the frame (Plate 1). Its performance was more than acceptable (as long as the screens on which the film was projected were not too large); to be on the safe side, many producers of cinematic equipment – Lumière included – were selling their products in versions compatible with both Lumière and Edison equipment. The objection raised by the Lumière brothers to the Edison system was that too many perforations were bound to make the film too fragile to withstand repeated use. Their point was well taken. Over time, it became nonetheless evident to all that the Lumière perforation had two disadvantages of an entirely different nature. First, no matter how carefully the intermittent system was calibrated, the captured or projected image was not as steady as the one in Edison's film with four perforations; keeping the picture in focus was also problematic, as the film had a tendency to wave within the aperture gate of the camera or projection equipment.

To make things worse, Lumière's perforations were subject to greater wear and tear. In some surviving nitrate copies of Lumière films, perforations are cracked or otherwise damaged at the lower edges. This is because a single pair of perforations had to endure the burden of receiving the transport mechanism's claw (Fig. 23) that penetrated the holes every time it pulled the film down the aperture gate, one frame at a time. Had the lower margin of the perforation been flat, the mechanical stress provoked by the claw's downward movement would not have had the same effect; a round edge, on the other hand, was sooner or later bound to crack. This happened also to the Edison perforations, but not to the same degree; when it did, it was evenly distributed along four perforations instead of one. Dickson's design was partly based on the principle of redundancy: if one perforation was partially damaged, the others would come to the rescue and do the job; when broken, a Lumière perforation had no backup option.

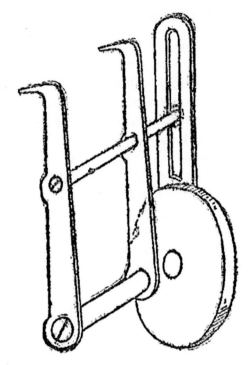

Fig. 23 Claw mechanism for film movement across the camera aperture gate. Source: Private collection.

The Lumière brothers must have been conscious of the trouble ahead, judging from the eight round perforations on each side of the large-format film they proudly presented in Paris at the 1900 Universal Exhibition (Plate 21). There were other factors behind the eventual demise of Lumière's system (including Robert William Paul's early adoption of the Edison perforations – at a different frame rate than Edison's – when the dice was still rolling), but the redundancy factor was decisive enough to warrant the quadruple perforations their remarkable endurance at a time of constant technological change. Because of their size, the Edison perforations were generally unsuitable to small non-theatrical formats. Many different perforation shapes and positions were used over the years for amateur films; some examples are shown in Plates 6, 7, and 16.

The battlefield of film perforations is littered with unorthodox and quickly forgotten schemes, such as those of Max and Emil Skladanowsky in their dual projection system (Fig. 18 and Plate 20); Ambroise-François Parnaland's 35mm films (Phono-Cinéma-Théâtre, 1900), with three symmetrical perforations between frames (Fig. 180); and the British company Prestwich (three round perforations in films of 35mm format). Some uncertainty remained throughout much of the silent film era about the position of the four Edison perforations in relation to the frames of 35mm stock; as late as 1919, film treatises were listing four different layouts, ranging from perforations aligned to the space between two frames, to those located at an equal distance between the frame line (Fig. 24). The latter prevailed, and became the norm in film manufacturing worldwide.

The shape and size of film perforations varied from one company to another until about 1904. Often closer to squares than rectangles, the holes were generally smaller than those found in prints of the later period (Fig. 25a). A major player in the film technology business, the Chicago-based Bell & Howell Company (established by Donald Bell and Albert Howell in 1907), suggested a slightly

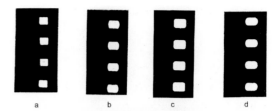

Fig. 25 The shape of perforations in 35mm film stock of the silent era: (a) small-gauge perforations, before c. 1905; (b) Bell & Howell; (c) Kodak Standard, for positives only; (d) Pathé.

different kind of perforation, with straight top and bottom edges, and rounded sides (hence the nickname, 'barrel' perforation). It was used for both positive and negative films (Fig. 25b) until 1924, when Kodak introduced a rectangular perforation with rounded corners – generally called 'positive perforations' or KS, 'Kodak Standard' – for positive projection prints only (Fig. 25c). Since then, negative elements continued to have Bell & Howell perforations, while most projection prints used the Kodak Standard.

The differentiation between positive and negative perforations was justified by the fact that negative stock requires maximum precision in image registration, but is used only a few times (for shooting and printing only), while a positive print must be able to run many more times through equipment of varying design and physical condition, therefore requiring a greater degree of adaptability to different situations. A proposal to unify the two kinds of perforations (the Dubray-Howell system) was greeted with limited consensus. From 1905 to the late 1920s, Pathé used perforations of a distinctive quasi-oval form, similar to the Bell & Howell shape, but with rounded corners (Fig. 25d). Camera negatives of 35mm films by the Biograph Company (Fig. 26), and some negatives of French and Italian films of the late 1900s to the mid-1910s, have a single perforation on each side of the frame (Fig. 27).

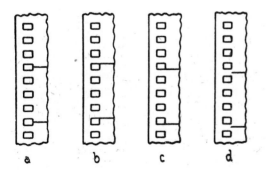

Fig. 24 Film perforation layouts in relation to the frame line. Source: Hans Schmidt, *Kino-Taschenbuch für Amateure und Fachleute*. Berlin: Union Deutsche Verlagsgesellschaft, 1926, p. 161.

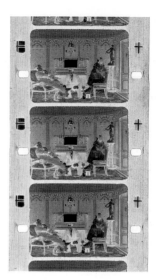

Fig. 27 35mm camera negative with single Bell & Howell perforation on each side of the frame. Unidentified Max Linder film, Pathé, c. 1913. Source: Courtesy of Laurent Mannoni.

Edges

There are images in motion picture film stock that were never meant to be seen by an audience. Production companies had been fighting against film piracy since the very beginnings of cinema, generally with modest if not dismal results; plagiarism and illegal duplication were so widespread at the turn of the twentieth century, especially in the United States (Siegmund Lubin and Edison were among the main culprits), that any given film could not only be imitated shot by shot and then distributed as an original work, but also duplicated from release prints and then presented as a film made by another company.

Georges Méliès aggressively fought against this practice by inserting the logo of his company (Star-Film) on the main title of his films – a tactic soon followed by almost everybody else – and by incorporating it within the set as early as 1896; he also resorted to applying his signature on the film leader, and to punching and embossing the logo on all positive prints (Fig. 28). His scheme

Fig. 26 *Fighting Blood* (D.W. Griffith, Biograph, 1911). Unassembled 35mm camera negative on nitrate stock, with a single perforation on each side (top frames) and handwritten annotations on titling ('as the night passes'), tinting ('amber'), and length of the section. Source: George Eastman Museum.

Fig. 28 *Le Maestro Do-mi-sol-do* (Georges Méliès, 1905). 35mm nitrate positive. The 'Star-Film' trademark, embossed onto the film, is shown with low-angle light refraction. Source: George Eastman Museum – Davide Turconi/Josef Joye Collection.

was effective only up to a point, as some competitors were persistent enough to manually erase the Star-Film logo from every single frame of a pirated negative (either by scratching the logo off the emulsion, or by covering it with ink) before reprinting it at will (Fig. 29a–b).

In 1896, Lumière inaugurated another anti-piracy measure. The idea consisted of inscribing the producer's name along the edges of all positives, between the perforations (Fig. 30), with the aid of an ingenious method that was virtually immune from forgery: commercially available printers were built in such a way that they could duplicate individual frames, but not necessarily the margins of film stock. The core component of a 1905 printer used by Pathé for its edge inscriptions was a shallow film sprocket, very similar to those used in cameras and projectors. An incandescent lamp was placed over its

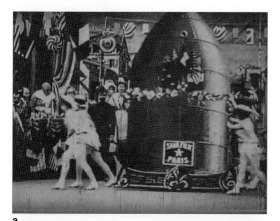

a

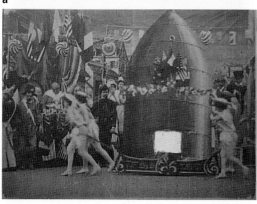

b

Fig. 29a–b *Le Voyage dans la lune* (Georges Méliès, 1902), tableau no. 26, in a 35mm nitrate print from Star-Film (a) and in a pirated version from Edison (b), with the Star-Film logo removed from each frame. 35mm acetate positive (a) and nitrate positive (b). Source: George Eastman Museum.

Fig. 30 Edge markings on a 35mm nitrate positive of [*96ème de ligne en marche*], variant of a Lumière film (catalogue no. 191, March 1896) with the same title. Source: Cinémathèque française.

centre. A stencilled ribbon with the inscription to be transferred onto the film stock was placed between the perforations; as the film was passed through the machine, the light sensitized the emulsion between the sprockets, thus printing the inscription on the film's edges (Gaumont went even further by replacing the stencilled strip with a tiny film upon which clear letters were printed on a black background). The wording or numbers on the stencilled strip could be changed from time to time, as required by the producer. The operation was completed immediately after perforating the film stock; a French manufacturer of film equipment, Joseph Jules Debrie, patented an edge printing machine where the film stock was also passed through extremely fine brush rollers in order to remove the tiny particles of celluloid dust created by the perforating equipment.

Pathé's technique was far more successful than previous attempts to prevent the illegal duplication of release prints; other companies were quick to adopt it for their own films. The system worked so well that Eastman Kodak began applying it to film manufacturing (Fig. 31 and Appendix 2): the company's first edge inscriptions appeared in 1913. Pathé had initially inserted a date after its corporate name; the idea was soon abandoned, possibly because films with an older date would no longer be marketable. In the summer of 1914, Kodak took the further step of printing symbols alongside the company's name in order to identify the manufacturing date of the film stock.

In line with Kodak's secretive policies, the meaning of the symbols was not revealed. By 1916, all Kodak prints were constellated by a cryptographic set of symbols and geometric figures, according to periodic combinations known only to Kodak employees. The coding system was further expanded in the following years with different symbols for Kodak's plants in Great Britain and

Fig. 31 *A Daughter of Two Worlds* (James L. Young, 1920). 35mm nitrate positive. Note the Eastman Kodak 1920 edge code on the right side of the film. The fragment reproduced here, photographed in 1994 at the George Eastman Museum, has decomposed and is no longer extant. Source: George Eastman Museum.

Canada, as shown in Appendix 2. It was rigorously followed for the entire silent film era and beyond, with subtle refinements and additions, including a specific code to indicate whether the stock was manufactured in the first or the second semester of any given year.

Splices

A crucial prerogative of motion picture film is that it can easily be assembled manually – with or without the aid of equipment – in a roll comprising two or more consecutive strips; in their original forms, both the camera negatives and the projection prints of most silent films included dozens, hundreds, often thousands of joins. Their shape and position varied according to the type of material (positive or negative) and the splicing equipment being used, but the basics of the technique were essentially the same for all materials (Fig. 32).

Fig. 32 A cement splice in an unidentified film (1899) made on Lumière stock [*Re-enactment of scenes from Victor Hugo's* Notre-Dame de Paris]. 35mm nitrate positive. Source: George Eastman Museum.

repeated use of the finished work through printing and projection machines.

Various formulas were used for the creation of splicing cement, most commonly a compound of film base (without emulsion) melted with acetone or ethyl acetate (Fig. 33); other recipes involved raw film stock dissolved in acetone and ether, or amyl acetate and acetone, or collodion and banana oil (isoamyl acetate). For some reason, acetone and ether in equal parts seemed preferable for splices to be made on stencil-coloured prints from Pathé. Unsurprisingly, splicing cement from the Eastman Kodak Company was hailed as the very best in the professional market; non-flammable stock required yet other cement formulas, variously described in technical publications of the silent film era.

From the viewpoint of film editors and projectionists, specialized knowledge was no substitute for individual taste and craftsmanship. The quality of the uncoated film base to be mixed with the other chemicals for a perfect splicing cement mattered more to them than anything else. Their

At one end of the film, the emulsion is carefully scraped off the edge of the cellulose base with a fine blade. Because the emulsion covers the entire surface of the positive or negative stock, it is necessary to apply this operation to the entire width of the film, including the margins and the areas adjacent to the perforations; doing otherwise would compromise the strength of the splice. At the end of the other strip to be attached, the base is slightly scraped to roughen the surface of the cellulose and eliminate all grease and dirt from the edge to be joined. The reason for these preliminary stages of the splicing process is that the two ends of the film should not be merely attached to each other: they must be welded together in order to sustain

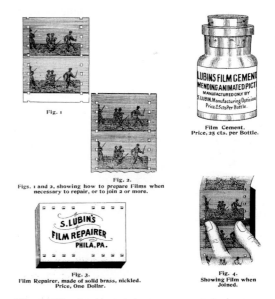

Fig. 33 The basic technique and equipment of film splicing. Siegmund Lubin catalogue, Philadelphia, 1898, p. 25. Source: Cinémathèque française.

preferences were heavily influenced by the evaporation speed of the cement: the faster the rate, the more imperative it was to act quickly and with the greatest degree of accuracy. Particular care was required in scraping the film emulsion only on the area to be joined; removing any more would result in flashes of white unexposed film appearing at the top or bottom of the screen during projection. In an attempt to discourage exhibitors from tampering with film continuity, Metro-Goldwyn-Mayer applied embossed markings (such as 'EX MGM') on each joint of its prints for some 1920s productions to certify that the splices were made at the studio.

High-performance film cement commercially available in small glass bottles from major manufacturers such as Bell & Howell and Eastman Kodak had a camel-hair brush attached to the cork; this enabled the adhesive to be applied evenly without smearing the adjoining portions of the frame. The strength of a splice also depended on the time required for keeping the two ends of the film pressed together, ranging from five to thirty seconds. On average, one minute of work was needed to achieve a good result on a positive print; more time could be required in negative cutting. To obtain a clean cut between the chosen segments, a frame from each piece of film had to be removed; this is why editors left at least two extra frames at both ends of each section.

Film projectionists did not have such luxury. Their main obligation was to get the prints ready as quickly as possible for the next show, which is why their splices were often weak and haphazardly made in the middle of a frame, rather than between frame lines. Joints made with film cement were irreversible: in the event of an error, the print had to be cut and the splice done again from scratch, with the ensuing loss of at least another frame on each side of the joint. If successful, the splice would be cleaned with alcohol to ensure removal of all residual cement. Initially implemented by hand or with rudimentary equipment (Fig. 34a–c), splicing was made faster and more accurate with precision tools for print assembly and in the projection booth (see Chapter 4). The shape and position of film splices will be the object of further analysis in Chapter 14, in the context of print inspection and authentication.

Fig. 34a–c Manual splicing of 35mm film. Source: The Modern Bioscope Operator. London: Ganes, 1910, pp. 10–12.

Chapter 3

Chroma

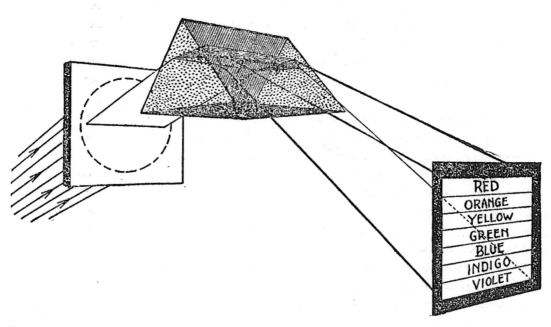

Fig. 35 Production of the colour spectrum by means of a prism. Source: Carl L. Gregory, Motion Picture Photography. New York: Falk Publishing Company, 1927, p. 33.

Decades of neglect and misinformation have nurtured the popular belief that silent films were all made in black and white. This prejudice began to wane as an increasing number of properly restored films became available to the public; it has been dispelled once and for all among cognoscenti, but is still engrained in the mind of the general public. Its most revealing symptom is the enduring tendency to deprive certain kinds of films of the appellative 'in colour' just because their prints included shots or sections in monochrome tints, such as blue, orange, or green. According to this line of thought, a film is 'in colour' only insofar as it resembles colour films of the modern era; a silent Technicolor film easily fits this category; a tinted film does not; a hand-painted copy is somewhere in between, but because the colours had been applied manually, the case is treated as something special, an exception to the rule. The earliest cataloguing records of some film museums and archives listed beautifully tinted and toned prints as being in black and white; they were copied onto black and white stock, and seen as such by later generations of viewers.

In the mid-1980s, when silent cinema was emerging as a topic of scholarly interest, film historians were surprised to find that black and white film was far from the norm in the early twentieth century. They could not have known otherwise, unless they had seen a nitrate print or read a technical manual from the silent film period: the majority of films commercially distributed at that time were indeed in colour, either in part or in their entirety, but collecting institutions had not preserved them as such (the reasons for this will be explained in Chapter 12). A comparative analysis of surviving nitrate film prints and catalogues for film exhibitors shows that audiences had a very diversified chromatic experience throughout the silent era; that until the early 1910s some films were available in two versions, black and white and colour, at different prices; that colour was used more frequently for dramatic subjects and documentaries than in comedy; last but not least, that the presence or absence of colour was only marginally influenced by a film's production values.

A treasure trove of information on this subject was provided by Italian film historian Davide Turconi, who took a large number of nitrate clips from a collection of early films he was researching in the 1960s. The prints had been previously acquired in Switzerland by a Jesuit priest, Josef-Alexis Joye, whose story will be told in Chapter 10; what matters here is that Turconi's 23,491 nitrate frames represent almost eight hundred different films, mainly from the 1906–15 period, and that at least one colour technique appears in about 60 per cent of the fragments. Of these, 82 per cent include tinting; 13 per cent stencilling; 7 per cent toning; 1.4 per cent tinting and toning combined; 2.6 per cent black and white and tinting on the same print; 0.23 per cent hand-colouring. Several frames display other combinations of colour processes (the percentages add up to more than 100 per cent because two or more techniques appear in different sections of the same print).

This statistical information cannot be regarded as a faithful mirror of the entire history of silent film colour, but the sheer size and chronological scope of Turconi's fragments from the Joye collection give enough credibility to this particular survey: taken as a whole, the nitrate frames cover about the first half of the history of silent cinema. They represent all film genres and all the major countries and production companies of the period. A much smaller (2,254 frames) but equally beautiful collection of the same nature at the Österreichisches Filmmuseum in Vienna, named after Edith Schlemmer, offers similar results. These treasures demonstrate that colour was by all means a normal occurrence in silent cinema, as long as the term 'colour' is understood in its broadest sense, including monochrome tints. These colours contributed in a significant measure to the aesthetic experience of the films in which they appeared.

Hand-colouring

The first manifestations of colour in film virtually coincide with the birth of cinema. Motion picture projection was initially regarded as a magic lantern show achieved by other means: this is how technical manuals from the turn of the twentieth century were presenting it. The main difference between decorating a glass slide and a flexible strip of cellulose was that the latter was a much more demanding process, not because the frames are so small (miniature painters had done miracles with even tinier surfaces), but because there was no way to make the coloured area look uniform and steady when projected as consecutive pictures on a big screen.

By addressing this initial challenge through trial and error over the next three decades, many inventions unrelated to each other found their synthesis in a single, highly successful colour process that emerged at the dawn of 'sound' cinema. Each main episode in this chromatic itinerary can be regarded as a small piece of an intricate puzzle leading to a synthesis of art, science, and entrepreneurial vision, and to a shared view of what 'natural colour' should look like in a photochemical moving image. Technicolor did not prevail over its competitors in the late 1920s because it was better than the other techniques: its eventual victory was the result of a compromise between money, chemistry, and public taste.

The earliest hand-coloured films, in which some areas of the black and white frame were covered with a maximum of six or seven different aniline dyes applied through tiny brushes, had turned a disadvantage into a golden opportunity. As it was impossible to paint several consecutive frames in exactly the same areas, the pioneers of cinema found a perfect subject for their imperfect paintings: a female dancer, symmetrically swirling her clothes in the air. The 'serpentine dance', presented in 1894 by the Edison Kinetoscope Company as *Annabelle Butterfly Dance*, was the first in a vast repertory of single-shot views on this theme (Plate 31a), based on a stage attraction launched by Loïe Fuller around 1891; in some of these films, the dancer's white veils were tinted by hand with half a dozen hues, in an attempt to simulate the effect of the changing lights projected onto the ballerina during her live performances. It was a brilliant sleight of hand: as the shape of Annabelle's dress was necessarily irregular, colour could be freely applied to its surface. Doing so against a black background would also ensure that the smudges would not be visible on screen, as the aniline dyes appeared only where the celluloid was transparent.

Other early attempts with this technique were made by Lumière (Plate 30) and, in Great Britain, by Robert William Paul. Film pioneers understood that hand-colouring was more effective in the depiction of visual events where contours are uneven and constantly shifting, like smoke and flames released by a volcano. Eager as he was to enhance the magic of his films, Georges Méliès used this technique to astonishing effect, as in *Le Palais de mille et une nuits* (*The Palace of the Arabian Nights*, 1905), with its ample strokes of brilliant dyes, often endowed with a golden glow pervading the entire frame. *Le Royaume des fées* (*Fairyland, or the Kingdom of the Fairies*, 1903), one of Méliès' pictorial masterworks, displays a chromatic complexity with no equal among extant hand-coloured nitrate prints: the flamboyant beauty of its palette has been appropriately compared with those of medieval miniatures. This certainly has something to do with the exquisite sense of detail and the choice of delicately woven colour patterns; their abstract beauty also functioned as an indicator of a mythical atmosphere, reminiscent of nineteenth-century European books of fables.

Hand-colouring was a very expensive and time-consuming process, unsuitable for distribution of film prints on a large scale. Applying colour onto the print required a special bench fitted with an aperture the size of a single frame. The film was lit from below, viewed through a magnifying lens, and advanced frame by frame by means of a foot pedal. Aniline dyes were spread over the frame with the appropriate brushes; when the foot pedal was pressed, the next image appeared, and the worker repeated the same stroke of colour until the scene was finished. A trained hand could move the brush rhythmically and very rapidly; movements across the frame were the hardest to work on. It was also very important to ensure that the shape and intensity of the brushstroke remained constant. According to a 1912 estimate, a skilled hand-colouring team could complete ten to twelve metres (about thirty to forty feet) of positive stock in an average working day. The figure could be much higher or lower, depending on how many different colours were to be applied on any given number of prints, and on the deadline for their delivery to exhibitors.

As a rule, each worker (generally female) was assigned the task of applying a single colour on each print. For time-saving purposes, the same positive copy could also be painted by two or more women, working at a distance of two or three metres (six to ten feet) from each other, so that the aniline dyes had enough time to dry in between. Despite the best possible efforts, no two copies could ever be identical, which made them all unique; errors or incompetence, however, sometimes led to medi-ocre results, as in some hastily painted copies of *Le Raid Paris–Montecarlo en automobile* (Georges Méliès, 1905), probably forged by distributors. By that year, Méliès' main competitor, Charles Pathé, had found a cheaper and far more efficient alternative to the manual application of colour. Hand-colouring did not disappear altogether: there are occasional instances of its use in the 1920s and well into the sound period, as shown by Gustav Brock's evocative splashes of colour on the projection prints of several Hollywood produc-tions, such as Erich von Stroheim's *Foolish Wives* (1922) and *Lonesome* (Paul Fejós, 1928).

Stencil

Around 1905, colouring by hand was almost completely replaced by a new mechanical system, based on the same techniques used for wallpaper and colour postcards. This system, known as 'stencil colouring' ('*au pochoir*' in French), involved two distinct steps. The first required cutting a different stencil for each colour to be used in the film (Fig. 36). These stencils were then transferred to a machine that automatically applied the colour to all positive prints. The number of stencils could vary from a minimum of one to a maximum of five or six for the same scenes. In its early stages, stencilling was done manually, using a precision blade or a sharp needle to cut the matrix frame by frame from a positive print that had been sacrificed for this purpose. The

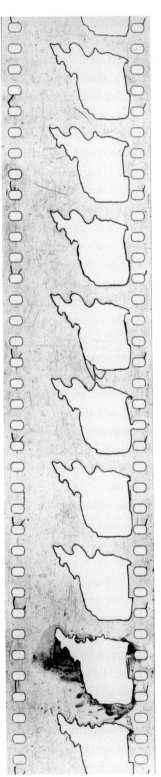

Fig. 36 Matrix for stencil-coloured film. Uncoated 35mm nitrate film, Pathé, c. 1910. Source: Courtesy of Laurent Mannoni.

operation was as difficult and time-consuming as the hand-colouring process, but had the advantage that it only needed to be done once for each colour. The stencils were then immersed in hot water or a hypochlorite solution in order to completely dissolve the emulsion. This treatment allowed an easier application of the colour without scratching the positive prints, or shrinking the stencil (this would have compromised a perfect registration between the stencil and the projection print).

Manual cutting of the stencils was soon replaced by a semi-automatic device similar to the mechanism of a sewing machine, with the cutting needle operated by an electromagnet. In a third phase of development, film technicians no longer cut the matrix directly, but worked instead on a bench parallel to it, with a reference print. The area to be stencilled was traced with a stylus connected through a pantograph to a cutting needle that carved the identical shape on a strip of raw film stock. To ensure that the stencil cut would exactly match the area to be coloured, the cutting needle worked only when the stylus was touching the reference print. At a later stage, the task was further facilitated by moving the pantograph stylus on enlargements of each frame, projected against a sheet of polished glass.

A system of such complexity required highly specialized personnel, who were trained for several weeks before being allowed to enter the production workflow (Fig. 37). Even then, a highly experienced worker could rarely exceed the ratio of about three feet, or one metre, of cut stencil per hour. While the use of unprocessed film stock in the pantograph stencil process eliminated the intermediate step involved in removing all film emulsion for the gelatin, it did require the operator to stop frequently and verify the results. Manual cutting was still preferred in the creation of stencils for very large areas of the frame: alternate frames were cut from two separate stencils, because a single matrix would have been too fragile

to be used repeatedly. Conversely, hand-colouring continued to be used for the tiniest areas of the frame, too small for stencil cutting, such as the dancers' red ribbons in *L'Écrin du Radjah* (*The Rajah's Casket*, Pathé 1906), as seen in Plate 39.

In the final step of the stencil colouring process, the application of aniline dyes to projection prints was almost entirely mechanical (Fig. 38). In most colouring machines, a sprocket system matched the matrix to the black and white print; all the copies of a particular scene were joined and matched with the stencil, rotating in a continuous loop. The dyes were then spread one by one on the film by a loop of velvet, moving in the opposite

Fig. 37 Stencil cutting laboratory. Pathé, c. 1910. Source: Frederick Arthur Ambrose Talbot, Moving Pictures. How they are made and worked. London: Heinemann, 1912; Philadelphia: J.B. Lippincott Co., 1914, p. 288.

Fig. 38 Stencil printing at the Pathé laboratories, c. 1910. Source: Frederick Arthur Ambrose Talbot, Moving Pictures. How they are made and worked. London: Heinemann, 1912; Philadelphia: J.B. Lippincott Co., 1914, p. 289.

direction to the advancing film. This band was fed past a rotating brush immersed in a tank of aniline dye; the amount of dye transferred from the rotating brush to the velvet band was adjustable, depending on the depth of the brush in the tank. To ensure colour uniformity, the velvet band coloured only three frames at a time; in a further improvement, the colour was sprayed onto the velvet band rather than dipped or brushed into the feeding mechanism.

The procedure was rather slow in its initial phase (before the introduction of the pantographs, each worker could cut only an average of about 250 frames per day, corresponding to 5 metres, or 16 feet, of a single matrix), but also very accurate. The matrix for a single colour could be assigned to a team of technicians; a group of ten workers could finish the job in less than one week, rather than the two months required by a single person for one reel (1,000 feet, or 300 metres) of stencil. When all the stencils were ready, the production process became much faster, averaging 25 metres, or 80 feet, of stencilled positive stock in a working day on each colour, a threefold increase in productivity from hand-colouring. It was still an expensive process that could be handled only by a large staff: Pathé would not invest so much effort unless the film was struck in at least two hundred copies, and sold at higher costs to exhibitors.

As the technology of the process evolved over the years, stencilled prints became available at lower prices, with chromatic palettes of hitherto unmatched subtlety, equally effective in fairy tales (Plates 36 and 39), domestic comedies, scenic views, and in other subjects where hand-colouring had once excelled (Plate 38). Realism and abstraction seemed to merge effortlessly in the warm surfaces of the walls in an ancient castle; in the uniform expanse of a blue sky; in the soothing tones of a living room; and in the emerald texture of the ocean, spangled with white sails

on the horizon, with no colour bleeding over their profiles. The only significant challenge to Pathécolor – the name under which the system was known in the early 1910s – came from Gaumont, whose films rivalled the competitor in boldly matching stencil to other colour techniques; the brief triumph of Pathé's invention coincided with the rise of 'natural colour' as a term of reference for film technology at the turn of the decade. The seductive power of the stencil process added a further touch of legitimacy to cinema as a fictional document of history, as seen in Pathé's Film d'Art series and in the literary adaptations of its sibling, the Film d'Arte Italiana (1909–12).

The meticulous neutrality of stencil-coloured prints, reminiscent of the academic painting in those years, was a reassuring departure from the dreamlike hues of the fairy tales that made Pathé and Méliès so famous; a cursory comparison of La Légende du fantôme (A Trip to Davy Jones' Locker, Segundo de Chomón, 1908), a stencilled masterpiece from Pathé, with a Film d'Arte Italiana production of the same period such as Francesca da Rimini (Ugo Falena, 1911) amply illustrates how the same technique of film colouring could be moulded to subversive or conservative ends. Regrettably, the difference between the two can barely be appreciated in reproductions: hand-colouring and stencilling, the most tactile expressions of silent cinema, are also the most elusive to the efforts of film preservation in achieving accurate reproductions of the originals. Abruptly dismissed after 1914, stencil colour sporadically reappeared in European films of the mid-1920s (Cyrano de Bergerac, Augusto Genina, 1923).

Tinting

A much simpler way to endow the cinematic image with a colour effect had been in place for more than a decade before stencilled prints reached the zenith of their commercial life. The first release copies uniformly tinted across the surface of the projected image appeared well before the end of the nineteenth century; one of the finest instances of this process is a British short, *Fire!* (James Williamson, 1901), celebrated for its bold editing technique. Much of the film's footage is in black and white; it becomes red in the sequence where flames have engulfed a building, threatening the life of its occupants. With the sudden appearance of a single colour, the drama unfolding in *Fire!* took on an extra element of suspense for the audience of its time, as it did when the same effect had been applied to magic lantern slides. Tinting was achieved by either brushing the aniline dye on the emulsion of the print (Plate 32), or more commonly by immersing the film stock in a tank where the colouring agent was diluted in water, a method that became standard in the production chain during the silent era (Plate 28).

Aniline colours are coal tar-based synthetic dyes that are water soluble; unfortunately, they are also light fugitive, meaning that they are susceptible to fading or being altered by temperature and humidity (film manufacturers did extensive research to come up with dyes that would not affect the stability of the gelatin layer and were stable enough to withstand the effects of repeated projection through a very hot and intense light source). Prints designed for tinting were processed with a slightly higher contrast than those to be projected as black and white copies. A third option for tinting, the manufacture of pre-tinted stock, was offered in the 1920s by major manufacturers like Eastman Kodak (nine tints available in 1921), AGFA, and Pathé. Sonochrome, a special set of tinted stock launched by Kodak around 1929, deserves mention as the product of a transitional phase in which the aesthetics of tinting were applied to early sound film: the softness of Sonochrome's palette, presented as a chromatic atlas of emotional moods (Fig. 39 and Plate 49), was designed so as not to interfere with the photoelectric cell of the soundtrack reader.

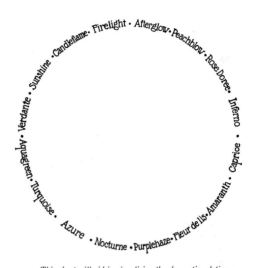

This chart will aid in visualizing the chromatic relationships of the sixteen Sonochrome tints in the hue cycle. The tints range from NOCTURNE, a cold violet-blue, to INFERNO, a fiery red tinged with magenta. Between these two on one side lie the purples PURPLEHAZE, FLEUR DE LIS, AMARANTH, and the purple-pink CAPRICE, on the other side the cool blues and greens from AZURE to VERDANTE, the warm yellows and oranges from SUNSHINE to AFTERGLOW, and the pinks PEACHBLOW and ROSE DOREE.

Fig. 39 Descriptive chart of the Kodak Sonochrome pre-tinted stock, *c.* 1929 (see Plate 49). Source: New Color Moods for the Screen. Rochester: Eastman Kodak Company, n.d. [ca. 1929].

Tinting is found in about two-thirds of surviving nitrate prints made during the silent era, mostly in the 1908–25 period; the percentage is higher if we include black and white copies with tinted intertitles, normally seen until 1914 as indicators of corporate identity and as deterrents to plagiarism: red tinting was a trademark of Pathé's title card, blue-green for Gaumont. The apparent decline of this technique during the late silent era may be attributed, among other things, to the growing attention bestowed upon new colour technologies such as Technicolor; in all likelihood, however, fewer tinted prints were made after 1925 because the personnel of film laboratories became aware that the added layer of colour on the base and the emulsion was smothering the subtle black and white gradations of panchromatic negatives; born with orthochromatic stock, tinting was not ideally suited to complement the subtler shades of grey registered by the new negative emulsion (orthochromatic film was still used for release prints). Tinting was applied to the positive film stock by assembling all the shots to be immersed in the same colouring bath. The tinted footage was then inserted in each release print according to the intended colour scheme: splices had to be made at every change from one colour to another, or from tinted to black and white stock and vice versa. The splicing process will be discussed in more detail in Chapter 14.

Filmmakers frequently turned this editorial necessity into a creative resource, as in interior scenes where a character enters a dark room (shown in black and white or blue) and turns on the light (the shot becomes tinted in amber). On other occasions, tinting plays a pivotal role in defining a dramatic situation. An instance of this is a scene in *The Lonedale Operator* (D.W. Griffith, 1911) where the daughter of the station master (Blanche Sweet) is threatened by two men in a train depot: to protect herself and the money in the room, she turns off the light and holds a nickel-plated monkey wrench in her right hand, pretending it is a gun. Her ruse succeeds. The glint of the metal object in the semi-darkness confuses the tramps, and their hesitation gives the girl's fiancé enough time to arrive for the providential last-minute rescue. In the many black and white reproductions of this film, the tool in the woman's hands is easily recognizable, and it seems absurd that her antagonists would fall for the trick. In fact, it is the viewer who is deceived, as the print is missing a deep blue tint simulating the darkness of the night, indirectly suggesting that the outlaws fail to realize what Blanche is actually holding.

Tinting positive stock in different hues without cutting it into pieces was by all means possible (it achieved remarkable effects, such as in the aforementioned transition from blue to amber, in order to show the coming of daylight), but also

very cumbersome and labour intensive; uncut nitrate prints of silent films with multiple tints are therefore comparatively rare (Plate 34). There are no splices, for instance, in a nitrate print of *The Four Horsemen of the Apocalypse* (Rex Ingram, 1921) during the shot of a woman singing the 'Marseillaise' while the image shifts from blue to black and white and red, alluding to the colours of the French flag. The effect was probably obtained by consecutively immersing portions of the footage in the same shot into different tinting baths without cutting the positive print (Plate 37a–c).

In 1916, Eastman Kodak published the first promotional book on tinted and toned film. The example was followed by Pathé and AGFA; their books and brochures contained actual samples of nitrate stock. The first known AGFA catalogue of tints and tones is dated August 1925; another one, with a much broader range of coloured nitrate frames, was distributed a few years later. Four revised and expanded editions of Kodak's manual were published between 1918 and 1927. Pathé produced a single volume, a striking compendium of tinting techniques whose nitrate samples vividly illustrate the degree of sophistication reached by this technique in the mid-1920s. Taken as a whole, these books are also revealing for the wealth of technical information they shared with the readers. Chemical formulas were not so secret; the magic was somewhere else, mostly in the smooth balance between the grading of the negative (p. 253) and the density of the tinting solution.

The examples of *Fire!* and *The Lonedale Operator* may give the impression that tinting and toning were used mainly to imitate reality. This was not necessarily the case. Analysis of surviving nitrate prints has revealed that monochrome images were equally employed for anti-naturalistic purposes, ranging from the description of emotional moods or atmospheres (red as a symbol of fear or unbridled passion) to sheer pictorialism, with no other motivation than the visual pleasure derived from embellishing the views in seemingly arbitrary variations. Different tints or tones may be applied to various shots in an exterior scene to act as discreet visual rhymes to accompany the film's narrative (a 1912 film by Georg af Klercker, *Dödshoppet från cirkuskupolen* [*A Fatal Decision*; or *The Great Circus Catastrophe*], offers a good demonstration of this).

Light ochre or amber tints were also uniformly applied throughout the entire length of projection prints, in the belief that they would lend a feeling of comfort and warmth to the viewing experience, or help conceal poor camerawork or film processing. This approach was frequently followed for copies destined for the non-theatrical and amateur market. The single-tint approach – supplemented by blue tints for nighttime scenes only when absolutely necessary – was a last resort stratagem for Poverty Row companies committed to giving their films a more dignified look; productions of this kind are sometimes notable for showing a certain degree of variety in the tinting schemes of the first reels, followed by fewer or no tints in the rest of the production.

Subterfuges of this kind were unnecessary in slapstick comedies, whose producers made no apologies for frequently releasing their films in black and white copies, as they were convinced that audiences were watching these shorts for reasons other than their colour schemes. These practices should be regarded as broad tendencies rather than rules systematically adopted by the global industry throughout the silent era. One of the main lessons to be learned from comparing two or more nitrate prints of the same film is that their tinting and toning schemes are rarely matching. When a production company sent the second negative of a new production to its overseas distributor, there was no guarantee that the original tints and tones would be reproduced exactly as instructed, and they often weren't.

Film audiences in each country also had their own preferences with regard to colour palette; some tinting and toning dyes may have been temporarily out of stock, or not available at all outside the country of origin; a foreign distributor may have wanted to cut corners in budgeting laboratory work, and so on. Three copies of *The Cossack Whip* (John H. Collins, 1916) with different tinting and toning schemes were found in the United States, Canada, and Great Britain. It would be very hard to assign the status of 'original version' to only one of them; all are equally authentic, in the sense that they are historically faithful reflections of the cultural and economic situations in which they were made and seen.

Toning

A subtler range of monochrome variations could be achieved with toning, a technique borrowed from still photography and introduced in film shortly after tinting. Positive prints were immersed in a chemical bath where the silver contained in the emulsion was replaced by a coloured compound that affected only the darker areas of the image. The rest of the gelatin surface remained colourless. As the chemical reaction occurred only in the presence of silver salts, the perforated edges of a toned nitrate print are not coloured (Plate 35); conversely, the film stock of a tinted print is coloured all over (Plates 33 and 34). This unmistakable visual cue is enough to tell the difference between tinted and toned prints; only a little extra attention is needed in those prints where the two techniques are combined with each other. Because it affected the chemical composition of the emulsion, toning could be applied only to photographic images of impeccable sharpness; anything less would have resulted in a vague but unpleasant haziness in the picture.

The toning dye was a coloured metallic salt, applied in the course of a process that could involve a single dye bath (direct toning), or two. In the two-baths version of the process, an uncoloured salt substituted the silver in the emulsion, which was subsequently treated with the pigmented salt. Mordanting, also known as dye fixing, was a variation of the toning procedure where the silver emulsion was replaced by a non-soluble silver salt; this metallic salt itself was only dimly coloured, or had no colour at all; its role was to function as a mordant, fixing the pigment in the next chemical bath. The intensity of the colour was directly proportional to the amount of mordanting material, which corresponded in turn to how much silver was originally contained in the emulsion. There is no obvious visual clue to tell the difference between toning and mordanting; nevertheless, an experienced eye can discern subtle but beautiful variations that escape a cursory look at the print. A case in point is silvered dark grey toning, whose unique atmospheric resonance is often mistaken for a very slightly faded black and white emulsion.

When tinting and toning were applied on the same print, their juxtaposition could produce results of outstanding beauty, as seen in *Maudite soit la guerre!* (Alfred Machin, 1914) and in many other films made between the mid-1900s and the late 1920s (Plate 29). European companies, especially Pathé and Gaumont, were unrivalled in their ability to blend the two techniques for the sake of both realism and fantasy. They went as far as adding stencil colour to tinted or toned prints (Plate 38), further multiplying the dazzling array of possibilities offered by the permutations of techniques and their respective colours. There were elements of unpredictability in this *ars combinatoria*: since prints had to be toned before being tinted, there was always a chance that the two chemical processes would interfere with each other in unforeseeable or destructive ways. Tinting and toning recipes were tested long before going into production, but laboratory technicians were fully aware of the risks they were taking. The 1922 edition of Eastman Kodak's tinting and toning

manual cautioned that toning and mordanting should not be applied to prints made for long-term preservation, as the gradual alteration of the emulsion was deemed inevitable, and its longevity impossible to forecast.

Kodak technicians strongly advised that high-quality conservation elements in black and white should be made for reference before toning and mordanting were applied to all release prints. Time has proven the Rochester scientists right, as the remaining extant copies of toned nitrate prints are relatively few, and definitely more vulnerable to decay. Let's now translate this empirical evidence into managerial language. Film manufacturers and entrepreneurs knew very well that the commercial life of a new film rarely exceeded two years (slightly longer in the early years of cinema, when films made in 1897 could still be available for sale in the 1904 catalogues of their producers); making them look beautiful was far more important than providing for their survival.

The combination of tinting and toning was therefore a potential liability, as projection prints could start decaying before the films had ended their profitable tours in theatres around the world. Conversely, pre-tinted film stock proved to be very stable when immersed in the developing and fixing baths. Colours were not as beautiful, but they were not altered by the heat and light of the projection equipment, not even after several screenings. The benefits of this innovation were soon to be felt in the non-theatrical market, where commercial films of the recent past continued to enjoy a long and often successful life in the form of 16mm prints.

Synthesis

Colour dyes applied directly onto positive prints dominated the scene until the late years of the silent film era. Their hegemony was challenged from the outset by several inventors, entrepreneurs, and scientists who tried a completely different route, employing a wide range of mimetic processes aimed at reproducing reality as seen by the human eye (hence the inaccurate but effective term 'natural colour', used to define them as a whole). These techniques, developed from the very beginnings of cinema, drew upon earlier experiments in the field of photography, namely by James Clerk Maxwell and Louis Arthur Ducos du Hauron. 'Natural colour' was achieved in cinema through so-called additive and subtractive processes.

Additive colour synthesis is obtained by green, blue, and red lights mixed with each other; when projected together, the light resulting from the addition of the three primary colours is pure white. When mixed in equal proportions, each two of the primary colours produce secondary colours: yellow (green plus red), cyan (green plus blue), and magenta (blue plus red). Conversely, subtractive colour is generated by pigments, inks, and dyes mixed with each other to absorb (that is, subtract) specific wavelengths of light. When superimposed on each other, the result of the subtraction of all the secondary colours (yellow, magenta, and cyan) is pure black. If combined in equal parts, each two of the secondary colours produce primary colours: red (magenta minus yellow), green (yellow minus cyan), and blue (magenta minus cyan).

The point of departure of additive colour systems is total darkness; subtractive colour systems start from pure white light. In 1898, British photographer William Friese-Greene began researching 'animated natural colour pictures' in two different ways. The first was to expose two or three consecutive images through coloured filters in succession. The black and white film derived from the negative was then projected (at double or triple projection speed) through rotating filters with the same colours used at the time of shooting (a Swiss scholar, Barbara Flückiger, calls this the 'temporal synthesis' approach). The other idea was to capture two or three images at the same time (hence the term 'spatial synthesis') with multiple lenses or beam-splitter prisms, and to have them individually tinted according to fixed patterns (Plate 40), or projected through coloured filters. Friese-Greene's pioneering work was of little or no consequence at the commercial level, but its theoretical foundations were of enormous importance in the development of the early Technicolor systems.

A third option for additive synthesis, predicated upon the recording or display of red, blue, and green dots or stripes arranged in regular or irregular patterns, was studied in photography and found some application with motion pictures. A collaboration between a French entrepreneur, Albert Keller-Dorian, and the astronomer Rodolphe Berthon resulted in the invention of lenticular film, where the cellulose film base functioned like a net of embossed microscopic lenses on a black and white film exposed through a trichromatic filter; when shown through a lens with vertical sections in green, blue, and red, the projected image revealed the three colours combined with each other. The patent for lenticular film was acquired by Eastman Kodak in 1915 and marketed to the amateur film community as Kodacolor, a special brand of 16mm film stock. Eastman Kodak also developed a subtractive process called Kodachrome, through a research project conducted by John G. Capstaff. Initially conceived in 1913 for still photography, the system was later adapted to motion pictures. A unique feature of its earliest version was the use of three film elements instead of two: a camera negative; a master positive; a duplicate negative turned into a positive with emulsions on both sides of the film stock.

Concerning $1,000 (1916) was the first fiction film made with the Kodachrome camera: its two lenses (one installed above the other) exposed negative stock, two frames at a time, through green and red filters (Plate 41). From the resulting positive, a printing apparatus with a beam splitter projected the alternate frames with the latent colours onto a negative stock covered with emulsion on both sides, ensuring that the two complementary images were in perfect registration with each other. A tanning developer hardened both emulsions; after bleaching away the silver, the unhardened portions were dyed red-orange on one side of the film (for the images taken through the green filter), and blue-green on the other (for the images taken through the red filter), thus turning the negative into a projection print. As the United States entered into World War I, the experiment was put on hold. Kodachrome's commercial life began only in 1922 under a different process developed five years earlier by Leopold D. Mannes and Leopold Godowsky Jr, with a mixed response from the industry, as competition was much fiercer than before. The concept of tanning, softening, and treating separate emulsions with different dyes would, however, find a more fertile application with Technicolor.

The dazzling patchwork quilt of early colour film is made of other similar devices and patents, scattered across the silent era in dozens of variations on the above themes. The vast majority of them never found an audience, let alone a marketplace; the only traces left by many of them are drawings and a few machines, with no actual films to look at. In the early years of cinema, additive systems took the lead in the competition for 'natural colour'; two front-runners in the race, Kinemacolor and Chronochrome, were novelties that achieved considerable success between 1908 and 1913 but disappeared from public sight soon after the curiosity factor had waned. Born as yet another

additive process, Technicolor was also doomed to fail if its founders had not turned their attention to other existing colour technologies, reinventing them as a technological marvel of lasting consequences for the film industry. The winner's story is so deeply intertwined with those of the defeated that a fully coherent narrative would have to include far more characters than those mentioned here. What follows only gives the broad strokes of a much larger and dramatic colour tapestry, yet to be explored in all its scope and depth.

Kinemacolor

The most successful 'natural colour' system of the early silent era was commercially developed in Great Britain between 1908 and 1913 on the initiative of an American-born film producer, Charles Urban. Back in 1897, Herman Isensee had discovered that colour separation could be obtained with tinted filters installed on a revolving shutter in front of the camera and projection lenses. The idea was further explored by other British film pioneers, including Edward Raymond Turner, Frederick Marshall Lee, William Norman Lascelles Davidson, and George Albert Smith; their research and patents provided the basis for Urban's Kinemacolor: standard 35mm black and white film stock was immersed in a sensitizing bath in order to make it reactive to the red wavelengths of the visible spectrum. A camera equipped with red and green filters on the revolving shutter recorded the pictures (Fig. 40a–c); the resulting film with alternating gradations of black and white was projected with the same colour filters (Plate 42). Both the camera and the projector had to run at 32 frames per second, as the images shown at the speed commonly used at that time (16 frames per second) would have been perceived as intermittent green and red flashes (experiments with an added blue filter required a threefold faster projection speed, 48 frames per second).

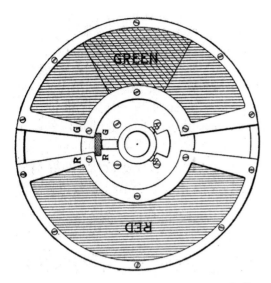

Fig. 40a Scheme of a shutter with coloured gelatin filters for the Kinemacolor process. Source: David S. Hulfish, Cyclopedia of Motion Picture Work. Chicago: American Technical Society, 1914, vol. I, p. 269.

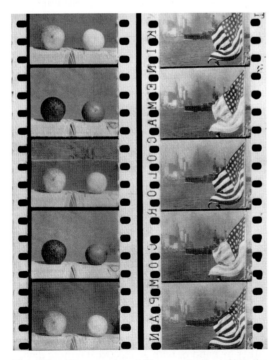

Fig. 40b–c Two samples of Kinemacolor films. Note the alternation in the black and white grading of the 35mm nitrate positives. Source: Courtesy of Laurent Mannoni.

Urban's decision to forego the blue filter was due to the distressing 'fringe' effect derived from the imperfect alignment of the alternating colour images, particularly acute in scenes with faster action; camera movements had to be kept very slow, or excluded altogether. Kinemacolor's 'natural' chromatic world was therefore a pastel-like blend of green, reds, and a brownish tinge reminiscent of Lumière's autochrome photography process (patented in 1903 and marketed four years later). Blue and violet were virtually absent from the projected image; white light tended to yellow, another colour otherwise scarcely visible on the screen except in various shades of orange. A slight amount of blue could be added to the green filter; blue was also present in the electric arc light of the projector. The overall effect was pleasing enough to make Kinemacolor a sensation with audiences of the early 1910s, who greeted its chromatic effects with qualified enthusiasm. The company's 1913 catalogue lists over four hundred titles available to exhibitors; dramatic subjects represented a meagre percentage of the total output (some fiction films were made by a Kinemacolor affiliate in the United States). The predominance of non-fiction titles is explained by the fact that the Kinemacolor system worked at its best in direct sunlight, and offered disappointing results with artificial lighting.

Kinemacolor's catalogue was emphatic in its assertion that the system was compatible with normal 35mm projection equipment, as it used 'film of the standard size and perforation', 'one lens of the ordinary kind', and 'one machine for both colour and black-and-white projection' (p. 12). While not altogether inaccurate, the claim was far-fetched. It was not an easy task to install a special rotating shutter in some projectors; their light sources had to be stronger to compensate for the added filters; last but not least, there were not enough films to allow continuous programming in the same format over an extended period of time. Kinemacolor equipment was licensed to hundreds of theatres – about 250 of them in Great Britain alone – as special attractions, mostly for a few months, with rare instances of tenures extended over a year or two. Trade journals reported complaints from audiences suffering from eyestrain caused by image flickering during prolonged viewings.

The undeniable charm of Kinemacolor's chromatic pageants such as *The Coronation Durbar at Delhi* (1912) also had a heavy material cost, as the screening time of a standard reel of film required twice the amount of footage in a Kinemacolor production because of the doubled projection speed. All these drawbacks contributed to the eventual demise of the system after its last public shows in 1918, exactly as had happened to other colour processes based on similar principles. There is an ironic postscript to this unhappy ending. The only way to reproduce the effect of Kinemacolor pictures on modern film stock without using the original equipment is to reproduce the colour of the filters on the print itself, making it look like a Friese-Greene film (Plates 43a–b). The 'betrayal' of the original process is compounded by the need to use red and cyan (instead of red and green) in order to provide a more plausible imitation of the Kinemacolor image on the screen.

Chronochrome

The issues of projection speed and colour registration were among the main topics covered in a presentation held in Paris on 15 November 1912 at the Société française de photographie, dedicated to a new two-colour additive system from Gaumont. It was called 'Biochrome'. A few months later, a three-colour version of the same additive process was launched under the name 'Chronochrome', with great acclaim on both sides of the Atlantic. An agent of Eastman Kodak attended with some trepidation the New York premiere in June 1913, as the company had assisted Gaumont's effort with the creation of a special panchromatic film on cellulose diacetate stock (see p. 27), sensitive to the full range of the visible spectrum. Unlike all other 'natural colour' processes designed so far, Chronochrome displayed a wide-ranging colour scheme with a black and white film of standard 35mm format. Instead of the two-colour rotating filter in the Kinemacolor apparatus, Gaumont's additive process employed a triple lens fitted with green, red, and blue filters in the camera and the projector, each picture being recorded in three black and white frames of different gradations (Plate 44a). When overlapped in projection, each with its respective filter, the three frames with their corresponding latent colours merged into a single trichrome picture.

A unique feature of the Chronochrome system is the height of its 35mm film frame, reduced from the 18mm in standard silent prints to 14mm, equal to a 1:1.71 aspect ratio. The panoramic look was meant to facilitate alignment of the converging projection angles, and to reduce the amount of film stock needed in cameras and projectors: with its narrower frames, a Chronochrome film used 2.25 times the amount of film stock of a conventional 35mm print, rather than three times as much, as would have been required with three frames of standard size for each picture. The central lens with a red colour filter was stationary; above and below it, the lenses with green and blue filters were adjusted vertically and horizontally, either by hand or with an electrical remote device controlled by a technician sitting in the auditorium. When properly in register, Chronochrome films are admired for the variety and brilliance of their colours. Pictures of inanimate objects captured at close range possess a startling three-dimensional look; the exquisite tonal harmony of outdoor scenes is especially striking where there are vast expanses of primary colours, as in the sea against a blue sky. The magic was dissolved in the blurred renditions of fast movements and small objects seen at long distances, exactly as had happened with Kinemacolor.

Gaumont's and Urban's additive colour systems required extra light to compensate for the filters: with its 33 per cent rate of light absorption, Kinemacolor used 250 per cent more electric power than a normal film projection; Chronochrome was even worse, as its blue filter alone absorbed almost one-third of all the available light from the projector's lamphouse. The fatal drawback of Gaumont's otherwise brilliant technique had to do with its mechanical design: Chronochrome films could be screened at the 'standard' speed of 16 frames per second, but were incompatible with conventional 35mm projectors because of Chronochrome's multiple exposure system (three frames projected at the same time) and aspect ratio; moreover, it was not possible to adapt the triple-lens device to any other projection equipment. Like all proprietary 'natural colour' systems of those years, Chronochrome was allowed to shine only on a very narrow commercial horizon, and for a very brief period of time. Its catalogue of available films was only a small fraction of what was being offered by Kinemacolor. With very few exceptions, such as the one-reeler *Un Conte d'Alsace* (*Heart's Memory. A Simple Alsatian Story*, 1920), Chronochrome was used exclusively for non-fictional subjects. It was deservedly praised in the early 1910s as a speciality item for high-profile venues, sometimes with the extra attraction of phonograph sound (an updated version of Gaumont's Chronophone system,

further described in Chapter 9). Ten years later, after a brief resurgence at the end of World War I (*Le Défilé de la victoire*, 1919), it was gone. As with the Kinemacolor process, Chronochrome films can be shown with modern film equipment only by recreating the effect of the projected image on the print itself, with the primary colours already combined in a single frame (Plate 44b).

Handschiegl

A revolutionary method for the mechanical application of colour to projection prints appeared in 1916 on the initiative of Cecil B. DeMille, who first used it for his epic *Joan the Woman*, premiered at the end of that year. Its inventor, Max Handschiegl, was working in St Louis, Missouri, as a photoengraver; in collaboration with DeMille and with his cameraman, Alvin Wyckoff, he conceived a new colour system derived from the lithographic process, by far the most ambitious ever designed up to that point. Its colours were also very beautiful to look at: surviving nitrate prints with the Handschiegl process (also known as the Wyckoff–DeMille process) are reminiscent of the chromatic nuances in glasswork by Victor Horta, René Lalique, and other designers of the Art Nouveau movement. Only a small number of films were made using this system, but it is appropriate to describe the process here because its basic concept was later borrowed by Technicolor for another experiment that changed the destiny of the company – and of cinema as a whole – at the end of the silent era.

In the preliminary stage of the Handschiegl process, a black and white print was used as a positive matrix for each colour (three colours was the maximum allowed for the same scene), as in the stencil method. Instead of cutting it, however, the emulsion of the area to be coloured was painted over, one frame at a time, with a special masking liquid. Once dried, the matrix was duplicated into an intermediate negative: the hidden area showed up on this duplicate negative as a transparent outline, while the rest of the frame retained the silver salts of the emulsion's reversed image. The exposed portions of the emulsion are less soluble than the unexposed areas: by immersing the print in a fixing solution of tanning bleach, the exposed gelatin was solidified in such a way as not to absorb any colouring agent. The unexposed section remained viscous and transparent.

After being fixed, washed, and dried, the internegative was immersed in a bath containing an aqueous colouring solution. The tinted film stock was then cleaned to eliminate any excess of colour dye, so that only the permeable areas retained the tinting. This new matrix was laid on top of a black and white print of the corresponding footage, in perfect register and with enough pressure to transfer the tint from the duplicate negative to the positive. To facilitate the transfer of the colour dye, the positive was treated with an emollient solution that moistened its emulsion, allowing it to absorb the tint from the internegative matrix. The internegative was therefore used as a sort of stamp that left its imprint on the projection copy. This delicate operation could be performed only twice, for the very same reason why a stamp cannot leave a clear impression unless it is periodically re-inked. Every two transfers, the duplicate negative had to be dipped again in the colouring bath.

The fixing solution for the duplicate negative also had a limited lifespan, as it began to dissolve after about forty positive prints had been stamped. At that point, the tinting solution would gradually bleed throughout the emulsion, rendering the internegative of no further use as a matrix: another one had to be created, by repeating the procedure outlined above. For this and other reasons, the Handschiegl process could only be

used in relatively short scenes, and was not suitable for a printing process on a large industrial scale; Handschiegl personally supervised the creation of every matrix, closely monitoring all phases of the production workflow. His source of inspiration, lithography, can be easily translated in cinematic terms: one strip of nitrate cellulose served as printing stone; another one – the projection print – replaced paper as the recipient of the coloured image.

About twenty feature films with this colour system (alone or in conjunction with toning, or with an early Technicolor process) were produced between 1916 and 1927, the year before Handschiegl's premature death. The technique relied on craftsmanship of the highest order, even more so than with hand-colouring and stencil because of the chemistry involved. To the uninitiated eye, Handschiegl tints can be mistaken for those of stencilled films, but their subtler translucence and textures brought a special atmospheric quality to the scene, or to the graphic designs of title cards where the colours were sometimes applied.

The pastel-like luminosity of the Handschiegl image is especially effective in those settings where natural elements like fire and water are predominant. A case in point is offered by the final sequence of *Joan the Woman*, where Geraldine Farrar's body is enveloped in flames and smoke; in *The Ten Commandments* (Cecil B. DeMille, 1923), the Egyptian army pursuing the Jews is first obstructed by a wall of fire, then drowned in the Red Sea, with the Pharaoh and his horse plunged in a dazzling splash of emerald green. The glowing yellow of a golden tooth in Erich von Stroheim's cursed masterpiece *Greed* (1925) must have had an indelible effect upon its audiences, insofar as they had a chance to see it on one or more of the versions released throughout the film's tormented life in theatres of the silent era (Plate 45).

When projected onto the big screen, Handschiegl colour has an astounding evocative power that no reproduction in any medium and format can possibly emulate. At their best, modern copies make it look like a faint stencilled film; vague but somehow more faithful impressions can be derived from looking at a nitrate copy on a manual film inspection bench. Stencil colours could only exist as clear-cut silhouettes; by using a brush instead (on the positive matrix), Handschiegl had achieved lithography by other means, and reconciled hand-colouring with mechanization. The chemicals involved in Handschiegl prints make them more vulnerable to decomposition, as shown in surviving elements. Their impermanence is yet another proof of cinematic colour's intrinsic status as simulacrum of an unattainable visual experience, a chromatic event belonging to spectators who cannot relate its story. The point was lyrically expressed in 1994 by filmmaker Derek Jarman: 'I know that my colours are not yours. Two colours are never the same, even if they're from the same tube. Context changes the way we perceive them' (*Chroma*, pp. 42–3). His unequivocal verdict can be read as a humbling counterpoint to film preservation: 'I prefer that colours should float and take flight in your minds'.

Technicolor

When Herbert T. Kalmus and his associates established the Technicolor Motion Picture Corporation in 1915, its early steps were not too different from those documented in many other half-forgotten patents from the period. The future arbiter of chromatic taste in the film entertainment industry began its corporate life with three different systems developed over the second half of the silent era. They are often referred to by a numbering sequence, simply to indicate their chronological order: no. 1 (additive), no. 2 (cemented), no. 3 (two-strip dye-transfer). Technicolor no. 4, a three-strip dye-transfer process, fully belongs to the sound film era.

The first Technicolor system (1916) was the only one developed by the company on the basis of the additive synthesis principle; behind the lens of its camera was a beam splitter that divided the light into two separate colour records (red and green) on every other frame of the same 35mm negative. Projectors had to be specially equipped with two lenses coated with colour filters, aligned in such a way that the two complementary images were superimposed on one another. The only film made with this additive process, *The Gulf Between* (Wray Physioc, 1917), failed because of a malfunction of the registration device, with wide colour fringes appearing on the screen.

Undeterred by the failure, the company's investors continued to provide financial support to their research staff. Technicolor's first camera using a subtractive process (1921) was inspired in part by an earlier patent by Arturo Hernandez-Mejia (Colorgraph, 1916). As in the previous Technicolor system, a beam-splitting prism separated the light into alternate colour records (again, red and green), with two frames exposed at the same time (Plate 46); in this case, every other latent image on the negative appeared upside down, so that the bottom edges in each pair of frames were in contact (Fig. 41).

The printing process of Technicolor no. 2 was also very different: each of the two colour records was reproduced on a separate reel; the two positives were then cemented to each other's base, resulting in a thicker film where each side had its own emulsion. The latent red and green frames were tinted, respectively, with green and red dyes. Once combined in projection, the two subtractive records conveyed an image of limited but pleasing chromatic range, as seen in Metro Pictures'

Fig. 41 Technicolor Process no. 2. *The Black Pirate* (Albert Parker, 1926). 35mm nitrate negative. Every other image is reversed, with the bottom edges of the two frames in contact. Source: Courtesy of Kevin Patton, BFI National Archive, London.

The Toll of the Sea (Chester M. Franklin, 1922), with a lesser fringe effect than the one suffered by the previous system. The film worked so well with theatrical audiences that the production company had a hard time meeting the demand for extra prints. Films produced in the new Technicolor process could be shown on any standard projector, with no extra lenses or filters required.

Over twenty feature films and a handful of shorts were made with sequences shot in this groundbreaking process; the masked ball scene in *The Phantom of the Opera* (Rupert Julian, 1925) and a fashion parade in *Irene* (Alfred E. Green, 1926) are among the highlights of this second phase in Kalmus' chromatic adventure. By the time Douglas Fairbanks made his first appearance in a Technicolor film, *The Black Pirate* (Albert Parker, 1926), however, everyone agreed that the price to pay for two positives glued to each other was extremely high. Release prints were susceptible to heavy curling, the cause of an ongoing nightmare in the projection booth, as operators were often frustrated in their attempts to maintain the picture's focus.

Due to their differing chemical structure, the emulsion and the base of a motion picture film are subject to different rates of shrinkage. Keeping them together on a single strip was hard enough; no adhesive could guarantee that four layers (two bases and two emulsions) would stay in perfect registration over an extended period of time. Last but not least, a projection element with the emulsion on both sides of the print was more likely to suffer from scratches after repeated screenings. As in all other two-colour subtractive systems, the second Technicolor process was particularly weak in reproducing yellow, blue, and purple on the screen.

The turning point came in 1926, when Kalmus and his staff came up with a brilliant synthesis of the additive and subtractive processes developed by Technicolor and its many competitors over the previous two decades. A camera with two separate negatives exposed them simultaneously, through a single lens, splitting light into a red and a green record. Instead of using the two combined negatives to make positive prints, the new system involved the creation of two positive matrices with a thicker emulsion (hence its laboratory nickname, 'relief film'), each imbibed with the respective toning dye. The matrices were then pressed in quick succession on a special kind of unprocessed film stock with a softened emulsion, very similar to the lithographic process (and to the Handschiegl colour system). To ensure an exact registration of the dye imprints, the matrix and the blank film were stretched upon a 35mm-wide steel pinbelt.

In dramatic terms, *The Viking* (R. William Neill, 1929) – the first feature film made with the Technicolor no. 3 (in technical terms, 'two-strip dye-transfer') process – was a rather mediocre film, but from a purely visual standpoint the new system worked beautifully; even more so in a stronger picture like *Redskin* (Victor Schertzinger, 1929; see Plate 47), where the difference between the monochrome world (tinted amber) of the white people and the chromatic culture of the Native Americans (in glorious Technicolor) was so striking as to leave little doubt about the future of Kalmus' company. Technicolor no. 4, a three-strip version of the same dye-transfer process, was devised in the early 1930s. It dominated the market for decades, until its decline in the 1970s and definitive disappearance in 2002.

Technicolor's warm tones and subtle control of colour saturation were critical to the achievement of a smoother, more versatile palette; after the flawed results of the first two systems, the overall effect of the third on the audiences of the late silent period seemed to finally transcend the technological rationale of the technique. One could still argue about *Redskin*'s imperfect colour registration, its blue skies leaning towards green, the muted yellows of some scenes, the problems in rendering flesh tones. These issues were discussed as matters of taste rather than mechanics. After many years of frustrating efforts, a colour film process had achieved the goal of making 'invisible' the technology that produced it.

Technicolor wasn't a priori the best contender in the race: it prevailed over Charles Urban's Kinemacolor, William van Doren Kelley's Prizma (first developed in 1916 as an additive system, then as a double-coated subtractive colour film in 1919: see Plate 48a–b), and all the other competitors primarily because its scientists, managers, and investors kept trusting each other's determination to succeed in spite of repeated setbacks and false starts. Even more importantly, they did so for an extended period of time. They were persistent enough to learn from their own mistakes, rather than withdraw in fear of continuing failures or financial losses. By earning its authority through constant trial and error, Technicolor defined the terms of engagement between 'natural' colour for the big screen and its audiences for many years to come. Hundreds of worthy experiments held in the same period are now obscure footnotes, chromatic utopias of silent cinema.

Chapter 4

Machines

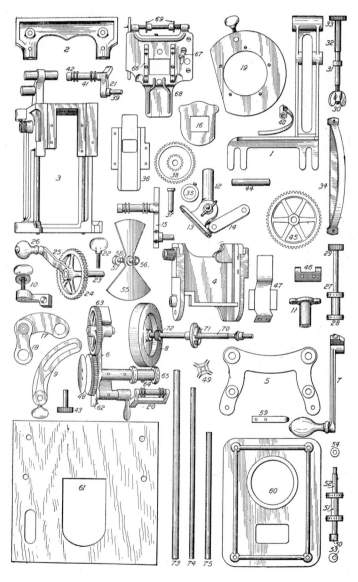

Fig. 42 Parts of the Power's Cameragraph No. 5 film projector. Nicholas Power Company, New York, 1908. Source: David S. Hulfish, Cyclopedia of Motion Picture Work. Chicago: American Technical Society, 1914, vol. I, p. 196.

Taking sequential photographs on a flexible strip of celluloid had at least two challenges: devising a mechanism to move the film at regular intervals through an optical recording instrument, and ensuring that the consecutive images would be perceived as a steady flow when exhibited in quick succession. A third requirement – controlling the amount of light allowed through the lens – had already been met with the introduction of the iris diaphragm, although there is no certainty on who invented it (Fig. 43). Photographers and scientists had undertaken research on these topics since 1870, often for educational purposes or pure research. Their names and their devices are celebrated as the founding fathers of cinema: among them are Eadweard Muybridge in the United States, Étienne-Jules Marey (Chronophotographie, 1882) and Georges Demenÿ in France, Ottomar Anschütz (Elektrotachyscop, 1887) in Germany, and Louis Aimé Augustin Le Prince, who worked in Great Britain and the United States before disappearing (16 September 1890) in mysterious circumstances.

By the time Edison's Kinetoscope and Lumière's Cinématographe were seen in action, the key mechanical issue had been more or less resolved. One of the solutions was borrowed from the sewing machine's traditional design: the film was intermittently pulled – one frame at a time – by metal pins moving in and out the film's perforations; in other equipment – including the Cinématographe – the same traction

was achieved by a claw with two or more prongs (Fig. 44). Image stability took longer to be fully managed: it was still a problem in 1908, both for cameras and projectors, at a time of rapid growth in the film industry. Exhibitors had more than their share of trouble, as they realized that intermittence might be good for cinema, but also a potential nuisance to the public. Picture flickering, steadiness, and luminosity remained major concerns for cinematographers, theatre operators, and audiences throughout the silent film era. Much of the technological history of silent cinema is epitomized by these variables. A fourth concept, speed, brought them all together, with music accompanists joining the debate.

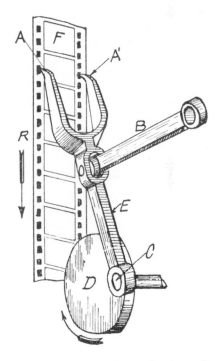

Fig. 44 The intermittent movement of a claw pulling the film, one frame at a time, from the feeding to the take-up magazine of a motion picture camera. Source: Rathbun, John B. Rathbun, Motion Picture Making and Exhibiting. Los Angeles: Holmes, 1914, p. 21.

Fig. 43 Phases in the movement of the diaphragm in a film camera. Source: Private collection.

Cameras

Many of the cameras and projectors from the silent film period are beautiful objects to behold, and a true pleasure to see in action: some of them stand out as eye-catching jewels of craftsmanship (Plate 23a–c). The two types of machines functioned in very similar ways, albeit with mechanisms of various kinds. An ingenious two-wheel movement called the 'Maltese cross', developed in 1896 by René Bünzli and Pierre-Victor Continsouza (Fig. 45), was the most widely adopted for film projectors (Figs. 46 and 47 illustrate how the mechanism works), but there were many others; one of them, generally referred to as the 'Geneva' drive (often confused

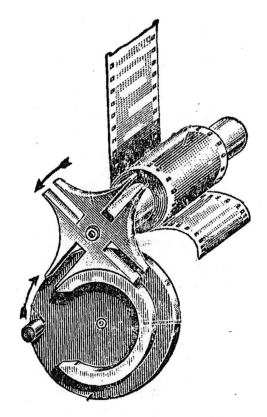

Fig. 47 The 'Maltese cross' mechanism in relation to a 35mm sprocket and film. Source: Hermann Joachim, Die Kinematographische Projektion (Halle [Saale], Wilhelm Knapp, 1928) [Guido Seeber and F. Paul Liesegang (eds.), Handbuch der Praktischen Kinematographie. Band III: Die Vorführung des Films. 1. Teil], p. 29.

Fig. 45 The 'Maltese cross' mechanism. Source: Cinémathèque française. Photo by Stéphane Dabrowski.

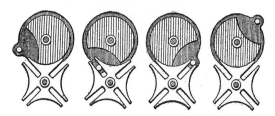

Fig. 46 The movement of the 'Maltese cross' mechanism. Source: Private collection.

with Continsouza's Maltese cross), takes this name because of its resemblance to those used in mechanical watches from Switzerland (in fact, the camera's intermittent device is quite different). In order to prevent the light from exposing the emulsion while the strip was moved to the next position, the pins or claw that controlled the film's progression within the cameras and in most projectors were connected to a rotating disc with one or more blades (Fig. 48), covering the lens or the aperture gate until the following section of the strip was firmly in place. To compensate for the movement at both ends of the intermittent mechanism in the projector (and in some cameras), the threaded film was arranged in two

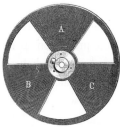

Fig. 48 Two- and three-blade shutters. Source: Hermann Joachim, Die Kinematographische Projektion. Halle [Saale], Wilhelm Knapp, 1928, p. 41.

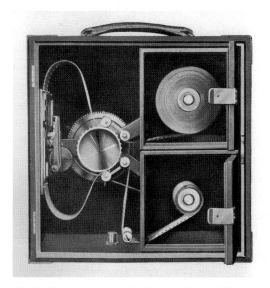

Fig. 49 Threading path of the film negative in a Williamson camera, Great Britain, 1910. Source: H.M. Lomas, Picture Play Photography (London: Ganes, 1914, p. 92).

opposite loops so that for each segment added to the top loop, another one was removed at the bottom (Fig. 49). They were called 'Latham loops', as the original idea was attributed to Woodville Latham, who patented it in 1886.

These operating principles are of the greatest significance in the history of cinema, as the consecutive images had to be duplicated and exhibited exactly as they were taken (many film printers also have a transport mechanism and a shutter). The Lumière brothers understood this from the outset, as shown by their Cinématographe, which could

adequately perform all three functions. In the Lumière camera, printer, and projector – as well as in most other machines of the silent era – the film was run through the equipment's gears with a hand crank. This meant that the operator was in complete control of the speed at which each frame of the film was exposed to the light; the rate could be as slow as 10 frames per second or below, and increased to 40 frames and beyond.

Turning the crank at a faster rate would give a more accurate rendition of the movement in the projected image, but also use a longer strip of expensive film stock for the same running time; the financial burden was actually doubled, as the camera speed and the projection speed were supposed to be one and the same (as will be shown later, this was not necessarily the case). It was generally agreed that, once some precautions were taken to reduce flicker, 16 frames per second were sufficient for a good film projection. In most camera equipment, this corresponded to two turns of the crank for each second, a rhythm sometimes achieved by humming, whistling, or mentally singing a familiar tune while shooting. Motor-driven cameras – activated by spring mechanisms or electric power – were in use before Lumière (by Marey and Edison) and afterwards (by the American Mutoscope & Biograph Company for its 68mm films); they remained the exception until 1919, when Bell & Howell introduced its 2709B model, followed by others by Debrie, Gillon, and Éclair in the early 1920s.

There is something almost magical about number eight and its multiples in the history of cinema. Fig. 50 shows the unity of measure of this mystique, a tiny but fundamental piece of engineering that embodies the consensus reached by film manufacturers in the 1900s on the standard shape and size of motion picture stock. It's a sprocket, a metal object of cylindrical shape with two sets of sixteen or thirty-two teeth protruding from the edges (its centre is hollow because

Fig. 50 A sixteen-tooth 35mm film sprocket. Source: Private collection.

the film's emulsion would otherwise be scratched through continuous friction with the surface). There are eight sprocket holes on both sides of a 35mm film, and 16 frames per foot. Sixteen images were individually exposed to light for one second inside the camera and during projection (in 1917, the Society of Motion Picture Engineers tried, unsuccessfully, to make this an industry standard). The number of teeth in camera and projector sprockets varies greatly from one model to another, but sixteen and thirty-two appear more frequently in film machines of the silent era.

The rapid and ongoing movement of the film and the registration pins or claws behind the aperture gate was a potential source of trouble, as it could adversely affect the quality of projection prints and negatives. The slightest irregularity in the mechanism or in the film perforations would prevent the camera or projector from keeping the consecutive images in perfect register, causing the projected picture to jump up and down, or even laterally, on the screen. Moreover, motion picture stock is not an inert piece of plastic: it is a thin, fragile, multilayered ribbon whose organic components shrink and expand – both in length and width – with changes in temperature and

humidity. When put in a projector, each frame of the film was briefly exposed to extreme heat. If the projection speed was too slow, or the film remained stuck between the light source and the aperture gate, the frame would instantly burn (if its base was cellulose nitrate) or melt (if it was diacetate).

A very slight 'breathing' effect – that is, a constant but almost imperceptible vertical and horizontal shift – in the projected picture was, and still is, considered normal (as opposed to current digital projection, where the image is absolutely steady), but the phenomenon was often more pronounced and severely disruptive in the earliest years of cinema. Manufacturers of motion picture cameras competed for years to address this problem. Picture instability plagued the viewing experience for more than a decade; in late 1907, the Italian production company Itala-Film inaugurated its trademark logo of a veiled woman holding a light, the rays of which form an inscription – the French word *fixité* – to signify that the work presented under that brand was rock-steady on the screen. Until and sometimes beyond the early 1910s, major production companies such as Vitagraph, Biograph, Gaumont, and Pathé preferred to make their own film equipment. As time went by, the soaring demand for projection machines drove manufacturers in Europe and North America to compete for leadership in the international market.

Lenses

Pathé, Ernemann, Prestwich, Prévost, Moy, and Debrie's 'Parvo' were the most popular cameras in the mid-1910s, with Pathé as the undisputed leader in the professional market, soon joined by Bell & Howell and by the Mitchell Camera Company in the United States. A major breakthrough came in 1911 with Bell & Howell's

2709 camera, whose success was largely based on a revolutionary mechanism with fixed registration pins (instead of ones that moved in and out of the film's perforations): in each advance of the frame, a 'shuttle gate' clenched the film and moved it towards the stationary pins. The long-time dominance of the 2709 model would not be challenged until 1920, when a Mitchell camera with a sophisticated focusing mechanism became the preferred option in the Hollywood studios.

Shortly after Kodak's introduction of 16mm stock, Bell & Howell presented in 1923 a spring-wound camera for amateur filmmakers ('Filmo'). This proved so successful that its 35mm equivalent ('Eyemo') was marketed two years later: it was praised by professionals for its versatility in newsreel shooting, aerial shots, and all circumstances where hand-held camerawork was required. Semi-automatic cameras (first launched by Gaumont with the Chrono de poche in 1900) became the rage in the amateur market, with Kodak and Pathé promoting an increasingly broad variety of models at relatively moderate costs. The best machines, however, remained quite expensive throughout most of the silent period: as of 1919, prices ranged from US$35 for the cheapest cameras in substandard formats to US$1,000 and more for the high-end models.

A major factor in assessing the cost of a camera was the quality of the lens and, in the feature film era, the viewfinders and turreted lens systems that allowed for the rapid change of up to four different lenses, each with its corresponding focal length. Focal length is the measurement of the distance between the lens and the point where it projects a focused image on the surface of the film within the camera. The normal focal length of a 35mm motion picture camera lens is 50mm. A lens with a longer focal length than 50mm has the effect of magnifying the scene and making the background appear closer to the subject; a shorter focal length lens captures more peripheral information and visually pushes the background away from the subject.

Lenses are basically prisms with a curved surface (Fig. 51). Their raw components were the same as those employed for glass: sand, soda, potash and lime (sometimes mixed with barium and lead), melted at extremely high temperatures; the resulting solid was very slowly cooled for about four days, broken into pieces, finely ground to obtain a curved surface as desired, and polished to make it perfectly transparent. Lenses were sold as separate items from the body of the camera. The average lens was of short focus to allow greater depth of field. The most common motion picture camera lenses in the late 1910s had a maximum aperture rated at f/3.5, a standard measure of how fast the light travelled through the lens. Such lenses required filming by natural sunlight. The higher quality lens manufacturers such as Carl Zeiss in Jena, Germany, and Bausch & Lomb in Rochester, New York, eventually offered lenses at the end of the silent era in speeds as fast as f/2.3 or even f/1.5, suitable for shooting interior scenes with electric incandescent lights, giving cinematographers much more flexibility in lighting scenes for special effects.

Don't be fooled by the mediocre – if not appalling – look of many silent films available today

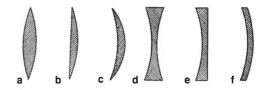

Fig. 51 The main types of lenses used in film cameras and projectors. From left to right: (a) bi-convex; (b) plano-convex; (c) concavo-convex (or positive) meniscus; (d) biconcave; (e) plano-concave; (f) convexo-concave (or negative) meniscus. Converging lenses (a–c) are thicker in the middle than at their edges; Diverging lenses (d–f) are thinner in the middle. Source: Bernard E. Jones, How to Make and Operate Moving Pictures. New York and London: Funk & Wagnalls, 1916, p. 75.

through modern copies or transfers. By and large, their clarity, texture, and richness of detail were outstanding, even by current standards. One of the best cinematographers in the early years of cinema, Gottfried Wilhelm ('Billy') Bitzer, was so proud of the 1902 Zeiss Tessar lens installed in his Biograph camera that when he and D.W. Griffith abandoned the Biograph Company in 1913, and Griffith asked him to leave it behind, Bitzer almost balked at the prospect; it was only after trying a Pathé camera built in 1905 by Pierre-Victor Continsouza that he reluctantly agreed to go along with it. Zeiss and Bausch & Lomb had already been in the photography business for many years, and the diaphragms of their lenses could be adjusted with the greatest degree of subtlety one would have expected in a still camera of the period. If the late G.W. Bitzer had known how today's audiences were seeing most of his films from the 1908–13 period, he would probably have been appalled. There are, fortunately, enough exceptions to prove what extraordinary artistry he displayed when painting with light on a celluloid strip through a wooden hand-cranked box.

Processing

The look of a silent film on the big screen was greatly influenced by the expertise and skills of technicians in the developing room (Fig. 52). In this sense, laboratory work could emphasize, improve upon, or diminish the quality of the images captured by the camera negative on the set, very much akin to what could happen with photographs in a darkroom. In very broad terms, the processing of motion picture film is similar to the gelatin dry-plate method in still photography, the main difference being the equipment used for long strips of cellulose. The most common workflow was known in colloquial terms as 'rack and tank': the exposed film roll or cartridge was extracted from the camera and wound on wooden frames of various configurations and sizes (Fig. 53 and 59). With orthochromatic film, this was done in a room with deep amber or red light, so as not to further expose the stock. The racks were consecutively dipped into four different vertical tanks, each of

Fig. 52 Preparing exposed film stock for processing. Éclair Company, Fort Lee, New Jersey, 1912. Gelatin silver print. Source: George Eastman Museum.

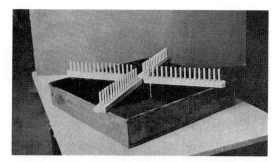

Fig. 53 Tray and star-shaped rack for film processing, c. 1912. Source: Carl L. Gregory, Motion Picture Photography. New York: Falk Publishing Company, 1927, p. 368.

them containing the chemical substances and water required for each processing step. The temperature of the developing baths was strictly controlled and kept constant, as the slightest variation affected the final outcome (Fig. 54a–f). The first tank was filled with film developer, whose main active ingredients were metol and hydroquinone; in the jargon of film laboratories, their combination was referred to as MQ developer.

When the motion picture film rolled in the camera, the light coming through the lens activated electrons in the silver bromide of the emulsion. Once immersed in the developer, the silver bromide exposed to the light was transformed into metallic silver. This operation lasted for about ten minutes, during which the racks or the liquid were occasionally agitated in order to bring fresh chemicals in contact with the emulsion. The progress of the development could be followed with the naked eye in the red light of the room, thus enabling the technician to determine whether the film had to be kept in the tank for a longer or shorter period of time (to enhance density, or to cut it back). Conversely, panchromatic film processing occurred either in total darkness or under a very dark green light. This applied only to the development of the film negative; positive prints were still made on orthochromatic stock, and could be processed under red safe light.

As soon as the film was fully developed, the rack was moved to a second tank where the chemical process triggered in the previous one was stopped by acetic acid, a very strong form of vinegar. The film stock remained there for about a minute, during which time the acetic acid also removed the residual developer that would otherwise contaminate the chemicals in the ensuing bath. The third tank contained a fixing agent, sodium thiosulfate, commonly referred to as 'hypo' because it was known as hyposulfite of sodium when British polymath Sir John Herschel introduced it in 1819. Four or five minutes are needed in the fixing bath, during which time the hypo eliminates all the creamy-coloured silver bromide that was not exposed to the light in the camera, leaving behind only the metallic silver image and the clear gelatin binder formerly mixed with the silver bromide of the emulsion.

Once fixed (or 'cleared', in laboratory jargon), the film stock was finally moved into a fourth tank filled with running water, where it remained for about twenty minutes to ensure that all chemicals from the previous bath were dissolved (a separate washing agent recommended by Kodak helped the water flow away without leaving spots on the emulsion). British film pioneer Cecil M. Hepworth deposited in 1898 the patent for a very sophisticated system for the entire path of film developing, which even included a perforating machine, a printer, a dryer, and a rewinder that could operate both before and after the developing baths (maybe also including those required for tinting and toning); unfortunately, no example of this brilliant invention is known to have survived. Between 1906 and 1907, Gaumont and Pathé secretly developed an experimental system (Fig. 55) for continuous film processing in consecutive baths (contrary to Hepworth's visionary scheme, no printing or perforating was involved). This technology, borrowed from

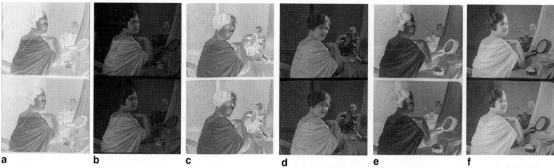

a   b   c   d   e   f

Fig. 54a–f The effects of different processing temperatures in developing baths on negative film with same exposure: (a–b) 14–15°C; (c–d) 18°C; (e–f) 23°C. 35mm nitrate negatives of unidentified film. The positive images have been digitally created for this book. Source: AGFA Kine-Handbuch, Teil IV, Film-Muster-Tabellen (n.l. [Wolfen], n.d. [ca. 1929], 3 vols.; English translation, Kine Handbook (n.l. [Wolfen], n.d. [ca. 1929], Table I).

Fig. 55 Léopold Löbel's concept of a prototype machine for continuous film processing of positive films in consecutive baths, c. 1910. Source: Léopold Löbel, La Technique cinématographique. Paris: Dunod et Pinat, 1912, p. 263.

similar equipment used for the mass production of photographic postcards, would eventually become standard in film laboratories worldwide (Fig. 56 and 57) but had a very slow start after Éclair's first patent submitted in 1912, and did not become widespread as quickly as expected.

Fig. 56 Continuous film processing in consecutive baths. Multiplex Debrie, Paris, c. 1925. Gelatin silver print. Source: Cinémathèque francaise.

Fig. 57 Film developer (detail) at the Haghefilm Digitaal laboratories, Amsterdam, 2015. Source: Photo by Juan Vrijs.

The photo reproduced in Fig. 58 documents two phases of the developing process. On the left, a man is winding the exposed film onto a wooden rack for processing. To facilitate his job, the rack is installed on a floor stand, where it revolves on its horizontal axis. Behind him, note the light creamy-coloured unexposed film stock,

ready for immersion in the developing bath; on the right, another man holds a rack where some images are beginning to appear on the emulsion. This photo could only be taken in a workspace with a red safe-light source. The image reproduced in Fig. 59, on the other hand, was made in normal light: a technician is inspecting a rack of developed, fixed, and washed film in front of what looks like a window. At this point, the film stock was ready to be removed from the rack and transferred for drying on large cylindrical racks with wooden slats (Fig. 60). On the far left of the drying room shown in Fig. 61 there are some empty processing racks; at the very back of the room, a man is unwinding film from one of these racks onto the slowly revolving cylinders, with the aid of the same kind of floor stand previously used to prepare the exposed stock for the developing process. Before the introduction of Kodak's washing agent, the dried film was wound on another drum of smaller size, covered with a

Fig. 58 Processing exposed film stock on wooden racks by immersion in developing tanks. Rothacker Film Manufacturing Company, Chicago, c. 1912. Source: Austin C. Lescarboura, Behind the Motion Picture Screen. New York: Munn, 1919, p. 209.

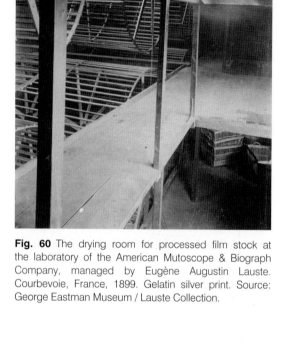

Fig. 60 The drying room for processed film stock at the laboratory of the American Mutoscope & Biograph Company, managed by Eugène Augustin Lauste. Courbevoie, France, 1899. Gelatin silver print. Source: George Eastman Museum / Lauste Collection.

Fig. 59 Inspecting processed film stock after the developing bath. Source: Austin C. Lescarboura, Behind the Motion Picture Screen. New York: Munn, 1919, p. 205.

fine cotton cloth, on which the film was polished to remove all residual stains left by water after evaporation.

The procedure described here applied to both negative and positive motion picture stock (Gaumont had employed its own system since 1905, with film stock being developed in tubes rather than tanks, and dried in warm ventilated closets instead of rotating drums). There is no significant difference between the two types of film in the theory and practice of film processing, other than the final result: two black and white images with opposite tonal values. Projection prints to be tinted or toned were subject to at least one additional bath (see Chapter 3) before being forwarded to the assembly room. Given

the extremely limited range of film stocks available during the silent era, the darkroom was both the cinematographer's only opportunity to correct mistakes in the camerawork, and the place where its interpreters, working with little or no light, had the almost absolute power of making it look beautiful or ugly (Fig. 62a–f).

Printers

Once ready for printing, the processed negative was taken to another laboratory for the creation of projection prints in the required number of duplicates (Fig. 63). In theory, this could be easily done by exposing the positive stock against a light source of uniform intensity through the entire

Fig. 61 Drying room with revolving drums for processed film stock. Source: Austin C. Lescarboura, Behind the Motion Picture Screen. New York: Munn, 1919, p. 205.

set of negatives (the 'one-light' system); practice, however, suggested that every shot or group of shots had been exposed or maybe processed differently, therefore requiring a specific amount of light in the printing process. Two competing viewpoints emerged on this issue. On the one hand, laboratory technicians argued that the burden of responsibility in providing a properly exposed negative was up to the cinematographers; consciously or not, they were underplaying their own role in film processing. In response, cameramen argued that it was up to the processing and printing laboratories to obtain the best possible illustration of their work.

Both parties had valid reasons for their claims. They could have gone even further by acknowledging their mutual dependence in giving shape to the cinematic image in its path from the camera to the big screen. Something may have gone wrong at the time of shooting because of bad weather, failure of the lighting equipment, or other mishaps beyond the cameraman's control. In the darkroom, impure water, poor chemicals, or the wrong temperature in the developing baths could ruin a flawlessly exposed negative. Careless printing was no less detrimental to the quality of the final product than over- or underexposing the negative in the developing bath.

The compromise they reached was as simple in its premise as it was effective in its concrete application. By printing two or more short

Fig. 62a–f The effects of different exposures of negative film stock with the same processing method: (a–b) underexposed; (c–d) correct exposure; (e–f) overexposed. 35mm nitrate negatives of unidentified film. The positive images have been digitally created for this book. Source: AGFA Kine-Handbuch, Teil IV, Film-Muster-Tabellen (n.l. [Wolfen], n.d. [ca. 1929], 3 vols.; English translation, Kine Handbook (n.l. [Wolfen], n.d. [ca. 1929], Table I.

segments of the same footage at different light levels, or by comparing the negative with a set of other negatives of varying density against a light source, the technician could determine the correct printing time for each section of the negative on a case by case basis. The negative was threaded in a printing machine (Fig. 64), in contact or near an unexposed strip of positive stock, with the two emulsions facing each other in front of a rectangular gate almost exactly as

Fig. 63 The printing room at the Éclair Company. Fort Lee, New Jersey, 1911. Gelatin silver print. Source: George Eastman Museum.

large as a single frame of film (its area was in fact slightly smaller; as a result, the printed frame was often surrounded by a tiny dark edge).

At each stop of the two overlapping strips of film through an intermittent mechanism, a properly calibrated beam of light was briefly projected through the negative, exposing the positive strip for the required time; the frames of both films were then pulled down together, bringing the next couple of frames in front of the same aperture gate, ready for the next flash of light. Frame by frame, the rolls of processed negative and unprocessed positive were paired from beginning to end. The positive stock was then ready to be developed and processed, more or less like the negative, with the addition of tinting and toning if and as required.

With the aid of notches cut onto the edge of the negative and special converters (Fig. 65), rolls containing multiple shots of changing densities could be automatically printed as varying intensities of light were flashed into the aperture gate. Along with picture steadiness, the greatest virtue of the 'step-by-step' or 'step printer' process in its fully developed form was the impeccable sharpness of the positive image during projection. It was also a time-consuming operation: a Duplex

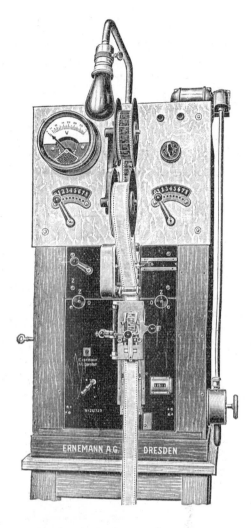

Fig. 64 Step printer. Ernemann-Werke, Dresden, c. 1910. Source: Karl Friedrich Forch, Der Kinematograph und das sich bewegende Bild. Vienna and Leipzig: A. Hartleben's Verlag, 1913, p. 218.

step printer (made in Brooklyn, New York), one among the best available in the market, was designed to work at no more than 15 feet of film per minute. Bell & Howell introduced in 1911 a revolutionary printer (Model D) based on an entirely different principle – the continuous movement of the coupled rolls in front of a light source. Running at 60 feet per minute, it dramatically improved productivity and decreased production costs to such a degree that the film industry embraced Model D in the early 1920s as the preferred way to produce positive prints on an industrial scale. What did not change was the working environment, still immersed in the dim glow of ruby lights.

The hegemony of continuous printing did not go undisputed, which is why it took almost a decade for it to prevail over the Duplex machine. A trained eye could easily detect that the positive image produced by a step printer was of superior quality compared to its faster and cheaper competitor. It is generally believed that the beauty of a nitrate silent film print of the 1910s can be attributed to the richer texture and razor-sharp definition of orthochromatic film, later replaced by the subtler but softer look of panchromatic stock, with the silky depth of its black and white emulsion that was so dear to Josef von Sternberg.

This is only half of the explanation. A Danish-born artist, Hendrik Sartov, is credited for

Fig. 65 Léopold Löbel, automatic converter. Établissements Filmograph, Montrouge, France, c. 1920. One of the first machines specifically designed for film grading. The device controlled the amount of light at the printing stage. Source: Cinémathèque française. Photo by Stéphane Dabrowski.

having introduced D.W. Griffith to soft-focus cinematography; his style influenced French filmmakers such as Abel Gance, Germaine Dulac, and Marcel L'Herbier. Sartov's first surviving film under Griffith's direction, *Broken Blossoms*, was released in 1919, when continuous printing had only begun to assert its dominance in the film industry. Have a look at a good 35mm print of *Way Down East* (1920), and compare it with a print in the same format of Griffith's feature films of 1915 and 1916. All projection prints of *Way Down East* were struck on a Bell & Howell continuous printer; they are vastly inferior to the photographic quality of *The Birth of a Nation* (1915) and *Intolerance* (1916), both released through copies created with the step-printing technique. Sartov was not responsible for this, but the film's soft photography is not all his making, either.

Projectors

Antoine Lumière, father of Auguste and Louis, made a terrible mistake in thinking that there was no commercial future for the moving picture. Edison's genius was equal and maybe superior to theirs in some respects. The Lumière brothers, however, had excelled him through their visionary concept of cinema as a collective spectacle, and with a machine that could function as a camera, as a printer, and as a projector, all in one piece of equipment. Their intuition had given them a formidable advantage over competitors, but they waited a whole year before deciding to make the Cinématographe available to the public.

By the time they did so in the spring of 1897, it was way too late: the market had already been flooded by a plethora of models, most of them endowed with imaginative names (Animatograph, Héliocinégraphe, Théâtrographe) and sometimes

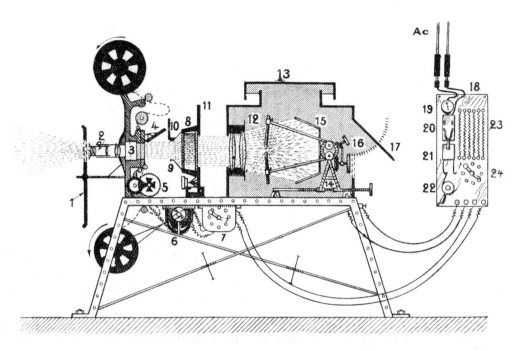

Fig. 66 Schematic lateral view of a basic film projection equipment, c. 1912: 1. blade shutter; 2. lens; 3. aperture gate; 4. automatic fire shutter; 5. Maltese cross intermittent mechanism (magnified); 6. electric motor; 7. rheostat; 8. & 9. cooling tank (filled with distilled water); 10. dimmer (frosted glass); 11. light shield; 12. condenser; 13. lantern; 14. lantern adjuster; 15. reflector; 16. carbon arcs adjuster; 17. ventilation panel; 18. electricity panel; 19. ammeter; 20. electric switch; 21. circuit breaker; 22. commuter; 23. resistance; 24. resistance handle. Source: Jacques Faure, L'Entretien et l'exploitation du cinéma. Comment on tourne, comment on fabrique, comment on exploite un film. Paris: Éditions de 'Sciences et Voyages', n.d. [ca. 1925], p. 7.

strange designs, yet indebted to Lumière's ingenuity in exploiting the idea that a strip of consecutive photographs can be projected through the same mechanisms used in order to capture them. Early film practitioners were paying an indirect tribute to the Lumière legacy by conceding that the projector is essentially a camera in reverse.

This sweeping assertion must be interpreted as a statement of principle rather than an empirical truth. Both cameras and projectors have an intermittent gear that moves the film past an aperture gate; both require a shutter to block the light while the movement is taking place, one frame at a time; both have a feeding and a take-up reel (projectors of the late 1890s let the film unspool in a basket instead of a reel). In one case, the film registers a latent image by receiving natural or artificial light from an outside source; in the other, the image is reflected back onto a screen only by artificial light, and made visible to the human eye in magnified form. Like most cameras, projectors of the early silent era were generally hand-cranked (Fig. 67). Projection speed could be changed almost at will; automatic models driven by electric power had been available since the first decade of the twentieth century, but did not become widespread until the 1920s.

In the camera, the shutter was generally placed behind the lens; in film projectors of the early silent era, it could be installed at either end. The camera and the projector shared the same kind of sprockets, claws, pins, and aperture gates, together with their constellation of belts, springs, and pulleys, as normally found in most mechanical works. Behind the analogies and the symmetries lies a wide array of subtle differences, and the devil is in the details. The devil in question is, again, light. Motion picture cameras embraced it by imitating the concurrent movements of expanding or contracting the iris (with the camera's diaphragm, as shown in Fig. 43) and blinking (with the shutter). Mirroring these actions for the screen was not such a simple affair.

With plain but appropriate metaphors, the two fundamental components of a film projector were respectively called 'lamphouse' or 'lantern' (the counterpart of sunlight) and 'head', as the brain decoding the image into a projected motion picture. An aperture gate, finely cut to exactly

Fig. 67 35mm film projector 'Ernemann I' with three-blade shutter. Krupp-Ernemann, Dresden, 1909. Source: Hermann Joachim, Die Kinematographische Projektion (Halle [Saale], Wilhelm Knapp, 1928) [Guido Seeber and F. Paul Liesegang (eds.), Handbuch der Praktischen Kinematographie. Band III: Die Vorführung des Films. 1. Teil], p. 214.

reproduce the shape of the film's frame, was located along the axis of the light source and the projection lens; the film was threaded vertically in the projector, with the images upside down – in compliance with the camera obscura principle (Fig. 68) – and pressed against the edges of the aperture gate with two parallel 'shoes' (as they are called by projectionists, although they actually resemble a tiny pair of skis or sledges) on both sides of the print, over the perforations (Fig. 69).

The optical features of a projection lens were somehow less demanding than those required for the camera, but its focal length had to be carefully chosen in relation to the size of the screen and the distance between the screen and the projector (the 'throw'). In a typical configuration, the projection lens is a metal cylinder with two sub-components at each end: facing the film, a bi-convex lens and a concave-convex lens (negative meniscus); facing the screen, a bi-convex and a plano-concave lens cemented to each other so as to resemble a single thicker lens (Fig. 70).

At the top and bottom of the 'head', the feeding and take-up magazines revealed the first substantial difference between the camera and the projector, introducing an obsessively recurring theme of the silent film era. In the camera, the roll of unexposed film had to be protected primarily from light; in a 35mm projector, the main enemy was fire. The early habit of letting the film in free fall into a basket under the projector (Fig. 71) without a take-up reel

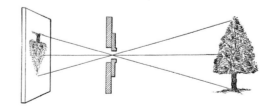

Fig. 68 Reversed and inverted image in the camera obscura or 'pinhole' effect. Source: David S. Hulfish, Motion-Picture Work. Chicago: American Technical Society, 1915, p. 13.

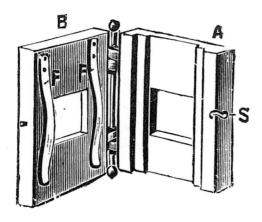

Fig. 69 The typical structure of an aperture gate for film projectors, c. 1920. Source: Hermann Joachim, Die Kinematographische Projektion (Halle [Saale], Wilhelm Knapp, 1928) [Guido Seeber and F. Paul Liesegang (eds.), Handbuch der Praktischen Kinematographie. Band III: Die Vorführung des Films. 1. Teil], p. 51.

was a recipe for disaster: when unspooled like spaghetti, nitrate stock is much easier to ignite. Around 1906 and possibly earlier, the areas where the film was brought towards the lens and then rewound after leaving the aperture gate were protected by round or square fireproof containers (the first known – non-fireproof – film cartridge as a distinct part of a projector was seen in the

Théâtrographe, used in 1896 by Méliès in his Théâtre Robert-Houdin). At the end of each metal enclosure there was a tightly coupled pair of metal cylinders through which the film was passed; the two rollers were arranged so closely to each other that, if the film burned, the flames would not penetrate into the cabinets and reach the main body of the reel on either side of the projector (Fig. 72). In such an occurrence, only a couple of feet of film would be lost, with little or no danger for the projectionist and the public. The operator would turn off the lamphouse or move it away from the aperture gate, mend the film, rethread it, and resume the show within a few minutes.

The 'fire valves' or 'fire rollers', as they were called, were not the only precautions taken against fire in the body of the film projector. Another safeguard was a semi-automatic curtain in the form of a metal sheet, better known as 'fire shutter', located between the light source and the film. The shutter was triggered whenever the projection speed decreased beyond the threshold of overheating the celluloid strip. This mechanism, often made mandatory by public authorities, was supposed to prevent the fire altogether; when properly functioning, it normally did. When in good working order, a projector

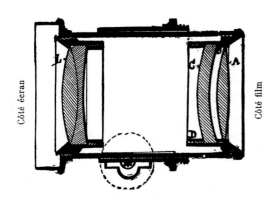

Fig. 70 Cross-section diagram of a Petzwal projection lens, c. 1910, with the left side of the lens facing the screen. Source: Léopold Löbel, La Technique cinématographique. Paris: Dunod et Pinat, 1912, p. 69.

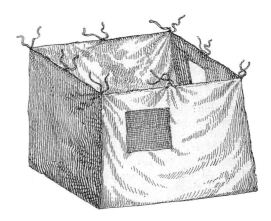

Fig. 71 Take-up basket for 35mm film, placed below early film projectors, c. 1898. Source: Guglielmo Re, Il cinematografo. Milan: Hoepli, 1907, p. 15.

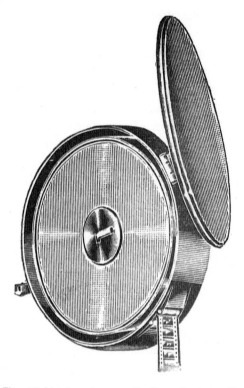

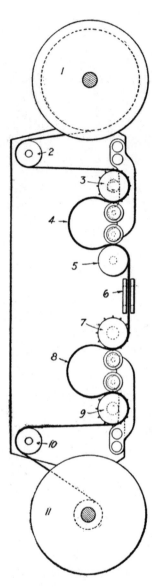

Fig. 73 The typical threading path in a 35mm film projector, c. 1910: 1. feeding reel; 2. idler roller; 3. feed sprocket; 4. upper feed loop; 5. film steadier; 6. film aperture gate; 7. intermittent sprocket; 8. lower feed loop; 9. lower feed sprocket; 10. idler roller; 11. take-up reel. Source: David S. Hulfish, Cyclopedia of Motion Picture Work. Chicago: American Technical Society, 1914, vol. I, p. 123.

Fig. 72 Metal enclosure with 'fire rollers' for 35mm film projection. Source: Hermann Joachim, Die Kinematographische Projektion (Halle [Saale], Wilhelm Knapp, 1928) [Guido Seeber and F. Paul Liesegang (eds.), Handbuch der Praktischen Kinematographie. Band III: Die Vorführung des Films. 1. Teil], p. 190.

with fire rollers and a fire shutter should have been enough to avoid any incidents during the motion picture show. We shall soon discover how the chronicles of silent film are telling a very different story.

After leaving the feeding reel cabinet and fire traps in the upper part of a 35mm projector, the film (threaded so that the emulsion faces the light source) passes through at least two sprocket drums at each end of the aperture gate (Fig. 73). Their role is twofold: first, they jointly contribute to an orderly trajectory of the perforated stock to and from the light source of the projector; second, they control the film's tension while it is moved down the aperture gate by the intermittent mechanism.

In film projectors, the 'Maltese cross' movement was often enclosed in an oil tank, with the dual aim of reducing the wear and tear of the mechanism, and muting its relentless clatter during the show. As in many film cameras, the film is threaded in the projector with a 'Latham loop', located both above and below the aperture gate (marked as 4 and 8 in Fig. 73); its function, described earlier in this chapter, is of crucial importance in ensuring a smooth and uneventful passage of the film through the implacable pins or claw of the intermittent mechanism. Take the 'Latham loop' away, and the film will sooner or later break, with dire consequences.

Shutters

The speed at which the film was projected was the cause of yet another concern. The negative stock had been exposed at a ratio of about 16 frames per second (with great variations over time and in different countries). This was good enough for recording images onto the emulsion; not so for the viewer, who was subject to an annoying flicker, the result of breaking down the continuity of natural movement into a discrete sequence of individual images. In the camera, the only purpose of the blade shutter was to ensure that light would not impress itself upon the emulsion while the film was moving across the aperture gate at regular intervals; in a projector, something more than that was needed to address the side effects of interrupting the light flow at every movement of the film across the gate. Replicating at the time of exhibition what had been done during shooting wasn't enough.

Oskar Messter in Germany and the American Mutoscope & Biograph Company in the United States had devised in 1903 their own modified versions of the camera's blade shutter by subdividing it into two or three sections. One of the segments, wider than the others in earlier applications of the device, performed the function of concealing the frame from the light of the lantern while the film was being moved into its next position. The other blades, sometimes called 'dummies' (Fig. 74), temporarily occluded the light source from the print during

small fractions of a second for a wholly different purpose: the more frequent is the alternation between light and darkness, the easier it is for the eyes to perceive a continuous movement. One could conceivably use blade shutters with even four or more narrower sections, but then more light and a greater rotation speed in the blade shutter would be needed to compensate for the reduced rate of projection.

In a projector equipped with an ordinary two-blade shutter, about 50 to 60 per cent of the light reaches the screen; three-blade shutters allow only 40 to 45 per cent of the light, thus requiring more powerful light sources to make up for the loss. It is also possible to narrow the area of the 'working' blade (the one that covers the aperture gate while the film is moving); if pushed too far, however, a trimming of the blade – or its imperfect registration with the intermittent movement – results in a ghosting effect caused by the projection of a frame while it is still in motion: in film projection, each frame must be absolutely still when it is exposed to the light. A clever method for reducing flicker without extra loss of light was to use two disks rotating in opposite directions

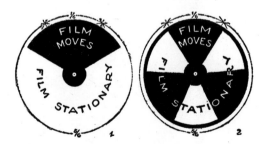

Fig. 74 Single- and three-blade shutters in a film projector. In the three-blade configuration, one blade covers the aperture gate while the film moves through the projector from one frame to the next; the other two blades prevent the light from reaching the screen when the film is stationary. Source: Private collection.

(Fig. 75); the one-third reduction in the time necessary to cover and uncover the beam (the cut-off period itself didn't change) was offset by more complex and delicate mechanisms.

The shape and width of blade shutters for film projectors changed considerably from one model to another (Fig. 76), but all functioned in more or less the same way. In the early twentieth century, the optical effect they pursued was called 'persistence of vision', a common yet inadequate term to describe a complex phenomenon related to the brain's decoding of visual impressions received by the human retina (the 'phi effect'). The employment of a two- or three-blade shutter means we never see a film in its entirety while it is projected: in fact, the actual photographic images of a cinematic event are presented to us for about half of its running time; the rest is darkness. 'The camera opens and shuts, open and shuts with equal time – so half of everything you do isn't seen,' D.W. Griffith told actress Lillian Gish in 1913. 'Then take away the sound, and you lose another quarter.' The

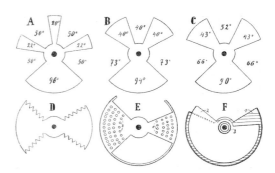

Fig. 76 Experiments in blade shutters for film projectors. Source: Karl Friedrich Forch, Der Kinematograph und das sich bewegende Bild. Vienna and Leipzig: A. Hartleben's Verlag, 1913, p. 52.

inaccurate but poignant remark was meant as an advice on how to perform in front of the camera (Gish recalled the episode in her memoir *The Movies, Mr. Griffith and Me*, 1969, p. 96): 'What's left on the screen is a quarter of what you felt or did,' he added, ' – therefore, your expression must be four times as deep and true as it would be normally to come over with full effect to your audience.'

There is a profound lesson to be learned from this deliberate effort towards incompleteness in a visual experience: the convergence of human perception and mechanics is an aesthetic phenomenon in itself, as exemplified by Dziga Vertov in his incomparable film essay *Chelovek s kinoapparatom* (*The Man with a Movie Camera*, 1929). This was especially true in the first two decades of silent cinema, when films were usually exhibited on hand-cranked equipment. Even when the first motor-driven projectors were introduced in 1908, initially with little or no success, most of them were equipped with rheostats allowing operators to control projection speed, and to monitor amperage. Blade shutters also remained a necessity for many decades after the silent era, when film projection speed was set at 24 frames per second.

Film exhibitors had a vast range of shutters, lenses, and sprockets to choose from. The leading brands differed from one country to another. They usurped each other's throne whenever they could

Fig. 75 Film projector with dual three-blade shutters, partially overlapping. Monarch Moving Picture Machine, Dearborn Novelty Company, Chicago, *c.* 1907. Source: Cinémathèque française. Photo by Stéphane Dabrowski.

throughout the first three decades of the twentieth century, as they would do afterwards. Some brands recurred more often than others, depending on the period: Williamson, Urban, and Walturdaw in Great Britain and its colonies; Ernemann and Messter in Germany; Pathé and Gaumont in France; Edison, Lubin, Motiograph, then Power's Cameragraph and Simplex in the United States. Pathé was the projector of choice in Russia and the Soviet Union until the 1920s, when its design inspired the creation of a domestic model, called Rus', for permanent venues. The hugely popular mobile projector GOZ (Gosudarstvennyj opticheskij zavod, the State Optical Factory) was used in factories and villages. Rus' and Ukrainec were the most common in the Soviet territory, but the old, pre-revolutionary Pathé no. 2 projector was still leading the game in the land of the Bolsheviks. It was supplanted only after December 1926, when the import of foreign projectors was banned and the new Tomp-4 model became the standard Soviet film projector. Simplex, Powers, Urban, and Ernemann projectors imported from Europe and the United States to Japan were gradually superseded by local brands, such as the Komitsu-Royal from the Komitsu Kogyo industries, founded by Hori Kumasaburo in 1918.

Lanterns

The film projector's lamphouse (or lantern) had much in common with those utilized in magic lantern shows. The most important changes after the earliest years of cinema involved the type of light source being used; the lantern's power to generate light also increased, as the theatres grew in size and capacity. Before the introduction of electric light in film theatres, at least five different systems were available to projectionists, all of them based on the notion that a solid with a high refractive index such as calcium hydroxide

(caustic lime) emanates light when brought to very high temperatures. In oxyetheric light, a small cylinder of lime encased in a glass tube was made incandescent with a flame created by a mixture of oxygen and ether. The same process was followed for oxyhydrogen light, with compressed oxygen and hydrogen; in oxycalcic light, with oxygen on a flame produced by alcohol.

When oxygen was not available, it was obtained by thermal decomposition of potassium chlorate, or by dissolving sodium hydroxide (caustic soda) in water. A viable substitute for compressed hydrogen at the turn of the century was acetylene gas; this option was soon abandoned because the light produced by it was very weak, and the vapours released by commercial acetylene had an unpleasant smell. Despite their intimidating terminology, these systems were not necessarily dangerous if handled responsibly (that was not the case in 1897, as will be explained in Chapter 6, when the gases of a oxyetheric light generator engulfed an entire projection hall in Paris). They were not, however, very efficient; they were also quite cumbersome (as seen in Fig. 77) and expensive.

Carbon arc light, introduced in France by Léon Foucault and Jules Deboscq in 1857, was used for film exhibition in the first decade of the twentieth century, and soon became the norm in all projection booths equipped with electric power (Fig. 78). It was affordable, of compact design, and guaranteed a far more powerful light than all its predecessors, as long as the screen was not too large or too far from the source. The arc lamp is run by electricity passing through two carbon pencils or rods – one positive, one copper-coated negative – of varying length (from 7 to 22 inches, or 18 to 56 centimetres) and diameter (from 6 to 16 millimetres, or 0.24 to 0.63 inches, but generally around 6 or 7 millimetres, or 0.24 to 0.28 inches), brought in close proximity to each other at a carefully calibrated angle until a very powerful

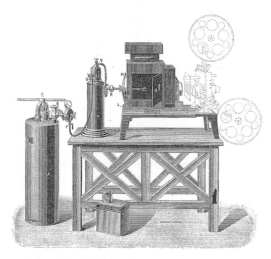

Fig. 77 Film projection by oxygen light. Elgé-Reflex system, Gaumont, c. 1905. Source: Léopold Löbel, La technique cinématographique. Paris: Dunod et Pinat, 1912, p. 67.

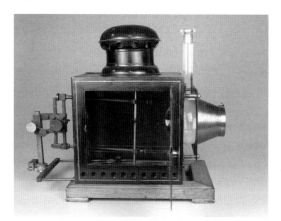

Fig. 78 Lamphouse for film projection (Alfred Molteni, Paris, c. 1895) with carbon arc rods, from the Lumière cameraman Francis Doublier. The arc rods shown here, coated with a copper jacket, were manufactured in the mid-twentieth century. Source: George Eastman Museum.

light in the shape of an arc is formed by a ball of plasma and incandescent carbon particles at the end of the positive rod.

On the back of the lamphouse, a concave silver-coated mirror (Fig. 79) reflects the light towards the film projector's aperture through a set of lenses (Fig. 80), normally two plano-convex condenser lenses with the curved surfaces opposite each other, concentrating the light upon a small rectangular

gate, whose area is equivalent to a frame of the projected film. The positive rod with the burning plasma is directed towards the reflector. The projectionist ensured that the distance between the rods remained constant by adjusting their position at short intervals until they were almost entirely consumed (at which point they had to be replaced); the operation was manually performed with knobs regulating the carbons' position, or by an elaborate motorized device.

The quality of the projected light depended upon several factors, beginning with the material from which the carbons were made, to the projectionist's skill in keeping them properly aligned, and the kind of electricity being used (direct or alternate). Carbon rods lasted for about one hour each; they were burned at about twenty minute increments, and had to be checked at each reel change. If the arc was too short, it started sputtering; if the rods were too far away from each other, the electricity could not bridge the gap, and the arc was interrupted. The first carbon rods for film projection were not

Fig. 79 Concave mirror for film projection lanterns. Établissements Demaria-Lapierre, Paris, c. 1909. Source: Léopold Löbel, La technique cinématographique. Paris: Dunod et Pinat, 1912, p. 11.

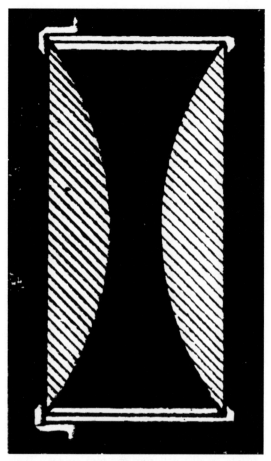

Fig. 80 Cross-section scheme of a condenser with two plano-convex lenses. Source: Léopold Löbel, La technique cinématographique. Paris: Dunod et Pinat, 1912, p. 10.

particularly effective, as the light had a noticeable yellow cast. Their performance improved after 1919 with the inclusion of rare earth elements in the core of the positive carbon rod; the resulting light was twice as bright as the one produced before.

Over the years, carbon arc light became even brighter, about forty times more than it was at the beginning. Light colour also improved by shifting from yellow to blue emissions, ideal for the blue-sensitive orthochromatic film stock. Early carbon arcs could be activated by both direct and alternate electricity; projectionists were in favour of direct current, as it minimized flicker in the

light source (in both cases, rectifiers took care of the issue). The heat it generated was reduced by water cooling systems located between the condenser lenses and the aperture gate.

The superior quality of carbon arc projection for film exhibition was unrivalled throughout the silent era, and remained as such for at least forty years after the advent of sound. Attempts were made with incandescent bulbs from the mid-1910s, with the prospect of dramatic savings in energy (25 per cent less electricity than required with carbon arcs), lower maintenance, and reduced heat, but it was clear from the outset that the best lamps available at the time would not be powerful enough for projection on large screens. Incandescent light was therefore relegated to non-theatrical venues and the amateur market, and never managed to go beyond those boundaries.

Only in the 1970s did carbon arcs began to be threatened by xenon light, so called because electricity goes through a bulb containing xenon gas at high pressure. Xenon eventually conquered the film projection market (and retained its dominance at the dawn of the digital era), but its ancestor did not disappear as quickly as oxyetheric light had in the 1900s. In the second decade of the twenty-first century, carbon rods were still in production; at the time of this writing, a very small number of theatres make use of them for their programmes. Research has shown that carbon arc light produces a slightly warmer image than xenon. Its main limitations were related to maintenance and safety: the rods produced a great deal of dirt, often extending to the projection booth, and the lamphouse required constant cleaning. They also emitted highly toxic fumes when in use, making ventilation a necessity.

Reels

In the beginnings of cinema, films consisted of a single shot and were no longer than about 65 feet, or 20 metres. This is because the containers for unprocessed film in the camera were extremely small, such as in the Cinématographe Lumière. Film stock was sold in tiny cans made of tin, cardboard, or brass whose diameter was generally between 7 and 8 centimetres, or 2.8 and 3.1 inches (Fig. 81); the rolled film had no core, due perhaps to its very limited length. Over time, the capacity of camera cartridges began to increase, and more models featured removable casings to facilitate loading and unloading of the film stock. By 1912, film manufacturers were selling negative and positive stock in rolls ranging from 160 feet (50 metres) to 400 feet (120 metres); the latter became the standard size of the raw film stock from the Eastman Kodak Company, a practice that continued for the rest of the twentieth century and beyond. The roll was wrapped in thick tin-coated black paper to protect it from the light when taken out of the can. As larger rolls became the norm, film cores made their first appearance. They were made of wood, had a diameter of 3 inches (7.6

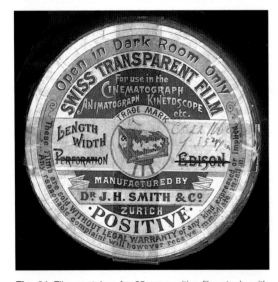

Fig. 81 Film container for 35mm positive film stock, with a capacity of 22 metres, or 72 feet, of film. John Henry Smith and Jakob Heusi, Switzerland, 1897. Cardboard and lithograph on paper, 7.5 × 4cm. Source: Cinémathèque française.

centimetres), and were also used for operations such as winding, unwinding, and sometimes projection.

In the early 1910s, as the normal running time of a fiction film reached the ten- to fifteen-minute threshold, diversification in the length of reels for camerawork and projection took its definitive form. Positive stock and release prints were shipped and projected in spools of approximately 1,000 feet (about 300 metres); in some countries, projection prints were consolidated into reels of 2,000 feet (about 600 metres), a practice which remained rare during the silent era but eventually became the norm worldwide, except in a few countries, including China and the Soviet Union. Film exchanges and theatres received them in round or square tin cans, enclosed in sturdy metal boxes of cubic or cylindrical shape, with one or more handles (Fig. 82). By the time they were projected, film spools had found a permanent residence in the reel holders made of sheet iron or oxydized brass and would not abandon them again for the rest of their natural life (projectionists used the word 'reels' for these objects, as distinct from the film copies). Their existence and material configuration is important for multiple reasons, beginning with the fact that projection prints would be shipped from one venue to the next in that form, with or without cans. This is how museums and archives have often found them over the past decades.

The encasing of positive prints in these metal holders was both a blessing and a curse: for the projectionist, they were easy to handle in projection and rewinding without the risk of dropping the film's core section (the funnel of loose film created by this common occurrence takes for ever to put back into place); the multiple circular or trapezoid holes on their sides made the metal structure substantially lighter; they also made the task of spooling the film into the projector much

Fig. 82 Fireproof shipping case for 35mm reels, c. 1910. Source: Projections fixes et animées, cinématographes, agrandissements, appareils & accessoires. Supplément au Grand Catalogue de Projection no. 1. Paris-London: Romanet & Guilbert, ca. 1910, p. 91.

easier, and were of great help to the operator in locating the splices that joined one short film to another. On the other hand, when the film was left there for a long time in unsafe environments, the contact between the nitrate stock and the rust that developed in reel holders of lower quality contributed to the physical decay of the projection copy. This kind of decomposition occurs most often on the edges of the print, in the areas where it was in contact with the metal, and in the core section of the reel holder (sometimes made of a metal sheet wrapped around a wooden core), where the head or tail end of the film was tightly wound.

The familiar countdown leader in film prints of the sound era was unknown to projectionists of the silent period; for that matter, there was very little or no blank film leader in the heads and tails of most projection copies, at least until the mid-1900s, which is why the beginnings and ends of surviving nitrate positives are so often mutilated and heavily scratched (the only protection given to a print at the time of shipping was

a cardboard band wrapped around the reel, to prevent the first coils from slipping loose in the container). Release prints started with main title cards, if any; in the early years, they ended with the last shot of the film. Intertitles with texts signifying 'End of Reel One', 'Reel Two', and so forth appeared as soon as the barrier of 1,000-feet, or 300-metre, productions was finally broken: they were designed both as markers for the operator, and as information for the audience, sometimes regarding an intermission in the show (see p. 176). As will be explained in Chapter 15, these title cards should therefore be treated as an integral part of the film, and incorporated – if extant, or if their exact placement is known – in new viewing copies (specific titles designating 'The End' of the film were gradually introduced in the mid-1910s). In some countries, projectionists received information sheets or cards with brief descriptions of the beginnings and endings of the reels. They were provided only for selected feature-length films.

Another reason for the importance of reel holders (or just 'reels', as they were called when they contained a print) in the study of silent cinema is that they are a useful indicator of the potential duration of the show, well before the rise of feature-length films. As early as 1908, the catalogues of major production companies and manufacturers of film equipment were offering reel holders of various sizes (Fig. 83), generally painted in black, ranging from 300 metres, or 1,000 feet, to 400 and 600 metres (1,300 and 2,000 feet respectively), all with a slot along the width of the core section to allow the head or end tail to be secured during projection or rewinding. The film reel was placed on a keyed spindle of the projector (supply or take-up), aligning the slot in the reel with the key on the spindle. Once the reel was engaged, the outboard end of the spindle was pivoted 90 degrees to lock the reel in place. Split holders were in commercial production before 1910 to facilitate film handling (Fig. 84).

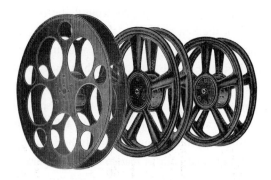

Fig. 83 Film reels of various sizes for 35mm film. Source: Léopold Löbel, La Technique cinématographique. Paris: Dunod et Pinat, 1912, p. 100.

A 600-metre, or 2,000-foot, reel could incorporate enough short subjects for 33 minutes of film projected at a speed of 16 frames per second; in a projection booth equipped with two machines installed side by side, the exhibitor could therefore show an entire programme of almost 70 minutes in just two reels, without wasting any time in replacing one short reel with another. It is hard to determine when booths with dual projection equipment became common practice; it may be surmised that this coincided with, or immediately

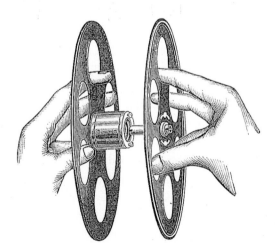

Fig. 84 Split holder for 35mm film, c. 1910. Source: Projections fixes et animées, cinématographes, agrandissements, appareils & accessoires. Supplément au Grand Catalogue de Projection no. 1. Paris-London: Romanet & Guilbert, ca. 1910, p. 91.

followed, the rise of feature-length films, but there is conflicting evidence on this point. The only certainty is that the option of having two projectors in the same booth was at least taken into consideration around 1906 or 1907, as soon as the first permanent venues for film exhibition made their appearance. Operators had thought about it even earlier, when there were no booths to speak of.

Tools

In addition to cameras, projectors, printers, and light sources, the two most important pieces of equipment in the film industry were the film splicers and the perforating machines. The latter ceased to play a significant role in the work of film producers only when – after perforation gauges were standardized – manufacturers of film stock began providing their clients with negative and positive material that had already been perforated. In the first two decades of cinema, however, film perforation was frequently the filmmaker's business, an integral part of the production workflow. Perforating machines of various kinds specifically made for film stock were commercially available from the late 1890s, but they were far from being accurate even if used with the utmost care, as audiences would painfully observe during projection; a decade later, progress in this field had been so swift that film laboratories could choose between perforating machines of great reliability from Debrie, Prévost, Lux, Bell & Howell, and many others (Fig. 90).

Raw and processed film stock was perforated in rooms with closely monitored levels of temperature and humidity, as the organic components of the material were such that every abrupt fluctuation in the atmosphere of the working areas would have resulted in some shrinkage along the length and width of the sensitized rolls. To eliminate dust particles from the air, working areas had constant filtered air exchange; residues of perforated celluloid were so dreaded by film technicians that recourse to brushing machines after perforation was considered mandatory.

Film splicing equipment was no less fundamental, and it remained as such throughout the entire commercial life of motion picture film. No projection booth in a first-run theatre could operate without at least one; the same applied to the assembly lines where all the different sections of the film were joined (mostly by female personnel), either shot by shot or by colour section, as per the producer's instructions, with the aid of continuity sheets or annotations on the film leader (Fig. 26 and Fig. 85). All processed negatives and projection prints were put together by hand, one at a time, in dedicated areas equipped with manual or semi-automatic rewind benches, magnifying glasses, and a splicer (Fig. 86). This, at least, was the theory; in fact, both the editing staff and the projectionists were accustomed to splicing film without any mechanical tool. Experienced technicians knew very well how to make impeccable splices, but they were often in a hurry: this was particularly true for the staff of film exchanges and for projectionists, endlessly coping with open splices, torn footage, and ravaged perforations in the prints they were supposed to put together, rewind, and disassemble on a daily basis.

In light of all this, it is no wonder that manufacturers of film equipment were competing for the fastest and most accurate splicing device.

Fig. 86 A cement splicer for 35mm film. Duplex Machine Company, Brooklyn, New York, *c.* 1920. Source: George Eastman Museum.

Regardless of their complexity, all models had to satisfy three basic requirements: keeping the film steady while the joint was made; ensuring perfect registration with one or more sets of pins, either fixed or retractable; cutting (sometimes also scraping) two ends of film stock in a way that guaranteed maximum adherence after the film cement had been applied. The most sophisticated equipment for film splicing on a large scale was built by Bell & Howell, whose contribution to motion picture technology deserves to be ranked alongside Eastman Kodak's.

At a time when the number of film negatives and release prints was dramatically increasing, Bell & Howell patented an automatic splicer (for film exchanges, laboratories, and assembly lines; it would have been too big for a projection booth) of outstanding precision. Its amazing speed of operation was made possible by a set of pedals enabling the technician to perform multiple tasks that would have otherwise required at least twice as much labour. Another feature that distinguished Bell & Howell's automated model from the others was a heating unit on the upper part of the machine's pedestal, maintaining the splicer's plates, cutters, and

Fig. 85 Markers for print assembly. *La Grotte des supplices* (Alfred Machin, Pathé, 1912). India ink on 35mm nitrate negative. Source: Private collection.

scraper blade at a constant maximum temperature of 49°C (120°F). At that temperature, the splicing cement would dry much faster than normal, ensuring a perfect adhesiveness of the binder with the film joints without damaging their emulsions.

Throughout the silent era, Bell & Howell realized a visionary concept of vertical integration in film equipment technology by covering all aspects of production where mechanical apparatus was involved: Bell & Howell cameras, printers, perforators, splicers, and rewinders formed a corporate chain of irresistible appeal to the film industry for many decades to come. The company stopped short of including professional projectors in their commercial strategy, but played an important role in the market for amateur and non-theatrical projection equipment. The usual suspects – Pathé, Gaumont, Ernemann, Debrie, and a few others – came close to achieving the same goal; nonetheless, these companies represent only the tip of an iceberg whose imposing size is documented by the hundreds of catalogues, brochures, and price lists showcasing an astonishing array of equipment and tools for all imaginable purposes.

Fig. 88 Automatic film measurer for 35mm stock. International Camera AG [ICA], Dresden, c. 1910. Source: Hans Schmidt, Kino-Taschenbuch für Amateure und Fachleute. Berlin: Union Deutsche Verlagsgesellschaft, 1926, p. 160.

An encyclopedia of motion picture equipment in the silent era would be as immense and exhilarating as one about the silent films themselves. There were cameras activated by compressed air (Fig. 87), to be used in aerial views; projectors

Fig. 89 Hand-cranked machine with magnifying lens for viewing 17.5mm film. Ernemann-Werke, Dresden, c. 1912. Source: H.[ans?] Lehmann, Die Kinematographie. Ihre Grundlagen und ihre Anwendungen. Leipzig: B.G. Teubner, 1911, p. 83.

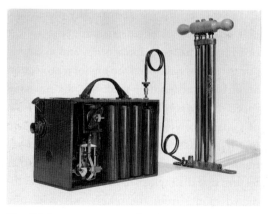

Fig. 87 Aeroscope camera, first built in 1909 by Polish inventor Kazimierz Prószyński. Cherry Kearton Ltd, London, 1912. Source: George Eastman Museum.

with auto-rewind mechanisms; film measurers for rewind and inspection benches (Fig. 88); toothed rulers to verify accuracy in the perforation of film stock; portable devices for individual film viewing (Fig. 89); reel holders that would emit a sound to alert the projectionist that it was time to stop or change projectors. Many of these artworks of film technology exist in private and public collections, still waiting to find their rightful place of honour in the history of silent cinema.

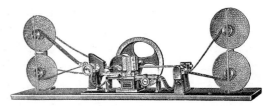

Fig. 90 Perforating machine 'K3' for 35mm film stock. Kurt Schimpf, Berlin, c. 1910. Copied from a similar machine by James Williamson, this perforator punched one pair of holes per frame. An original piece is preserved in the Kodak Collection at the National Media Museum, Bradford, Great Britain. Source: Hans Schmidt, Kino-Taschenbuch für Amateure und Fachleute. Berlin: Union Deutsche Verlagsgesellschaft, 1926, p. 58.

Chapter 5

People

Fig. 91 A crew member and an actress of the Star-Film Company flirting on the set of *Les Quat' cents farces du Diable* (*The Merry Frolics of Satan*, Georges Méliès, 1906). Méliès is seen from behind, on the left of the image. Gelatin silver print. Source: George Eastman Museum.

Tradition, culture, politics, and religious beliefs influenced the daily life and work of film artists, technicians, entrepreneurs, and audiences worldwide, as they do in all other spheres of human activity. These issues have shaped the existence of silent cinema in profoundly different ways from one geographic area to another, to such an extent that any generalization is bound to hide or distort the specificities of each particular context. It is important to keep this in mind when comparing the intense scholarship in North America and Europe (as shown in the bibliographic sources at the end of this volume) with what is known about Asia, South America, and especially Africa, a continent where fewer written records are available on the interactions between people and moving images in the first decades of the twentieth century.

In the formative years of the artificial moving image, inventors, scientists, producers, camera operators, and exhibitors were often one and the same person. The first divisions of labour occurred, as one would expect, by entrepreneurial decision: Edison was the first to do this, with W.K.L. Dickson and his research team; soon afterwards, Auguste and Louis Lumière recruited a small group of cameramen whose task was to take the Cinématographe around the world, carry an adequate supply of unprocessed rolls, take motion pictures of notable or exotic places, events, and people. Eventually, these nomad filmmakers had to come back home. They did not exhibit their work right away: all negatives were to be handled by Lumière's personnel in the city of Lyon, and the resulting copies premiered to a local audience before being shown elsewhere. That was the rule.

Lumière's strategy highlights a chronic dilemma faced by many pioneers of cinema: exercising full control over their own works while reaching (through film duplication) the widest possible audience. Every now and then, until the mid-1910s, film producers entertained the thought that both objectives could be achieved by retaining ownership of the camera and projection equipment. This is exactly what the Lumière brothers did in 1896. Once the negative had been processed at the company's headquarters, the resulting copies were entrusted to authorized dealers who were, however, neither the owners of the prints nor the projection equipment, let alone of any raw stock. Authorized projectionists carried the Lumière apparatus to the exhibitor's venue at an agreed date; they turned the crank, but also checked attendance records, as the dealer was expected to pay a hefty portion (50 per cent) of the earnings for each show, as well as the projectionists' salary.

The scheme could not succeed for long, and it didn't (the embargo on the sale of film equipment, projection prints, and raw stock for the general public was lifted in May 1897). Its overarching goal was to prevent the creation of a parallel production line: Georges Méliès claimed that the Lumière company rejected his request to buy a Cinématographe machine with the excuse that there was not much to be gained from a toy of such uncertain future; a more credible reason for the refusal was Lumière's attempt to deny a potential competitor the opportunity to set up a business of his own, which is precisely what Méliès tried to do as soon as he was able to acquire, in 1896, a different piece of equipment from British film pioneer Robert William Paul. Another ill-fated variation on this story would occur in the United States with the creation in 1908 of the Motion Picture Patents Company. Its failure to impose film technology upon its clients, however, proved far more traumatic.

Amateurs

There is another justification for Lumière's protective stance: the new product had far exceeded not only their expectations, but also the range of commercial possibilities they thought it could offer. The fact that the Cinématographe would be effective for theatrical showings on a systematic basis dawned on them only after the euphoric responses to public demonstrations of the equipment. There is some degree of uncertainty about whether its original aim was public exhibition, domestic use, or both. Whatever the case, the Cinématographe was instantly greeted as an admirable synthesis of performance, versatility, and economy of design. This view was so unanimous that it is hard to draw a clear demarcation between those who expressed it for personal or professional reasons.

Fig. 92 A film exchange library for 28mm copies. United States, *c.* 1919. Source: The New Premier Pathéscope. Boston: The Pathéscope Company of New England, 1919, p. 28.

By turning the crank of a Lumière camera – or, for that matter, of any other similar apparatus in the late nineteenth century – people were enjoying themselves as much as those who were watching them in action. The irresistible impulse to look at the camera is documented by countless street views, taken everywhere at the turn of the century.

From the perspective of what is now called 'amateur cinema', the history of non-theatrical motion picture making is commonly subdivided into three periods. From 1896 to the late 1900s, shooting or showing films was at once a very private passion and a commercial endeavour. Why the business aspect took the lead so soon may be explained by the significant cost of 35mm apparatus, unsurprising to studio photographers (who promptly seized the opportunity to expand their business) but well outside the range of households living on a modest budget. Moreover, the various small film gauges promoted in the early years by Gaumont, Ernemann, Messter and by the British

pioneers of cinema (p. 31) all qualify as 'amateur formats' in hindsight, but this was not always taken for granted by their makers. In a time span of less than two years, for instance, the Birtac (Birt Acres, 1898) and the Biokam (Alfred Darling and Alfred Wrench, 1899), both on 17.5mm stock, were presented as low-cost alternatives to 35mm, thanks to a frame of comparable size to Edison's. Popular as it already was at that time, 35mm film had not yet been universally accepted as a standard format.

The second period – from about 1908 to the late 1910s – saw the emergence of a new concept for film distribution. Once a consensus was reached on 35mm as the theatrical format of choice, amateur cinema became a synonym for equipment of even more compact design than the Cinématographe. Edison took this approach to the extreme with his 22mm Home Kinetoscope film, whose frames (arranged in three vertical columns) were among the smallest ever seen at the time. Pathé followed the opposite path with 28mm film stock (Pathé-Kok), much closer to 35mm and suitable for projection on larger screens. While promoting their respective systems, Pathé and Edison inaugurated the practice of reissuing commercial films for non-theatrical exhibition. Those who wished to experience cinema at home could then become filmmakers (by capturing treasured moments in their lives, or by creating their own fictional subjects) but also spectators, purchasing or borrowing copies of mainstream productions – mostly in abridged form – for an evening of domestic entertainment. Amateur film formats also brought cinema to schools, religious communities, and to remote areas of the world (including colonies) where no permanent venues for film exhibition were available.

From the late 1910s, Pathé and Eastman Kodak transformed this ancillary business into

Fig. 93 The delegates of the International Conference of Film Producers and Manufacturers held in Paris on 2–4 February 1909. Gelatin silver print. Jean-Jacques Meusy has identified the participants as follows (see also Fig. 14a–b): Source: George Eastman Museum.

Akar, ? (Lux) – 24
Ambrosio, Arturo (Società Anonima Ambrosio) – 7
Arribas, ? – 9
Austin, ? – 49
Barker, Will G. (Warwick Trading Company) – 8
Bernheim, Émile (Lux) – 33
Bollardi, Riccardo (Saffi–Luca Comerio) – 23
Bromhead, Alfred C. (Gaumont Ltd. Great Britain) – 26
Brown, ? – 29
Chesneau, E. (Éclipse) – 18
Comerio, Luca (Saffi–Luca Comerio) – 35
Cricks, George H. (Cricks & Martin) – 27
De Beaulaincourt, Roger (Le Lion) – 14
Duskes, Alfred (Duskes) – 15
Eastman, George – 43
Effing, ? – 19
Gandolfi, Alfredo (Ambrosio) – 2
Gaumont, Léon – 45
Gifford, William S. (Eastman Kodak, Great Britain) – 47
Helfer, Charles – 5
Hepworth, Cecil M. – 17
Hubch, ? – 21
Jourjon, Charles (Éclair) – 4
May, Ernest, Sr. (L'Éclipse-Radios) – 38

May, Paul Jr. (L'Éclipse-Radios) – 3
Méliès, Georges – 44
Méliès, Paul (Star-Film US) – 6
Messter, Oskar – 30
Olsen, Ole (Nordisk) – 31
Ottolenghi, Camillo (Aquila Films) – 22
Pathé, Charles – 42
Paul, Robert William – 16
Prévost, Alphonse (Pathé) – 32
Promio, Alexandre (Théophile Pathé) – 28
Raleigh, Charles (Raleigh et Robert) – 37
Reader, Ronald (Vitagraph) – 11
Robert [Robert Schwobthaler] (Raleigh & Robert) – 10
Rogers, George H. (Eclipse) – 41
Rossi, Carlo (Cines) – 12
Sciamengo, Carlo (Itala-Film) – 1
Smith, ? – 48
Stow, Percy (Clarendon Film Company) – 40
Unidentified – 13, 34
Urban, Charles – 46
Vandal, Marcel (Éclair) – 36
Williamson, James (Williamson Kinematograph Co.) – 25
Winter, ? – 39
Zeiske, Erich (Deutsche Bioskop) – 20

a distinct branch of their companies by establishing libraries of film titles available for rental or purchase at moderate fees in the Pathé-Baby (9.5mm), Pathéscope (28mm), and Kodascope (16mm) film formats, providing their clientele with detailed catalogues of short or feature-length works, and with the equipment necessary to show them (Fig. 92). It is hard to overestimate the number of people around the world who discovered and cultivated their own passion for cinema through these finely packaged reels (Plate 24a–b) without ever having set foot in a motion picture house. This vast community included children, who often became competent cinephiles without knowing it (among them was British historian and filmmaker Kevin Brownlow, one of the foremost experts in the history of silent cinema). Small gauges also triggered a swift increase in the production and distribution of non-professional pornography, limited until then to the more affluent private clubs and brothels that could afford the luxury of 35mm equipment for their 'smoking parlours' or *serate nere* ('black soirées', as they were called in Italy).

Younger viewers, their parents, and schoolteachers also learned the basic principles of the cinematic apparatus with toy projectors, miniature tinplate machines for film loops of a few seconds each, showing animated drawings (Plate 51) or individual shots from comedies, features, cartoons, and educational subjects. Germany had been a leader in this field since 1897: Ignaz and Adolf Bing, Ernst Plank, Johann [Jean] Falk, and George [Georges] Carette, all based in Nuremberg, should be regarded as the earliest film animators. They were renowned for their chromolithographic loops of thirty to sixty frames, multicoloured prints, mostly made (without a camera) through the same lithographic printing methods employed in the nineteenth century for the mass production of magic lantern slides.

Entrepreneurs

The business scheme devised in 1896 by the Lumière brothers for their Cinématographe could not last for long, but their failed experiment is a good illustration of how blurred were the boundaries between film investors, artists, distributors, and exhibitors at the beginnings of cinema. Camera operators, on the other hand, acquired a distinct professional identity almost from the start: some of them were studio photographers; others had a background in optics, or played a role in the development of camera and projection equipment before turning their acquired expertise into a full-fledged profession. As soon as they began to shoot fictional scenes, they were also in charge of staging them: aside from Méliès (who was sometimes behind the camera in the early days of his career) and some British pioneers, the distinction between cinematographer and film director slowly came into being only about a decade after the invention of motion pictures.

Once neglected by film historiography, the role of women in both the creative and the managerial phase of the filmmaking process has garnered long overdue attention in cinema studies. Anita Loos, Alice Guy-Blaché, Lois Weber, Esfir' Shub, Grace Cunard, Germaine Dulac, Nell Shipman, Constance Talmadge, Elvira Notari, and Jeanie MacPherson are only a few among the most notable personalities who asserted their position in the industry, well beyond the boundaries of acting roles. Each of the other phases in the production and exhibition chain had a distinct gender balance. In the film laboratory, for instance, responsibility for processing negative and positive stock with chemical compounds was largely a prerogative of men (Fig. 94); female workers were assigned to printing, stencil and hand-colouring, assembling projection copies, and performing quality control on the finished products (Fig. 95); this is because

Fig. 94 Preparing chemicals for film development in the laboratory of the American Mutoscope & Biograph Company. Courbevoie, France, 1899. Gelatin silver print. Source: George Eastman Museum/Lauste Collection.

Fig. 95 Female workers assessing the quality of release prints before distribution. Biograph Company, New York, 1909. Gelatin silver print. Source: Museum of Modern Art/Film Stills Archive.

women were thought to be more efficient in repetitive and methodical jobs requiring the greatest possible accuracy over long working hours. This is precisely what film projection was all about, but projection booths were inhabited almost exclusively by men.

Regarding all the male producers, exhibitors, and distributors (as shown in Fig. 93, there were no women at the helm of the 1909 international summit in Paris), their intertwined biographies reveal the degree to which they stumbled upon the film business by sheer chance rather than by design, under the most diverse and sometimes bizarre circumstances. Carl Laemmle, co-founder of the Universal Film Manufacturing Company, began working in retail shops and was about to devote himself to the chain store business before finding his vocation in cinema. Samuel Goldfish (later known as Samuel Goldwyn), also a father of the American film industry, was originally a garment salesman. Film producer Jesse L. Lasky had been an apprentice reporter for a newspaper in San Francisco before joining the gold rush in Alaska. He studied music and served as a band conductor in Honolulu, managed the Folies-Bergere in New York, and presented musical acts for vaudeville theatres, where he met Benjamin Albert Rolfe, soon to enter the film business.

One of the greatest film producers of the silent era, William Fox, was a Hungarian émigré who left a lucrative business in New York to buy a nickelodeon parlour; as the penny arcade phenomenon was about to fade, he acquired or built motion picture houses, then bought films to be distributed in the venues he owned, and finally established a production company in 1915. A similar professional trajectory applies to Marcus Loew, the uneducated son of a poor Polish couple, who began by purchasing penny arcades and eventually became the owner of one of the largest chains of film theatres in the United States. Film producer Harry M. Warner and his three brothers were also from Poland. To a large extent, the Hollywood film empire was built by immigrants; many were of Jewish lineage, but worked hard to secularize their commerce and assimilate into American culture (non-immigrants played a greater role in film exhibition outside metropolitan areas of the United States).

This kind of career pattern does not belong exclusively to the commercial history of cinema in the United States. One of the giants of the burgeoning film industry in Europe, Charles Pathé, was supposed to inherit his parents' professional lives in the butchery trade, but he was possessed by the demon of adventure. He joined labour migrants on a ship to Argentina, tried a number of jobs with no success, failed in the marketing of a bleaching machine and in the trade of South American parrots before discovering Edison's phonograph at a fair in Vincennes in 1894 and soon afterwards the Kinetoscope during a trip to London; deeply fascinated by both inventions, he was eager to make something out of them. Two of the major film producers in Italy, Arturo Ambrosio and Giovanni Pastrone, encountered cinema as they were earning their living respectively as a studio photographer and an accountant. In a way, they were all explorers of an unknown territory whose boundaries had not yet been drawn, and rules had not been written. They, too, were pioneers. They had all the energy, ruthlessness, and instinct necessary for their entrepreneurial vision.

Financers

The achievement of that vision required, of course, money. The financing strategies for building a film production studio in the silent period are currently known only in their broadest terms, and would deserve further investigation. In essence, they did not differ much from the establishment of any legitimate business: the owner of a motion picture firm invested the company's profits to build a production stage or a theatre, generally with supplementary help from a lending institution, and tried to cover the debts as soon as possible through the income derived from newly released films. Financing individual pictures was another matter, as companies were producing many of them on a regular basis, and needed sufficient time to recoup the costs through distribution. The budget for a new film could range from very small amounts of money to astronomical figures, depending upon its length, the human and technical resources needed for its completion, the year when the film was made, and where it was produced. Information on this topic is currently limited to a few countries, and in most cases (with some notable exceptions, such as the Reliance-Majestic studios in Hollywood during the mid-1910s) to feature-length films of the late 'silent' period.

In a typical cost breakdown for a feature film made in the United States at the heyday of the silent era, a quarter of the budget went on the performers' salaries, as should be expected at a time when the star system was in full swing. Another 10 per cent each was allocated to stories (including literary rights) and screenplays, and to directors, cameramen and their crew: therefore, the so-called 'creative' side of the project accounted for almost half of all production expenses. Management, editing, titling, and other studio overhead items were the second most important budget line, 20 per cent of the total, closely followed by the construction of the sets (films of the western genre were generally much cheaper to produce); the rest was spent on location shooting and transportation (8 per cent) and costumes (3 per cent). Raw film stock accounted

for more or less 5 per cent of the total, depending on how many prints were struck. This does not take into account the general operating budget for the production company as a whole, its headquarters, personnel, and administration. In the 1920s, it took between one and two years before the film completed its commercial life and the company had secured all its returns.

The financing of such a complex and often costly project was the result of a negotiation between a banker and the producer, who asked for a loan to cover the production budget in part or, sometimes, in its entirety. This was more likely to happen if the lender had proof that a film with a major star and director would be released through a distribution company of solid reputation. The banker demanded that the loan was to be liquidated within a short period of time, usually four months. In special cases, banking limits were extended to half a year and beyond, but would not exceed eight months. Financing agencies did not make their decisions without due diligence: before lending large sums, they wanted details of cast and director, storyline and screenwriter, not to mention the organization's structure as a whole. The biggest lenders went as far as to send senior managers or representatives to see other films previously made by the artists to be hired for the project.

The bankers' enquiries generally stopped at the threshold of the company's corporate policies and the technical aspects of the productions, which they felt were not their concern. On some occasions, however, a bank or a consortium of financial institutions would take the leap and participate more directly in the production company's governance or management structure. In that case, film producer and investor could be one and the same person, with all the opportunities and all the risks involved wherever creativity, entrepreneurship, and financing are merged under the same roof. Syndicates (they are now called 'limited partnerships') and credit corporations were important forms of film financing in the United States; Paramount, Cecil B. DeMille, Metro-Goldwyn-Mayer, and others formed their own financing subsidiaries, lending money to producers. Some celebrities (including Gloria Swanson and John Ford) made attempts at self-financing their films, but eventually retreated to financing syndicates. The strict discipline imposed by Thomas H. Ince and the Famous Players-Lasky Corporation upon production budgets was praised by bankers as a model in the industry (in 1927, the actual cumulative cost of all the feature films produced by Famous Players-Lasky was only $3,000 above the initial budget).

A global history of film financing during the silent era remains to be written, but there are many instructive stories in the best scholarly literature on national cinemas in North America (Janet Staiger in *The Classical Hollywood Cinema*, 1985) and Europe (Stéphanie Salmon on Pathé, 2014). A particularly striking tale involves a coalition of bankers who virtually took over film production in Italy after the end of World War I, with dire consequences for the industry in that country (its cinematic output collapsed within less than a decade). In the United States, independent production was the only avenue for African American talents, as shown by the films of Oscar Micheaux. The rediscovery of his creative work by film archives, museums, and the academic community in the 1990s opened a long-neglected chapter in silent film history (the cinema of ethnic and linguistic minorities in other countries, notably India and the Soviet Union, is also a fertile ground for research).

Writers

Preparing a film was initially an art of improvisation. There was no such thing as screenwriting, not just because films were so short:

concepts were developed more or less in the same way they are now, with embryos of ideas coalescing around a few words scribbled on scrap paper, or even kept and nurtured in the brains of their creators. This does not mean that filmmakers were careless about their projects: Méliès is credited as having been the first to adopt the term 'scenario cinématographique' for *A Trip to the Moon*, and many of his contemporaries were as conscientious and organized as they are today, but it took some time before they felt the need to articulate in written form the details of their intuitions.

A very large number of texts prepared for silent films exist in collecting institutions under different forms, but they are 'screenplays' only in a heavily mediated sense of the term, because they were often compiled for a variety of purposes: the so-called 'continuity' lists deposited by the Biograph Company at the copyright office of the Library of Congress are shot-by-shot transcriptions of the action and the title cards as they were seen in release prints. The Bibliothèque Nationale de France holds similar documents – also submitted for copyright protection – pertaining to over fifteen thousand films made between 1907 and 1923, but their status as pre-production scripts is not always clear. These pages are, at least, typewritten, but when D.W. Griffith was given his first directorial assignment in 1908 for *The Adventures of Dollie* at Biograph, his cameraman Billy Bitzer was working from handwritten notes taken on the fly, sometimes on the back of used envelopes.

Griffith was an aspiring stage actor. He had an intimate knowledge of printed and unpublished theatre scripts (he even authored some), but neither wrote a script during his entire career, nor worked with someone else's screenplay unless he was forced to do so when the Hollywood studio system imposed its rules upon him. His longest film, *Intolerance*, consisted of 2,203 shots and intertitles (as of 24 June 1916), but its intricate narrative structure remained intact in his mind from beginning to end; when he decided to extrapolate the modern and the Babylonian episodes of the film for two shorter features, *The Mother and the Law* and *The Fall of Babylon* (both released in 1919), Griffith excised the footage he needed from the original camera negative of *Intolerance*, re-edited the stories (with the addition of new title cards), made all the prints he wanted, and later reassembled the full version of *Intolerance* from his own phenomenal memory. It is true that Griffith's production method was a rare exception by the standards of the time: well before *Intolerance*, the layout of theatrical screenplays had been widely adopted – with some modifications – by the film industry, with the crucial additions of numbered scenes and the separation between interiors and exteriors, both necessary to set up the shooting schedule by locations and settings, rather than in the chronological sequence of events in the story.

Many of the original scripts of silent films known to survive today are related to feature films produced in the United States; as in North America, most of what is known about film production in the rest of the world points to an ongoing dialectic between tradition and innovation in the relentless search for new or unusual narratives and themes. A small independent firm, Embarrassing Moment Pictures, went as far as to offer a financial reward in 1927 to those who would submit a real-life situation that was interesting and awkward enough to be depicted on celluloid: one of the films resulting from the public contest is preserved at the Library of Congress. The thirst for storytelling among production companies was so pervasive that no stone was left unturned at every level, ranging from the recruitment of full-time writers to open-ended invitations to submit original scripts (journalists were a privileged category in both instances). One of the most prolific genres in film literature of the silent period is

'photoplay' writing ('photoplay' and 'photodrama' were the preferred terms from the early 1910s in English-speaking countries): it was second only to handbooks on screen acting, an eloquent indication that the scriptwriter's role was one of the most coveted in the motion picture business. By the time cinema had become an industry, it was widely assumed that one could be handsomely paid by simply presenting a clever storyline to the executives of a well-established studio.

The first known screenwriting instructions were published in France by Edmond Claris for the periodical *Ciné-Journal* (1909), by Epes Winthrop Sargent in the United States for *The Moving Picture World* (1911), and by Émile Kress for *Cinéma-Revue* (1912). Sargent was also the author of the first book entirely dedicated to the subject, *The Technique of the Photoplay* (1912), prompting a true avalanche of introductory or specialized manuals, at a time when the demand for new stories to be brought to the big screen was reaching its peak; more than one hundred treatises appeared in the United States alone within a decade. By then, the average length of a motion picture script had risen to at least fifteen typewritten pages per reel of film, allowing greater depth in the definition of narrative details and character psychology.

With the steady rise of feature-length subjects, the screenwriting process saw a momentous change in its workflow. Major companies established full-fledged scenario departments, whose employees were engaged in four distinct areas of activity. A team of reading 'scouts' evaluated novels, short stories, plays, and unsolicited manuscripts (Fig. 96); the most promising ideas were transcribed into plot summaries for further consideration; in the next step of the selection process, the synopsis was broken down into a scene-by-scene narrative 'continuity'; if accepted, the text was finally rewritten in expanded form as

Essanay

Your manuscript is returned for the reason checked below:

1. OVERSTOCKED.
2. NO STRONG DRAMATIC SITUATIONS.
3. WEAK PLOT.
4. NOT OUR STYLE OF STORY.
5. IDEA HAS BEEN DONE BEFORE.
6. WOULD NOT PASS THE CENSOR BOARD.
7. TOO DIFFICULT TO PRODUCE.
8. TOO CONVENTIONAL.
9. NOT INTERESTING.
10. NOT HUMOROUS.
11. NOT ORIGINAL.
12. NOT ENOUGH ACTION.
13. NO ADAPTATIONS DESIRED.
14. IMPROBABLE.
15. NO COSTUME PLAYS, OR STORIES WITH FOREIGN SETTINGS DESIRED.
16. ILLEGIBLE.
17. ROBBERY, KIDNAPPING, MURDER, SUICIDE, HARROWING DEATH-BED AND ALL SCENES OF AN UNPLEASANT NATURE SHOULD BE ELIMINATED.

Yours very truly,
ESSANAY FILM MFG. CO.,
Studio and Laboratories
1333 Argyle St.   CHICAGO, ILL.

Fig. 96 Form rejection letter in response to unsolicited screenplays. Essanay Film Manufacturing Company, Chicago, c. 1915. Source: Private collection.

a shooting script, complete with intertitles. It was a well-paid and highly respected job, earning the authors a prominent mention in the main credits of the finished film.

Production

With his customary pragmatism, Cecil B. DeMille used to distinguish between three types of film director. There was the one whose reputation was so well established as to have the liberty of choosing the project and shooting the film without any external interference; another would receive a manuscript to be turned into a film, evaluate its potential, and make or suggest changes for further

discussion with the producer; then, DeMille wrote, 'there is the director to whom you say, "Take this manuscript out and shoot it just the way it is written and do not change anything"' (*The Story of the Films*, 1927, p. 124). It's a rather cynical but accurate portrayal of the profession at the dawn of the studio system.

The last two categories of DeMille's candid assessment, on the other hand, may also apply to the work of other creative personnel in silent film production, namely those now called 'set designers'. The term appeared in the United States only at the end of the 1910s, as part of the studio system's new corporate lexicon, but this activity had always been part of the filmmaking process. In the early years of cinema, when the scenes were staged with basic furnishings and painted backdrops, there were people in charge of selecting, arranging, and sometimes making them, securing their stability on the set, and tailoring their look to the specific needs of the situation. For more than two decades, a legion of handicraft workers left an indelible mark on motion pictures without ever being noticed.

These anonymous carpenters and painters were following the orders of company owners, production managers, photographers; their activity was more closely supervised by directors of greater ambition or authority, who wanted to add nuances to the physical space of the action. The cinema studios' craftsmen came from a variety of professional backgrounds, including theatre, vaudeville, circus, and fairgrounds: they were skilled in drawing upon canvases, building wooden frames, installing doors or windows at very short notice, as they were accustomed to do in their former jobs. In some respects, their work was somewhat easier than before, because they did not have to worry about scene changes, except when required in elaborate fairy tales and trick films; as painters, they developed a special talent for monochrome

Fig. 97 Backdrop painters at work in the Pathé studios, c. 1910. Source: Frederick Arthur Ambrose Talbot, Moving Pictures. How they are made and worked. London: Heinemann, 1912; Philadelphia: J.B. Lippincott Co., 1914, p. 105.

surfaces, as the chemistry of orthochromatic film stock narrowed their palette to variations of grey for decorated walls, imaginary landscapes, and flat renditions of three-dimensional objects (Fig. 97).

The *trompe-l'œil* technique of faking depth and chiaroscuro was well known by the early masters of set design. They often saved their employers money by using the same furniture or painted backdrop in different productions. Pathé, Ambrosio, Nordisk, Vitagraph, and others could do so with minimal or no changes in interior scenes from one film to another (some of their films can be identified by their wallpaper, cupboards, and assorted ornaments). In many Pathé and Gaumont films of the 1905–10 period, characters are seen walking up and down the same staircases and landings over and over again; they pretend to access different floors, but the set is one and the same (at times, stage assistants were clever enough to add or replace a small object in the scene to reduce the awkward feeling of having watched the same action multiple times).

Over the years, audiences began to lose their patience nevertheless. Camera operators, too, were growing restless, as their equipment was invariably placed at a 90-degree axis in relation to the set. Italian producer and filmmaker Giovanni Pastrone

broke the spell by introducing three-dimensional architectures especially built for studio shooting. He did so for *La caduta di Troia* (*The Fall of Troy*, Luigi Romano Borgnetto, 1910), a film in two reels. Historic dramas and epics were extremely popular at the time; audiences had been so accustomed to painted renderings of temples and fortresses that their newly discovered sense of volume and depth in the archaeological settings around the Trojan horse was a sensation worldwide.

An average work in every other respect, *La caduta di Troia* is remembered as the film that dislodged the hegemony of perpendicular sets, paving the way for the dynamics and stagecraft of diagonal views. Studio carpenters finally had their chance to think in architectural terms, and seized the opportunity in other visions of classical antiquity, from *Quo Vadis?* (Enrico Guazzoni, 1912) to *Cabiria* (Giovanni Pastrone, 1914), and in D.W. Griffith's *Intolerance*, whose gigantic walls were built and decorated with the contribution of Italian immigrant labourers experienced in theatrical set design. *Cabiria*'s no less imposing interiors were presented to the audience through majestically slow and sinuous movements of the camera. Pastrone's historical epic shares with *Intolerance* the status of cinematic legend, but the one-reel crime story *An Attempt to Smash a Bank* (Lewin Fitzhamon, 1909), a Hepworth production with no less elaborate tracking shots between two adjacent sets, would deserve a place in their company.

Had his films enjoyed wider circulation at the time of their release, Russian filmmaker Evgenij Bauer would have made an impression on world audiences as lasting as Pastrone's and Griffith's celebrated creations. Much remains to be discovered about the personnel assisting him with the columns, mirrors, and curtains in the films he directed for the Khanzhonkov company between 1913 and 1917 (*Posle smerti* [After Death], 1915, is a breathtaking case in point). Their scenes do not possess the evocative grandeur of *Cabiria* and *Intolerance*, and yet are memorable for their subtle interaction between camerawork and the perspective and depth of the films' exquisite interiors. The set designs of Bauer's decadent dramas stand comparison with the work of other great artists of the 1920s: Robert Mallet-Stevens in France, Ben Carré (*The Blue Bird*, Maurice Tourneur, 1918), and William Cameron Menzies in the United States are among the best known, together with the architects of Fox studio productions (*7th Heaven*, Frank Borzage, 1927), German film expressionism, and *Metropolis*.

Silent cinema is a pictorial art based upon the theatrical tradition: our memory of its best achievements is partly dependent upon the physical look of the world in which their fictional characters lived. It is no exaggeration to say that the aesthetics of set designs functioned as virtual trademarks for several production companies of the early 1910s such as Vitagraph, Deutsche Bioskop, Gaumont, Cines, Nordisk. Their unnamed construction crews were the true architects of silent cinema, well before the Hollywood studio system included their names in the main or final credits of its films.

Acting

To put it mildly, the acting profession was generally regarded with ill-concealed suspicion in the nineteenth century. Reprobation would be a more accurate term to define this attitude, but the truth of the matter is that, in the eyes of the beholder, the performer had two distinct personalities: on stage was the fictional character we could engage, sympathize, or identify with. When the performance was over, the same woman or man was someone who belonged to a world of dubious moral standing. This prejudice was rooted in a popular belief that had originated many centuries

earlier; cinema made it more tangible only because it was applied to a form of expression with no cultural credentials, just another attraction as entertaining as a country fairground, vaudeville theatre, and the circus.

Lumière's and Edison's first performers were either non-professionals who were asked to execute brief actions (such as sneezing, having an argument over a game of cards, or upsetting a gardener intent on watering plants), or vaudeville professionals paid to display their talents in front of a camera: Annabelle Whitford's serpentine dance, May Irwin and John C. Rice playing a romantic couple (*May Irwin Kiss*, 1896; see Fig. 98a), Eugen Sandow flashing his muscles, and so on (the term 'cinema of attractions', coined around 1985 by Tom Gunning and André Gaudreault, refers to the presentation of these spectacles as episodic

Fig. 98a *May Irwin Kiss* (Edison, 1896). Frame enlargement from a 35mm triacetate positive. Source: Library of Congress.

Fig. 98b *Something Good – Negro Kiss* (Selig, 1898). Frame enlargement from a tinted 35mm nitrate positive. Note the Lumière perforations from the negative source. Source: Courtesy of Dino Everett.

views without a narrative context). Most of the other people depicted on screen were regarded as 'artists' only in the most basic sense of the term, if not improvised accomplices of film pioneers' experiments. It is not yet clear whether or not the workers returning home in *Sortie d'usine* (Louis Lumière, 1895, five versions) or the travellers getting off the train in *Arrivée d'un train à la Ciotat (France)* (Louis Lumière, 1896–7, three versions) had been told beforehand that they were about to be filmed.

When early film producers began looking for real professionals, all they could find were people who were earning a modest living with travelling theatre companies of little or no reputation. D.W. Griffith, an ambitious but not very talented young actor, ended up in the offices of the Edison and Biograph companies in late 1907 only because he badly needed a job and another actor, Max Davidson, had told him he would be paid reasonably well for relatively little effort. One of Italy's greatest divas of the silent period, Francesca Bertini, was the daughter of a stage property master and a theatre comedian of very humble origins. In either case, there was nothing glamorous about entering the cinema business. Quite the contrary: at the inception of the silent era, the public status of a film actress was only a few notches above that of a prostitute, unless she was married or went to the producer's office in the company of her mother. Being an immigrant, on the other hand, could be an asset in disguise; many stars of silent cinema (and countless extras) were hired precisely because of the exotic 'touch' in their gestures, manners, and complexion.

It is in this volatile environment that film performers became the messengers of a new art form. They had no tradition to draw upon, other than the popular theatre, its long-standing repertoire, and the recognized codes of its acting styles in the respective countries where the performers

had learned their craft (exaggeration, a common approach to acting in the early years of cinema, was slowly relegated to slapstick comedy and replaced by a more subdued behaviour in front of the camera; not so in Italy, where female players of the mid-1910s – the 'divas' – turned facial and body contortions into a peculiar language of emotional torment). Screen performers of the 1900s were further disadvantaged in that producers had no intention of listing their names in the films' title credits, afraid as they were that celebrity would be an incentive to requests for higher salaries.

Around 1908, two concurrent events drastically changed the rules of the game. In France, performers from the legitimate stage theatre were so intrigued by the new medium that they were easily persuaded by the Pathé company to offer their services for period dramas such as *L'Assassinat du Duc de Guise* (Charles Le Bargy and André Calmettes, 1908); in the United States, an actress from the Biograph Company, Florence Lawrence, became so popular as 'the Biograph Girl' that the discovery of her real name was only a matter of time. Two years later, when Danish theatre actress Asta Nielsen became an international celebrity following her starring role in the erotic drama *Afgrunden* (*The Abyss*, Urban Gad, 1910), the ancient curse on the profession began to crumble. Acting in a film had not only conquered the status of a respectable job: if all went well, it could also be a highly lucrative business for both the performer and the film production company.

When another stage celebrity, Sarah Bernhardt, appeared in *Queen Elizabeth* (Louis Mercanton and Henri Desfontaines, 1912), film stardom had reached the point of no return. Screen performers such as Max Linder and Musidora (Jeanne Roques) in France; Ruan Lingyu in China; Theda Bara, Rudolph Valentino, Lillian Gish, Buster Keaton, Clara Bow, Harold Lloyd, Constance Talmadge, Gloria Swanson, and William S. Hart in the United States; Lyda Borelli, Leda Gys, Rina De Liguoro, Emilio Ghione, and André Deed in Italy; Asta Nielsen and Valdemar Psilander in Denmark; Vera Karalli in Russia; Betty Balfour, Clive Brook, Henry Edwards, Chrissy White, and Ivor Novello in Great Britain; Henny Porten, Marlene Dietrich, and Emil Jannings in Germany – to name only a few – drew the masses to film theatres (the silent film careers of other major stars like Greta Garbo, Ivan Mozzhukhin, and Pola Negri spanned different countries and continents); some of them, especially women, became far more powerful than their employers, or became directors and producers themselves.

Within less than a decade, this trend reached global proportions, transforming cinema into a major driving force of public opinion. Adult female, male, child (Peggy-Jean Montgomery, later Diana Serra Cary, the real name of her screen character Baby Peggy), and animal stars (such as a German Shepherd dog, Rin Tin Tin) shaped the destiny of the world's film industry in the 1920s. Surviving images of the crowds assembled in front of Charlie Chaplin, Mary Pickford, and Douglas Fairbanks during their public appeals to support the United States' intervention in World War I, the funerals of Russian actress Vera Kholodnaya in Moscow (1919) and actor Rudolph Valentino in New York City (1926) give only a faint idea of the sheer magnitude of a phenomenon with no equals in the cultural history of the twentieth century.

Scholarly research in the United States has explored in depth the circumstances and issues related to the work of African American performers in silent films (Fig. 98b), and highlighted the significant acting roles played by members of ethnic minorities, such as Lillian Margaret St Cyr ('Red Wing') and her husband James Young Deer, also a notable film director of westerns in the early 1910s. Sessue Hayakawa and Tsuru Aoki, two great screen personalities of the silent era, were discovered by film producer Thomas H. Ince for their previous theatrical experience

in local Japanese communities of the West Coast. Films produced by Ince for the New York Motion Picture Company are notable for the depth and range of acting roles given to Native Americans.

Makeup

The change in public perception of screen performers from characters of questionable repute to objects of public worship is reflected in the proliferation of books published from the mid-1910s about screen personality, film acting methods (Fig. 99), and advice on how to find a job in the

EXPRESSION

MARIE DORO
IN
"DIPLOMACY"

Courtesy of Famous Players Film Company

Left to right:

1.   —Desire, love, longing, ardor, pleading.

1. MARIE DORO—Uncertainty, doubt, hesitation, perplexity, wavering.

Fig. 99 Marie Doro in the leading role of *Diplomacy* (Sidney Olcott, 1916). The page is taken from Jean Bernique's *Motion Picture Acting for Professionals and Amateurs* (1916), a catalogue of emotions for display in front of the camera. Source: Jean Bernique, Motion Picture Acting for Professionals and Amateurs. n.l.: Producers Service Company, 1916, p. 97.

Fig. 100 A violinist accompanies actor Wallace Reid during his performance in front of the camera, c. 1920. Source: Jacques Faure, L'Entretien et l'exploitation du cinéma. Paris: Éditions de 'Sciences et Voyages', n.d. [ca. 1925], p. 75.

studios. A barely disguised form of fan literature, this specialized genre provided sets of instructions on the technique of makeup, the choice of costumes to be worn at auditions, and the archetypes of cinematic expression derived from pantomime: arrogance, dismay, terror, joy, and trepidation found new codes as they were meant to be captured by the camera (to assist performers in their efforts, musicians were sometimes employed to play on the set with appropriate mood music [Fig. 100]).

A leitmotif of these manuals is the difference between stage and screen performance, the merciless scrutiny of the lens in those scenes requiring prolonged close-ups, and the imperative to shift from one kind of emotion to another within a few seconds, as film shooting rarely followed the natural sequence of events in the story. Those who aspired to be chosen for an acting role supposedly had to forget the rules they had learned or heard about in the realm of stage performance. Watching as many pictures as possible before registering for an audition was also recommended. These instructions were implicitly addressed to those readers identified by the authors as the core audiences of film theatres: young men and women with little or no acting experience and boundless ambition.

In North America and Europe, white actors had their faces painted in dark tones ('blackface') to perform characters of African descent (Fig. 101), a practice rooted in theatre and vaudeville. Some manuals on film performance contained derogatory remarks on racial minorities: 'the [acting] work affords them an opportunity to live their savage days over again, and they are not slow to take advantage of it', wrote Ernest A. Dench about Native Americans in *Making the Movies* (1915, p. 92); 'to act as an Indian is the easiest thing possible, for the redskin is practically motionless' (p. 94). Statements of this kind did not make any particular impression at the time, as they reflected views that were widely shared by the public opinion; even more so in Europe, where the subject had long been incorporated into the rhetoric of orientalism, colonies, and the exotic.

The need to relieve the film performer from the burden of theatrical tradition was especially felt in the use of makeup. 'Do not overdo it' was a recurring piece of advice given to the uninitiated, and it took time before the message was fully understood. Until the late 1910s, heavily marked character lines were still accepted, but they had to be applied with restraint, and white highlighting on the face was suggested only to experienced players. By 1920, theatrical makeup was banned altogether from the set. Faint carmine lipstick was allowed for lips, but grease paint was no longer used for hair, eyebrows, and moustaches, except for slapstick comedy.

Cameramen preferred a yellow tinge on the face to better control lighting, with spare touches of blue pencil to enhance expression in dramatic situations; a uniformly pale look soon became the preferred way to conceal skin imperfections. Actors were used to applying makeup by themselves, which is why their fingernails look so stained in those title cards or detail shots where they are holding letters and telegrams; the tradition came

Fig. 101 The cast and crew of the Star-Film Company's 'American Wildwest' unit. Gaston Méliès is the man with the white moustache, under the banner. Sulphur Mountain Springs, California, 4 July 1911. Gelatin silver print. Source: George Eastman Museum.

to an abrupt end as soon makeup artists found a permanent place in the studio system.

Hairdressers brought an additional set of variations to the expressive codes of screen performers. For female characters, curly hair conveyed a more or less pronounced sexual innuendo; beards, moustaches, and sideburns played the same function for their male counterparts. In this respect, theatrical conventions continued to exercise an important function in defining the cinematic identity of the human body throughout the silent era. A similar influence could be discerned in clothing and gowns, although its echo faded away in the early 1920s. The chromatic balance of jackets, shirts, and trousers was monitored with the

same degree of attention paid to makeup and set designs, but there was a more intractable handicap for the human body itself: blue eyes looked quite eerie on screen because orthochromatic film registered them as white. This strange and cruel liability ceased to exist with the introduction of panchromatic film stock, whose emulsion no longer discriminated screen performers on the basis of their genetic attributes.

Post-production

Of all activities occurring after filming on the set or on location, editing and titling were those where the artistry of their practitioners was most widely respected and publicly acknowledged. It took years for this to happen, as both assembling negatives and writing texts for intertitles were initially seen as important but undemanding endeavours, requiring only a practical understanding of narrative logic and sufficient technical skills. For some time, the task of an editor was basically a complement to directorial work, the execution of a set of instructions established at an earlier stage of production; the first filmmakers frequently edited their own negatives with no external help.

Before the editing process evolved into an artistic discipline of its own, the length of a shot was simply measured and written down on a sheet (or at the end of each negative segment, as seen in Fig. 85) to be used for the assembly of release prints or negatives. In the 1910s, when the length of fiction films extended to multiple reels, the creative relationship between filmmakers and negative cutters took on a more intimate, at times symbiotic, connotation. In practical terms, their dialogue did not always happen in front of the rewind bench: editing instructions could be delivered on paper or even through sound recordings, as was the practice in some major companies. The material aspect of the job, however, was only the initial step of a sometimes very complicated process.

Silent films were frequently shot in two negatives (Fig. 102a–b), either with parallel cameras – sometimes with different types of lenses – or by shooting the same scene twice. This was necessary to create two versions of the same film for domestic and foreign markets, in those countries whose film industry was important enough to warrant an export distribution strategy. Aside from the method and accuracy required to keep track of so many short segments of negative film in the working area equipped with viewing devices, rewinds, and film synchronizers (to ensure that negatives of the two versions were the same length), editors and directors had to discuss which shot or group of shots would be used for one or another version; as the shooting angles of the views taken with contiguous cameras were slightly different, the criteria for selection were severely limited by the need to maintain visual consistency within each sequence.

It was also desirable for the editor and the director to preview the film together in the screening room, where changes were to be discussed, decided upon, and meticulously documented. This enabled the editor to become a sort of alter ego of the filmmaker, a trusted sounding board on which to clear doubts and resolve dilemmas

Fig. 102a–b Filming the same scene with two adjacent cameras: *La Femme rêvée* (Jean Durand, 1929). Digital scans from 35mm nitrate negatives. Source: Courtesy of Gaumont.

before the finished product was submitted to the producer (who may have already joined them in the projection room anyway).

A similar pattern can be detected in the preparation of film titles. As soon as their number began to increase, with longer texts and drawings or optical effects, film titling became an art form in its own right, with dedicated staff specialized in turning plain sentences into lyrical or comic utterances. Some screenwriters and film directors – including a young Alfred Hitchcock – started their careers by writing texts for film titles; peppering them with jokes and saucy allusions was a common resource for making slapstick comedies look funnier (before taking up directing, the great American filmmaker Gregory La Cava became an expert in this), or to inject an extra element of interest into an otherwise unremarkable plot. From the mid-1910s, a pictorial commentary was often added to the text;

once printed on a large sheet of paper, the title was given to a draughtsman in charge of embellishing it in a manner that was deemed coherent with the content and atmosphere of the film.

Title artists, too, earned a mention on the credits of major film productions in the United States, therefore playing a small but recognizable role in their public presentation (Fig. 103). Sadly enough, they achieved much greater visibility than their colleagues in charge of designing the promotional material (Fig. 104), posters, and lobby cards to be displayed on theatre fronts and around town; millions of people worldwide – many more than those who actually viewed the films – looked at

Fig. 103 A title artist at work. Unidentified studio, United States, *c.* 1918. Gelatin silver print. Source: George Eastman Museum.

Fig. 104 Publicity card for the Cinématographe Lumière, *c.* 1896. Lithograph on cardboard with 35mm nitrate frame insert, 58 × 92mm. Source: George Eastman Museum.

this artwork without a second thought about their makers (publicity departments of production and distribution companies are still relatively unexplored in the silent cinema of most countries). A fast-growing community of connoisseurs is actively seeking these rare lithograph prints, mostly printed on flimsy and highly acidic paper, as expensive collectors' items; the same can be said of production stills made to promote the films or to document their creation. Many of them are very beautiful, and the names of their makers are sometimes known, but a comprehensive history of their ephemeral art has yet to be written (Fig. 105). Ironically, these and other extremely fragile objects are financially worth more than surviving nitrate prints of the films they were meant to advertise.

Between film editing and film promotion there is the long and very delicate process of making projection copies for general release. The technical personnel involved in this activity are certainly not forgotten in this brief account. Many thousands of male and female workers manufactured, processed, hand- or stencil-coloured, and assembled the negatives and prints (Fig. 106); they are the first women and men encountered in this book (Chapters 3 and 4); others will be found in the film studios and laboratories to be visited in Chapter 6. If there is a slim chance that their names may be retrieved some day from the corporate records of production companies, chemical plants, and theatre chains, an even greater number of those who actually printed, dispatched, and posted the beautiful single or multi-sheet placards that adorned

Fig. 105 O'Galop (pseudonym of Marius Rossillon), promotional poster for the Société du cinématographe automobile. France, 1905. Lithograph on paper, 104 × 163cm. Source: George Eastman Museum.

Fig. 106 Laboratory for the assembly of film negatives and release prints. Biograph Company, New York, 1909. Gelatin silver print. Source: Museum of Modern Art/Film Stills Archive.

the walls of cities and villages around the world have left no trace of their lives.

Workers

It is now time to meet the hosts of the audiences who saw these posters and decided to attend the motion picture show. In answer to a statistical survey held in 1924 at the Kinema Theatre in Fresno, California, patrons said that the second most important reason for choosing this venue was the 'courtesy' of its staff (over 18 per cent of the responses); seat comfort came as a close third, at almost 18 per cent; the beauty of the auditorium was fourth, at 15 per cent of the total (we will soon find out what they thought of the films). Whatever the significance of this specific study, evidence suggests that the quality of service staff played a major role in the public perception of a cinematic event. Experts in the sector identified two categories of employees: the 'back', which included the projectionists and the musicians (along with those responsible for other aspects of the actual show); and the 'front', defined as the overall activities held in conjunction with the service and administrative end of the theatre.

'Front' and 'back' do not reflect the topographic location of employees' work (the two terms and concepts are borrowed from the operation of a conventional 'live' theatre). With the exception of projectionists, musicians, and theatre managers, very little is known about the identity and social background of theatre personnel – let alone their salaries – in different countries and periods in the history of silent cinema; the demographic data available so far provides scant indication of their gender balance, and is limited to a few geographic areas with better coverage by scholarly research.

For the purposes of this book, our attention goes primarily to the 'back' – that is, to those who actually performed the motion picture show. This statement, however, should be qualified by the recognition that film exhibitors – especially those of a first-run theatre – would have vehemently disagreed with this resolution. From their point of view, the smile of an usher, the cleanliness of the auditorium, and the beauty of the billboard on which the films were advertised were as important as the films themselves. For the patrons, the outstanding service of theatre personnel was as important as the lights that constellated the auditorium, the evocative decorations on its walls, and the mood of the music performed during the show.

In various degrees, this holistic approach to film exhibition was widely shared among film exhibitors around the world, even though there were huge differences in its manifestations from one country to another, and in theatres of different sizes and importance. The names of the women and men who worked in silent film theatres as valets, electricians, publicists, or cashiers are rarely known, but no serious study on the presentation of silent cinema can ignore the role they played in its growth as a social and cultural phenomenon.

In a first-class picture theatre of a major city, staff interacting with the public were obliged to wear a corporate uniform of some sort. Box-office staff were almost invariably female; their duties included maintaining the pleasant appearance of the booth, possibly with one or two vases of flowers displayed in a prominent position, and keeping an eye on suspicious behaviour at the entrance of the building. Women were also hired as coatroom supervisors; as full-time nurses, in permanent attendance during the show, ready to escort patrons to first-aid rooms with emergency kits; as maids in charge of the ladies' powder room equipped with dressing table items; and to assist children. Larger theatres had streetmen to handle crowds in the lobby and the pavements, and librarians who managed the theatre's collection of music scores. Theatres of more modest ambition provided a selection of these amenities, or only a few, or none at all.

The five functions of the 'front' – engineering, housekeeping, maintenance, service, and advertising – were flanked by a business office, whose chief worked in close collaboration with the floor manager. The advertising department was responsible for all signage and printing, either in liaison with film distributors, or for the production of programme brochures distributed to patrons in premium seats. Publicity managers also kept in touch with the chief projectionist regarding the scheduling of film trailers to be screened before the main programme. This brings us to the 'back' of the theatre, where one or more people in a sealed room were responsible for achieving the ultimate goal of the filmmaking process.

Projectionists

The most important job in motion picture exhibition was, by a long stretch, the most ingrate of all. It was solitary, repetitive, dangerous, physically and mentally demanding, often very unhealthy, and poorly paid. The success of the show was almost entirely dependent upon it, and yet the life of many projectionists could only be described as

a claustrophobic ordeal in the most literal sense of the term. Until the early 1910s, the booth was so small that one wonders how a person could have worked in it for long hours: a cabin 6 feet long, 8 feet deep, 7 feet high (2 by 2.5 metres, with a ceiling barely over 2 metres tall) was considered more than adequate for the task, but there were portable booths (Fig. 107) as small as 4 by 4 feet, 6 or 7 feet high (an area of less than 2 square metres, slightly over 2 metres tall); a box of 1.60 by 1.36 metres (about 5.5 by 4.5 feet) was decreed in 1908 as the minimum legal size for film theatres in Paris.

These coffins for the living will be described in more detail in Chapter 6. It is no wonder that a 1905 article by Baxter Morton in *Scientific American* ('Fires from Moving-Picture Exhibitions', 5 August 1905, p. 102) would attribute so many disasters to the fact that an operator 'may become faint or giddy from the heat or from escaping gas'. In a memoir published in the Soviet Union in 1928 (Vsevolod Vasiliievich Chaikovskij, *Mladencheskie gody russkogo kino* [Infant Years of the Russian Cinema], p. 10), it is recalled that 'sometimes the box became so intolerably hot that the projectionist used to go out and sit for a while in the auditorium', in which case the show must have come to a halt every now and then. Programme schedules in Japan were so

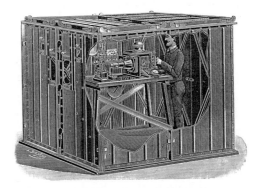

Fig. 107 Cross-section of a 1908 portable projection booth, c. 1907. Source: Cinematografi Pathé Frères. Milan: Pathé, 1908, p. 77.

demanding that projectionists were submitted to gruelling shifts, requiring them to learn how to crank projectors with their feet while eating.

Given such dreadful conditions, it is no surprise that projectionists were among the first in the film business to organize themselves into unions. The first known entity of this kind was established in San Francisco in 1904. It was followed in April 1907 by the National Association of Cinematograph Operators in Great Britain, and by the Opérateurs Cinématographistes de France in 1908. The British union's charter was drafted with the best intentions: its declared goals were to 'protect and promote the interests of qualified operators, and to raise the status of their profession'; to encourage best practice in film exhibition, and 'establish a standard of proficiency by a qualifying examination'; to create a register of certified operators, entitled to benefits commensurate with their skills; last but not least, 'to secure the recognition of a minimum rate of pay' for their services. Most of these initiatives were stymied by those theatre owners who vigorously opposed professional licensing; as of 1910, only two hundred projectionists were officially enrolled in the union, a tiny fraction of the estimated four thousand operators in the entire country.

Projectionists' wages also compared unfavourably with other kinds of manual labour: in France, non-unionized projectionists earned 40 to 45 francs per week in 1910 (against 60 to 70 francs for union members); 25 to 30 shillings per week was the norm in Great Britain, less than plumbers and electricians. The situation was even worse in the United States, where rampant competition allowed film exhibitors to find labourers for as little as 15 dollars per week, with higher salaries reaching 22 dollars a week for shifts of eleven consecutive hours (without a break).

All sorts of technical codes and bureaucratic regulations were promulgated for the protection of public safety, with little concern for projectionists: in 1908, booth ventilation was recommended in Paris theatres 'when possible'; this was made into law only in 1927, when 8 cubic metres became the mandatory minimum size for a projection booth. Over the years, the increasing rate of fatal accidents involving untrained labourers in unsafe working conditions resulted in a backlash against film exhibitors; emboldened by this, projectionists' unions became much stronger, exerting a tighter control over the recruiting process and more stringent safety rules. Film projection was a favourite topic of technical literature, a signal that the position was in great demand and that exhibitors recognized its importance, despite their reluctance to accommodate the workers' needs, and their opposition to higher wages.

By the end of the silent era, the projectionist's job was surrounded by an aura of mystery and awe, compounded by the extremely secretive stance taken by the members of their guild. Once motivated by safety concerns, the projectionists' protective attitude towards their working environment became legendary. To say that the projection booth had all the marks of a male-owned territory is an understatement: it was a place where masculine authority over the machine was exercised with the same mixture of pride and exclusiveness shown by car, boat, and locomotive pilots. Insofar as there was enough room for them to intrude, uninvited staff and casual visitors entered the booth at their own risk. Alone in a mostly airtight, soundproof and fireproof booth, the projectionist was absolute master of his secluded kingdom. The entire show – with its lights, its live or synchronized music, and the speed at which the audience would see the film – was taking place under his authority, something he would not surrender or share with anybody.

On the other hand, projectionists rarely showed much reverence towards the objects to be exhibited: in the absence of a splicer, a broken film was often mended by licking its ends and joining them before threading it again into the projector's gears. Some technicians cared more than others about the longevity of release prints, but no one expected nor particularly wanted them to last for ever. Scratches on the film emulsion were as normal to projectionists as abrasions on a worker's skin after long days of manual labour. Day after day, night after night, with no other interlocutor than the noise of the projector and the hiss of the carbons in the lamphouse, the projectionists had ample time to think, observe, touch, and listen to the sprockets as they engaged with the film's perforations, familiarize themselves with the apparatus, learn to interpret the slightest variations in the behaviour of its lenses, gears, and light sources with the same remote benevolence bestowed by a lonely *deus ex machina* upon its unknowing subjects. Occasionally, projectionists went beyond the call of duty by rescuing discarded prints, or at least keeping individual frames for future reference: the first guerrilla activists of film preservation.

Musicians

If film projection gave a somewhat stable occupation to a vast number of people who were learning their craft on the fly, an even larger population of musicians was employed at the service of sound accompaniment to motion pictures. In the United States alone, according to statistics, more than one hundred thousand people were reported to be active in the music business at the beginning of the twentieth century. Their ranks grew exponentially in the following decades; thanks to cinema, new job opportunities became available to those who could not find a role for themselves in theatres, concert and dance halls, or vaudeville. They were not necessarily the most talented, but their influence was steadily increasing over time; trade unions representing

their interests became more powerful, and salaries were often raised to respectable levels.

In large cities of the United States in the late 1920s, the earnings of music performers for silent films could reach an average rate of 70 or 80 dollars per week; according to music composer and conductor Hugo Riesenfeld, about half of the players was paid 100 dollars. A first violin's annual income ranged from $7,000 and $10,000 per year; film theatre organists were frequently paid even more, with annual incomes of $6,000 to $20,000. The reputation of Japanese film exhibition venues was habitually dependent upon the celebrity and skills of their *benshi* performers: the most famous were lavishly remunerated for their acting and singing, which was regarded – with good reason – as an integral part of the show (we shall return to them in Chapter 9).

Wages to those musicians who provided their services in small towns and rural areas were not as generous. Any music teacher or amateur living in the provinces could be given a chance to secure a job in a picture house, and not all audiences were as sophisticated as those of the big cities; but large theatres were being built even in relatively small communities, and group performances were not at all uncommon outside the major urban centres. In the 1924 statistical survey mentioned earlier in this chapter, over 28 per cent of the patrons attending the Kinema Theatre of Fresno, California, responded that they chose that venue because of the music being played, with only 10 per cent indicating the films being shown as the reason for their visit. Four years later, a university teacher conducted similar research in another area (not identified in the report), and discovered that music was the main attraction for no less than 43 per cent of the patrons; the pictures themselves ranked third at 17 per cent, behind seat comfort (24 per cent).

It would be imprudent to take these figures as representative evidence of how audiences felt about music worldwide and across the years, but they clearly suggest that musical accompaniment was not an ancillary component of the filmgoing experience as the term 'accompaniment' might lead us to believe. The range of options available to exhibitors – aside from the adoption of mechanical instruments – was not limited to vertical pianos and orchestras of different sizes. Organ music was extremely popular in some countries; a large number of film theatres in North America proudly featured the Wurlitzer Unit Orchestra, an organ with a sound so powerful, and endowed with such an extraordinary ability to reproduce a wide variety of instruments, as to deserve the popular nickname of 'mighty Wurlitzer'. The majestic look of its console with multiple keyboards and countless switches was highlighted in some venues by placing the instrument on the platform of an elevator that would slowly rise from beneath the orchestra pit, with the organist playing, as the show was about to begin: theatrical effects of this kind can still be experienced in surviving picture palaces of the United States.

Even in venues of humble profile, it was considered normal to have a percussionist sitting near the piano player to inject an extra touch of rhythm during action sequences, and for imitations of natural sounds. Noises could also be creatively integrated into the show, with individuals or groups placed behind the screen employing a wide array of objects to imitate everything: rain, thunder, waves, trains, car horns, sirens, birdsongs (Fig. 108). Manuals of theatre management offered basic instructions on how to achieve these effects, berating those exhibitors who did not make at least an effort to add a note of realism to the action portrayed in the film.

The skills and personal taste of these noise or music performers was, admittedly, an object of sustained debate. Newspapers, magazines, and trade journals of the silent era are peppered with reports of untalented or careless pianists

Fig. 108 Performers of sound effects behind the screen of a projection hall, *c.* 1910. Illustration from a Yerkes Manufacturing Company catalogue. Source: Reproduced in Gaumont Co. Catalogue of Moving Picture Apparatus and Accessories. The Chrono Moving Picture Machine. The Chronophone Talking Pictures, n.l. [New York], n.d., [ca. 1912], p. 30.

who would not only miss important cues in the action, but sometimes blatantly ignored the film's storyline; caricatures and cartoon strips on this theme were keen to expose the carelessness of absentee sound-effects technicians, together with the casual behaviour of pianists who would show up only a few seconds before the interval, or pay more attention to their own appearance than to the film being screened. As in any concert hall, the public could witness either talent or mediocrity, depending on how much they paid to attend the show. With the abrupt end of the silent era, this became a moot point: hundreds of thousands of people around the world suddenly found themselves unemployed, the first victims of a technological revolution that redefined the experience of cinema through recorded sound on film.

Audiences

Determining how many people went to motion picture shows during the silent era is virtually impossible until the early 1920s at least, but there is plenty of circumstantial evidence suggesting that their numbers grew very quickly immediately after the invention of cinema. By the mid-1900s, the new medium had become a worldwide sensation. We do not yet have global statistics on a chronological basis, but it can be roughly estimated (based on the very uneven appraisals published in the period) that in the late 1920s about 5.7 billion tickets per year were sold in the United States (the figure was 4.75 billion in 1919); 364 million in Great Britain, 348 in France, 310 in Germany, 260 in Italy, 190 in Japan. This means, on average, 15 million people entered a cinema somewhere in the United States in one day, a little more than 10 per cent of the country's entire population; one million in Great Britain (2.1 per cent of the population), 800,000 in Germany (1.25 per cent), 950,000 in France (2.4 per cent), 700,000 in Italy (1.8 per cent), 500,000 in Japan (0.95 per cent).

Despite the much lower percentages outside North America, these are staggering figures on a global scale: if the numbers are correct, they add up to a worldwide total of almost ten billion tickets sold each year, before the advent of sound film. In the virtual absence of statistical information until 1918, we are left with the presumption that the number of tickets sold since the beginnings of cinema must have steadily increased every year, at least until the outbreak of World War I on the European continent, and that the United States box office was heavily affected by the 1918–19 influenza pandemic that killed over half a million people in the country (around seventy-five million victims worldwide).

It is far more difficult to ascertain who the viewers were, where they went to see films, and their identities (in terms of gender, social status, and ethnicity). Over the years, film scholars have put considerable effort into figuring out the demographic profile of film audiences during the silent era. The humble origins of cinema as a fairground or vaudeville attraction, and its spectacular growth in the first decade of the twentieth century as a cheap form of entertainment, were seen as supporting evidence of a linear trajectory in the evolution of public attendance.

In a nutshell, the scenario runs as follows. When moving images were a novelty, their clientele was drawn almost exclusively from the working class; in some countries, cinema was a catalyst of social integration for immigrants and ethnic minorities; around 1903, producers and exhibitors felt it necessary to attract a more diverse constituency, especially in the major urban conglomerates; viewers from the middle class were gradually brought in by virtue of a broader gamut of film genres and subjects, ranging from literary adaptations to melodrama, science, and edifying themes; the strategy paid off after 1913, when feature-length films earned the attention of dominant bourgeois taste. At that point, with the blessing of a small but vocal elite of artists and intellectuals, cinema achieved the kind of respectability needed to transcend class divisions and become a global phenomenon.

This oversimplified picture is not altogether inaccurate. It is true that a film programme was the best entertainment option (aside from the pub, the saloon, the fairground, or the dance hall) for those who could not afford the theatre or the music concert. It is also true that educated people often regarded cinema with sheer contempt, as shown by the answer of one respondent to a survey on the film experience conducted by an Italian journalist of the early 1910s: 'Sir, I am a gentleman.' According to research carried out in New York City in 1910, 72 per cent of the total audience was reported as being of lower income, and 25 per cent from the 'clerical' class.

These figures, however, can be misleading if they are not observed from other perspectives. Women and children were the core audience groups; more than two-thirds of the motion picture houses' patrons were between 15 and 25 years old. As for minorities, their integration into the film theatre community of some countries was uneven at best: in the United States, racial segregation against African Americans was the norm, either within the theatres' seating arrangements, or in specific neighbourhoods (Jacqueline Stewart's 2005 study *Migrating to the Movies* is a classic on this subject); before World War I, immigrants of Chinese, Italian, Slavic, and Irish descent could be treated with the utmost scorn, as shown in several films of the period (a 1914 film by D.W. Griffith, *The Escape*, goes as far as portraying Irish people as the carriers of genetic diseases), and it is hard to imagine that the derogatory portraits conveyed in these pictures were ignored by the interested parties.

Much of what is currently known about film audiences in the silent era is the outcome of research projects undertaken in Europe and North America, with the United States, France, Germany, Great Britain, Russia, and the French-speaking region of Canada occupying the leading positions. What these studies had in common until the late 1990s was a strong emphasis on urban populations, and yet 70 per cent of the film theatres operating in the United States around 1910 were located outside the cities. Fewer forms of collective entertainment were available in rural communities, thus making cinema a very attractive option to all, regardless of their social status.

Emilie Altenloh, author of a flawed but pioneering study on film spectatorship (a 1913 dissertation, published in the following year), drew her conclusions from an investigation of cinema audiences in a single German city, Mannheim. She concluded that young and unmarried people represented a substantial portion of filmgoers, and that boys were more likely to go to the picture house because girls had work to do at home. Another woman, Matilde Serao, wrote in 1916 one of the most perceptive assessments of film spectatorship (aptly titled 'A Spectatrix Is Speaking to

You') from a female perspective. Around the same period, German-American psychologist Hugo Münsterberg applied his theories to the analysis of cinema as a social phenomenon. Later scholars have frequently drawn their conclusions from conceptual frameworks based on the notions of modernity, gender, and class divisions.

Fertile as they are, these approaches offer a necessarily partial view of the subjective and interpersonal dynamics that brought people to motion picture shows. Differences in the ethnic, linguistic, and social identities of all the nations where cinema was experienced during the early twentieth century were just too pronounced to impose terms like 'bourgeoisie' or 'modernity' with sufficient accuracy upon the behaviour of a picturegoer in, say, Tokyo as opposed to one from Montevideo (Yuri Tsivian's magisterial 1994 study on early film reception in Russia is an eye-opener in this respect). In many countries, the most coveted theatre seats were located on the floor; in others, like India, well-to-do spectators regarded them as utterly inappropriate to their status, and chose the upper balcony instead. Organ music was cherished in the United States, not much so in Europe. Standing up and singing the national anthem before the show was mandatory in certain nations (short films were made and exhibited for this specific purpose, with a waving flag in a single extended shot); elsewhere, the same practice would have provoked the loudest catcalls.

The list of examples could go on, together with a wide range of very plausible but also very uncertain explanations of what may or may not have been specific to the cinematic experience, as opposed to attending a church function, a sporting match, or a drinking spree at the bar. Many forms of social behaviour outside work had no relationship with cinema; too little is known about them to allow anything more than conjecture on why people chose one or another for their leisure time. This is not to diminish the importance of sociological research on spectatorship; the habits and motivations of film audiences – in particular outside the metropolitan areas, and in territories other than Western Europe and the United States – are only beginning to be explored, and much can be learned from systematic work in these regions, as long as we keep in mind that the knowledge to be drawn from the surviving evidence is bound to remain fragmentary at best, and to sometimes contradict our own assumptions on what the world looked like in the early twentieth century.

What is beyond doubt is that, in a few years, cinema was exercising a profound influence on culture, morals, and politics, prompting a fierce and persistent debate on matters of education, propaganda, and censorship. The arguments could occur within the film theatre itself: talking during the show, either in reaction to what appeared on screen or to music and lecturers, was the norm until the rise of feature-length film (and beyond, at least in some countries outside North America and Europe, where the etiquette of music concerts became a sign of distinction for the most refined patrons of a motion picture show). Theatres were privileged places for welcome or unwelcome seduction, trysts, and plain lovemaking. The most avid filmgoers kept souvenirs of their experiences in scrapbooks filled with items such as newspaper clippings, ticket stubs, and autographed photos of their favourite stars.

There were people who felt that cinema was detrimental to their vision. Image instability, especially flickering, was the main culprit of real or imaginary diseases, from ordinary conjunctivitis to its newly discovered variation, 'cinematophthalmitis'. Physicians agreed that it didn't permanently damage the retina, but some remedies were in order, such as waving hands with open fingers in front of the eyes while watching the film, wearing glasses with blue-coated lenses during the show,

or applying eyedrops with a solution of cocaine or adrenaline chlorhydrate. Scientists of the early twentieth century urged producers and exhibitors to do something about jittery projection and the unpleasant effects of slower projection speeds. To assist those patrons who were particularly subject to teary or red eyes, Gaumont was selling in 1906 a charming and totally useless placebo, a special fan with tiny holes, to be agitated sideways before the eyes in the course of the screening (Fig. 109).

While the political thoughts of film audiences could not be detected by statistical means, they could at least be influenced for ideological ends. Newsreels were so popular that they could provoke riots in theatres if their subject matter

Fig. 109 Perforated fan to reduce the flickering effect in film viewing. Gaumont, Paris, c. 1905. Source: Catalogue des appareils Gaumont, January 1906, p. 35.

was controversial enough to warrant fist fights among young male populations. The first film school, VGIK (Vsesojuznij gosudarstvennij institut kinematografii kinematografii [All-Union State Institute of Cinematography]) was established by Soviet decree in 1919, soon followed by a similar institution in Italy (the Istituto Luce, founded in 1924 by the Fascist government), but authoritarian regimes were not alone in understanding that the new medium could be instrumental in controlling mass opinion. When D.W. Griffith arrived in London on 7 April 1917 for the British premiere of *Intolerance*, Prime Minister Lloyd George, Queen Alexandra, and Winston Churchill welcomed him with the pomp and circumstance normally bestowed to a head of state. A day earlier, the United States had joined the war against Germany, and Griffith was hailed as a messiah of the long-awaited intervention. In those years, it was not difficult to believe that cinema could change the world.

Interpreters

Surrounded as it was by the indifference or the sheer contempt of mainstream culture, cinema lived its first decade in relative isolation from the arts community. This does not mean that intellectuals were unaware of its mass appeal, as testified by penetrating and often imaginative commentaries from major personalities such as Maksim Gorkij in Russia and Guillaume Apollinaire in France. Film criticism in the modern sense of the term did not appear, however, until motion pictures attained such popularity that public opinion could no longer ignore it. Most of the first public statements about the aesthetic value of individual films were written by the filmmakers themselves, generally as codas to plot summaries where the pioneers of cinema chanted the praise of their own work. These texts are found in early film catalogues, with

descriptive notes following each title (*Dislocation mystérieuse*, 1901, is described by Georges Méliès as 'one of the best and most mysterious films ever produced' in the English-language version of his 1903 catalogue, p. 22). Around 1907, as the first trade journals exclusively devoted to film were established in Europe and the United States, these narratives found their way into densely printed pages featuring detailed lists of the titles available for distribution.

Around the same time, notes on specific films made timid appearances in newspapers and magazines. The first film review in *Variety*, published on 19 January 1907 – sixty-nine words in all – was dedicated to a Pathé film, *Émouvant voyage de noce* (*An Exciting Honeymoon*, 1906), described as a mixture of 'comedy and "chasing", besides a melodramatic touch'. Critical analysis was basic at best ('the fun is amusing', wrote the reviewer), with frequent references to the public's reaction ('the picture [was] well worked out and the audience remained in its seats until the close'), but very early on there were also remarkable instances of theoretical insights on how cinema should be seen, and what it could become; over the years, these normative or utopian visions would grow into coherent and at times complex systems of thought. Special consideration was given to the photographic quality of the works: unsteady or poorly processed pictures were the objects of explicit and at times colourful grievances. References to music performances were rare; a modest share of attention went to acting styles. Most of the commentaries focused on storylines, with occasional remarks about controversial or morally questionable scenes. As the identity of the filmmakers was not announced in the credits, the only two terms of comparison available to commentators were the names of production companies, and their nationalities. French melodrama and Italian comedies were regarded as the standards of excellence; colour was deemed worthy of mention only in particular cases.

By the time feature-length films from Italy and Denmark were exported all over the world in the early 1910s, the critical vocabulary had reached a certain degree of sophistication in trade periodicals. The sensation caused by Italian costume epics shook the status quo: Enrico Guazzoni's *Quo Vadis?* was a box-office triumph of such magnitude as to persuade *The New York Times* to publish its first film review on 22 April 1913, with references to sound accompaniment and to the viewers' response (the plight of Christian martyrs 'is managed in a way to bring gasps of horror from the audience'). Readers of the *New York Times* would have to wait more than six months before another commentary appeared in its pages: it was a much shorter article about a German film, the biopic *Richard Wagner* (Carl Froelich, 1913), reviewed on 21 November; two weeks later, on 9 December, *The Inside of the White Slave Traffic* (Frank V. Beal, 1913) represented the newspaper's third foray into film criticism, with an unexpected glimpse at demographics: 'a large proportion of the audience was composed of young girls from 16 to 18 years of age. Fully two-thirds of the audience were women'.

Spectacle, biography, and sex paved the way to film journalism; its most creative and ambitious practitioners did not wait long before presenting themselves as screenwriters. Just when Europe was about to be engulfed in the carnage of World War I, an Italian film producer and a French writer provided – in separate contexts – two key ingredients for what was bound to become the double identity of film criticism. Giovanni Pastrone, a young film entrepreneur based in Turin, lured an influential poet of the time, Gabriele D'Annunzio, to lend his name for the creation of *Cabiria*, attributed to D'Annunzio himself but actually directed by Pastrone under the pseudonym Piero Fosco. Soon afterwards, Louis Delluc saw a film by Cecil B. DeMille (*The Cheat*, 1915), and was sufficiently impressed to declare in his 1919 article 'Le Cinquième art' (published in *Le Film*) that the world was 'witnessing the birth of an extraordinary art form'.

From different perspectives, Pastrone and Delluc legitimized cinema as a new tool for artistic expression. Their influence spread around the world like wildfire, providing film criticism with two formidable sources of inspiration: cinema as an alternative form of theatre, and as an entirely different medium, obeying aesthetic rules of its own. An avant-garde intellectual, Ricciotto Canudo, had boldly announced it in 1911 as 'the sixth art'; he later acknowledged that dance should be included in the count, thus making cinema the seventh art in human history. The tension between cinema as popular entertainment (the present) and as the ultimate synthesis of all the other arts (the conditional future) would be an ongoing theme for thousands of writers who succeeded Canudo and Delluc in the following decades. Their influence still reverberates in the current reincarnations of film theory and criticism.

Chapter 6

Buildings

Fig. 110 The entrance of the Cinéma Pathé in Redessan, France (1,185 inhabitants in 1906), as it appeared in 1988. Source: Private collection. Photo by Karel Dibbets.

The artists, musicians, audiences, and critics introduced in the previous chapter barely knew that many thousands of workers had been active behind the scenes, far removed from film theatres and studios, to create the material conditions for the existence of cinema. The sheer complexity of the process involved in manufacturing motion picture film on a large scale required a vast amount of space, energy, materials, and qualified personnel. In order to meet the skyrocketing demand of raw stock, each of the three major companies in the business – Kodak, Pathé, and AGFA – built factories of such imposing scale that they soon resembled small industrial towns, with lodging, refectories, and health care services for their staff. The first manufacturing plant, established in 1896 by Eastman Kodak in Rochester, New York, grew to the size of a small town ('Kodak Park', 400 acres) by the end of the 1920s (Fig. 111). By that time, the factory was operating continuously throughout the year, twenty-four hours a day; a smaller manufacturing unit was set up in Australia in 1908.

In 1916, Kodak had 8,218 employees in Rochester alone; by 1928, the number had soared to 11,347 (there were over 20,000 workers worldwide, a fourfold increase from 1907), and it continued to grow in the following years, inside and outside the United States. In Germany, the AGFA laboratories were initially located in Treptow, near Berlin, adjacent to the company's existing facilities for photographic products; three years later, in 1909, they were moved to Wolfen, in the Bitterfeld district, with the goal of producing thirty million feet of film per year. The company's managers had wildly underestimated the increase

in film production worldwide: before the outbreak of World War I, the annual output at AGFA had reached ninety million feet; at the end of the silent era, that figure had to be multiplied several times. In 1920, cinema was already the fifth largest industry in the United States.

What the three members of the motion picture stock oligopoly had in common was their need to create their infrastructures in areas that would offer an abundant supply of clean water and natural reserves for electric power. Kodak found both in the Genesee River and its waterfalls in western New York State; in 1929, AGFA's personnel of 5,350 chemists, engineers, and manual labourers used the electricity generated by burning in a day more than 600 tons of lignite drawn from the open-air coal fields of Bitterfeld; a direct railway service connected the excavation site to the factory's main entrance, branching into four lines that served as the plant's transportation network for the people and the ingredients needed to the creation of sensitized film stock. In the mid-1920s, over 20,000 cubic metres of water were required for a normal day of operation in the various departments of AGFA's technical headquarters. A great portion of the energy and water were used for removing dust particles from the air – dust is the main enemy of raw film stock – and for moisture and temperature control: 800,000 cubic metres of air were pumped in and out every hour.

In the 1920s, Pathé, AGFA, and Kodak also each divided their film manufacturing activities into nine departments, with separate buildings or dedicated areas, arranged to facilitate the workflow: producing the photographic emulsion; creating the film base; preparing it for coating; applying the emulsion to the base; slitting the films into strips; perforating the film stock; marking its edges; verifying the final product; packing it to protect the raw stock from light and making it ready for delivery. These buildings covered most of

Fig. 111 Aerial view of the Eastman Kodak manufacturing plant in the United States. Rochester, New York, 1923. Photographic glass slide. Other film factories were operated by Kodak in Australia, Canada, and Great Britain during the silent film era. Source: George Eastman Museum.

the manufacturing plant's territory; its topography was constellated by a larger number of warehouses, private dwellings, and ancillary services.

The most important of all – strategically placed in one or more areas of the factory – was the fire station; its personnel worked in shifts around the clock. The huge amount of highly flammable and toxic materials stored, handled, and processed over such a vast surface made this preventive measure an absolute imperative, despite the obvious fact that no fire brigade would have been able to do little more than circumscribe the effects of an explosion (no such accident of great magnitude was ever recorded by the three companies). Smoking was categorically prohibited everywhere, both inside and outside the premises.

The pumping heart of the manufacturing plant was the generator, a power station whose capacity would have been enough to provide electricity to a mid-sized town. It's an apt comparison, because all other buildings – aside from the administrative offices, the repair and maintenance workshops, the dining rooms (at AGFA, men and women had their meals in separate halls; a luxury version was reserved for the company's officials), and the research laboratories (chemistry, engineering) – were designed to serve the private and communal needs of the personnel. Near the AGFA plant, a residential area for employees had its own hospital, a maternity home, a swimming pool, plus a polyclinic and X-ray facilities, all provided by the company.

This blend of pitch-perfect capitalism and social welfare was a peculiar aspect of all three giants of film manufacturing. It was more pronounced at Kodak, where everyone on the company's payroll – without exception – were offered free college education for their children, very generous retirement plans, and received part of the company's annual dividend in proportion to their salary: for them, a thriving film industry meant a higher bonus at the end of the year. In the mind of George Eastman, this was a powerful incentive to loyalty, longer tenure in the job, and productivity. In exchange, everyone at Eastman Kodak was required to comply with the strictest corporate secrecy: access to the plant's entrances and buildings was subject to uncompromising security policies.

Studios

Film production, the first point of arrival of film stock from the manufacturing plant, had two parallel beginnings. One occurred in the open air, with the Lumière brothers and their cameramen shooting their earliest films in urban or rural locations in France and around the world. The other happened in a tiny, ugly building erected by Thomas Alva Edison in 1893 on the premises of his laboratory in West Orange, New Jersey, for the relatively modest sum of $637.47, the equivalent of about $17,000 in 2017. Two of Edison's employees, W.K.L. Dickson and Jonathan Campbell, found it so crammed and uncomfortable that they compared it to a police van, commonly known at the time as the 'Black Maria'. The name took hold, and was subsequently attached to the first film production studio ever built.

For eight years, until Black Maria's closure in January 1901, a variety of artists and sportsmen – actors, magicians, boxers, acrobats, dancers, strongmen – posed in front of the camera for the creation of single-shot films to be viewed in Edison's Kinetoscope. Entirely covered with black tarpaper, the Black Maria had a movable roof to allow sunlight into the studio; underneath, a system of circular rails made it rotate in order to capture the best available light. After 1895, Edison followed Lumière's example by making films on location, but the die was cast: filmmaking needed a permanent home in which to flourish, regardless of the weather.

The popularity of iron-and-glass buildings in France and Great Britain since the mid-nineteenth century inspired film producers to adopt this kind of structure for their studio shooting. The one constructed by Georges Méliès at Montreuil-sous-Bois in 1897 (Fig. 112) was 6 metres high, and initially had a square base of 17 metres on each side, and a wooden skeleton (soon replaced by metal). All other major producers followed his example, with ever larger and more sophisticated designs; Selig Polyscope Company's studio in Chicago, 179 feet in length and 80 feet wide, was one of the largest in the United States during the early 1910s. Two or more different scenes could be staged simultaneously under the same roof, enabling a dramatic improvement in the daily output of exposed camera negative (Fig. 113). Glazed glass and a blind wall at the end of the proscenium soon became the norm; Méliès further modified the original design of his studio, giving its floor plan a telescope-like profile.

The introduction of movable shutters to control light levels in the building during the brightest days made life easier for camera operators, but exacerbated a problem that had become apparent from the very beginning of interior shooting: the studio was essentially a greenhouse, intolerably hot in the summer and very difficult to heat in the cold season because of its sheer size. Ventilation ports and mechanical fans brought modest improvements during hot weather; as for the winter, the best solution was to reduce or pause film production altogether, which also took account of the fewer hours of useful daylight available.

The era of iron-and-glass studios came to an abrupt end as soon as more efficient and affordable systems for electric lighting were invented, but other drawbacks had meanwhile become painfully evident in this architectural concept. The studio had originally been thought of as a space reserved for the stage and the camera. Before shooting, the studio floor served as a versatile workshop in which to paint backdrops, instruct carpenters on how to

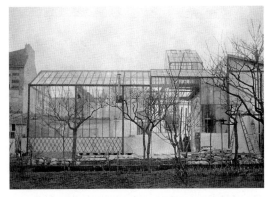

Fig. 112 The east façade of Georges Méliès' first production studio in Montreuil, built in 1897. Gelatin silver print. Source: Cinémathèque française.

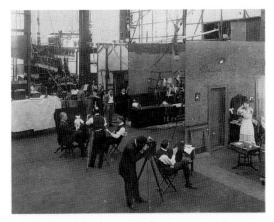

Fig. 113 Filmmakers, performers, and technicians at work in the Biograph Company studios. The Bronx, New York City, c. 1913. Gelatin silver print. Source: George Eastman Museum.

build the set, rehearse stage machinery as needed (Fig. 114). Costumes, props, and furniture could be stored in nearby rooms (Fig. 115), together with mechanical and electrical equipment. This may have been good enough in the pre-industrial age of cinema; the methods of film production, however, had evolved to a point where this type of approach was no longer adequate for the requirements of filmmakers and their technical crew.

What was missing in the old studio configuration could be defined as the real estate for an

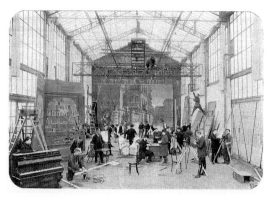

Fig. 114 Personnel at work at the Pathé studios, c. 1910. Source: Frederick Arthur Ambrose Talbot, Moving Pictures. How they are made and worked. London: Heinemann, 1912; Philadelphia: J.B. Lippincott Co., 1914, p. 112.

Fig. 116 Shooting a scene in front of the audience at the Universal studios, California, c. 1916. Source: Rob Wagner [pseud. of Robert Leicester], Film Folk. "Close-Ups" of the Men, Women and Children Who Make the "Movies". New York: The Century Company, 1918, p. 96.

Fig. 115 The wardrobe room at the Selig Polyscope studios. Edendale, California, c. 1910. Source: Frederick Arthur Ambrose Talbot, Moving Pictures. How they are made and worked. London: Heinemann, 1912; Philadelphia: J.B. Lippincott Co., 1914, p. 113.

Fig. 117 Exterior set by Storm V. Boyd Jr for *The Vampire* (Robert G. Vignola, 1913). Cliffside Park, New Jersey, September 1913. Gelatin silver print. Source: George Eastman Museum.

ever-expanding division of labour: dedicated areas in which to shoot miniature scenes and special effects; develop and print the footage; verify its quality in a projection room; let performers apply their own makeup; provide wardrobe assistants with enough space and sewing machines to make alterations to costumes and gowns (in 1918, the Universal studio even had a dedicated area where visitors were invited to observe the filming process, as seen in Fig. 116). Moreover, some scenes could not be shot indoors because they were just too big to fit into a conventional studio. Poverty

Row companies and entrepreneurial talents had learned how to recreate an indoor scene practically anywhere (Fig. 117), covered when necessary with cotton cloth to diffuse the light from above. Building large sets in the open air was not difficult per se. The question was how to consolidate interior and exterior shooting in a single, multifunctional, efficient production entity.

The layout reproduced in Fig. 118 shows an ambitious but ill-fated attempt to address all these questions. It was designed in 1914 by the Photo-Drama Company, a consortium of American and Italian producers instigated by George Kleine, a film distributor who had envisaged the creation of a huge studio complex at Villa Boriglione in Grugliasco, a

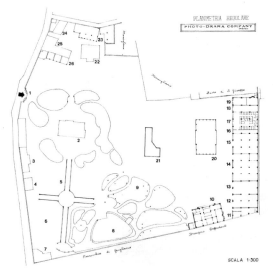

Fig. 118 Map of the Photo-Drama Company studio complex. Grugliasco, Italy, 1914. Source: Library of Congress/The George Kleine Papers.

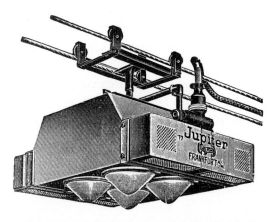

Fig. 119 Studio lighting unit on suspended cables. Jupiter-Kunstlicht, Frankfurt a.M. and Berlin, *c.* 1924. Source: Hans Schmidt, Kino-Taschenbuch für Amateure und Fachleute. Berlin: Union Deutsche Verlagsgesellschaft, 1926, p. 102.

small town near Turin, at the time a major centre of film production in Italy. The glass studio still played a central role in Kleine's vision, but it was integrated with a wide array of storage facilities, workshops, laboratories, dressing rooms, administrative offices, even a refectory for catering services.

Photo-Drama's integrated studio facility had an artificial basin, a lake, a garden, a pine forest, a garage, and enough space in which to build temporary sets in exteriors. The outbreak of World War I put a dramatic end to Kleine's dream, and plunged the Italian film industry into a crisis with long-term consequences, but the concept behind the aborted project did not die altogether. Improvements in lighting technology triggered the resurrection of this idea. Hollywood in the United States, and Neu Babelsberg in Germany, brought it to fruition in the 1920s. Their newest studios were buildings of an innovative kind, where glazed glass was no longer a necessity. A brief detour from industrial landscapes to the history of light sources will help to explain why these buildings changed so radically.

Lighting

One of the earliest forms of artificial lighting in the film studio was the arc lamp, arranged in rows of five or ten above the set, or on the sides and sometimes at the front. These had to be arranged with great care, their parabolic reflectors shaded with glass or linen screen, so that their light would diffuse more evenly, but they had the advantage of being very compatible with orthochromatic film emulsion because of their blue-white emissions. The beginning of the end for the 'glass roof' concept of studio architecture came in the early 1900s, when mercury vapour tubes revolutionized interior shooting after their first appearance in large office spaces. Peter Cooper Hewitt, an electrical engineer from New York, had found a way to produce light by using an electric arc through vapourized mercury in glass tubes of 3 inches (7.6 centimetres) in diameter and 3 feet (about 90 centimetres) in length.

The Cooper Hewitt tubes were considerably more efficient than incandescent light: they produced far less heat, and could easily be installed in racks to be hung from the ceiling, or placed vertically – generally in groups of eight – on movable stands around the set (Fig. 120). At the time of their introduction for filmmaking purposes in 1905, mercury vapour tubes were not deemed suitable for domestic use: their light was very rich in blue and ultraviolet emissions, and had almost no red. Their glow was therefore very unpleasant in everyday life (the problem was fixed in the 1930s with a coat of phosphor inside the tube), but it was a true blessing for the orthochromatic stock, whose emulsion could perfectly capture green and blue and was totally blind to red.

In the early 1910s, Maurice J. Wohl and two German émigrés to the United States, the brothers Johann and Anton Kliegl, developed self-feeding carbon arcs that produced a highly concentrated light, ideal for dramatic effect (to the delight of Cecil B. DeMille and his cinematographer Alvin Wyckoff). Powerful as they were, their performance on the set was marred by at least two collateral effects. Compared to the Cooper Hewitt tubes, they were extremely hot. Furthermore, their ultraviolet rays were so strong that a condition known as 'Klieg eyes' (without the final 'l') – in medical terms, actinic conjunctivitis – could give performers swelling and redness of the eyes.

No matter how carefully maintained, these lights were also subject to flickering (this was so pronounced that in some German and Russian films of the mid-1910s there appeared to be a lightning storm raging around the set) and produced an inordinate amount of dirt from the incandescent ends of the carbons. In the tightly enclosed lamphouse of a film projector, heat, dust, and ultraviolet rays could be kept under control; not so in the open space of a film studio, although leaded glass panels that captured ultraviolet light were eventually fitted onto the reflectors to reduce optical strain for the players. Electric cables were not making things any easier, proliferating as they were in intricate webs around the set. On the positive side, technically savvy personnel of some production companies had found a way since 1920 to adjust light positioning with remote controls driven by electric motors.

With their smooth, relatively cool, and highly uniform flood of blue-green light, the Cooper Hewitt panels prevailed over the intense but

Fig. 120 Cooper Hewitt lights in the Triangle Film Corporation studio. Culver City, California, 1917. Gelatin silver print. Source: George Eastman Museum.

messy brightness of their carbon arc antagonists well into the late 1910s, when incandescent lamps filled with nitrogen and activated by a filament of tungsten began to be used for close-ups. Long shots were not as simple to achieve with this light, as tungsten bulbs were so faint that extra voltage had to be pumped in to make them effective. The overload of electric power also served a more fundamental objective: the actinic quality of incandescent bulbs was extremely low (the word 'actinic', derived from the Greek for 'beam' or 'ray', was widely used in early photography to indicate the light captured by the sensitized emulsion; actinic lights were used in developing and printing laboratories). Tungsten light was rich in red emissions; to make it compatible with orthochromatic stock, it was installed in blue-tinted bulbs. The red emissions were further reduced by adding extra voltage to the tungsten filament, giving it the maximum possible brightness.

The introduction of portable lighting units for studio and location shooting (Fig. 121) provided further impulse to innovation. A famous stage actress with a keen interest in 'natural colour' cinematography, Maude Adams, made an appeal to the General Electric Company to improve their products for the advancement of the film industry. It was more than a publicity stunt: General Electric's new Mazda lamps – so called in reference to the Zoroastrian god Ahura Mazda, 'light of wisdom' in the sacred language of ancient Iran – were significantly more powerful than all their predecessors. Despite their superior strength, the improved bulbs would not have been enough to determine a real change in studio lighting without the demise of orthochromatic stock. Panchromatic film did not require all the precautions applied to its precursor; it reacted to all the colours of the visible spectrum, including red.

In the late silent era, Mazda lamps gradually replaced the Cooper Hewitt mercury vapour tubes and became the dominant force in studio lighting. They were cheaper to install and operate; they could be conveniently mounted on trolleys and moved around the studio; they did not demand as much electricity as their competitors' models. They also did not produce the crackling sound characteristic of arc lights. This was not yet an issue in 1927, at least not until microphones began to appear on the set.

Fig. 121 Electrical equipment and generator for location shooting. Brunton Studios, Los Angeles, *c.* 1920. Gelatin silver print. Source: George Eastman Museum.

Laboratories

Once production was completed, the camera negatives were dispatched to the processing and printing laboratory. To the casual observer, the only noticeable feature of this building was the scarcity or total absence of windows, an obvious precaution against possible damage to the exposed film stock. The interior of the building did not differ much from any other facility for photographic processing, other than the larger size of some working areas (darkroom, drying room) where substantial quantities of material had to be processed. The floor plan reproduced in

Fig. 122 shows, in simplified form, the ordinary configuration of a film processing department. Near its centre, a tortuous path guided the workers from the well-lit inspection, shipping, and packing area to the almost complete darkness of the developing and printing rooms.

The doors connecting the laboratory (on the upper right of the floor plan) where film stock was washed after processing and the wider area containing the rotary drums for drying the film stock are about twice the width of the other entrances, so that the film developing racks could be expediently moved across different areas. The gooseneck aperture that connected the developing room to the rest of the workspace was sometimes integrated or replaced by a darkened turntable booth (Fig. 123), for extra precaution against dust particles or accidental leaking of light from the adjacent room.

At this stage of film production, the sensitized film stock was not only the material expression of the filmmakers' work: it was also an invaluable and extremely perishable financial asset, to be protected at the very least until all projection prints had been struck from the assembled negative. In this building, the precautions against fire were even stricter than before, precisely because any loss of the finished work, however unassembled, would have brought the financial investment in the production to a catastrophic end. Safety came first, but it was no longer the only reason for caution.

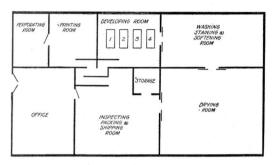

Fig. 122 Floor plan of a film processing laboratory, United States, c. 1910. Source: David S. Hulfish, Cyclopedia of Motion Picture Work. Chicago: American Technical Society, 1914, vol. II, p. 141.

No less critical was the secure handling of all negatives and their safeguarding against dust and light streaks; film technicians knew that excessive exposure of the unprocessed negative to the red or blue-green light of the developing room had to be avoided, as the sensitized stock would have been subject to irreversible fogging of the images. In the 1920s, these problems were compounded by a general tendency to bring developing plants closer to urban areas, where dirt and atmospheric pollution tended to be higher.

Industry practitioners had debated the respective virtues and shortcomings of constructing buildings for film development on the ground floor only, or stacked along three or more floors. According to the former viewpoint, predominant in the early decades of cinema, concentrating all the operations on the ground floor was a safer option

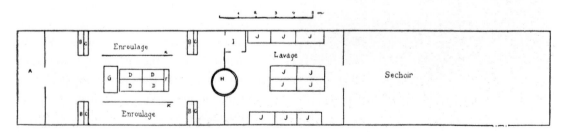

Fig. 123 Floor plan of a film processing laboratory, France, c. 1910. Note the turntable booth (H) separating the darkened room (left) for the developing tanks from the washing and drying rooms on the right. Source: Léopold Löbel, La Technique cinématographique. Paris: Dunod et Pinat, 1912, p. 250.

because it reduced to a minimum the human and financial risks connected to the physical transfer of film stock from one room to another. Over time, the advantages of a multilayered processing plant had persuaded many film technicians to take this route. Their theory was that the upper floor could be dedicated to the preparation and mixing of the chemicals for the processing baths; once ready, the liquids would flow into reservoirs installed in the floor underneath, and be filtered while descending through the pipes. At the end of their useful life, the developing baths were pumped into recycling tanks. The fixing baths would go to another room

or to a basement for the capture and recycling of the unused silver (Fig. 124).

In either case, special attention was paid to the materials used to seal or paint the surfaces of most processing areas. Concrete floors were waterproof and easy to wash, but also prone to corrosion, with the consequent release of harmful dust. Lacquered paint was recommended for the walls of drying rooms, whose floors were preferably made of ceramic tiles. As the film stock's delicate itinerary in the processing plant was approaching its end, precautions could be relaxed a little. There were no special requirements for the interior design of perforating rooms (Fig. 125), other than a more generous supply of ruby lights for handling unexposed film, and a seamlessly even floor, facilitating the removal of any cellulose dust generated by the perforation machines. In the assembly rooms for release prints (see Fig. 106 on p. 112), the main requirement was an orderly arrangement of the furniture and containers where smaller film rolls were to be sorted, retrieved, and spliced together to form complete prints. In a properly equipped workspace, the job was facilitated and its quality improved by the use of two light sources: a table lamp above the bench, and a light source from beneath, seen through a sheet of finely polished glazed glass.

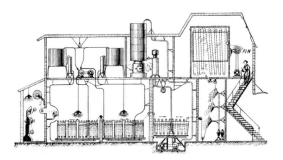

Fig. 124 Schematic view of a film processing plant on two floors, c. 1915. Source: Adapted from Jacques Faure, L'Entretien et l'exploitation du cinéma. Comment on tourne, comment on fabrique, comment on exploite un film. Paris: Éditions de 'Sciences et Voyages', n.d. [ca. 1925], p. 27.

Theatres

Early cinema was a nomadic show that made use of fairground pavilions, community halls, churches, brothels, schools, vaudeville theatres, and any other permanent or temporary space where a projector and a screen could be installed; this was the norm until about 1905 or after, when the first dedicated venues were built. We only have a very approximate notion of what projection rooms looked like before cinema put an end – at least in the urban areas – to its itinerant life of the first ten years and took permanent residence in specially designated

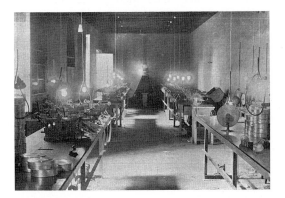

Fig. 125 Film perforating room. Cines, Rome, c. 1910. Source: Frederick Arthur Ambrose Talbot, Moving Pictures. How they are made and worked. London: Heinemann, 1912; Philadelphia: J.B. Lippincott Co., 1914, p. 66.

buildings. What is known about them comes mainly from photographs and illustrations of the period, from the personal testimony of spectators, and to a good extent from our own imagination. By describing cinema as a fairground attraction, we assume that it appeared in a more or less improvised hall (often a tent), with someone standing by a projector installed in close proximity to an audience sitting in front of the screen (Fig. 126).

Seating must have been of the simplest kind: portable chairs, wooden benches, maybe stools, except in those venues where the cinematic event was intended to satisfy the curiosity of affluent audiences. It must also have been a noisy room: the projector and its lighting apparatus; the projectionist's chatter while the machine was being cranked; the loud response of the public to the events depicted in front of them on a white surface; sometimes music. To dispel any impression of a 'golden era' in film exhibition, it must be added that a screening room was also likely to be a smelly place; manuals for entrepreneurs included automatic or pneumatic sprays to purify the air.

This speculative portrait of film shows at cinema's beginnings excludes all other places where moving images were available for individual viewing in peephole machines such as the Mutoscope and the Kinetoscope. These devices had their own

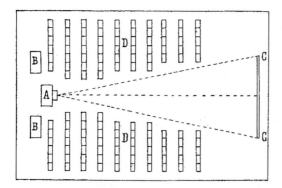

Fig. 126 Floor plan of a projection hall in the early years of cinema: front projection. Source: Vittorio Mariani, Guida pratica della cinematografia. Milan: Ulrico Hoepli, 1916, p. 253.

architectural settings, too, but they were either only one among many attractions (in penny arcades, filled with other coin-operated curiosities on the busiest streets or amusement parks of American cities and towns), or were lined up in rows along the walls of public spaces that looked like cafés or expanded living rooms. The first motion picture house in Persia, opened in 1905, was both a theatre and a Kinetoscope parlour. Instead of chairs, patrons of the 'Cinema' theatre in Tehran used simple rugs, as they would do in a mosque; Edison's viewing machines were installed in the lobby. Unlike in most other countries, the clientele came from the upper echelons of society (amidst fierce opposition from religious authorities).

Cinema's initial foray into a stable theatrical environment was made possible in the United States by vaudeville, a form of live entertainment featuring a variety of unrelated short acts (song, dramatic theatre, dance, burlesque, acrobats, magicians, impersonators, and trained animals). Films projected on a big screen became part of the programme, and they worked so well that producers soon reclaimed a space of their own, dedicated exclusively to motion pictures. Harry Davis, owner of one of those theatres, called it 'Nickelodeon'. It happened in Pittsburgh. It was June 1905.

In the United States, these places were called 'storefront theatres' because their design was almost identical to those of department stores: there was no separation between the pavement and the auditorium, other than a box-office booth flanked on either side by two entrances, a few feet away from the pavement line. In addition to a large sign to indicate the name of the theatre, its façade often displayed hundreds of electric lights ('electric theatre' was another common name for the venue), either white or in bright colours. Once inside the theatre, patrons found themselves in a plain rectangular room (Fig. 127), with a screen at the opposite end, normally flanked by a vertical piano and sometimes a percussion instrument.

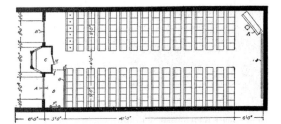

Fig. 127 Floor plan of a small storefront film theatre. United States, c. 1910. The auditorium is 47 feet long by 22 feet wide (14 by 6.5 metres); the screen is 13 feet, or 4 metres, long. Source: David S. Hulfish, Cyclopedia of Motion Picture Work. Chicago: American Technical Society, 1914, vol. II, p. 177.

The auditorium was filled with as many chairs as possible, with a central aisle in between, as in a stage theatre. At the back end, there was an elevated projection booth on one side or at the centre, near the box office, and two parallel walls to prevent the

outside light from interfering with the show when someone entered the room. It was taken for granted that the height of the screen and the projector should be such that patrons could walk up and down the aisle without affecting the image on the screen.

The storefront theatre was nothing more than the adaptation of an existing space to the requirements of cinema; within five years, entrepreneurs made great strides in designing theatres specifically built for the newborn medium. Their capacity swiftly increased, in response to the explosion of public demand; orchestra pits replaced the vertical pianos; as cinema acquired some sort of cultural legitimacy, its residence became a palace (Fig. 128). Exhibitors unchained their creativity by giving their venues the most attractive and at times ingenious names, from Aérogyne to Zanzibar. It would be interesting

Fig. 128 The entrance of the Parisiana Theatre. Petrograd, Russia, 1915. Gelatin silver print. Source: Courtesy of Peter Bagrov.

to browse an international dictionary of all their variations: the longest known (forty-five letters) is the French tongue twister Lentielectroplastic-romomimocoliserpentographe, seen in 1902 at the entrance of a cinema in Bordeaux.

By the mid-1920s, architects and entrepreneurs were competing to have the most extravagant façades, ceilings, and lobbies. Their luxury transformed the filmgoing experience into a feast for the eyes to be experienced well before the film programme itself had started. Large cities were not the only beneficiaries of this architectural bonanza: some of the most beautiful cathedrals of cinema were erected in small towns, like exclamation marks in otherwise nondescript urban conglomerates.

As the silent film era was approaching its twilight, the number of venues had soared at an astonishing speed. The Film Daily Yearbook estimated that

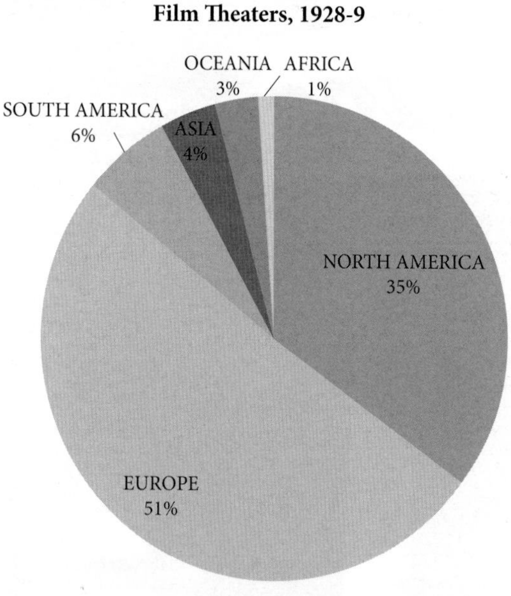

Chart 1 Geographic distribution of film theatres in the late silent era, 1928–9. The cumulative figure for South America includes British, French, and Dutch colonies. All projection venues of the Soviet Union are incorporated in the overall count for Europe (for a list of sources, see Table 1 on pp. 135–136).

in 1928 a total of 57,341 of theatres worldwide were regularly showing films (over 20,000 in the United States alone, ten times more than in 1907); a German handbook published at the dawn of the sound era reports an overall figure of 64,550. Davidson Boughey's The Film Industry (1921) was perhaps off the mark in claiming that there were already 87,000 cinema theatres operating at the time, but he may well have included in his count the semi-permanent projection venues of community halls, schools, and parishes (especially in Italy, with its expanding network of non-commercial theatres run by the Catholic Church). The very definitions of 'permanent' and 'temporary' projection halls are very elusive, and cannot be uniformly applied to all countries at all times in history.

Bearing in mind these caveats, it is safe to infer from the best available statistics that about 61,000 picture houses were active between 1928 and 1929 around the planet. About half of them were located in Europe (see Chart 1). At that time, world population was approaching the two billion mark: one theatre for every 32,000 people. Given an average capacity of 350 patrons for each venue (a highly cautious estimate, as will be explained shortly), there would have been over 21,800,000 film seats worldwide, a ratio of one to ninety-two inhabitants. The data reproduced in Table 1 do not include itinerant exhibitors in regions like India, sub-Saharan Africa, and the vast expanse of the Soviet Union, where temporary venues often outnumbered those operating on a permanent basis. In all likelihood, the total number of wandering show people who brought cinema to churches, classrooms, and rural areas of all continents will never be established with any plausible degree of approximation.

Auditoriums

A visual indication of how cinema had grown as a popular form of entertainment in just two decades

Table 1 World Film Theatres, 1928–9 (Estimated)*

Afghanistan 1	Germany 4,203–5,150	Nicaragua 14
Albania 3	Great Britain 3,760–4,366	Norway 252
Algeria 112	Great Britain – Misc. territories 50	Palestine 12–20
Andorra 1	Great Britain – Straits Settlements 35	Panama 30
Angola 4	Great Britain – Guyana 10	Paraguay 8
Argentina 349	Great Britain – Gibraltar 3	Persia 30
Australia 1,300–1,431	Greece 138	Peru 60
Austria 723–757	Guatemala 20	Philippines 268**
Belgium 797–1,000	Haiti 6	Poland 508–510
Belgium – Congo 10	Honduras 9	Portugal 120–130
Bolivia 16	Hong Kong 5	Portugal – Açores Islands 7
Brazil 1,300–1,350	Hungary 427–535	Portugal – Misc. territories 10
British Guiana 12	Iceland 6	Puerto Rico 125
British West Indies 18	India 320–400	Romania 300–450
Bulgaria 90–131	Iraq 11	San Marino 2
Cambodia 4	Irish Free State 150–200	Siam 45
Canada 1,000–1,100	Italy 2,000–3,225 **	South Africa 150–425
Ceylon 3	Japan 1,000–1,172	Soviet Union (Europe) 4,839–6,259 ***
Chile 150	Korea [Chōsen, Japan] 32	Soviet Union (Asia) 153***
China [including Manchukuo] 115–145	Laos 1	Spain 1,500**
Cochinchina 14	Latvia 95	Spain – Canary Islands 15
Colombia 200	Lebanon 3	Spain – Misc. territories 5
Costa Rica 8	Libya 5	Sweden 1,016–1,385
Cuba 400	Liechtenstein 1***	Switzerland 265–298
Czechoslovakia 720–1,068	Lithuania 46	Syria 15–20
Danzig (Free City of) 10	Luxembourg 21	Tahiti 9***
Denmark 270–350	Madagascar 10	Taiwan [Japan] 70***
Dominican Republic 10	Malta 16	Tanganyika 10
Dutch East Indies 205	Mexico 700	Tannu Tuva 2
Dutch West Indies 3	Monaco 7	Tonkin 6
Ecuador 25	Mongolia 2	Transjordan 3
Egypt 45–60	Morocco [France] 41	Tunisia 47
El Salvador 35	Morocco [Spain] 11	Turkey 60–102
Estonia 60	Mozambique 5	Ukraine [Soviet Union] 1,185***
Fiji 6	Netherlands 228	United States 18,000–20,500
Finland 235–239	Netherlands – Guyana 5	Uruguay 105
France 3,354–4,039	New Caledonia 6	Venezuela 30
France – Guyana 3	Nigeria 5	Yugoslavia (Kingdom of) 344–427
France – Misc. territories 43	New Zealand 175–443	Zanzibar 5

Sources: The Film Daily 1928 Year Book (New York: The Film Daily, 1928), p. 9; *The Film Daily 1929 Year Book* (New York: The Film Daily, 1929), p. E; Alexander Jason, *Handbuch der Filmwirtschaft. Europäische Statistiken und Verzeichnisse seit 1926. Band II: Film-Europa* (Berlin: Verlag für Presse, Wirtschaft und Politik, 1930), n.p. [pp. 34–5]; Nikolai Lebedev, *Ocherk istorii kino SSSR, Tom 1: Nemoe kino* (Moscow: Iskusstvo, 1965), p. 268; *Semnadtsatyi syezd Vsesoiuznoi Kommunisticheskoi partii (b), 26 janvaria–10 fevralia 1934: stenograficheskii* otchet (Moscow: Partizdat, 1934); Odile Goerg, Fantômas sous les tropiques: aller au cinéma en Afrique coloniale (Paris: Vendémiaire, 2015); Jean-Jacques Meusy (letter to the author, 15 June 2016); Annette Ling, 'Das Kino im Wirtshaus "Rössle" in Schann', Jahrbuch des Historischen Vereins für das Fürstentum Liechtenstein, no. 103 (2004); Sikminji-sidae-ui-Youngwha-Gumyeol, 1910–1934 (Seoul: Korean Film Archive, 2009); Karl Wolffsohn (ed.), Jahrbuch der Filmindustrie (Berlin: Verlag der 'Lichtbildbühne', 1928); Le Tout-cinéma. Annuaire général illustré du monde cinématographique (Paris: Filma, 1929); Kazuo Yamada (ed.), Eiga no jiten (Tokyo: Gōdō Shuppan, 1978); Glenn Reynolds, Colonial Cinema in Africa. Origins, Images, Audiences (Jefferson, NC: McFarland, 2015); Howard Yang (Taiwan Film Institute, Taipei; letter to the author, 21 May 2018); Erlendur Sveinsson (Kvikmyndasafn Íslands, Reykjavik; letter to the author, 11 May 2017). Some figures have been compared with those provided in Annuaire général de la cinématographie et des industries qui s'y rattachent (Paris: Cinémagazine/Publications Jean Pascal, 1927), with the earlier statistics on French colonies published in Annuaire général de la Cinématographie française et étrangère (Paris: Éditions de 'Ciné-Journal', 1917–1918), pp. 218–221, and with a later census reproduced in Isidro Satanowsky, La obra cinematográfica frente al derecho (Buenos Aires: Ediar, 1948), Vol. 2, pp. 141–5. With few exceptions (notably New Zealand and South Africa, where there are major discrepancies between different sources), when more than one estimate was found for the same country, the highest and lowest figures are indicated here. Temporary venues and itinerant exhibitors are not included in the count; it is acknowledged, however, that the very definition of 'temporary venue' is subject to different interpretations.

* The data reproduced in this chart are purely indicative. Figures vary considerably according to the sources and the criteria for the estimates.

** The highest figure includes venues administered by the Catholic Church.

*** Includes semi-permanent venues such as stage theatres, hostels, taverns, workers' and village clubs (when more than one figure is listed, these venues have been included in the highest count). The figures for Taiwan are a conjectural median between data published online by Wanshun Shih (http://map.net.tw/theater/distribution/a/) and Daw-ming Lee (http://w3.tkgsh.tn.edu.tw/97c219/). The lowest figure for the Soviet Union is to be integrated with the one for Ukraine.

since its emergence comes from the blueprints and architectural designs of motion picture houses. In the mid-1910s, a 'small theatre' of the United States was defined as a venue with 400 to 1,000 seats; by the same accounts, the capacity of an 'average' large theatre was between 1,200 and 1,800. The figures were generally lower in Europe: the most prestigious venue in Stockholm, the Röda Kvam, offered 900 seats in its auditorium; in Russia, the Pikadilli and the Parisiana of St Petersburg (Petrograd), and the Kolizey and the Forum in Moscow, could accommodate 700–800 patrons each, but one of Germany's landmark venues, the Apollo-Theatre in Düsseldorf, had no fewer than 3,500 seats; the Gaumont-Palace in Paris (5,500 seats) was advertised as the largest film theatre in the world. Each picture house had a single auditorium; venues with more than one screen were the exception in the silent film era.

Architects and engineers struggled to fully appreciate the differences between a cinema and a conventional theatre or concert hall, and initially underestimated the special challenges involved in designing a space for an audience placed in front of an elevated screen (the first known book in English entirely dedicated to the construction of a cinema, dated 1916, pays little attention to projection booths and their equipment). Given the frequent alternation of motion pictures with song, dance, and other attractions (see p. 132), large picture houses also needed stages big enough to accommodate live presentations. In the early years of film theatres, the main concerns were public safety and compliance with municipal or state regulations on the handling of nitrate film; the aesthetics of the theatre and its acoustics were addressed only in a later phase of the project.

Predictably enough, the first major change to the traditional floor plan of a theatre was the proliferation of security exits. More substantive variations derived from the awareness that the traditional horseshoe seating layout adopted for stage theatres and concert halls was inadequate for cinema, as it was important that spectators could not only count upon a properly sloped floor and a staggered seating arrangement, but also be placed as close as possible to a perpendicular axis in relation to the screen. The ratio between the width and length of the film theatre changed accordingly, with floor plans shaped like more elongated rectangles. Seats were arranged in broad curves, or almost straight in narrower spaces (Fig. 129).

There were also limitations to be taken into account in determining the desirable depth of the auditorium: two opposing viewpoints on the subject were expressed throughout the silent film era. Architects and exhibitors were pushing for a maximum distance of 150 feet (46 metres) between the projector lens and the screen; projectionists insisted that no picture could ever be pitch perfect beyond a distance of 75 feet (23 metres). There was no agreement, either, about the minimum allowable distance, although it was generally felt that there was no point in running a film theatre with a 'throw' of less than 35 feet (11 metres). Technical handbooks of the mid-1910s mentioned an average length of 14 to 25 metres (46 to 82 feet) and a width of 7 to 16 metres (23 to 52 feet) as the most common for projection halls in Europe.

Much depended, of course, on how many cubic feet or metres were available in the first place for the construction of a new motion picture house. Over time, theatre owners reluctantly agreed that the first rows in the auditorium should not be placed

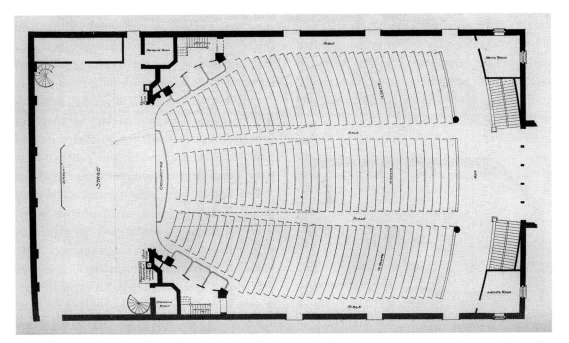

Fig. 129 Floor plan of a typical picture palace. United States, *c.* 1915. Note the width of the screen, about 4.5 times shorter than the auditorium's total width. Source: Arthur S. Meloy, Theatres and Picture Houses. New York: Architects' Supply & Publishing Company, 1916, p. 5.

too close to the screen, as its proximity would have made image flicker too painful to bear for any extended period of time. An orchestra pit located between the screen and the audience took care of the problem in larger venues; a false stage was the only useful alternative to this, except perhaps leaving enough empty space in front of the screen to fit a small group of music or sound-effects performers.

With some good mathematics and enough common sense, it proved fairly straightforward to adjust sight lines to the needs of a cinema audience. Conversely, no compromise was possible about the angle of projection in theatres with one or more balconies (Fig. 130): a projection axis of 20 degrees to the screen was considered the limit beyond which imperfect focus and picture distortion (the 'keystone' effect) would spoil the viewing experience. In the United States, the Society of Motion Picture Engineers adopted an even stricter approach by declaring in the early 1920s that the angle of projection should not exceed 12 degrees (SMPE's standards were subject to refinement over the years). Architects obliged, as long as they were free to express themselves in the unbridled imagery of their interior designs. Film theatres in North America were unsurpassed in their breathtaking fusion of classical antiquity, baroque, and

orientalism in interior decorations (Plate 52); their counterparts around the world were often as elegant, but somehow more restrained in their style.

Exhibitors, engineers, and designers were far less inclined to confront two other issues – both related to the comfort of their patrons' viewing experience – where previous knowledge of theatre design was of little or no help. For audiences of the silent film period, eyestrain was an extremely serious matter: books, articles, and letters to trade journals of the time made very frequent mention of this syndrome. Flicker was regarded as the main culprit, but there were also misgivings about the contrast between the darkness of the theatre and screen luminosity; Eastman Kodak had even published a brochure on this subject in 1921. The imperative of almost complete obscurity in the picture house was often questioned (out of physiological or moral concerns about social behaviour), and proposals to install systems for indirect light over the auditorium or right above the screen were brought forward from time to time. Experts in the field went as far as suggesting that indirect light could be strong enough to allow someone to read a newspaper while the film was running, with no significant loss to the quality of the show.

It is not yet known how often the advice was put into practice, but there is reason to believe that no clear consensus was ever reached on this point; the debate was put to rest only with the introduction of sound on film and the increase of projection speed, with the consequent reduction of the flickering effect. There was another type of complaint from the public: temperature and humidity levels in film theatres were often distressing, unbearable at times. This had nothing to do with the size of the auditorium; everybody knew that any space with a very high ceiling demanded the use of costly equipment to keep the place warm in the winter and cool during the summer. The real difference between a picture house and a theatre or concert hall was, to put it plainly, its exhibition schedule.

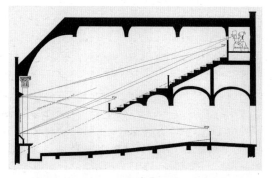

Fig. 130 Sight lines and angled projection throw from the projection booth to the screen in a typical picture palace. United States, c. 1915. Source: Arthur S. Meloy, Theatres and Picture Houses. New York: Architects' Supply & Publishing Company, 1916, p. 22.

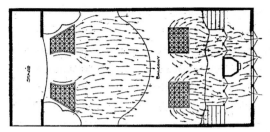

Fig. 131 'Monsoon' cooling and air exchange system in a large film theatre. United States, c. 1920. Source: James R. Cameron, Motion Picture Projection. An Elementary Text-Book. New York: Theatre Supply Co., 1921, p. 172.

Fig. 132 Installing a portable screen for film projection, c. 1907. Source: F. Paul Liesegang, Handbuch der praktischen Kinematographie. Leipzig: Edition Liesegang's Verlag, 1908, p. 184.

Conventional venues for the performing arts were open to the public a few hours a day, and were often closed in the summer; conversely, most film theatres offered their programmes for ten hours or more, without interruption, on a daily basis (all year long in many countries), and were frequently filled to capacity. The cumulative effect of the body temperature and sweat released by thousands of patrons from late morning to midnight – combined with the heat generated by light sources and by the building itself during the hot summer months – is not too hard to imagine. In the interest of good business and public safety, there was no choice but to make theatre ventilation more effective – especially in the balconies – by dramatically increasing the frequency of air exchange (Fig. 131). It was quite possible to do so; it was only a matter of money.

Screens

The images seen by film audiences of the late 1920s were 25,000 to 60,000 times the size of a 35mm frame. This simple calculation should be enough to remind ourselves that screens are almost as vital to cinema as the films shown upon them; their indispensable role in the motion picture show is too often underrated, if it is mentioned at all. In the beginning, screens were portable and relatively small: town halls, churches, fairground tents, and other temporary venues offered

itinerant projectionists little or no other choice (Fig. 132). Surprisingly enough, screen size did not change much when cinema became sedentary. It may be assumed that the capacity and shape of a projection hall would be primary factors in determining the size of the rectangular surface upon which films were to be shown. On average, however, the size of the screen was noticeably smaller than one would expect by comparing it with theatre's capacity (see Fig. 129 on p. 137); the Rivoli Theatre in New York could accommodate 2,200 people, but its screen was merely 20 feet (6 metres) long and 15 feet (4.5 metres) high. By the standards of the period, it was already too big: barring unusual circumstances, a length of 18 feet (5.5 metres) was the preferred limit (the minimum being 10 feet, or 3 metres) in the 1910s.

Before attributing this restraint solely to the presumed weakness of the projectors' lanterns, it is best to remember that the Lumière brothers had installed a huge screen (69 by 53 feet, or 21 by 16 metres) for a presentation of their 75mm films at the 1900 Universal Exhibition in Paris. An even bigger screen (100 by 75 feet, or 30 by 23 metres) – arguably the world's largest for its time – was erected to celebrate the 1919 Methodist Missions Centenary in Columbus, Ohio. Both

structures had been built as short-term attractions for special occasions; the gargantuan screen
of the Methodists stood at the centre of an open-
air temporary venue. A most likely reason for
the relative modesty of screen size in permanent
theatres of the silent film period was indeed the
imperative to enhance picture brightness, but
there was also the concurrent priority to reduce,
insofar as possible, the eyestrain derived from
optical defects in the picture and flickering at
lower projection speeds. It has been argued that
another motive should also be taken into account:
in the early 1910s, it was believed that pictures
should be 'life-size', rather than 'larger than life'.
Human figures were supposed to look as real as
if they were performing live on stage. Even after
close-ups were introduced and embraced as
powerful expressive tools, audiences were reluctant to give them free rein on a very big screen.

There is good value in this theory, but let's
consider a more pragmatic explanation. Theatre
owners wanted to fill the house, and they knew
that the front seats would be far less appealing if the
projected image was too large, given its loss of detail
and the eyestrain caused by following the action
from right and left, top and bottom of the image.
Empty seats in an otherwise packed theatre made
no sense to film exhibitors. Hence, they maintained
that the front row should be no closer than 21 feet
(6.5 metres) from an 18-foot screen, and that little
more than 100 feet, or about 30 metres, should separate it from the last row. A screen length of 15 feet
(4.6 metres) was the norm in the first decade of the
twentieth century; once stretched from 18 to 24 feet
(5.5 to 7 metres) two decades later, it seemed that
the silent screen had finally found its golden ratio.

Nevertheless, as early as 1908 the Pathé catalogue of film equipment and supplies was proudly
featuring seven screens of different sizes, ranging
from 2.70 by 2.30 metres (9 by 7.5 feet) for the tiniest model (at a bargain price of 17 francs) to 12.60

by 9.70 metres (41 by 32 feet) for the most expensive one (285 francs), at aspect ratios between
1:1.17 and 1:1.30. They were made of two-layered
canvas, with eyelets to ensure proper tension when
installed on a wall or within a portable frame,
sold separately. The frame, provided with its dedicated suitcase for ease of transport, had a twofold
purpose. The first was to enable film projection
in temporary venues, such as schools, conference
halls, or other areas for public recreation. The
second is linked to rear projection by transparency, an alternative form of exhibition practice in
the early days of cinema, in places where the screen
was located in the middle of the room, between the
projector and the audience (Fig. 133).

To achieve the desired effect, the screen surface
had to be made uniformly wet by adding a solution of 15 per cent glycerin added to the water in
order to prevent evaporation, plus some starch to
maintain the correct light reflection. In vaudeville theatres, where cinema was one among many
attractions in the show, screen mobility was both
a necessity and a stagecraft resource. It was called
a 'sheet' in the United States, and was treated
more or less like a drop 'curtain' (also a common
term for screens in the 1900s), to be lowered
when films were projected on stage, and maybe

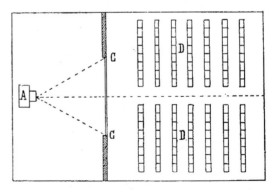

Fig. 133 Floor plan of a projection hall in the early years
of cinema: rear projection. Source: Vittorio Mariani, Guida
pratica della cinematografia. Milan: Ulrico Hoepli, 1916,
p. 254.

allowing actors and acrobats to prepare their next act behind it. However practical, the system had a major drawback: the incessant rolling and unrolling of the fabric between shows would eventually result in wrinkles and waves on the surface of the screen. The issue was resolved with the application of a sturdy roller at the bottom of the fabric (in 'olio drop' curtains), ensuring that the screen was properly stretched.

A pioneer of German cinema, Oskar Messter, pursued a radically different route in his attempt to achieve a three-dimensional effect with the beautiful but short-lived Alabastra films (1910), shown on a oblique screen made of glass, where projected figures moved against the background of an actual theatre stage (Fig. 134). Messter's innovation was the epitome of a trend towards integration between the projection surface and its surroundings: as cinema was finding a dedicated space where it could be experienced as a self-contained spectacle, the screen became part of its architecture. A blank wall in front of the seats, opposite the projector, was good enough: a white plaster surface, either made smoother with sandpaper or with the application of a very thin layer of muslin, provided more than adequate light diffusion and reflection.

These were only the first among several variations on the theme. In addition to the plain cloth screen, quite acceptable in terms of light diffusion but generally poor in reflecting it, exhibitors could choose between paint (preferably on a foundation of plaster, cement finish, or stretched cloth) made of either zinc white and white lead, or a mixture of slaked lime and chalk, then commonly known as Kalsomine; plain white chalk; sand-blasted mirrors; and any white surface treated with finely powdered glass, aluminum, or other metallic compounds. Painted screens were the favourite, because of their excellent performance in theatres with higher viewing angles. Their maintenance was easy and inexpensive. The addition of faint yellow or flesh tint pigments to soften the look of the projected picture was suggested by some manufacturers in the mid-1910s, but never took off on a large commercial scale.

In those years, film theatre owners were keen to focus the viewers' attention towards the screen with the aid of decorative or functional elements, as in traditional stage theatres. It all began with a gilded frame, more or less elaborate depending on the exhibitor's ambitions, a logical consequence of the desire to surround the motion pictures to be displayed with an aura of sophistication and prestige. Projectionists, too, had their say, and it wasn't about fancy stuccos painted in gold: in their view, a black outline was a better way to enhance the film's pictorial brilliance through contrast with the surrounding darkness.

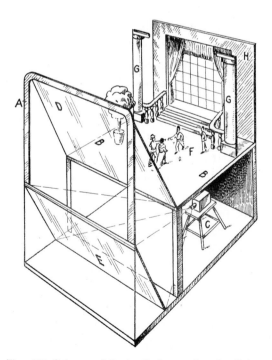

Fig. 134 Scheme of the projection system for Oskar Messter's 'Alabastra' films, 1910. The image is reflected onto a glass screen from a projector and a mirror located below the stage. Source: Oskar Messter, Mein Weg mit dem Film. Berlin-Schöneberg: M. Hesse, 1936, p. 81.

Matted black borders were indeed not as attractive as their baroque equivalents. To make everyone happy, film theatre managers adopted them both, with the black outline functioning like a passe-partout or mount for the framed image (its corners were often rounded, like the camera's and the projector's aperture, for a more pleasing effect), and the gilded frame as its outside ornament. This combined approach ratified the function of the 'moving picture' as the centrepiece of the theatre's interior design, not unlike a cherished painting in a family's living room (Fig. 135). With an imaginative twist of perspective, J. Stuart Blackton remodelled his Vitagraph theatre in New York by creating a set around it, in the guise of an artist's studio, with the screen inscribed in a verandah's frame: 'a window on the world', as Blackton called it.

Determining the appropriate height of the screen in relation to the seats brought the comparison with the other arts to a crossroads. If film had to be a theatrical performance pursued by other means (and if there was a stage in the auditorium), it would have made sense to lower the bottom of the image as close as possible to the floor; if it was to be enjoyed as a framed 'picture' on a wall, an average height of 6 feet (less than 2 metres) was

the most desirable, compatibly with the shape of the auditorium and the position of the seats. In most countries, the 'hanging picture' configuration prevailed, with or without gilded frame.

When asked to include an orchestra pit in their drawings for a new theatre, architects were mindful that the musicians' lights should not interfere with the projection, and moved the screen up a little further. Curtains covering the screen were not the norm in dedicated film theatres of the silent era. When present, Austrian-style, 'olio drops' (common in vaudeville theatres of the United States, therefore used as projection screens in themselves), or traveller curtains were never open before the show: as in stage theatre and opera, the screen only appeared when the film performance began. Regardless of its height, size, and spatial relationship to the rest of the theatre, cinema viewers were presented with much more than an empty canvas: it was a natural landscape, waiting to be filled with artificial illusions. From their different perspectives and with their respective skills, interior designers and film projectionists were working together to make them look beautiful.

Booths

The heart and soul of a silent film theatre was a tiny room, normally located at the top of the building or between one of its balconies, rarely on the ground floor (except in some storefront theatres of the nickelodeon era). It was inaccessible to all, except for projectionists and theatre managers (only when strictly necessary, and with circumspection: talking to the pilot required some tact). During the show, the only visible evidence that it existed at all was a cone of light coming from behind; for those who worked inside, it was a hermitage of obsessive discipline. The space was thermally and acoustically insulated from the rest of the theatre (concrete or brick walls and ceiling were suitable to both); for safety reasons, wooden booths were wrapped in

Fig. 135 The screen and proscenium of the Saxe's Alhambra Theatre in Milwaukee, Wisconsin,1911, as shown in a postcard. Lithograph and stencil colour on paper. Source: Private collection.

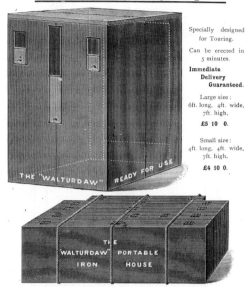

Fig. 136 Portable projection booth, c. 1907. Source: The "Walturdaw" Bioscope Specialities. London: The Walturdaw Company, 1909, p. 43.

asbestos. Those made of iron, as was frequently the case in the early years, were as good as ovens (Fig. 136). Ventilation pipes released the heat and fumes of lamphouses, but such luxury was often not extended to projection staff. Concern for the booth's design was virtually nil, to the extent that printed guidelines on how to build motion picture houses mention the subject with the dutiful conciseness of an afterthought; their authors showed some concern for the booth's floor, with a preference for thick slabs of concrete, to avoid vibrations during projection while the operator was moving around during the change of reels. Otherwise, lumber would be coated in asbestos like the rest, with sand or cork placed under the projector to absorb the tremors.

The indifference towards this working area is also reflected in the rather unattractive names

attached to it: 'projection room' was its formal denomination in most of the English-speaking world, but common language called it 'projection booth' or, in Australia, the 'bio box' (an abbreviated reference to the early term 'bioscope'). French and German idioms didn't fare much better with their respective words, 'cabine' and 'Vorführungskabine'. The best theatres made it spacious enough for a more dignified appearance, but these were exceptions; as a rule, the projection booth hardly qualified as a room. It provided enough space to stand by the machine, change reels, and store small quantities of film, nothing else.

Such a grim reality feels like a retribution for what happened in the very early years of cinema, when the projectionist stood behind the audience and was visible to all, like a magic lantern operator: on one of those occasions, on 4 May 1897, a fire erupted during a motion picture show at the Bazar de la Charité in Paris. A total of 126 people were burned or suffocated to death, and the authorities panicked. Nitrate film had nothing to do with this horrific event. The explosion was caused by mishandling of the oxyetheric lamp used for the show: it was called 'Securitas' (Fig. 137), a model built by Alfred Molteni in 1895. Too much ether gas had been let out of its container, filling the entire area of

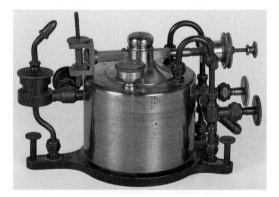

Fig. 137 Oxyetheric lamp 'Securitas' (Alfred Molteni, Paris, 1895). A human error in the handling of this model was the cause of the catastrophic fire at the Bazar de la Charité film screening in Paris on 4 May 1897. Source: Cinémathèque française. Photo by Stéphane Dabrowski.

the pavilion where the screening was taking place. The projectionist lit up a match: minutes later, the place had been reduced to ashes and charred bodies. Following the catastrophe, cinema was deemed a pernicious thing in itself (an outright ban was seriously taken into consideration); its apparatus was seen as dangerous, too, and was moved as far away as possible from the audience.

It was, by all means, the right thing to do, but the stigma attached to the material source of the cinematic event would never go away. Many other fires devoured film theatres (250 victims in Acapulco, Mexico, 1909), laboratories (Hepworth, 1907), and studios (Thanhouser, 1913; Lubin, 1914; Éclair at Fort Lee, 1914; Famous Players, 1915; Ince, 1916), all involving nitrate film. Its segregation took the form of an elevated fireproof chamber, located behind the auditorium. In a typical venue, the projection booth featured one or two projectors (Fig. 138) – more in larger theatres – flanked by a magic lantern projector (sometimes also called a 'stereopticon' in English-speaking countries) for the display of glass slides during intermissions and for publicity. In front of each projector, two small rectangular ports were cut into the wall (normally with a sheet of

Fig. 139 Manual film rewinder. Walturdaw Company, London, 1908. Source: Price List of Everything Required for the Bioscope Business from the Theatre to the Films. London: The 'Walturdaw' Company, 1908, p. 51.

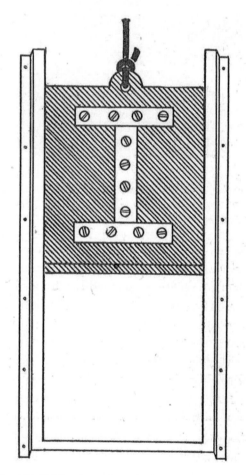

Fig. 138 The projection booth of the Pikadilli Theatre in St Petersburg, Russia, 1913. Gelatin silver print. Source: St. Petersburg State Archive of Photo and Phono Documents.

Fig. 140 Wall fire shutter for projection port. Source: Frank Herbert Richardson, Motion Picture Handbook. A Guide for Managers and Operators of Motion Picture Theatres. New York: The Moving Picture World, 1916, 3rd edition, p. 223.

non-reflective glass), one for the projector's lens, the other for the projectionist to verify that the picture was correctly framed and in focus.

The only furniture in the room consisted of a rewind bench – mostly vertical (Fig. 139), sometimes equipped with a splicer – and fireproof cabinets for film storage before and after projection; another closet was available for tools and supplies. The projection room's door, either sliding diagonally (to ensure it was automatically closed) or opening to the outside, was constructed of fireproof material, like everything else in that area. A separate door, preferably leading to the outside of the building, was introduced in some countries during the late silent era; it later became mandatory, as it is today. A metal or asbestos fire shutter placed above the projector's port was connected to the equipment through a mechanism that moved it down like a guillotine (Fig. 140), further isolating the room from the rest of the theatre in case of fire.

When designing a new venue, sensible theatre owners provided for running water and a toilet (Fig. 141). The latter was especially important whenever only one projectionist was working in the booth, often for shifts of several consecutive hours; as for the water basin, it was partly to suggest that projectionists should periodically wash their hands, heavily soiled with oil from the projector mechanisms and with carbon dust while adjusting the rods of the carbon arc lamp (handling reels with dirty hands was also not good for the print). It was believed that the presence of a chair or tall stool at the side of each machine, in front of the viewing port, would greatly enhance the projectionist's overall performance and encourage attention to detail during the show; theatre owners and the projectionists tended to think otherwise, because of the limited space available and of the other duties to be carried out while the film was running.

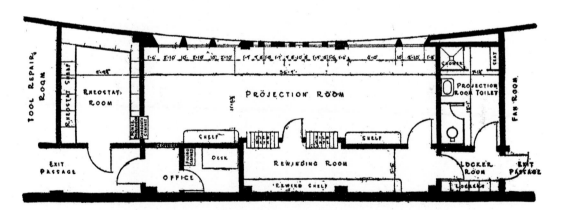

Fig. 141 Layout of the projection room at the Paramount Theatre in New York, 1926. Source: Harold B. Franklin, Motion Picture Theater Management. New York: George H. Doran Company, 1927, ill. 12.

Chapter 7

Works

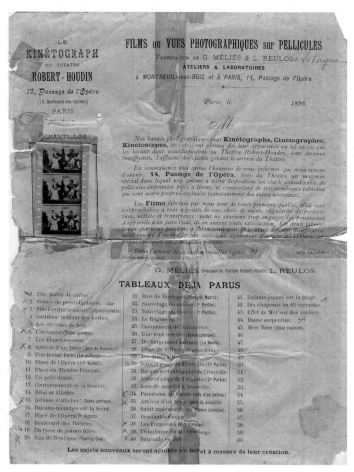

Fig. 142 The first Méliès catalogue, 1896. The document includes a sample of actual 35mm nitrate frames from a Star-Film production. Source: Courtesy of Laurent Mannoni.

Strictly speaking, we will never know exactly how many films were made during the silent era: amateur filmmakers rarely left a record of what they did, and only a few of their productions survive to this day. The overall number of works commercially released, on the other hand, can be determined with a certain degree of approximation: the aggregate data provided by all the national filmographies published so far suggest a total figure of more than 152,000 shorts and features. An important piece of the puzzle still missing from the overall picture of silent film production is the vast and insufficiently explored terrain of non-fiction shorts; this is no small gap, considering how prolific were the companies that specialized in this genre. The documentary and newsreel output of major film companies in countries like France, the Soviet Union, and the United States has been partly covered, allowing for a cautious optimism about the reliability of the existing estimates. By allowing a 5 per cent margin of error in the statistics, we reach a grand total of almost 160,000 individual titles, a figure we can feel reasonably comfortable with once all the necessary caveats have been taken into account. It is an enormous number of films, an average of about five thousand per year (more than ten thousand films were made in 1913 alone).

The trajectory described in Chart 2 gives no indication on the volume of film distribution business in general (how much positive stock was printed and circulated for general release); it has no pretence of accuracy, and is only a generic indication of worldwide trends in film production between 1894 and 1928 (silent films were produced in some countries well into the mid-1930s). It is clear enough, however, to illustrate a steady rise and then a brief pause in the mid-1900s, followed by a dramatic growth until 1914; by an equally abrupt fall during World War I; by a slower decline around the years of the 1920–1 economic depression in the United States; and by a slower but uninterrupted increase until the beginning of the sound era. On the basis of the filmographic information available, it is estimated that roughly half of all the films produced during the silent era were made in Europe (Chart 3).

Length

In broad terms, each of the above phases corresponds to a moment in history: the rise of pre-industrial filmmaking; a period of crisis,

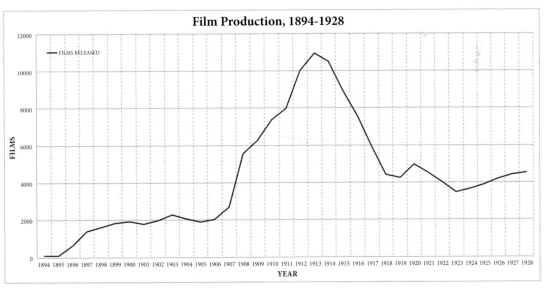

Chart 2 Estimated number of commercial films produced in the silent era, 1894–1928 (for a list of sources, see Bibliography, pp. 366–370).

Films Produced, 1894-1928

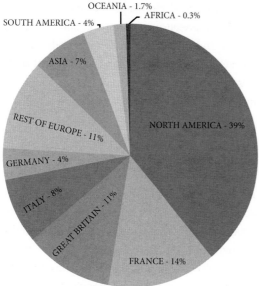

Chart 3 Geographic distribution of the commercial films produced in the silent era, 1894–1928 (for a list of sources, see Bibliography, pp. 366–370).

caused by a growing imbalance between stagnant consumption and the offer of new products; a major surge in demand for more subjects, and in corporate initiatives to respond accordingly; the abrupt collapse of the European market during the war years; the rise of Hollywood. This timeline matches with the transition from one- and two-reel films to the feature-length format: the shift occurred in the early 1910s, reaching its peak almost exactly at the point where European production and distribution were crippled by the war. When the crisis was over, short films had been redefined as ancillary attractions of the show.

If one were to draw another line indicating the average length of a commercial film over the same period of time, we would see it climb from the beginning to the end of the silent period. The first productions by Lumière and Edison were about 20 metres (65 feet) long, corresponding to less than one minute of projection. By 1908, films of 300 metres (1,000 feet) had become the norm in

the industry; shorter subjects, often of non-fiction genres, were called 'split reels' because two of them could fit into one standard reel. Increasingly averse to the prospect of squeezing their narratives within the boundary of fifteen minutes or less of screening time, filmmakers began to make films twice as long, often in opposition to producers and theatre owners, who were afraid that audiences would reject the two-reel format. They were wrong: the public response was so enthusiastic that film directors felt encouraged to go even further by presenting films in three or more reels in the early 1910s. A harbinger of things to come was *The Story of the Kelly Gang* (Charles Tait, 1906), an Australian film in four reels, now surviving only in scattered fragments. European companies spearheaded the innovation, taking overseas markets by storm with *Afgrunden* (four reels) and *Quo Vadis?* (nine reels). By then, the irresistible rise in popularity of the feature-length film had reached the point of no return. Until the early 1910s (when the Famous Players Film Company used it to differentiate its products from those of the affiliates to the Motion Picture Patents Company), the term 'feature' did not refer to the running time of the film, but to its distinctive qualities as the centrepiece of the programme; D.W. Griffith quickly adopted the word for his films soon after leaving Biograph.

The longest silent feature films ever made are probably *La Roue* (1923) and *Napoléon*, both by Abel Gance, and Erich von Stroheim's *Greed*, a much revered cause célèbre in the annals of cinema. Stroheim had assembled an eight-hour version (forty-two reels) that was never officially released. It may well have been nothing but a rough cut: Stroheim himself reduced it to twenty-four reels, but the executives of Metro-Goldwyn-Mayer were still aghast at the film's inordinate narrative span; after a failed attempt by Rex Ingram's editor Grant Whytock to create an eighteen-reel version (to be possibly split in two parts), the company ordered that *Greed* be reduced to a ten-reel abridgement of a mere 10,607 feet (3,233 metres). The palm for the longest silent film ever seen as intended by its creator is therefore a disputed contest between *La Roue* and *Napoléon*, the latter released in two versions of approximately 540 and 240 minutes (it must be reckoned that Gance had originally planned to distribute the longest version as a 'series' in six or more instalments, and that he had a similar intent with *La Roue*; film 'serials', made of self-contained episodes, are also excluded from the competition, as they were not exhibited in a single show). Japanese films of the late silent era were sometimes in the same league as Gance's and Stroheim's, but without their accompanying controversy and fanfare: *Ai yo jinrui to tomo ni are* (Love, Be with Humanity), a 1931 family drama directed by Shimazu Yasujiro, runs for 241 minutes when screened at 18 frames per second.

Genres

Early writings on the history of film have often described the evolution of subjects and themes in silent cinema as a linear process leading from the real-life views of the Lumière brothers (a train arriving at the station, workers demolishing a wall or leaving a factory at the end of the day) to fictional works of increasing complexity and depth. This chronological outline was forthright but also inaccurate, as it ignored the fact that the action of most Edison films of the mid-1890s was staged (*Joan of Arc*, 1895) and that the first screening of Lumière films included a comedy (*Arroseur et arrosé*, 1895). Edison productions of 1894–6 encompass dance (*Fatima's Coochee-Coochee Dance*, 1896), sports (*Corbett and Courtney before the Kinetograph*, 1894), acrobatics (*Luis Martinetti, Contortionist*, 1894), and romance (*Interrupted Lovers*, 1896); the prominence of what is now called 'documentary' in the bulletins of film pioneers should therefore not be regarded as absolute. Lumière's *Les Dernières cartouches* and

Méliès' *Bombardement d'une maison*, both made in 1897, are dramatized versions of an episode in the Franco-German war of 1870, two different *tableaux vivants* derived from the same canvas (1873) by Alphonse de Neuville, a famous military painter of the time. Méliès went even further by presenting his very accurate rendition of a royal ceremony in Westminster cathedral on the very same day of the actual event (*Le Sacre d'Édouard VII*, first shown on 9 August 1902).

Before surrendering to the temptation to call this film a fake newsreel, it should be acknowledged that the word 'genre' was largely unknown to filmmakers of the early silent era, and that it is applied today with a large degree of hindsight. Production companies were certainly using terms like 'drama' or 'comedy' to present their films; a cursory look at their bulletins of the mid- to late 1900s, however, should suffice to appreciate that their descriptive categories have changed considerably over time. The Pathé catalogue of 1906 listed no fewer than twelve of them. Among the featured 'series' – this was the heading of each section – were comedies, trick films (not on a par with Méliès, except for those by Segundo de Chomón), dances and ballets; 'documentaries' were more aptly announced in Series 1 as *Scènes de plein air*, separately from sports and acrobatics (Series 4); drama, second only to comedy in quantitative terms, did not include the Passion of the Christ (Religious and Biblical Scenes, Series 10), fairy tales (Series 9), or the retelling of historic events. Series 5 is a conglomerate of three different 'genres': documentary (military manoeuvres), actuality (ceremonies, parades, and other notable events), and reconstructed episodes of the past. Historical subjects were seen as distinct from everything else, regardless of their status as fiction or non-fiction.

The eleventh series of the Pathé catalogue covered all films to be projected with gramophone recordings: their actors could perform comedy, drama, or music acts, cutting across all narrative boundaries. *Scènes diverses* (Series 12) ended the book with a potpourri of shorts that would not fit into any of the previous sections. A single page at the beginning of the book, called *Titres annonces*, was dedicated to another kind of oddity, each with a running time of one minute or less: they were miniature items, made to notify the audience about intermissions, changes of programmes, forthcoming matinées, or just the fact that the last show was over, and it was time to say goodnight. Some of these films are tiny cinematic gems; few titles of this kind, all from European companies, are known to survive (Fig. 143). Series 6, *Scènes grivoises d'un caractère piquant*, deserves special attention: it stands right in the middle of Pathé's repertoire, but a caption under the title points out that children should stay away from the screen.

This section made no apologies for the films' patently erotic nature, an obvious source of attraction to male audiences. Sex had been a staple of the photography business for years, and it was inevitable that its portrayal in cinematic form would find a lucrative niche in the business. Pathé, a stalwart of cinematic decorum, had openly exploited the theme since the early 1900s (the other giant of French cinema, Gaumont, apparently did not).

Fig. 143 *Buona sera, fiori!* (Giovanni Vitrotti, 1909). Frame enlargement from a 35mm nitrate positive of the German-language version. Source: Eye Filmmuseum.

Saturn-Film, a company based in Austria, was solely dedicated to this type of productions: its founder, Johann Schwarzer, marketed his films in various trade journals between 1906 and 1910. A much more explicit anti-clerical farce presumably shot in Italy, *Saffo e Priapo* (made sometime between 1921 and 1922), was long attributed to Gabriele D'Annunzio. Pornography flourished at the margins of the public sphere throughout the silent era; its depiction of sexual intercourse reached at times surprising extremes, both in content and in the language of title cards. A short film from France, *La Maîtresse du Capitaine de Meydeux* (*The Exclusive Sailor*, or *Cast Ashore*, attributed to Bernard Natan, 1924), is one of the earliest known extant films depicting homosexuality in explicit terms.

The burgeoning popular demand for fictional subjects was accompanied by a gradual shift of non-fiction to the sidebars of theatres' programmes. By and large, these films remained short (one reel, sometimes half) as feature-length production was becoming the norm; their contents increasingly diversified over time, with the resultant emergence of specific strands in the early 1910s: educational, scientific, and industrial films; advertising; scenic views, travelogues, ethnographic documents; and vehicles for political or religious propaganda. Born with J. Stuart Blackton, Émile Cohl, and Segundo de Chomón in the first decade of the twentieth century (with an amazing precursor from Russia, ballet dance teacher Aleksandr Shiryaev, around 1906), animation joined the ranks of subsidiary attractions (Walt Disney began making film cartoons in the early 1920s; the first animated 'feature', dated 1917, is Quirino Cristiani's *El Apóstol*, an Argentinian production). The magic of single-frame (Figs. 144 and 145), high-speed, and stereoscopic cinematography was a regular feature of technical manuals; early experiments with 3-D films are preserved in France and the United States (Plate 50).

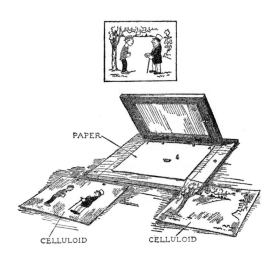

Fig. 144 Composite celluloid cells for animation films, *c.* 1915. Source: Private collection.

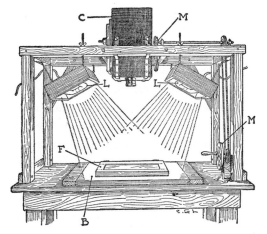

Fig. 145 Camera and lights arrangement for animated film, *c.* 1915. Source: Private collection.

Cartoons and comedy shorts, produced in very large numbers throughout the silent period, were by far the most successful; their commercial life was often much longer than that of dramatic features, and sometimes continued well into the early sound era in the form of reissued versions, with added music and voice-over soundtracks. Another format in which short films had an enduring appeal was the serial (mostly made in France and the United States), whose instalments were generally distributed in two- to four-reel episodes of varying number. Serials should not be confused with dramatic films in multiple parts ('series'), released over an extended period but composed of feature-length sections (*Les Misérables*, Henri Fescourt, 1925).

Short films retained their prominence also as vehicles of information. The French term *actualités*, defined by the 1904 Pathé catalogue as 'scenes of general and international interest', evolved into more systematic forms of visual information about recent events, with single reels containing about eight to twelve sections – each preceded by a descriptive title – on topics such as crime, accidents, politics, sports, and fashion. Popular demand for cinema journalism grew to such an extent that these occasional productions rapidly evolved into dedicated series, sometimes called 'animated newspapers', even though they did not contain animation scenes in the technical sense of the term. 'Pathé – Faits divers', soon to become 'Pathé Journal' ('Pathé Weekly' in the United States), appeared first in 1908, prompting competitors to follow suit in France ('Éclair-Journal', 'Gaumont Actualités', 'Éclipse-Journal'), Germany ('Messter-Woche', 'Eiko-Woche'), Great Britain ('Topical Budget', 'Gaumont Graphic', 'Warwick Bioscope Chronicle', 'Pathé's Animated Gazette'), the United States (Universal's 'Animated Weekly', Vitagraph's 'Monthly of Current Events') and elsewhere between 1910 and 1912. The Mutual Film Corporation created a sensation by persuading General Pancho Villa to cooperate in filming the Mexican revolution for its 'Mutual Weekly' journal.

With the outbreak of World War I, public interest in this type of news coverage had attained such a global scale that governments were soon to exploit it as a powerful tool for propaganda:

'Sascha-Messter-Woche' (1914–18) portrayed the conflict from an Austro-Hungarian perspective; the Soviet government did the same in 'Kino-Nedelia' (1918–19), then commissioned Dziga Vertov's 'Goskinokalendar' (1925) and 'Kino-Pravda' (1922–5); 'Giornale Luce', a creation of the Fascist regime, began in 1927. They were now called 'newsreels' in the English-speaking world, with 'Hearst Metrotone News' as their most influential voice in the United States. Countries of relatively modest film output had one or more newsreel series, such as 'Rossi Actualidades', 'Sol e Sombra', 'Cine Jornal Brasil', and 'Cine Revista Mineira' in Brazil; 'Jornal do Condes' and 'Jornal Central' in Portugal; 'Actualidades Argentinas', and 'Film Revista Valle' in Argentina; and 'Australasian Gazette' in Australia.

Once firmly established as the centrepiece of the motion picture show, the feature film underwent a process of further specialization into an ever-increasing range of moods and variations. Some of them flourished within specific cultures, like the *kengeki eiga* (sword films) in Japan and the expressionist *Kammerspiel* drama in Germany; others grew as purely national phenomena, but proved so popular as to cross their native boundaries. The western, born in the United States, found clever and at times inspired imitations in Europe; an Italian non-professional actor, Bartolomeo Pagano, was so charismatic in his role as the benevolent muscular hero Maciste that action films featuring strongmen appeared in France and Germany throughout the 1920s; monumental depictions of the ancient Roman world, also admired in Italian productions, were sometimes borrowed by filmmakers in Germany and the United States. The multiplicity of themes in the same film points to an important aspect of film genre in silent cinema: some modes of expression had clear-cut labels, as illustrated by the Pathé catalogues; others, like actualities and trick films, were more fluid (critics and trade journalists played a role in this, as they did in later years with the film noir genre). Thematic boundaries were so blurred that a film could be 'animated', 'educational', 'industrial', and a comedy, all in one.

Theatrical, literary, and biblical adaptations, generally praised for their intellectual or devotional ambitions, knew little or no cultural barriers other than religion or politics (Pathé's and Gaumont's episodic films about the Passion of the Christ were probably the most widely circulated in all continents, well beyond the early years of cinema); on the other hand, audiences of some countries in the 1910s had a profound dislike for happy endings in the feature films imported from abroad. In response to this, alternate reels with tragic outcomes – known as 'Russian endings' – were occasionally created to replace the finale. During World War I, distribution of the many feature films where German military officers were depicted as sadistic criminals was understandably limited to the Allies' market.

Complex as it is, this picture would not be complete without mentioning two of the most peculiar instances of regional cinema. At a time of profound crisis in the Italian film industry after the war, Neapolitan producers released low-budget melodramas of a pronounced vernacular style. In some countries, itinerant filmmakers recruited the population of a given town or village for the making of fictional or factual subjects, also with shoestring budgets. Once processed and edited, the footage was presented to the community in its local theatre, in improvised screening halls, or in the open air. Elsewhere, mostly in urban areas, a minuscule but committed group of intellectuals had the ambition to make cinema without any connection to traditional storytelling. Italian artists of the Futurist movement were among the first, soon followed in France by the Surrealists and by a young émigré from Spain, Luis Buñuel.

Fig. 146 Cover of *L'Illustration* (Paris) vol. 66 no. 3396 (28 March 1908), for the article by Gustave Babin 'Les Coulisses du cinématographe'.

Tricks

When he made *Un Chien andalou* (with Salvador Dalí, 1929), Buñuel must have remembered Méliès: the film includes disappearances, abrupt substitutions, and objects with a life of their own. In this sense, Buñuel's subversion is firmly rooted in cinematic tradition (Fig. 146). Camera operators knew from the start that optical effects reproduced on glass negatives could be equally applied to animated views. The most common, obtained by exposing the same negative twice or more, had long been exploited in photography for a variety of purposes, ranging from scientific experiments to ghostly portraits of the deceased. In a motion picture camera, the 'film ribbon' (as it was called in the late 1890s) only had to be run backwards, and then unspooled again in front of a different subject. In doing so, early filmmakers discovered that cinema had also empowered them to modify the natural course of time: this was the first 'special effect' of cinema, all the more extraordinary as it only required

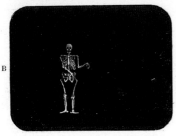

Fig. 147 Superimposed images in *The Haunted Curiosity Shop* (Walter R. Booth, Great Britain, 1901), a Robert W. Paul production. Source: Frederick Arthur Ambrose Talbot, *Moving Pictures. How they are made and worked*. London: Heinemann, 1912; Philadelphia: J.B. Lippincott Co., 1914, p. 203.

turning the crank in reverse mode, or just slowing it down.

The anecdote concerning an audience panicking in front of the projected image of a train approaching the camera in a Lumière film may or may not be apocryphal, but the sight of a demolished wall standing up again all by itself (*Démolition d'un mur*, Lumière, 1896, in two versions) must have been greeted with genuine bewilderment by early film audiences. One of the most bizarre trick films in the first decade of cinema, *Créations renversantes* (*Marvellous Reversing*, or *Stunning Creations*, Ferdinand Zecca, 1905), consists of a single scene – with one splice on the negative – showing a man methodically smashing a set of dishes on a table. When done, the protagonist retrieves the dishes one by one, now perfectly intact.

Producing a silly film like this with a straight face, long after Méliès had enchanted the world with much subtler inventions, shows the extent to which the most basic optical illusions could exercise an irresistible appeal on the audiences of the time. One of Méliès' greatest works, *Le Mélomane* (1903), was made by rewinding the film six times – seven exposures in all – inside the camera to produce an imaginary performance of the British anthem 'God Save the Queen' with singing heads on a pentagram, an astonishing feat of mathematical precision. Other pioneers of cinema, from James Williamson in Great Britain to Gaston Velle and Segundo de Chomón in France, used photographic effects for surreal and humorous exploits, or to evoke the dreamlike atmospheres of fairy tales. Master cartoonist Émile Cohl also experimented with animation combined with live acting in *Clair de lune espagnol* (*The Man in the Moon*, or *The Moon-Struck Matador*, Étienne Arnaud, 1909).

Whenever possible, early film producers resorted to stratagems borrowed from the theatrical tradition: Méliès himself did not hesitate to use invisible cables, floor trappings, and machineries in which

the camera played no role other than registering the events unfolding on the stage. For underwater scenes, or to simulate the climbing of walls, the performers crawled on the floor, on top of a painted backdrop, with the camera placed above them on a perpendicular axis (Figs. 148 and 149). There was no particular need to manipulate the film stock inside or outside the camera for illusions based on perspective and depth of field. In *Le Rêve du trottin*

Fig. 148 The shooting of an underwater scene in *La Sirène* (Louis Feuillade, Gaumont, 1907). The camera was placed above the painted backdrop, perpendicular to the floor. Feuillade is seen at the centre, standing in front of actress Christiane Wague. Source: Frederick Arthur Ambrose Talbot, Moving Pictures. How they are made and worked. London: Heinemann, 1912; Philadelphia: J.B. Lippincott Co., 1914, p. 227.

Fig. 149 The underwater scene in *La Sirène* as it was intended to appear on the screen. Source: Frederick Arthur Ambrose Talbot, Moving Pictures. How they are made and worked. London: Heinemann, 1912; Philadelphia: J.B. Lippincott Co., 1914, p. 226.

Fig. 150a–c *Le Rêve du trottin* (Gaumont, 1908): how an optical effect for the film was achieved. Source: Gustave Babin, 'Les coulisses du cinématographe', in L'Illustration, vol. 66, no. 3396, 28 March 1908, p. 212.

(Gaumont, 1908), the figurines that appear on the back of a suitcase are moving in real time behind the scene. The camera was stopped only to allow studio personnel to replace the suitcase lid with cut-outs of appropriate shape (Fig. 150a–c).

In the 1911 manual *Le Cinématographe scientifique et industriel. Traité pratique de cinématographie*, Jacques Ducom identified no fewer than twenty different types of special effects in cinema. He was actually listing many variations of six basic methods: using traditional stagecraft, recorded by the camera during the action; rewinding the film, as in *Le Mélomane* and *Créations renversantes*, or altering its cranking speed; opening or closing the camera diaphragm (for dissolves and cross-fading); displacing or altering the point of view, as in *Le Rêve du trottin* and *La Sirène* (Louis Feuillade, Gaumont, 1907), with or without mirrors (they were used by J. Stuart Blackton in 1909 for *Princess Nicotine; or, The Smoke Fairy*, a canonical work of early 'trick' cinema); superimposing two negatives upon each other, as was allegedly the case in *The Haunted Curiosity Shop* (Walter R. Booth, 1901, Fig. 147); or cutting the negative or positive stock to manipulate time, sometimes in conjunction with one of the other techniques. There is proof that splicing film for expressive purposes was known to Lumière (many early films apparently made of a single shot were in fact composed of different segments joined together); Méliès, however, elevated the mechanical act of cutting and splicing film to a complex art form, an astounding synthesis of poetry and synchronicity (his most elaborate trick films have an average of one splice every forty-four frames of negative).

Film historian Jacques Malthête has identified four main types of splices on negative film stock.

Resumption splice: the film was broken or jammed inside the camera, or something went wrong during shooting. The operator stopped the camera; if needed, the film was rethreaded, and the action restarted from where it was a few moments before the incident. After processing, the negative was cut to remove the defective frames and resume continuity.

Repair splice: the negative was broken or otherwise damaged at a particular point during film processing. The defective section was removed, and a new splice made to join the ends of the negative.

Extension splice: two or more pieces of negative were joined to each other to make the film longer (until about 1903, motion picture cameras could rarely accommodate more than 20 metres, or 65 feet, of film).

Retouch splice: this is the only type of splice on the negative that was planned ahead of shooting. It was used in 'trick' films by removing frames from both ends of a shot in order to achieve the optical illusion. For example, when Méliès transforms himself into a ballerina in *L'Impressionniste fin-de-siècle* (1899), the effect of substitution could only be achieved by cutting the images corresponding to the end of Méliès' jump and those at the beginning of the dancer's leap.

Double exposures required two splices on the negative, also decided upon in advance. The film section with superimposed images was created separately, and spliced into the negative at the beginning and the end of the double exposure. This was done for budgetary reasons: a mistake in achieving a perfect double exposure would have entailed remaking the entire scene.

Languages

Before the mid-1910s, when the United States began to play a hegemonic role in the film industry, worldwide audiences regarded France, Denmark, and Italy as the driving forces of quality programmes. French cinema took the lion's share of the market – both in Europe and overseas – until the outbreak of World War I, when production companies based in New York, Los Angeles, and Chicago took advantage of the political crisis and in particular of the embargo imposed upon film distribution among enemy countries. European cinema never fully recovered from this traumatic reversal of fortune: by the end of the conflict, Hollywood was the undisputed leader in film theatres of all continents. This is all the more remarkable if one considers that an international distribution network for European films had been in place well before 1910, when Pathé, Gaumont, and other major companies had branches or delegations in many countries: even a maverick like Georges Méliès had been releasing his films in the United States through his New York office since 1903. Title cards in foreign languages for European films were edited into the release prints, with identical fonts and graphic designs as in the originals; odd phrases and spelling errors were fairly common. To avoid the slow and risky process of dispatching projection prints around the world, many companies of the early 1910s instead shipped a second negative to their overseas representatives, who would then make as many projection copies as needed.

These negatives had no intertitles. One positive or negative frame of each original title card (known as 'flash title' because it would be barely visible on screen if projected as such) was spliced into the foreign distribution negative at the appropriate place, so that workers in the print assembly line could easily figure out where to insert its equivalent in a foreign language. Production companies provided the original and translated title lists to their distributors or agents, who were responsible for typesetting, filming, processing, and incorporating the new intertitles into the positive copies. In many instances, fonts and graphic designs differed from those of the domestic versions, and sometimes included the corporate names of local distributors (often with a mention of their geographic location); it is therefore possible to see a silent film made in the United States with title cards referring to a Spanish or a Czech corporate firm: this is something to keep in mind in the process of authenticating archival prints, as further explained in Chapter 14. On other occasions, a negative with all the translated titles in the company's original fonts was created by the producer and shipped with the picture negative in a separate reel. In rare instances, bilingual title cards were made for communities of diverse cultural backgrounds (Fig. 151).

Major companies of the late Hollywood era were proud to tell journalists that their films were translated into thirty-six or more idioms. In 1927, the offices of Paramount-Famous-Lasky Corporation were compiling and sending title lists in languages such as Hindu, Armenian, Gaelic, and Javanese to 115 foreign exchanges serving seventy-five countries in the world, where the company earned 25 per cent of its average gross revenue. Separate title lists were also compiled for countries like England and Australia, whose expressions and idiomatic terms were different from those adopted in the United States. The films' release titles could also be modified for the same reason.

Fig. 151 Bilingual title card (in Mandarin and Norwegian) from *Pan si dong* (Darwin Dan, 1927). Digital scan from a 35mm nitrate positive. Source: Courtesy of Norsk Filminstitutt, Oslo.

It must be added that the best intentions to meet the demands of worldwide audiences were sometimes thwarted by situations beyond the producers' control. Once a film was received in a foreign country, local distributors who presumed to have a better knowledge of their public were keen to make editorial changes not only to the pictures (including their tints and tones), but also to their textual components. They excised any title cards they felt were redundant; they altered or rewrote them altogether; they changed their positioning within the reels, so that the plot would be drastically altered; in numerous instances, they added new intertitles in dialogue scenes, turning them into longer conversations between the characters.

Whether or not distributors had been contractually allowed to do all this, the chances that someone would be resourceful enough to compare the foreign version with the original were extremely slim: the limited benefits to be derived from such a monitoring exercise would not have been worth the effort. French, Italian, and Hungarian release prints of feature films produced in the United States during the 1920s tend to be on the verbose side when viewed against the domestic versions; conversely, many intertitles of European films shown in other continents were removed from projection prints, in the belief that their absence would enhance an otherwise stilted narrative flow.

Intertitles

There is an unspoken but widespread belief that the title cards of a silent film have a special status within the overall work because they mainly or exclusively consist of written words rather than real or artificial events unfolding over time. The fallacy of this line of reasoning is proven by the simple fact that titles (often referred to as 'intertitles', 'title cards', or otherwise) were filmed like everything else, with cameras, film stock, and lighting sources; their production obeyed different protocols, and was chronologically distinct from the shooting of the live action or of animated scenes, but this is not a good enough reason to treat them as separate from the cinematic event as a whole.

The first films had no titles or intertitles at all. With or without a live presenter who would announce the next title to appear on screen, motion pictures were often preceded by magic lantern slides describing the content of what the audience was about to see next. The separation between the title and the actual film also allowed projectionists to change reels while the slides were being shown. Even then, the title on display from a magic lantern slide was an element of continuity rather than disjunction in the context of the early motion picture show.

It took very little time for production companies to understand that the hassle of alternating between films and glass slides could be avoided altogether by printing the titles on the film itself. After a very brief period during which titles on film stock were made available separately from the main body of the work, filmmakers tackled the issue of how to create textual inserts that were pleasing to the eye and easy to read. At the very beginning of the twentieth century, intertitles of Pathé films were laid out on an off-white background (Fig. 152), in a clear reference to the tradition of the printed page; Méliès cleverly integrated some titles of his early films into their set designs. Soon afterwards, however, the benefits of creating title cards with white text on a black background became evident to all: their contrast was much easier to tolerate than black over white, especially when increasingly complex narratives mandated the inclusion of titles between scenes.

There were many techniques for filming titles; three in particular are worth mentioning here. In the earliest method, adopted mainly in English-speaking countries and soon abandoned because

of its crude results on the big screen, movable white letters were pinned to a soft black surface with horizontal grooves all across its width, placed vertically in front of the camera. Soon afterwards, individual characters in matted copper or zinc were arranged on a wide horizontal bench, sometimes slightly tilted to facilitate work, with the camera perpendicularly placed above the surface to be filmed (Fig. 153); the movable letters were eventually replaced with a printed sheet with black letters over a white background.

Fig. 152 *Le Fer à cheval* (Camille de Morlhon, 1909). Frame enlargement from a 35mm polyester positive. Source: Associazione Culturale Hommelette.

Fig. 153 Making title cards at the Pathé studios, *c.* 1910. Note the cameraman at work above the set. Source: Frederick Arthur Ambrose Talbot, Moving Pictures. How they are made and worked. London: Heinemann, 1912; Philadelphia: J.B. Lippincott Co., 1914, p. 157.

It was enough to shoot one or a few frames, as they could then be duplicated in the desired amount with the same printing process used for the rest of the film. One of these frames was often attached to the negative of a given shot, indicating where the title was to be inserted; otherwise, the placement of a title was signalled by a sequential number reproduced at one corner of the title card itself and on the tail of the matching negative section. Flash titles and numbering systems were especially important for projection copies with title cards in languages unknown to the personnel in charge of print assembly.

Illiteracy was widespread in many areas of the world during the early twentieth century: this prompted the adoption of title cards with short texts reproduced in large capital fonts (Fig. 154). This precaution was abandoned in the early 1910s for longer and complex sentences in uppercase and lowercase fonts, but filmmakers kept paying attention to the amount of time needed by different audiences to read the same text. One second per word was regarded as the standard ratio; longer reading times were applied in some regions throughout the entire silent film era. Each title card was also an opportunity to promote the producer's name or trademark as a benchmark of quality (Fig. 155), and to remind picture house patrons about the title of the film they were watching (Fig. 156).

The function of title cards evolved in parallel with the narrative structure of the films themselves. Most early intertitles simply announced what was about to happen in the next shot or sequence; gradually, other forms of written information emerged. Titles began to appear in dialogue sequences; aside from sporadic cases where the name of the speaking character was spelled out as in the script of a play (Fig. 157), conversations were reproduced as they would be in print, with hyphens or quotation marks, sometimes in italics. The element of

Fig. 154 *Vie et passion de N.S. Jésus Christ: passion et mort* (Ferdinand Zecca, 1907). Frame enlargement from a 35mm triacetate positive. Source: Library of Congress.

Fig. 155 Title card from *Shelkovaia pautina* (Yuri Yurievskij, Russia, 1916) with the logo of the film's production company, Drankov. Frame enlargement from a 35mm nitrate positive. Source: Gosfilmofond of Russia.

Fig. 156 *The Debt* (director unknown, Rex Motion Picture Company, 1912). Frame enlargement from a 35mm triacetate positive. Source: Library of Congress/Dawson City Collection.

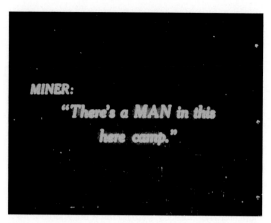

Fig. 157 Dialogue intertitle from *The Spoilers* (Colin Campbell, 1914). Frame enlargement from a 35mm triacetate positive. Source: Library of Congress.

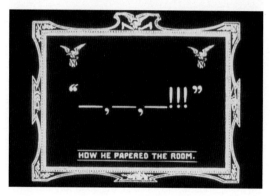

Fig. 158 *How He Papered the Room* (director unknown, Vitagraph, 1912). Frame enlargement from a 35mm triacetate positive. Source: BFI National Archive.

sound also made its appearance, with smaller fonts for whispered sentences, huge block letters for shouting, single words appearing one by one for enhanced dramatic or rhetorical effect (as in many Soviet films), and visual effects to reproduce intonation. Intertitles were becoming 'moving images' in their own right; after learning how to evoke noises, technologies, inarticulate sounds, and states of mind (as they had done since the early 1910s; see Fig. 158 and Fig. 159), their makers embraced the possibilities offered by narrative titles for commentaries or witticisms (Fig. 160), and by static or dynamic graphic designs added to or superimposed onto the texts.

The boundaries between 'title' and 'motion picture' became increasingly blurred (Fig. 161) as still images of letters, telegrams, and handwritten messages were replaced by live action shots showing the hands of those who were holding them: more than substitutes for intertitles, they were discursive elements of the narration. Intertitles also were set to move when too long to fit onto a single card. Swedish filmmakers of the 1910s did not mind showing two or more consecutive titles with no live action in between,

Fig. 159 *The Raven* (Charles J. Brabin, 1915). Frame enlargement from a 28mm diacetate positive. Source: George Eastman Museum.

Fig. 160 *The Wishing Ring, an Idyll of Old England* (Maurice Tourneur, 1914). Frame enlargement from a 16mm triacetate positive. Source: Library of Congress.

Fig. 161 *The Girl Without a Soul* (John H. Collins, 1917). Frame enlargement from a 35mm triacetate positive. Source: George Eastman Museum.

Fig. 162 *Hedda Gabler* (Giovanni Pastrone, 1923). Frame enlargement from a 16mm triacetate positive from the release version for Hispanic countries. Source: Cineteca del Friuli.

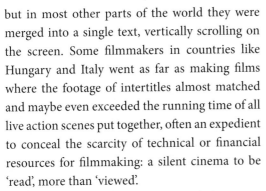

Fig. 163 *Blue Jeans* (John H. Collins, 1917). Frame enlargement from a 35mm triacetate positive. Source: George Eastman Museum.

Fig. 164 *The Chamber Mystery* (Abraham S. Schomer, 1920). Frame enlargement from a 35mm triacetate positive. Source: George Eastman Museum.

but in most other parts of the world they were merged into a single text, vertically scrolling on the screen. Some filmmakers in countries like Hungary and Italy went as far as making films where the footage of intertitles almost matched and maybe even exceeded the running time of all live action scenes put together, often an expedient to conceal the scarcity of technical or financial resources for filmmaking: a silent cinema to be 'read', more than 'viewed'.

French and Italian producers of the 1920s were keen to incorporate titles into live action for dialogue (Fig. 162), voice-over, or sung music. Metro Pictures had attempted to do so for the narrative title cards in *Blue Jeans* (John H. Collins, 1917), superimposing the text to the image (Fig. 163); a lukewarm reaction from the audience put an end to this experiment. Abraham S. Schomer took the highly unusual step of covering parts of a live action shot in *The Chamber Mystery* (1920) with dialogue balloons (Fig. 164). German filmmakers of the Weimar period went back to the early days of film and dispensed with titles altogether, persuaded that cinema should be a form of purely non-verbal expression, free from any connection with literature.

Copies

The number of prints made for a commercial film varied enormously in the course of the silent era, depending on the importance attributed to the work, its actual or expected success, and the size of the intended market (prints struck and rented for non-theatrical use are even more difficult to assess in quantitative terms). Between 1896 and the late 1900s, when copies were available for purchase, prints were made upon request. In its 1905 catalogue for exhibitors in the United States, the Star-Film Company distinguished between three categories of products: in the first, some films of the 1896–1902 period – all made with a single camera – are listed only by their title, catalogue number, length, and retail price. No duplicate negative existed for those early productions, as they were apparently no longer in great demand.

Part Two of the catalogue featured the most popular films made by Méliès in the same years. Exhibitors could obtain them either as high-quality prints made from the camera negative (they were shipped from Paris within four weeks after the order), or in cheaper and readily available but poorer duplicates struck from a second-generation negative created for the company's New York office, opened in March 1903. At the end of the previous year – after A Trip to the Moon – Méliès had begun to make his films with two cameras running simultaneously; one of the two original negatives was dispatched to New York, providing North American customers with excellent copies in a shorter period of time, and to combat piracy by submitting domestic prints for copyright protection at the Library of Congress. These are the films listed in Part Three of the Star-Film catalogue. Méliès' method was quickly imitated by others, and became standard practice for many production companies of the silent era.

There are statistical records on how much raw (that is, unprocessed) film stock was manufactured in France, Germany, and the United States in the 1920s. Information on the volume of positive film stock distributed for release around the world, on the other hand, is available to a much more limited degree. The corporate records of Pathé are so detailed as to enable us to determine that, for instance, 5,722,568 metres (18,774,829 feet) of processed film were produced by the company during the month of February 1913, including 521,920 metres (1,712,336 feet) in stencil colour, a much lower percentage than one would have expected only a few years earlier.

We know very little (with the partial exception of the Turin-based company Itala-Film) about how much positive film was made in Italy at any time during the silent period, and virtually nothing on the output of production companies in countries like the Soviet Union, India, China, Japan, and in South America. On the basis of the extant documentation, an average of fifty to one hundred prints were struck for a fiction film produced by a major European company around 1910. Comparable figures appear in the records of Nordisk Film at the heyday of the motion picture industry in Denmark (1910–14), with peaks of 200 or more release prints, as in the case of Den hvide Slavehandel II (In the Hands of Impostors, August Blom, 1911), an international box-office hit.

Other films of the early silent era existed in only one or two copies, or were not printed at all from their negatives (therefore, they were never seen by an audience) because nobody ever requested them for a public screening, as was the case with some Edison 'actuality' titles. On average, a 1914 Keystone comedy was released in a little over thirty prints; Charlie Chaplin's Dough and Dynamite fared a little better with forty copies; forty-one for His Trysting Places. According to Chaplin himself, 135 copies of the first film he made for Essanay,

His New Job (1915), had already been booked by film exhibitors by the end of shooting.

Chaplin's meteoric rise is eloquently illustrated by *The Floorwalker*, released by Mutual in May 1916, when seventy-five prints were needed for New York City's theatres alone. By the end of 1926, the number of film theatres in the United States had been estimated at 20,500. To cover such a large number of screens, a Hollywood major could not meet the demands of film exchanges with less than an average of 200 prints for a feature-length film, 150 being the minimum for a production of lower profile. *The Big Parade* (King Vidor, 1925) and *The Covered Wagon* (James Cruze, 1923) were released in about 250 to 400 prints for the domestic market only.

It is still unclear how often, and how many, additional prints were made after a film's initial release; some information is available in the United States about the number of copies struck from negatives for overseas distribution, averaging 140 for major firms at the end of the silent film era (European producers never managed to do the same with their own films in North America). The glaring disproportion between this figure and the modest percentage of total revenues reported for Hollywood feature films abroad can be explained in strategic terms with the following example. Great Britain – the world's foremost colonial power, with a huge reservoir of actual or potential audiences – had imposed in 1927 a quota system (the Cinematograph Films Act) whereby a fixed percentage of motion pictures released in its theatres had to be produced within the British Empire. According to executives in Hollywood, major companies were fighting this legislation with quality, pushing new films into the global market without seeking any short-term financial advantage, in the hope to persuade the public that their products were the best. Cinema, the ultimate propaganda tool of the early twentieth century, was promoting itself. The strategy paid off within

a decade or two, and we are still witnessing its effects.

Commerce

Setting up a motion picture show seemed like a relatively simple business in the early years of cinema. Anybody with a keen interest in film exhibition could browse through the catalogue of a manufacturer, pick the most appealing subjects, and purchase a copy of the film. As the case of Lumière's business model demonstrates (p. 93), there could be obstacles along the path. When all went well, however, exhibitors bought all the film prints they could afford, then used them for as long as they wanted until they were either too worn out to be of any use, or had been seen so frequently to be of no further interest for the same audience.

This, of course, was a matter of little or no concern to itinerant showmen, as the public changed at every venue. Positive film stock could, in any event, be given a second life by splicing it into another damaged print of the same film, or by inserting it as supplementary footage into another film on a similar topic: a surviving print of the French production *Un Drame en mer* (*Tragedy at Sea*, Gaston Velle, 1905) includes documentary footage showing British seamen at work. At some unknown point in time, an exhibitor or a projectionist must have thought that there was no harm in adding a touch of realism to Pathé's original story, as few would have noticed the discrepancy between the non-fictional material and the rest of the film.

In their negotiations at the 1909 Paris conferences (Chapter 2, p. 25), film entrepreneurs had long debated – with the steadfast opposition of exhibitors, who had not been invited to the meetings – the idea of putting an end to this practice with the introduction of film rental under the direct control of production companies. In this scheme, individuals could no longer purchase prints, let alone loan them out to third parties as they pleased (something they had been doing since the beginning of the century); instead, exhibitors would borrow them from the producer, show the films at fixed dates and in compliance with previously agreed financial terms, then send them back to the owners (or their designated representatives) for loan to the next venue. It was a time when permanent film theatres were gradually replacing fairground shows; their audiences demanded that programmes were changed very frequently, but exhibitors had neither the inclination to amass large amounts of flammable reels in their warehouses, nor the time necessary to negotiate their sale to second-hand dealers. As a result, the same films were being shown over and over again; the supply of new films was therefore hampered by the slow consumption of the old ones.

This, at least, was the theory. In blunt terms, film producers and manufacturers had no interest whatsoever in prolonging the commercial life of a print beyond what they regarded as an acceptable time frame (normally around four to six months). Enabling any second-, third-, or fourth-run venue to show the same film any further than that would have meant losing an opportunity to occupy precious screen real estate with new products; film rental was a powerful incentive to maintain a steady flow of fresh material, with the added value of better control over the company's assets and the authority to dispose of those prints whose commercial age and physical condition were such as to compromise the quality of the picture and, consequently, the reputation of its maker. A formidable player in the film business began to emerge at this point: the film distributor, a designated intermediary between the offer from producers and the demand by theatrical exhibitors (the transfer of power from the exhibitor to the distributor and studio was an important facet of early cinema,

and one of the defining concepts of the 'classical Hollywood cinema' system).

In short, early capitalism was already reclaiming its right to control the rate of obsolescence of its products. For a brief period, between 1907 and 1909, Pathé had tried to implement a vertically organized, integrated distribution of its films through one of its subsidiaries, Pathé Omnia, by maintaining a tight grip on the production chain from beginning to end: its ultimate goal was to manufacture the raw stock, produce films, and then exhibit them in company-owned theatres on an exclusive basis. The scheme would have worked well if the public demand for motion pictures had not soared so much as to make it wholly impossible for Pathé to offer as many new films as were needed in those years. This became even clearer to production companies once the rental system was introduced: they needed distribution outlets to handle their business, either on an exclusive basis or as part of a broader group of corporate entities. These outlets, called 'film exchanges', were in charge of negotiating contracts with the theatres, dispatching prints and receiving them back after the shows, inspecting the copies upon return, and making them ready for the next booking.

The film exchange was the pulsating heart of the distribution business, and its beat was fast, especially at night, when the shows were over and the exhibitor had to make quick decisions on what to show next. The peak hours for a film exchange of a major company were from 7pm to 2am in the morning. It was preferably located near the area where most first-run theatres were concentrated, or in proximity to train stations, where prints could be swiftly sent off to as many venues as possible around a metropolitan area. In bargaining for the rental of a major motion picture, exchanges often made recourse to an unpopular and contentious trade mechanism called 'block booking': in exchange for a popular title obtained at favourable terms, the theatre owner agreed to show a number of films of lesser importance. Harsh as it seemed, this rental procedure was not completely unfair to the exhibitor, who could not possibly find the time to look at films from many different companies to schedule the theatre's programme with enough advance. By offering the exhibitor a range of products of acceptable quality, the film exchange would earn a chance to establish a relationship of mutual trust. Both parties had an interest in the smoothest continuity for their business.

If the exhibitor could not afford to betray its patrons by feeding them with mediocre or outright awful films, film exchanges were constantly under pressure to make as much profit as possible from the pictures provided to them, and had no interest at all in force-feeding their customers with pictures they would be ashamed of promoting. A finished film could not lie dormant on the distributor's shelf for too long: in the late 1920s, its negative depreciated at the average rate of 80 per cent of the investment after the first year. The remaining 20 per cent of its original worth was liquidated within the following twelve months; by the beginning of the third year, the only value left was, quite literally, the amount of silver on the negative's emulsion. A day in the life of a film exchange, with its whirlwind traffic of theatre managers signing contract forms, film projectionists dropping off film cans and picking them up for the next day's show, and technicians frantically rewinding, splicing, or mending damaged prints must have been a spectacle to behold, second only to the havoc of a newspaper room in the minutes before going to press with the morning edition. Prints that had officially reached the term of their natural life sometimes found their way into the second-hand market, an unofficial remnant of the long-defunct practice of direct sales, largely ignored by the mainstream trade.

Copyright

Every time a new technology or mode of expression sees the light, the law is generally unprepared to cope with all the implications of the newcomer's appearance in the public world. There is nothing strange about this. Legislation is fundamentally based on the lessons of the past, and on principles that have been applied to existing and often long-established areas of knowledge and human action. The moving image is no exception, as it presented a whole set of properties for which there seemed to be no adequate tool for interpretation. Legal authorities promptly asserted their control over film exhibition by applying the same moral and safety codes already in place for other forms of public entertainment; the outcry that followed the 1897 tragedy at the Bazar de la Charité (see p. 143) gave them the perfect opportunity to enforce drastic restrictions in the use of projection equipment. Matters were far more difficult when it came to defining film per se, both as a physical object and as a product of the intellect. Over three decades, jurisprudence tried to catch up with the irresistible ascent of the new entity in culture and society; much progress was made over the years, but cinema never ceased to be a matter of controversy. In some areas, the debate continues to this day.

Protection of intellectual property had been enforced in some countries long before the invention of cinema. In 1787, a clause of the Constitution of the United States was proclaimed 'To promote the Progress of Science and useful Arts, by securing for limited Times to Authors and Inventors the exclusive Right to their respective Writings and Discoveries.' Creators were originally given the right to earn profit from use of their own works by third parties for a limited period of time (fourteen years) by submitting a request for copyright protection.

The intellectual property could be extended only once, for the same amount of time; after that, the work would become part of the public domain, and everyone was allowed to use it for the benefit of human progress; unfortunately, the word 'limited' included in the clause was exploited as an argument in favour of extending the monopoly for much longer periods of time. In the meanwhile, filmmakers and legislators of the United States had to decide upon the evidence to be presented in the copyright application. Books, theatre plays, and music were easy to handle, as it was enough to submit a copy of the published work to the Library of Congress, where copyrighted works were deposited. No comparable repository, however, existed for rolls of films, and the Library of Congress struggled to find a rational solution to the new challenge.

As a practical measure, it was deemed useful to register the motion picture films as photographs (they were even formally incorporated in the Library of Congress' Prints & Photographs Section between 1961 and 1978): after all, a 35mm projection copy is indeed a sequence of tiny gelatin silver 'prints'. This very logical way of thinking was at odds with the fact that a film was also a cumbersome and flammable object that could not be read like a book, or looked at like a daguerreotype. Over the years, librarians and copyright officers took various approaches to

what should constitute the object of legal deposit, ranging from a more or less detailed written transcript of the film's content, to the provision of actual rolls of 35mm film printed on paper (sometimes with perforations) instead of celluloid (Fig. 165). The latter option, intermittently adopted between 1895 and 1916, made it possible to preserve on a relatively stable carrier a beautiful collection of early films, known as the 'Paper Print Collection' at the Library of Congress.

Still, the number of titles submitted for copyright protection was growing at such an exponential rate that librarians reverted to textual descriptions, or to a combination of typewritten continuities and individual clips or frames for each shot. A similar procedure (with the addition of one or a few strips of frames reproduced on photographic paper) was implemented at the Bibliothèque Nationale in Paris after the French copyright authorities took notice of the avalanche of new productions being released in France. Avant-garde poet Guillaume Apollinaire told a funny anecdote about his visit to the French national library, where he was trying to look at some prints: 'Ten films! ... No, Sir, we are still not equipped to grant access to that kind of stuff ... The library would look as if it has been infected by some kind of tapeworm' (Pascal Hédegat [pseudonym of Guillaume Apollinaire], 'Le Cinéma à la Nationale', *L'Intransigeant*, 1 March 1910, p. 2).

While bureaucrats and archivists were struggling with the unwelcome guest (they eventually resigned to erecting dedicated vaults for them), lawmakers could not reach a consensus on the legal nature of the new beast. Only one type of activity is involved in writing a novel, painting a canvas, or taking a photograph; not so with cinema, as its existence is dependent upon the joint efforts of writers, camera operators, and other creative and technical personnel, under the supervision of a financing agent. If the motion

Fig. 165 Paper print. *Le Roi du maquillage* (*The Untamable Whiskers* [US title], or *The King of the Mackerel Fishers* [UK title], Georges Méliès, 1904). 35mm positive on photographic paper. Source: Library of Congress.

picture is a dramatic work, the story itself must also be regarded as a primary ingredient of its cinematic expression (this viewpoint was emphasized in the English-speaking world by the term 'photoplay', indicating the hybrid nature of the product). By the end of the silent era, the prevailing opinion was that a new film is an original work in its own right, not to be confused with anything else that may have contributed to its achievement, and whose identity is distinct from the sum of its sources and components.

The definition of a film as self-contained entity raised the question of who should be legally called its author. Two opposite theories were widely discussed in national and comparative terms during the silent era. Advocates of the multiplicity or divisibility of rights were persuaded that a certain number and categories of people involved in the production of a film were entitled to share its legal rights; conversely, according to the indivisibility principle, the director or the producer were the only individuals who could claim sole ownership of the film. A significant majority of scholars endorsed the second line of thought; producers were the most frequently recognized 'authors' from a legal standpoint. There was also an ongoing discussion on what were the author's privileges as the owner of a film. Special emphasis was given to patrimonial rights within and outside the film industry, including the option to assign, sell, reproduce, and reutilize the work; and to moral rights, from the inclusion of the author's name on the film credits to the prerogative to cut, expand, or modify the content of the creative work, and to exercise control over the conditions of its exploitation.

The most famous controversy in the legal history of silent cinema occurred between 1908 and 1915 in the United States with the creation of the Motion Picture Patents Company (MPPC), a powerful consortium of film producers, distributors, and film manufacturers who tried to enforce a monopoly over the use of cameras, film stock, and projectors in order to prevent the proliferation of competitors. The ruthless enforcement of the alliance faced a backlash when independent producers transferred their operations to Hollywood in order to steer away from Edison's aggressive and at times violent imposition of its patents; Eastman Kodak's decision in 1911 to begin selling film stock to non-MPPC members was another blow for the cartel, whose plans were finally denounced as illegal by a federal court decision in October 1915.

Elsewhere in the world, moving images found their place in the intellectual property laws of over twenty countries during the silent era. The list does not include France, whose legislators felt no need to include the word 'cinema' in the various amendments to the 1793 decrees on the protection of literary and artistic works (on 11 March 1902, legislators added architecture, sculpture, and decorative arts to the list, but not motion pictures). The earliest mention of film in the context of a national legislation has been found in Japan (3 March 1899); Spain addressed the issue only as a matter of industrial (not intellectual) property in 1929, at the beginning of the sound era.

Censorship

In most countries of the world, various forms of regulations and restrictions regarding the content and exhibition of silent films were in place for the protection of public order and morality. The principles governing these decrees were no different from those enforced in other areas of culture and entertainment; they were at times spelled out in painstaking detail, and the motives behind their application are not always clear. In broad terms, the main objects of censorship were the display of images contrary to the decency of individual and collective behaviour, the dignity of the nation, and the international relations between governments.

Severe limitations were also imposed upon the depiction of events perceived as offensive to the police, the army, the bureaucracy, and the judiciary arm of the government; the portrayals of perverse or repugnant acts; the glorification of blasphemy and evil. Images of violence and cruelty were so strongly condemned that direct portrayals of murder and suicide were often not allowed at all, or, if they were, in very elliptical ways (as in the breathtaking finale of a 1912 short by Harold Shaw on the theme of child abuse, *The Land Beyond the Sunset*, one of the masterpieces of early cinema). An emblematic instance of directorial self-restraint is a climactic scene of *The Cossack Whip* where a prison guard takes his own life with a revolver. As the man is about to pull the trigger, an optical mask covers half of the frame: all we see is the gun smoke floating in the air (Fig. 166a–b). 'Poison and its use should be kept out of any play,' wrote Eustace Hale Ball in *The Art of the Photoplay* (1913); 'it is too apt to suggest deviltry to weak minds or vicious' (p. 45).

The categories of prohibited images and title cards were subject to ongoing scrutiny and refinement over the years. No legal sanction fell on the Edison shorts *Execution of Czolgosz with Panorama of Auburn Prison* (1901) and *Electrocuting an Elephant* (1903), respectively a semi-fictional re-enactment of a capital sentence and a very real chronicle of an animal being killed. In the early 1910s, on-screen graphic violence against humans was out of question; this privilege was denied to animals until the end of the so-called 'cinema of attractions', as shown by a gruesome Éclipse production (*Duel sensationnel*, 1908) where a crowd observes a bull and a tiger slaughtering each other within a cage. By the 1920s, when filmed cockfights were tolerated only in travelogues, censorship had targeted

Fig. 166a–b *The Cossack Whip* (John H. Collins, 1916). Frame enlargements from a 35mm polyester positive. Source: George Eastman Museum.

many other sensitive topics: adultery, normally judged from a male perspective, but also hypnotism, magnetism, mesmerism, or other forms of psychological threats to innocence, and any hint at presenting mafia, hooliganism, and witchcraft in a positive light.

The censors' reformist zeal was directed in particular against crime films like *Zigomar, roi des voleurs* (Victorin Jasset, 1911), whose appearance in Japan elicited a furious response from public authorities. Slapstick comedy was, on the contrary, a relatively safe haven for freedom of expression. The exhilarating vulgarity of the second reel in *Springtime Saps* (Leslie Goodwins, 1929) is so flagrant as to raise the suspicion that censorship officers never bothered to see it; this could hardly have been the case for a brazen parody on drug addiction, *The Mystery of the Leaping Fish* (John Emerson and William Christy Cabanne, 1916), given the reputation of its leading player, Douglas Fairbanks, in the role of Coke Annyday.

Official censorship of silent films could occur before production (through an approval process for the original scripts), or at the time of their release; even retroactively (when a new legislation was applied to older works still in circulation). Regulations were sometimes jointly implemented at the national, regional, or municipal level. Most countries in Europe enforced them with great perseverance. Controls were particularly strict in Germany and Italy; also in Sweden (Fig. 167), where films were given different colour codes for each of their authorized audiences (red censorship cards for general admission, yellow for viewers of over 15 years of age; white was reserved for productions to be banned altogether).

As in the Swedish example, many censorship boards kept meticulous records – in the form of file cards, instructions sheets, or inventories – of the scenes, individual shots, and intertitles to be amended or deleted (as seen in Chapter 11, these documents are invaluable sources for historical

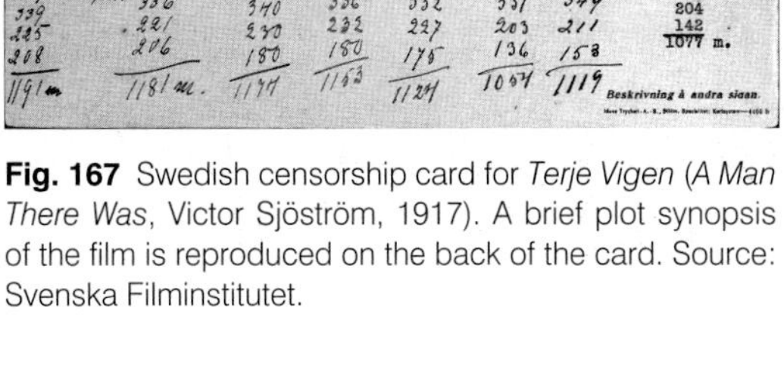

Fig. 167 Swedish censorship card for *Terje Vigen* (*A Man There Was*, Victor Sjöström, 1917). A brief plot synopsis of the film is reproduced on the back of the card. Source: Svenska Filminstitutet.

research). Swedish officials were especially hostile to close-ups and details of intimate, upsetting, or contemptible situations; to ensure compliance with their directions, every single projection print in Sweden received a stamp of approval after thorough inspection of the footage. Censorship in Turkey was equally stern, but exercised its authority only in matters of religion. Canada, New Zealand and Australia had their own governmental bodies for film review, independent from Great Britain. In Honduras and Costa Rica, censorship boards included the head of a family (normally the father).

Japanese film censorship extended its reach beyond the realm of film production and public safety in the theatres. Among its most contentious measures taken in the course of the silent film era were the total exclusion of children from motion picture houses (1917), leading to a sudden drop of 40 per cent in box-office revenues nationwide; and segregated seating for three categories of patrons: single men, single women, and married couples (similar kinds of discrimination were enforced for religious and racial reasons – either by custom or by decree – in India and the United States). In line with the importance attributed to *benshi* performances as an inherent part of the cinematic work, players were subject to a thorough investigation of their morals, social backgrounds, and politics before being allowed to work. Censorship was, in this case, directed at *benshi* performers' troublesome habit of improvising, as further explained in Chapter 9.

Two countries where cinema was a major driving force of economy and society, Great Britain and the United States, had no government censorship at all. The British Board of Film Censors started its official deliberations in 1913; it emanated from the motion picture industry itself, working in collaboration with the Home Office ('native customs in foreign lands abhorrent to

British ideas' was one of the reasons for banning a film). The film industry of the United States achieved self-governance through the National Board of Review, born in 1909 in response to the closure of all motion picture theatres ordered by the mayor of New York City, George B. McClellan Jr, on the grounds of the allegedly rampant immorality of cinema. In the words of Wilton A. Barrett, Executive Secretary of the Board in 1926, the organization consisted of about 'three hundred people reviewing films … before they are released for general exhibition to the public'. In strong opposition to any form of legal censorship, the Board was 'in favor of the constructive method of selecting the better pictures', encouraging producers 'to make the finest pictures and exhibitors to show them, and the people in general helped to a response to the best that the screen has to offer' ('The Motion Picture in Its Economic and Social Aspects', 1926, p. 175). Hailed as a fulfilment of freedom of speech as guaranteed by the Constitution of the United States, this kind of preventive self-censorship was not taken as gospel by individual states and municipalities, where local Boards of Review had their say in approving the films in their intact form, dictating amendments, or prohibiting public showings within the respective territories. For this reason, audiences of different states may have seen very different versions of the same film.

Plate 1
Cinématographe Lumière. *Inauguration par Guillaume II du monument de Guillaume Ier* (4 September 1896), Lumière catalogue no. 221, 35mm nitrate positive. Source: Private collection.

Plate 3 Veriscope. *Corbett vs Fitzsimmons – Heavyweight Boxing Match* (Enoch J. Rector, 1897), 63mm nitrate positive. Source: George Eastman Museum.

Plate 2 Gaumont Chronophotographe. *Avant l'assaut: le mur* (Georges Demenÿ, 1896), 60mm nitrate positive. Extant prints of this format have shrunk to about 58mm in width. Source: George Eastman Museum.

Plate 4 Unidentified film and format (United States?, c. 1916), 11mm positive (base undetermined), formerly referred to as 'Duplex'. Source: George Eastman Museum.

Plate 5 Edison Home Kinetoscope, United States, 1912–16. Unidentified film, 22mm diacetate positive. Source: George Eastman Museum.

Plate 6 Ernemann-Kino, Germany, 1903. Unidentified film, 17.5mm nitrate negative. Source: George Eastman Museum.

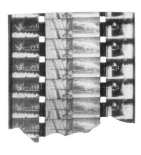

Plate 7 Messter Kino-Salon or 'Salon-Kinemesster', Oskar Messter, Germany, 1908. Unidentified film, 35mm diacetate positive. Source: George Eastman Museum.

Plate 8 Duoscope, 1912. Unidentified film, 17.5mm nitrate positive. Source: George Eastman Museum.

Plate 9 American Mutoscope & Biograph. Unidentified film [*Procession in Italy*] (c. 1899–1905), 70mm unperforated nitrate positive. Source: George Eastman Museum.

Plate 10 American Mutoscope & Biograph. *French Acrobatic Dance* (1903), 70mm paper print for Mutoscope equipment. Source: George Eastman Museum.

Plate 11 Filoteo Alberini. Unidentified film [*Street Scene, Rome*] (1911), 70mm nitrate negative. Source: George Eastman Museum.

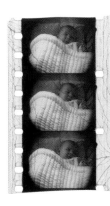

Plate 12 Pathé-Kok, 1912–20. *Fifty-Fifty* (Allan Dwan, 1916), 28mm diacetate positive with three perforations per frame on the left, one on the right. The North American standard of this format (Pathescope, 1917) has three perforations on each side of the frame. Source: George Eastman Museum.

Plate 15 Chrono de poche, Gaumont (1900), 15mm unprocessed film stock. Source: George Eastman Museum.

Plate 13 Cine Kodak. Shooting test by William C. Vaeth on reversal film (May 1920), 16mm diacetate positive. Source: George Eastman Museum.

Plate 16 Movette Camera Company, United States, 1917–c. 1927. Unidentified film (c. 1918), 17.5mm positive. Source: George Eastman Museum.

Plate 17 Pathé-Baby or Pathex. *Le Travail des éléphants aux Indes* (c. 1922) (reissue of *Travail des éléphants de l'Inde, 1910*), Pathé-Baby catalogue no. 288, 1923, 9.5mm diacetate positive. Source: Cinémathèque française.

Plate 14 *Madame Baron présentant le Graphophonoscope* (Auguste Baron, France, 1899), 50mm nitrate positive for synchronized projection with phonograph recording. Source: George Eastman Museum, courtesy of Vincent Pinel.

Plate 18 Carlo Rossi, 'Duplex' film, Italy, 1910. *Milano dalle guglie del Duomo* (Luca Comerio, 1910), 35mm nitrate positive. Source: Museo Nazionale del Cinema – Fondazione Maria Adriana Prolo.

Plate 21 Lumière film for the 1900 Universal Exhibition, Paris, 75mm nitrate positive. Source: Courtesy of Vincent Pinel.

Plate 19 *Bains de la Jetée de Pâquis, Genève* (Casimir Sivan, Switzerland, 1896), 35mm nitrate positive with non-standard perforations. Source: George Eastman Museum.

Plate 22 Pathé-Rural, France, 1926 seqq., unidentified 17.5mm film with one square perforation on each side of the frame. This format was also used for Pathé-Rural/Pathé-Nathan early sound film. Source: George Eastman Museum, courtesy of Vincent Pinel.

Plate 20 *Das boxende Känguruh* (Max Skladanowsky, Germany, 1895), 55mm nitrate positive. Perforations and splices are reinforced with metal studs. Source: George Eastman Museum.

Plate 23a–c Moy & Bastie 35mm camera. Ernest Francis Moy and Percy Henry Bastie, London, 1909. Source: George Eastman Museum.

Plate 24a–b Container and reel for Kodascope 16mm film. Brass, aluminum, and lithograph on paper, diameter 18cm. Source: Private collection.

Plate 25 A reel of nitrate positive film with tinted sections. Source: George Eastman Museum.

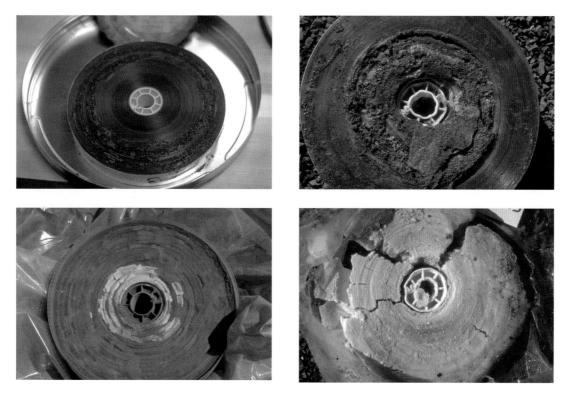

Plate 26a–d Stages of chemical decomposition in 35mm nitrate film. Source: George Eastman Museum.

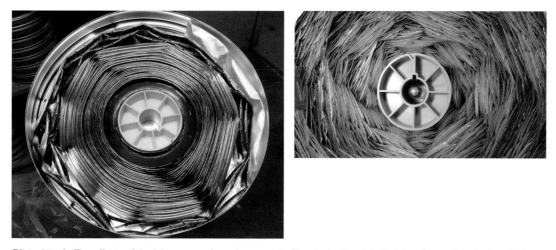

Plate 27a–b The effects of the 'vinegar syndrome' on acetate film stock. The detail is taken from a tinted print of *Trilby* (Maurice Tourneur, 1914), 28mm diacetate positive. Source: George Eastman Museum.

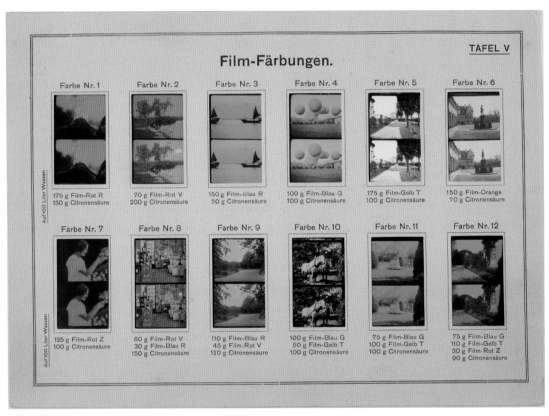

Plate 28 Tinting in dye baths. AGFA, Germany, c. 1928. Actual samples of 35mm nitrate film are included in *AGFA Kine-Handbuch – Teil IV, Film-Muster-Tabellen* (s.l. [Wolfen]: n.d. [c. 1929]), Table V. Source: Private collection.

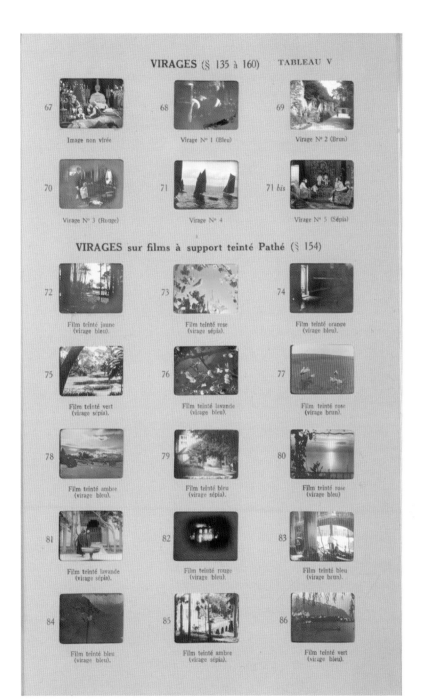

Plate 29 Examples of toning (frame samples nos. 67–71 *bis*) and toning on pre-tinted stock (nos. 72–86), in Louis Didiée, *Le Film vierge Pathé. Manuel de développement et de tirage* (Paris: Établissements Pathé-Cinéma, 1926), Table 5. Source: Private collection.

Plate 30 Hand-colouring. [*96ème de ligne en marche*], variant of a Lumière film with the same title (catalogue no. 191, March 1896), 35mm nitrate positive. Source: Cinémathèque française.

Plate 31a–b Hand-colouring. *La Danse du feu (Haggard's 'She'/The Pillar of Fire*, Georges Méliès, 1899), 35mm nitrate positive and black and white duplicate. Source: George Eastman Museum.

Plate 32 Tinting by manual or semi-automatic brushing. *Das Schmiedelied aus Siegfried* (Messter-Gaumont, 1905?), 35mm nitrate positive for synchronized projection with phonograph recording. Note the irregularities of the red tint on the edges of the print. Source: George Eastman Museum.

Plate 33 Tinting by dye bath. *Padre* (Gino Zaccaria and Giovanni Pastrone, 1912), 35mm nitrate positive. Source: Private collection.

Plate 34 Tinting by consecutive dye baths. *Ballet mécanique* (Fernand Léger and Dudley Murphy, 1924), 35mm nitrate positive. Source: Eye Filmmuseum.

Plate 35 Toning. *La Fiancée du maître d'armes* (Gaumont, 1908), 35mm nitrate positive. Source: George Eastman Museum.

Plate 36 Stencil colour process. *Fée aux pigeons* (*Pigeon Fairy*, Gaston Velle, Pathé, April–May 1906), 35mm nitrate positive. Source: Private collection.

Plate 37a–c Multiple tinting. The colours of the French flag in the 'Marseillaise' sequence of *The Four Horsemen of the Apocalypse* (Rex Ingram, 1921), 35mm triacetate positive. Source: Courtesy of Kevin Brownlow.

Plate 39 Stencil and hand-colouring. *L'Écrin du Radjah* (*The Rajah's Casket,* Pathé, April–May 1906), 35mm nitrate positive. Note the irregular shape of the hand-coloured scarves on the dancers' shoulders. Source: George Eastman Museum.

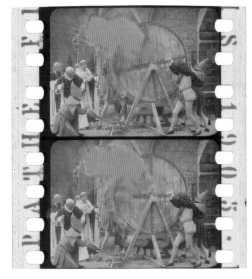

Plate 38 Toning and stencil. *Les Martyrs de l'Inquisition* (*Martyrs of the Inquisition*, Lucien Nonguet, Pathé, November 1905), 35mm nitrate positive. The red cloud in the scene is coloured with the stencil process. Source: George Eastman Museum.

Plate 40 William Friese-Greene three-colour system. Unidentified film, *c.* 1909, 35mm nitrate positive. Source: George Eastman Museum.

Plate 41 Two-colour Kodachrome process. *Concerning $1,000* (director unknown, Eastman Kodak Company, 1916), 35mm nitrate positive. Source: George Eastman Museum.

Plate 43a–b Kinemacolor process. *The Scarlet Letter* (David Miles, Weber & Fields Kinemacolor Company, 1913). (a) Frame enlargement from a 35mm nitrate positive (note the different density in some areas of the middle image); (b) Frame enlargement from a 35mm polyester positive. Source: George Eastman Museum.

Plate 42 Kinemacolor projector. George Albert Smith and Charles Urban, London, *c.* 1912. Source: Cinémathèque française, photo by Stéphane Dabrowski.

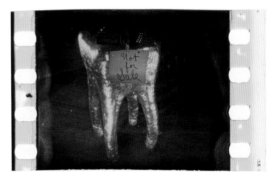

Plate 45 Handschiegl process (also known as Wyckoff–DeMille process). *Greed* (Erich von Stroheim, 1925), 35mm nitrate positive. Source: Seaver Center for Western History Research, Natural History Museum of Los Angeles.

Plate 44a–b Chronochrome Gaumont. *Paris Fashion. Latest Spring Hats* [English release title] (France, c. 1913), 35mm diacetate positive. Black and white panchromatic film, to be projected through a triple-lens vertical unit with blue, red, and green filters. The lenses were converged in order to produce a single colour image, recreated here digitally from a scan of three frames of the film. Source: George Eastman Museum.

Plate 46 Technicolor process no. 2. Two-colour subtractive prism, filters, and film gate, removed from the camera. Technicolor Motion Picture Corporation, 1921. Source: George Eastman Museum.

Plate 47 Technicolor process no. 3. *Redskin* (Victor Schertzinger, 1929), 35mm nitrate positive. Source: George Eastman Museum.

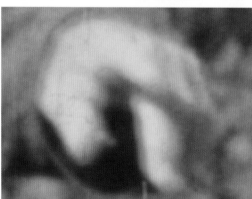

Plate 48a–b Prizma colour process. *A Day with John Burroughs* (director unknown, World Film Corporation, 1919), 35mm double-coated nitrate positive, with red and green toning. The detail shows the fringing effect caused by imperfect colour registration between the two emulsions on the opposite sides of the print. Source: George Eastman Museum.

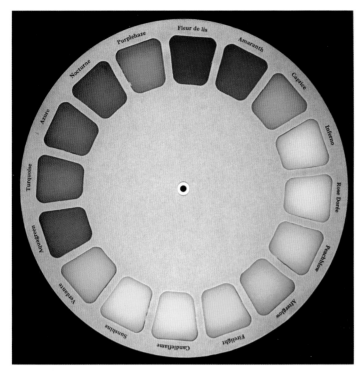

Plate 49 Kodak Sonochrome (*c.* 1929). Cardboard disc (25.5cm) with samples of pre-tinted film stock. Source: George Eastman Museum.

Plate 50 William T. Crespinel and Jacob F. Leventhal, stereoscopic film process, possibly from *Plastigrams* or *Stereoscopiks* (William T. Crespinel, *c.* 1924), 35mm nitrate positive. The composite image is viewed through anaglyph glasses. Source: George Eastman Museum.

Plate 51 Frames from a chromolithographic loop (Nuremberg, Germany, *c.* 1898), reproducing a section of a film by Georges Méliès, *Séance de prestidigitation* (1896), 35mm nitrate print. Source: Archivio Carlo Montanaro.

Plate 52 Mural painting in the entrance lobby, Loew's State Theatre (now Landmark Theatre), opened in 1928, Syracuse, NY. Source: Private collection.

Plate 53a *Verdun, vision d'histoire* (Léon Poirier, 1928). Frame enlargement from a 35mm polyester positive. Source: Cinémathèque de Toulouse.

Plate 53b *Apocalypse – Verdun* (Isabelle Clarke and Daniel Costelle, 2016). Reframed and colourized digital scan of the Poirier film. Source: Clarke Costelle & Co (CC&C).

Chapter 8

Show

Fig. 168 A fictionalized screening of *Cabiria* (Giovanni Pastrone, 1914) with live orchestral accompaniment, as seen in the feature-length film *Maciste* (Luigi Romano Borgnetto and Vincenzo Denizot, 1915). Frame enlargement from a 35mm nitrate positive. Source: Eye Filmmuseum.

An eminent film historian, Charles Musser, is among those who most insistently pointed out that the story of film cannot be studied independently from the way in which films were shown. This is especially true in the case of silent cinema. Its performance began with the act of turning the crank of a projector, whose presence near the audience was a boulevard 'attraction' in itself:

Fig. 169 Admission ticket for 'Edison's Life Motioned Pictures and Phonograph Exhibition'. Biomotoscope Company, Bay City, Michigan, 1897. Lithograph on yellow paper, 9.2 × 4.3cm. Source: George Eastman Museum.

the earliest film exhibitors appealed to the public's willingness to believe that the new spectacle was a scientific device, the utopia of artificial reality permanently etched for posterity. The status of cinema as entertainment available to all, so cheap as to rapidly establish its prominence in popular culture of the early twentieth century, is one of the most cherished truisms of film history: in the United States, the very word 'nickelodeon' – with its direct reference to the five-cent coin – has become the symbol of a time when 'going to the pictures' could be decided upon by just fumbling in one's pocket or purse for small change (Fig. 169).

Tickets

This may well have been the case, but it is important to keep in mind that a 1905 nickel was no laughing matter for lower-income families, considering that a worker's annual salary at the time was about 400 US dollars: in that year, 5 cents corresponded to almost 1 dollar and 50 cents in 2017; the national average cost of one pound of sugar was 4 cents; one pound of coffee, 16 cents. By the mid-1920s, in the same country, admission prices for film theatres had risen to a nationwide median of 25 cents (equal to 3 dollars and 50 cents in the early twenty-first century), and that

included the rural areas of the nation; newspapers and trade journals denounced the excesses in this upward trend, with New York City's leading venues routinely charging a minimum of 50 cents up to 2 dollars and 20 cents. Back in 1915, on the inaugural premiere of *The Birth of a Nation* at the Liberty Theatre in Manhattan, the 2-dollar entrance fee had established an all-time record.

The value of a cinema ticket during the silent period in relation to the cost of living is not easy to assess, as it must take into account a wide array of variables. Among them are the value of the currency, the geographic location of the theatre, its commercial prestige, the different rankings of the seats, the time of screening, and the inflation rate (especially in Europe during the 1920s). The 1899 Russian film poster reproduced in Fig. 170 makes mention of prices ranging from 20 kopecks to 1 rouble and 25 kopecks. The cost of a film theatre

Fig. 170 Announcement of a Lumière Cinématographe screening in Tambov, Russia, 14 February 1899. Lithograph on paper, 50.8 × 61.9cm. Source: George Eastman Museum.

ticket in France was between 1 and 9 francs in 1923 (1 franc of that year equalling 1.03 euros in 2015), but it soared to somewhere between 7 and 25 francs during the 1929 inflation. In the French colony of New Caledonia, where a seat in the stage theatre of the capital Nouméa was worth between 2 and 5 'francs d'outre mer' ('overseas francs'), a picture show in 1897 cost 3 or 4 francs, depending on the seat (Fig. 171). Admission prices in Italy around 1914 ranged from 10 cents to over 1 lira; in Germany, from 20 pfennigs to 1.5 marks; in Great Britain, 4 pennies to 1 shilling or more; in India, 2 or 3 annas (in smaller towns it would be 2 annas, whereas in Bombay, Calcutta, and Madras, the cost would vary from 2 to 4 annas, depending on the location of the cinema and whether it showed first- or second-run films). A decade later, ticket prices for Harold Lloyd's *The Freshman* (Fred C. Newmeyer and Sam Taylor, 1925) at the Royal Opera House in Bombay ranged from 6

annas to 3 rupees and 6 annas for the best seats; at the Virginia Theatre of Champaign, Illinois, the same film was offered for 15 to 50 cents.

These figures are nothing but mute cyphers if they are not checked against the average pro capita or household income in a given region of the country being considered, at the time of the ticket's purchase. This kind of analysis has been conducted so far in some geographic areas (notably by Jean-Jacques Meusy and Jean-Claude Seguin); additional research is needed to draw any conclusions on a comparative basis. The mercantile nature of this subject should not be dismissed as trivial: to understand film spectatorship as a global phenomenon, it is important to put into context the financial implications of attending a motion picture show in a provincial area of Mexico or New Zealand, Poland or Québec, Maharashtra or Egypt, at the same time in history, in venues of different appeal to different social strata. Difficult as it may be, this kind of investigation would help us to look at silent cinema from the perspective of those who paid money to witness the new and wonderful invention that reshaped the public's imaginary worlds at a time of dramatic social and cultural transformation.

Fig. 171 Newspaper advertisement for a film screening in Nouméa, New Caledonia. *La France Australe*, 7 April 1897. Source: Courtesy of Jean-Claude Seguin.

Schedule

The structure of motion picture shows underwent a slow but constant change over three decades. In the early years of cinema, a programme could last as little as fifteen minutes to one hour depending on the country, the location of the venue, and the time of year. Schedules varied accordingly, with some theatres showing forty or more programmes from morning until late evening, while others only screened a handful. With the rise of feature-length films, differences in schedules from one place to another became less pronounced; it was not unusual for a picture house in a city of medium size to begin projecting films in the late morning, and to continue with no interruption for the rest of the day. In the first permanent theatres, the responsibility for managing the show was largely in the hands of the projectionist, who operated the film equipment but also supervised the transitions from one part of the programme to the next. Wherever film was the only ingredient of the presentation, there was little or no need for a theatre manager. Turning the lights off and on at the beginning and the end of each programme was basically all that had to be done; a floor manager was required only in those venues where film shared the stage with other attractions, as happened in vaudeville shows.

In theatres exclusively dedicated to films, the programme sequence followed a preordained scheme, alternating various narrative forms and moods. A regular show of the late 1900s consisted of scenic views, documentaries, dramatic subjects, and comedies, carefully blended with the goal of avoiding thematic redundancies and boredom in the audience. The very concept of 'programme', however, should be understood in its looser sense when applied to early cinema. In some venues, a cluster of short films could be presented as a stand-alone show, followed by an intermission; in others, there was no temporal gap between the beginning of a programme and its reiteration. Patrons could pay their admission fee and enter the theatre at any time during the show, regardless of whether a drama, comedy, or cartoon was being screened. Spelling out the exact sequence of a forthcoming programme was not at all unknown to early film exhibitors, but became standard practice only in the early 1910s. By and large, this change coincided with the introduction of multi-reel films; even then, continuous programmes did not disappear all of a sudden. While the projection schedule for a given feature-length film was provided and advertised well in advance, it was understood that the viewer had no obligation to enter the theatre before the main attraction had appeared on the screen. For many audiences, feeling free to decide when to join or leave the show was one of the most beloved aspects of the film-going experience (in most countries, this practice – a long-lasting echo of the vaudeville tradition – continued until the late twentieth century).

Another defining property of the early cinematic event was the protean nature of film programming itself. At a time of rising demand from the public, with new productions being released at a breakneck pace, theatre owners took pride in changing pictures on the screen as frequently as possible. They did not necessarily show a whole new set of films every day, but wanted to introduce at least one fresh attraction, and to constantly reshuffle the existing batch so that their most loyal clients would always get the impression of watching a different programme every time they entered the theatre. Attending a motion picture show more than once a week was not at all unusual; theatre entrepreneurs knew this, and tried to respond as quickly as they could to keep their patrons happy. By the 1920s, when feature-length film was in full swing, smaller or cheaper picture houses in the United States were still faithful to the old practice of updating programmes on a daily basis; doing so twice a week was common in venues of mid-range towns. First-run theatres projected the same main feature for a full week or more, depending on their patrons' response. In large cities, they always had multiple venues to choose from, often concentrated in the same streets.

Early film exhibitors were the first curators in the history of cinema: by constantly renewing their offerings with the insertion, substitution, or rearrangement of a given sequence of titles, they were engaged in a constant dialogue with their audiences, endeavouring to better understand their tastes, anticipate their wishes, interpret their likes and dislikes. Theatre owners cultivated their clients; film producers listened to both; from a distance, filmmakers were paying close attention to all. It was a hectic, very stressful business: the average commercial life of a fiction film rarely exceeded two or three weeks. After a month, a new film was regarded as old hat, good for distribution in peripheral markets such as rural communities, schools, and remote areas where audiences did not particularly care about the novelty factor (a famous case in point, the Canadian town of Dawson City, a former centre of the Klondike Gold Rush, will be discussed in Chapter 12). As seen earlier (p. 164), a film's extended longevity could become a liability, because it was preventing fresh celluloid blood from entering the competition.

Slides

In most North American venues of the mid-1910s, the opening of a typical motion picture show consisted of projected glass slides promoting local stores and merchandise, or related to the activity of the theatre itself. These handcrafted or photographed still images (often also hand-painted) included references to forthcoming attractions, directions on proper conduct in the auditorium (no spitting on the floor; ladies must remove their hats; no disturbance from babies and small children), or generic references to the theatre's exhibition policies (how often titles were replaced, what kind of films would be shown on a given day of the week). Live or mechanical sound accompaniment often started in advance of the magic lantern show itself, while patrons were finding their seats. Lights were dimmed just before the slide show, and were brought further down at the beginning of the first picture. Good practice suggested a smooth transition between slides and film with the aid of an optical dissolve mechanism to avoid any glare from the lights on screen. When the show was over, a gradual fade-out was preferred to an abrupt ending; slowly increasing the level of theatre lights while the last projected images were seamlessly brought down to black was a matter of distinction and pride for the theatre owner.

When the first part of the programme was followed by a music interlude, the booth operator matched the tunes with song slides, or took advantage of the pause to rewind the film and prepare the projector for the next reel. This depended on how many technicians were on duty, and how many projection machines were installed in the theatre. The alternation of motion pictures, glass slides, and a live music act was inherited from the vaudeville era, but also fulfilled a practical purpose: in addition to rewinding and changing reels, the projectionist needed time to readjust the carbon rods in the lamphouse; the musicians who were playing throughout the day needed some rest every now and then; exhibitors were keen to use the break for selling candies and refreshments, a practice greeted with enthusiasm by younger audiences. To make the song more audible, ventilation in the room often had to be turned down or off altogether, sometimes with dire consequences for the patrons' well-being. One major instance of a programme where sound, glass slides, and cinema were merged into an organic whole during the silent era is a production from the United States, *The Photo-Drama of Creation* (Charles Taze Russell, 1914), in four parts. The total running time of this extraordinary work of religious propaganda – a huge international success – was approximately eight hours.

Prolonged exposure to publicity slides – especially between films – was unwelcome in picture houses, as patrons were impatient to watch the next part of the programme; advertisements were highly profitable for theatre owners, but had to be showcased in very moderate doses. Other kinds of magic lantern projection before the shows were acceptable as long as no single slide remained on display for too long and the complete set was changed frequently enough to avoid tedium or irritation among regular customers. This tension between showmanship, financial incentives, and technical constraints made film exhibition in the early years of cinema a delicate balancing act, whose risks were compounded by the uneven quality of the films being shown.

All around the world, films from Europe were the core ingredients of a high-quality theatrical offering: until the early 1910s, no reputable programme was conceivable without at least one French production; Italian comedies and period dramas were also in great demand. Only three American companies were popular enough to compete with them: Edison, Biograph (largely thanks to Mack Sennett's slapstick comedies and D.W. Griffith's dramas), and Vitagraph, a reliable supplier of good family entertainment. Conversely, the penetration of films from the United States into overseas cinemas was initially modest, with Vitagraph posing the only serious challenge to Pathé and Gaumont until the outbreak of World War I.

Intermissions

When the first permanent venues for film exhibition were established around or after 1905, theatre owners were quick to install two projectors whenever they could. Their decision was based on the available space and on financial considerations, but these concerns were not limited to the size and cost of the machines. Two hand-cranked projectors could not be handled by a single operator; early motorized models (pp. 82–83) were not deemed reliable enough to allow one technician to prepare the reel on the second projector while the first one was running, as the light sources had to be constantly monitored. As long as live acts – with or without musicians –

were perceived by exhibitors and their audiences as useful or welcome breaks between two reels of film, there was little advantage in purchasing another piece of equipment and hiring an extra person for the job. It should be noted in this regard that the legacy of programme structures in stage theatre and vaudeville was felt in many countries throughout the entire history of cinema, down to the late 1920s and beyond: the alternation between stage attractions and film shows persisted even in picture palaces, where the practicalities of reel change were not a matter of concern. In these venues, song and dance hardly qualified as 'intermissions' in the show.

The introduction of dual projection systems in the early years of cinema was rarely driven by the need to change reels rapidly between films: metal arms attached to the feeding and take-up mechanisms of a projector easily allowed 2,000 feet (600 metres) to run at a time in a single reel, the equivalent of at least half an hour of screening. With two projectors, the exhibitor was instead free to decide when to stop the show, thus making live performances optional: the slow decline of the vaudeville legacy in film exhibition began by applying the principle of redundancy to the equipment for film projection. Charles Francis Jenkins and Thomas J. Armat had done so from the very beginnings of cinema, when they used two projectors for their first show of the Vitascope to a paying audience in September 1895.

It would take three decades for the cycle to be complete, but its path was clear from the outset. Entrepreneurs were initially cautious in exploiting the opportunity: some of them installed the second projector only as a backup, in the event of a malfunction of the other machine. Then, as soon as they felt there was no point in leaving the spare equipment idle, they took the big leap. By 1912, the majority of film theatres in the United States had two projectors in the booth. This does not mean that continuous shows of feature-length films became the norm all at once across the world. The trajectory that led to the uninterrupted show of a multi-reel picture followed a slow and at times uncertain course: even from a technical perspective, there was no fixed rule on how to achieve the transition between consecutive reels.

For many years, the appearance of a title card indicating the end of a reel was the most common signal to projectionists for the next one to start. Other methods were used from the mid-1920s, such as lengthening the last title card of a reel and repeating it at the beginning of the next, a practice implemented by Metro-Goldwyn-Mayer in 1924; supplying projectionists with instruction cards describing the last shot or intertitle in each reel; installing mechanical or electric bells activated by the increasing centrifugal force of the reel at the end of its run. Projectionists had their own methods, too, from the insertion of a coin between the last coils of film (the operator was alerted by the noise of the coin falling from the reel cabinet), to the crude cross-shaped scratches applied on the emulsion of consecutive frames ('changeover cues' in the form of small circles scratched on the upper right corner of the frame, alerting projectionists of an imminent change of reel, were introduced by Metro-Goldwyn-Mayer in 1930).

As the length of narrative film grew to two or more reels in the early 1910s, many exhibitors and their audiences remained loyal to the fragmented structure of early film shows. In 1913, film theatres in Japan equipped with a single projector began their shows with a long spoken explanation (*zen-setsu*) of the forthcoming feature; at the end of each reel, lights were brought back up in the auditorium and a formal announcement was given about the intermission and the imminent start of the next section.

Narrative discontinuity was often an integral part of the presentation, not unlike the acts of a stage play (in some German feature films, title cards for the heads and tails of each reel are so beautifully designed that they may have been something more than ordinary visual cues for projectionists). The most intriguing case in point is offered by Sweden in the 1910s, when the equivalence between film reels and theatrical 'acts' was so deeply felt that the length of each reel and the projection schedule itself were dictated by the dramatic structure of the work, rather than by the standard size (1,000 feet, or 300 metres) of the reel or the capacity of the machine.

Blodets röst, a 1913 film by Victor Sjöström, was divided into four reels of respectively 484, 508, 479, and 355 metres (1,588, 1,667, 1,572 and 1,165 feet). At the end of a section, theatre lights were turned on; the audience would read the programme, discuss the film, purchase candies from vendors who walked up and down the aisles. The exceptional longevity of the single-projector system in Swedish cinemas (the first known Swedish theatre with two projectors was inaugurated in late 1918) and its stubborn survival into the early 1920s suggests that intermissions were more than a passing fad in the cinematic culture of that country. One cannot rule out the possibility that this and other practices were employed elsewhere in the world during the feature-film era, regardless of the number of projectors in the booth.

Programmes

There is a widespread notion that the structure of an exhibition programme in the post-World War I period of silent cinema was more or less the same throughout the world, with a feature-length film as the show's centrepiece and a number of ancillary items before and after its presentation. The assumption is fundamentally correct; nevertheless, seemingly small details in the evolution of film programmes over the years and in different countries are sometimes of great significance. Mentioning them all would be a daunting task, as the variations are often very subtle, and require a deep knowledge of the culture and society of each country in order to be fully appreciated. The following two examples from France and Japan should provide an idea of the wide range of possibilities, with the understanding that more than one exhibition framework could be adopted in different theatres of the same country at any given period of the silent film era.

In France, mainstream theatres of the 1920s were not the only places where films were shown every day: in large cities, for a very modest sum, a casual viewer could go to smaller venues where programmes consisted of weekly newsreels – popular alternatives to the daily newspapers – distributed on a regular basis by the major producers of the time. Their forty-minute schedule, run uninterruptedly throughout the day, was divided in two sections of approximately twenty minutes each. In other theatres, vaudeville sketches continued to be presented as parallel offerings, more or less as in the early years of cinema. In many countries, 'presentation acts' remained an important component of a cinema programme; in Japan, they were the main reason why people were eager to attend the picture show.

First-run theatres in French cities during the post-war silent era began the show with a live orchestral performance consisting of one to three pieces. The music was played with full or dimmed lights in the theatre while patrons were finding their seats or browsing the printed programme, if available. As lights were turned off, the projection began with a one-reel scenic subject or travelogue, followed by a comedy in two reels and by a weekly newsreel, sometimes integrated with a lightweight magazine-style supplement on fashion, sports, and other assorted curiosities. This brought an

end to the first part of the show; its running time was slightly less than one hour, with or without the inclusion of the orchestral introduction. The intermission would occur at this point, with the lights turned up again for about five to fifteen minutes.

The show resumed with the orchestra performing a grand overture, signalling the imminent start of the programme's main feature. With few exceptions, the feature film (French or foreign) was shown in its entirety with no interruption. The closing attraction was another comedy in one or two reels, except when the feature film was particularly long, or of special distinction. Cartoons, when available, were included early in the schedule; so were the weekly serials, replacing the opening two-reel comedy. Programme templates of this kind and their variants – twelve reels of film, for a total running time of three hours – were common in North America, Western Europe, and the British colonies. In some countries, national anthems were played before or after the show, often in conjunction with a brief film or a slide depicting the national emblem (see p. 118).

The twelve-reel model was also adopted in Japan after World War I, with a more nuanced programme layout. This included a one-reel documentary and a two-reel comedy, as in France; in this case, the place of honour was split between a dramatic subject (five reels), a serial (four reels, presumably two consecutive episodes shown side by side), and a shorter action feature (two or three reels). Whatever the programme sequence, it seems that the hierarchy of its components was not as clear-cut as in Europe and North America, given the relatively small difference in footage between the three main attractions; it is to be presumed that showing a longer feature drama (six reels instead of five) made it necessary to settle for shorter films in the other categories.

This was, however, only one of three distinct types of programme schedules, all implemented in Japanese venues of the post-war period.

In the second programme template, sixteen reels were shown instead of twelve, for a total running time of four hours. The main attraction was a Japanese drama, preferably set in modern times, accompanied by another five-reel feature from abroad and by a smattering of comedies, scenic views, documentaries, or cartoons. The difference between this and the three-hour programme was a sharper demarcation between the two main attractions, with priority given to a domestic production. The third type of programme pushed this tendency even further with a five- to six-hour show (twenty to twenty-two reels or more) that also included a one-reel Japanese modern drama, a one-reel Japanese costume drama or *kabuki*, and a five-reel foreign or serial film. Obviously, only three shows of this kind could be held during the day, beginning at dawn and proceeding well after midnight (with the consternation of public authorities, who eventually felt compelled to intervene).

We do not know whether or not this punishing schedule represents the *nec plus ultra* of film exhibition in the silent era, as more research needs to be undertaken in other geographic areas, but the case of Japan is emblematic because it unequivocally reflects an insatiable public demand for cinema: over 153 million tickets were sold in that country during 1926, more than twice as many as its overall population (60 million). All over the world, people were filling theatres to their capacity, and the average size of the venues was growing in parallel to their numbers. It would be interesting to compare the duration of film programmes in different nations: unfortunately, the main evidence on this comes primarily from newspaper and trade journal reports about special events, rather than for average shows. The running time of a film programme was generally measured by the number of reels (of standard size) being shown, multiplied by ten or fifteen minutes, round figures representing the plausible duration of one reel's unspooling through the projector. Journalists made their calculations accordingly, but were neither uniform nor consistent in their claims. It is time, therefore, to examine to what degree the actual running time of a silent film could deviate from the generic criterion adopted so far.

Movement

Few aspects of the silent cinema experience are as contentious as the question of the rate at which films were projected and seen by audiences of the time (as exemplified in Fig. 172). One reason why the topic has been so divisive is that the debate

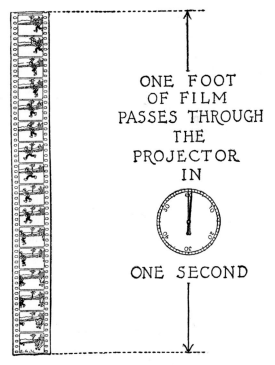

Fig. 172 The 'standard' speed of cinema, as described in the 1920s. Source: Private collection.

has direct implications on how silent films should be seen today. The terms of reference for such discussion will be addressed at the end of this book; for the time being, let the facts speak for themselves.

France: Georges Méliès indicated in the Star-Film catalogues that *A Trip to the Moon* should be projected at 14 frames per second. According to the same catalogues, another film by Méliès, *La Légende de Rip Van Winckle* (*Rip's Dream*, 1905), was to be shown at an even slower rate, 13 frames per second. One year later, in *La Théorie et la pratique des projections*, Guillaume-Michel Coissac mentioned 23–26 frames per second as the average speed in film projection, twice what Méliès recommended for his major works (a 1897 book by Georges Brunel mentioned an even higher average rate, forty to forty-five seconds of screening for a film of 23 metres, or 75 feet, in length, corresponding to about 28 frames per second); in another authoritative manual published in 1912, Léopold Löbel declared that the normal projection speed is, 'for very well known reasons, 16 frames per second', adding that negative and positive film should run at an identical speed in cameras and projectors (*La Technique cinématographique*, p. 149).

Germany: in 1902, the same year of Méliès' *A Trip to the Moon*, film producer Oskar Messter suggested a projection speed of about 17 frames per second; in 1928, his opinion had slightly changed (20 frames per second); meanwhile, however, musician Gottfried Huppertz had written an orchestral score for Fritz Lang's *Metropolis*, requesting that the film be shown at the breakneck speed of 28 frames per second (Fig. 173). The musical instructions for another German silent feature, *Alt-Heidelberg* (Hans Behrendt, 1923), ask for various projection speeds, ranging from 14 to 24 frames per second, with eighteen changes of speed throughout the show (24 being the 'normal'

speed, according to a music cue sheet). *Die kinematographische Projektion*, a manual published in 1928, contains a conversion chart with film speeds ranging from 16 to 75 frames per second.

Denmark: deeply upset by what he regarded as an appalling presentation of his film *Kærlighedens Almagt* (*The Power of Love*, or *Sealed Lips*, 1919) at the wrong projection speed, director Anders Wilhelm Sandberg became involved in a quarrel that was reported by various newspapers of the period. Billed at the Gammel Kongevejs Biografteater in Copenhagen with a running time of one and a half hours, the film was over in about fifty minutes. Sandberg, who was attending the show, had stormed into the projection booth with a lit cigar, asking the projectionist to slow down;

Fig. 173 Piano score for *Metropolis* (Fritz Lang, 1927). Gottfried Huppertz, composer. At the top of the page, the handwritten note: 'Projection speed: 28 [frames per second]'. Source: Stiftung Deutsche Kinemathek, Berlin.

in contempt, the operator apparently turned the crank even faster, at which point Sandberg made a big scene in the auditorium, urging patrons to join his protest. He could not bear to see his work mistreated that way, and had no intention of acquiescing any further. The police were summoned to the theatre. Sandberg blamed its owner for trying to squeeze as many shows as possible into a single day; his description of the film projected at high speed is painfully funny to read (lovers bumping heads instead of kissing, dancers jumping like fleas in a frying pan). The projectionist, in turn, accused Sandberg of having put everybody's life at risk with his cigar in a nitrate booth (according to some patrons, he was drunk). Sandberg's reckless behaviour cost him a fine of 4 kronor.

United States: the first known instance of a motor-driven projector approved for use in a film theatre (December 1908) is documented in New York City, but in 1911 this kind of equipment was still prohibited in most of the country, apparently because of the risks associated with the absence of constant monitoring of the machines during projection. Convinced that film projectionists should be recognized as the artists in charge of achieving the best quality in the motion picture show by turning the projector's crank at the appropriate speed, Frank H. Richardson proposed in 1912 the construction of a special platform in every projection booth, connected to an electrical sensor that would automatically turn off the projector whenever the technician stepped away from the podium's floor. This would have ensured that the projectionist remained 'absolutely anchored right there beside his machine, where he should be, every moment the machine is running' (*Motion Picture Handbook*, 2nd edition, p. 367); four years later, by Richardson's own admission, only one state had adopted his proposal (with some modifications).

Rhythm

Back to the basics: for many years in the silent era, cameras and projectors were hand-cranked. Because the movement of the film through the equipment depended upon a manual operation, it was subject to changes and fluctuations; as seen in Chapter 4, motor-driven equipment had been available since the first decade of the twentieth century, but was not widely used until the 1920s. These machines allowed the rate at which pictures were taken and shown to be controlled. In spite of the repeated attempts to reach consensus on a uniform speed for cameras and projectors, no worldwide standard was ever achieved until the introduction of sound on film; at best, professional organizations were able to issue suggestions whose content varied considerably over time; their effects were negligible and transitory at best, with no echo beyond the respective national boundaries. In isolated instances, projection speed was the object of legally binding parameters; with the known exception of one country (Japan), their application was never closely monitored.

This summary in the past tense must be integrated with another factual observation about present beliefs on how silent cinema was seen by its original audience. It is commonly assumed that the average projection speed increased over the years, according to a linear path leading from 16 frames per second to 24, soon to become the standard projection rate for sound film; so, if the film was made early in the twentieth century, its audience must have seen it projected at a lower speed; the closer we get to the year 1929, the higher the projection speed. The range between 16 and 24 frames per second was thought to represent the normal gamut of film projection speed in the silent era, aside from the Kinetoscope (about 40 frames per second), the early American Mutoscope & Biograph films (30 frames per second), and various additive colour systems requiring higher projection speeds. These sweeping statements should not be dismissed altogether; the problem with their indiscriminate application is that they fail to consider where the film was made and shown, why it came to exist, and who was responsible for its production or exhibition. Tackling these questions is very important, because it may bring very different answers about the projection speed of the very same film.

A distinction must be made at the outset between the running speed of the negative film stock within the camera and that of the positive film in the projection equipment. In the silent film era, the two did not necessarily coincide. The camera operator decided, or was asked, to turn the crank at a given speed (often twice a second for a camera with 32-teeth sprockets), knowing very well that the prints struck from the negative may or may not be projected at the same frame rate. Some cinematographers were working on the assumption that there would be a perfect match between camera (or 'taking') speed and projection speed; others presumed that the film was going to be projected faster, maybe in order to bring more energy or comic zest to the action, maybe for other reasons; or slower, to make its mood more contemplative.

If the expectation was that projectionists would exhibit the film at a speed of 16 frames per second, it was a good idea to turn the camera crank a bit slower than twice a second for a hectic car chase, a horse ride, or a slapstick scene; conversely, the crank was turned at least three times per second or more if the sequence was to be viewed in slow motion. If projection speed were kept uniform throughout the show, fewer frames exposed to the camera lens in a given shot would accelerate the action; more frames running through the lens within the same time span resulted in a very leisurely and equally abnormal visual record of the same events.

This primer on film projection speed serves as an introduction to the cast of characters taking part in the debate. Each of them had a specific view of what the appropriate speed should be, and was reluctant to compromise. For the cinematographer, a taking speed was correct when it properly exposed the negative film emulsion in the camera. Under normal light conditions, sixteen frame exposures per second were just fine, but there was room for negotiation. If the light source were so weak as to underexpose the negative, camera speed would be decreased; if too bright, it had to be increased, so that the film would not be overexposed (see Fig. 62a–f on p. 74).

So went the theory. Major fluctuations in camera speed had to be avoided within the same production, as the finished film would have been a patchwork of shots requiring various projection rates. For film directors, the right speed was as important as the correct framing, acting, lighting, and editing; those who particularly cared for the visual rhythm of their films went as far as to provide detailed instructions for projectionists, either on the film itself (before the main credits, as in the title card reproduced in Fig. 174), or with other printed materials: in his advertising for *Home, Sweet Home* (1914), D.W. Griffith asked

Fig. 174 A title card from *The Love Flower* (D.W. Griffith, 1920). Frame enlargement from a 35mm triacetate positive. Source: Private collection.

that 'the running time for the picture should be 16 minutes for the first reel, 14 to 15 minutes for the second reel and from 13 to 14 minutes for each of the other reels. The last reel, however, should be run slowly from the beginning of the allegorical part to the end.'

Overcranking

We shall never know how film projectionists responded to this kind of directive, but their working conditions were generally so dire that only a minority of them was likely to pay much attention to the filmmakers' pleas for accuracy. To put it bluntly, the projectionist's definition of what constituted a correct projection speed was heavily influenced by managerial deliberations on how many programmes could be squeezed into a single day. This intent was translated in an equally blunt formula: the faster, the better. Projectionists had the power, but not necessarily the authority, to make a film look beautiful or ugly with the deceptively simple act of turning the crank of their machines, or adjusting the rheostats that controlled the variable speed mechanism.

Some film directors romanticized the figure of the projectionist with epithets like 'the orchestra conductor of the show': the truth of the matter was that the baton they held in their hands was actually moved by the theatre owner. Despite this, film projectionists were accountable to their audiences, who had no one else to blame if the images on the screen were running too fast or too slow. There are scant oral history records of what the average patron thought was the ideal projection speed; most of the surviving documentation is nothing but a litany of complaints, largely about excessive speed. Very few, if any, of the grievances had anything to do with the narrative pace of the film; what mattered most was the time required for reading the title cards.

As if this wasn't enough, projectionists had to cope with the artists in charge of live sound accompaniment. They, too, had their own opinions on projection speed, and were often so adamant about it that brawls could sometimes occur between performers, projectionists, and theatre managers, with the film director's view sometimes heard in the far distance. It is here that the competing views of all the players in the game of projection speed could lead to a collision course. No one had absolute control over the matter, because they all depended upon each other; moreover, each of them could act against the will of the other interlocutors. Griffith could not possibly have the final word on projection speed in all the theatres where *Home, Sweet Home* was being shown; his cinematographer, Billy Bitzer, had no say, either, on the calibration and intensity of the light sources employed in each piece of projection equipment; not all projectionists cared about Griffith's instructions, and who knows how musicians felt about them anyway.

There is yet another theme in this already convoluted plot: in some countries, especially the United States, there was a widespread belief that it was a good idea to project film at a speed that was slightly faster than the camera speed, no matter what the story was about; if 16 frames per second was the speed at which the photographer had taken the film, a projection speed of 19, 20 or 21 frames per second was deemed perfectly acceptable, and actually more desirable than a perfect correspondence between camera speed and projector speed. This had nothing to do with comedy, romance, or action scenes in particular. Two lines of argument to support this claim were brought forward. The first – unsupported by any empirical evidence – was that there was no point in trying to reproduce 'natural' movement by photomechanical means, as machines are not imitations of the human eye, and their way of 'interpreting' image reproduction is fundamentally different.

A second, perhaps cynical but more persuasive justification for higher projection speeds was invoked with the involuntary complicity of the public: over the years, exhibitors had been increasingly pushing projectionists for faster speeds in order to increase the number of daily shows; audiences had become so used to seeing films in this way that they were led to believe (or had become accustomed to thinking) this is what motion pictures looked like in general; therefore, it would have made no sense to ask cinematographers to increase camera speed, as this would only have resulted in a further increase of projection speed, thus perpetuating a vicious circle. In other words, if a fake representation of movement has become engrained in the public mind as a truthful one, let the fake prevail. Aside from making exhibitors happy, this also had the advantage of reducing flicker and compensating for the glare generated by the more powerful light sources and semi-reflective screens adopted in North America and Europe during the 1920s.

While this strange drama of psychology and technology was unfolding, the ultimate decision maker on projection speed – money – entered the scene to pronounce its last verdict. Film stock was an expensive item; in some countries, it was only available in very limited supplies. What had given Robert William Paul and the Lumière brothers a decisive advantage over Edison was their ability to persuade audiences that 16 frames per second was an acceptable projection speed, good enough for a motion picture and requiring less than half the amount of film stock used for Edison's Kinetoscope. Film producers liked 16 frames per second because it was good enough for them too, with no waste of costly raw stock, processing, and developing.

Actors and cinematographers were no less satisfied, as faster filming speeds would have required much more light on the set, which was difficult to keep in balance and very stressful for the performers' eyes. In short, almost everybody had some reason to be pleased, including theatre managers, who could keep tailoring projection speed to their needs, and the public, largely unaware that the debate had occurred at all (only film manufacturers would have been delighted to manufacture more film stock for the same running time of a film). Little, if anything, changed in the lives of the projectionists, who continued to struggle with the hectic schedules imposed by film exhibitors, and with the demands of music directors on how to adapt projection speed to their scores.

Undercranking

Projection speed was a byproduct of corporate policies as much as of artistic ambitions and public taste. In some countries, however, other imperatives prevailed over everything else in the form of legal provisions. In Japan, film stock was so scarce that shooting and projection speeds were kept at between 7 and 14 frames per second, with 12 frames per second as the norm in the mid-1910s. There were, of course, severe consequences to such a drastic (and unsafe) approach. Films were often overexposed; when they were projected at 8 frames per second, audiences complained that actors were moving on the screen like grasshoppers (an emerging star of Japanese cinema, Tachibana Teijiro, became famous for his ability to move around in slow motion on the set by listening to the cranking sound of the camera); running a single reel of film imported from Europe often took more than twenty minutes.

The situation came to a turning point in 1915, when three production companies gained permission to film the enthronement ceremony of Emperor Taishō at the Kyoto Imperial Palace. Two of the accredited cinematographers turned the crank at such a slow speed that the resulting film, once projected at a higher frame rate, offered a less than flattering portrayal of the sacred procession. Public authorities ordered the immediate confiscation of the negative and of all positive prints, to be subsequently incinerated. Since then, all films about the imperial family had to be projected at slower speeds. At the end of World War I, on the initiative of film critics and eminent filmmakers such as Kinugasa Teinosuke, camera and projection speeds were gradually conformed to the standards adopted in Europe and North America. Faster frame rates were not just a matter of aesthetics: in the late Japanese silent era, the Police Security Bureau established specific parameters for the projection speed of silent films (20 frames per second), in an unprecedented attempt to contain the inordinate length of the programmes. One of the declared goals was to bring people back home from film theatres earlier in the night.

Similar measures were adopted in the Soviet Union for entirely different reasons. During the Tsarist regime, the average projection speed in commercial theatres was consistent with common practice in the rest of Europe and North America: a 1916 manual by Moisei Aleinikov and Iosif Yermoliev explicitly mentioned the familiar 16 frames per second standard. Ten years later, another textbook by Pavel Radetskij provided three alternative definitions of 'normal' speed (18, 16–20, and 16–25 frames per second). Soviet authorities took a stricter approach by ordering on 21 May 1921 that projection speed must not exceed the rate of 25 metres of film per minute (equal to 21.9 frames per second). The instructions were confirmed in two documents issued to the Office for Political Enlightenment on 20 February and 11 June 1928, pointing out that the 'artistic perfection of a film is also dependent upon projection speed', and that 'peasants who have never seen a film respond with laughter to images of any kind if they are projected faster than

normal' (the letter from Vladimir Meshcheriakov to the Directorate-General for Literature and Publishing is preserved at the Russian State Archive for Literature & Art [RGALI] in Moscow, Collection 645, Register 1, Preservation Element 531, Leaves 174–6).

An intriguing distinction is made in these documents between the 'normal' projection speed in commercial venues, as opposed to the projection speed required for artistic reasons: 'masses are not informed that the artistic perception [of a film] depends upon the speed of the film's movement in the projector ... normal projection speed is caused by commercial, not artistic or ideological reasons'. Films are projected faster than they should be, so that 'film theatres ... can have one extra show in the evening. In the end, patrons are those who suffer because of a low quality presentation.' Projection speed also affects 'the physical condition of the film: every year Sovkino loses more than one million rubles because of the premature deterioration of the prints'; moreover, 'distribution outlets (especially Sovkino) are not interested in enforcing the normal projection speed because they receive a percentage of the income from every screening; the more screening sessions in a day, the more money they earn'.

The projection speed established by the Soviet committee came with a barrage of sanctions and technical provisions: all projectors were to be equipped with an automated mechanism that prevented the film from being shown at a speed faster than 25 metres per minute (21.9 frames per second); if the projectors were not modified within an agreed deadline, they would be taken out of service; the Central Board of Sovkino had the right to summarily dismiss the person responsible for not complying with the orders, and to suspend all financial support to the theatre where the infraction had occurred.

Ambiance

The emotional mood of a motion picture show was determined not only by the theatre's physical appearance and by the balance between the various components of the programme, but also by a sense of expectation generated by the acoustic and visual environment surrounding the audience. Wherever possible, exhibitors were keen to add a further element of attraction by projecting coloured light on the screen before, after, and even during the show. In those theatres where a vertical or horizontal curtain was in place, the traditional rule that no screen should ever be seen empty began to find its place in the rhetoric of showmanship, but spotlights with colour filters did more than prepare for the curtain to open or rise: they were used as a chromatic complement to the film itself, like another layer of tinting applied on the print during its projection.

This kind of stagecraft was reserved for important films in selected theatres, mostly in large cities. It is mentioned here only as another indication of how film producers and directors were keen to showcase their work in the form of special events, with more than motion pictures and music. To a greater or a lesser extent, silent cinema always was a performing art. Its core element – film projection – was surrounded by other coordinated actions involving booth operators, artists, technicians, managers, and their supporting staff all around the theatre. The premiere of D.W. Griffith's *Intolerance* at the Liberty Theatre in New York on 5 September 1916 included half-clad Babylonian dancers, large braziers with burning frankincense at each side of the stage, and an abundance of tinted spotlights: a total of 134 people were employed for the occasion. This convergence of people and electric machinery, of natural and reproduced life, in the name of a live dramatic performance is the essence of 'silent cinema' as a watershed episode in the history of visual culture.

It is not necessary to validate the point by looking only at the most wonderful or celebrated manifestations of the new medium: the gala premiere, the landmark film, the large orchestra. For more than thirty years, people watched film history projected in the humblest and least appealing venues. There is a natural inclination to focus upon the most exceptional achievements of an art form – in this case, the films, the people, and the places where cinema revealed itself in all its silent glory. They are also better documented, which makes them easier to recall; so much more is known about what happened during these shows, precisely because they were special. They were the shining stars in a galaxy made of many other projection halls where none of the added values described so far – the orchestra, the dancers, the scenic effects – were even remotely close to the viewers' cognitive horizon.

As mentioned earlier, film theatre patrons were rarely upset by variations in projection speed, unless its deviation from the norm was blatantly disrupting their viewing experience. Their margin of tolerance must have been very high, considering that films were projected as fast as 32 frames per second during the afternoon or evening shows in some theatres. If the films were just too long to fit within the allotted schedule, even if screened at outlandish speeds, exhibitors cut them down to the desired length, either by trimming shots here and there, or by discarding entire reels. Torrential rains of scratches on the emulsion, and hiccups in the action caused by repair splices from previous shows – both due to poor operation and maintenance of the equipment – were so common that viewers took them as a matter of course, not to mention the holes and heavy markings applied by projectionists on the last frames of each reel, to alert them of an imminent change to the other machine.

The majority of film theatres were sparsely decorated rooms with minimal heating in the winter, basic or no ventilation in the summer, and wooden seats or benches to accommodate patrons. From 1896 to the early 1910s, motion pictures taken from the front or rear of moving trains were popular fairground attractions: to enhance the simulation, Hale's Tours and Scenes of the World (1904–11) exhibited around the world these 'phantom rides' – a reference to the imagined point of view of a flying ghost – in theatre cars that tilted and vibrated like real trains. Many temporary venues in exteriors (they were called 'airdomes' in the United States) had no chairs at all. In tropical areas, open windows let the air flow in, together with noises, lights, and smells from outside. Eating, sleeping, and spitting on the floor were common sources of grievance, dutifully followed by warnings from the theatre management. Meanwhile, in a corner of the projection hall, under the screen or behind a curtain, other people were busy preparing words, noises, and music for the silent films about to be screened. Their work is often described as live accompaniment, but viewers did not necessarily see it as a subsidiary part of the programme. The presence of these artists was actually one of the main reasons why people had paid an admission price to attend the picture show.

Chapter 9

Acoustics

Fig. 175 Maud Nelissen, a music composer and performer for silent films, explains the Fotoplayer. Eye Filmmuseum, Amsterdam, 2009. Source: Courtesy of Maud Nelissen.

According to a long-established view among film historians of the late twentieth century, silent cinema was never silent. This is both plainly untrue and entirely accurate, depending on what is meant by 'silence'. One of its greatest interpreters, the American composer John Cage, would probably have laughed at anyone claiming that a silent film could ever have been viewed in the total absence of sound.

Centuries of theatrical and musical tradition had acknowledged the audiences' role in shaping the acoustic background of the show:

people talked, jeered, maybe slept and snored, or commented upon what was happening on stage, taking for granted that the admission price they had paid entitled them to express their thoughts about the performance through vocal and noise signals. Even if they didn't, something else would invariably fill the space with sounds, either emanating from the room or reverberating from its exterior: a fan on the ceiling, a sneeze or a cough from the lobby, life on the street outside the theatre, or maybe a distant whirr from the projector booth. This environment was part and parcel of the collective experience of a film, one of the reasons for being in a motion picture house: the feeling that the breath of life could be quietly heard in solitude, in the company of strangers.

In a more conventional sense of the term, 'silence' was not at all unknown to silent cinema; before dwelling upon the absence of live or artificial sounds deliberately produced for the show, however, we should accept the fact that any distinction based on their casual or intentional occurrence is inherently flawed. The utterance of a disgruntled viewer and the whisper of a fan are both the direct or mediated results of conscious actions: one is the spoken response to an event, the other a byproduct of the intent to provide temporary relief from the heat in the auditorium. The fact that neither of them was designed to be part of the screening event is not a good enough reason to ignore their effect on the viewers' experience.

Once these caveats are accounted for, there is enough evidence in support of the view that some motion picture shows had no 'performed' sound at all. In his impressive study of film exhibition in the United States (*Silent Film Sound*, 2004), Rick Altman indicated that, until at least 1910, the production of live sounds for cinema was not a universal practice. In the nickelodeon era, films were alternated with magic lantern slides of illustrated songs; musicians were called on the stage to provide a suitable accompaniment to these tunes, not to the films. Film projection resumed when the song was over, allowing the players to take some rest. Ten or fifteen minutes later, a signal from the booth alerted them that the reel was coming to its end, and that it was time for them to get back to work with the next song.

In the early years of cinema, films were often presented with the aid of spoken words, gramophone records, or mechanical instruments. Live, automatic, or recorded sounds could all be heard during the screening, or be absent altogether; it didn't really matter, because the real music was to be played elsewhere in the programme. There was no single epicentre for the show: the combination of songs and slides was important enough to align film at the same level with its non-cinematic counterparts. This cohabitation did not abruptly cease to exist when cinema asserted its dominance in the theatrical event.

As musicians shifted their attention from the illustrated songs to motion pictures in the early 1910s, magic lanterns continued to be used in projection booths. There were divergent opinions on which films should be kept entirely silent: some argued that comedies were better suited to sound effects; others believed that any interference to cheering, responding, and laughing at the actions unfolding on the screen was to be avoided; whether or not travelogues and scientific films had music accompaniment at all is largely a matter of speculation. As production companies began distributing music cue sheets for their films, some musicians took the printed instructions at face value by playing music intermittently, with long stretches of silence between sequences, or used the suggestions to punctuate the action only when they deemed it appropriate.

Confusion on the subject was exacerbated by conflicting views of what pianists and orchestras were supposed to do while the film was running.

Commentators had mixed feelings about music improvisation for cinema, but were appalled by those screenings where solo or ensemble performances sounded like concert programmes in disguise, with separate pieces and movements being played irrespective of what was going on in the film. Some experts argued that longer pauses were not only acceptable but also desirable, as the public needed time to reflect upon what they were seeing, with no aural distraction. Intermittent music was sometimes caused by sheer necessity, as theatre owners with limited financial means were working consecutively in the ticket office, in the projection booth, and at the piano for lack of dedicated personnel.

As illustrated by these few examples, it is plainly impossible to summarize music accompaniment for silent films in a single formula. To assume that exhibition practices in India, Japan, Russia, and Great Britain were more or less the same at all times would be like pretending that people of different countries always followed the same rituals at mealtimes throughout history. Even at a time when sounds for silent films were routinely produced in theatres around the world, there were still places where no one expected to hear anything during the show, other than their own sighs, catcalls, or applause.

Voices

In the beginning was the word, often preceded by shouts. Audiences had been used to both for a long time in magic lantern shows, as the human voice was a regular part of the slide projection event, with or without music. Before and after the birth of cinema, what was said remained basically the same: notices of forthcoming views, lectures, and all sorts of interpretations, either declaimed from a script or improvised; dramatized renditions – when the topic was appropriate – providing added

value to the visual experience. There was plain reading from the screen, because many slides contained textual information and there was a high illiteracy rate in some communities. Barkers at the entrance of projection halls were lecturers, too, only of a more outspoken kind.

The various performing styles did not necessarily require different talents; in fact, the lanternist, the speaker, and the promoter were often one and the same person, given the proximity of the magic lantern operator to the public. As we know, this did not last for long in motion pictures, except in non-theatrical contexts, but lecturers never disappeared altogether from public sight. Showpeople of the African continent, Jewish immigrants to New York, Catholic missionaries in Indonesia, and rural entrepreneurs all over the world cultivated this exhibition format well into the late 1920s and beyond, outlasting silent cinema by several decades.

Acting as both lecturer and projectionist was still the norm in classrooms and religious gatherings in the 1920s; everywhere else, exhibiting films and accompanying them were two separate jobs, linked only by gestures and instructions from the speaker to the man in the booth. In vaudeville programmes, this kind of interaction could be one aspect of the lecturer's role as coordinator of the show, where stage directions coincided with verbal signals to the public. The extended range of options available to the lecturer in a picture house is the most compelling evidence that the cinematic event had all the attributes of a theatrical happening from the very beginnings of cinema. Behind this generalization lies a complex reality made of very diverse and at times conflicting approaches to the same action of talking to an audience while a film was being projected.

The purpose of the talk could be to present a research topic with moving images used to illustrate the case in a conference-like fashion, as in the visually arresting medical films (1908–28) by Italian neurologist Vincenzo Neri. A live speech could also comment upon the films themselves, or explain them for dramatic, edifying, or liturgical reasons: the stations in the Passion of Christ, as told by Gaumont, Pathé, Lubin, and many other companies of the silent era, were ideally suited to the spoken word (Pathé sold its episodes separately, allowing exhibitors to tailor the structure and duration of the show to their specific needs).

In between, countless variations on the above paradigms may have qualified the live performer as an instructor, a storyteller (Elias Burton Holmes, who allegedly coined the term 'travelogue' for his live shows about his voyages around the world), a voice-over similar to the invisible narrator of a sound film, or an opera singer (two of them accompanied the short film *Boris Godunov*, produced in Russia by the Khanzhonkov company in 1912), in *recitativo* style, at the threshold between speaking and singing. Moreover, the hierarchy between cinema and commentary could be reversed: it seems that British pioneer James Williamson made some of his films in the expectation that they would be shown with a lecturer, and modelled their structure accordingly. The distinction between lecture with screening, and film with live commentary, is severely tested by the 'red lectures' of Bolshevik activists in the Soviet Union, who were both presenting facts and instructing on how they must be interpreted.

Finally, the job of a lecturer was also to make the unknown more intelligible and accessible to the public: translating title cards of foreign releases; explaining behaviours and values of remote cultures; paraphrasing the films' messages with the rhetorical tools of the oral culture of a given community. At once messengers, instructors, and mediators, lecturers were the voice-over narrators of early cinema. French-speaking scholars sometimes call them *bonimenteurs*, but the term was rarely, if ever, employed at the beginning of the twentieth century, *conférencier* being a preferred, more dignified title, incorporating the functions of information and entertainment in the motion picture show. Other terms, such as 'barker' or the Italian *imbonitore*, are borrowed from the fairground tradition and were applied by extension to cinema in a colloquial sense.

Benshi

The live spoken commentary to fiction and non-fiction silent films found a unique and highly sophisticated expression in Japan. This kind of accompaniment evolved over the years, both in style and technique, and could differ enormously from one location to another. In the early years of cinema, a typical show in Japan was preceded by a verbal explanation of what was about to be presented. As films reached and eventually went beyond the fifteen-minute threshold, the announcements became actual performances, often by as many as seven or eight people, presenting the characters' dialogues in parallel to the projection; these actors became known as *benshi*, a term that originally referred to political orators of distinguished eloquence. In line with the rejection of realism that dominated Japanese cinema of the 1908–18 period, *benshi* ensembles were not expected to mimic, let alone synchronize, what was being said in the films' dialogues: their goal was to achieve a full integration between the commentary and the action, in a constant shift between counterpoint (reflecting upon the events as they unfolded on screen before the audience) and subjectivity (giving voice to the characters' inner thoughts and emotions). The use of male performers (*oyama*) for female roles was considered entirely appropriate.

Benshi performances included live or recorded musical instruments – namely the shamisen, with its three strings and elongated neck – and sound effects borrowed from the kabuki theatre. *Rensageki* ('chain drama'), a popular variation on this exhibition format, alternated brief film screenings and feisty interactions between the players and the audience. The nature of musical accompaniment also changed over time, depending on the location of the theatre (metropolitan or regional) and the nature of the programmes (domestic or imported films). In the late silent film period, there was a preference for solo piano accompaniment to *benshi*. A piano was also used in many venues featuring shamisen and traditional percussion: these groups were referred to as *wayō*, literally meaning 'Japanese-Western'.

The *benshi* style is heavily indebted to the legacy of kabuki. Its *gidayu* singers, and the *joruri* narrators of the *bunraku* puppet theatre, reflected a popular taste for expressive storytelling that had developed in Japan since the seventeenth century. This technique of oral performance extends even beyond the theatre, to popular literature like the *kōdan* (its tales of epic battles and their heroes are known as *kōkashu*), from as early as the twelfth century. Pictures and scrolls were often displayed during the shows; in 1801, Ikeda Kumakichi went a step further and introduced projected pictures (*utsushi-e*) into the performance, paving the way for the use of magic lantern equipment. Stories from the *kabuki* and *bunraku* traditions were narrated in conjunction with multicoloured slides, frequently shown side by side on paper screens; the repertoire was soon expanded with *kōdan*, with comic acts (*rakugo*), and later with episodes from contemporary life. Once the shamisen music was added to the formula, all the basic components of *benshi* were already in place, well before the arrival of motion pictures in Japan.

One of the first showpeople of cinema, Ueda Tsunejiro, introduced the Edison Kinetoscope and its animated views as the machine made its first appearance in Kobe (1896). Presenters of the Vitascope and the Cinématographe in early 1897 behaved no differently from European and North American speakers; their declamatory talents, however, had nothing to do with the entirely new performing style that emerged around 1907. Its enormous popular acclaim in the following years was bound to play a major influence in Japanese film production for the next three decades. *Benshi* artists of the late silent period delivered their lines with the aid of plot summaries and dialogue scripts, often provided by the studio, with ample room for improvisation when the opportunity arose; earlier on, *benshi* artists prided themselves on their 'authorship', creating their own texts to perform. They were required to possess superior skills as dramatists or comedians, and to demonstrate great versatility in the use of their voices: the gentle whispers of a young woman, the stately intonation of a samurai warrior, the ominous depth in the words of a villain, and the shrill voice of a child had to be equally mastered with a seamlessly natural eloquence (*kowairo*). In the so-called 'mother dramas', a *benshi*'s grief-stricken soliloquy could be so intense as to bring an entire audience to tears.

The art of *benshi* as a group performance was deemed unsuitable to contemporary dramas and especially to foreign films, generally shown with a single *benshi* player and instruments; *wayō gassō* – 'Japanese-Western ensemble' – was a common form of accompaniment for American and European works. The audience's general dislike for intertitles in domestic productions, and the labour involved in film titling, were among the reasons for this. Aside from interfering with the commentaries, title cards were seen as disruptive of the narrative flow: *benshi* players had a strong predilection for very extended shots that enabled them to demonstrate their skills, and the increasing use of cross-cutting in American films of the

1910s was incompatible with their fluent, unhurried dialogue with the moving image.

Audiences were so fond of *benshi* artists that the most charismatic personalities were revered as objects of public cult, often ensuring the success of a film by simply associating its exhibition with their appearance on stage. The reputation of a motion picture theatre was heavily dependent on that of its *benshi* ensemble, whose virtuoso leaders were contracted on an exclusive basis (their names were advertised at least as prominently as the films being shown). The *benshi* presentation format was successfully exported to other countries such as Thailand, Korea, and Taiwan. It was also very popular in Hawaii and with Japanese communities along the West Coast of the United States.

A new generation of filmmakers tried to make Japanese films more competitive by adapting their style to the models of Europe and the United States. They encountered a fierce resistance from the *benshi* star system, whose celebrities acquired even greater power as ensemble shows were replaced in the 1920s by solo performances. Films running for four or more hours were accompanied by individual players working in tandem until the most famous artist was called on stage to enact a key sequence. The authority of *benshi* masters was so great that producers and screenwriters had to take their opinions into serious consideration. When sound cinema reached the shores of Japan in the early 1930s, *benshi* workers went on strike. They could not prevent their own eventual demise, but the public supported them long enough to allow more silent films to be made until the late 1930s, when the rest of the world – with the exception of China and the Soviet Union – had long been accustomed to the sound of recorded music and dialogue. Roughly between 1930 and 1938, several Japanese productions were made as silents but distributed with post-synchronized soundtracks of music scores, sound effects,

and popular songs (this hybrid format was called *saundo–ban*).

The chronicles of cinema make mention of two other forms of live performance: in Brazil, short films of musical pieces were accompanied by singers located behind the screen (this genre, known as *filme cantante*, made its appearance from 1908 to 1911); around the same period in the United States, groups of three to six actors developed their own scripts and recited them during the show, in some cases removing all the intertitles from the prints to allow themselves more expressive freedom (they could do so, of course, only at a time when reels could be purchased and carried from one venue to the next). Dialogue accompaniment, sometimes improvised by local and amateur stage actors, had a brief but sparkling life until the early 1910s, when complex narratives and the introduction of film rental put an end to this practice.

Noises

In addition to a drum, *benshi* players had a pair of small wooden clappers at their disposal. It was used parsimoniously, to underline both physical events and dramatic turning points in the action. Compared to what film audiences witnessed in most other parts of the world, their set-up for sound effects was a model of restraint: of all the influences exercised by stage theatre on silent cinema, none was as pervasively manifest as the reproduction of all sorts of noises, either natural (a galloping horse, thunder, the cry of a baby) or artificial (trains, cars, telephones). Shaking a large piece of sheet iron made the thunder feel uncannily real; dried peas in a canister helped to evoke a train ride or rainfall; these and other artifices had been used behind the scenes since the Baroque era, reaching such a degree of sophistication that the humble art of backstage performance had become not only a harbinger of avant-garde music, but also a prosperous business in itself.

Both in Europe and North America, corporate entities were competing for the most diverse and ingenious array of manually operated devices, where plain materials like wood, cork, sandpaper, and rope could be elevated to the rank of unlikely instruments in a music concert, alongside keyboards, strings, voices, winds, and standard percussion. In a catalogue for the North American market, Gaumont encouraged the use of the 'realistic sound effects for moving pictures' on sale from the Yerkes Manufacturing Company of New York, available in a full-fledged series of thirty-four instruments, or in a shortened set of basic items. The company's founder, Henry A. Yerkes, deserves to be remembered as one of the greatest precursors of 'concrete' music (Fig. 176).

Performers of sound effects stood behind the screen (see Fig. 108 on p. 116), alone or in groups

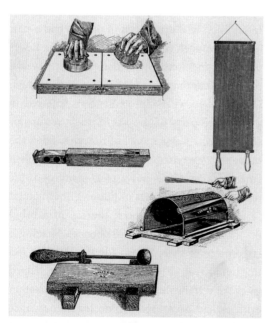

Fig. 176 Instruments for sound effects. Yerkes Manufacturing Company, New York, c. 1912. Source: Gaumont Co. Catalogue of Moving Picture Apparatus and Accessories. The Chrono Moving Picture Machine. The Chronophone Talking Pictures, n.d., [ca. 1912], p. 28.

of as many as fifteen people, and tampered with the most unusual and sometimes bizarre contraptions; in a telling demonstration of how blurred were the boundaries between instrumental and vocal performance for silent films, exhibitors were recruiting their sound-effects personnel on the basis of their ability to imitate as many animal languages as possible, including those of birds, insects, domestic and wild beasts. Witnessing their efforts must have been a sight to behold. Audiences didn't (insofar as the players remained invisible to them), but were so excited about what they heard that commentators felt some concern about the immoderate use of flashy or unnecessary tricks.

The most frequent criticisms levelled at sound effects pertained to timing and volume: if played out of synch, a dog's bark or a car crash would spoil the dramatic situation or make it unintentionally hilarious; when overwhelmingly loud, the sounds disconnected the audience from the emotional texture of the film, to the detriment of its appreciation. Neither the producers nor the exhibitors wanted that. Redundancy was another problem: listening to the horns of automobiles in an urban setting was entirely appropriate, unless the entire story was taking place in the streets.

In a rational world, these matters would have been settled by the application of discipline and common sense. In philosophical terms, the question was whether sound effects should imitate reality, or give resonance to human emotions by eschewing naturalism. It was even suggested that a film's atmosphere may be enhanced by making noises in counterpoint mode: refraining, for instance, from sound effects in pivotal moments of the story, or applying them as punctuations to wistful or plaintive pauses in the action, such as a distant bell in a death scene. Another option was to dispense with sound effects altogether, letting the piano evoke the murmur of water flowing down a stream, or the violin imitate the song of a nightingale. This is what happened in the late 1910s, when the profligate use of sound effects became unfashionable; slapstick comedies remained exempt from the embargo, to the audiences' delight.

Another compromise was reached in the last decade of silent cinema, when organs and automatic instruments resurrected the old practice in a more impersonal form, under the strict control of mechanics and their operators. John Cage would have been pleased to know that 'noise' was almost never used as a substitute term for 'sound' effects in silent cinema, except by the Futurists. A leading figure of the movement, painter Luigi Russolo, had used objects and noise machines since the 1910s (his *intonarumori*, also known as 'rumorharmonium', 'rumorarmonio' or 'Russolophone', was patented in France in 1922), but it all happened too late: Russolo's live accompaniment to *La Marche des machines* (Eugène Deslaw, 1927) presumably took place when silent cinema was just about to become the object of history.

Automata

Sound effects could also be created with mechanical instruments, operated either manually or by electric or pneumatic power. A French patent for the Ciné Multiphone Rousselot, one of the earliest machines of this kind, was deposited in 1907. Other companies jumped at the opportunity, beginning with Pathé in 1908; a year later, in Great Britain, the Alleflex was believed to produce more than fifty sounds of different kinds. These were only the early steps for an industry that flourished at least until the 1920s, and continued to be active until the end of the silent era. In the United States, its products – known as theatre photoplayers – were equipped to generate both noises and music (one of their earliest examples was the Soundograph, a hand-

operated cabinet of sound effects, made in 1910 for nickelodeon theatres).

There was nothing particularly new about the design of these wonderful objects: automatic sound machines had been manufactured and played for many years, well before the invention of cinema. What differentiated the novelties from their predecessors was that these machines were not coin operated, as in the case of musical contraptions built for public entertainment. Photoplayers were also very compact, as they were supposed to be placed right in front of the audience, preferably below the screen: for this reason, their profile was often low and very wide. Despite their complexity, these marvels of precision engineering were also remarkably sturdy, as theatre owners kept them functioning for long hours, day after day, and hurried or careless operators did not always treat them with kindness.

The widespread appeal of mechanical devices for silent film music was not limited to theatres with a modest budget: Guazzoni's *Quo Vadis?* was premiered in April 1913 at a prestigious first-run venue, the Astor Theatre on Broadway, with an automated orchestral player. By purchasing these machines (at prices ranging from about US$1,500 to more than US$10,000 in the early 1920s), exhibitors no longer had to negotiate salaries with the musicians, or deal with their union delegates. The investment was attractive to theatre owners also because it released them from the duties of managing personnel who could misbehave, leave for another job, be late for the show, or fall sick. Last but not least, patrons could not complain about a poor performance, question the versatility of the players, or bemoan the limitations of their repertoire.

The core component of the machine, an automatic piano, provided impeccable reproductions of music recorded on piano rolls, available by the thousands. The supply was virtually endless, ranging from classical music in the public domain to fashionable tunes of the moment, at prices rarely exceeding the 1 dollar threshold in 1918. The Filmusic Company in Los Angeles marketed a catalogue of Picturolls especially made for film theatre shows. Two compositions for mechanical devices to be played with silent films were created by German composer Paul Hindemith: *Vormittagspuk* (for a 1928 film by Hans Richter), and *Felix der Kater im Zirkus* (1927), made to accompany a Felix the Cat animated short and played on a Rhythmonome, an invention by Carl Robert Blum.

The main manufacturers of machine music equipment for silent cinema were based in the United States, France, Germany, and Great Britain. Q. David Bowers, author of a monumental book on the subject, estimated that about eight to ten thousand pieces were sold between 1910 and 1928. The simplest models, with little or no noise effects, consisted of an upright automatic piano, supplemented by gears and pipes that reproduced the sounds of a few instruments such as violin, flute, and mandolin.

In their cheapest forms, music machines did not require any human intervention other than the roll change and normal maintenance. More expensive varieties of the product featured dual mechanisms that allowed piano rolls to be changed manually or automatically without interruption in the music. The operator could also rewind the perforated paper roll, or fast-forward it to a given point, as required by the action in the film. A mammoth version from the American Photo Player Company of Berkeley, California, was a masterpiece of craftsmanship: its 6.5-metre (21-foot) oak console included a bewildering array of xylophones, bass drums, cathedral chimes, castanets, bird whistles, and other assorted instruments; with its 195 reeds and 412 pipes, the Fotoplayer Style 50 produced more powerful sounds than those of a large theatre's organ (see Fig. 175 on p. 188).

Equipment of such scale required a well-trained operator. The best manufacturers of automatic players for motion picture houses offered basic or advanced courses for their personnel, and provided regular maintenance as required by the machines' intricate network of cables, springs, and wheels. Sound cinema mercilessly brought all this commerce to an abrupt end. The names of some companies remained familiar long after the disappearance of these clockwork orchestras: Wurlitzer (based in North Tonawanda, New York) had little reason for concern, thanks to its solid reputation in organ and keyboard instruments; another firm, Seeburg, turned to another kind of automated music instrument, the jukebox. Bulky as they were, photoplayers seemed to have vanished from public sight despite the keen interest of collectors (a beautiful piece is preserved at the Eye Filmmuseum in Amsterdam); this is all the more surprising in that other types of mechanical instruments from the early twentieth century are relatively easy to find. It was later discovered that the largest machines had slept undisturbed in their original locations: instead of removing or destroying them, real estate owners had sometimes buried them behind walls, unknowingly securing their survival. Futurists were not so lucky: Russolo's 'rumorharmonium' is considered lost.

Scores

Orchestras appeared in film projection halls sooner than is generally thought: on the promotional poster for a Lumière screening (14 February 1899) held in the city of Tambov, about 500 kilometres (300 miles) south-east of Moscow, it is announced that 'the orchestra will play during the programme and through the intermission' (see Fig. 170 on p. 172). Between 1900 and 1914, Albert and Sarah Corrick toured New Zealand, Australia, and South-East Asia with their six daughters and one son as the Corrick Family Entertainers. The children were trained both as a choral group and as instrumentalists (piano, organ, violin, flute, piccolo, cello, saxophone, mandolin, cornet, and percussion). Each family member could play several instruments as accompaniment to the silent films purchased or made by the Corricks for their popular tours (a collection of 135 prints used for the shows is preserved at the National Film and Sound Archive of Australia).

According to Harold B. Franklin, a theatre manager operating in the United States, music for silent films 'should have plenty of contrast, with plenty of colour and novelty in harmonic treatment'. Its function was fully integrated into the other components of the show: 'the soft lighting of the auditorium, the soothing music – bringing about almost a hypnotic state – give the picture on the screen an almost dreamlike quality. In such an atmosphere, the patron is able to concentrate on and live with the characters on the screen.' The music itself 'is at its best when it is an accompaniment. It should never dominate the scene, but subtly blend the senses'; in its ideal form, the cinematic event 'should be followed almost as at an operatic performance' (*Motion Picture Theater Management*, p. 281).

This illuminating and somewhat lyrical declaration of faith in the motion picture show as an all-inclusive feast for the senses was published in 1927, when the art of film exhibition had reached such a level of refinement that no major production could be conceived without an original orchestral score or, at the very least, an adaptation of existing musical pieces carefully blended in a cohesive whole. It should be noted that Franklin managed a chain of prestigious motion picture palaces, where orchestral music was an integral part of the offerings. Commissioned scores to be performed by large ensembles were primarily aimed at luxury venues like the Gaumont-Palace

in Paris, the Ufa am Zoo in Berlin, and the Paramount Theatre in New York. From there, the new music composition or collage travelled with the film in its original version or in abridged form, either as an adaptation for smaller ensembles or as a transcription for piano soloist.

True to his vocation as a pioneer, Georges Méliès was interested in providing musical settings for his films; no score for *A Trip to the Moon* is known to exist, but there is one to be performed with *Damnation du docteur Faust* (*Faust and Marguerite*, 1904), compiled by Georges' brother, Gaston (Fig. 177). The earliest known original score for a large orchestra (forty-one elements) was written by Herman Finck to accompany *Marie-Antoinette*, a ten-minute film produced by Pathé in late 1903; it precedes by almost five years a more famous piece composed for *L'Assassinat du Duc de Guise*, another one-reeler from Pathé

Fig. 177 The original piano score (English version) by Gaston Méliès for *Damnation du docteur Faust* (*Faust and Marguerite*, Georges Méliès, 1904), adapted from Charles Gounod's opera *Faust* (1859). Source: Archives françaises du film / Centre National de la Cinématographie.

(as part of the Film d'Art series). Pathé added an extra touch of gravitas to its period drama with a little help from a venerable personality of classical music, Camille Saint-Saëns, who authored a chamber music work for the occasion. Its critical and popular success inspired Russian composer Mikhail Ippolitov-Ivanov to write the music for a Drankov production, *Stenka Razin* (Vladimir Romashkov, 1908), from a popular folk song associated with the story.

The circumstances of Pathé's efforts on *L'Assassinat du Duc de Guise* are worth retelling as an emblematic case study in silent film accompaniment. Saint-Saëns was no stranger to theatre music, but he was 73 years old and his active career was coming to an end; André Calmettes and Charles Le Bargy were smart enough to entice him with the prospect of a relatively short piece for piano, harmonium, and strings (later published in a slightly expanded form as *Opus 128 pour cordes, piano et harmonium*). In trying to give his composition a thematic range of sufficient breadth, the elderly maestro had to face a constraint that would become typical of film music production in general. Saint-Saëns watched each scene of the finished product – fortunately for him, it was structured into long narrative segments with little or no editing – and devised its music as quickly as he could, structuring the piece into brief movements, exactly like a concert format. Pathé's idea was to premiere the work with Saint-Saëns as conductor, in a programme also featuring a poetry recital, a choreographed scene, and other films; everything was ready, when Saint-Saëns left Paris and delegated the task to his colleague Fernand Le Borne. As a token of gratitude, Saint-Saëns dedicated a piano reduction of the suite to him.

This episode highlights a fundamental challenge in composing film music: the time allowed for completing a score is generally very limited, and famous artists don't like to be rushed. Giovanni

Pastrone realized this at his own expense when trying to apply the concept of Calmettes and Le Bargy's film to his three-hour epic of the ancient world, *Cabiria*, whose production occupied the Italian director for much of 1913. In those times, it was hard enough to bring the highest ranks of the classical music sphere in contact with film entrepreneurs, snubbed or despised as they were by the cultural elites. After having managed to recruit Gabriele D'Annunzio in exchange for an exorbitant honorarium, Pastrone used the poet's name to persuade a notable composer of the time, Ildebrando Pizzetti, that his film had genuine artistic ambitions.

Shortly after agreeing to join the project, Pizzetti realized that he could not possibly complete a three-hour vocal and symphonic score at such short notice; all he had managed to write was a ten-minute piece for baritone, choir, and orchestra, *Sinfonia del fuoco*, for a spectacular sequence in which children are sacrificed to the god Moloch. As *Cabiria*'s premiere was looming, and with only sixty-five pages of orchestral music in hand, Pastrone had no choice but to accept Pizzetti's suggestion of enlisting his collaborator and former student Manlio Mazza, who miraculously delivered the remaining 624 pages of music score on time for the film's premiere on 18 April 1914.

This remarkable feat could not have been accomplished in the way Harold B. Franklin would have hoped for thirteen years later. Mazza's music for *Cabiria* is 'synchronized' to the action only in the loosest sense of the term, helped in this by the film's slow narrative pace. As for the *Sinfonia del fuoco*, Pizzetti made no particular effort to match the music with the action, as there was very little of it in the scene. Pastrone was so painfully aware of this that he re-edited the sequence in 1931 for a new release of the film with recorded sound, inserting additional shots of a priest singing the *Sinfonia*'s sacred hymn in front of worshippers at the Carthage temple. In essence, Pastrone had adapted the film to the score rather than asking Pizzetti to do the opposite, as one would expect from a director with grand artistic ambitions.

To a certain extent, film composers and conductors of the silent era followed the very same pattern when preparing for an orchestra performance in a motion picture theatre: as a rule, the rehearsal process involved a dialogue between the conductor and the projectionist, who was instructed to accelerate or slow down the projection speed in order to better adapt the tempo of the orchestral score to the rhythm of the film and to the timing of its most notable events. When no change in the metronome settings or in the speed of projection was enough to obtain the desired results, the conductor asked the projectionist to remove as much footage as was required by the score. The editing of a film could therefore continue on individual prints, well after the date of general release; when this happened, neither the director nor the production company could do much to intervene in the process.

The first official public showing of D.W. Griffith's *Intolerance* was accompanied by a 46-piece orchestra and a choir of sixteen voices; in the Netherlands, Johan Gildermeijer made *Gloria Transita* (1917), an operatic drama that required performers to stand beside the screen and follow the characters' lip movements. Sadly, the list of personalities from the pantheon of classical music who had some association with silent cinema is extremely short; the names of Erik Satie (*Entr'acte*, René Clair, 1924), Darius Milhaud (*L'Inhumaine*, Marcel L'Herbier, 1924), and Arthur Honegger (*La Roue; Napoléon*, both by Abel Gance) are among the best known. Paul Hindemith wrote a score for *Im Kampf mit dem Berge* (Arnold Fanck, 1921), but he preferred to be credited under the pseudonym of Paul Merano. Austrian-born composer Hugo Riesenfeld, one of the most prominent names

(together with Ernö Rapée, Gottfried Huppertz, and Giuseppe Becce) of silent film music as an art form, had no hesitation in pointing out where the problem lay: namely, the length of a major studio production 'requires as much music as an opera. Think of the physical effort of writing such a work! The life of even important films hardly exceeds two years. It is then put aside and forgotten.' Is there an ambitious talent, Riesenfeld argued, who would be willing 'to devote his best effort and energy to something whose death is doomed before its birth? From what I know of composers, they would rather starve with the hope of creating a great symphony that will live through the ages' ('Music and Motion Pictures', 1926, p. 61).

Instructions

For a first-class picture house of the United States in the 1920s, the cost of an orchestral accompaniment was roughly equal to that of the film rental itself. To help exhibitors save some money (and possibly also reduce the risk that films were tampered with in the projection booth during the rehearsal process), production companies offered compilations of popular or classical music especially made for their new feature-length releases. Other firms supplied vast repertoires of multipurpose music scores printed in separate orchestral parts for generic use in film accompaniment, covering a range of moods, emotions, and dramatic or comedic situations.

Pre-packaged music suggestions were sold to exhibitors in the form of printed scores, normally four to eight pages, commonly known as 'cue sheets' because they contained indications on where a change in the music was supposed to take place during projection, and when specific events in the story were expected to receive special attention from orchestra conductors and soloists. Cue sheets sometimes included specific instructions on projection speed. Each tune was represented by one or two lines of musical notation; when the same piece of music was to be repeated, one or two bars served as reminders. As in most orchestral scores for silent film, some cue sheets also reproduced the texts of intertitles corresponding to the beginning or the end of a musical section.

Above each transcription of the first bars (often referred to as an *incipit*) in a suggested tune, the cue sheet reproduced the title of the music piece; at the bottom right corner of the sample, another caption mentioned the music publisher's name. At that point, the orchestra conductor, the organist, or the pianist had all the information they needed to look out for the orchestral or soloists' parts. Any motion picture house in good financial standing could afford a respectable music library of its own: during the silent film era, music parts were sold at extremely low costs because they were constantly in demand, and printed in very large numbers; first-run theatres held collections of several thousand printed scores, with full-time librarians in charge of acquiring, cataloguing, and making them accessible upon demand to resident performers.

With all the required music scores or cue sheets compilations in hand, the conductor and performers could begin the rehearsal process; as a rule, barring unforeseen issues with the film to be screened, a single rehearsal with projection of the entire work was deemed sufficient, and indeed was often all that was possible, due to performance schedules. Cue sheets began to be produced by major film companies around 1915, but were widely adopted only from the early 1920s. They were more popular in North America than in Europe and in the Asian continent; music libraries of varying sizes, however, existed in film theatres almost everywhere.

In the scenario described above, it is assumed that every music part listed in a cue sheet was available when needed; even in a theatre with a large music library, this was not always the case. No experienced musician would be daunted by occasional gaps in the film theatre's collection: as a cursory reading of the *incipit* revealed what kind of music was suggested, the performer would retrieve other pieces of a similar mood, and adjust them to the rest of the compilation. In the unlikely event that few or no pieces were available, artists would use their own creativity, working with music scores they had at home, or purchasing enough parts from the nearest music store to get the job done. When nothing else was at hand, a direct reading of the cue sheets themselves, or a quick look at the musical suggestions reproduced in recent issues of trade journals – with the occasional touch of impromptu mode – were enough to meet the needs of the moment.

Improvisation was more than a last resort in case of an emergency: some degree of flexibility in music performances for silent films was the norm for pianists and organists, working alone or in tandem with a percussionist or a violin player (piano and violin played leading roles in the literature of cue sheets). This was true, nonetheless, only up to a certain point. Music improvisation entirely based on memory and personal talent was not a default option during the silent era of cinema, but happened often enough – especially with theatre organists – that professional music journals such as *The American Organist* took special notice of those cinema musicians who displayed this ability well, as improvisation was (and continues to be) a standard part of the music conservatory organ curriculum.

Recordings

From the outset, Edison produced films with the clear intention of making them talk. The solution to one-third of the equation was well on its way in 1877, when Edison's phonograph proved that sounds could be recorded and played back on the same device. By 1894, the photographic carrier of consecutive images had found its definitive shape. The next step was to shoot a film while the phonograph was capturing the sounds of the action, which is what Edison did around the same year with the help of W.K.L. Dickson, who played a barcarole from Robert Planquette's light opera *Les Cloches de Corneville* (1877) on a violin while two male colleagues from the laboratory danced in front of the camera (Fig. 178). There is no proof that the film and the wax cylinder phonograph resulting from production in the Black Maria studio were ever played together, but the experiment was successful enough to persuade Edison in April 1895 to launch his Kinetophone, a combination of the Kinetoscope and a phonograph player: patrons listened to the sounds by means of earphones while watching the film through a peephole viewer with a magnifying glass (Fig. 179).

In the following year, Pathé made its first attempts to match projected motion picture films with phonograph discs played on a Berliner Gramophone. A group of synchronized shorts was presented on 28 April 1900 at the Universal Exhibition in Paris under the collective title

Fig. 179 Edison Kinetophone, 1894–1900. Gelatin silver print. Source: George Eastman Museum.

Phono-Cinéma-Théâtre, featuring Sarah Bernhardt in *Hamlet* and other celebrities in the French show business (Fig. 180). The prestige series was shown across Europe after a lukewarm reception in France; Charles Pathé's main rival, Léon Gaumont, followed his path in 1902 with the Chronophone, barely recouping the investment at the box office; better results were achieved in Germany by Oskar Messter's Biophon system. The stage was set for a brief period of fierce competition, culminating in 1906 with Gaumont's phonograph amplified by compressed air (the Elgéphone, whose first letters were a phonetic transcription of Léon Gaumont's initials) to synchronize the company's *phonoscènes*, and with Messter's aggressive campaign in Denmark, Austria, Bohemia, and the domestic market, where about five hundred Biophon machines were sold between 1907 and 1910.

Fig. 178 [Dickson Experimental Sound Film], 1894. Frame enlargement from a 35mm triacetate positive. Source: George Eastman Museum.

Fig. 180 Phono-Cinéma-Théâtre. *Air de Roméo et Juliette* (Ambroise-François Parnaland, France, 1900). 35mm nitrate positive for synchronized phonograph recording, with three non-standard perforations on the frame line. Source: George Eastman Museum, courtesy of Vincent Pinel.

Alice Guy (later Guy-Blaché), arguably the first female film director, made several films for Gaumont from theatrical acts or songs with notable artists of the time; Messter produced similar works at breakneck speed. Taken together, the two companies had enough material and expertise to dissuade others from entering the arena. As shown in the inscription on a film leader (Fig. 181), Messter and Gaumont entered into a collaborative venture by agreeing not to export their projection and gramophone machines in each other's country, but other problems were obstructing their plans for further expansion in this area. Synchronization was so flawed that cameras had

to be kept far enough away from the players to conceal the frequent mismatch between their lip movements and the sound. Instead of having their voice recorded while singing or speaking in front of the camera, performers were playing against phonograph recordings previously made.

Exhibition of these films was also rife with technical difficulties. As proven by Gaumont's Elgéphone and later, from the same company, the Chronomégaphone, making the sound audible in a large auditorium was not the main issue (Fig. 182); managing the distance between projection booth and phonograph player behind the screen, on the other hand, remained a matter of major concern in the 1900s. The mechanical or electrical cabling systems used in connecting two pieces of equipment at the opposite sides of the auditorium (Fig. 183) were cumbersome and often unreliable; once the performance had begun, projectionists maintained the film and the phonograph record in synch to the best of their abilities with a control device nicknamed 'orchestra conductor'. Leaving the projection booth during the show to address a malfunction in the phonograph player was out of the question without extra personnel; precise as it could be (Fig. 184), perfect registration was often thwarted by uneven supply of electric power.

Within months of the 1900 Universal Exhibition, merging the two components of the talking picture into a single object had been theorized or put into practice by German and British researchers (William Du Bois Duddell, Hermann

Fig. 181 The film leader of *Das Schmiedelied aus Siegfried* (Messter-Gaumont, 1905?). 35mm nitrate positive for synchronized projection with phonograph recording. Note the shape of the smaller perforations with rounded corners, common until 1905. Source: George Eastman Museum – Davide Turconi/Josef Joye Collection.

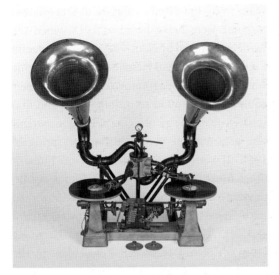

Fig. 184 Cue frame to be placed in front of the projector's aperture gate for synchronization with a phonograph recording of *Le Boxeur des Folies Bergère* (Gaumont Filmparlant, *c.* 1913). Frame enlargement from a 35mm triacetate positive. Source: Gaumont Pathé Archives.

Fig. 182 Chronomégaphone, a phonograph player system for synchronized film in large projection halls. Amplification for both turntables was achieved with compressed air. Gaumont, France, 1911. Source: Cinémathèque française.

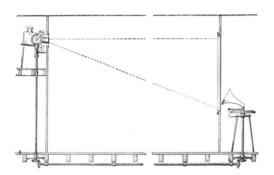

Fig. 183 Cross-section of a projection hall with synchronized sound film equipment, *c.* 1910. The power shaft connecting the projector to phonograph player is visible under the theatre's floor. Source: David S. Hulfish, Motion-Picture Work. Chicago: American Technical Society, 1915, p. 248.

Theodor Simon, and Ernst Walter Ruhmer) who worked independently from each other towards the same goal. Ruhmer's research on his Photographophone (1900) was further developed in 1906 by the French inventor Eugène Augustin Lauste, who patented a machine that could capture images and sounds simultaneously on the same strip of 35mm film.

None of this made a difference in the short term: between 1904 and the end of the decade, film producers and entrepreneurs in Great Britain (Cinephone), the United States (Picturephone, Photophone, Lubin's Cineophone, Cameraphone), and Italy followed the path pursued by Messter, Pathé, and Gaumont with their own products, in the hope of securing a niche in the market. Giovanni Pastrone, in particular, invested time and money around 1908 at the newborn Itala-Film in the production of short films to be accompanied with recordings of brief excerpts from the classical repertoire. Around 1913, Edison made one last attempt at reviving his Kinetophone through an aggressive marketing campaign.

After reaching its peak between 1910 and 1913 with Gaumont's improved version of the Chronophone (the company offered more than 700 *phonoscènes* to be played with commercially available phonograph records, and about 250 *filmparlants*, recorded on stage while shooting the films), synchronized cinema was no longer a fashionable item. Its fortune languished for

Fig. 185 Tri-Ergon 42mm film with lateral soundtrack. Hans Vogt, Joseph Benedikt Engl, and Joseph Massolle, Berlin, c. 1925. Source: Courtesy of Laurent Mannoni.

years while the distant rumbles of a revolution to come were being heard in 1918, when the work undertaken by Hans Vogt, Joseph Benedikt Engl, and Joseph Massolle on photographic soundtracks was beginning to bear fruit; their equipment for sound recordings on 35mm film separate from the picture (the Tri-Ergon system) was presented in Berlin during the spring of 1921. The process was later tried on films of other formats, with picture and soundtrack on the same strip of film (Fig. 185). Others worked in the same direction throughout the silent film era: Eric Tigerstedt in Finland and Germany (1914), Valentin Ivanovich Kovalenkov in the Soviet Union (1920), Axel Petersen and Arnold Poulsen in Denmark (1922), Sven A. Berglund in Sweden (1922, Fig. 186). The breakthrough came between 1923 and 1925 with Lee de Forest's Phonofilm (its optical soundtrack adjacent to the picture was decoded by a photoelectric cell) and by Theodore W. Case, who made several sound film tests in Auburn, New York, where his laboratory was located.

Fig. 186 Experimental sound recording on film (Sven A. Berglund, 1922). Frame enlargement from a 35mm nitrate positive. Source: Svenska Filminstitutet, Stockholm; gift of the Deutsches Filminstitut, Frankfurt, 2010.

One of his shorts – depicting a canary in a cage against a black background – was shown to film producer William Fox, who was so impressed by the clarity of the high-frequency pitch in the recorded birdsong that he decided to adopt Case's system for his Movietone films (the canary film is still extant). In the midst of an acrimonious fight between Lee de Forest and Case, who were once collaborators, Warner Bros. released *Don Juan* (Alan Crosland, 1926), starring John Barrymore. It was a sudden and triumphant comeback for phonograph film sound. Prints were synchronized to several 33⅓ rpm records of 40 centimetres (almost 16 inches) in diameter, played on a gramophone (attached to the projector) with a stylus running from the centre to the edge of the shellac disc: the Vitaphone system. Undaunted by the technological turmoil, Pavel Grigorevich Tager was pursuing in the Soviet Union his own research on a variable density soundtrack (1926); a few months later, Fox proudly presented Charles Lindbergh, Benito Mussolini, and George Bernard Shaw in their own words ('Movietone News', April 1927).

The race between soundtracks and phonograph records lasted for another eighteen months; by the end of 1927, sound on film prevailed. A brief but raging worldwide chaos engulfed the film industry. Producers hastily added soundtracks to films that had just been completed with no sound recordings; a similar fate befell reissues of dramatic features and slapstick comedies of the recent past, perceived all of a sudden as grotesquely remote by the very same people who once enjoyed them as silents. Within a few years, audiences would find it hard to believe that films could ever have existed in any other form than the 'talkies'.

Chapter 10

Collections

Fig. 187 A group of 35mm prints in a street shop. Mumbai, July 2017. Source: Courtesy of David Farris.

According to a dramatic formula adopted since the 1980s by the film community to raise awareness of the urgency to preserve the cinematic heritage, about 80 per cent of all silent films have been lost because of neglect, natural decay, and the intentional destruction of negatives and prints. After decades of research and painstaking efforts by archives and museums worldwide, the estimate should be revised in both a positive and a negative sense. The encouraging news comes from the International

Federation of Film Archives (its acronym, FIAF, stands for Fédération Internationale des Archives du Film), representing non-profit collecting institutions committed to safeguarding, restoring, and making accessible the history of cinema. As of March 2018, a database of silent films held by FIAF institutions listed 52,074 existing titles from the 1894 to 1929 period. Taking the presumed 160,000 silent films made during the silent era as a point of reference (p. 147), this means that close to one-third of them have now been rescued, albeit not necessarily preserved (Chart 4 illustrates their chronological range). Almost two-thirds are of European origin; together with those from North America, they account for more than 95 per cent of the total, as shown in Chart 5.

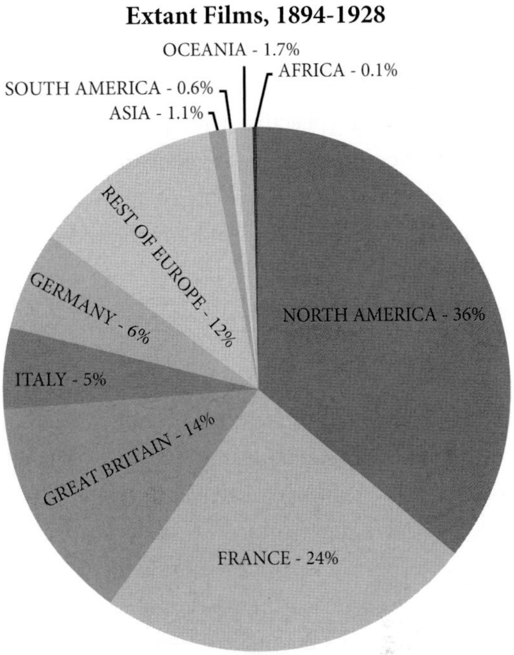

The inventory is by no means complete, as there are collections of silent films held outside the FIAF constituency; moreover, some FIAF affiliates do not contribute regularly to the database, or don't participate at all. On the other hand, the production of many silent films may not be documented yet, and not all the existing filmographies may have been taken into account. If both

Extant Films, 1894-1928

OCEANIA - 1.7%
AFRICA - 0.1%
SOUTH AMERICA - 0.6%
ASIA - 1.1%
REST OF EUROPE - 12%
GERMANY - 6%
ITALY - 5%
GREAT BRITAIN - 14%
NORTH AMERICA - 36%
FRANCE - 24%

Chart 5 Geographic distribution of surviving silent films, 1894–1928.

assumptions are correct, the two figures balance each other: there is a theoretical chance that one out of about every three films made during the silent era will be seen by a modern audience. If

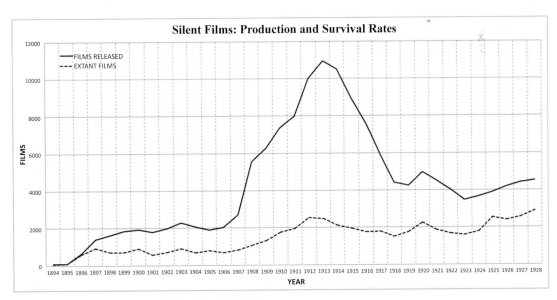

Chart 4 Estimated survival rate of silent films, 1894–1928.

one considers that fewer than 2,000 surviving titles were documented in 1962, the achievement of the FIAF community over half a century should be hailed as a collective triumph of initiative and perseverance. The many other titles held by for-profit companies contribute to an even more optimistic picture of the silent films rescued so far.

Destruction

The sheer number of film prints that suffered a very different fate starkly contradicts this reassuring outlook. Supposing that an average of fifty to eighty prints were struck for each film – a conservative guess, based on the comparative analysis of film distribution worldwide (p. 162) – it may be surmised that the number of copies made in the silent era ranged somewhere between 7,500,000 and 12,000,000 over three decades: even by picking the lower estimate as a point of reference, and by factoring in the multiple prints that exist for some films, the rate of survival drops to 0.43 to 0.69 per cent, an almost insignificant fraction of the total (it would be even lower if we included in the count all the amateur films and prints made for the non-theatrical market, whose numbers will probably never be ascertained), meaning that for every 1,000 prints made, at least 995 have disappeared. Multiply the above numbers by the footage of each film – from 20 metres, or 65 feet (Lumière and Edison), to 2,500 metres, or 8,000 feet (a feature film of the late silent era) – and we reach the astronomical figures of almost 40 billion feet or 12 million kilometres of film that went up in smoke, thirty times the distance between the earth and the moon – not even counting the film negatives.

Vague as it is, because of the number and magnitude of the variables involved, the estimate gives an eloquent idea of the fate suffered by nitrate prints after they ceased to be profitable to their owners. The destruction of silent cinema was a phenomenon of massive scale, compounded by the inherent fragility of the medium. In the frenzy of their working schedule, film projectionists were often unable or unwilling to spend the time necessary to properly care for projection prints, nor were they particularly interested in what happened to them after they had left the projection booth. They knew that prints were replaceable, and had little incentive to keep them in pristine condition, other than their own professional pride or the watchful eye of a responsible theatre manager. Defective, unclean, or poorly maintained projection equipment did the rest.

If handled with care, a nitrate or diacetate cellulose film could be shown hundreds of times without significant damage to the object and to the viewing experience; in reality, its useful commercial life was much shorter. It all depended, of course, on what distributors and exhibitors thought were the minimum standards required to keep their patrons pleased with the look of the pictures: in the United States, where image quality was regarded as a key factor of customer satisfaction in theatre management, a 1927 film was withdrawn from circulation after having been exhibited fifty-nine times on average, with a minimum of forty screenings and a maximum of seventy-five in mainstream theatres with qualified personnel committed to best practice. In the same year, a manual published in the Soviet Union (Nikolai Spiridovskii, *Gibel' filmy. Porcha filmy i mery preduprezdeniia*, p. 3) lamented that 'before World War I [a print] could be exhibited for a period between 250 and 300 days, while nowadays it lasts only for 134 days of screenings', at least twice the number of shows in North American venues. It's not that St Petersburg's projectionists were more competent than their comrades in San Francisco; in all likelihood, the margins of tolerance on what constituted an acceptable print were just very different.

Regardless of the country and the theatre's standards of excellence, a single screening could inflict irremediable harm to a print's emulsion without affecting the mechanical condition of the object (base and perforations); for most audiences of the silent film era, a heavy rain of scratches on the projected image was absolutely normal in second- and third-run picture houses. In those venues, worn-out prints were crudely patched with makeshift splices, staples, and sewing thread (when no splicer or cement was available), then exploited until they literally fell apart, making it impossible to run them through the projector's sprockets without posing a threat to safety in the projection booth and nearby auditorium. Despite the recurring pleas by authors of projection manuals (in the United States, Frank H. Richardson was particularly outspoken in this respect), the problem was so endemic as to inspire 'The Film Prayer', a one-page instructional sheet distributed in 1920 among exhibitors and film exchanges on both sides of the Atlantic (it was often placed inside film canisters): 'I am celluloid, not steel. O God of the machine, have mercy', the imploration goes. 'If a careless hand misthreads me, I have no alternative but to go to my death.'

A catalogue published in 1908 by the British company Walturdaw enumerates with clinical precision the most likely causes of print combustion: the film could break below the projection aperture; 'the feed mechanism may become jammed and inoperative; it may lose its hold on the film; the crank may become loose of the shaft of the feed mechanism, so that its turning will not feed the film forward'; a small piece of celluloid could be torn off the print 'and lodge in the projection aperture, where it will be exposed to the full heating effect of the light; or the operator may stop turning the crank of the film feed mechanism for any one of a variety of reasons'; the operator's attention could be 'suddenly distracted, and he may forget to keep the film feed mechanism in motion; or he may stop the feed of the film intentionally and neglect to cut off the light' (p. 27).

Decay

As pointed out by the anonymous writer in the Walturdaw catalogue, nitrate prints could burn during projection because of the 'intense heat produced where the light is condensed upon the film. This heat is sufficient to ignite the film at the projection aperture if the light is allowed to rest continuously upon one portion of the film for a few seconds.' The projector's aperture is the point where 'the film is most apt to take fire, and in almost every instance the ignition takes place because a portion of the film is held stationary at the projection aperture for a time.'

Chemistry teaches that the silent film heritage was also decimated through a natural process, with little or no human intervention. Because it is largely made of organic materials (animal bones and cotton), nitrate film stock starts shrinking and decomposing from the very moment it is manufactured. Its decay can be considerably delayed if the film is kept at a cold temperature and low relative humidity (the colder the environment, the better for the film, as long as fluctuations in temperature and humidity are kept to a minimum); otherwise, the pattern of spontaneous self-destruction can be slowed down, but is irreversible: hence the slogan 'nitrate won't wait', once fashionable among film curators.

Shortly after processing (as noted in film manuals of the 1910s), the nitrate cellulose stock begins to contract, both in length and width; when the shrinkage rate has exceeded 1.15 per cent, projection is already problematic because the distance between perforations has decreased beyond the tolerance of the steel sprockets' teeth in most projectors. Along its inevitable path to oblivion, nitrate film releases several gases – notably nitrogen dioxide – that interact with the surrounding air and with the water contained in the gelatin to form nitrous and nitric acids. The clusters of silver salts embedded in the emulsion are gradually corroded by these acids, with the ensuing destruction of the photographic images they once formed. As the emulsion begins to melt, the print emits an increasingly strong and pungent odour, vaguely reminiscent of camphor and chocolate; unwinding the sticky coils of a nitrate reel in this condition is a very bad idea, as the emulsion will detach itself from the base (there are methods for temporarily avoiding this in the laboratory, right before print duplication).

At this stage, the film still seems relatively intact: the external appearance of a nitrate print may not necessarily reveal that the worst has already occurred within the object (Fig. 188). It is only later in the process that decomposition manifests itself on the surface of the reel. When detected, it is pointless to proceed any further: the film footage underneath is almost certainly gone for ever. The rate at which all this happens is not at all uniform (even within the same reel), and is impossible to predict, but it is certain that high temperatures accelerate the chemical reaction: a film stored for decades in a hot and humid environment has fewer chances of surviving for long, even if transferred to storage vaults with the best possible climate control.

It all sounds like the grand finale of a cheap horror story. Bubbles of a dark, viscous matter (Plate 26a) appear in correspondence with the decomposing areas (sections treated with toning solutions are especially vulnerable); the dense lump gradually spreads all over the reel (Plate 26b) until it solidifies into a brown crust. In the terminal phases of decay, the film is reduced to a cylindrical brick, covered by a thick layer of very fine brownish powder (Plate 26c), or to a crumbling biscuit of white-yellow crystals (Plate 26d).

This gruesome picture should not be construed as a reason for avoiding archival prints altogether. There is no harm in handling nitrate film, as long as common sense is deployed and all the necessary precautions followed: this includes, among other things, avoiding flames and excessive heat

Fig. 188 *Elettra* (director unknown, Aquila Films, Italy, 1909). Frame enlargement from a decaying 35mm nitrate film fragment. Source: George Eastman Museum – Davide Turconi/Josef Joye Collection.

RULE 2

If you find a nitrate film, do not try to unwind it!
Contact a film museum or archive immediately.
Its staff will advise on how to handle it
without endangering yourself and the artefact.

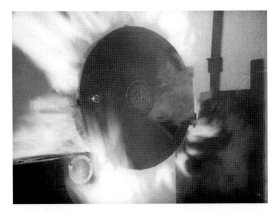

Fig. 189 Nitrate fire in a film projector, as demonstrated in *This Film Is Dangerous* (Ronald Haines, 1948). Frame enlargement from a 35mm triacetate positive. Source: Imperial War Museum.

in the inspection room. A nitrate film in mint condition ignites at a temperature of 170°C (338°F); a decomposing film can spontaneously burn at much lower temperatures, down to 41°C (105.8°F). When stored on a large scale in a very hot climate, in sealed cans, and no air exchange in the vaults, nitrate film can explode. There is absolutely no way to douse the flames, as the cellulose nitrate gives off the oxygen that feeds the fire even if submerged under water, covered in sand, or sprayed with extinguishers of any kind, whether using carbonic acid or other substances.

Two documentaries, *Das Verhalten von brennendem Nitrofilm gegenüber Löschmitteln* (1975), produced by the Österreichisches Filmarchiv, and *This Film Is Dangerous* (Ronald Haines, 1948), dramatically illustrate the destructive power of nitrate stock when it is not properly handled (Fig. 189). These films do not fully convey the extreme risks involved in being anywhere close to a large quantity of nitrate film if it bursts into flames. Frightening as it is because of its abruptness and violence, the fire in itself is not the main reason why you should beat a hasty retreat. The real danger comes from the deadly smoke emitted by the burning nitrocellulose: if inhaled, its toxic cloud can kill humans and animals

within minutes. Over the decades, countless prints of nitrate films were lost because of incompetence, neglect, irresponsible budgetary cuts, or exceptionally adverse circumstances. A chronological list of the worst catastrophes is included in Roger Smither's nitrate encyclopedia, also titled *This Film Is Dangerous* (2000); others have occurred since the publication of that book, such as the one that affected the Cinemateca Brasileira in São Paulo on 3 February 2016.

Before continuing the story of nitrate film, a very brief digression is in order regarding another troublesome aspect of film chemistry. The diacetate stock used in the silent era – mainly for the amateur market – is called 'safety film' because it is not as volatile as nitrate. Its base burns very slowly, and is difficult to ignite (even more so with triacetate film, which basically just melts). Much to their dismay, film archivists of the mid-1980s discovered that all acetate film is also subject to an irreversible decay process, known as 'vinegar syndrome' because of the strong acidic smell given off by the deteriorating film. Decomposing reels on a diacetate base tend to transform into multi-pronged stars (Plate 27a–b). In the final chapter of the 'safety' film's material life – this also applies to triacetate film stock of the sound period – the photographic emulsion remains more or less intact (contrary to what happens with nitrate film), but the cellulose base is so warped and crumbly that the chances of preserving a film in such a desperate condition are very slim.

Disposal

Newspapers, magazines, and journals of the silent era provide ample evidence of the many fires that occurred during motion picture shows, often with dramatized illustrations of the tragic fate that befell their victims. Health and safety concerns, however, had little (if anything) to do with the destruction of millions of silent film prints in the course of the twentieth century. The demise began because, until about 1907, anybody could buy film prints and do whatever they liked with them: fairground exhibitors, community leaders, and all sorts of entrepreneurs and even private citizens with no commercial intent only had to find a production company's catalogue, pick the titles they were interested in, have enough money to purchase the copies they wanted, and the films would become their sole property. They could edit, collate, exploit, keep, or discard the objects they purchased, at their own will, very much as they would with a book, a photograph, a printed music score, or the script of a theatre play.

That is exactly what they did, and explains why many piano and orchestral parts of Jacques Offenbach's operas were used to wrap grocery merchandise once they were no longer needed for public performances. Virtually no one thought of them as cultural objects deserving a repository of their own. They were not meant to last. They were disposable. A large number of silent films disappeared this way, without drama, as would be expected when dealing with any everyday tool of an ephemeral nature, like a newspaper, a pencil, or a tramway ticket. It should be pointed out that some 'junked' prints continued to be shown in semi-official or informal distribution contexts. As late as 1946, the Italian entrepreneur Roberto Pallme bought 35mm nitrate copies of silent films from local distributors and showed them to his family, neighbours, and war refugees in his house at Torre del Greco, near Naples. Incomplete or drastically altered versions of popular titles were exhibited in the Dutch East Indies, the Philippines, Persia, and other Middle Eastern countries, long after their original release (re-edited copies of *Intolerance* were shown in Tehran to glorify Cyrus II; in the Soviet Union, D.W. Griffith's epic was bestowed new title cards, turning it into an indictment of capitalism). The non-linear cultural life of

these prints constitutes an intriguing chapter in the history of global film circulation.

In theory, the film producers' initiatives in 1909 to replace the direct sale of projection copies with a rental regime under direct corporate control (Pathé had begun doing so in 1903) could have facilitated the survival of a greater number of films. Their fate was actually the opposite: the protocols discussed at the conferences in Paris were designed to give producers a greater degree of control over their products by removing battered copies from the market, withdrawing titles from circulation when they were no longer profitable, and creating an ongoing demand for new films; from Eastman Kodak's perspective, this was also an expedient way to make sure that fresh film stock would be requested from the company at a time of seemingly unstoppable growth in the industry. The business model was also advantageous to distributors, who became essential players in what looked like a perfect arrangement for all parties involved.

In their plans, obsolescence was a pivotal component of the overall scheme: the physical condition of a print mattered only insofar as it could generate revenue. After that, the 'film' asset was nothing but a cumulative 'print' liability, an impediment to the injection of new product, and a novelty turned stale in a world where a 1905 film was already regarded as old hat by 1908 standards. There were just too many old prints lying around projection booths. It was time to get rid of them and to instigate a more dynamic cycle of ever-changing supply.

The destruction of unwanted projection copies was not carried out methodically, but it certainly was presented with great pride in a news item published by *Ciné-Journal* (28 May 1910, p. 4): 'One of the main reasons for the current crisis in the film industry of our time is the existence of old, battered prints, unworthy of being projected any further.' According to the French magazine, 'it is in the best interest of exhibitors, of their public, and of the producers to gradually wipe out all such copies from the market. Is there a better way to do so than incineration?' To this end, a group of production companies that included Ambrosio, Éclair, Itala-Film, Lux, Raleigh & Robert, Vitagraph, and others 'has decided to undertake the progressive annihilation of those awful reels'.

To prove they meant business, some members of the consortium staged 'a bonfire of films rented in the past few months, now unsuitable for public exhibition … All filmmakers are strongly urged to come witness this voluntary *auto da fè*,' a flamboyant allusion to the burning of heretics during the Spanish Inquisition in the fifteenth century. *Ciné-Journal*'s article ended with an even more ominous metaphor: film destruction as 'a work of commercial hygiene'.

With his customary entrepreneurial acumen, Charles Pathé went even further, excusing himself from the fireworks display to take advantage of a recycling opportunity. In his memoirs, Pathé recalls the time when, following the Paris negotiations, he was trying to free himself from Eastman Kodak's supremacy in the production of motion picture stock. The manufacture of film base on an industrial scale required an amount of celluloid that was well beyond his means, both in terms of technology and the raw material required for such a project. 'In the following eighteen months,' writes Pathé, 'I asked my sales agents abroad to purchase all the copies of old films they could find. The prints had their gelatin scraped off the base, which was then re-emulsioned after polishing it to remove all scratches' (*Souvenirs et conseils d'un parvenu*, 1926, p. 119; reproduced in *Écrits autobiographiques*, 2006, p. 79).

Not at all pleased by Pathé's intentions, Eastman denounced to journalists the mediocre quality of rejuvenated stock (judging from the foggy brownish base of extant nitrate prints of this kind, he was absolutely right); undeterred, Pathé recycled almost 100,000 metres (300,000 feet) of nitrate base per day, with an estimated loss of one hundred thousand projection prints in one and a half years. He thus achieved his dual goal of finding the celluloid he needed, and of withdrawing all the outdated films from theatres and fairground halls worldwide to make room for new ones to be rented to the very same venues. As of 1909, half of the projection prints distributed by Pathé had been obtained from recycled material.

The cellulose emergency did not last for long. By 1912, after a series of tests conducted during the previous year, Pathé began manufacturing his own film stock, reaching a daily output of 170,000 metres (almost 560,000 feet), with no need to harvest used nitrate reels from around the world. The path to decimation of early silent cinema had only begun. Another surge of iconoclasm followed in the mid-1910s: the rise of feature-length films was a death sentence by proxy for thousands of shorts whose commercial value had become close to nil, with the notable exceptions of slapstick comedies, cartoons, and some non-fictional subjects. There was no incentive to keep newsreels, although the first signs of interest in stock footage material emerged in the course of World War I, mainly for political propaganda.

Still, this was nothing compared to what was about to happen at the dawn of sound film. By the mid-1930s, theatres solely equipped for the exhibition of silent films were on the verge of extinction. It took longer outside Western Europe and North America (silent cinema was especially resilient in Japan, China, India, and the Soviet Union), but production companies of the developed world did not waste time in clearing their vaults of all projection prints with no soundtracks, suddenly deprived of any value to their audiences, even if they had been made only a few months earlier. Some of these prints survived only because they were deemed suitable for so-called 'sonorization', a process involving the addition of music, noise effects, and sometimes voices, to a film originally produced as a silent; this is what happened to *Sunrise: A Song of Two Humans* (Friedrich Wilhelm Murnau, 1927), released in many North American theatres with a Movietone soundtrack (the full-frame version was distributed everywhere else).

Understandable as it was from a purely financial perspective, this modus operandi took its toll upon posterity. Most producers followed it to the bitter end by abandoning or destroying the negatives of their own films (true to himself, Méliès paved the way in an outburst of despair by burning them all in the garden of his property at Montreuil, in 1923), as they did with projection prints. Fortunately for us, a few companies behaved otherwise. They left the matrices alone for a variety of reasons, from mere procrastination to the remote hope of a residual profit in an unspecified future. While these negatives represent a minuscule percentage of the more than fifty thousand silent films resurrected so far, their survival should not be treated as a mere accident of history.

The Biograph Company kept the negatives of many one- and two-reelers of the 1908–12 period; some were reissued shortly afterwards, when feature-length films were emerging and the firm was on the brink of collapse (the negatives were later acquired by the Museum of Modern Art in New York). After all, these elements could be retained at a negligible expense to their owners: they did not take up much storage space, there was no reason to dispatch them to different locations over time, and they required no special maintenance. When the negatives of the British company Mitchell & Kenyon were found in 1994 at a demolition site, they occupied just three metal containers.

The camera negatives of the fiction silent films produced by AB Svensk Filmindustri, by its earlier incarnation AB Svenska Biografteatern, and by other Swedish studios it acquired in later years, were dutifully kept by their owners. To protect the matrices from potential harm while World War II was raging, the company moved them from downtown Stockholm to the suburban area of Aspudden, at Vinterviken, next to the Nobel plant for the manufacture of dynamite. Something went wrong in the inspection room of Svensk Filmindustri's warehouse. The entire collection went up in flames (Nobel had nothing to do with the disaster).

The fire happened on 22 September 1941. Ten years later, in February 1951, Eastman Kodak introduced its non-flammable triacetate film stock. In a promotional volume published in 1983, *The Book of Film Care* (p. 45), the company was adamant in its recommendation that 'when nitrate base negatives have been duplicated, they should be destroyed'. Banned in the projection booths of most countries, nitrate films were again regarded as a threat to public safety. Those allowed to keep the remaining copies were often asked to burn or recycle them after duplication onto another carrier. The practice, enforced in modern times at major collecting institutions such as the Gosfilmofond of Russia, the Library of Congress, the British Film Institute, and the Bundesarchiv in Berlin, resulted in the loss of unique nitrate prints that had so far been spared from annihilation in earlier decades.

It is very important to be clear on this point: silent films of historic or aesthetic significance have been saved in the form of facsimiles by the same cultural institutions that subsequently destroyed the originals. These institutions had previously rescued the artworks in their native form and could have kept them as such, had they wanted or had they been allowed to. It may be argued that some silent films could be classified as 'art' more than others, in which case we should revisit both film history and the history of art in general, beginning with those works made for reasons unrelated to what is called 'art': cave paintings, medieval icons, the films of Georges Méliès and his contemporaries. What survives to this day has been spared by human passivity, blissful neglect, and by people who thought that silent cinema deserved to have a future.

Rescue

When the organizers of a gala event held in celebration of Georges Méliès at the Grande Salle Pleyel in Paris on 16 December 1929 looked for films to be screened in honour of the rediscovered genius of early cinema, all they could find was a handful of 35mm prints, including *A Trip to the Moon* (as shown in Chapter 12, we know exactly which nitrate copy of this title was screened for the event). None of these prints came from archives or museums, because there were no institutions of this kind at the time. The nitrate reels had been found by individuals who acquired them in flea markets, or from retired fairground exhibitors, often at risible prices. They bought them for the same reason why others might acquire an old gramophone, an atlas from the nineteenth century, a curious piece of furniture, an anonymous painting, or a music manuscript. They were collectors. Without them, the history of silent cinema would largely be written *in absentia* of its most important objects.

Film preservation as a cultural enterprise is the outcome of these people's own initiative. In the only general history of film archives and museums published so far (*Les Cinémathèques*, 1983), film curator Raymond Borde chronicles the many aborted attempts since the 1900s to set up entities of this kind, mostly in Europe. They all failed because they were designed as institutions from the start, noble aspirations translated into action by decree, without a curatorial driving force behind them. The earliest advocates of film preservation were filmmakers: W.K.L. Dickson was the first, in his book *History of the Kinetograph, Kinetoscope*

and Kinetophonograph (1895): 'The advantages to students and historians' derived from keeping a record of notable events, he wrote, 'will be immeasurable. Instead of dry and misleading accounts, tinged with the exaggerations of the chroniclers' minds, our archives will be enriched by the vitalized pictures of great national scenes' (pp. 51–2).

In the same vein, British pioneer Robert William Paul should be credited as the founder of the first film repository. It apparently consisted of one nitrate reel. In a letter dated 21 July 1896, he requested that the British Museum includes his own 'animated photographs' of London as part of its permanent collection. The museum took only one print, together with Paul's instructions on how to protect it (in a sealed box – not a good idea to begin with – with an engraved metal plate reproducing the film's title). No further exchange is known to have occurred between the institution and the first activist in the history of film preservation.

Throughout the silent film era, private endeavours and the impersonal rules of collecting bodies remained at odds. Archives of long-standing tradition such as the Bibliothèque Nationale in Paris and the Library of Congress were given the task of acquiring films as creative works, but they agreed to do so mainly for legal reasons (understandably, the Bibliothèque Nationale was happy to relinquish this duty to other institutions as soon as possible). Bolesław Matuszewski, a Polish photographer who had worked in France, wrote in 1898 two seminal articles for the newspaper *Le Figaro* – later reprinted as separate booklets – where the key principles of film preservation are outlined with extraordinary foresight.

In Matuszewski's view, cinematic works should be given to the care of public institutions, and made accessible to all in projected form. Original negatives would be conserved as a matter of priority, through an agreed protocol for mandatory legal deposit to be promoted and executed by all national governments. Matuszewski's texts (*Une Nouvelle source de l'histoire, création d'un dépôt de cinématographie historique* and *La Photographie animée, ce qu'elle est, ce qu'elle doit être*) drew favourable comments without having the slightest effect at the time of their publication. Thirty years elapsed before Matuszewski's ideas found expression in the work of others who may have never heard his name. They probably had only a generic notion of what an archive for cinema should look like. Many were cinephiles, students, and aspiring filmmakers.

Many years earlier, however, when silent cinema was a blossoming industry, others had begun to collect prints of silent films with totally different goals. Jean Desmet was a Dutch film distributor who kept in his warehouse about a thousand nitrate prints of films from the 1906–15 period. He was reluctant to let them go after their commercial exploitation. Desmet's decision to retain his copies was inspired by a mixture of prudence, avarice, and hope that they could still earn him some profit in the future. When he made a fortune in the real-estate business, the nitrate prints stayed with him as cherished toys until his death in 1956.

Another case in point was that of Jesuit abbé Josef-Alexis Joye (1852–1919), who in the early 1900s acquired a large number of prints from the second-hand market in his native country of Switzerland, and in Germany. The films were used for his lectures at the Borromäum, an educational institution he had established in 1898 to support the local Catholic community. Joye treated the prints as instructional tools to be used in his Sunday classes to orphans, working-class families, and recent émigrés in his parish. By virtue of Joye's charitable efforts, one of the major sources for the study of early cinema is now available (most of the surviving elements are held at the BFI's National Archive; a vast collection of original nitrate frames from the same prints, assembled by Davide Turconi, is preserved at the George Eastman Museum).

The stories of Jean Desmet and Josef Joye are only two of the many instances in the early chronicles of film collecting: Kawakita Kashiko in Japan, Albert Fidelius and Gerhard Lamprecht in Germany, Mario Ferrari and Maria Adriana Prolo in Italy, James Card and William K. Everson in the United States, John and William Barnes in Great Britain, Henri Langlois in France, Vladimir Pogačić in Yugoslavia, and Einar Lauritzen in Sweden are among the most eminent champions of the collective effort to save the silent film heritage, but they represent a minuscule avant-garde within the much larger community of people who spent their lives in retrieving and caring for the same flammable reels that were so feared, ignored, or despised by everyone else.

Shelters

Most of the scattered attempts to establish official repositories for film in the course of the silent era had shared Matuszewski's emphasis on cinema as a visual chronicle of the world (notable places, events, personalities). This was also the view of George Bernard Shaw, who suggested in 1915 that it may also be beneficial to match the camera's views with sound recordings; and of actress Sarah Bernhardt, who saw cinema as an opportunity to keep a durable trace of her performances.

This approach was expressed by the core mission of the Arkiv for Films og Fonogrammer in Copenhagen, founded in 1913 with the declared aim to produce 'living portraits of famous people, whose historical value is worth transmitting to posterity', and of the film collection at the Imperial War Museum in London, where documents and images of military operations were the exclusive focus of interest. The separation of fictional and non-fictional films as objects of preservation was enforced by national governments throughout the twentieth century, and continues to this day in many countries (Rossijskij gosudarstvennij arhiv kino-fotodokumentov, a Russian State Documentary Film and Photo Archive at Krasnogorsk, is distinct from the Gosfilmofond of Russia, located in Belye Stolby; the original elements of Dziga Vertov's silent films are at Krasnogorsk).

Much of the credit for a more ecumenical approach to the preservation of film history (with no distinction between fiction and non-fiction, art or document) must be ascribed to collectors and film lovers with a strong emotional investment in the objects of their passion. Bengt Idestam-Almquist, a Swedish journalist who signed his writings under the pseudonym 'Robin Hood', co-founded what may be considered the first film archive in the modern sense of the term. He created the Svenska Filmfundet with his friend Lenny Stackell, later joined by two young cine-philes, Gunnar Lundquist and Einar Lauritzen, whose methodical work ethics and research skills quickly turned an amateur's adventure into a small but efficient institute for film conservation.

Josef Goebbels, Propaganda Minister of the Third Reich, was also an avid and competent cine-phile. A great admirer of Eisenstein and of Soviet cinema in general, he was determined to persuade Adolf Hitler that a national archive of cinema was urgently in order: in a decree issued on 18 December 1933, he prohibited the destruction of any 'negative film, whether fiction, non-fiction, cultural, educational, advertising, sound or silent, without explicit authorization' from the competent authorities. Goebbels' perseverance was rewarded with the creation of the Reichsfilmarchiv, inaugurated on 29 January 1934 with a core collection of 1,200 titles 'of historic and cultural value'. In the same year, the VGIK film school in Moscow began collecting fiction films to be used in its educational

programmes: VGIK's fast-growing archive of nitrate prints eventually became part of what is currently known as the Gosfilmofond of Russia.

The archival projects launched in Sweden, Germany, and the Soviet Union were preludes to an avalanche of landmark events in 1935, an *annus mirabilis* in the resurrection of silent cinema. Three years after the publication in Great Britain of a report titled *The Film in National Life* (1932), by a favourable turn of events (Parliament had no specific 'vision' on the subject), the House of Commons gave the newly born British Film Institute the mandate to establish a collection of prints to be preserved or made available for screening. Initially called the National Film Library, the entity was later renamed the National Film Archive (it is now called the BFI National Archive). Its overall collection as of September 1936, after a year of activity, consisted of 807 reels: 275 titles (241 of which had been produced in the silent era, almost 90 per cent of the total) 'for permanent preservation' – corresponding to 727 reels – and 58 films (80 reels), mostly educational shorts, for non-commercial exhibition (only to BFI full members, and exclusively for classrooms and film societies). Thirteen of these, all silent films, were copied from the 'preservation' list.

Like the Reichsfilmarchiv, the National Film Library was run entirely with public funds; its young archivist, Ernest Lindgren, was well aware of the need to achieve a careful balance between cultural vision, empirical knowledge, and account-ability in a discipline whose parameters had not yet been clearly drawn. He is now celebrated as one of the founders of film curatorship as a profession. The first curator of the Film Department at MoMA in New York, Iris Barry, was also British. Her collection policy (17 April 1935) issued at the inception of MoMA's Film Department – it was co-signed by her husband John E. Abbott, Director of the museum's Film Library – put a strong emphasis on the artistic significance of the works to be acquired, the quality of their preservation elements, and the importance of presenting film history in a global perspective.

The year 1935 also marked the founding of a film society called Cercle du Cinéma, the brainchild of two young cinephiles in Paris. Georges Franju and Henri Langlois were, respectively, 23 and 21 years old. Asked for advice, film scholar Jean Mitry suggested that it would be good to acquire classics of cinema to be exhibited over time in a dedicated venue. Mitry had already tried to establish a film archive in 1927, to no avail. Franju and Langlois had better luck, thanks to the financial support of Paul-Auguste Harlé, editor of a trade journal: the Cinémathèque française was officially registered on 9 September 1936 as a private non-profit association.

Jean Mitry agreed to be in charge of the film collection, but it soon became clear that Langlois was the entrepreneurial soul of the new entity. Langlois' formidable energy, diplomatic skills, and personal charisma brought the Cinémathèque française to a prominent position in the fast-growing community of film archives and museums. The effects of Langlois' whirlwind proselytism to the cause of cinema would soon be felt at the international level. A major consequence of his efforts – aside from the steady progress in the rediscovery of silent films – was the flourishing of a cinephiles' network around the globe, with the ensuing creation of film archives in countries where many collectors like Langlois had been operating in relative isolation, unaware of what their European and North American colleagues were doing.

This sudden awakening of interest in cinema as a source of cultural history prompted a flurry of initiatives in the second half of the 1930s. Inspired by the example of VGIK, the Fascist regime in Italy had given birth to a national filmmaking school, incorporated within the Centro Nazionale

di Cinematografia on 13 April 1935; to assist the students in their courses, film scholars Luigi Chiarini, Umberto Barbaro, and Francesco Pasinetti provided them with a 35mm film library (mostly of silent films) of considerable size and scope, tragically dispersed at the time of the Nazi occupation in 1943. A silent film star of Mexican cinema, Helena Sánchez Valenzuela, received in 1936 a presidential mandate to run the Filmoteca Nacional, only to see her efforts thwarted by the political regime that came to power soon after the appointment (undaunted, Sánchez toured South America to promote the cause of film preservation). The Cinémathèque Royale de Belgique/Koninklijk Filmarchief, a dominant force in the film preservation community after World War II, was born in 1938 thanks to the joint efforts of a documentary filmmaker (Henri Storck), a film critic (André Thirifays), and a left-wing politician (Pierre Vermeylen).

Almost half a century of cinema had elapsed in the meantime. By 1942, when the Library of Congress had begun to receive 35mm film prints of American films on a systematic basis for the purposes of copyright registration, much of the world's silent film heritage had already disappeared. Film museums, archives, and schools were eagerly safeguarding what was left of it; their ranks included administrators, scholars, technicians, and other professional or amateur practitioners committed to its future survival. Many of them were collectors, too, but that did not prevent them from talking to each other with the vocabulary of film curatorship. Once they understood that they all wanted one and the same thing, their leaders felt the need to strike an alliance.

Institutions

When film archivists began exchanging notes on what they were doing, it did not take long for them to find strong similarities in their respective situations. All of them had started from scratch, with no established curatorial tradition to rely upon, scarcely noticed by public opinion, often with limited resources and scant technical knowledge. A legal vacuum surrounded film as an object of preservation and cultural use: collecting institutions were acquiring other people's creative works without asking their permission. The prints were, in a sense, what may be called 'abandoned property', but this did not automatically grant the right to exhibit them to the public. Archival holdings initially consisted of a very small number of titles, mainly domestic productions; important as they were, their chronological and geographic scope was not wide enough to provide an accurate record of film history as a whole. Langlois, Barry, Lundquist, and their colleagues needed each other to fill the gaps.

Shortly after the formation of the Reichsfilmarchiv, the Nazi regime hosted an International Film Congress in Berlin from 25 April to 1 May 1935, attended by a thousand delegates from the film industry. Twenty-four nations were represented (unsurprisingly, several others had boycotted the event). Discussions held within a working group on film preservation at the conference resulted in a call for action, which included 'the setting-up of a film repository in each country for the collection of films of cultural, educational, and scientific value or showing the development of film art'. The memorandum also urged producers in each country to 'deliver a free copy of each of their films to the Repository. Each Repository would compile a catalogue of educational films and the various repositories would have contact with one another.'

In a crucial coda to the memorandum drafted by the preservation committee, it was stated that 'as far as possible, a copy of all films produced in the respective countries, educational and otherwise, should be kept'. The message could not have been clearer. The fact that it had been promulgated in a country ruled by a dictatorial regime could not be ignored; nevertheless, Iris Barry and John Abbott included Berlin in their European trip during the summer of 1936, carefully planned with the intent of meeting colleagues around the continent, gathering information on cinematic holdings in various countries, and acquiring projection copies for MoMA's fledgling Film Library. It was an eventful journey, for them and for the cause of film preservation.

Their itinerary covered all the cities and institutions where the history of cinema – that is, silent cinema – had become a matter of cultural concern. They visited the National Film Library in London (and met Lindgren, whom they liked), the Svenska Filmfundet in Stockholm, and the Reichsfilmarchiv, where they met its first director, Frank Hensel. They also went to Moscow, where they were confronted with the ideological differences between the United States and the Soviet Union; they then reached Paris, and were warmly greeted by Langlois and Franju, who were seeking an opportunity to expand the Cinémathèque française's holdings of American cinema.

Barry and Abbott were equally hopeful that their mission would result in the acquisition of European films for MoMA; unimpressed by their experience in Moscow and Stockholm, they found more responsive interlocutors in Hensel, Langlois, and in Olwen Vaughan, the BFI's Secretary since 1935 (Lindgren was too much of a junior staff member to take part in the negotiations). The four institutions they represented agreed to exchange some prints on a trial basis, and it all worked fairly well: Abbott did not fail to notice that the twenty-nine copies of German films received from the Reichsfilmarchiv were impeccable, as opposed to the battered prints received from the other collections.

Galvanized by the results of their collaborative experiment, Vaughan, Hensel, Abbott, and

Langlois met again in Paris at the end of May 1938. After two further meetings in June, FIAF came into being (although the agreement was signed on 17 June, the creation of FIAF was not publicly announced until the end of October, as all parties wanted the approval of their respective administrations or governments). It was agreed that FIAF would coordinate all the activities related to safeguarding the cinematic heritage; foster the development of film collections and related artefacts (stills, posters, scripts, set designs) among the Federation's members; encourage the creation of film archives in other countries, thus expanding FIAF's institutional network; promote and facilitate research on the history of the medium; and guarantee the free circulation and exchange of prints within the archival community.

The latter objective was admittedly the main focus of interest for Abbott and Langlois, who were looking for a legitimate framework in which to pursue their efforts to strengthen MoMA's film collection. The five points of FIAF's charter were preceded by the clause that membership was reserved exclusively to non-profit archives and museums: this was both a legal precaution and a political message to the film industry, the implicit assurance that neither FIAF nor their affiliates intended to challenge the rights of copyright owners.

The founding members of FIAF had different opinions on how to inform the public of their initiatives. Most of them took for granted that FIAF affiliates with an exhibition programme had the option, but not the obligation, to explain to their audiences where they had obtained the prints. Langlois was resolute in demanding that any information about the holdings of the Cinémathèque française would be restricted to the Federation's members (confidentiality was a cornerstone of FIAF's statutes and rules). The very use of the word 'access' in FIAF's internal proceedings met

the fiercest resistance until the early 1990s: in a 'Manual for Access to Film Collections' published in FIAF's *Journal of Film Preservation* at the end of December 1997, active access was still defined from the viewpoint of the archive, with 'the selection of films put together according to its own agenda (programming)', while 'passive access means that the archive generally waits until an individual or a group approaches it with a list of requests' (p. 6).

In sharp contrast with Langlois' concerns, the BFI's film cataloguing unit published between 1960 and 1966 a three-volume set on the National Film Archive's holdings of silent films. One of the greatest film historians of all time, Jay Leyda, worked with FIAF in the same decade to create a union catalogue of silent short films. Since its beginnings, the soul of the Federation had multiple incarnations: the film archive in service of its citizens (BFI) and of the national interest (Reichsfilmarchiv); the film museum as a cultural forum (Cinémathèque française) and a showcase of artistic achievements (MoMA). Despite all the overlaps and cross-pollinations, the four genetic codes remain at the core of all institutions where moving images are protected and exhibited on a non-commercial basis. The two main collecting strands are also still there: preserving all films of a certain kind (the archive), and selecting the best or the most representative (the museum).

When the four godparents of film preservation met in Paris, the world was heading towards a tragedy of unprecedented scale. Frank Hensel was talking to people from countries that were about to become enemies; upon his return to the United States after signing the FIAF protocol, Abbott had to confront a delegate from Will H. Hays – President of the Motion Picture Producers and Distributors of America – and justify his involvement with the Reichsfilmarchiv. The greatest achievement of FIAF's pioneers, and their most enduring legacy, is the unwavering non-political stance they adopted in all the debates and deliberations on how to preserve film, at a time of enormous upheaval in the international community. After 1945, when the Cold War was raging, film archivists and curators from the communist bloc were allowed to travel with relative freedom in and out of Western Europe and North America. Their colleagues from other countries could attend FIAF meetings in Moscow, Sofia, Budapest, and East Berlin, where the Staatliches Filmarchiv der DDR hosted the first school of film preservation.

Since then, the number of collecting institutions dedicated to film has grown exponentially. Many other regional, national, and multinational associations are now pursuing the same aspirations that Lindgren, Langlois, and their eminent contemporaries (from Jacques Ledoux at the Cinémathèque Royale de Belgique to Jerzy Toeplitz in Poland, Sam Kula and Robert Daudelin in Canada, and Manuel Martínez Carril in Uruguay) had nurtured in the formative years of the Federation. Rather than treating them as heroes of a nostalgic past, it would be more appropriate to recognize how much cinema they managed to save, with no formal background and no teachers other than themselves and their peers. FIAF was their only professional outlet, a window onto the world of film preservation. For purely chronological reasons, much of what these explorers of the cinematic legacy managed to save for posterity belongs to the silent film era, which is why they deserve to be mentioned here.

Collectors

An unspoken but noticeable point of disagreement among the first members of FIAF was the ultimate purpose of their mission. The field was almost evenly split between opposite viewpoints on what film archives and museums should do: for some, including Langlois and his colleague James Card (the first film curator at what was then called George Eastman House), films were to be saved in order to be exhibited, with the collecting institution as the learned arbiter of public taste; for Lindgren, Ledoux, and others, preservation came first – ideally, this was a prerequisite of their availability for public screening and bona fide research. Lindgren, in particular, was often mocked for wanting to preserve films for a 'posterity' that was always perceived as being many decades away.

Those who tried to reconcile the two positions could find themselves on a collision course with one faction or the other; only Ledoux was successful in giving equal weight to both imperatives. He did so at the expense of his personal relationship with Langlois, whom he regarded as an egocentric maniac; when the French filmmakers of the nouvelle vague (François Truffaut, Alain Resnais, Claude Chabrol among them) sent him a telegram in March 1968, asking to join them in the protest against Langlois' expulsion from the Cinémathèque française, Ledoux drafted a terse response: 'If you were able to watch cinema in Brussels it is because I am not the Langlois of Belgium. A film archive belongs to the public, not to a collector. Down with the cult of personality. Down with the Langlois mythology.'

Langlois was not the exclusive target of Ledoux's indictment: his outrage was directed against those who, in his opinion, were treating film copies as their private possessions by misusing the power that derives from a position of leadership in a film archive or museum (Ledoux was a tyrant in his institution, but no one could accuse him of putting himself above the collection). Many curators of the first generation began as collectors; unable or unwilling to establish an emotional distance from the objects bequeathed to the care of a cultural institution, they maintained their former habits and disregarded conflict of interest as an unnecessary nuisance. Film collectors were often driven in equal measure by their own predilection for certain genres, performers, or periods of film history, as well as by an unquenchable instinct for secrecy, exacerbated by an inherent mistrust of bureaucracy and the corporate world in particular. Aware that many films in their possession were under copyright, they operated at the margins of legality at a time when the material ownership of a print could be construed as a crime. It was also a collector's habit to make copies of theatrical films in amateur formats, as they were easier to project, occupied less storage space, and could be exchanged at lower shipping and laboratory costs.

The illegal reproduction of copyrighted films was punishable with a jail sentence, but this did not dissuade collectors from saving thousands of titles that would otherwise have been lost for ever. All they could afford to do, unfortunately, was to duplicate them on prints of lesser quality than the originals. Preservation was part of their vocabulary only in the broadest sense of the term: primarily, what they wanted was to have physical control of the film reels and to project them at will, either for their own pleasure or for their audiences. The schizophrenic bond between collectors and curatorship starts here, in this clash of competing goals over the same object of desire.

From the collectors' perspective, the film archive was an unwelcoming place where their passion would be frozen in a heartless grid of rules and procedures aimed at preventing people from enjoying cinema. Archivists and curators reciprocated in spades, looking down on cinephiles' amateurish behaviour as the opposite of the discipline and rationality required by the new profession. For many years, MoMA regarded 16mm reduction copies as non-collection material, good only for circulation in classrooms and other non-theatrical

venues; in retaliation, private collectors lamented the gradual deterioration of MoMA's stunning tinted and toned nitrate print of *A Kiss for Cinderella* (Herbert Brenon, 1925), praising film collector and historian William K. Everson for having made a 16mm copy from it before it was too late. When both parties finally resumed a more constructive dialogue in the 1990s, many opportunities for a fruitful alliance had already been lost.

Production companies did very little, if anything, to save their silent films until the 1970s. This sad appraisal may be given a positive twist by acknowledging that some producers refrained from destroying their assets, thus contributing to film preservation through inaction. Gaumont and Pathé had the foresight to build nitrate film vaults in the suburbs of Paris, but had limited success in protecting their early flammable elements (Léon Gaumont also tried to preserve his film equipment, largely destroyed after a corporate meltdown). Other major firms went as far as allowing 16mm duplication of some titles, as occurred with *The River* (Frank Borzage, 1929) and *Beggars of Life* (William A. Wellman, 1928) before the nitrate elements disappeared.

Collectors, archives, and museums are responsible for the survival of the vast majority of the silent films we can see today. The corporate world belatedly woke up in the last quarter of the twentieth century, realizing that the assets were silent but not worthless after all. At that point, collecting institutions were invited, asked, or forced to open their vaults and make copyrighted films available again for commercial purposes. Silent cinema as a fringe benefit of the home video business was often the result of work done by others, at their own expense and risk, over many decades. More often than not, legal rights owners are harvesting a soil that had been patiently tilled by someone else, at a time when hardly anybody in the industry cared about it.

Chapter 11

Evidence

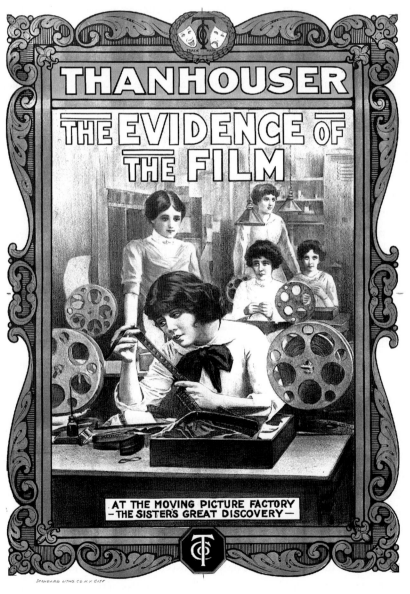

Fig. 190 Promotional poster for *The Evidence of the Film* (Edwin Thanhouser and Lawrence Marston, 1913). Lithograph on paper. Source: Private collection.

Much of what we know about silent cinema comes from the direct experience of the films themselves: to understand what they mean, we should watch as many as possible. There is, however, a wide array of other resources that provide us with important information on what those films are, how and why they were made, the ways in which they were distributed, the intended or involuntary consequences of their exhibition for culture, economy, and society. It is possible to do research on silent cinema without ever seeing a silent film, although there is a severe risk that the knowledge derived from this kind of enquiry will be hampered by the absence of its ultimate point of reference. When studying the demographics of film audiences in a given territory, it would be good to have at least an impression of what kind of works were shown in the film theatres of that area. Familiarity with their interior design is not a requirement for studying camera placement in early cinema, but a formal analysis of fiction films made before the feature-length era would probably benefit from a basic awareness of seating arrangements in a typical picture house of the period. The more we learn about the context, the better.

The assortment of documents and objects known and available for scrutiny in this field has become so vast that no single person can examine them all in detail; as the tools for scholarly enquiry become more sophisticated, new documentation resources keep emerging, with their wealth of invaluable data. A preliminary distinction between two kinds of research tools may be of some guidance in this seemingly endless ocean of information. The raw facts gathered from the creative works (including, but not limited to, images, objects, and written words) made in the period being considered – in our case, the years from the 1890s to the late 1920s – constitute the traces of a past we are trying to make sense of, primary

evidence collected and arranged in an orderly fashion for the sake of translating the traces into concepts. The later attempts by others (through books, articles, memoirs, letters, interviews, and other reports in various forms) to describe or explain these facts is secondary evidence that improves, corrects, or disproves our perception of the past. A tinted and toned nitrate print, a silent film theatre still standing, a Kinemacolor projector, a manuscript letter by its inventor, and a 1912 film catalogue are all pieces of primary evidence; a black and white duplicate of the same nitrate print, a journalist's interview in 1955 with the owner of a picture palace, an essay on the Kinemacolor process are examples of secondary sources.

In our domain of enquiry, primary and secondary sources are defined by their chronological terms of reference. A journal entry by Abel Gance about his first trip to the United States is a primary source for Gance's biography, and a secondary source on the people and places he visited; the history of cinema published by Maurice Bardèche and Robert Brasillach in 1935 is by all means a secondary source about the silent films they had seen, but it is very much a primary source on French film criticism and historiography and its relation to right-wing ideology. Similarly, the recorded soundtrack of a live music performance for Murnau's *Sunrise* is a primary source on silent film music because it was actually heard by audiences of the period when the film was released; it is also a pale acoustic rendition of what the performance by the Roxy Theatre Orchestra must have been for those who witnessed it, and in this sense it should be considered a secondary source.

For the purposes of this book, priority is given here to the basic primary and secondary sources commonly used in film studies and curatorial work about silent cinema, with the awareness that they are only signposts of a much larger, more intricate, and culturally diverse atlas of the cinematic event.

Just as all good maps should have an index, it is useful to look at how each silent film is given a name, a birth date, the name of its parents (when known), and has a story to tell. These identity cards, and the family trees they are attached to, are the stuff filmographies are made of.

Stories

For more than five years after Edison and Lumière began to sell their films, projection prints had no main credits. To promote their works, production companies distributed catalogues of the titles available to exhibitors, first in the form of flyers and brochures with minimal information, then with booklets – sometimes updated on a periodical basis – with photographs and descriptions of the films, mostly consisting of plot summaries or explanations of the events depicted for the screen. The aim of the synopses was twofold: persuading the exhibitor to purchase a copy of the film, and providing the means to advertise it to its potential audiences. The page reproduced in Fig. 191 shows an entry from the Pathé catalogue (German edition) of November 1907, one of the largest to appear in the early years of cinema. Pathé consistently adhered to a narrative style based on neutrality and restraint, more so than many competitors. Other company writers (often the filmmakers themselves) had no hesitation in touting the pictorial or dramatic qualities of the film on offer, often resorting to lyricism and hyperbole to embellish a storyline that could otherwise be reduced to a much shorter text.

Second to none in the art of illusions, Georges Méliès resorted to elaborate and often humorous rhetoric to single out the virtues of his numerous trick films, occasionally drawing the reader's attention to their technical innovations or virtuosity. Longer texts by other film producers, also used for inclusion in copyright records, bloated the

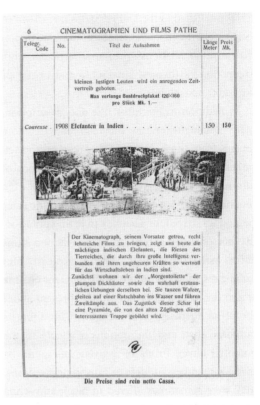

Fig. 191 *Les Éléphants de l'Inde* (Pathé, 1907) in the German edition of a Pathé catalogue, November 1907, p. 6. Source: Stiftung Deutsche Kinemathek, Berlin.

narrative to the point of expounding background events, motivations, and emotions nowhere to be found in the actual film. Poetic licence, a frequent prerogative of film catalogues and bulletins in circulation until the early 1910s, turned the film synopsis into a small literary genre in itself. Here is the seed of a dual phenomenon that was about to emerge with the rise of multi-reel films: the film series derived from mass literature (Louis Feuillade's *Fantômas*, 1913), and the motion picture converted into a derivative text, presented either as a stand-alone volume or in episodic form for newspapers and popular magazines. In a further twist of cross-pollination between the moving image and the written word, imaginary characters involved in filmmaking or filmgoing activities (such as the Motion Picture Girls, in a series published in the United States from 1914 to 1916) were the juvenile heroes in popular fiction that bore no relationship to any particular film, except for its themes, situations, and exotic or perilous atmospheres.

In addition to the film's title and description, many catalogue entries included one or more images from the film (normally taken on the set, rather than from the film itself). The names of filmmakers, writers, and members of the cast were mentioned only on rare occasions, but some early catalogues strived for accuracy in listing noteworthy personalities appearing in non-fiction films about sports and politics. What makes early film catalogues so useful in the study of silent cinema is also the factual information they present about the prints themselves: the length of the film; its purchase cost; and the options available to the potential buyer. Prints of a given title could be made with either Lumière or Edison perforations; they were sometimes offered in black and white copies or in hand-coloured or stencilled versions (at a higher price).

For high-budget productions, the Star-Film catalogue went as far as to specify their running time, thus offering precious evidence of the recommended projection speed. Like most other companies, Méliès assigned a sequential number to each film he made (with few exceptions): his indexing system was slightly more elaborate, as it attributed one number to each 20 metres (65 feet) of film; longer films were therefore given two or more numbers. For instance, the catalogue entry for *Les Fromages automobiles* (*The Skipping Cheeses*, 1907), 80 metres (260 feet) in length, is accompanied by the numbers 925–928. The importance of these and other reference codes in print identification will be further considered in Chapter 14.

Major companies arranged their catalogues by genres (their denominations and properties changed in the course of time, as seen in Chapter 7). Over the years, certain titles could be withdrawn from circulation, or the numbering system changed. To avoid confusion, Biograph, Pathé, and others devised an even simpler way of ordering prints, consisting of a single code word attributed to each title. As purchases were often made via telegraph, one word per title saved the client money, and simplified the negotiations between exhibitors and print providers: a cable to Pathé with the words 'Baba', 'Appétit', and 'Avide' meant that the client was looking for *Arrivée d'un train en gare* (1900), *Roman d'amour* (*Love Story*, 1904), and *Le Langage des fleurs* (*The Language of Flowers*, 1905). With the rise and rapid growth of exhibitors' trade press from the mid-1900s, film catalogues gradually surrendered their former role to journals: by 1915, they were a thing of the past for owners and managers of picture houses or print exchanges. Not so in the non-theatrical business, where catalogues of films available in abridged versions for amateur formats continued to be published on a regular basis well into the 1920s.

Periodicals

When film exhibition began the shift from its itinerant life in fairgrounds and vaudeville houses to more permanent venues, a new and fast-growing community of professionals felt the need to have a forum for debate, promotion, and information on a regular basis. Until then, their concerns had found limited room in the printed columns of existing periodicals dedicated to popular theatre and music; by 1907, however, these outlets were no longer adequate to the demands of a rapidly expanding business. Within two years, all countries where there was a film industry had at least one weekly, bi-weekly, or monthly publication devoted exclusively to its activities. They were trade journals in the strictest sense of the term, with theatre owners and entrepreneurs as their intended readership. Value judgements about recent films appeared in those pages mainly to highlight their performance at the box office. The bulk of editorial content was dedicated to brief production and exhibition reports, equally succinct news items on matters of technology, public education, safety or censorship regulations, theatre management.

The core element of attraction for subscribers was the list of new releases issued by production companies and distributors on a more or less regular basis, following a format similar or almost identical to the one used in corporate film catalogues. For some time, the reputation of a trade journal was largely measured by the amount of space allocated to this section. Many producing and distributing firms would also publish one or more pages of paid advertisements, often with lists of recent releases. Over time, plot summaries were integrated and eventually accompanied or replaced by commentaries. Whether they were signed with real names, pseudonyms, or mere initials, their authors soon emerged as influential voices in the expanding galaxy of film criticism. Some writers became film practitioners – mostly as screenwriters – or at least garnered a wider reputation as authorities in their respective areas of expertise, from dramaturgy to technical matters. Reviews of new films could include observations on the quality of projection, with particular emphasis in the early years on the plague of image unsteadiness.

Despite their original aim to serve mainly as publicity outlets for the film industry, the circulation of trade journals grew to the point of attracting non-specialist readers. Their eager attention to news items on forthcoming films and leading personalities of the big screen contributed to the rise of the star system, as seen in the numerous letters addressed to the journals' editors, published in dedicated sections of expanding length and importance from the early 1910s. It is through these texts that the influence of film as a harbinger of cultural change can be observed in all its magnitude, as much as in the elaborate designs of those pages where motion picture celebrities and their new productions were presented with great fanfare. At a time when film literature mostly consisted of manuals for projection technicians and amateur performers or writers, trade journals were living encyclopedias of cinema in its making, multifaceted and often exhilarating mirrors of an ongoing dialogue between the artists, the producers, the exhibitors, and their customers.

Next to the films themselves, these publications are the best sources of knowledge for those who wish to acquire a comprehensive understanding of silent cinema. An eminent film curator and historian, Eileen Bowser, used to say that she would have happily traded all her film books for a complete run of *The Moving Picture World*, arguably the most authoritative trade journal in the United States during the silent film era. Original copies of this and other periodicals are now rare and valuable collectors' items. The good news is that they are often available in reproduced form, at little or no cost; the bad news is that their densely printed pages can indeed be searched electronically or with microfilm, but not explored as they were in the early twentieth century. History and anecdote, the meaningful and the insignificant, ruthless financial logic and raw emotions mingled together as images and texts stockpiled upon each other, seemingly unable to keep pace with the hundreds of new films and picture houses opening every week all around the world.

Much of what is known about silent cinema comes from these miniature portraits of collective taste as a work in progress. A myriad fragments of evidence are scattered across other kinds of ephemera: daily newspapers; weekly bulletins for leisurely or sensational reading; magazines about science, religion, politics, education, sports, fashion, and unqualified gossip – all had something to say about motion pictures. Cartoons and caricatures, in particular, form a distinct genre of commentary: as shown by Stephen Bottomore in his matchless compendium on the subject (*I Want to See This Anny Mattygraph: A Cartoon History of the Coming of the Movies*, 1995), public perception of the new medium was commented upon in these drawings with a sharp eye and an intelligence rarely found in all the serious printed matter about cinema.

Bureaucracy

The films announced and described in trade journals had been previewed by others beforehand, for the sake of protecting law, morality, and the national interest (the work of these officers was explained in Chapter 7). By and large, censorship boards kept a written record of what they did. Their proceedings had no particular secret to conceal, but rarely appeared as publications in the traditional sense of the term; most of them were kept in ministerial, judicial, and police archives (with few exceptions, they are now generally available to the public). They are printed checklists, typewritten pages, or manuscript cards where the approval, rejection, or abridgement of a new film production found its formal ratification in a wide variety of protocols and formulas. The detail of these statements was also variable, depending on where and when the review process had taken place.

For researchers on silent cinema, censorship papers are invaluable sources of information – well beyond the immediate purpose of their creation – as they may contain factual and quantitative data missing from other primary or secondary sources. Among them are the exact lengths of individual reels; accurate descriptions

of the films, sometimes shot by shot; and full transcriptions of the intertitles (both before and after censorship review). Curators and archivists who are trying to reconstruct silent films available only in foreign release versions, modified reissues, or incomplete prints are extremely happy when they find out that someone else had been patient enough to copy every word from a title card, and to make a note about its placement within the print. So much the better if the title lists and continuities came straight from the production companies.

As for the act of censorship itself, the reasons for its enforcement were so many, and so diverse, that some deletions and corrections are hard or impossible to fathom without a thorough knowledge of the culture, politics, and morals of the time in a given country. Much depended on the degree of diligence or zealousness of the individuals in charge of viewing the finished products. Archival documents often describe in painstaking detail the cuts imposed upon sequences, individual shots, or even parts of a shot, as when a scene depicting acts of violence or disrobing was trimmed, if necessary, of only a few frames. In many official reports, approval of a film was contingent upon the amendment or the outright removal of one or more title cards: concerns about their wordings, and the motivations behind the required changes, can be either fascinating to read, or utterly cryptic, or both.

Another hurdle for researchers is the fact that censorship could be applied to a film more than once, sometimes well after its release, or be tailored to the political situation of the moment. The intertitles of *Maciste alpino* (Romano Luigi Borgnetto, 1917), an action film about World War I (still raging at the time of its production), were modified in light of the changing circumstances in the conflict. The official date of approval for a film's official release is, in several instances, the main point of chronological reference, but it may not correspond at all to the time when the film was made or first exhibited to a paying audience. In such cases, the approved version of a film can have little resemblance to what people had seen until then, and a surviving print does not necessarily reflect the alterations and cuts required by the censors. Like any other piece of evidence, a censorship document must be interpreted on a contextual basis.

Delving into the administrative records of national, local, or corporate bureaucracies in control of silent cinema production and exhibition is a complex but worthwhile exercise, abundantly rewarded with information unlikely to be found in published sources. It should not be too difficult, for instance, to draw a historical atlas of the motion picture houses established and operating in any township, wherever a permit was needed to show films publicly. Safety regulations required theatre owners to submit textual or visual information about the structure, the capacity, and the floor plan of their intended venues; annual permits issued by fire departments may be of help in determining if and when a theatre was expanded, modified, or closed.

Useful pieces of information can also be retrieved from reports and documents created by police stations, hardware factories and retail shops, schools, hospitals, trade unions, actors' and photographers' guilds, charitable associations, lawyers' and coroners' offices, as well as any other place where accounting, budgets, and some sort of statistical information was kept for whatever purpose. The list of potential sources in this area is virtually endless, but special mention should be made at least of street maps, topographic plans for city zoning, patent records, telephone books. Depending on what one is looking for, no aspect of human activity that has left a paper trail is too small to be ignored.

Commentaries

A distinctive feature of cinema is that its inventors and spectators began reflecting on the nature and possibilities of the new medium from its very inception, as had already occurred with photography, maybe with a greater sense of urgency (a theme briefly discussed at the end of Chapter 5 in this book). Assembling a bibliography of all publications related to film that appeared between the 1890s and the late 1920s is a daunting but not unattainable task. Much depends on whether or not the list should include catalogues and brochures for the sale of film or related equipment; revised and enlarged editions of the same work; and the many volumes on magic lantern shows where film projection was discussed in a separate section or in an appendix.

One of the earliest French specialists in film history, Guillaume-Michel Coissac, compiled in 1932 an inventory of 151 books about cinema for the eleventh edition of the yearbook *Le Tout-Cinéma. Annuaire général illustré du monde cinématographique*. His bibliography, consisting almost exclusively of books and articles for French-speaking readers, offers some indications on the range of topics most frequently covered by the existing literature: out of the 149 entries (another 2 were dedicated, respectively, to special reports and to *Le Tout-Cinéma* itself), 30 are devoted to film technology; 20 to professional handbooks of various types; 14 to film history; 10 to cinema as a tool for education; 18 are evenly split between film criticism and theory; 29 titles are general introductions; business, censorship, memoirs, and legal matters account for the few remaining titles.

Coissac's register does not include catalogues of films and film equipment, and contains only two works of fiction about cinema; by the author's own admission, his survey was nothing more than a preliminary attempt at presenting what he had found in the course of his own work in an orderly fashion. The recurring themes of his bibliography should also not be assumed to reflect editorial trends in other countries (for instance, there was a higher ratio of handbooks about acting and screenwriting in the United States than elsewhere). What can be inferred from *Le Tout-Cinéma* is that many witnesses of cinema's birth felt the urge to document the story of its evolution, like proud parents of a very special child.

These chroniclers were resolute in their belief that the emerging medium could be beneficial to culture and society, a powerful agent of democracy and progress. By explaining the technology and the industrial processes that made cinema possible, journalists and experts in the new field made their readers not just the beneficiaries of a wonderful invention, but active partakers and advocates. In political terms, this meant that moving images could be particularly effective in serving different forms of populism, from nationalist movements to egalitarian ideologies. Any programme with a connection to these subjects could be an occasion for quarrels, protests, and fist fights during the show. Film producers, directors, performers, and practitioners have left a rich corpus of memoirs, providing vivid and often absorbing portraits of their times and personal experiences.

Religious authorities initially treated cinema with suspicion, portraying it as an invention of the Devil, and then embraced it as a devotional tool. Socialist regimes hailed it as the fulfilment of a revolutionary utopia before turning it into a propaganda weapon. The vast majority of books about the effects of motion pictures upon collective life are dedicated to a few crucial questions: the influence of cinema on morality and public order; its potential role in education, science, and professional training; the opportunities and threats presented by the 'photodrama' – as it was

called in English-speaking countries during the mid-1910s – in relation to theatre. Some doctors asserted that watching films could be harmful to the eyes, and suggested methods to diagnose and treat the patients (some of their concerns have been described in Chapter 5).

A small but resolute minority of intellectuals detected in cinema an art form in its infancy, and tried to make sense of its early achievements; *The Crisis of the Film*, a 1929 pamphlet by John Gould Fletcher, was already discussing its downfall. Within three decades, books about film had already gone full circle in interpreting the meteoric trajectory of cinema from scientific experiment to mass entertainment. Reading books about film, however, was an occupation reserved for a tiny percentage of the audience. Being mindful of this does not imply diminishing the importance of published writings on cinema during the silent period: it is only a reminder that the viewpoints they represent were minority voices in a community of hundreds of millions of viewers around the world. We are listening to these elites only because the printed pages reproducing their thoughts are still extant. The voice of all the others can be heard only in the letters they wrote to film journals, and in what remains of their private diaries, correspondence, and other personal possessions.

Ephemera

Scholarly research has identified some materials as being especially relevant to a better knowledge of silent cinema (they are often referred to as 'ephemera': not by any means to diminish their importance, but to simply indicate that – like the films themselves – most of these artefacts were intented for use over a very short timespan). Two categories of objects in particular have rightfully earned a privileged status in this field of research. A large number of music scores and cue sheets are now available for study in public libraries worldwide. All major collecting institutions devoted to the history of cinema have original documents and phonograph recordings about the sounds of the silent film era. Many libraries and conservatories are richly endowed with them, although they have almost exclusively been explored by musicologists and music performers. This is a pity, because so much can be learned from these materials even without possessing a thorough knowledge of music notation. Cinema was the subject of many popular tunes; there were also operettas such as *Filmzauber* (music by Walter Kollo; libretto by Rudolf Bernauer and Rudolf Schanzer, 1912), *Die Kino-Königin* (music by Jean Gilbert; libretto by Georg Okonkowsky and Julius Freund, 1913), and *La signorina del cinematografo* (1915), adapted from Charles Weinberger's *Der Schmetterling* (1896).

The other major harvesting field is provided by literature, in the form of novels (see pp. 225–226), short stories, articles, and memoirs inspired by the cinematic event, or intended as meditations on the nature, virtues, and presumed threats of the new medium: Luigi Pirandello's *Quaderni di Serafino Gubbio operatore* (1925) is among the most celebrated texts of this kind. This and many other writings in this vein have been collected in anthologies and critical editions, as testimonies of the fascination exerted by film among intellectuals. Maksim Gorkij's article 'Beglye zametki. Sinematograf Lyum'era' ([Fleeting Notes. The Lumière Cinematograph], 4 July 1896) is widely regarded as the first text on cinema published by a renowned artist; another Russian author, Pyotr Demianovich Ouspenskij, wrote a novel informed by the concept of repeated projection of the same film (*Kinemodrama – Ne dlia kinematografa*, allegedly drafted in 1905) to illustrate his metaphysical theory of cyclical time. The book was published only in 1917 in Petrograd, then reissued in English by its author under the title *Strange Life of Ivan Osokin* (1947).

Posters, production stills, lobby cards, and graphic designs used to promote new releases occupy the opposite end of film culture's pantheon. After a brief period when films were publicized by simply reproducing their titles or by announcing the show as a whole, lithography was the medium of choice for posters, often produced in multiple versions and sizes. Many of them are beautiful artworks in their own right. In the late twentieth century, nitrate prints could be bought in flea markets at a relatively modest price (they are collected only for reproduction onto safety film or other media); conversely, film collectors can spend considerably more for original posters – particularly if they are related to famous films – because of the intrinsic beauty and antiquarian appeal of their designs.

The financial value attributed to these objects is, of course, proportional to their rarity (the very flimsy and fragile acidic paper on which they were printed contributes to their low survival rate); exquisite as they may be, production stills are not as profitable – no matter how great their photographers may be – because so many of them are in circulation. Here is an intriguing and not so obvious contradiction: regardless of their cost and availability, works that were conceived as ancillary products are treated as cherished memorabilia, more than the original works they advertised. A film and a poster are both printed artefacts that were distributed in multiple copies; the hierarchy between the two derives from the fact that one of them requires a mechanical apparatus in order to be exhibited.

There is no big money to be made from the sale of nitrate film elements: those who accept them in their care should actually be compensated for the monetary effort required to properly safeguard the prints in climate-controlled vaults, and to ensure their preservation in the long term by duplicating the originals onto more permanent carriers. For a variety of reasons (including legal rights over public exhibition), the chances that a nitrate copy will ever reach a market value remotely comparable to that of other artworks like paintings or sculptures are extremely slim, even if the film in question was *London After Midnight* (Tod Browning, 1927), the complete version of Stroheim's *Greed*, or some other coveted treasures of cinema.

Once referred to with the perfunctory label of 'non-film' objects, the vast collections of publicity photographs and posters held in film archives and museums have begun to receive the scholarly attention they deserve. The same applies to the film cameras, projectors, and other pieces of equipment preserved in collecting institutions around the world. Film curators have rarely been indifferent to the machines behind the creation of cinematic events; sadly enough, a long-embedded tradition of implicit or deliberate separation between arts and crafts and the humanities has prevented researchers from drawing knowledge about cinema from the technology that made it possible in the first place. Another cause of its past neglect is that no pictorial representation, computer simulation, or other second-hand description of these machines is a substitute for the physical contact between the apparatus and its user: to fully understand the turning of a crank at regular intervals, one has to feel its weight, the effort required to make it rotate, the smoothness of the gears connecting it with the shutter and intermittent device of the camera or the projector.

Film curatorship is belatedly addressing the question of how film technology should be taught as a hands-on practice in a workshop setting that provides the necessary acquaintance with the sprockets, light sources, and lenses used for filmmaking and projection in the silent era. Useful as they may be, all professional manuals, manufacturers' catalogues, and patent descriptions of how

films were shot, developed, printed, assembled, and projected (together with the surviving corpus of historical papers and manuscripts on the optics, physics, and chemistry of cinema) are bound to be mute cyphers for those who have not manually engaged with the real things they refer to, not unlike the sailing instructions given to someone who has never been on a boat. As great novels and operettas, film machines are not really 'ephemera' at all (metal, wood, and glass are far more durable than cellulose): they are mentioned here only because they have been undeservedly treated as such, victims of the Platonic notion of cinema as a purely mental phenomenon.

On a more familiar front, much can be done with the smithereens of historical evidence put together by film and theatre professionals or anonymous filmgoers, either for work or as a hobby. They collected newspaper clippings, postcards, leaflets, ticket stubs, letters, and photographs with real or stamped autographs of film stars, sometimes even nitrate film clips; all of them were carefully laid out on the pages of albums or notebooks, like sprawling diaries of all the hours spent in the protecting darkness of motion picture houses. From an archival perspective, scrapbooks have been regarded for many years as unwieldy time capsules, vast repositories of data assembled in often subjective, capricious, or utterly random fashion. The concurrent evolution of library science, new technologies, and social history has prompted a resurgence of scholarly interest in these hybrid carriers of historical evidence.

One of the best examples of this archival 'genre' is the Robinson Locke Collection at the New York Public Library, a mammoth set of 1,016 volumes and 2,215 portfolios on American musical and dramatic artists, assembled from the 1890s to about 1920 by the owner and editor of an Ohio newspaper, *The Toledo Blade*. Not all scrapbooks of the silent film period are as satisfying as those compiled by

Locke and his associates, but the patience required to look at these handmade montages of other people's lives can be repaid in ways that are much harder to obtain by other research methods. In their apparent chaos, these fragmentary micro-histories also offer a uniquely immersive experience of the times in which the compilers kept a trace of their own memories of cinema.

Histories

Over the years during the silent film era, many of these people wrote down their recollections in a more systematic form. Dickson's example in 1895 (p. 215) was followed by other narrative accounts of varying length and ambition, published all over the world in books, pamphlets, and articles for popular magazines. It would be more accurate to call them chronicles than histories: their goal was to establish a direct connection between the animated views and their non-cinematic forerunners. In broad terms, the history of silent film historiography can be subdivided into three periods. The first, spanning approximately two decades, is predominantly a history of film technology. Virtually all introductory books and manuals on cinema production and projection compiled until 1914 contain at least one chapter or section where the origins of the moving image are described in some detail.

The milestones and protagonists of these proto-histories had been identified from the start: the Thaumatrope (1825), a cardboard disc with two strings attached to the margins along its diameter, and two complementary pictures drawn or printed on each side (as the strings are quickly twirled between the fingers, the two images blend into one); the Phénakistiscope (Joseph Plateau, 1833), also a cardboard disc, with radial slits and a series of pictures showing a dozen or more phases in the movement of figures to be viewed

by spinning the disc around its centre in front of a mirror; the Zoetrope (1833), a rotating cylinder with vertical slits and a band of consecutive images placed around the inside; Charles-Émile Reynaud's Praxinoscope (1877), where the slits were replaced by a circle of mirrors at the centre of the cylinder (in the 1892 Théâtre Optique, a further development of his invention, Reynaud applied the images on a longer ribbon and projected them onto a screen); and so on.

These books were, by and large, evolutionary histories of so-called 'pre-cinema' (the prefix attached to 'cinema' was a signal of their teleological stance; hence the authors' predilection for the word 'primitive' as a qualifier of early film). Some of them went back in time far enough to mention Plato's cave and Athanasius Kircher; others had chapters on magic lantern shows and the 'Chinese shadows' created by the artful movements of hands and objects in front of a light source; for most of them, the watershed between prehistory and history was marked by the experiments of Étienne-Jules Marey and Eadweard Muybridge, where sequential photographic images made their first appearance. With them, the history of cinema was introduced as the science of creating optical illusions by mechanical means. Writers were particularly keen to reveal the details of how the 'magic' of motion pictures is created, from mermaids swimming in front of painted backdrops (Fig. 148) to optical effects (Fig. 150a–c). One of the most popular illustrations in early cinema literature describes the making of a scene involving a man whose legs are amputated in a car accident. The mutilated man was real; the photograph was reproduced in several journals and books after its first appearance in L'Illustration on 28 March 1908 (Fig. 146).

With two books published in the mid-1910s, Robert Grau's The Theatre of Science (1914) and Vachel Lindsay's The Art of the Moving Picture (1915), and with the writings of Louis Delluc in

France, film historiography saw a major shift from the production and exhibition process to the discussion of past cinematic achievements. This new phase coincided with the rise of feature-length films: an essential ingredient of storytelling – the segmentation of time into periods – was finally in place, enabling a chronological trajectory to be drawn from cinema as a scientific discovery to its narrative development in the one-reel format and its eventual triumph as a 'photoplay'. Lindsay's goal was to develop a critical lexicon for motion pictures; Grau wrote mainly about producers and performers rather than specific films; taken together, the two works are the epitome of all film histories to come: cinema as an industry, and as a mode of aesthetic expression.

A peculiar manifestation of early film historiography was its desire to establish a pantheon of its most important works. *Quo Vadis?* and *The Birth of a Nation* were among the first entries of a 'film canon', measuring sticks for all the other films to come. Historians and journalists found several ways to make cinema flirt with posterity. The 'national' canon included films recognized as classics within a specific territorial community: Robert Wiene's *Das Cabinet des Dr. Caligari* (1920) for Germany, *Cabiria* for Italy, *Körkarlen* (*The Phantom Carriage*, Victor Sjöström, 1920) for Sweden. The 'auteurist' canon stemmed from the reputation of individual directors; their films were 'canonical' by proxy, because of the names attached to them (in this respect, almost any film by D.W. Griffith deserved special attention). There was also a 'temporary' canon, made of films widely acclaimed in the months immediately following their release, as shown in books dedicated to the best pictures of a given year or season.

The advent of sound triggered a third phase in film historiography by *force majeure*: as silent cinema no longer existed, its obituary required a suitable list of names, tendencies, and objects of devotion. Other types of film 'canon' emerged: notable works by 'pioneers' of cinema, categorized according to real or imaginary groupings (the 'Brighton school' in Great Britain, German expressionism, the dichotomy between Lumière's realism and Méliès' tricks). Titles, names, and labels were repeated from one history to another, with corrections and mistakes added or perpetuated from time to time. Some histories of cinema published in the following decades also qualify as 'canonical': those by Benjamin Hampton in the United States, Jean Mitry, Maurice Bardèche and Robert Brasillach in France, Rachael Low and John Barnes in Great Britain, Roberto Paolella in Italy, Jerzy Toeplitz in Poland, Ulrich Gregor and Enno Patalas in Germany are among the classics in the field. The towering achievement emerged between 1946 and 1975 with the publication of *Histoire générale du cinéma* by Georges Sadoul. Many historians have improved upon Sadoul in terms of individual topics, but no general history of silent cinema has yet surpassed this monumental work.

Inventories

In researching and recounting their version of the facts, the pioneers of film history had at their disposal the same catalogues and journals available to film exhibitors in the pursuit of their business. These documents were used to draw synoptic charts of the cinema's past in the form of alphabetical or chronological lists of titles. The earliest ones are particularly fascinating to read, because they are like tentative maps in the cartography of a new art form, cautiously drawn by its navigators at the beginning of their journey. In scholarly terms, filmographies should be treated as secondary sources (film inventories made by producers, distributors, and exhibitors had different purposes); in essence, however, their content is supposed to faithfully reproduce the information found in primary sources, with no extra intervention other than a specific methodology for assembling them, and the possible addition of commentaries. Given the frequent use of filmographies in the study of silent cinema, and their intended objectivity as mosaics of factual knowledge, their evolution as learning resources deserves some attention. Those who compiled them were rarely, if ever, entirely neutral in their intentions; their impartiality was an aspirational goal, to be measured against the nature of the materials they were working with and of the instruments designed for their dissemination in textual form.

Filmographies first appeared as supporting evidence to the writings of journalists and scholars about filmmakers and production companies in the first decades of cinema. It is hard to determine when the word 'filmography' was first used, but it is certain that completeness or scientific accuracy were rarely the main objectives of these lists. From the standpoint of their authors, what really mattered was to bring the readers' attention to the fact that certain people, corporate entities, or nations were responsible for the creation of significant works, or had to be remembered simply because they made them in large numbers.

By current standards, the very term 'filmography' applied to lists of this kind may be seen as a misnomer, preceded as they were by sentences such as: '1910 – about forty films, including … '. Titles were often squeezed alphabetically into dense paragraphs; their spelling was sometimes incomplete or incorrect; there was confusion between the dates of production and release; the same films may be found twice when reissued at different times; wrong attributions were not uncommon. It didn't really matter: the important thing was that the artist or producer in question made 'about forty' films in a given year – that is, many of them in a short time span.

As the history of cinema was turning into an object of academic interest, film scholarship resumed the job in the 1940s with the aim of making the lists as complete and accurate as possible. Researchers had realized that a closer scrutiny of film catalogues and trade journals could generate more exhaustive and reliable inventories through a careful comparison of dates, names, and titles. The main virtue of these collections of data is their reliance upon primary sources, diligent transcriptions of rare documents at a time when public libraries were paying scant attention to their potential value. Georges Sadoul paved the way with his Méliès filmography, commissioned in 1947 by the British Film Institute as part of a series that included similar works by Theodore Huff (on Charlie Chaplin) and Seymour Stern (on D.W. Griffith). The Museum of Modern Art followed the same path in its monographs about D.W. Griffith and Douglas Fairbanks. With admirable restraint, the title of the BFI's series ('An Index to the Creative Work of … ') was unequivocal in defining the ambitions and the limits of the project: a comprehensive record of film productions, presented in the form of a directory.

Another filmographic trend emerged in the 1950s, directly inspired by the French movement of the nouvelle vague. If some directors (such as Fritz Lang, John Ford, Alfred Hitchcock) made so many great films, it was only appropriate to look at their oeuvre as a cohesive whole. If only three or four titles were widely recognized in the work of other filmmakers (such as Gregory La Cava, William Dieterle, Allan Dwan), maybe it was time to discover more about them and appoint these artists to their rightful place in the annals of film history. Establishing a complete list of their works was a way to celebrate them as 'auteurs', kindred souls in a distinguished cohort of acclaimed or underrated visionaries. 'Auteurist' filmographies were the reference works of the true cinephile:

being able to demonstrate a thorough knowledge of every film in the list was a proof of loyalty to the cause of cinema.

In the wake of this effort to present an exhaustive record of the masters' creative output, Jean Mitry conceived the first project of a universal filmography. Between 1963 and his death in 1988, Mitry published thirty-five volumes of his *Filmographie universelle*, with the declared goal of documenting all the films ever made. His herculean undertaking was both prophetic and premature, in the sense that it foresaw the possibility of intellectual control over the entire history of cinema at a time when too little was known about the chronology of film production in many countries outside Europe and the United States. Mitry's dream was later resumed by Alan Goble's *International Film Index, 1895–1990*, first published as a book (1991), then on a digital disk (1995), before appearing on the Internet in 2004, when many other digital resources were competing for the same goal.

Filmographies

The main problem with Mitry's filmography was that too many people – often inexperienced volunteers – were asked to transcribe whatever they could find in the catalogues, journals, and books available at the time, without the training and knowledge needed to determine the value of every piece of collected information; as in earlier attempts, the same film could be registered twice in different years, just because it had been reissued (maybe even under a different title). The most significant flaw of the *Filmographie universelle* was that its entries were not connected to their sources, mentioned as a whole at the beginning of each volume. Unable to find out where exactly the information was coming from, readers had no other choice than to take each entry at face value.

The imperative to document filmographic provenances was a source of inspiration for George C. Pratt, one of the unheralded champions of objectivity in historical research on film during the 1970s. Pratt was instrumental in the creation of the first chronological instalment in *The American Film Institute Catalog of Motion Pictures Produced in the United States* (1995), a filmography on the early films produced and distributed in the United States (Pratt's 1973 book *Spellbound in Darkness* remains one of the greatest works on silent cinema in general).

Another manifestation of Pratt's approach to harvesting evidence about cinema was a British publication, the *Monthly Film Bulletin*, born in 1934 as a reference tool for film exhibitors. Its editorial policy was the exact opposite of Mitry's, in that it was based upon a strict adherence to the data provided by primary sources: cast, credits, plot summaries, and length were taken from release copies. The primary objective of the *Monthly Film Bulletin* was to report on the films distributed in Great Britain, but its finely printed pages were offering more than that. In its deliberately stern, unglamorous way, the British Film Institute's *Bulletin* was a filmography in progress. The history of cinema it aspired to write was disguised as a cataloguing form with critical annotations. Had it been published worldwide in the first thirty years of cinema, Mitry's utopia would have been much closer to its achievement.

Very few silent films were featured in the pages of the *Monthly Film Bulletin* until its virtual demise in April 1991, when it merged with another BFI film periodical, *Sight & Sound*. Nevertheless, this seemingly neutral assembly of names, synopses, and succinct commentaries must be mentioned here because one can feel the echo of its encyclopedic spirit in André Gaudreault's *catalogue raisonné* of all the films shown at the seminal Brighton conference on early cinema held in 1978 under the auspices of the International Federation of Film Archives, a milestone in the history of silent film studies. A detailed description of the 548 archival prints shown on that occasion appeared in the second volume of *Cinema 1900–1906: An Analytical Study* (1982), co-edited with Roger Holman. With his project, Gaudreault initiated the short-lived but fertile dream of the 'analytical' catalogue, based on the principle of an in-depth scrutiny of individual prints (with written sources in a supporting role) and of their unique status as archival objects. This is a 'filmography' in the most literal sense of the term, cinema translated into words according to selected variables such as editing patterns, camera placement, optical effects.

Analytical filmographies fulfilled only part of their promise, as their authors were mainly focused on moving images available in the form of duplicate copies. The physical evidence (splices, perforations, edge codes) of the original prints, their colour techniques, material history, and provenance were seldom discussed, if at all, given the difficulty in obtaining access to nitrate copies at that time. Another drawback of these otherwise heroic efforts was the disproportion between the amount of text devoted to the most meticulous explanation of the events occurring in the films, and the number of titles to be covered by the filmography itself. Its purported virtues – precision and exhaustiveness – became liabilities: lack of time, budgetary constraints, and the sheer exhaustion of the authors meant that the filmography was never achieved. At best, it was the sampler of a complete work that would never see the light, thus contradicting the very essence of the endeavour.

Unable or unwilling to measure their goals against the work required to accomplish them, some researchers became engulfed by intellectual paralysis after having gathered huge amounts of data. Fearful that relevant pieces of information might still be waiting to be uncovered somewhere, these scholars preferred to abstain from publishing their filmographies at all, rather than blaming themselves for not having conducted a more exhaustive research into all existing sources (the current absence of an analytical filmography on Charlie Chaplin has something to do with this syndrome). Another alternative to failure is to refrain from undertaking a filmographic project in the first place: non-fiction has been one of the most neglected areas in this kind of endeavour, partly because – until at least the mid-1990s – its subject matter was deemed unimportant or unattractive. The harder truth is that information on these films is more difficult to retrieve, as trade journals paid more attention to dramatic works in reporting about the latest releases. The lack of an authorial identity also did not play in favour of these chronically underrated creations. Film actualities, scenic views, newsreels, educational and scientific films are much better known today, but reliable filmographies remain scarce.

The intrinsic flaw of analytical filmographies was that they were treated as substitutes for the actual viewing of films at a time when it was difficult to see them outside archives and museums, with no specialized festivals to speak of. Many collecting institutions were reluctant about, or even opposed to, loaning their copies, although 16mm circulation prints were made for classroom or non-theatrical use. Silent films were seldom shown on television, except for slapstick comedies and a small repertoire of classics. To compensate for the absence of reference copies, illustrated books about specific films had been published since the mid-1940s (with a photograph for each shot, a sequential number, and a descriptive caption). In the United States, the Grove Press produced in 1969 a faux-leather clamshell box containing 120 photographic slides representing the complete works of Sergei Eisenstein. *L'Avant*

RULE 3

A filmography is more useful and reliable
when each piece of information
is accompanied by a mention of its source.

---

scène cinéma, a French journal created in 1961, features complete texts of dialogues or intertitles for one or more films in each of its monthly issues. The importance of these limited but necessary replacements of the actual works began to wane only much later, with the introduction of technologies for mass reproduction of moving images through electronic or digital means.

Once relieved from the obligation to repeat with words the visual and narrative content of motion pictures, filmographies found new vitality in the form of databases. Their inherent flexibility enables the information they contain to be revised, integrated, and corrected, but this privilege does not make them necessarily more authoritative, which is why most website search engines on silent cinema are not filmographies at all. They are practical reference tools to be used with a great deal of caution, insofar as no mention is made of the sources of the information (an outstanding example of best practice is the Pathé filmography by Henri Bousquet, now on the website of the Fondation Jérôme Seydoux-Pathé). Modern works may not be a matter of concern, given that there is plenty of data about them everywhere (with all the challenges entailed in their ubiquity); this is not the case for silent films, whose primary sources are the documents and objects described earlier in this chapter, as well as the prints themselves. Filmographies of silent cinema can never be called complete, because each of them is a response to a specific type of question. Being a constant work in progress is an integral part of their cultural identity.

A filmography can be browsed with some degree of confidence when a piece of evidence is provided to support each of its components. It is not enough to claim that a given title was released in two versions, black and white and with stencil colour: a statement of this kind should be accompanied by the indication of where this information was found, and when it was produced. Similarly, in writing that a two-reel film made in 1912 had a running time of twenty-four minutes, it is essential to declare who made such an estimate. The figure may have appeared in a producer's catalogue. Maybe it derives from the assumption that 16 frames per second was the average projection speed of a 1912 film, in which case the author of the filmography must take responsibility for what is only a plausible hypothesis. Either way, the reason for the statement should be made unequivocally clear.

Databases

No single method works for all filmographies: the scope, depth, and purpose of the compilation process determines their structure. A filmographic entry may consist of one word or number, a few lines, a paragraph, or several pages, depending on the intended use of the tool. All of them are made of two or more of the following components:

(a) the single or multiple name given to the creative work (the title);

(b) the moment in time when the work was made and shown (the date);

(c) the place where it was created (the origin);

(d) the people who made it (the artistic and technical personnel);

(e) the corporate entities involved (the production company);

(f) the distribution of the film (the release agency);

(g) its public exhibition in different times and places (the show);

(h) its surviving elements and their provenance (the objects);

(i) the main title, if any, appearing on extant prints (if different from the official title).

The first five categories of data (also the sixth, if a film was released only once) are invariable, as they apply to all the prints of a silent film, whether it is extant or not. Once established, these data can be integrated by additional facts or figures to enhance detail and context on what is already known. The last two categories describe the material evidence of the film, as expressed by the negatives, prints, and production documents (if any) that are held by private and public institutions. These documents are sometimes linked to the seventh category, describing the commercial itinerary of the objects over time. A double bind connects categories (h) and (i) to all the others: for instance, if a given film was produced in 1910 by Vitagraph, it is to be expected that the logo of the firm will appear in the intertitles and somewhere on the set (some examples are shown at p. 296).

Conversely, the examination of prints and negatives can offer opportunities to integrate or correct the data retrieved from other sources: an alternate or foreign release title, an uncredited actor, a shooting location never mentioned in production records, even the events unfolding in the film. Filmographies may contain two kinds of descriptive summaries at the same time: one drawn from original manuscripts or published documents (with mention of the source), the other made through the actual viewing or inspection of the copies (with mention of who wrote it and of the print viewed). A reliable film synopsis is important both as an *aide-mémoire* and as an identification tool, especially when it mentions the names of characters in fictional works. When an incomplete or fragmentary copy has no title card, this is how a silent film can often find its correct attribution.

The value of a filmography is defined, among other things, by the exactness of its chronological sequence. No matter how the inventory was designed, the order in which the films appeared on the market should be made unambiguously clear. As in most scholarly studies, this book cites all films by the date of their release, but this is only one among the many legitimate options to choose from. The release date indicates when a film was made available for commercial exhibition, which often corresponds to the moment of the first encounter between paying audiences and the finished work in different theatres at around the same time. Useful as it is, this criterion is rife with exceptions and caveats. The production of a film (script, shooting, title cards, negative cutting, print assembly) may have occurred days, months, or years before its appearance on the screen. Once completed, films could be shown to invited or paying audiences on a trial basis, or presented at gala soirées well ahead of their release. Some filmmakers and producers went even further by first exhibiting their films in selected venues (the roadshow theatrical release) before general distribution.

Censorship boards also played a role in subverting our chronological rules: their members could review an existing film at various points in time, imposing cuts and alterations as required; in those countries where this practice was delayed by legislative inaction, the approval process often occurred several years after a film's first appearance. For commercial reasons, the same film could also undergo multiple releases over time, sometimes with a different title. On other occasions (as in some slapstick comedies of the 1910s), the reissue could be almost exactly the same as the original, with a few frames trimmed at the beginning and end of each shot, in order to adapt the film's editing to the swiftest pace of more recent productions. Filmmakers did their part by modifying, dismembering, and reassembling film negatives during the commercial life of their own work.

To further complicate matters, films could be distributed in foreign countries with entirely new designations, frequently using projection prints made from negatives that varied in length, editing, camera angles, and narrative structure from their domestic siblings. These nations had their censorship agencies, too, with bureaucrats imposing their own cuts and revisions to what had already been cut and revised before. Again, intertitles could be deleted; others were added where

the action should have spoken for itself; characters' names were changed, according to the whims of local distributors and the predilections of their clientele. In short, the same 1913 film can be a very different thing, in different places, at different times. Its release date does not automatically tell us what the film was like, except perhaps in the intentions of its makers.

Filmographies can and should be the ideal places for a timeline of all such deviations from a non-existent 'original' film as a singular entity; in its essence, their compilation is a necessary but never-ending task, as definitive as a minute-by-minute verbal report on the life of a cloud. The scholarly study of silent cinema has always thrived upon the orderly illusion of catalogues and indexes. If they are still assembled today, it's because creativity sometimes wants a dictionary of its own history. Like all knowledge, a filmography is only as good as the use we want to make of it.

RULE 4

When presenting information on an archival print,
always keep clear the distinction
between material and visual evidence found on the copy
and information drawn from other sources.

Chapter 12

Duplicates

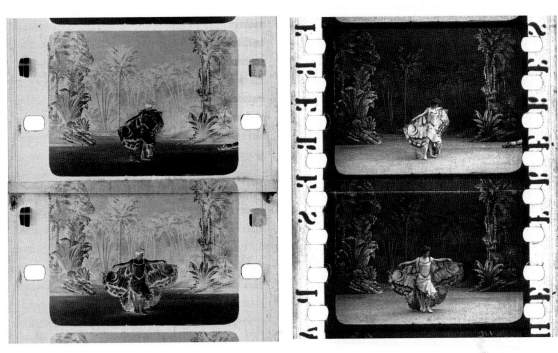

Fig. 192a–b *Le Charmeur* (Pathé, 1907). 35mm nitrate negative and positive. Note the cement splice and the single perforation on each side of the negative. Source: Courtesy of Céline Ruivo, Cinémathèque française.

'The nitrate originals should be used when they're negatives to get the best possible prints; the original positives should be looked at as long as they can be put through projectors. Otherwise you're not talking about films, you're talking about facsimiles.' These words are from a 1977 *Image* interview with James Card, who regularly showed nitrate film at the George Eastman Museum's Dryden Theatre in the 1950s while struggling to collect the funds necessary for their duplication onto more stable carriers.

Many colleagues would have cringed at his bold statement, but there is an uncomfortable truth in what he said (p. 29). A three-volume promotional book distributed by German film manufacturer AGFA at the end of the 1920s, showcasing actual samples of 35mm negative and positive frames on nitrate cellulose base, is a good illustration of Card's viewpoint: so far, the condition of all nitrate frames in the extant copies of AGFA's manual is no less than astonishing (Plate 28). The sharpness, translucence, and vibrancy of the images are matched by the pristine condition of their photochemical carriers.

As seen in Chapter 3, other companies in Europe and the United States – notably Pathé and Eastman Kodak – produced similar booklets to advertise their products. Many of them are still preserved, although their quality can hardly be compared with that of their German counterpart. Several prints and negatives of films made between 1896 and 1908 by Lumière and Pathé, by the British company Mitchell & Kenyon, and by the Biograph Company of New York are in such good condition that they could be safely handled with the appropriate equipment. What is so special about the AGFA frames is that they are reminders of a lost opportunity: had the films they document been stored in ideal conditions of temperature and humidity from the very moment of their creation, the prints could probably have been exhibited today. Their progressive obliteration in the ensuing decades was a likely but not inevitable event. The duplication activity known as 'film preservation' is a belated attempt to make amends for past negligence.

Strictly speaking, the best way to preserve a film is to keep it in good shape for as long as possible, so that it can be safely projected and seen by everyone. Unfortunately, most of the silent films held by museums and archives in nitrate copies are in such bad condition that this is almost never an option; they are therefore conserved only for the purposes of creating new duplicates. To call copying 'preservation' is quite a conceptual stretch, even more so in the case of the equally common term 'film restoration'. A nitrate print can be cleaned, repaired, and reinforced – certainly not restored like a Rembrandt canvas or an ancient monument.

The attempt or pretence of 'restoring' a silent film is applied to only one part of the creative work, the visual information contained in a carrier that can no longer be used for display. Much of the rest – the original carrier, but also the equipment used for the projection – is gone. In his 1997 book *De vergankelijkheid* (published in English as *The Way of All Flesh*), Dutch biologist Midas Dekkers takes the point another step further by arguing that 'one can no more restore an area of natural beauty – or a painting or a tugboat – to its original state than one can turn women into the little girls that they once were; conserving is ambitious enough' (p. 94). He adds: 'old paint fades in light, varnish cracks, linen decays, layers of dirt hamper viewing' (p. 95). With paintings, at least, dirt can be removed from the surface; doing so from the emulsion of a film makes little difference, except before copying its images onto something else.

Conservation

Brash as it is, Dekkers' pronouncement is well suited to the dilemma facing film curators and archivists. 'Film restoration' is the unavoidable misnomer for another kind of activity. In taking the duplication process at its epicentre, film preservation as a whole is a necessary mistake: it can be a useful one, as long as it allows us to learn from its pursuit by reducing its side effects to a minimum, without misleading the audience who views the results of this contradictory, highly complex, and incessant effort to capture the essence of an art form through its imitation.

The best way to make sense out of this seemingly paradoxical endeavour is to push its inconsistency even further, acknowledging all the other things film preservation *cannot* do. Even in the hypothetical case that silent films were reproduced without the slightest loss of visual information, they would be copied on a film emulsion that is substantially different from those (particularly the orthochromatic) used in the first three decades of the twentieth century; the available colour film stock commercially produced today would be almost the only option for recreating tinting and toning effects, stencil, and hand-colouring (tinting by immersion in dyed solutions is possible, but very costly). The new prints would be struck on a polyester base, whose refraction index is different from that of nitrate and diacetate film stock. Projectors from the silent era still exist and could be repaired, but at least one of their core components – the carbon arc lights, whose rods must be constantly replaced – are increasingly hard to find. Modern screens are made of materials and textures that are different from those in use during the silent era.

Given all these handicaps, one might wonder what is the point in seeking authenticity at all, as so many variables are well beyond anybody's control. 'The dividing line between restoring and forging', writes Dekkers (*The Way of All Flesh*, p. 97), 'is vague and shifts with time.' There is only one answer to this objection: copying film on film is the most effective and the least expensive option for long-term preservation, in addition to conserving the original prints. It is also the least inaccurate rendition of film history. Duplication on the same type of medium and carrier does, at least, comply with the basic principle of motion picture exhibition during the silent era (and beyond) – the projection of successive frames of individual images at regular intervals on a flexible photographic carrier – thus preserving the mode of perception that is a prerogative of the cinematic event (an intriguing signal of interest for this non-revisionist approach to film preservation occurred in May 2018 at the Festival de Cannes, where a 70mm print of Stanley Kubrick's *2001: A Space Odyssey* was proudly presented by film director Christopher Nolan in its 'unrestored' version).

All in all, film conservation – as applied to either the original prints or their duplicates – should be regarded as of paramount importance for a collecting institution, very much in the spirit of what museums do with other cultural artefacts.

Duplicating prints must not be construed as a convenient substitute for the safeguard of collection objects in the long term. To call film conservation the indicator of a 'conservative' (or, in a fatuous variation on the theme, 'fetishist') approach sounds like a convenient rhetorical excuse to bypass the issue: at a time when the moving image is increasingly treated as a docile commodity to be altered and manipulated at will, the act of allowing film to live on its own terms – protected from the hubris of those who pretend to rewrite its material history, or ignore it altogether – may in fact become a culturally subversive gesture. Film conservation is the heart and soul of film preservation. Everything else, as James Card said, is indeed about making facsimiles. It is only by extension (in the photochemical domain) that the term 'preservation' is applied to the act of copying visual information from one carrier or medium to another. Once 'preserved', the images must be 'conserved' so that they are permanently available for projection in their intact form.

The only actual benefit of duplicating nitrate prints onto new film stock – aside from the fact that the nitrate prints may not be projectable and cannot be replaced with others of the same vintage – is that its polyester base is relatively more stable (its tensile strength is actually so strong as to break the projector's gears if it is not properly threaded). When kept in the appropriate conditions of temperature and humidity, its expected longevity can be measured over very long periods of time. This conjectural virtue is the best available answer – other than taking the digital route – to the imperative of enabling future audiences to watch films. Projection prints are made for exhibition in a live cinema performance; their physical existence as part of a technology, with its specific historical framework, is a requisite of the motion picture show. Deprived of this context, prints are mute objects: not silent films, but inert visual content wrapped in plastic rolls. They might just as well be pixels.

> **RULE 5**
>
> The goal of film preservation is to ensure
> the permanence of cinema as a performing event.
> Safeguarding moving image carriers
> is an essential component of the process,
> not its exclusive concern.

Budgets

Making film prints for preservation also has a strategic purpose that is worth mentioning here. If assessed in the long term, the cost of storing film in photochemical form is much lower than maintaining digital files through their periodical migration and upgrade. Once a film is protected on film, digital copies can be made on demand, for the purposes of general access. What the two forms of duplication have in common is that they are both very costly. On a large scale, both endeavours require financial investments whose magnitude is often beyond the means of non-profit organizations.

Contrary to popular belief, a film preservation project in either photochemical or digital form cannot be easily quantified in budgetary terms, as there are many variables to be considered: the condition of the original material; the time required to prepare it for laboratory work; the nature of the source elements (positive or negative, colour or black and white, 35mm, 28mm, or 9.5mm, and so on); the intended quality of the outcome (printing methods with film or pixel rates with digital); the labor involved in obtaining the desired chromatic balance and contrast; and the infrastructure necessary to guarantee the longevity of the preserved work. The cost of a digital 'correction' job is normally calculated by the time necessary to intervene on each frame of a film, multiplied by the number of frames in the complete print; this could vary enormously, depending on the available technology and the degree of refinement demanded by the project.

A major difference between photochemical and digital laboratory work is that the latter can be pushed to extremes in the time applied to the cleaning and grading of each frame, shot, or sequence; hence the astronomical cost for the 2011 digital version of *A Trip to the Moon* (p. 9). It is possible, of course, to do the same work at a much lower cost (this can happen only if the source material is in pristine shape, which is rarely the case for a silent film), but its quality is much lower, too. Conversely, laboratory work in the analogue domain yields to fixed technical parameters: in general terms, its budget is comparatively easier to forecast.

The copyright law in France has a providential clause in its definition of a film as a 'print'; at the present time, to secure legal protection, producers must deposit a 35mm projection copy of their films. This is good news for film preservation, as it motivates copyright owners to protect their photochemical assets in the original formats (the requirement extends to digitally born works, which is a source of controversy). The governments of countries like Great Britain, France, Norway, Sweden, the Netherlands, and Australia have been very generous with institutions in charge of preserving the national film collections in their respective countries. Over the years, however, film archives and museums have become increasingly reliant upon the support of private donors. The Library of Congress (with the David W. Packard Campus of the National Audio-Visual Conservation Center) and the British Film Institute (with the J. Paul Getty Conservation Centre) are two leading examples of partnership between public repositories and their benefactors.

In early 2012, the Svenska Filminstitutet took over the operations of the last surviving commercial film laboratory in Sweden for the purposes of continuing its own preservation work, in compliance with the principle of identity between the original medium and format of the carrier, and its reproduction on film for long-term conservation. The success of these projects is predicated upon the commercial availability of motion picture film stock from the two main companies that currently provide it on an industrial scale (Eastman Kodak in the United States, Orwo in Germany); in the early 2010s, artists like Tacita Dean, Christopher Nolan, and Quentin Tarantino have made themselves heard in support of this vision of the future of cinema. With a similar intent, photochemical film preservation will be discussed in the following pages in the present tense. It is hard to predict for how long this will remain a possibility.

Generations

It is to be presumed that most of the digital versions of *A Trip to the Moon* mentioned at the beginning of this book were created from one or more of the best surviving copies of the film. As of 2018, seven nitrate elements of first or second generation (six prints and one negative) were known to exist:

1. A complete black and white positive of first generation from the personal collection of film journalist and historian Maurice Bessy (1910–93). The copy is now at the Cinémathèque Méliès in Paris; this is one of the sources for the digital version presented at the Festival de Cannes in 2011.

2. An incomplete duplicate negative of second generation (made in 1929 on AGFA, Pathé, and a third unidentified stock), received by the Archives françaises du film from the estate of film exhibitor Jean-Placide Mauclaire (1905–66). The opening scene (the astronomers' congress) is missing; evidence shown by the fourteen sections of the negative suggests that three different sources were used for its creation.

3. An incomplete positive of second generation, tinted and hand-coloured (on AGFA stock, 1929), also from the Mauclaire collection at the Archives françaises du film, derived from the 1929 duplicate negative mentioned above. This was the print shown by Mauclaire on 16 December 1929 at a gala held in honour of Georges Méliès in Paris. Mauclaire's material is the second element used in the creation of the 2011 digital version.

4. An incomplete hand-coloured positive of second generation (a pirated copy from Spain), found by the Filmoteca de Catalunya, the third source for the 2011 digital version, the most extensively used for that project.

5. An incomplete black and white positive of second generation, from the David Eve Collection at the George Eastman Museum. This is also a pirated copy, distributed by Edison in September 1902 after the Star-Film logo had been removed from each frame of the twenty-sixth tableau in a duplicate negative (Fig. 29b).

6. A positive fragment of undetermined generation (47 metres, or 154 feet) in the Will Day Collection at the Cinémathèque française, on deposit at the Archives françaises du film.

7. A tinted positive of yet undetermined generation, with title card in German, held by the Eye Filmmuseum in Amsterdam.

There was also a black and white print (possibly of second generation; the end was missing) at the Museum of Modern Art in New York. It was donated by the widow of an American film exhibitor, Jean-Aimé 'Acme' LeRoy; some evidence indicates that LeRoy had received a duplicate negative of the film from a British film exhibitor, Will Day, who also owned a nitrate print. MoMA made a print for Henri Langlois, who did not have one at the Cinémathèque française. The nitrate, unfortunately, is no longer extant (the sixth element in the nitrate inventory just outlined is included in Part 3 of the Pathe Pictorial compilation by Will Day, *The Evolution of the Film*, made in 1928).

We do not know if all the existing prints on film of *A Trip to the Moon* are derived from these elements. The above list reproduces some of the available information on what is known about their origins: who owned them, when they were made, where they were shown. Each of these prints has a story to tell. Every copy of a film appearing on a screen – as a print or in digital form – has a story, too. It is not an abstract entity brought to the present after a logical path designed by history on behalf of posterity. It is the survivor of a complex, often random process of selection, not much different from a Darwinian evolutionary scheme. Considering the limited number of prints struck for a film of the early years, and taking into account the variety of factors contributing to their loss or decay, the very existence of a silent nitrate copy may be seen as something close to a miracle.

By their nature, miracles tend to occur in extraordinary situations. A group of nitrate prints (the Uhl Collection, now at the Library of Congress) was found in 1987 inside a barn in the rural community of Temperance, Michigan; they belonged to the grandfather of Robert Uhl, a 23-year-old student at the University of Toledo, Ohio, who alerted one of his professors, Scott Nygren, about the discovery. For no apparent reason, most of the decomposing copies of feature films were lacking the first or the last reel. It was later determined that the missing reels had been used by some local kids for a rather

daring form of fireworks display, in which the film was removed from the cans, unspooled, then ignited at one end of the leader – a very dangerous game, and a spectacular sight to behold.

No less astounding was the discovery in 1978 of a large number of nitrate reels under an abandoned ice-hockey rink in Dawson City, Yukon, the most unlikely repository for a time capsule of silent cinema. The severe cold temperatures in northern Canada, and the unusual protection given to the prints in the underground shelter – uncovered by an excavator half a century after their burial – contributed to the physical survival of more than four hundred of these long-forgotten relics. The films had been left there at the end of their commercial life, as they were not deemed worth the expense of returning them to the distributors.

The temperature shock caused by the fortuitous retrieval of so many projection copies from near-arctic permafrost, and their abrupt exposure to sunlight and humidity, contributed to the melting of the emulsion close to the surface of many reels in their metal containers. Duplicates from the nitrate prints in the Dawson City Collection at the Library of Congress are still showing the scars from the rescue operation, in the form of decayed emulsion fluttering at the vertical margins of the frame during projection, as shown in Fig. 193 (Bill Morrison's 2016 documentary *Dawson City: Frozen Time* is an artist's interpretation of the events).

Amazing as they are, these episodes are not isolated examples of where film preservation begins. Nitrate prints can turn up anywhere, from construction sites to landfills and basements; they are often found when it is too late to give them shelter. What has safely reached the vaults of museums and archives is only the tip of what used to be a slowly thawing and volatile iceberg, most of which no longer exists. Its sheer dimensions may be better appreciated by turning it upside down and viewing it as a genealogical tree, at the apex

Fig. 193 Image loss from the melting of film emulsion in a 35mm nitrate positive of *The Half-Breed* (Allan Dwan, 1916). Frame enlargement from a 35mm triacetate positive. Source: Library of Congress/Dawson City Collection.

of which are the camera negatives used to make distribution prints at the time of a film's commercial release.

It would have been appropriate to illustrate the point by using *A Trip to the Moon* as a real-life case study, but the film was so hugely successful that we have no idea of how many prints were made over the years; the following scenario should serve as an imaginary but plausible substitute to what could have been applied to Méliès' masterwork, had we known the exact number of negatives and projection copies produced over time. Let us imagine, for argument's sake, that two parallel black and white camera negatives of an American feature film were made in 1914, following the practice described in Chapter 5. The first negative was to be used for the domestic market; for the purposes of this demonstration, we shall assume that the second negative was recut before being dispatched to London for overseas distribution.

In our fictional account, we will suppose that nineteen positive prints (tinted and toned) were made from the first negative (A) in the United States, while sixteen copies of the edited version

were struck abroad from the second negative (B), with title cards translated into various languages and with different tinting and toning schemes for each country in which the film was shown (only print 22 is in black and white, as a distributor decided to leave it as it was). By the end of World War I, both camera negatives had vanished. After being dormant for a decade, one of the 'domestic' projection prints was used in 1925 to create a duplicate negative (C) for a reissue of the film.

Genealogy

The second chapter in our simulated 'material history' of the film continues with the discovery of a corporate document, proving that twelve positive copies, all in black and white, were struck from the duplicate negative of second generation (C). In 1936, a private collector found one of these prints, liked the film very much, and made another duplicate negative (D) in addition to three prints: one for private use, the other two for trade with fellow collectors. Another decade elapsed. The collector disappeared from sight; so did the three nitrate prints derived from the 1925 negative (D). In 1948, an independent distributor took possession of another copy from the 1925 reissue with the intention of renting it to local film societies. Some footage was removed because of wear and tear at the beginning and end of each reel; a cheap laboratory took the nitrate print, from which yet another duplicate negative (E) and ten abridged copies were hastily made.

The image on the new duplicating element and the resulting prints was cropped on one side: the laboratory's machines had been set up with aperture gates for the reproduction of sound films. One of these prints was borrowed in 1952 by a film club, whose owner kept it long enough to send it to another laboratory and make a 16mm reduction negative (F). Five projection prints came out of this process; four were sold to schools and film libraries after removing some title cards from each copy (their racial slurs were deemed inappropriate); the fifth was kept intact.

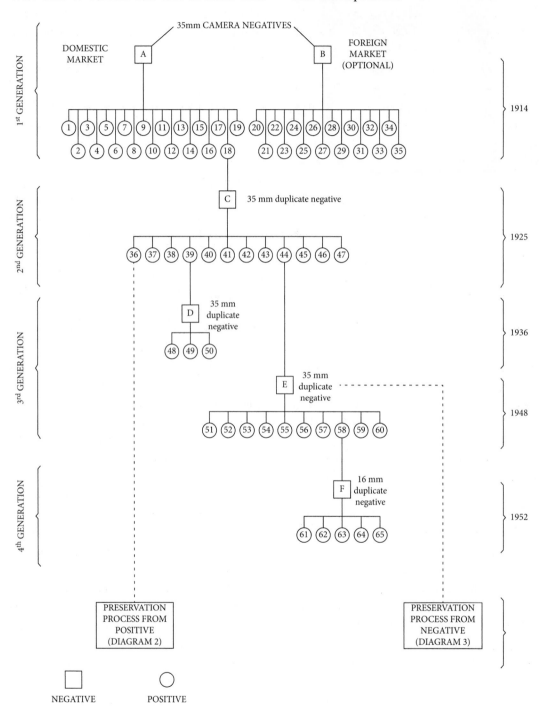

Diagram 1 Print generation in history.

The story could go on until the present time, but it is best to interrupt it at this point; its plot is visually represented in Diagram 1.

All in all, our film came to exist in six negatives (A–F) and sixty-five prints, five of which were made on 16mm stock. The scenario described above may look excessively complex; in fact, it is the over-simplified mirror of a very plausible reality. Many silent films were subject to a much larger number of duplications, and in most cases there is no way to determine how many prints were made at any given step of the process, nor can we reconstruct its actual chronology. It is equally impossible to tell whether or not the story is over; for that matter, someone may have bought one of the 16mm prints in a flea market, put it through a digital scanner, and downloaded it on the Internet. Once a film exists, the trajectory of its reincarnation into duplicates becomes anybody's guess; the only type of work where the principle does not apply is amateur or avant-garde cinema, as its makers rarely made more than one print and had no reason or the financial means to strike extra duplicates. *Ballet mécanique* (Fernand Léger, 1924) and *Un Chien andalou* are among the few exceptions to this.

No reliable census of all the film reels in circulation during the silent period (and beyond) can be conducted. We are only left with the conjecture that some films were never reprinted from the original negatives after their initial release, and that very few titles proliferated into a vast number of replicas of ever more unsatisfactory quality than their predecessors. A perfect case in point is the early work of Charlie Chaplin, whose shorts made for Keystone, Essanay, and Mutual between 1914 and 1917 were scattered around the world in so many copies of various formats that we will never be able to have an exact count of them. First-generation prints of the pre-feature period in Chaplin's career are extremely rare, and mostly survive in a very battered condition. An unspoken rule of film preservation is that the chances of finding a nitrate copy of a silent film in good shape are inversely proportional to its commercial success: the more the film was projected, the worse its prints are bound to appear, unless the negative still exists, in which case it all depends on whether or not it has been properly handled in previous times.

Two preliminary observations can be drawn from the hypothetical saga outlined so far. Should we be holding a 35mm copy of *A Trip to the Moon* in our hands, we could now begin to appreciate that its position in the genealogical tree of the film's duplication history does matter, because it explains why the print is in black and white, and not in colour; why its title card appears different from those of other prints; why it is complete or not. As for our imaginary film, watching it as a 1948 print (number 52 in Diagram 1) would have told us very little of how copy number 4 appeared in 1914, given the many previous steps undertaken to generate projection copies from the negatives, and the duplicate negatives from projection copies made at a later time.

Each of these steps (the making of a negative and the subsequent creation of one or more prints) corresponds to a print 'generation'. In each duplication cycle with a photographic process, some percentage of the visual information in the previous copy – a smaller or greater amount, depending on the quality of laboratory work – is lost for ever (modern film technology can only reduce the gap without eliminating it altogether). Think, for instance, of a projection copy derived from a tenth-generation negative: the cumulative effect of the previous nine generations in the latest reproduction cycle should give a rough idea of the disparity between the film's appearance on the screen and the look of a print made from the original camera negative.

The frame enlargement of Fritz Lang's *Metropolis* reproduced in Fig. 194 (a) is taken from a 35mm nitrate positive print of first generation.

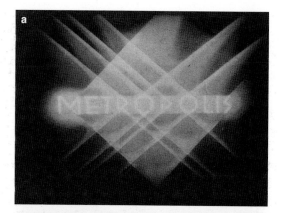

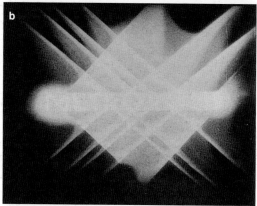

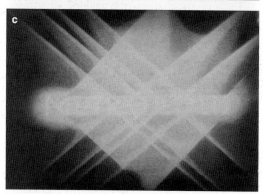

Fig. 194a–c The main title of *Metropolis* (Fritz Lang, 1927). From top to bottom: (a) 35mm nitrate positive of first generation, tinted; (b) 35mm triacetate positive, 1987; (c) 16mm triacetate positive, 1954. Sources: [a] National Film and Sound Archive of Australia; [b], [c] George Eastman Museum.

The second frame enlargement (b) is from a 35mm triacetate print of unknown generation, possibly the third, made in 1987. Frame enlargement (c) shows the same frame as it appears in a

16mm print made in 1954. The difference between the first and the last in the series is palpable. It is impossible to tell how many generations came before the reduction copy: it can take many of them – or just a single careless printing job, such as the one shown in Fig. 195 – to turn the picture into such a poor surrogate of the prints in the top rank of the genealogy tree, a far cry from what *Metropolis* was in 1927. On the other hand, there is not much visible difference between (b) and (c), in that the title card is barely readable in both; the 35mm's coarseness and contrast are surprising for a print that should, in theory, look much better than a 16mm duplicate.

There are at least two possible reasons for this. First, the processing of the 35mm copy may have been less than adequate; second, the 16mm print may have been struck from an earlier source than that used for the 35mm positive. There is a lesson to be drawn here: film format is important, but its generation also counts when comparing different elements of the same title. Non-theatrical prints may represent the best available materials for some silent films, and be in much better shape

Fig. 195 Frame enlargement from a 16mm triacetate positive of *The Navigator* (Donald Crisp and Buster Keaton, 1924) showing a printed-in 'double' frame line next to the upper edge of the frame, a common flaw in film duplication work of the mid-twentieth century. Source: George Eastman Museum.

than beaten or incomplete 35mm duplicate prints made several years later.

When searching for the best existing elements of a film, collecting institutions pay attention to both print quality and print generation. Camera negatives are generally the most coveted objects, but they give no indication of how the films were tinted, toned, or stencilled, something which can only be gathered from release prints. Curators are justifiably excited when they find copies struck directly from the camera negatives, because their images are sharper. In many cases, print generation can also be inferred from the frames' right and left margins, where the printed-in profile of sprocket holes from previous negatives and prints is sometimes partially visible (Fig. 196a–d).

No first-generation copies are known to exist of *Sunrise*, which explains the uneven quality of all surviving prints known so far; whatever is left of *The Blue Bird* is a far cry from the lovingly tinted and toned copies originally made from the camera negative. When faced with these realities, collecting institutions have no other choice than to settle for what they have, in the hope that elements of better quality will eventually emerge. On rare occasions, their patience is rewarded by sheer coincidence, as happened in 1981 when a beautiful 35mm nitrate print of *La Passion de Jeanne d'Arc* (Carl Theodor Dreyer, 1928) was retrieved from the basement of a mental hospital in Norway.

Matrices

What we have described so far is the 'material history' of the film, a multilayered account of what happened to the creative work as a whole and to the physical components created for its duplication and exhibition. As shown earlier, each generation has its own story to relay, and each individual member of any given generation could tell even more, should it be given a chance to

Fig. 196a–d Print generation as seen through the profile of sprocket holes. *The Voice of the Violin* (D.W. Griffith, 1909). 35mm nitrate positive (a). The black areas on the right and left margins of the frame (b) are from the 35mm camera negative, which has a single Edison perforation per frame on both edges of the film stock. Negative and positive perforations have both overlapped the area occupied by the image. In the 35mm polyester positive of second generation (c), the sprocket holes of the nitrate positive are still evident, while the single perforations in the negative are barely visible. The margins have been cropped in the 16mm triacetate positive (d), of unknown generation. Source: George Eastman Museum.

speak for itself; taken collectively, all these voices would form a sprawling cacophony of cuts, splices, rewinds, and a brief but intense period of travels around the world. For the sake of argument, it shall be assumed that one of the elements shown in Diagram 1 – print 36, a nitrate positive – has been found somewhere, formally acquired by a museum as part of its permanent collection, and believed to be the only extant one for that title, the sole remaining witness of the film's material history. The lonely messenger of what the creative work once was becomes the protagonist of a totally different story, unfolding in what is referred to as the art and technique of film preservation.

For some time, Print 36 will be lonelier than ever. Being the only known print of that film, it is withdrawn from public access. It may or may not be projectable, but that doesn't matter: even if the print was made of polyester and with minimal scratches, curators would refrain from projecting it because there are no others left, and any further damage would diminish or compromise the chances of seeing the film again in the distant future, many centuries from now. This print is now a matrix, the only substitute for the original camera negatives, now lost. Archives call it a 'master positive' for this reason, even though it was originally not meant to play such an important role. This is where curatorial judgement makes its first appearance in the material history of the film. Should the copy not be unique, its archival denomination would not necessarily change; as this is the nitrate print of a silent film – a rare object by definition – it is likely that the archive would treat it as a matrix anyway. It may be more complete, or in better condition than the others. A second nitrate copy held elsewhere may belong to later generations (prints 51 to 65 in Diagram 1). A third one, whose condition and archival status are unknown, may be kept in a vault with no climate control and high relative humidity. All three are 'master positives' for as long as they are irreplaceable.

Until the early 2000s, it was customary to allow the exhibition of an archival print as long as there was a film preservation element – that is, a negative – derived from the matrix. Should the projection print be ruined, another could be made. Reliant upon this very sensible theory, museums and archives kept showing the same copies until they became so damaged as to be almost unusable. They rarely had the financial means to make new ones; it was easier for them to seek support for an entirely new project than for a replica of what was already done. Once a common practice among collecting institutions, this rule of thumb can no longer be applied without a careful assessment of its implications. Whether in colour or black and white, an archival projection print is never easy to replace. Even if a preservation negative is available or its whereabouts are known, there is no guarantee that a new print will be as good as the old one. Moreover, making a new print is indeed a very expensive business, and there is no abundance of funds for film archives and museums.

Important as they were, Charlie Chaplin's early films remained unpreserved for a very long time precisely because there were so many projection prints around, and everyone thought they would have been easy to replace. By the time collecting institutions became aware that very few preservation negatives had been made of Chaplin's films, much of the damage to the existing prints had already been done (many years elapsed before the problem was partially remedied). The temptation may arise to take the digital route and forego preservation altogether; a response to this is given at the end of this chapter and explained throughout this book, but it must be remembered that the tension between ethics and convenience is a leitmotiv of the debate on how to give film history the protection it deserves.

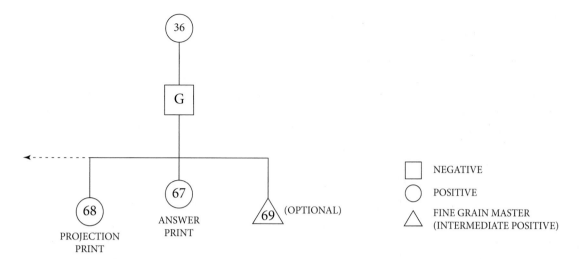

Diagram 2 Film duplication path from a projection copy.

Prints

A schematic representation of what 'protection' means in photochemical terms is provided in Diagram 2. The digital equivalent of this process is much simpler at its preliminary stage, as it basically entails the scan of the nitrate element and its transformation into pixels. Matters become far more complex in the ensuing phases, as data obtained from the 'raw scans' – the first outcome of the non-photochemical work for print duplication – are manipulated and translated into other digital formats (or new 35mm prints) that are suitable for exhibition and access.

Prints

Print 36 is cleaned, repaired, and put in cold storage. As soon as financial resources allow it, the print is taken to a laboratory and a negative element (of the same format, when possible or required by the nature of the project) is produced. Duplication by photographic means is achieved with contact printing (the positive and the negative are continuously run through the printer) or step printing (each frame of the film is separately exposed in front of the duplicating element), following the same process described in Chapter 4. The latter method is much slower, but it is far more accurate, especially when the source material is heavily damaged or shrunken.

In a broad sense, the laboratory process follows the same path adopted in the silent era: a duplicate negative (known also as a 'preservation negative') is struck from the master positive. The first copy derived from this negative is called an 'answer print', as it will reveal whether or not the preservation negative has reproduced the images of the matrix with a sufficient degree of accuracy. The most delicate part of this phase, commonly referred to as 'timing' or 'grading', is a shot-by-shot or section-by-section measurement of the amount of light needed to give each portion of the film the correct exposure (a 'one-light negative' is so called because it was uniformly exposed to the same amount of light; in the digital domain, only the term 'grading' is used).

When all the necessary corrections have been made, the preservation negative is used to make one or more positive copies. Their technical names are dependent upon the context in which the prints are created: 'show print' or 'release print' in the laboratory; 'viewing print', 'reference copy', 'projection print', or 'access copy' in the museum or archive. Some of these terms have more than one meaning ('reference print', for instance, may describe a copy that is not good enough to qualify as a 'projection print' but can be studied on a machine for individual viewing). Their common denominator is that the prints they refer to are not subject to the same restrictions imposed upon access to the master elements – in this imaginary case study, print 36 – because accidental damage or gradual wear and tear on the exhibition copy will not compromise the survival of the film.

The preservation negative can be used for further copying as required, but not carelessly: if the negative is damaged or destroyed, it may not be possible to produce another one because its matrix has further decomposed in the meanwhile, or no longer exists. Making at least two projection prints – one for screenings in the museum, the other one for loan – helps to delay repeated use of the negative; best practice recommends taking the extra step of duplicating the negative onto a low-contrast positive, whose emulsion is different from those of the projection prints (it is called a 'fine grain master' or 'intermediate positive' – element 69 in Diagram 2), to be used as an emergency backup, and ideally a 'duplicate negative' or 'intermediate negative' (not reproduced in Diagram 2) from the fine grain master.

The great advantage of this redundancy method is that the preservation negative is never touched, as all projection prints are made from the duplicate negative; the obvious drawbacks are a slight loss of visual information in the second-generation print for projection, and the extra costs involved. Production and distribution companies of the late twentieth century used to create several intermediate negatives, given the very large number of

projection prints for general release. Collecting institutions have no such obligation, but they don't have much money to spend, either: unless a given title is in great demand, archives and museums rarely go beyond the making of a fine grain master. Most of them cannot afford even that: their project comes to completion when a new projection print has been created, in the hope that nothing will happen to the newly created negative. This is the average basic scenario of a film preservation project.

The vast majority of extant silent films were found as projection prints. In the infrequent event that the surviving element is a negative (such as item E in the genealogical chart), the preservation workflow begins with the creation of a fine grain master (element 66 in Diagram 3). This is a necessary extra step with respect to the printing process from a positive: it is possible to make a projection copy directly from the archival negative, and some institutions do this as well (the quality of the resulting print can be exceptional if the negative is a first-generation nitrate in good condition), but the goal of the preservation process is to generate a new negative on a more stable carrier for the future creation of new viewing copies. The intermediate negative made from the newly created preservation element (the fine grain master) is the printing source for the answer print and – if the negative has been approved – one or more projection prints, as shown in Diagram 3.

In a narrow sense, a preservation negative (from a master positive) or fine grain master (if a negative is the best surviving material) is the minimum requirement for the protection of an endangered film. It is not 'preserved', as it cannot yet be seen (in the absence of a projection print), but the risk of its complete oblivion has been temporarily avoided. Archives and museums with limited budgets have sometimes made recourse to this emergency option, in hope of better times. Other collecting institutions do the same before

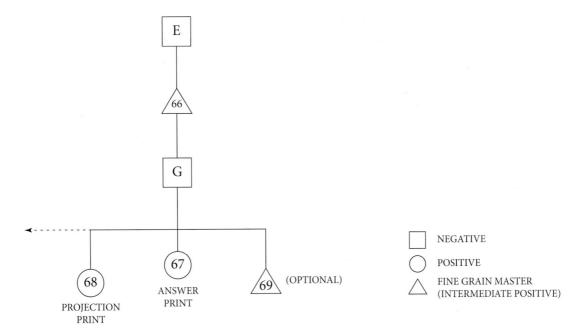

Diagram 3 Film duplication path from a negative.

delivering their work by digital means: the nitrate material is duplicated onto a more stable film carrier, which is used exclusively for the creation of access elements on other media.

Nitrate film – positive or negative – can also be scanned directly into digital files and then left to its own destiny. Producers of digital 'restoration' projects are very keen to do the scanning work from original elements (even when they have already been copied onto new photochemical elements, or have not yet been preserved) because they belong to an earlier printing generation, thus ensuring a more accurate reproduction of the source image (if the nitrate material has not started to decompose). This, however, does not fulfil the minimum requirements of film preservation, particularly if the source is decaying and no photochemical duplicate has been made. Digital scanning from unpreserved nitrate can be of great help in film preservation if its final outcome is a new set of negative and positive film elements;

otherwise, this approach only satisfies the needs for immediate access, to the detriment of the film's availability in the long term. The original material may never be preserved at all, in the belief that a set of digital files is enough to guarantee its permanence for posterity.

Dyes

So far, we have deliberately ignored the fact that some of the prints in the genealogical tree of Diagram 1 were tinted or toned. Archives and museums have ignored it, too, for many years, as they did not have the money or the technology required to imitate their colours with sufficient accuracy. For both reasons, copying tinted, toned, stencilled, and hand-coloured prints onto colour film stock was out of the question until the early 1970s. This situation improved only slightly with the introduction of Eastmancolor, whose emulsion was so chemically unstable that two of its three layers (yellow and cyan) were notoriously subject to fading after a few years if the prints were not kept at very low temperatures.

Eastmancolor's crude imitations of the original dyes, combined with budgetary constraints, were more than enough to persuade film curators that reproducing silent films in black and white, regardless of their chromatic palette, was better than nothing. Many of the nitrate prints they copied have vanished for ever. Much as we regret the permanent loss of their often beautiful colours, we must be grateful to all those who preserved so many films to the best of their ability under such difficult circumstances. Plates 31a and 31b, taken from a nitrate positive and from a black and white duplicate, offer ample evidence of how heavy was the compromise they had to accept, and of how much has become invisible in thousands of titles now surviving as monochrome shadows of what they once were.

The situation has dramatically changed since then, but the problem continues to haunt film curators and laboratory technicians. Processing methods allow the colours of silent cinema to be recreated with better approximation, and yet they are not quite the same. Colour film emulsion in negatives and prints of the early twenty-first century is apparently more stable than in motion picture stock of previous decades, but will eventually fade like that of all its predecessors: its inevitable decay can be slowed down only by storing acetate negatives and polyester prints in refrigerated vaults where temperature and humidity are kept as constant as possible. Digital technology has managed to emulate some colours of silent cinema – stencil and hand-colouring in particular – in ways that are precluded to photochemical processes; still, there is something missing in the chromatic palette of silent films as seen through modern reproductions in general, whether by analogue or by non-analogue means.

Laudable and necessary as it is, the objective of accurately replicating the colours of silent films on a systematic basis – that is, from the vast collections of original elements held by film museums and archives worldwide – is no less illusory than it was in the early days of colour film preservation. The evidence of this wishful thinking is best appreciated by looking consecutively at a nitrate print and its duplicate on the big screen (less so with a side-by-side comparison of the physical objects over a light bench or from computer monitors, as the discrepancies are truly revealed only at the moment of projection). Another problem is that the human brain has an extremely short and highly subjective chromatic memory: those who claim that some early Technicolor films may or may not be reproduced to their satisfaction are only fooling themselves if they saw the originals a few weeks before.

Reproductions of colour films from the silent era by photochemical means fall under four basic categories:

1. *Tinted and toned prints* may be copied with standard negative and positive (black and white or colour) film stock. The resulting duplicates can provide accurate imitations of the originals. In the case of colour stock, there is no guarantee that both the negative and the positive will keep their chromatic balance for a very long time. This may not be a major issue in the case of a positive copy, as more prints can be struck as needed; unfortunately, the same process of slow but irreversible decay affects the negative as well. As an alternative, it is possible to reproduce the tinted or toned original onto a black and white negative, specially graded for its subsequent exposure to one or two colour filters in the creation of positive prints. This technique, known as 'Desmet system' or Desmetcolor, is named after Belgian preservation specialist Noël Desmet,

who developed it in the 1990s. Its main advantage is the greater stability of black and white preservation negatives, compared to their colour equivalents. Within certain limits, the Desmet process is suitable for the duplication of nitrate prints with tinting and toning combined (similar attempts have also been made with stencilled and Handschiegl prints), but the results are not necessarily as good as those attainable with colour negatives.

Tinting and toning can also be applied to a black and white positive with the same methods and formulas used in the silent film era: Czech specialist Jan Ledecký has done so, often with remarkable effects, since 1979 (a proof of his craftsmanship is the beautiful 2016 restoration in 35mm format of Alexandre Volkoff's *Kean*, 1924, on behalf of the Cinémathèque française). Much can be learned on this subject from the corporate research and technical manuals of the silent period, although many dye compounds of the early twentieth century are no longer in use, or are prohibited by the law because they are considered toxic; fortunately, other options are available to film technicians. A single 35mm copy to be tinted or toned by immersion in dye baths requires extra time and meticulous work in the laboratory, but the effort is amply rewarded by the chromatic quality and relative stability of the projection prints.

Each copy obtained through Ledecký's method is unique, very much like the original elements it derives from, the only difference being that transitions in tinting and toning do not require splices in the new projection prints. Doing so would mean processing several rolls of positive film by their respective colour dyes, then assembling the projection prints according to the procedure shown in Chapter 3. While the same method could easily be followed in principle, a projection print with hundreds of splices is neither desirable in itself nor ideal for repeated use. Film cement does not work with polyester stock; the only alternative to adhesive tape is a special kind of splicer where the two ends to be joined are melted together by an ultrasonic signal.

2. *Copies coloured by hand or mechanically* (as in the Handschiegl process, or by stencils) are reproduced with the standard techniques involving the use of colour negatives and positives. The rare attempts to manually apply transparent dyes on black and white safety prints with the aid of tiny brushes and magnifying lenses have attained modest results at best. Intriguing as they may be, these experiments in hand-painting early films are of limited value in an archival context.

3. *Black and white negatives* of films that were to be released as tinted, toned, stencilled, and hand-coloured prints can only generate photochemical copies in black and white (their images can, of course, be 'colourized' through digital reproduction, but the results are an educated guess at best, if not a figment of the colourist's imagination).

4. *Projection prints made with additive processes* such as Chronochrome (p. 56) or Kinemacolor (p. 54) were also in black and white; their chromatic life began as the prints went through projectors equipped with coloured lenses, or with colour filters applied to the blade shutters.

Many of these negatives and prints can be duplicated to produce convincing simulations of what originally appeared on the screen. The copies made for this purpose are no longer 'duplicates' in the true sense of the term. If they derive from nitrate negatives, these prints have received their tinting on the basis of the information available from secondary sources, or from nitrate prints of other films. Reproductions on colour stock of Kinemacolor and Chronochrome films are doubly unfaithful to the originals: first, because they are not in black and white as the original copies were; second, because they altogether bypass the mechanical and optical characteristics of the machines that were needed to view their colours. What is lost in translation here is the essential role of the projector in the making of a motion picture show. The black and white elements of these films should be duplicated exactly as they are, and projected with the same kind of apparatus. Everything else is acceptable and maybe desirable for the sake of presenting these films to modern audiences when no original equipment is available, as long as this compromise is not confused with film preservation.

RULE 6

A film is preserved when it is permanently available
in a medium and format as close as possible to the original.
Film projection is the ultimate fulfilment of this goal.

Chapter 13

Lacunae

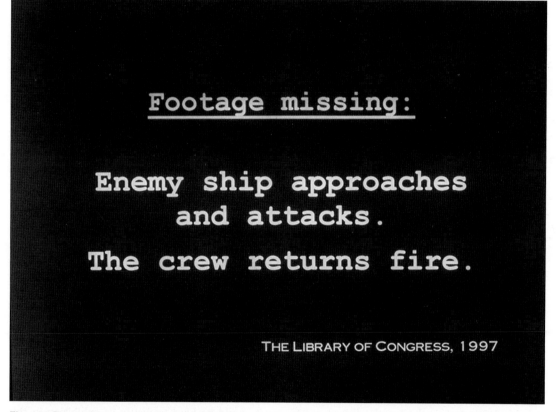

Fig. 197 Title card from the 1997 reconstructed version of *The Blue Eagle* (John Ford, 1926). Frame enlargement from a 35mm triacetate positive. Source: Library of Congress.

The previous chapter described how to preserve silent films as they have been found, regardless of their material condition. To continue with the example of print 36 as part of the genealogical tree in Diagram 1, nothing has yet been said about the physical state of the imaginary film element. We don't know whether it had been well maintained or carelessly projected, kept intact or savagely cut by censors, stored in a relatively cool and dry warehouse or left at the mercy of humidity and mould in the corner of a basement. Nitrate prints are very rarely found in the same shape as they were at the beginning of their commercial life; in those rare instances when this has happened, the most frequent reason is that the prints had been forgotten more by accident than design, early enough to spare them the perilous nomadic life of their siblings.

Another explanation for the almost pristine condition of some elements is that the prints could not be projected with conventional equipment: the original Chronochrome films at the George Eastman Museum were found almost intact by virtue of their unusual ratio between frames and perforations (Plate 44a), unsuitable to normal 35mm projectors. Film negatives are only slightly more fortunate than projection prints, in that they were generally cut and assembled just once, rarely changing domicile after reaching their second destination (the company's film vault). As seen in Chapter 10, this doubtful privilege found its counterpart in the routine destruction of the matrices, when their financial worth was reduced to the raw cellulose base and the silver of the emulsion. What is missing from all these objects, and what is being done to compensate for the gaps, is the theme of this chapter.

A film may be defined as 'complete' or 'incomplete' in (a) material, (b) narrative, and (c) optical terms. The criterion most commonly used is of purely quantitative nature: the length of the surviving element is measured against that of the finished film, as announced by producers and distributors at the time of its first release. So, if the 1903 Star-Film catalogue lists *A Trip to the Moon* as being 260 metres (in the French edition), or 845 feet (according to English-language edition) in length, it is to be hoped that the found print measures exactly the same. The numbers almost never match: the vast majority of extant nitrate prints and negatives are shorter than they were originally. *A Trip to the Moon* is no exception: there are about 13,520 frames in 845 feet of film; 13,375 were apparently scanned for the 2011 version, meaning that about 9 feet (or 2.7 metres) of film

are missing, barely above 1 per cent of the total. All things considered, the loss is very marginal in this case.

Film curators are so accustomed to this discrepancy that they call a 5,000-foot (1,524-metre) film 'complete' even if the surviving copy is 4,960 feet, or 1,512 metres, long. If they do not worry too much about it, it is because they are aware of all the alterations that may have affected negatives and projection copies even before the film's release. Prints were manually assembled. Censors were on the alert. Producers were often comfortable with footage counts rounded to whole reels, instead of feet or metres; the nitrate print of a film advertised as being in five reels will therefore be deemed complete if its actual length is close enough to the target of about 4,500 feet, or 1,400 metres.

The only other numerical count applied to an original film element is related to the splices detected on the material, as some of them may indicate that the print or negative suffered a break at some point, and had to be repaired (with the probable loss of one or more frames). The five-reel print is indeed qualified as incomplete if one reel is missing, but also when the absence of a section, however short, affects the comprehension or flow of the events registered on film. Should the brief shot of the rocket in the eye of the moon be missing from our copy of *A Trip to the Moon*, the print would certainly not be called complete (and it would be hard to justify its exhibition in this form), even though the shot's length is less than 6 metres, or 20 feet, of the total. To be 'complete' in narrative terms, a nitrate print should also be free of spurious elements, such as images or title cards unrelated to the original work.

This proviso highlights a major dilemma in film preservation, as it is well known that film exhibitors of the early years had total freedom to add, subtract, interpolate, and substitute titles and shots as they pleased, often taking pieces of films and inserting them in other prints for a variety of reasons. As creative works expressing the intention of their makers, these films are very much incomplete and are not authentic; nevertheless, they may be coherent and authentic 'complete' works in another sense, in that they represent the intentions of someone other than the director or the producers. We have no right to ignore, let alone suppress, the evidence of their decisions. These films should be preserved – therefore also seen, if so desired – exactly as they have been found. Not doing so would be equal to distorting or obliterating a piece of history.

Principles

This possibility raises the crucial question of how to determine whether or not a film should be preserved, and why. The above example shows that there are multiple factors involved in such a decision; each of them, alone or combined with the others, contributes to the assessments made at the curatorial level on when and how to tackle a new preservation project. In her short but fundamental essay 'Some Principles of Film Restoration' (1990), Eileen Bowser – a former curator at the Museum of Modern Art – has outlined five main goals and objectives:

1. Preserving the negative or positive film element exactly as it was acquired, with minimal or no corrections, regardless of its completeness and internal structure.

2. Bringing the film to a condition as close as possible to how it was seen by its audience at the time of release.

3. Presenting a version of the film in which the original intentions of the artist or the commercial entity that produced it are fully achieved.

4. Ensuring access to the film in a form that can be appreciated by a contemporary audience.

5. Using the film as the source material of new creative works, adapted or derived from the original.

A sixth category – preserving the film as it has been experienced by later audiences – has been proposed by some authors, but this is actually a variation on the first and the fifth categories. In deciding that a print should be formally acquired, a collecting institution makes a commitment to preserve it regardless of the film's version, generation, or material status; had it been otherwise, the print would not have been accepted as part of the archive's or museum's holdings. There is a hierarchy in Bowser's list of objectives: the first precedes all the others because it upholds the main imperative of all cultural repositories – safeguarding and making accessible the traces of history and culture as they have come to us, protected from any further interferences and distortions. Before altering the evidence of a film (as it has reached us in its material form) in order to achieve one or more of the other four objectives, the first one must be met. Bowser articulates this ethical imperative in three overall principles:

1. All film preservation processes must be reversible.

2. No alteration should be made to the collection artefact after its acquisition.

3. The preservation work should be documented, so that others are allowed to evaluate the choices made and the procedures chosen, and take corrective action if necessary.

A great advantage of preserving and making accessible a silent film in its original state (the first in Bowser's list of objectives) is that it satisfies the three requirements all at once. There is consensus among curators and scholars that it is necessary also to keep a detailed record of the main actions taken during the preservation process in the film or digital laboratory, but this promise has almost never been fulfilled. Film technicians are especially reluctant to document it in writing; as for curators, they are often unable or unwilling to go beyond generic or perfunctory reports. Preserving all the individual components of a film reconstruction in their unaltered form and internal sequence guarantees at least that everybody in the future – curators, scholars, technicians, as well as the general public – can extrapolate individual pieces of the puzzle and deconstruct or reconstruct it in its reproductions (the reversibility principle) without erasing the original evidence (the non-alteration principle). In this sense, the most passive approach to film preservation – not as paradoxical as it seems – is the best guarantee of its longevity. Film restorations come and go. With or without them, the original structure of the film object (and, yes, its visual content, should the work be digitally born) must be left unchanged.

New complications arise as soon as the above principle is applied to the print to be preserved from the perspective of its optical appearance. The copy in our possession may not be missing any footage and yet be incomplete in a different sense, as the images embedded in its emulsion have been ravaged by careless handling in projection, adverse environmental conditions, and the chemicals used for processing. All the frames of the film have survived, but are no longer in pristine condition: the images may have been cropped during duplication in order to add a soundtrack at the time of the film's reissue (in which case, 10 to 12 per cent of the image is lost, as seen in Fig. 198a–b); they

may lack the tints and tones applied to previous versions of the same film; they may show too much contrast, or have lost all their sharpness after several printing generations; finally, there may no longer be any image to look at, because the emulsion is gone. The body of the film has been physically damaged, or it has been photographically reduced to a ghost of itself. These 'qualitative' lacunae are no less significant than the missing footage, as they profoundly affect our rational and emotional response to the film. They are also painful to watch,

Fig. 198a–b *Ben-Hur* (Fred Niblo, 1925). 35mm triacetate positives of (a) the original release version and (b) the 1931 re-release with variable density soundtrack. Source: George Eastman Museum.

RULE 7

A film should be preserved in its original condition
before undertaking any further action about its contents,
so that future audiences can exercise their right
to see it in unaltered form.

as we are mourning their withered or devastated beauty, rather than their sheer absence. Observing a decayed image on the big screen is harder to forget than a missing shot, sequence, or reel.

When a nitrate print arrives at the premises of a collecting institution, it is normally inspected, measured, and cleaned before entering the vaults; after that, it is periodically checked to verify its shrinkage rate and chemical stability; perforations and splices are carefully repaired or reinforced before duplication. This is the starting point of the preservation process; much can happen in the course of its long and convoluted path. There is one area where film preservation must surrender to the status quo: in the photographic domain, print generation cannot be reverted (there is no way to make a 16mm print of fifth generation look as good as a first-generation copy).

All in all, film preservation confronts a dual test dictated by history: from a diachronic perspective – the unfolding in time of photographs projected in sequence – print 36 is 'incomplete' in the sense that some images recorded by one of the camera negatives – (A) in Diagram 1 – are no longer there. Should another print or a negative of another generation be found somewhere, reintegrating the visual content that is missing from print 36 in a new combined film element would be part of the preservation work. In its synchronic approach – each photographic frame considered as a discrete visual unit, closely related to the adjacent ones – the goal is to remove the effects of the mechanical damage inflicted upon the print, and at least some of the harm suffered by its previous generations. A third test, emanating from film preservation's own ethical standards, is giving film history more material to dwell upon.

Scratches

Predictably enough, scratches are a matter of major concern in film preservation. They are the symbols of what makes silent cinema look so decrepit, with film archives and museums trying hard to get rid of the wrinkles through cosmetic or plastic surgery. To better understand this cause of so much trouble, the comparison may be pushed a step further: scratches are tiny grooves carved onto the skin of the film, on both sides of the print or negative, provoked by intermittent or continuous friction with particles of dust, or with some components of the projection or printing equipment. If very deep, scratches on the base can accumulate dirt over time (a cross-cut view of this is schematically shown in Diagram 4). Before digital technology was applied to film preservation, scratches were a big problem for film laboratories, as nothing could be done about those made on prints or negatives of previous generations (commonly referred to as 'printed in'). The solutions available in photochemical work to eliminate or reduce them are therefore limited to scratches directly affecting the print or the negative to be duplicated. In most silent films, scratches on the *base* appear as black or white lines on the screen, depending on whether they were inflicted, respectively, upon positive or negative elements. It should be noted that scratches were sometimes applied intentionally to the camera negatives in order to achieve visual effects, such as lightning and rain in *King Lear* (Vitagraph, 1909; Fig. 199).

When a film emulsion is scratched, small portions of the visual information carried by the print or the negative have been scraped away and cannot be recovered by photomechanical means, unless the scratch is extremely light (in which case, the emulsion can be softened so that it expands slightly, thus filling the affected area). If the scratch is on the *emulsion* of a positive film, it will show as a clear line during projection. If it is made on the negative's emulsion, it will appear as a dark line on the positive copy struck from its matrix. In prints

Fig. 199 *King Lear* (William V. Ranous, 1909). The rain effect was obtained by scratching the film's camera negative. Frame enlargement from a 35mm triacetate positive. Source: BFI National Archive.

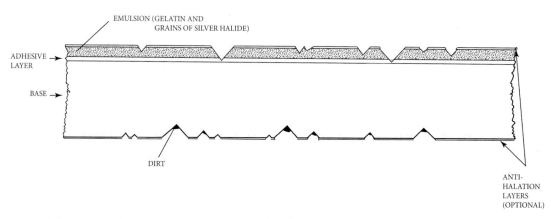

Diagram 4 Section of a film element with scratches on the base and emulsion sides.

with multilayered emulsions (such as those of Technicolor films), scratches can show up in different colours, depending on the depth of the abrasion.

Scratches on the base of the film are somewhat easier to treat, because no visual content was removed from the emulsion. The projector's light does not travel in a perpendicular direction across the surface of the print; in forming slightly different angles, the light's refraction against each groove on the base of the positive film generates a shadow, seen as a dark irregular line in the projected image. Any dirt or dust deposited into the groove makes this line appear more pronounced. Dirt and speckles of dust can be removed before printing and projection through various cleaning methods (at present, best practice calls for ultrasonic cleaning in a chemical bath). At the printing stage, there are two techniques for reducing or preventing the appearance of base scratches on the duplicate. In the first method (now infrequently used), known as 'light diffusion', the light source used for printing is directed from a variety of angles, so that the greatest possible amount of light reaches the grooves at a 90-degree angle as it does with the remaining flat surface of the film stock. No chemicals are required in this process, but the resulting image exhibits a lower contrast, and sometimes looks foggier than the original.

The second method, called 'wet gate printing', is far more effective. It requires a printing device where the optical gate is enclosed in a box containing a chemical substance so transparent that it fills the grooves, making the base appear smooth and free from scratches, just long enough for the light of the printer to pass through in a perpendicular direction. This is the best way for transferring scratched film into duplicates of excellent quality by photochemical means (only the very deepest grooves may leave a residual trace of their presence). Digital technology achieves the same in a completely different way, with the extra benefit of identifying and erasing scratches, dust, and

dirt 'printed in' from previous film generations. With this powerful advantage over its predecessor, computer software forcefully entered the field of film preservation by enabling the photographic process to be replicated or bypassed.

The film scanner takes a digital picture of each frame at the required pixel rate (or 'definition'); through algorithms or manual interventions, the missing or altered portions are filled until the image is reconstructed. Digital transfer of motion picture film can either be an intermediate step of the photochemical process, or an end in itself. In the first case, the scanned film frames are 'corrected' before being transferred back onto positive or negative film; otherwise, the digital frames are used as master elements to reproduce the film in as many formats as required. A simplified version of the process is shown in Diagram 5.

Hybrids

It is worth repeating what a digital scanner does to a film. It makes reproductions in binary code of photochemical images. Each frame of the print or negative is now a 'file'. Each group of files (a shot, a sequence, a reel, or the entire film) has become one or more 'folders'. The duplication of photographic frames into digital images has major consequences at both the technical and the curatorial level. The reproduction process has also profoundly changed in conceptual terms: when digital is used as an intermediate element for image correction, the film is turned into data, and the data are later reverted into grains of silver bromide. The result is, by all means, a copy made with photochemical techniques, but it is no longer the mirror of a photochemical emulsion. It is a replica of pixels. Because it will be watched in the form of single photographs projected at regular intervals, it is fair to keep calling it 'cinema'. The source of the cinematic event, however, is

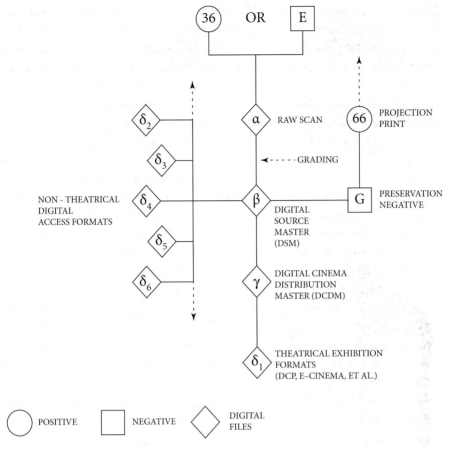

Diagram 5 Film duplication path in the digital domain.

something different. This may not be noticed because the pixels are extremely small (when it is, the residuals from the digital process are called 'digital artefacts', an inadvertently ironic exchange of roles between the tangible and the intangible); nevertheless, a projection print of this type is the product of a transplant process, a hybrid between two distinct forms of visual expression.

There is good value in this cross-pollination method. A digital scanner can run nitrate prints so damaged (such as those where the perforations are almost all gone) that photochemical copying would be extremely difficult, if not impossible to achieve. The possibilities of digital intermediate processes are equally impressive in the reproduction of stencilled films. Where

tinting and toning are combined, colour grading by digital tools succeeds where the Desmet method (pp. 256–257) sometimes fails. There are limits in what photochemical wet-gate printing can do to reduce the effects of scratches on the film's emulsion and base; conversely, the only boundaries to the use of digital software in solving the same problem are purely of a budgetary nature.

As explained in the previous chapter, digital work on images from a print or negative is often very expensive and time-consuming, but for a film laboratory it is not a matter of money: by definition, photochemical reproduction does not go beyond revealing or hiding visual content. Making the best use of both worlds – analogue and digital – by combining them in the film preservation process has dramatically improved the look of silent cinema in duplicate form. On the other hand, as long as the collecting institution's policy is to remain faithful to the original medium both in its conservation and its public exhibition, not all silent films require digital intermediate work. A nitrate print in good condition can be duplicated on film, employing the same techniques used before digital came into being.

The technological and curatorial landscape of film preservation is entirely different where silent cinema migrates to pixels in order to be exhibited in digital form. As noted earlier, a digital scanner is basically an automated machine that takes pictures of individual film frames and translates them into a binary code. Some of these machines work extremely fast. Nitrate film requires them to run at much slower speeds. Digital, too, has its own wet-gate process, where film is either immersed or drenched in a chemical substance while it goes through the scanner. The result of this preliminary step is a set of files and folders called 'raw scan', consisting of thousands of digital images, one for each frame. The data are then converted into the formats required for various access platforms, and that is where the digital journey of silent cinema confronts its first important obstacle. As of 2018, projectors installed in commercial theatres could handle digital files to be projected at the same frame rate of all current productions – that is, 24 frames per second or more. The projection speed of most silent films was slower than that. This is not an impediment to the projection of motion picture film in modern theatres, as the equipment for variable speed control is commercially available, not very expensive, and relatively easy to install.

For a short period in the late twentieth century, some collecting institutions thought it best to make prints of silent films that could be run at the standard rate of 24 frames per second in commercial theatres. The trick was achieved by optically 'stretching' prints that were originally projected at slower speeds. Some frames (from the nitrate source, or from the preservation negative) were printed twice at regular intervals: one frame every five to imitate a projection speed of 20 frames per second; one every three for 18 frames per second; and so forth. Aside from being an outright falsification of film as an object (once 'stretched' to imitate the projection speed of 16 frames per second, a nitrate print of 5,000 feet, or 1,500 metres, would be duplicated onto a safety copy of 7,500 feet, or 2,285 metres), the result is awful to look at, with people and objects weirdly advancing in a jittery or dreamlike fashion.

The same kind of effect is painfully evident in the theatrical projection of a 1907 film in digital form; attempts to solve the problem by digitally 'merging' two frames into one at regular intervals have so far brought only marginal benefits (at present, variable speed control is not an option for digital projectors in commercial film theatres). Once copied into a raw scan, a silent film can be adapted to a given projection speed with methods that are similar to optical stretching by photographic means; if that doesn't work, another access file at a different speed can be created. Either way, once delivered in a so-called 'cinema package', the speed can no longer be changed. There are technical solutions to this, but – for the time being – silent cinema is not regarded as a sufficiently commercial asset to justify the investment that would be required on the part of the industry to address the issue.

Translations

Curatorial rules are not dogmas. Scratches are part of a print's internal history, but it would be foolish not to try to remove at least the most glaring ones, if at all possible. There is no harm in using pixels to repair what cannot be fixed otherwise, even if they are not grains of silver bromide. Nonetheless, the question of where film 'integrity' begins emerges in all its intricacy. When admiring a wooden table from the seventeenth century, scratches are so much a component of its 'aura' that its owner likes them to be perceived as part of the object's history, and would cringe at the prospect of someone smoothing its surface to perfection with sandpaper, thus significantly affecting the table's value. When an ancient mural painting is found in fragmentary form, fine arts specialists restore what they can, and leave the rest alone. Many of Sappho's poems, and the Aphrodite of Milos on display in the Louvre, are incomplete; much as it would be wonderful to read or see the rest, no one has a problem in admiring these works of art as they are now. The question of why film audiences cannot stand scratches and gaps in a silent film to the point of removing or filling them whenever possible is too complex to be shrugged off as an unnecessary philosophical musing.

A plausible explanation for the urge to improve what is defective is that cinema itself is a very pliable form of artistic expression. Its innate flexibility is comparable to that of music and oral literature. Monteverdi's opera *L'incoronazione di Poppea* (1643) survives in two very different versions, neither of which includes all the instrumental parts. There are so many variations on the ancient Indian epic *Mahabharata* (presumably crafted over more than a millennium, between the eighth century BCE and the fourth ACE) that no critical edition can be called definitive. Silent films have morphed over the years, too, for so many reasons and to such an extent that curators and scholars are sometimes unsure about their true identity. Their mutation continues to this day, even in those places – the archive, the museum – where the metamorphosis should be slowed down.

Every time a silent film is duplicated, some of its material history becomes hidden from sight, adding or subtracting a new layer to it (a digital reproduction makes it disappear altogether into an eternal present, one for each new migration; no

further stratification is allowed). Let's consider, for instance, the most elementary action undertaken by film curators when they preserve a silent film: restore, reconstruct, or recreate title cards. They do this, above all, because they feel they must. Nitrate prints have often survived with very brief intertitles, barely noticeable during projection when they are reduced to a few frames. Curators don't think twice about it, with good reason, as viewers must be given enough time to read. Therefore, laboratory specialists are encouraged to 'stretch' intertitles into longer strips of film, or more pixels, by applying the rule of thumb of one second of running time for each word in the text of the intertitle.

In a startling reversal of perspective, technicians are also asked on many occasions to excise all title cards of a silent film indicating the end of a reel and the beginning of the next. They generally do not hesitate in following the instructions because, since the early 1930s, the public has been accustomed to view a feature-length film as one uninterrupted flow of consecutive reels (with an intermission when needed). In the absence of countdown leaders and changeover cues (p. 177), the appearance of title cards such as 'End of Part One', 'Part Two' (and so forth) was perfectly normal for most spectators of the 1910s and 1920s. These intertitles were often crafted and designed as exquisitely as all the others, as it was expected they would appear on screen. In the name of accuracy, they should therefore be retained, and viewed as part of the show. If they are not, it's mainly in compliance with a viewing practice that rarely occurred in the silent period.

Harmless as it seems, this decision represents yet another step in the constant change of film as an artefact and as a creative work. It is hard to determine to what degree the presence of these non-narrative titles had an influence on film spectatorship. Without a thorough analysis of extant (and unaltered) projection prints, it is equally difficult to make assumptions on how long it took for people to read title cards. It is presumed that they could do so at the rate of one word per second, but the scant information at our disposal on this point is hardly enough to turn this hypothesis into a worldwide standard. Audiences may have needed more (or less) time to read intertitles in different countries, at different times in history. Useful as it is for practical purposes, extending the footage of title cards also discounts the fact that, at some point in time, a print was probably viewed in the exact same form in which it has been found. Maybe the nitrate copy had been progressively trimmed to the point that its owner felt it was no longer suitable for exhibition. It is equally possible that the print was shown for a long time exactly as it is now, with no complaints from the public. Some audiences liked intertitles as they provided a welcome respite from prolonged exposure to moving images, a source of visual fatigue (in the early years of cinema, when flicker and picture instability were serious issues). Others would have preferred to dispense with title cards altogether, as happened in Germany in the 1920s.

Looked at from this perspective, the routine direction imparted to film laboratories to 'stretch' intertitles is not so straightforward. It is taken for granted because title cards are too often treated as the 'soft' evidence of the film, rather than an integral component of it (p. 157). When this happens, title card engineering is not only an abdication to the reductive view of written words as accessories of silent cinema; it is a deliberate intrusion into the artwork, based on subjectivity and speculation. This is not to say that an illegible title card should remain untouched in all projection prints. Such an absurd decision, however, should not be countered by ignoring the implications of the corrective action to be taken.

Recreating, interpolating, or removing title cards is a favourite sport of film preservation specialists,

who have refined their tools to the point of perfectly replicating the fonts used in the original film. Eileen Bowser's fourth objective of film preservation – making a film 'more accessible' to contemporary audiences – comes to mind as the inspiration for the efforts taken in this respect. When the nitrate copy of a German film is found with title cards in English, much labour is put into bringing back the work to its original language, at the risk of forgetting that English-speaking audiences saw this film as well, and that the surviving material is a faithful representation of their own experience. The least that can be done in taking this curatorial licence is to insert a marker of some kind – preferably the full name of the institution (posterity won't remember all acronyms) and a date – at the margins of the title card (as shown in Fig. 197), to indicate that this section of the film does not belong to the source material. Casual viewers may or may not pay attention to it, but there is at least a guarantee that, sometime in the future, there will be no uncertainty about who made the change, and when.

Once this step is completed, it is worth asking what its collateral effects may be. First and foremost, it should be assumed that the nitrate print of the German film with English intertitles has been fully preserved, in compliance with Bowser's first principle of film restoration. There should be no room for doubt on this point: future viewers must be free to choose between the original copy of the film in a foreign language, or its domestic version in reconstructed form. As far as the new version is concerned, having located the original text and identified the correct font is not enough. Text legibility was taken into account when arranging printed words for the screen: how many words were reproduced in each line; whether they were centred, or aligned to the left, or justified; how large they were in relation to the entire frame, and how wide were the margins, top and bottom, left and right; what kind of line spacing was used.

These questions can rarely be answered without having a sufficient number of original samples available from other films – from the same production company and period – in support of the ambition to reconstruct what was lost. If the evidence isn't there, no text and no font are authentic enough to justify the claim of recreating 'original' intertitles. They have not been 'reconstructed', let alone 'recreated', and they might as well have been reproduced in a totally different font in order to stress the difference, instead of concealing it. When a nitrate print of *Blue Jeans* was found with Czech intertitles, James Card translated them into English and printed them as a typewritten text. They can't be mistaken for originals. Card had neither the money nor the inclination to be accurate, but he was at least (perhaps inadvertently) honest with his public by admitting that several sections of the original artefact had been removed, purely for the sake of convenience.

Fragments

Some experts in film restoration are particularly keen to recreate title cards for silent films because they feel empowered to make them look more 'authentic', especially if the original elements had intertitles in foreign languages, or none at all. There is no worse destiny for a silent film than to be found in an incomplete form (except perhaps being also unidentified). By and large, audiences are not interested in looking at truncated copies; therefore, it is much harder for collecting institutions to secure financial support for their preservation. Incomplete films are also favourite battlefields of the film restoration industry: to achieve proper recognition, a new restoration project on an important title must demonstrate that the resulting film will not only be more beautiful to look at, but that it also contains material (including intertitles) never seen before.

This inescapable mantra is the basis of many remakes in the history of film preservation, from

Napoléon (twenty-three versions to this date, including reissues) to *Metropolis*. When a film is preserved, the standard course of action is to look for all the extant copies, compare them with one another, and strive for the assemblage of the longest possible copy, which is normally assumed to be the one shown for the first time in the film's country of origin. Another glance at the fictional print 36 in Diagram 1 may help illustrate the troubles that lie ahead of this indisputably logical goal.

Another nitrate copy of the film has been found: it's print 22. It was struck from the negative that was sent to Europe for overseas distribution. It is not complete, but does include several shots that are missing from print 36. The copy is also in a sorry condition, parts of the emulsion having liquefied into a surreal gallery of distorted landscapes and faces, similar to the frame enlargement reproduced on p. 210 (Fig. 188). As it turns out, the material that has been rescued clarifies some digressions from the main plot, should the newly available sections be merged with print 36.

It is an interesting situation. The narrative thread in print 36 is clear enough to be understood, despite the absence of many segments contained in print 22. Physical damage to print 36 is limited to a handful of ugly splices in the midst of a shot, and some scattered areas of peeled emulsion. Conversely, there is so much decomposition in print 22 that no digital intervention is likely to make a difference; the print is in black and white, but it was struck from a camera negative. Where unaffected by chemical decay, this print is of exquisite photographic quality. As it comes from the second negative, however, all camera angles are different from those of print 36 (an example of this is shown on p. 109 [Fig. 102a–b]). Now that all the aspects of the dilemma have been spelled out, a decision must be made on how to handle it.

To add a further ingredient to the curator's predicament, the film to be restored is a revered icon of silent cinema. The discovery of print 22 was greeted with joy by academics and the media, and it is expected that a newer version of the masterwork will have its premiere at a major film festival before being made available to all. Given the significance of that title, it is likely that prints 36 and 22 will soon have a third sibling (after an explanation that the film is too important to remain split into two 'adjacent' versions). Maybe it will be called print 70 (derived from a new negative G or H, depending on whether or not print 22 is fully preserved), with conjectural tinting added to the black and white sections; maybe it will only be a digital master and its derivative copies produced in a variety of formats for public distribution (having been made in 1914, our imaginary film is in the public domain).

Should that be the case, two of Bowser's five goals and objectives of film preservation have been achieved. Two have not. One has a question mark attached to it. Print 70 or its digital avatar will not come anywhere close to the author's intentions, whatever they may have been. It will not resemble what audiences saw at the time of the film's release: not because of decomposition of the carrier, but because in the years of silent cinema a projection print very rarely combined materials from two different release versions (on the other hand, there were examples of silent and sound films where sections of two camera negatives were interpolated to make a single complete negative for distribution). A modern viewer may or may not be aware that there is already another projection copy (print 36) available to look at, and still be happy to see the film (print 70) in its Frankenstein version. Explaining the difference between this complete work of fiction and the incomplete authenticity of print 36 is up to the film curator.

Eileen Bowser's fifth objective of film preservation – the creation of an entirely new work– has therefore been met, albeit involuntarily so. As for the first (preserving the material as it was found), it can only be hoped that print 22 (made in 1914) had been protected exactly as it was before blending an intermediate negative with its 1925 second-generation equivalent. If print 36 was properly safeguarded, its permanence in the form of a preservation negative and of one or more projection prints will also be ensured, as the film had been seen in that version for many years until print 22 was found. In short, if both existing elements have been fully preserved before the merger, and can be viewed separately, Bowser's first objective of film preservation has been honoured. When writing about the fifth, Bowser probably had in mind something more akin to Giorgio Moroder's 1984 version of *Metropolis* – an abridged reissue of the 1927 classic by Fritz Lang, with Moroder's own music attached to the film – but print 70 would still be a good fit in this category.

Bowser's fifth point could also be optimistically regarded as an act of faith in film preservation as an experiment, a living laboratory of cinematic ideas. Its specimens are the stuff history is made of, fragments to be interpreted, challenged, combined, or ignored altogether. In a way, print 70 is precisely that: a new film, the expression of a vision that didn't exist before. The most extraordinary aspect of this process is that film preservation is largely performed as an art of camouflage: its success is measured by the viewer's ignorance of how it was achieved.

Fictions

For a long time, art historians have dwelled upon the respective merits of conservative and integrative restoration (one of the foremost authorities in this field, Cesare Brandi, wrote in 1963 an influential book on the topic). Judging by some of its most celebrated deeds, film preservation had aggressively pursued the integrative approach well before digital technology entered the debate. A new version of D.W. Griffith's *Intolerance* was presented on 2 October 1989 at the New York Film Festival. The project stemmed from a collaboration between MoMA and the Library of Congress after comparing the instrumental parts of the score for the official premiere of the film in New York on 5 September 1916 (some preview screenings had been held in California in the preceding weeks) with a scrapbook containing a nitrate sample of the first frame from each of the 2,203 shots and intertitles in the film, in the order designed by Griffith three months before the inauguration at the Liberty Theatre.

Preserved footage from other existing versions of *Intolerance* was edited according to the order in which the frames – deposited by Griffith at the Library of Congress for copyright – were displayed in the scrapbook; at every missing shot in the film, the corresponding 35mm nitrate fragment was stretched into a freeze frame, for a duration inferred from the notations in the orchestral score. In formal terms, the reconstructed film was a daring feat of scholarship; as a motion picture show, it was an awkward collage of cinema and non-cinema, all made of 'authentic' images but entirely artificial. Without the grandiose music setting by Joseph Carl Breil, it would also have been an unwatchable film. The continuity was correct and very complete, but Griffith's utopian act of faith in cinema as an agent of redemption for humanity had also been deprived of much of its emotional power and turned into an exasperating jigsaw puzzle of empathy and remoteness. MoMA's curators now call the 1989 reconstruction, quite appropriately, a 'study version'.

Many attempts have been made in the preservation of silent films to seek a compromise between 'integration', 'conservation', and the pleasure of viewing. The frame enlargement reproduced on p. 259 (Fig. 197) shows a title card from the Library of Congress' 1997 version of John Ford's *The Blue Eagle* (1926), providing information on the narrative content of the missing sections. Swiss film historian Hervé Dumont used production stills as substitutes for the lost sequences in *The River*; Rick Schmidlin

and Richard Koszarski worked along the same lines in their 1999 recreation of Stroheim's *Greed*, the victim of several consecutive mutilations before and after its release. Many of the films made by Griffith during the Biograph period (1908–13) survive in the form of unedited camera negatives without intertitles.

There is always an interesting reason for the incomplete status of archival prints, and their material evidence is in itself a product of history. The need to keep and preserve these sources of knowledge in unaltered form – which, in curatorial terms, is the only sound choice – should not discourage their application in reconstruction projects, as long as their rationale is explained with clarity and honesty. This kind of approach fully justifies the inclusion of a very brief fragment from *The Lost World* (Harry O. Hoyt, 1925), found in a heavily damaged copy, in other versions of the film where the final shot is missing (Fig. 200).

The Lost World's blessing is that the work is in the public domain. This is also its curse: any owner of one or more print elements feels entitled to modify its visual content (some recent versions include 'censored' title cards, due to the racist overtones in the original) without providing any notice to the viewer. Fortunately, this questionable approach to the 'integrative' method

Fig. 200 *The Lost World* (Harry O. Hoyt, 1925). Frame enlargement from a 35mm triacetate positive. Source: Národní Filmový Archiv, Prague.

is an exception. Multiple film sources were used for the reconstruction of *The Blue Eagle*; for the 2006 version of *Monte-Cristo* (Henri Fescourt, 1929), with sections from a French distribution print preserved by the Gosfilmofond of Russia, a copy with Dutch titles from the Stiftung Deutsche Kinemathek in Berlin, and a 17.5mm copy held in a private collection (an earlier version in 1993 merged two incomplete nitrate prints from the Národní filmový archiv in Prague). The reconstruction work on Fritz Lang's *Metropolis* over many years was dramatically enriched by the discovery of a 16mm reduction copy at the Museo del Cine Pablo Ducrós Hicken in Buenos Aires; the almost complete film (as of 2018, only a few shots were still missing) was shown at the 2010 Berlin Film Festival under the auspices of the Friedrich-Wilhelm-Murnau-Stiftung.

There was no way to bridge the gap between the visual quality of the previous versions and that of the very mediocre 16mm print in Argentina. Given the legendary status of the film, it didn't really matter, but digital technicians did their best to ease the transitions from one film generation to the other as smoothly as they could, without falsifying the difference between the many archival sources of *Metropolis*. When applied without the necessary restraint, the same integrative approach turns the cult of 'completeness' into ideology: a false consciousness and a false representation of history. The 2011 version of *A Trip to the Moon* presented at Cannes (p. 9) was put together with material from a pirated copy made in Spain well after the film's release, as shown by the poor printing job, the density of the nitrate base, the shape of the Edison perforations, and the hand-colouring style (the French flag in the last scene has the colours of the Spanish standard). The print from the Filmoteca de Catalunya is also incomplete; the black and white footage from two other sources (p. 245) was digitally 'colourized'

to blend it with the rest; the colour itself was enhanced to make it look brighter. Its contours were sharpened, too, as digital-born audiences are accustomed to see moving images that way.

The Filmmuseum München announced at the 2007 FIAF conference in Tokyo the screening of 'the very first (and even to film experts totally unknown) 3-D films by Méliès and Lumière' (*FIAF 2007 Tokyo Conference Program Guide*, p. 20). The false claim was prompted by the use of some films by Méliès that survive in elements from both negatives, taken from different angles and therefore suitable for the creation of stereoscopic films that Méliès never made (three years later, an article by Anne-Marie Quévrain and Jacques Malthête in the journal *Cinémathèque Méliès*, no. 28, March 2010, pp. 10–11 attributed the presentation to the French commercial archive Lobster Films). What happened to *A Trip to the Moon* at Cannes is a more insidious application of the same approach. Had this version been presented as a variation on a Méliès theme – another film, in line with the fifth section in Eileen Bowser's charter of film preservation – its appearance would not have raised any controversy. It would have been indexed as *Le Voyage dans la lune* (2011), a free adaptation from the 1902 film by Georges Méliès. The public would have enjoyed it anyway, just as it does the many other versions available in digital formats. If described this way, the remake would have hardly warranted its phenomenal budget, and it would probably not have earned a premiere at Cannes, as it is neither a restoration nor a preservation project, let alone a reconstruction. Another word, 'recreation', is a more appropriate definition of the 2011 video. The tiny glass jar held by the Technicolor specialist shown in the photo at the beginning of this book (Fig. 5, p. 20) contains one million copies of this fake: the DNA synthesis of a plagiarized second-generation copy of *A Trip to the Moon* with non-Méliès hand-colouring, digitally improved and applied to sections of black and white film stock.

It has been asserted that the genetic code of this concoction can be retrieved several thousands of years from now. Should this happen, viewers in the year 12,018 will be looking at something very different from what they think it is. The fact that they will be marvelling at the sight of a fake is not what we should worry about. The real problem is that there would be nobody to tell the story, as the Méliès visual DNA does not contain any information on how it was altered, and no one would therefore know that a falsification had taken place at all, thus making it impossible to reverse its effects. What happened to *A Trip to the Moon* is not very different from what has occurred to many other silent films, except for the fanfare that surrounded the pseudo-Méliès operation.

Media outlets are well accustomed to altering the chromatic balance, framing, and projection speed of documentary and newsreel footage borrowed from collecting institutions in order to make it look more appealing to their audiences (Plate 53a–b); the addition of bogus 'soundtracks' to silent films (marching soldiers, roaring crowds, train and car engines) finds no resistance from lending institutions with not enough time, personnel, and political clout to prevent the systematic breaches to the ethics of film preservation they otherwise promote in festivals and conferences. Observing this phenomenon as an organic process inherent to cinema, rather than as a mere victory of the marketplace over culture, can mitigate the vertigo effect derived from its widespread application to the relics of film history.

Terminology

The naked truth behind these and other exercises of *cinéma-vérité* in reverse mode is that the meaning of 'film preservation' is in the eye of the beholder: this is why a consensus on terminology around this activity is so hard to achieve. In this sense, there is a long way to go before cinema and the other arts can talk the same language. The following definitions are therefore intended only as broad terms of reference for further discussion.

Preservation is described in a film museum or archive as the overall complex of principles, procedures, techniques, and practices necessary for safeguarding the material evidence, restoring the content, and organizing the intellectual experience of cinema on a permanent basis.

The objects of film preservation are

(a) the physical carrier of motion pictures;

(b) the equipment used to project them;

(c) the darkened space where the projection occurs;

(d) the expertise and artistry of those who make it happen.

This definition acknowledges the manifold purpose of preservation work: making sure that the surviving artefact is not further damaged or modified; bringing closer to its original state; sharing it with an audience, in a manner consistent with how the artefact was meant to be exhibited. No laboratory work is sufficient to meet the above requirements if the film is presented without proper projection speed or aspect ratio, or if the source copy is altered, damaged, destroyed, stolen, or abandoned after printing. Duplication, restoration, conservation, reconstruction (when necessary), and theatrical projection are all constituent parts of preservation activities. Public access to duplicate copies is both a consequence and a requisite of the preservation process.

Duplication is the set of practices related to the creation of a replica of the moving image, either as a backup of existing original or preservation components, or as a means to project the creative work or provide access to it without jeopardizing its existence over the long term. While the duplication process is performed with the goal of obtaining a copy as faithful as possible to the source, such a process is a necessary but not sufficient requirement of film preservation, or of any film restoration project that is true to its name. The responsible use of duplication techniques (for example, a wet-gate printing or a digital scanning at very high resolution) may result in a satisfactory imitation of the source material. Other than removing the effects of physical damage, no further action is taken during the duplication work to bring the film back to its presumed original condition.

Conservation includes all activities necessary to prevent or minimize the process of physical degradation of the archival element, whether it is newly created (a preservation negative, a digital scan, a projector, a film theatre), or part of an existing body of objects. An underlying principle of this process is that conservation activities should be carried out with the minimum possible intervention or interference with the archival element itself. The ultimate goal of film conservation is to keep the creative work, in its current state, for as long as possible. Storing a nitrate print or a 1905 projector in a vault equipped with temperature and humidity control systems is part of the conservation process. In the digital domain, moving images are conserved through data migration on a periodical basis.

Restoration is the set of technical, editorial, and intellectual procedures aimed at compensating for the partial loss or degradation of motion picture film, with the aspirational goal of bringing it back to a state identical to its original condition. Removing alterations or manipulations detected on the film artefact (in the reproduction process), retrieving elements missing from it (with reconstruction practices), and reversing the effects of time, wear and tear on the optical and (in the case of sound film) aural content of the motion picture carrier

are all components of the restoration work. Taken individually, none of them is sufficient to meet the requirements of film restoration, which finds its quintessential expression in the projection event. The term 'restoration' in motion picture preservation has a different meaning than in most other artistic disciplines, in the sense that it generally involves the duplication of one or more source elements. In some circumstances, the original artefact may be projected if the physical condition of the object allows it (under the strict supervision of curatorial staff) without the risk of further damage; otherwise, a reproduction will be exhibited in lieu of the original.

Reconstruction is the editorial process enabling the creation of a new archival element (whose appearance is compliant with a desired version, regarded as authoritative) by interpolating, replacing, or reassembling segments within a single copy, or by the integration of elements retrieved from other copies. In the reconstruction of silent films, some segments (such as intertitles) are sometimes invented for this purpose. Because of their superficial resemblance to the critical edition of a manuscript or printed text, the principles and practices of film reconstruction are sometimes misconstrued as 'philology', a discipline pertaining to the interpretation of literary works. The term 'reconstruction' is also used in digital work to indicate the rebuilding of visual information in a damaged film frame or group of frames.

Recreation is an imaginary account of what the film would have been if, in the personal opinion of artists, curators, or producers, some or all of its missing parts had survived. This course of action is taken by using material directly or indirectly related to the film in order to provide a credible representation of its original concept. Without making any claim about the cinematic style of the original work, a recreation offers a fictional representation of the film's content.

No matter how carefully drawn and tested against other formulas, all the above definitions are confronted by the inescapable question of who cares about converting them into practice. No one is in control of terminology, but anybody can call a film 'restored' if there is a vested interest in saying so. Perhaps because of their inherent pliability, modest or negligible market value, and limited appeal to general audiences, the works of silent cinema lend themselves particularly well to this semantic anarchy. A significant percentage of these films are in the public domain. Many have been saved with governmental support, or through the generosity of private donors and foundations. Other silent films are legally owned by commercial entities, even when the film objects – prints and negatives – were saved and are preserved by others.

Most laboratories for the duplication of the moving image have been established with the goal of generating a financial profit; while some collecting institutions are capable of running their own technical facilities, all of them are reliant upon proprietary technology, which is also meant to earn dividends. Some corporate companies collaborate with film museums and archives, with tangible benefits for both, and for their audiences. The imbalance of power between the players, however, has affected the growth of film preservation as a curatorial discipline. Born as an industry, cinema continues to be part of it even when it deals with its own history.

Insofar as they are sold and bought, all artworks need a public or private forum in which to be displayed. Film preservation is unique only in that its marketplace is neither run by the artists (or their agents), nor influenced by curatorial authority (in museums and galleries), but is driven instead by its own infrastructure. There is a dangerous populist edge in the proclaimed belief that technology is a vehicle for a more democratic access to film history. This simplistic formula is, in fact, a rhetorical weapon to justify the very undemocratic imposition of one mode of spectatorship over another. There is no such thing as the 'ethics of film preservation' if the owners of its tools are to dictate what constitutes 'preservation' and what doesn't. There is, instead, an ethics of spectatorship; that, too, must be learned and protected. Rather than passively inheriting the history of cinema in whatever form it is being offered, its audiences have the right to question its modes of presentation, and should protect their freedom to pursue a film experience of their choice. The actions resulting from this stance are reflected in the following statement of intent:

Film spectatorship is the ultimate objective of film preservation: the art of observing the transformation of cinema over the course of time, and the discipline of coping with its consequences on culture and society. In monitoring the process, every reasonable effort will be made to cultivate, encourage, and participate in cinematic events for as long as possible; if they can no longer occur, their migration to another kind of visual experience will be interpreted and explained, so that the meaning of what has been lost can be fully understood by future generations. In doing so, the spectator takes a creative role that is comparable to what filmmakers did in the age of cinema.

By agreeing to this uncertainty clause, film audiences accept the responsibility of caring for cinematic events in the same way as they would help preserving a forest: keep the fire and the parasites away, help the trees to follow the path of their biological life, and create a safe environment for them, in the awareness that nobody can control their shape, nor predict what the landscape will look like a thousand years from now. This particular forest is made of silent films. In the next chapter, some aspects of its trees – each with its own cultural and technological DNA – will be examined at closer range in order to better comprehend how the forest evolves. Look at them. Touch them, if you can. You, the spectator, are the genetic memory of cinema.

Chapter 14

Traces

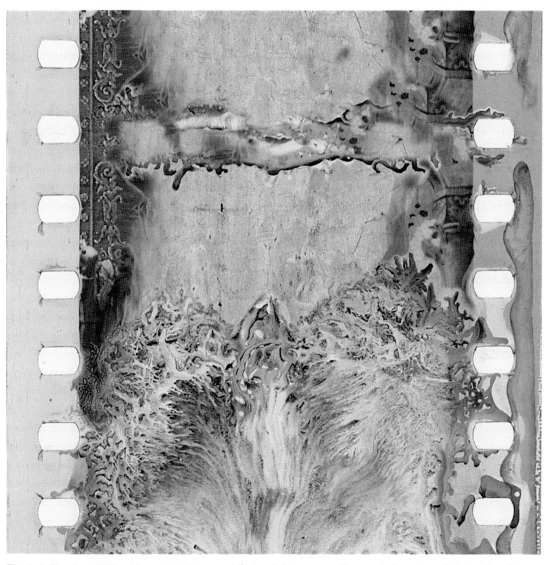

Fig. 201 *King Lear* (William V. Ranous, Vitagraph, US, 1909). Decomposed fragment of a 35mm nitrate positive. Source: George Eastman Museum – Davide Turconi/Josef Joye Collection.

From now on it will be assumed that you, fellow spectator, would like to see the objects that made silent cinema exist. Most of the non-profit collecting institutions dedicated to film provide on-site access to their collections. They do so by appointment, after a written exchange between the researcher and the person in charge of the viewing services. Some film archives and museums also have study centres and decentralized offices where digital copies of collection material not available on the Internet can be observed on a monitor; in these places, appointments are generally not necessary. Work on film stills, posters, books, journals, and historical papers follow procedures that are similar to those generally found in libraries or special collections of paper-based artefacts.

What will be discussed here are the protocols and practices recommended for the individual viewing of photochemical film prints in the context of a project related to silent cinema. There are venues (archives, museums, festivals) where these prints can only be viewed as part of a public exhibition (its preparation is referred to with the popular but reductive term 'film programming'), others in which the scholar has the option of seeing the film in a theatre (generally at a higher cost, because of the personnel involved), or on a dedicated viewing machine or inspection bench. Research fees vary according to the country and the type of institution; by statutory mandate, government-funded archives such as the Library of Congress are often required by law to provide this service at little or no charge.

Many collecting institutions dedicated to film have put their catalogue of holdings online, which greatly facilitates the preliminary research necessary to locate the prints to be viewed. Some databases, such as those of the Berkeley Art Museum/Pacific Film Archive, the BFI's National Archive, and the National Film and Sound Archive of Australia, are very comprehensive and relatively easy to browse. Those of Northern Europe – in particular, the Svenska Filminstitutet and Det Danske Filminstitut – are extremely generous in sharing digital versions of the films and useful documentation (scripts, production stills, posters). Others are more protective towards their holdings; students of silent cinema are nevertheless in a good position to find out more about them through the Treasures Database of the Fédération Internationale des Archives du Film (FIAF), accessible either by paid subscription or in all major libraries of the universities where there is a department of film and media studies. The database is far from complete, as some museums and archives have neglected or declined to participate in its development. With over 52,000 extant silent films inventoried as of 2018, however, more than a lifetime would be required to study them all. Other film elements are held by private and corporate collections around the world, sometimes also accessible in digital form.

There was a time when visiting a museum or an archive was the only way to watch silent cinema outside festivals and film societies. As the interest in this area exploded after the 1978 FIAF conference on early cinema in Brighton, collecting institutions felt the need to do a better job at assisting students and scholars in their research projects. From this standpoint, the digital versions of silent films made available over the web provided much welcome relief, as they alleviated the curators' and archivists' concerns about possible damage to the prints being requested for reasons that were at times superficial or mundane (Raymond Borde, founding curator of the Cinémathèque de Toulouse, was vociferously opposed to cinephile tourism in the archives).

By and large, on-site viewing is now limited to those silent films that remain unavailable in digital format; this means that individual access to photochemical prints of titles distributed online now requires a more plausible rationale than simple curiosity. Even in a public repository like the Library of Congress, asking to look at a safety 16mm print of *A Trip to the Moon* on a viewing table may warrant a modicum of explanation. Inspecting a nitrate print of the same film at the Archives françaises du film in Bois d'Arcy also demands some justification: compare such a request, for instance, to enquiring about an original 1646 copy of Athanasius Kircher's *Ars magna lucis et umbrae*, the precursor of all books on the cinematic perception.

Do not expect to encounter the same kind of courtesy and collaborative attitude from all film museums and archives around the world. Try instead to earn the trust and respect of the archive's staff by showing how serious your intentions are. Ask to read a copy of their Collection Policy. If they don't have one, you will at least know you are in no man's land. Explain in concise and accurate terms the rationale of your project; ask, if you can, for a letter of support from a reputable personality in the field; whenever possible, offer in exchange to share the knowledge you have acquired on the subject. The more you engage with your interlocutor, and demonstrate how important it is for you to look at a nitrate print, the greater are your chances of success.

Be flexible in your approach. If there is no way to look at nitrate prints (only on inspection benches), settle for safety copies of the same films, then show how diligent you are in handling them. No method of enquiry works by default: what opened all doors in one institution may keep them permanently locked in another one. If you are ignored or summarily dismissed by the employees of some archives or museums, don't take it personally: there are places where scholarly research is regarded as a nuisance or a threat. Finally, if you think that the look and feel of a nitrate or safety print are not worth all this effort,

you can always turn to the computer and embrace the safe anonymity of a digital file. So much can be learned from it, as long as you understand that it will be something different.

Repositories

Films, papers, posters, and other artefacts from the silent period are collected and preserved in virtually all countries where there was a cinema industry in the first quarter of the twentieth century. At the present time, FIAF has affiliates in seventy-five countries worldwide. The greatest number are in the United States (seven members as of March 2019); Great Britain and Italy follow with five FIAF members each, France and Germany with four, Spain with three (the census does not take into account FIAF 'associates', institutions with either no film collections or with goals that are tangential to the actual preservation of film). Most countries have national archives – within or outside FIAF – where moving images are acquired in a more or less systematic and permanent manner.

This section is largely dedicated to non-profit institutions that are part of FIAF, because they generally allow researchers to consult their collections. It is important to note, however, that silent films are also kept in many archives that do not belong to the Federation, as well as in private collections. Exploring their holdings may be difficult at times, but is no less gratifying than research in a public archive, once it is understood that the people who own these objects may be at times very secretive, or must take into account the commercial aspects of their activities. What follows is a brief overview of the places where silent cinema can be studied. It is by no means complete, and it does not cover all the types of collecting institutions; its only objective is to provide a basic orientation in the archival atlas of the moving image.

Most FIAF affiliates preserve original or duplicate elements of silent films; some institutions have more titles than others, but the value of a collection does not exclusively depend on its size. There are, for instance, archives with a very small number of film prints or negatives, and formidable libraries with rare books, papers, posters, and photographs. Others have neither films nor papers, but are unique by virtue of their collections of film apparatus. Rather than establishing a list of the most important museums and archives, it is useful to distinguish their objectives and structures, since these two factors determine the collection policies on acquisition, preservation, and public access; the types of objects made available for scholarly research; and the costs of the services they provide, if any. The institutional models outlined below are therefore given only for orientation purposes. They are not mutually exclusive, in that a collecting body may well belong to more than one category.

Museums of Technology

Film cameras and projectors of the silent period are found in almost every FIAF archive or museum, as well as in many private collections. Few institutions are specifically devoted to the history of film technology. The only large museum of film manufacturing and processing currently in operation is the Industrie- und Filmmuseum in Wolfen, Germany, located at the former headquarters of AGFA. The best collection of cinematic apparatus in the silent period is at the Cinémathèque française in Paris, followed by the George Eastman Museum in Rochester (formerly known as George Eastman House) and the Smithsonian Institution in Washington, DC; the Museo Nazionale del Cinema – Fondazione Maria Adriana Prolo in Turin, Italy (although its main strength is in the 'magic lantern' era); the Science Museum in London and the National Science

and Media Museum in Bradford, Great Britain; the Deutsche Kinemathek in Berlin; the Národní technické muzeum (National Technical Museum) in Prague; the François Lemai Collection at the Université Laval in Québec; and the Musée des arts et métiers in Paris. Basic information on the objects held by these institutions can be found online. The size of their collections is such that only a very small number of machines are on display; special arrangements are necessary in order to consult the other objects on site.

National Collections

Every major film archive or museum likes to be 'national', regardless of whether it receives ongoing support from a national authority or is in fact a private foundation. Most of the 'national' repositories for film are funded by governments: the National Film and Sound Archive of Australia, the Filmoteka Narodowa in Warsaw, the BFI National Archive, and Cinematek – Cinémathèque Royale de Belgique/Koninklijk Belgisch Filmarchief in Brussels are all 'national' film archives. Every now and then, public administrations feel compelled to save money by merging archives dedicated to film and recorded sound: the South African National Film, Video and Sound Archives in Pretoria, Kansallinen Audiovisuaalinen Instituutti in Helsinki, the National Screen and Sound Archive of Wales, and Ngā Taonga Sound and Vision in Wellington, New Zealand, are among the many hybrids of this kind. In other countries, cinema is amalgamated with books (the National Library of Norway, the Indiana University Libraries Moving Image Archive, the National Library of Scotland – Moving Image Archive) and the film industry (the Mediateca Regionale Toscana Film Commission in Florence, Italy, the Instituto Nacional de Audiovisual e Cinema in Maputo, Mozambique; and the Magyar Nemzeti Digitális Archívum és

Filmintézet in Budapest). Hungary is the first country whose national moving image archive included the word 'digital' in its formal title.

Some institutions are rightfully called 'national' because of laws requiring film producers to deposit preservation elements for copyright protection: the rule is applied, with many variations, at the Centre National du Cinéma et de l'Image Animée (CNC) in Paris and Bois d'Arcy, at the Cineteca Nazionale in Rome, and at the Motion Picture, Broadcasting and Recorded Sound Division – Packard National Audio-Visual Conservation Center of the Library of Congress in Washington DC and Culpeper, Virginia (no such obligation exists in Great Britain at this time). Following a long-established tradition, some nations are keen to separate films funded by the government – especially non-fiction – from everything else, on the basis of the old distinction between film as document or as creative work. This intriguing anachronism persists in countries like the Russian Federation (State Archives of Krasnogorsk), the United States (National Archives and Records Administration), and Australia (National Archives of Australia).

Film Museums

In the film world, the term 'museum' has a dual connotation. A sign at the entrance of the Österreichisches Filmmuseum in Vienna explains the first definition: 'The Austrian Film Museum is a cinematheque. Exhibitions take place on the screen.' Many institutions where film exhibition is the primary focus of activity call themselves 'museums' for the same reason, regardless of the size and scope of their collections. The Film Department at the Museum of Modern Art in New York, established in 1935, was the first: its charter provided it with the mandate to collect, preserve, and present the history of cinema as an art form. Other 'museums', like the Museo Nazionale del Cinema – Fondazione Maria Adriana Prolo in Turin, were given this name to underline their commitment to preserve and exhibit objects related to cinema: cameras, projectors, costumes, ephemera. In reality, most of these entities do both, as reflected equally in their official name and their extensive collections of films and cinematic technology (the Cinémathèque française – Musée du cinema in Paris; the George Eastman Museum; the Deutsche Kinemathek – Museum für Film und Fernsehen in Berlin).

University Film Archives

Since the 1960s, academic institutions in Europe and North America have set up collections of films with the official mandate to assist students and faculty in their research (the Wisconsin Center for Film and Theater Research in Madison, the Cinémathèque Universitaire in Paris, the Harvard Film Archive at Harvard University, the Yale Film Study Center in New Haven, Connecticut, and the Moving Image Research Collections at the University of South Carolina are typical examples of this service-oriented approach to archiving). While fulfilling its statutory obligation, the UCLA Film and Television Archive in Los Angeles does much more than this: its collection is among the largest in North America. Despite the relatively modest size of its collection (notable for its holdings of Soviet, Asian, and experimental cinema), the UC Berkeley Art Museum – Pacific Film Archive is widely regarded as home to one of the very best film exhibition venues worldwide. A unique feature of BAM/PFA is the presence of both the words 'archive' and 'museum' in its formal denomination.

Regional and Municipal Film Archives

A number of relatively smaller but very active institutions – mostly in Europe – have been established within autonomous or semi-autonomous administrative and linguistic entities. Among those with significant holdings of silent films are the Cineteca del Friuli, co-organizer of the Pordenone Silent Film Festival (Le Giornate del Cinema Muto); Culturarts–IVAC in Valencia, Spain, formerly known as the Filmoteca de la Generalitat Valenciana; and the Centro Galego de Artes da Imaxe in A Coruña, also in Spain. Other public and private film archives are the emanations of city governments, or are largely funded with public money from local authorities. Among them are the Fukuoka City Public Library Film Archive; the Cinémathèque de Nice; the Filmmuseum München in Germany, whose formal mandate is to collect and preserve the works of Bavarian filmmakers (but has a sizeable collection of silent films); the Fondazione Cineteca Italiana in Milan; the Fondazione Cineteca di Bologna (co-organizer of Il Cinema Ritrovato, a festival of film preservation); the Cinémathèque de Toulouse, the brainchild of Raymond Borde, a driving force of film curatorship in the late twentieth century; and the Cinémathèque de la Ville de Luxembourg, a cinephile sanctuary established by a maverick of film collecting, Fred Junck, in 1977.

Special Collections

On a stand-alone basis or as part of larger collecting bodies, some institutions are devoted to the acquisition, preservation, and exhibition of films on specific subjects: among the many cases in point are the Institut Lumière in Lyon, the city that gave birth to the Cinématographe; the Steven Spielberg Jewish Film Archive in Jerusalem, exclusively dedicated to the culture and history of the Jewish people; the Archivio Audiovisivo del Movimento Operaio e Democratico in Rome, born in 1979 with the acquisition of film materials from the Italian Communist Party; the Filmoteca

Vaticana, for film of religious and devotional subject; the Film Archive at the Imperial War Museum in London, where films on World War I and II produced in Britain, Germany, Russia, Italy, Japan and other countries are collected along with other visual documents of the military operations of British and Commonwealth forces from 1914; the same type of material is also preserved in Ivry, France, by the ECPAD – Établissement de Communication Audiovisuelle de la Défense.

Corporate Archives

The emergence of film archives administered by production companies is a relatively recent phenomenon, stemming from two parallel imperatives: earning profit from the assets of a corporate entity, and promoting an aura of cultural legitimacy about past achievements in the industry. These objectives sometimes become intertwined. When there is a serious intention to earn public credibility (with the added advantage of fiscal incentives), film producers set up foundations: the Fondation Jérôme Seydoux-Pathé in Paris, established in 2006, is an admirable illustration of this approach. In other instances, corporate archives are established and disbanded according to the whims of their proprietors. Universal Pictures opened an Archives and Collections branch in 1998; two years later, its director was summarily dismissed, and the branch realigned to the company's mandate. In 2011, a new entity called NBCUniversal Archives began to sell moving images from its collections. In the meanwhile (on 1 June 2008), a fire had destroyed between 40,000 and 50,000 of the company's 'assets', dating back to the 1920s, stored in the studio's premises.

Tragedies of this kind have occurred everywhere, in both commercial and non-profit repositories. The systematic preservation of commercially owned collections has rarely been a matter of priority; that is why, every now and then, production companies look for their 'assets' in non-profit archives and museums. By the time you read this book, the typology of film collecting institutions in general – as well as their ever-changing names – may have already shifted. It is normal for this to happen all the time, but its acceleration is palpable. In a brief but illuminating article published in 1999 in the *Historical Journal of Film, Radio and Television*, Jan-Christopher Horak wrote: 'with the establishment in the last five years of archives at Warner Brothers, Fox, Universal, and Sony, we have seen a sea change in the attitudes of the Hollywood majors. For the first time, the studios are concerned with their own history' (vol. 19, no. 3, p. 405). The extreme volatility in archival nomenclature, philosophy, and strategies is a sobering indication of how fragile these institutions are, two centuries after the invention of the medium they are committed to saving for the long term. Penelope Houston's question – when does posterity begin? – in her indispensable book on film archives, *Keepers of the Frame* (1994), is as valid as ever.

Provenance

The remainder of this chapter is addressed to those who do not mind taking the hardest route, and were granted permission to examine nitrate and safety prints of silent films in one of these repositories. If you are about to view a projection copy, you are fully entitled to ask when the preservation process took place. It is important for you to know this, as the physical condition of the print and its optical quality may not be what you expect: looking at a colour duplicate made, say, in 2015 from a nitrate print, with the technology available at the time, is one thing; seeing the same film in a colour duplicate struck in 1974 (or, for that matter, a black and white copy, as is often the case with reproductions made until the 1980s) is not quite the same thing. At the cost of jumping ahead in your relationship with the archive or museum staff, you might as well ask if anything is known about the origins of the source material. You must do so very tactfully, because this is a potentially sensitive topic. Strange as it may appear, this is something you cannot change and must therefore accept as a rule of the game.

Information on the source of acquisition does not appear in the cataloguing records accessible to the public. In many cases, collecting institutions do not even know when and how their films became part of their holdings. With admirable foresight, the BFI published in 1936 the first catalogue of its holdings, mentioning, when possible, the full name of the acquisition source. In spite of its unassuming design, the booklet is a tiny masterpiece of curatorial integrity. Few institutions, if any, followed the BFI's example (further editions of the National Film Archive catalogues no longer mention film provenance). For decades, many archives and museums did not keep accurate records of their transactions, or deliberately refrained from doing so; prints were acquired, donated, or found in the most diverse and often casual circumstances.

The first film curator of the George Eastman Museum, James Card, obtained many nitrate prints from a still photographer and stock footage dealer, John E. Allen Sr, as part of a standing agreement: Allen knew where to find the reels, Card bought them without asking too many questions. Documenting film acquisitions in detail, with the indication of their sources, their cost, and the conditions – if any – of the purchases became standard practice much later, when the bulk of the silent film collections had already become part of the institutions' history. Only the people involved would have been able to tell the story, but scholars and curators rarely thought about interviewing them on this topic before they retired or passed away.

As a result, archive personnel with a longer employment history often don't have much to say about their so-called 'core collections' of silent films, and sometimes are not too pleased to be reminded about it. Other organizations fare slightly better by virtue of the suffix 'museum' attached to their name: in this kind of collecting body, keeping track of an object's material genealogy has always been a matter of institutional pride. Still, the primary evidence available today on projection prints or negatives cannot be compared to what one may expect from repositories dealing with other types of cultural artefacts. The emergence of the silent film 'collection' as a coherent body of objects related to a specific person or corporate body is a relatively recent phenomenon. Its status as a 'treasure' has been acknowledged only from the mid-1980s, when Frans Maks, then Director of the Nederlands Filmmuseum (now Eye Filmmuseum), and his collaborator Frank van der Maden had the first intuition that the nitrate copies belonging to a film distributor of the early twentieth century, Jean Desmet, could be preserved and promoted as a distinct entity, rather than being assimilated into the rest of the institution's holdings (the Desmet project was continued in the following decade by Hoos Blotkamp, Eric de Kuyper, Peter Delpeut, and others).

Well before then, Davide Turconi had brought attention in the 1960s to the exceptional value of the Josef Joye collection in Switzerland, initially with scant response from archives and museums of the period; Joye's nitrate prints would deserve to be celebrated as much as Desmet's, but the path of their acquisition by the BFI was not as linear as the one followed by its Dutch counterpart. It was only in 1972 that a young British director, David Mingay, persuaded David Francis – then Curator of the BFI's National Film Archive – to save Joye's nitrate prints

(Mingay had found out about them while preparing his pioneering television series *The Amazing Years of Cinema*, aired in 1976; the collection was formally deposited in January of the same year).

It must be noted that information about the provenance of both the Joye and the Desmet prints is limited to the last episodes of their story: the earlier life of the nitrate copies they acquired remains unknown. When it comes to the silent films currently held by museums and archives, there rarely is a genealogical tree to speak of (the evidence on surviving nitrate elements of *A Trip to the Moon* reported in Chapter 12 is one of the exceptions, due to the reputation of the film). In the event that your question receives an answer at all, count yourself lucky if you find out something about the latest owner of the prints. If it doesn't, the other reason for the silence may be that the institution does not have permission to pass on such information, either for credible or questionable reasons.

The person in charge of access to the collection is not necessarily the same one who can divulge this kind of information. The film may have been deposited by a third party, in which case the museum does not own it, and must ask for formal clearance before revealing the name of the depositor. It may be that the donor did not wish to be identified, this being one of the conditions for the transfer of the print to the archive. Until recently, there was yet another reason for the reluctance to talk about acquisition sources: the film is under copyright. The fear of being accountable for the legitimate ownership of a silent film has now waned, but it has not disappeared altogether. Irrational as it is, this anxiety is the ultimate proof of how vulnerable collecting institutions are, or believe themselves to be, in the pursuit of their mission.

The early films made by Henri Joly and Ernest Normandin and collected in 1897 by Antonino Sagarmínaga are also a 'collection' in the fullest sense of the term. They are not under copyright, but it will be hard for you to see the originals (fortunately, the 35mm duplicates made from the collaboration between the Cinemateca Portuguesa in Lisbon and the Filmoteca Española in Madrid are accessible, and quite beautiful to look at). Prints such as these can be extremely fragile, and there comes a point in their life when the slightest shock in temperature and humidity, or a small oversight in handling them, can be fatal to their survival. Some prints on nitrate or diacetate stock have become like celluloid scrolls, so delicate that they can break into minuscule fragments, unusable for further duplication if not properly conserved.

Film elements of this kind are to be left untouched after copying for as long as the projection and access elements are adequate enough to make their retrieval unnecessary. Collection managers are good judges of what may be detrimental to the materials under their care. Alone or with the support of their staff, they periodically inspect every single reel of film to ascertain its condition and write detailed reports on each of them. They have such an intimate knowledge of print shrinkage, brittleness, and chemical instability that film curators rely upon their judgement when it comes to establishing preservation priorities. If these specialists determine that it is best to leave a nitrate film alone, it is because they want the object to have a longer life.

Protocols

As we are about to begin the physical examination of film prints, one more word of caution is in order about the respective rights and responsibilities of the researcher and those who have granted access to the collections. Archivists have a duty to facilitate your work, as long as the institution has the necessary resources, and should be supported in their effort to comply with its policies and protocols. The physical condition of the objects that are put at your disposal must never be compromised: preserving films is a very expensive business, and it should not be assumed that a damaged print would be easy to replace (it is possible, for instance, that a viewing print derives from preservation elements held by another institution). Requests to view films and related materials such as posters, correspondence, and production stills must be commensurate with the work entailed in making them accessible.

Retrieving a print from the vaults is definitely not like picking up a reference book from the stacks; each reel undergoes a time-consuming but necessary process that require pulling the object from the refrigerated vault, keeping it for at least one day in a temporary storage area so that it can adapt to different levels of temperature and humidity, and preparing it for viewing. All research projects that involve examining a large number of prints should

---

RULE 8

Scholarly work in a film museum or archive
involves a mutual agreement on the rights and duties
of the researcher and the institution's staff.
Both will contribute, in their respective roles,
to a better knowledge of the collection
through a responsible approach to its preservation.

be submitted with as much advance notice as possible, allowing film technicians enough time to inspect the materials as necessary. Also remember that all collection objects must be inspected again when your viewing session is completed, before they are brought back to their locations in the storage area.

There is obviously not a fixed rate at which films are viewed in the course of a research session: a single or 'double' reel of film (normally 1,000 feet, or 300 metres, for nitrate stock and 2,000 feet, or 600 metres, for safety prints: that is how most archives and museums store their film collections) can be examined in fifteen or thirty minutes, or may require an entire week if you are doing a frame-by-frame analysis. On average, two feature films of five or more reels, or about ten shorts of one reel each, occupy a full day of viewing or inspection. In planning your work, allow enough time for carefully setting up the reel through the gears of the viewing table; putting the print back in its archival container; stopping the machine to take your notes; seeking help from a research assistant if something is wrong; and for a second viewing of the film, if needed, in which case it has to be rewound (you should never do this yourself in 'fast rewind' mode on the viewing machine).

Asking for more prints than you can handle in a day involves unnecessary extra work for the archive's staff, and should be avoided out of consideration for your colleagues. Also, your study session would be reduced at best to a hurried and superficial browse through the film. Some practical experience and visual dexterity are required in handling and looking at nitrate film stock. Prints of this kind should not go through the sprockets of an automated viewing machine; you will be allowed to look at them on a manually controlled rewind bench where images are not projected, but seen instead with the naked eye or with a portable optical device against a cold light source. With time and patience, you will get used to following the basic events in the film without an intermittent mechanism.

Do not make photographs or video recordings of the prints being viewed without prior permission from a member of the staff. Frame enlargements will normally be allowed, as long as they are for personal use only and are taken under the supervision of a staff member. Approval from the institution is also required for publishing the images in any form. Taking the pictures first, and then asking to make use of them for individual or public consumption, is reprehensible and rude: publication for scholarly purposes is rarely denied, except on those occasions where legal restrictions are in place.

Food and drinks are strictly prohibited in the viewing areas and wherever prints are being stored, permanently or not. Should you want to take handwritten notes anywhere near the print, use a pencil instead of a ballpoint pen or a permanent marker. This said, there are other things you may want to bring along for your viewing session: a magnifying glass or a similar optical device (often provided by staff); a footage chart or calculator for determining running times at different projection speeds (a simplified version is shown in Appendix 1); one or more edge code tables – such as those reproduced in Appendix 2 and 3 – for print identification. Those who study cinema before 1915 should not forget to bring along a copy of Harold Brown's *Physical Characteristics of Early Films as Aids to Identification* (1990), an indispensable tool for all those who wish to examine the archival object in greater detail.

Senses

The museum's staff should provide you with archival gloves, but their use is not always mandatory. You will be asked to wear them if you need to frequently hold safety film stock: fingerprints, grease, and dust are very bad for viewing prints, and a curse to negatives, fine grain masters, and all preservation elements in general. Nitrate stock, on the other hand, has endured so many hardships before entering the archive that cotton gloves can actually be harmful to them, as broken perforations and loose splices may catch a thread in the fabric, inflicting further damage to the print, and scratching your fingers too, if you are not careful.

Nitrate prints (not the negatives) are delicate but resilient objects, accustomed to the human touch. Female hands have assembled them with the greatest care (see Chapter 5) to make them ready for distribution; film projectionists, almost always men, have wound, unwound, cut, spliced, and threaded them around metal sprockets and aperture gates many times over the years. They were generally much rougher with the prints than anybody else in the film business, but you should do precisely the opposite, and behave instead like technicians in a print assembly line. By the end of a working day, your fingertips may be rather soiled, that's all. Let the museum staff decide, on a case-by-case basis, whether or not you should wear gloves. Nitrate prints seen on a rewind bench are not at all dangerous, unless in a very advanced stage of decomposition, as shown in Fig. 201 (in which case you will probably not be allowed to come anywhere close to them), and will not self-combust in front of you in a cool and ventilated room if there is no flame nearby. When handling film elements in the final stages of chemical decay, film technicians wear protective masks, and inspect or rewind prints near a device that absorbs the dust and particles that may be released by the most heavily decomposed material (Fig. 202).

In working with film objects, you should use all your senses, except for taste. Lazy or inept projectionists have 'kissed' the print, French style, by holding a strip of film stock between their lips in order to determine which side is covered by the emulsion. For your information, it is the one that feels a bit rough and tastes vaguely sour when licked, something you should never do, however: once left upon

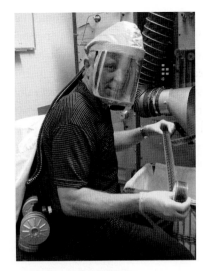

Fig. 202 Film preservation technician Juan Vrijs examines nitrate film at the Haghefilm Laboratory. Amsterdam, 2010. Source: Courtesy of Haghefilm Digitaal, Amsterdam.

the emulsion, the imprint of the lips is indelible because your saliva has impregnated the emulsion. The shiny side of a print is the base; the photographic emulsion has a duller surface. Holding a strip of film stock against any light source will be enough to determine this. The difference between base and emulsion is only slightly more difficult to ascertain in new polyester prints; a regular acquaintance with this type of material will gradually make this exercise much easier for you.

If done in moderation, there is also no harm in smelling a print (unless it's heavily decomposed): the scent of nitrate evokes a gentle blend of camphor and dark chocolate or cocoa; aged triacetate is on the pungent side, increasingly acrid when the print is irreversibly affected by the notorious 'vinegar syndrome' (see p. 211 and Plate 27a–b). The 'rancid butter syndrome' produced by the butyric acid in diacetate and triacetate stock, and the 'pisces syndrome' or 'rotten fish syndrome', believed to be the effect of chemical decay in the photographic gelatin, are generally found in film materials so badly damaged that you are unlikely to experience them directly.

At the early stages of the 'vinegar syndrome', the print may still be projectable, but its smell eventually becomes so overwhelming that you won't want to get near it. Film elements on 16mm diacetate stock – especially those distributed under the Kodascope brand for non-theatrical use – are all camphor and no chocolate, in part because they were stored in special cans equipped with a small damp cloth of rounded shape, periodically soaked with a mild camphor solution to prevent the print from becoming brittle.

Polyester stock, the most inert of all, has a faint nondescript smell of assorted chemicals. It is very easy to distinguish from its triacetate ancestor: if held against a light source, a polyester reel is semi-transparent (Fig. 203a), while acetate looks as solid as a black rock (Fig. 203b); so does nitrate, but the colour of its surface is unmistakably different. Prints with multiple tinting dyes have the appearance of muted rainbows (Plate 25). Nitrate stock has different thicknesses, depending on where the film was manufactured and sometimes

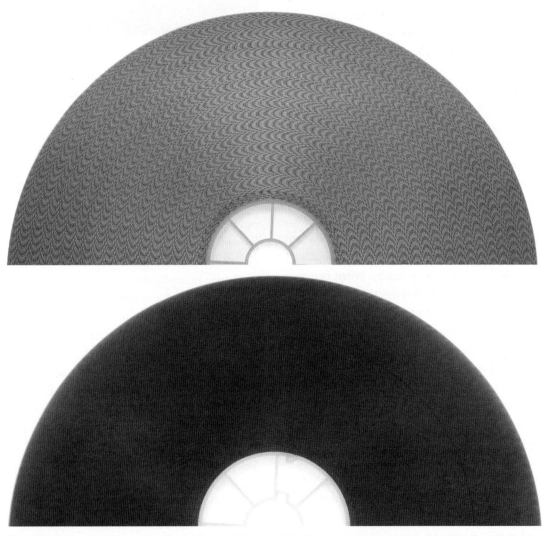

Fig. 203a–b A reel of 35mm polyester film (top) and triacetate film (bottom), seen against a light source. Source: George Eastman Museum.

on the company that used or produced it: early Cines, Ambrosio, Pasquali, and Pathé prints in good condition are rather sturdy to the touch; Gaumont's are somehow flimsier and convey a feeling of impending brittleness.

Then there's hearing. Here lies the gift of the greatest film projectionists, who can diagnose print condition by the purr or the crackle of a print through the sprockets of their machines. Every snap is a splice; when the noise in the projection booth becomes worrisome, it's because the print is very brittle or shrunken, and the teeth of the sprockets are eating into the perforations instead of perfectly matching their shape. To a small extent, the same applies when running an acetate or polyester print on a viewing table, where the path of the film is much simpler. The base of polyester prints seems to be immune from shrinkage; not so in the case of triacetate prints. If their noise becomes too loud, it is best to stop the machine and ask a research assistant to investigate the problem: the copy may have come closer to the end of its active life, in which case it should be kept only as backup material for possible preservation.

Winding through a nitrate print is relatively easy, as the only precept is to turn the crank of the manual rewind bench very, very slowly. If you hear a slight noise, similar to two sticky surfaces being detached from each other, the aural message is unmistakable: the emulsion is adhering to the adjacent film base. It is a bad sign. Stop running the film; rewind it to where you started from; even better, don't touch it at all, and inform a research assistant. The print will be sent back to the refrigerated vaults as quickly as possible. It is not too late to save the film by reproducing it onto another carrier (if this has not been done already), but time is running out. To avoid this kind of incident, archives tend to refrain from repeated access to unpreserved nitrate elements – except for periodical inspection – until they are selected for laboratory work.

Practice

Most film archives and museums are equipped for the visual and material investigation of their collections: viewing tables for safety copies, hand-cranked inspection benches and rewinders (vertical and horizontal) for all film formats, and special machines used in the comparative evaluation of prints and negatives. Viewing tables from Germany (Steenbeck and KEM-Elektronik Mechanik GmbH), the United States (RGI), Italy (Prévost), and France (CTM) are the most common (Fig. 204), although many firms that specialized in this kind of equipment are no longer manufacturing it or have disappeared altogether, which constitutes a growing problem in relation to the maintenance of these machines. When an employee at the Library of Congress shows the viewing table to a researcher, one of the first questions will be: 'Do you know how to use the Steenbeck?' There is, however, no mystery at all about its operation. Structurally, the Steenbeck viewer looks like any other editing table for 35mm or 16mm film utilized in the post-production process during the pre-digital era, with the added advantage that you don't have to worry about threading the print through the magnetic or photoelectric cell that reads the soundtrack. The instructions provided here can therefore be

Fig. 204 Viewing table for 35mm film. CTM, France, 2004. Source: George Eastman Museum.

applied to a Steenbeck machine and to almost every other similar piece of equipment.

Normally, you will be looking at prints that have already been prepared for viewing on this type of apparatus. The reels have been wound 'heads out' (from the beginning of the film, as opposed to 'tails out', its terminal part) around plastic cores with the emulsion out – that is, facing you. The same applies to archival film projection, where prints are often mounted on reel holders (not dissimilar from those available in the late silent era) and must have the emulsion out. There is no unanimous view among collecting institutions on whether film prints and negatives should be stored with the emulsion 'in' or 'out', but the only thing that matters in your case is that the film you are about to watch should have the emulsion facing you. If the emulsion is facing in (towards the plastic core), the image will appear on the small screen of most viewing machines flipped left to right, like a mirror image. If the reel is 'tails out', the image will appear upside down and, of course, you will be watching the film from the end of the reel to its beginning.

Do not attempt, for instance, to view the film in reverse mode or, worse, flip the whole reel (films elements are rather heavy objects, each 'double' reel weighing almost 5 kilograms, or 10 US pounds; the diameter of a 'single' reel of 1,000 feet, or 300 metres, with a plastic core is approximately 10 inches, or 25 centimetres; a 'double' reel of 2,000 feet, or 600 metres, is 14 inches, or 35 centimetres, wide). When a print is not properly wound, it is always best to ask for assistance from the museum's staff. They will take care of rewinding the reel in the right direction and orientation while you look at the next film in your list, or check your research notes. There are two other things you should never do: holding a reel only by the edges, as you would with a vinyl phonograph record (it is common practice not to wind the prints too tightly before putting them in storage); and unspooling the

beginning of the reel by hand to verify its contents. The first action may give you a very big headache, as the middle of the reel is likely to slip down to the floor in an unwieldy funnel of film stock. The second makes the print equally vulnerable to dust and scratches, most frequently seen at the beginning and the end of a reel.

The viewing table has a control device for viewing film at the standard speed of 24 frames per second (in some machines there are buttons or knobs for lower or higher speeds). The same handle also serves the purpose of slowing down or winding back the film; this can be done at a higher speed, but must be avoided with archival prints, as it increases the risk of scratching or otherwise damaging them permanently. Don't use the viewing table to quickly run through the film, as you would with a computer file or a magnetic tape. Never fall into the bad habit of 'seeing' more prints in a shorter period of time by rushing them through the viewing machine at an excessive speed to obtain the information you need. This procedure is of doubtful value as a research practice, and it endangers the collection object: when seen as a print, a film cannot be browsed like a book. Digital files are much better suited to this kind of activity.

If a change of direction is necessary while the print is running in the viewing machine, make sure that the switch is not abrupt, as too much tension on the print may tear it apart. Should a break occur for this or any other reason, or if you find an existing break or partial tear on the print, stop the machine immediately and call a research assistant. If no assistant is available and there is no time to wait, you may temporarily join the two ends of the print with a special adhesive white tape, normally found near the viewing table; even better, overlap the two ends, carefully advance the film in its direction of travel, and insert a piece of paper to correspond with the break, so that a technician can easily locate it and make the necessary repairs.

Prints are wound on plastic cores, sometimes (in 16mm copies) on reel holders of various sizes. Before you start watching the film, make sure that the take-up plate of the viewing table has a core or a reel holder of the same size. This will simplify the job of inspecting the print again when the viewing session is over, and avoid the trouble caused by a print that no longer fits into its archival container because the core is too large, or the reel holder is wider than the plastic or metal can. When you start to view the print, you must never use adhesive tape to secure the leader to the core, as this creates unnecessary tension when the film is rewound; if not promptly removed, the residual glue of the tape can also damage the print itself, and transfer to the sprockets and gears of the viewing table where the film will be examined next time. Conversely, do apply a short piece of adhesive white tape (folded upon itself at one end) to fasten the tail end of the film after viewing. Remember that, in general, film prints should not be wound too tightly (to avoid excessive pressure between the base and the emulsion of the nearby coil), but also not too loosely, as the film would be subject to scratching when projected or rewound; dust can easily penetrate into the reel; and the base may become warped.

Regardless of the archival status of the print you are watching, be mindful that it may be more precious than initially thought (the Argentinian 16mm print of *Metropolis* referred to in the previous chapter is a perfect case in point). Should you come to believe that the material is rare or unique (or, for that matter, that what was presented to you as a projection print is actually something else, such as a fine grain master), do not be greedy or foolish. Stop the machine, call the research assistant, and explain what you think. The curatorial staff will be grateful for your gesture, and you will gain the admiration and trust of your hosts. As you are nearing the end of the reel (that is, at the point where the print is joined to its protective

film leader), slow down the viewing machine, because there is always a chance that some adhesive tape is attached to the core. If that is the case, do not run the end tail of the film leader through the machine's sprockets and in front of the lens; instead, gently remove the leader from its path and secure its end to the body of the reel before putting it back into the archival container. When you have finished examining a reel, do not rewind it: a film technician will take care of that when inspecting the print before it goes back to storage.

Observation

This and the next two sections of the chapter provide a succinct outline of the evidence that may emerge by studying projection prints of silent films, based on their physical appearance, regardless of their visual content. The main difference between a nitrate or diacetate element and a replica on triacetate or polyester stock is that the traces left upon the object during its commercial life can be detected with a greater degree of accuracy in the original than in the facsimile. In this sense, it is preferable to examine – if that is still possible – the nitrate copy of a given title, rather than its duplicate. Photographic quality is not all: a modern projection print inevitably conceals some information carried in its matrix, inside and outside the edges of the frames. The colours of nitrate, and the respective shapes of negative (camera) and positive (printing) apertures can sometimes be deduced by approximation from a close analysis of more recent projection copies available in the museum's or the archive's film study centre. Either way, you are likely to learn more about the story behind these prints than with any other kind of reproduction.

In theory, it should not be impossible to achieve the same goal by digital means. Many copies created in this medium, however, are either of such poor definition or have been manipulated to such an extent that it is no longer possible to establish a direct connection between the translated image and its source. The photochemical duplicate of a nitrate print can be as unfaithful to its aspect ratio and to its tinting, toning, and stencil colouring as its digital equivalent, but everything else can only be hidden, not fabricated or distorted. Watching a silent film (either nitrate or diacetate) on a triacetate or polyester film print made in recent times is like observing it across one or more superimposed veils, one for each print generation. The goal is to see beyond the veil and to better understand what is, or was, behind it.

Previous chapters of this book have offered many examples of the sorts of alterations and mutilations silent films have undergone over time, for reasons ranging from neglect to morality, from authorial decisions to musical accompaniments, from language and culture to showmanship, from economic profit to exhibition schedules. In the absence of primary or secondary sources indicating who was responsible for these changes, and where they were implemented, there is just no way of knowing any more than is visible on the projection copies themselves. Original prints (and, to a lesser extent, their best photochemical duplicates) are helpful at the very least in making conjectures about how the changes were made, and the logic – if any – that was applied in their execution.

One thing is certain: no two prints of a silent film will tell exactly the same story. Depending on where and when the objects were found, some hypotheses can be formulated about their material history. The circumstances behind the physical structure and appearance of individual copies will almost never be known in all their details, but there is often an opportunity to make some sense out of their current condition. The lesson to be learned from film as an object is that its adventures are as revealing and compelling as the photographic images it carried so imperfectly and so stubbornly, against all odds, in the course of its existence.

Let's translate this principle in empirical terms. A film may have seen the light as its makers and producers intended, but it was never really finished: other people, in various capacities, left their imprint on all copies and negatives, redefining the film as an endless work in progress. Its ramifications extend to this day, through the activity of film preservation and through all past and future digital avatars of the same work. The first and foremost evidence of this ongoing process is the splice on the print or the negative. All those who handled film copies (for editing, censorship, or projection purposes, and for many other reasons) have almost always left this blunt testimony of their relationship with the objects in their possession.

A nitrate or diacetate copy from the silent film era usually shows one or more cuts (unless the film consists of a single uninterrupted shot). There are three basic explanations for this: (a) the film broke, and had to be repaired; (b) the contents of the finished film were intentionally altered; (c) separating and joining different pieces of film stock were necessary actions for the completion of a creative work. The first reason is self-explanatory: handling a film print for projection, inspection, or rewinding involves the risk of breaking it. Projectionists,

RULE 9

Every print of a film is a unique object
carrying its own physical, historical, and aesthetic evidence,
and should not be treated as identical
to other prints with the same title.

theatre managers, and distributors did not pay much attention to this during the silent era; in later years, tears and splices were accepted as inevitable, even within collecting institutions. Vincent Pinel, former curator of the Cinémathèque française, used to call projectors 'film manglers', alluding to their propensity to scratch, chew, and tear apart cellulose if they are not properly operated and maintained.

Cuts

The practice of deliberately cutting and splicing, on the other hand, has long been an object of intense scholarly research. In the early years of cinema, the very notion of connecting disparate pieces of motion picture stock for the sake of establishing a coherent chain of visual information was a revolution in itself, greeted with some hesitation or resistance before being assimilated into the filmmaking process. The basics of splicing technique (aligning and cementing two ends of film along the perforations) were in place well before 1900, following a brief but intense period of experimentation. None of the film joints made by other means could be as sharp, quickly made, easy to repeat, and permanent. The fifth requirement – being as invisible as possible during projection – revealed the virtues of a good junction between two strips of film beyond the realm of complexity in storytelling. Georges Méliès, who almost never had any inclination to think about 'editing' in these terms, was nevertheless the first pioneer of the film splice in its most inventive form, as seen in his 'artificially arranged scenes' populated with magic appearances and disappearances of objects and people, and with imaginary worlds of exquisite visual charm.

Méliès wrote in his memoirs that he had discovered the secret of these 'special effects' while shooting a view of the Place de l'Opéra in Paris. His camera allegedly had a malfunction at the precise moment when a carriage was passing in front of the lens. As cranking resumed, a hearse was in exactly the same position previously occupied by the carriage; once projected on a large screen, the optical 'transformation' had been achieved as if by magic. The anecdote may or may not be apocryphal, but Méliès must have found out from the very beginning of his career that the 'camera stop and substitution' trick he referred to could not have been obtained by simply interrupting the turn of the crank, and by making performers and objects change their positions in front of the lens: there would have been at least one overexposed frame – probably more – corresponding with the moment when the camera paused, thus spoiling the optical illusion. The only option was to process the negative, remove its overexposed frames, and join the two ends as required (see pp. 155–156). In the first decade of cinema, the negative was often left untouched, and the splice made on each and all projection copies.

Another type of editorial splice, also unrelated to conventional 'editing', was used in the assembly of release prints with coloured sections employing tinting, toning or mordanting, and stencilling. As seen in Chapter 3, all the shots to be treated with a certain colour or combination of tints and tones were processed together in a single negative, then separated and immersed in their respective chemical baths (changes in tinting within the same shots were possible, but rarely applied until the 1920s because of the technical hurdles involved, as seen on p. 50); release prints were collated by teams of female workers according to the instructions contained in a continuity sheet. The splices they made had an aesthetic function only in the loosest sense of the term, as these joints existed merely because film producers could not do otherwise. This important but very repetitive job was parodied in a German comedy short starring Lil Dagover

Fig. 205 *Tragödie einer Uraufführung* ([Tragedy of a Film Premiere], O.F. Maurer, 1926). Frame enlargement from a 35mm triacetate positive. Source: Stiftung Deutsche Kinemathek.

(Fig. 205), *Tragödie einer Uraufführung* ([Tragedy of a Film Premiere], O.F. Maurer, 1926), also known as *Wenn die Filmkleberin gebummelt hat …* ([When the Film Editor Got Confused …]), describing the fanciful or surreal effects of a young woman's distractions from her duty (title cards shown upside down, fiction film grotesquely mixed with documentary footage, chaotic jump cuts in the action).

These are the kinds of splices we know more about. By and large, they can confidently be called 'original' because there is no other plausible reason for their existence (some joints may have weakened over time; if reinforced or reconstructed, some discrepancy between them and the others should be apparent upon close analysis). The material history of all other splices is not as easy to determine. It is often possible to tell at least the difference between two pieces of film hastily glued together in 1918 by a frenzied projectionist to repair a break in the film, and the splice made by a film collector in 1954 to improve upon a sequence whose continuity did not seem logical enough to be left as it was, even though there was no evidence to support the alteration (this did actually happen on some occasions). Look at the shape of the splice as it appears on the nitrate print, or by transparency on its safety film duplicate. If all the junctions in a 1907 nitrate copy show as straight lines overlapping each other – always at the same intervals – except for a thicker one, where the corners at one end of the film have been slightly trimmed diagonally, it is very likely that the exception reflects a later intervention. Whether it is there to mend a break in the film, or because some other shots have been placed or excised in between, is up to you to decide.

It is also possible to apply this method on a modern viewing print, even if the object is perfectly intact: the profile of a splice made on the negative source always appears as a very thin clear area on the upper or lower margin of the frame (Fig. 206a); conversely, a splice in the positive copy of a former generation will show up as a darker line (Fig. 206b). The distinction is also valid when looking at third- or fourth-generation duplicates, the only difference being that it is harder to tell which print generation was affected by the cut on the print or the negative. As splices in the silent film era – especially in

Fig. 206a–b *Le Chevalier mystère* (Georges Méliès, 1899). 35mm nitrate positive. The cement splice on the edited camera negative (a) is visible as a light area on the upper section of a frame. The splice made on the projection print (b) appears as a dark line, located in this case between two frames. Source: George Eastman Museum.

the early period – were often made manually, there is little chance of identifying them with any greater precision on recent copies, unless a distinctive technique or equipment was used (p. 89). It is helpful to gain at least some familiarity with the most common mechanical splicers available in laboratories and film inspection rooms, if you are given a chance to see them in action.

Identification

One of the greatest pleasures and frustrations of studying silent cinema in museums and archives is that film collections are full of films still awaiting proper authentication. You will rarely see them widely disseminated in digital form, precisely because of their proud and stubborn anonymity. No stone is left unturned in the process of giving them a name: the face of an actress, a car's licence plate, the façade of a building, and even the briefest glimpse of a newspaper in the scene can be of help in determining the identity of a film. Still, in many cases, the images themselves are not enough to bring the mystery to a satisfactory solution.

This is where the evidence of film as an object can help disentangle so many seemingly insoluble enigmas. Looking at a print on a viewing machine gives the opportunity to observe and evaluate details otherwise difficult or impossible to capture during film projection in a theatre. Before describing some of them, it is worth mentioning those traces that can be detected on the screen, regardless of the format in which you are watching the film. If you are quick or patient enough when taking research notes, it is always a good idea to write down the non-narrative factual information – signs, numbers, alphabetical codes – revealed in the body of the picture and its intertitles. Corporate logos or other kinds of markers appear in more or less prominent form within the scene in a large

Fig. 207a–d Film company logos or names within the scene: (a) *Entre Calais et Douvres* (Georges Méliès, Star-Film, 1897), production still; (b) *J'ai perdu mon lorgnon* (*I've Lost My Eyeglasses*, Charles-Lucien Lépine, Pathé, 1906), 35mm triacetate positive; (c) *Viaggio in una stella* (Gaston Velle, Cines, 1906), 35mm triacetate positive; (d) *The Voice of the Violin* (D.W. Griffith, Biograph, 1909), 35mm nitrate positive. Source: [a] Courtesy of Jacques Malthête; [b] Library of Congress; [c] Museo Nazionale del Cinema – Fondazione Maria Adriana Prolo, Turin; [d] George Eastman Museum.

number of films made until the mid-1910s (Fig. 207a–d), and on title cards (the latter continued to be the norm for some companies into the 1920s). Intertitles may include the film's catalogue number, the sequential number of the intertitle itself, and even a language code, to guide the workers in print assembly (Fig. 208).

These visual clues are of vital importance for authentication and preservation: thanks to catalogue numbers, films without a main title can be identified and dated through a comparison with other projection copies and printed sources. Sequential numbers of title cards are also invaluable in ascertaining whether or not the print is complete. This tool should be used with caution,

however, as the absence of one or more intertitles is no decisive proof that something is missing from the print. Censorship boards may have required the suppression of one or more title cards before approving a film for public exhibition.

Producers and distributors removed intertitles – even after the film's official release – because they were considered to be confusing, redundant, misleading, or problematic; they could be moved or reshuffled within the film to clarify or change the storyline as was deemed necessary. This can be verified, for instance, with the parallel observation of domestic distribution prints of silent films made in the United States, and their Italian versions in the Roberto Pallme Collection at the George Eastman

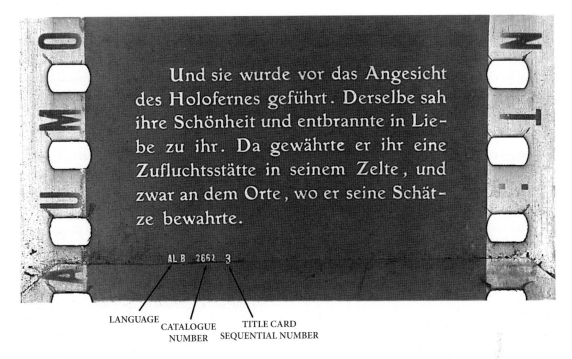

Und sie wurde vor das Angesicht
des Holofernes geführt. Derselbe sah
ihre Schönheit und entbrannte in Lie-
be zu ihr. Da gewährte er ihr eine
Zufluchtsstätte in seinem Zelte, und
zwar an dem Orte, wo er seine Schät-
ze bewahrte.

AL B 2652 3

LANGUAGE   CATALOGUE   TITLE CARD
                   NUMBER   SEQUENTIAL NUMBER

Fig. 208 *Judith et Holopherne* (Louis Feuillade, Gaumont, 1909). Frame enlargement from a 35mm nitrate positive. Source: George Eastman Museum – Davide Turconi/Josef Joye Collection.

Museum, an ideal case study on the commercial life of feature-length works outside their country of origin. Another treasure of silent cinema, the collection of Komiya Tomijiro at the National Film Archive of Japan – formerly known as the National Film Center – includes an English-language version of Jacques Feyder's *L'Atlantide* (1921) that is so beautiful (for the design and style of its English intertitles, as much as for its tinting and toning) as to make all other extant projection copies pale by comparison.

If there is no particular need to examine film prints to understand the meaning of these visual clues and variations from the main versions, much more can be discovered by holding a nitrate or diacetate print in your hands (beginning with the realization that a title card may not belong to the film at all, because it was added by some exhibitor long after the film's release). Many of these revelations emerge from a closer look at the areas surrounding the photographic images of the print

or negative. This is a unique opportunity, as such evidence is not reproduced in any other film or video duplicates you may be able to see in the future:

1. There is a tiny horizontal area between contiguous frames in the film element, positive or negative. This is the 'frame line': its thickness and shape are very variable, especially in projection copies made before the 1920s. The more you are able to inspect nitrate or diacetate prints, and compare their frame lines, the easier it will be to establish correlations between their appearance and the production companies that made those films; this is particularly helpful when there is no other way to identify a projection print. Some early films had no frame line at all, and their images are some-times overlaid at the top and bottom of the image.

2. In the corners between frame lines and perfora-tions, there may be numbers handwritten on the negative (therefore appearing as white on some

projection prints). These were used as reference aids in the editing process, in stencil colouring (Pathé), or as indications of the exposure required for printing. They are often found on films produced in the Soviet Union, and partially visible as almost imperceptible flashes at one corner or at the upper or lower margins of the picture during projection.

3. A small unexposed area around the image is often detected on projection prints, marking the gap between the profile of the camera aperture (the portion of negative film stock exposed to light at the time of shooting) and the slightly smaller one of the positive (or 'printing') aperture, as seen in the frame enlargements reproduced on p. 295, most notably at the right margin of the samples.

4. The shape or profile of the picture frame (the 'positive' or 'printing' aperture) is unique to some production companies of the early years.

5. The number, size, and shape of the perforations in film negatives and projection prints, as described in Chapter 2, may indicate the work of specific filmmakers and producers from the early years. The perforations of films made before 1905 can be used as identification aids, as no standard had yet been agreed upon in that period about their exact configuration (if you see a nitrate print with this kind of perforation, you can safely assume it was struck during the first decade of cinema).

6. The 'shadow' of the perforations, sometimes visible at the edges of the frame (Fig. 196a–d), is derived from negative or positive film elements of previous generations. The number of overlapping shapes and their clear or darker lines, next to the perforations of the copy being viewed, may help determine whether a projection copy was struck from the camera negative or from intermediate printing elements.

7. Inscriptions (known as 'edge codes') are often printed along the edges of projection copies and negatives, between the perforations (for an explanation of how these codes were printed on the film stock, see pp. 39–40). Many production companies tried to counteract the illegal traffic or duplication of their films by applying names, initials, or coded information that was subject to change over time (see Plate 38 and Appendix 3). Film stock manufacturers frequently adopted the same technique to indicate their corporate names, as well as the place and year of manufacture (see Fig. 31 and Appendix 2).

You should not expect to find much of the above in film elements from the silent era in formats other than 35mm: with the possible exception of 28mm prints, duplicates in amateur formats were generally too small to include more than the manufacturer's edge code. There are marks at the edges of 16mm frames that may indicate precisely what kind of camera was used for shooting in that format.

Another suggestion: never take any single piece of evidence from the print at face value, if it is not corroborated by other facts. For instance, the presence of a 1907 edge code from Pathé on a

---

RULE 10

Every piece of material or visual evidence
found in a film print or negative
should be used in comparative terms,
and is not conclusive proof of the film's identity.

projection copy is by no means conclusive proof that the film was shot or distributed in that year. All you know, for the time being, is only that this is a Pathé film, and that the copy in question was not printed in 1906 or earlier. The chances that the film was released in 1907 are actually very good, but you cannot be absolutely certain about this yet.

All information gathered from a direct inspection of nitrate prints should primarily help to eliminate other possibilities: in the Pathé 1907 example, the edge code narrows the focus to a single production company, and excludes all films produced by this company after 1907. The greater the range of evidence supporting a given hypothesis, the smaller the number of alternatives; inferences drawn from the facts collected so far are more plausible if you can show that different research tracks, jointly verified, corroborate your answer.

Film identification is a scholarly exercise where the art of doubting is cultivated with a detective's mind. Intuition, imagination, and scepticism are its main ingredients, blended with common sense and a knack for the seemingly nonsensical. If you recognize a scene from Charlie Chaplin's *The Face on the Bar Room Floor* at the beginning of a nitrate reel, do not assume that this is the film you are about to inspect: the first shots may be followed by excerpts from *Caught in a Cabaret*, *Gentlemen of Nerve*, and *Recreation*, all produced by Keystone in 1914, as in a 35mm nitrate copy held by the George Eastman Museum. The same kind of precaution should be taken with all prints of *Vie et passion de N.S. Jésus Christ*, one of Pathé's most successful productions of the early years, as you may witness a Crucifixion sequence in which Jesus reaches the top of a Golgotha from the 1902 edition of the film, is nailed to a cross from the 1914 remake, and dies in front of a painted backdrop from the 1907 version (with all the splices in between); a print with a similar content is preserved at MoMA in New York.

Memory

The value of doing research in a film archive or museum is largely dependent upon the accuracy and objectivity achieved in recording the information you have acquired, with a clear distinction between data collected from film elements and those drawn from printed or manuscript sources. The list reproduced in Table 2 describes the suggested contents of a spreadsheet to be filled out when examining the archival print of a silent film. In setting up your own database, some fields may be unnecessary to your purposes; others can be expanded, or added to the existing items, depending on the nature of the project (the seventh field – 'director' or 'cinematographer'– is one example among many, as your research may be more focused upon technical or creative personnel in the film other than those mentioned here). Most of the entries should be self-explanatory, in light of what has been discussed so far throughout the book.

The following anecdote may serve as an illustration of the importance of Fields 9 and 11 in the spreadsheet. A masterpiece of early cinema, *Suspense* (Lois Weber and Phillips Smalley, 1913) is preserved at the BFI National Archive. The film is hailed as a triumph of technical innovation and narrative tension: shots divided into three triangular sectors (with different action taking place in each, as shown in Fig. 209), bold positioning of the camera, a breathtaking editing style. When a scholar went to the BFI to view a projection print of *Suspense*, however, there was a conspicuously wrong note: in a scene halfway through the film, a man is seen standing in the middle of a road. He is lighting a cigarette, unaware that a car is approaching at breakneck speed behind him. Just as he is about to be run over by the vehicle, the next shot shows him safe and sound on the other side of the road. The researcher took note of this jarring gap in the narrative and mentioned the scene to a fellow student, who also saw the film

Table 2 Print Viewing Report

Print viewed at _____ Date _____

1. **Film title** (if known)
2. **Title on print** (if applicable; in parentheses if different from the release title in the country of origin)
3. **Archival title** (in square brackets if there is no title on the print, and its identity is unknown)
4. **Production company**
5. **Country of origin**
6. **Date of release** (or production, or censorship review)
7. **Director** (or cinematographer, for the films of the early period)
8. **Other credits** (as shown on the print)
9. **Archival source** (collector, collecting institution, or distributor of the print)
10. **Collection** (the print's provenance, if known)
11. **Location, inventory, or accession number**
12. **Viewing equipment** (rewind bench, viewing table, private or public projection)
13. **Medium** (nitrate, acetate, polyester film, etc.)
14. **Format** (35mm, 28mm, 17.5mm, 16mm, etc.)
15. **Colour process** (if applicable)
16. **Title cards** (their language and nature: original, reissued, reconstructed)
17. **Edge codes and markings** (if applicable)
18. **Original length** (if known)
19. **Length of the print**
20. **Projection speed** (as presented at the screening, or estimated by the viewer)
21. **Estimated running time**
22. **Notes**

Fig. 209 A split-screen shot from *Suspense* (Lois Weber and Phillips Smalley, 1913). Frame enlargement from a 35mm triacetate positive. Source: BFI National Archive.

but had a very different recollection of the episode. The man is run over by the car. The police arrive at the incident. Luckily, the man only suffered a few scratches and a big fright.

Upon further investigation with the Cataloguing Unit of the BFI National Archive, it turned out that there were at the time three copies of *Suspense* in the collection. Only one of them was complete, and this is not the copy the researcher saw. When the other student had looked at the same film, several years earlier, there may have been only one projection print available. Keeping a record of when the film was seen (at the top of the worksheet) can make a difference: a nitrate print, for instance, may be in wonderful shape today, but no longer be extant five years from now.

Film festival curators are understandably keen to show a film in its most complete form, but another scholar may think that there are distinctive elements of interest in other prints, incomplete as they may be. All three copies of

RULE 11

The 'original' film is a multiple entity,
fragmented over time into as many variants
as the number of surviving copies.

Suspense are 'authentic' in their own way, as the material history (that is, the provenance) of each is somehow connected to the condition in which it was found. This pluralist approach should be extended beyond film research in a museum or archive: whether you have seen Abel Gance's *Napoléon* with live music accompaniment, in the silence of a cubicle at the nearest film study centre, or in a digital format at home, it would help to know which of its twenty-three versions you are referring to, before discussing its narrative structure in a scholarly paper.

The example of *Napoléon*, one of the greatest cinematic events of all time, serves as a reminder that the individual study of silent films in an archival setting is not a substitute for their experience on the big screen. On a viewing table (or, for that matter, on your computer screen), you are entitled to dissect films any way you like: interrupting the natural course of their visual and narrative flow, making them run as slowly as a few frames per second, examining the same sections over and over again, going back in time to review some shots, sequences, or single frames, as you would do with sentences, paragraphs, or specific words when reading a book. You do this alone or in small groups, in a highly disciplined research environment. Paying audiences in a picture house never

experienced cinema that way. In an ideal world, it would be preferable to first watch a silent film on the big screen, with music (if appropriate) and without arbitrary interruptions, as this is how its makers thought it would be seen.

To push the metaphor suggested at the end of Chapter 13 a little further, participating in the public exhibition of a silent film before studying its content on a private basis is like discovering a new species of tree within the sensory landscape of its forest, with all the rational and emotional reactions attached to the film's appearance on the theatrical horizon. If seen on a rewind bench, *Pass the Gravy* (Fred L. Guiol, 1928) is a slapstick comedy; in a theatre, at the right speed, with a talented musician and an audience, it is half an hour of collective bliss. You may or may not be able to choose when this kind of encounter takes place, but it would be wonderful if you could be part of it sooner or later. Film curatorship is like a bird's-eye view of the cinematic event, the synthesis of all its components, enjoyed both from inside the forest – as shown in the previous chapters – and especially above its branches, in the company of other people. Such a communal approach to silent cinema is, by reflection, a creative work in itself. Film curators are, above all, devoted and discerning film spectators at the service of their fellow viewers.

Chapter 15

Curatorship

Fig. 210 Filmmaker and curator Peter Kubelka explains the nature of cinema by preparing mayonnaise in front of the audience. Österreichisches Filmmuseum, Vienna, 1995. Gelatin silver print. Source: Courtesy of Österreichisches Filmmuseum.

It is time to look again at *A Trip to the Moon*. You have encountered it at the beginning of this book as a film made by Georges Méliès in 1902; as one of the many titles preserved and available on 35mm copies from archives and museums; as a digital-born celebrity, presented on a large screen with the highest possible pixel rate available at the time and multiplied in a plethora of low-resolution siblings on personal computers; finally, as a ribbon of artificial DNA enclosed in a tiny glass container, one million little Méliès waiting to be decoded in an unfathomable future. In between, the film has existed as grains of silver halide scattered on a sticky surface made with pulverized remains of cattle. It has been put behind the lenses and through the metal sprockets of countless projectors. It has been unwound, cut, scratched, burned, repaired, edited, sold, and reproduced in a large number of copies (seven elements on nitrate stock, made between 1902 and 1929, have survived the ordeal to this day). Lecturers and musicians have provided all kinds of sounds to accompany its projection. Audiences have viewed it under the most diverse circumstances in complete, incomplete, or fragmentary prints, with or without colours. Private collectors, archives, and museums have preserved it to the best of their abilities, often spending large amounts of money to keep it in good condition and to create new and more stable elements to be conserved and viewed.

Film curatorship is both a method of observation and participation in these events. It is 'the art of interpreting the aesthetics, history, and technology of cinema through the selective collection, preservation, and documentation of films and their exhibition in archival presentations'. This definition was proposed in a book written by film curators with experience in museums and archives where silent cinema has a prominent place (*Film Curatorship: Archives, Museums, and the Digital Marketplace*, 2008, p. 231). There are specific issues confronting film curators who acquire, conserve, and show silent films on a systematic basis. Before discussing their concerns, it is appropriate to describe a curator's responsibility towards other people, and to society in general. A private pleasure and obsession by default, the act of collecting undergoes a radical change when it is reframed as an altruistic gesture. Curatorship begins here, at the point of convergence between reason and passion, pragmatism and moral responsibility. This final chapter will explore its components in the same sequential order.

Accountability

As a matter of principle, film curators are expected to develop and implement the cultural policies of film archives, private and public museums, festivals, and exhibition venues in general. They direct the acquisition, preservation, and presentation of film collections (this includes negotiating and approving film purchases, exchanges, or loans to other institutions). They are responsible for authenticating and evaluating the historical or aesthetic significance of the objects, on the basis of agreed parameters and in compliance with the institution's collection policies. Curators also conduct and oversee research projects related to the collections, with the goal of making them more accessible and better appreciated by the general public. Whether by choice or necessity, an increasing part of curatorial duties involves management and administration. The fact that some curators have considerable power in the cultural world does not make them dictators or arbiters of public taste; in fact, curators are accountable for their actions to their financial supporters, to their present audiences, and to future generations of citizens who will evaluate their work under the lens of posterity. They may or may not care about it, but the accountability remains, and it should not be taken lightly.

Curatorship has a long tradition in archives and museums, a testimony to the ongoing interaction between history and society. Curatorial values are not the outcomes of a quantifiable science. Their aim is to integrate three types of activities into a cohesive whole: selecting human artefacts to be preserved and made permanently available; cultivating the expertise necessary to evaluate and interpret them; building an infrastructure to protect and promote them as cultural manifestations of history. Curatorship is an intellectual bridge between the past and the future. Its corner-stone is the strategic vision necessary to decipher the traces of what has happened; to explain them to others as objectively as possible; and to anticipate the ways in which a given work may be understood and assessed by generations to come. The curator is a messenger who has the authority and the obligation to ensure that the message itself will foster memory and creativity at the same time.

The first imperative of film curatorship is to assure that the traces of history embodied by the works in a film collection will not be altered under any circumstance, be it of economic, political, racial, or religious nature. While new works may be achieved through the use of one or more existing items in the collections (curators who believe in the archive or museum as a catalyst of invention should always encourage this kind of activity), their creation will never be of detriment to the physical condition of the originals. In this respect, the archivist and the curator are powerful allies, in that they are both committed (the former from the perspective of a custodian of the artefact, the second from that of its interpreter) to the protection and availability of the work in its original form.

In addition to these duties, film curators are responsible for deciding the preservation procedures to be followed with the collection as a whole, or with some of its components. They gather advice from staff and outside experts about the costs of safeguarding, duplicating, or reconstructing archival films, and about the technical implications of the decisions to be made. Their mandate is to ensure that works included in the collections are preserved according to best practice, and that they can be exhibited for as long as possible in their native media and formats, ideally in their original state. The same applies to all other objects related to cinema: posters, photographs, documents, sound recordings, film technology, and so on.

The equal importance of acquisition, preservation, exhibition, and access is a pivotal feature of a curatorial vision. None of these activities, taken individually, should be pursued at the expense of the others. This may be compared to the balance of power between legislative, executive, and judiciary branches in a democratic regime: through a complex system of checks and balances, each component of the political system supports the others and ensures that no single player is allowed to have absolute power. While some agents (such as the judicial function) are also expected to act in complete independence from the political party or coalition holding office at a given point in time, all must comply with agreed rules in the democratic system.

Selection

The same holistic approach applies to the curatorial process as a form of cultural governance, in that acquisition of films and related documents or objects should comply with agreed collection policies that include provisions for preservation and exhibition; in turn, the preservation process must take into account the specific nature of the works acquired and the ability to show them over an indefinite future; demand for access to the collections will influence the choices made from time to time, without altering or compromising their underlying principles. A selective approach is, by far, the most important and the most demanding of all the skills a curator must possess. Curators make value judgements: not all films can be acquired, not all can be preserved; exhibiting them is another form of selection, as this decision is based on a careful assessment of what should or should not be shown, and of the reasons for the inclusion or exclusion of an artwork from the project under consideration.

These parameters apply within and outside institutional frameworks: being a freelance curator gives no special exemption from accountability to present and future audiences. History is the ultimate curator of the cultural heritage, as it determines (through a series of events ranging from social and economic trends to wars, genocides, and natural catastrophes) what posterity will be allowed to experience and what will disappear for ever. Curators don't have such an overwhelming power. They do, however, decide what should be preserved. This prerogative must be used responsibly, as it requires a refined sense of judgement, strategy, diplomacy, and foresight.

In formulating their viewpoint, curators give equal weight to a dual set of considerations. The first is the potential consequence of either failing to preserve a film soon enough, or not at all. When trying to determine the best course of action, both the archivist and the curator appraise the collection from a technical standpoint, and estimate the risk of physical decay of the films. The second set of criteria pertains to which of the films in need of preservation should be given priority. Choosing work A instead of B is not to condemn B to oblivion. It only means that under the present circumstances, given the existing body of works, and in view of a presumed future landscape of the collection, preservation of A comes first. The other one will have to wait.

This is by all means a value judgement as well, and the curator assumes a heavy burden in applying it in a sensible manner after consulting with the preservation technicians, whose knowledge of conservation practices is a necessary prerequisite of any informed curatorial decision. This is also what makes the curatorial profession so inherently complex, as it requires a multiplicity of talents, ranging from historical expertise to knowledge in technical and legal matters, managerial skills (the ability to reconcile conflicting interests and to allocate the staff's activities in the most effective manner), and proficiency in fundraising. How

to make such decisions without contradicting or betraying the notion of adherence to the original medium is only one of the many hazards facing film curatorship in the digital world.

The curators' responsibility is not limited to the development of a film collection according to the prevailing values of today's society. They must also represent the beliefs of cultural, political, and religious minorities, or ideals promoted by individuals and groups whose viewpoints are in direct conflict with the dominant trends of the present, or alien to the views of the curators themselves. In operational terms, this means that curators are expected to maintain a clear distinction between what the history of cinema 'is' and what it 'should be' in their opinion, showing an equal degree of commitment to the preservation of widely admired works and of films that are now despised because of their underlying ideologies, or have a lesser reputation than the canonical milestones so often mentioned in textbooks. This includes, for instance, unidentified films, or prints found in incomplete or fragmentary form, generally undervalued if not altogether ignored by public opinion.

By the same token, curators are responsible to posterity. Ideally, they should have enough intuition and sense of history to make conjectures on what the audience of a distant and therefore unimaginable future may ask from a collecting institution. The measure of success in the curators' endeavours is far more than the mere notion of 'completeness' in a film collection; it is the belated gratitude from their successors for having anticipated needs unforeseen by others during their time. In this context, the professional life of a film curator is profoundly affected by a recurring question: whether or not there is an aspect of cinematic culture which is being overlooked at present, but may become significant, useful, or desirable to the audience of tomorrow.

Orphans

The word 'neglect' is often used by film curators when discussing the past history of collection objects rescued from destruction. Lawyers call them, in more prosaic but equally effective terms, 'abandoned property'. An article published in the October 1950 issue of the journal *Industrial Marketing* referred to 16mm industrial sales movies as 'orphan films'; around 1993, the term began to find widespread acceptance in the archival community. It was initially applied to films that are out of copyright protection; the label was later extended to other items of no apparent commercial value: newsreels, silent films, avant-garde works, and instructional shorts. It could be argued that most films made before 1909, when the direct sale of prints was being replaced by the rental system through authorized distributors, were technically 'orphans' because they could be moved from one home to another before coming to the end of their natural life as physical objects. As many corporate entities of the silent era had made no offer to preserve their assets (or had ceased to exist altogether), collecting institutions could redefine themselves as orphanages of cinema history.

Over the years, film curators pushed the Dickensian metaphor even further. One aspect of the 'orphan' condition, in particular, applies to the films made in the silent era: many of them have been saved unbeknownst to their 'parents', who may or may not have been aware that their offspring still belong to them. When informed about their parentage, production companies are not necessarily interested in bringing them home, unless there is a financial incentive to do so. In such cases, collecting institutions find themselves in a strange situation: they are formally entitled to conserve these films, as they have legitimate possession of the physical elements (their rights often include the creation of new duplicate negatives and projection copies, emphatically excluding digital reproductions); they cannot exhibit, however, the preserved films to the public without permission from copyright owners, who normally charge a fee for each screening, even if they have done nothing to save the films and may not even have any positive or negative elements in their own vaults. Faced with this dilemma, film curators can hardly persuade administrators of their own institutions to disburse public or private funds for preserving silent films they are not allowed to show without compensation to third parties.

After a period of time (legislation varies according to the geographic area), some films no longer have an exclusive owner, and can be publicly exhibited without any limitation: like all other films by Georges Méliès, *A Trip to the Moon* entered into the Public Domain in 2008, seventy years after the death of its author. Freedom from copyright can be a mixed blessing, as other films and directors of lesser repute do not receive the same attention once their corporate ties are severed. As this vicious circle continues, many nitrate prints of silent films lie dormant in the vaults, with no easy solution in sight. They are 'orphan films' against all evidence: the identity and the whereabouts of their parents are often known. The spell is broken only when the parents agree to pay for preserving their own films, even though they will make no money out of them, or when a donor intervenes to assist the orphanage in pursuing its mission. The other major category of silent 'orphan' films encompasses all those nitrate and diacetate prints, copyrighted or not, that survive in fragmented or incomplete form. Like their siblings, they had been spared the fate they would have encountered after leaving a projection booth for the last time in their commercial life. So far, not many people are interested in giving them a second chance.

If the fragments belong to silent films already available in complete form, their only hope is to be either camera negatives or prints of first generation, in which case some curator may eventually want to incorporate them into a future preservation project (if the title in question is deemed worthy of it). It is a slim possibility, but it is better than the permanent limbo bestowed upon the multitude of tiny reels scattered in refrigerated vaults around the world, the debris of a film history that no one dares to discard once and for all, for the same reason librarians are reluctant to throw away individual pages of printed incunabula. A few institutions have celebrated this legion of the condemned by selecting the most beautiful fragments, preserving and showing them exactly as they are. In the late 1980s, the Nederlands Filmmuseum inaugurated a series called 'Bits & Pieces', consisting of several hundred unidentified fragments thematically assembled. It was a brilliant example of film curatorship, and a bold political statement on the cultural rights of 'orphan' films.

Diaspora

Film curators have put considerable effort into reconstructing the history of cinema in the country of their respective institution, regardless of its 'orphan' status. The manifest incongruity with their proclaimed notion of cinema as an art and an industry that transcends linguistic and cultural boundaries can be explained with the understandable desire to give national audiences a sense of ownership of their own cultural history. Corporate interests also play a role in this, albeit to a very marginal extent in relation to silent film. To be precise, the resulting process should be called 'diaspora', since it is a controlled exodus of nitrate prints from the places where they were legitimately sent in order to be seen by people of other territories. Collecting institutions in the United States – where this idea was born – chose the antonym 'repatriation' to describe this activity, defined as the process of bringing cinematic works back to their nation or community of origin for the purposes of collecting, preserving, and exhibiting them in the territory where they were made. In some geographic areas, repatriation is also meant to protect and promote the community's cultural and ancestral interests.

This seemingly harmless principle, derived from a long-established tradition in archaeology, ethnology, and the fine arts, is a nest of ideological assumptions (beginning with the word 'repatriation' itself, derived from the Latin noun *patria*, which translates as something like 'fatherland', 'native land', or 'homeland'). There are two players involved here: one is the person, governmental agency, or corporate entity seeking to resume possession of the films; the other is the individual or institution wishing (or expected) to give them away. Their agendas are not necessarily attuned to each other. Strictly speaking, only the voluntary act of returning films to another country should qualify as repatriation, as it reflects an intention and a subsequent action initiated by the donor or promoted by the recipient. There are other words to describe the forceful transfer of the objects from one to another.

The process of film repatriation is not linear, either; fairness, logic, and generosity are not always part of the equation. Attesting the citizenship of a cultural object is not just a bureaucratic decision. The motives behind it can be as decent as trying to have the films preserved and made available to all, or as pragmatic as treating film prints as a legal, budgetary, and material liability to get rid of. The irresponsible use of deaccession (the sanctioned disposal of collection materials), the absence of transparent collection policies, their deliberate manipulation or disregard by reckless archive managers and curators, are all concrete threats to the world's cinematic heritage. Film repatriation also calls into question the legitimacy of the concept of 'nation' as a cultural principle; the role of administrators and funding agencies in the repatriation process; and the value attributed to film as an object for the creative work it represents. The issue is emerging in the digital domain as well, despite the alleged irrelevance of the carrier in non-photochemical media.

In the neutral sense of the term, 'repatriation' could be renamed 'print exchange', which has been a common occurrence since the formative years of film archives and museums, as seen in Chapter 10. By agreeing to join forces with an international association, the first film curators were trying to prevent or at least contain the uncontrolled movement of film prints from one country to another for private or commercial interests. From the mid-1920s onwards, film collectors have routinely exchanged copies of silent films (particularly from France, Germany, the United States, Denmark, Sweden, and the Soviet Union), the very same titles coveted by museum and archive curators like Iris Barry and Ernest Lindgren for their own institutions. From their perspective, there was no cinematic 'diaspora' or 'repatriation' to speak of; all they wanted were projection prints of important works.

Cinema's most cherished treasures were therefore the first objects of curatorial trade; it was only when the size and scope of archival collections began to grow that the concept of repatriation emerged in the United States. The most ambitious project of its kind was the Library of Congress' return in the 1960s of the captured German, Japanese, and Italian films to their respective countries after World War II. The two main motivations behind the initiative were the pressure to reduce the size of nitrate holdings at the Library, and the awareness that there would have been

little chance for the institution to fully preserve the confiscated prints (the German collection alone consisted of 1,200 features, several thousand shorts, plus a complete run of Ufa newsreels of the Nazi era).

Repatriation

A second wave of film migration, in the opposite direction, occurred two decades later. By then, the word 'repatriation' had acquired a decidedly normative undertone. Its premise was the merging of two complementary agendas: from the recipients' perspective, it was the intention to fill the gaps in the national collection (represented here by a consortium of major archives and museums in the United States); from the giving end, it was the objective of either delegating to others the preservation of films deemed of secondary importance to the archive's curatorial charter, or finding a practical solution to the same issues highlighted by the repatriation of the World War II films to Europe, namely the inadequacy of storage space and the lack of financial resources for preservation.

Under these circumstances, the potential recipient would make the simple suggestion of lifting a financial yoke from another archive by transferring the works to their native grounds. By taking the prints into its collection, the receiving archive committed to preserving films that might have otherwise been left untouched for an indefinite period of time, eventually deteriorating beyond repair. After duplication, a copy of the preserved film would be offered to the donating archive, if so desired. In the 'golden age' decade of American film repatriation – from the mid-1980s to the mid-1990s – the response of the donating archives at the prospect of obtaining new prints of the preserved titles varied from one country to another. Several options were considered: the donating archive (that is, the 'host', or the 'source' archive) could receive a duplicate of the repatriated film as soon as it was preserved, at no charge to the institution; the donor could also agree to pay for the shipping costs of the viewing copies obtained in exchange, or have no interest in receiving anything in return, happy to make space in its vaults (oddly enough, another possibility – sending a projection copy of the foreign film upon request while retaining the original elements – was rarely contemplated as a full 'repatriation' by the receiving institution).

A pioneering instance of this curatorial trend is the series of five repatriation projects from New Zealand, Australia, and the Netherlands conducted from 1987 by the National Center for Film and Video Preservation at the American Film Institute. The first instalment of the endeavour was completed in 1988; the other four followed in the next decade. Their effects were profound and long-lasting: hundreds of silent films were identified in about five years of filmographic research; a cumulative total of 1,941 titles were brought to the United States and distributed among its major film collecting institutions; many of them were preserved; viewing prints were sent back to the donors. That's no small achievement, if one only considers the intricacies of the procedures for shipping several thousand cans of nitrate film across two oceans. From this viewpoint, curators like Jonathan Dennis (founder of the New Zealand Film Archive), Susan Dalton and Larry Karr at the AFI, and Hoos Blotkamp (Director of the Nederlands Filmmuseum) should be hailed as the true heroes of film repatriation in its noblest sense.

The argument for repatriation, however, can be turned upon itself on equally compelling grounds. Very few of the almost 900 prints in the Jean Desmet Collection from the Netherlands are of Dutch origin; nevertheless, this extraordinary corpus of films from the silent period was kept virtually intact and preserved almost in its entirety, thus giving its custodian organization – the Eye Filmmuseum – a golden chance to reassess the history of world cinema between 1910 and 1914. The Komiya Collection was painstakingly restored by the National Film Archive of Japan – under the direction of its Chief Curator, Hisashi Okajima – even if the vast majority of its titles are not of Japanese origin. Conversely, the National Archives of Canada had no hesitation in offering to the Library of Congress most of the Dawson City Collection, a large body of silent films from the United States (see p. 246). On that occasion, William O'Farrell – then in charge of the film collections at the National Archives of Canada – retained fiction films and newsreels pertinent to his country, and sent everything else to the Library of Congress.

The Josef Joye Collection was found in Basel, Switzerland. This treasure trove of international early cinema – 1,158 surviving titles in all at the most recent count – was moved in 1977 to the National Film Archive in London by the Jesuit group in whose name Joye acquired the prints during the first decades of the twentieth century (the Cinémathèque Suisse, renowned for its formidable international collection of feature films and a member of the International Federation of Film Archives since 1948, had no interest in it at the time; a small portion of the Joye Collection had been moved to Italy before the rest was transferred to Great Britain). To call this 'repatriation' is a misnomer; 'diaspora' would be more appropriate, as the Joye films – along with those of Desmet, Komiya, and others in their respective countries – belonged by all intents and purposes to the Swiss cinematic heritage. This is where the inherently flawed concept of film repatriation is subordinated to a higher imperative: safeguarding and preserving a film collection in peril, in the interest of a history of cinema without borders.

RULE 12

All prints of a silent film,
regardless of its country of origin,
are part of the cultural heritage
of the country where they were distributed
and seen by its audiences.

Technology

A large exhibition on the history of film cameras, projectors, and technical apparatus was curated by Laurent Mannoni at the Cinémathèque française in 2016. It was the most comprehensive show of its kind ever held until then, a magnificent display of rare and often striking cinematic objects. Over the years, many institutions have showcased similar apparatus on a temporary or semi-permanent basis in their galleries. These initiatives are not meant to replace the core mission of a film museum: its true 'gallery' is the projection room. Without it, film technology is deprived of its context. Another problem is that projectors and cameras should be touched and used, not only looked at. The quandary is yet unresolved. Seductive as it is, Mannoni's curatorial masterpiece is best interpreted as an urgent call to action.

Projectors and cameras are the tools of cinema. To be fully appreciated, they should be seen first and foremost as functioning mechanisms; if this is not possible, their operation should be at least explained in precise but accessible terms, or with accurate simulations. To expect that visitors of 'museums' on film technology will be excited at the mere sight of a Cinématographe from 1895 is like showing them a vintage car in working order without seeing it move around, or being allowed to take a ride in it. Knowing how a Lumière camera, printer, and projector works is important to understanding Lumière's films, and indirectly

helps to ensure that they are better appreciated in the future.

Silent cinema is preserved when it is exhibited with the apparatus it belongs to. Protecting, copying, and reconstructing film is not enough. Projectors can, and should, be preserved, duplicated, and recreated as well. All these goals can be met, as long as the equipment itself and the documents related to their manufacture and operation remain accessible. By virtue of their special

Fig. 211 Benjamin Walden (Hove, Great Britain), a student in the George Eastman Museum's annual workshop on manufacturing film stock, develops the 35mm film negative he has made and shot with an 'Eyemo' Bell & Howell camera. The photo was taken in a room with red safe light. Rochester, New York, 2016. Source: Photo by Nick Brandreth/George Eastman Museum.

relationship with the image carrier and with the art of displaying it on a large screen, film projectionists are de facto curators in action. Making nitrate film stock (and using it to make new films) is also possible, albeit in relatively small quantities, provided that the machines and the expertise are both safeguarded (Fig. 211).

Until recent times, technology was the big 'black hole' of film curatorship. Declaring that a silent film was restored by a given archive or museum tells only one part of the story: the collecting institution may have decided to give it a full conservation treatment, and probably determined how the preservation process should be implemented, but most of the real work – if not all – has been done in a film laboratory, generally a commercial company (some collecting institutions have film duplication facilities within their own premises; their capacity is often limited to black and white processing, as colour work requires more sophisticated and expensive equipment).

As a rule, the script goes more or less as follows: the archive resolves that a film should undergo preservation work and delegates a film laboratory to do so on its behalf. Aside from cleaning and repair, the laboratory refrains from any unilateral decision affecting the physical structure of the artefact. This rule is by no means inflexible: if, for example, a splice is too fragile to withstand the mechanical strain of the scanner or printing machine, a film technician may decide to open and rebuild the splice, or temporarily reinforce it with tape. A widespread practice (now strongly discouraged) in film laboratories involved cutting a frame from both ends and creating a brand new splice. What is lost in this case was a fraction of a second in screening time, and a useful piece of information on whether the break was recent or not, the result of an accident, or a deliberate editorial cut.

The film laboratory personnel are effectively in control of the duplication process until a set of digital files, or an 'answer print' – the first projection copy obtained through photochemical processing or from a digital intermediate (p. 253) – is made in order to evaluate the results. The definition of film preservation as an art and a science is more than a catchphrase: a good technician is often able to observe details or detect errors that may be invisible to curators. Contrary to the established view of the film laboratory as a 'service provider' fulfilling the clients' orders, its senior staff has an experience and a foresight sometimes beyond the reach of the archive's personnel (in many instances, curators feel compelled to ask laboratory people what to do when faced with a particularly difficult case); by all intents and purposes, the archive itself should be regarded as a 'service provider' to the taxpayer or other stakeholders, with the statutory mandate to act in the public interest. Commercial laboratories, on the other hand, are not bound by such obligations. Most of its technical experts do not feel an incentive to discuss what is relevant and what is not from a curatorial standpoint, as they assume that archive and museum employees have done all the required homework, or that it is not their business to interfere with them.

Film scholars have traditionally played a marginal role in this scheme. Barring a few notable exceptions, they have no other option than taking for granted that things are done properly, entrusting to curators the responsibility of decisions in which they could on some occasions, and quite legitimately, have their say. The flaw in such a course of action is the underlying belief that the temporary residence of a film print in the laboratory should not be the scholar's concern, in compliance with an inflexible (and, especially in the digital world, anachronistic) division of labour. According to this line of thought, scholarship is concerned with ideas to be drawn from the experience of a document made ready for analysis; how it was preserved has no significant effect upon the comprehension of its meaning. Such prejudice was reinforced both by the scholar's emotional distance from the practice of moving image preservation, and by the curators' protectiveness towards their own authority over the archive's operational protocols.

Harsh as it may appear, this picture is not a caricature of reality. If the overall map of visual culture is constantly redefined by the migration of moving images across a variety of media, its *genius loci* is the technological environment where the intellectual choices underlying these transformations are made on behalf of the viewer. So far, the debate on how silent cinema should be experienced has been mainly held between the archive, the museum, and the scholar; digital technology has brought them closer to other agents – the laboratory, the commercial distributor, and the user of moving images in the public sphere – in a more inclusive but inevitably fraught relationship with the notion of film history.

As seen in Chapter 11, the first building block in this cultural environment was laid out in 1978 at the FIAF conference in Brighton, where scholars were officially invited to co-curate a film programme organized by archivists. This part of the process is now well under way. The second step occurred during the following decades with the increased involvement of curators in the activities of film laboratories to ensure better control over the outcome of their preservation work. But this is precisely the hidden face of film preservation: the name of the archive appears prominently – and justifiably so – on the main credits of the restored film, while the organization technically responsible for it takes second place on the podium (both receive scant mention, or none at all, when the film enters the mainstream marketplace). To declare that a silent film available for viewing comes from a given archive or museum is not enough; insofar

as it wishes to make the duplication path transparent to the viewer, a collecting institution should acknowledge that film restoration is also the product of an expertise in action at the laboratory where the duplication work was achieved.

Events

Film projection is the ultimate goal of film preservation. That is where all the work involved in rescuing, acquiring, conserving, duplicating, and interpreting silent cinema finds its most complete and meaningful expression. It is only in a film theatre that curatorship can finally deliver its message, as other curators do when artworks are installed in museum galleries. No matter how much we know about the film, no matter how carefully it has been preserved and how beautiful the print is, silent cinema comes to life when the film object is brought into contact with the world to which it belongs: a large screen; projection equipment; one or more projectionists; live performers, be they musicians, lecturers, or other performing artists; a room designed for film exhibition; an audience. Taken individually, none of these components makes cinema exist. Together, they are so much more than the sum of all parts. One of the great film curators of our time, Alexander Horwath, expressed this concept in a speech he delivered at the Cinémathèque française on 14 October 2011 with a brief sentence of disarming eloquence: 'film is a tool of perception and of measuring movement in time and space'. Projection is the event that makes the measurement and the perception happen.

The event of silent cinema has a complexity of its own, but is not particularly difficult to perform in purely mechanical terms. Its basic technical requirements are the same as those for all other films exhibited in a curatorial context. The projection booth should have two machines in which the film reels are run in sequential order; the 'platter' projection system used by commercial theatres before the introduction of digital technology is not suitable for archival prints, as it increases the risk of scratching the film's emulsion, and requires joining and separating reels before and after every screening, with the consequent need to cut the film's heads and tails and the possible loss of a frame at the beginning and end of each reel. Even if that wasn't the case, the process of repeatedly joining and disjoining film is potentially harmful to the object. Unlike their commercial ancestors, archival prints are not replaced on a regular basis. Collecting institutions could never afford such a luxury, which also contradicts the essence of their mandate.

As the ultimate achievers of film preservation, film projectionists play a critical role in film curatorship. They have an intimate knowledge of the objects to be exhibited, and often know more about how they should appear on the screen than anyone else, curators included. Their profession is as important as that of cataloguing, preserving, and reproducing film. In order to exhibit silent films, they need two special tools: a variable speed device attached to the projector, and – in some cases – a three-blade shutter to install behind its lens whenever a film is to be shown at lower speeds. Skilled operators know how to procure an aperture gate for the correct aspect ratio in silent film projection: once it is ready, installing it before the show does not require more than a few seconds, if the correct lens is in place (a German filmmaker,

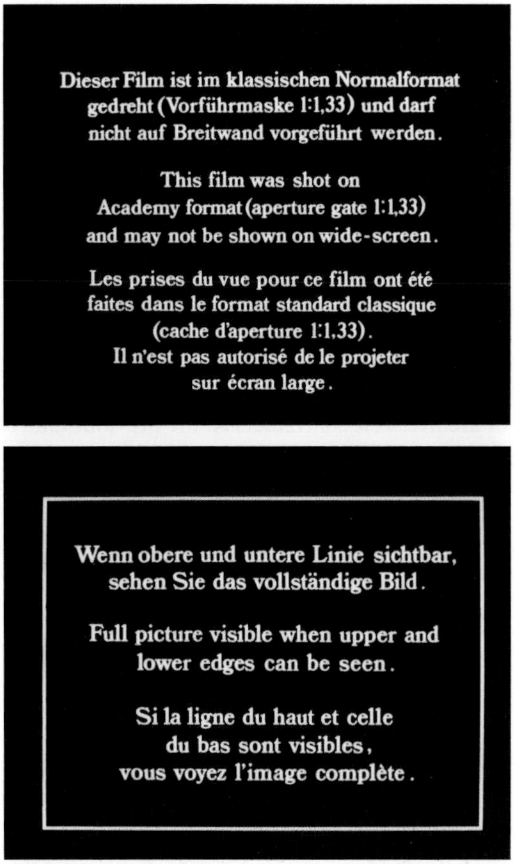

Fig. 212a–b The opening credits of *Parsifal* (Hans-Jürgen Syberberg, 1981). Frame enlargements from a 35mm triacetate positive. Source: Courtesy of Hans-Jürgen Syberberg.

Hans-Jürgen Syberberg, went as far as spelling this out before the main credits in one of his films, as seen in Fig. 212a–b). A pre-focusing test, film rewinding, and print inspection before and after

---

RULE 13

There is no such thing as a 'normal' wear and tear
of an archival print in a curated exhibition.
It is possible, beyond any reasonable doubt,
to project a film several times and return it to the vaults
in the same condition it was before each show.

projection are also curatorial acts, no less and no more than assessing the condition of a painting, a photograph, or a sculpture before and after their display in a museum gallery.

Projectionists are the curators' indispensable allies in the pursuit of their core mission. Among other things, they often are the best judges of whether or not a film has been properly preserved. Claiming that a projection print was never meant to remain intact upon repeated projections is a deplorable excuse in the context of a film museum or archive, as it contradicts all the previous efforts made to protect or reinstate the film's original appearance and to celebrate its 'aura' in front of an audience: it makes no sense to keep an archival print in cold storage with the expectation that it will last for centuries, and then be oblivious to its immediate future in a projection room. Film projectionists are co-protagonists in the curatorial process. Sooner or later, their professional title should more accurately reflect their contribution to the cinematic event in an archival or museum setting. Plainly put, they make it possible. Projectionists, too, are curators of film exhibitions. In particular, when showing silent cinema, they participate in its achievement by controlling film speed, by reducing image flickering when necessary, and by working in close contact with music accompanists, either directly or with the intermediary of a theatre manager. One way or another, they are all silent film performers.

Speed

When a silent film is presented to a live audience, it is assumed that a consultation has taken place beforehand between the curator, the projectionist, and the musicians about the speed at which the work should be exhibited. An important part of the discussion, when it occurs, is devoted to the search for a compromise between the technology involved

in the presentation, the imperative to faithfully represent a cultural phenomenon of the past (pp. 179–185), and the legitimate desire to make silent cinema a rewarding experience for today's public. Projection speed is the point where the three variables should meet. Regrettably, their convergence often results in a collision. The flexibility allowed by variable speed devices installed on film projectors is harder to achieve with digital media, whose software rarely provides for speed control during the show: as explained in Chapter 13, once a decision has been made on the frame rate at the time of transfer from motion picture film, the viewer is often stuck with it and must live with the choices originally made at the time of digital migration. The much despised and long-rejected habit of 'stretching' film in order to make it comply with the standard speed of 24 frames per second has come back with a vengeance in the digital domain, where the primary method for slowing down movement is to replicate some frames at fixed intervals at the time of duplication from the print source, with the resulting loss of the fluid progression that is typical of a cinematic display. Either way, at the time of this writing, the projection speed of a silent film in digital form is cursed by the inflexibility of the medium and by the inadequate means to modify it in real time, let alone without interrupting the show.

It may be surmised that the technological challenge will be met eventually (there are encouraging signs in this regard), or that projecting film on film will remain an option in the years to come. Even if that were the case, the correct projection speed cannot be treated as an exact science. In the silent era, the same film could be projected at varying speeds, depending on the venue and the time of show. There is also abundant evidence of other variables involved, from the cranking speed of the camera to the personal inclinations or needs of projectionists and theatre owners. Musicians wanted to have their say, too, and they often persuaded or forced projectionists to comply with what they thought was best for their orchestral scores. Two articles by James Card and Kevin Brownlow, both authoritative voices in this field, have long been regarded as the main points of reference on the subject. They were written, respectively, in 1955 and 1980. Their examples are largely drawn from films made in the United States, in the late silent era. As seen in Chapter 8, more knowledge has been unearthed since Card and Brownlow paved the way to a better understanding of this topic. Their conclusions are still fundamentally valid, but deserve to be updated and integrated with new facts and considerations.

If the intention is to view silent films as the hypothetical versions of an unknown past, fragmented into as many truths as the number of times the film was projected, the best we can hope for is that the filmmakers themselves had given specific guidelines on the speed they deemed preferable for the exhibition of their work. As for the instructions on projection speeds provided by music composers in their orchestral scores or arrangements for silent films, it is best to reflect on whether these directions were promulgated in the best interest of the film, of the music composed or assembled for the occasion, or both. A responsible approach to the search for historical accuracy brings to the forefront the fact that viewers of the silent era often watched films at higher speeds than those recommended by their makers, mostly because projectionists decided or were told to show them that way. In the photochemical era, it was generally agreed that slapstick comedies benefited from slightly faster projection speeds; the same could be said of action sequences involving horse or car chases, fights, and urban mayhem. How these rules of thumb should be applied has always been a matter of taste, whose criteria are subject to change over time.

Technical manuals from the period frequently insisted that projection speed should be as close as possible to the camera speed, but photographers were taking for granted that their films were bound to be projected at higher speeds anyway, and sometimes deliberately undercranked the camera accordingly. The more one delves into surviving documents on the subject, the more difficult it is to pinpoint a linear progression in the average cranking rate at any time in the history of silent cinema. As there is ample proof that projection speed was treated differently from one country to another and from one period to another, it should be conceded, once and for all, that the pursuit of 'true' projection speed on a wholesale basis is a chimeric endeavour. Directors, cameramen, exhibitors, projectionists, musicians, and audiences all had their views on what was right and what was not for each film in a motion picture show.

A possible way out of this quagmire is to learn as much as possible from the existing prints, papers, and trade periodicals of the period, and then tackle the question of what is the intended benefit of achieving the 'ideal' projection speed of a silent film. Understanding silent cinema means, among other things, trying to decipher the filmmaker's vision in light of our current perception of history. Each film has its own narrative rhythm and visual pace; it unfolds on the screen like a musical score, where the same notation can be interpreted according to the opinions of the performer. A variation of one frame per second will change the film and affect the way it is experienced.

If the goal is to highlight the cinematic event in all its emotional poignancy, choosing the appropriate speed becomes a matter of sensibility and discernment. Take an imaginary scene that actually belongs to many silent films: two lovers are hesitating before exchanging a kiss. How long they will wait before embracing each other is entirely up to the projectionist. The 'natural' speed of physical movement is always a good parameter to follow, but a long-term acquaintance with silent cinema teaches that a slight acceleration of the action can be beneficial to public appreciation of the film, if such a choice is made on a case-by-case basis rather than as a blanket rule.

This leads to the ultimate reason for caring about projection speed: curators want the silent film to 'speak' to its audience, to reverberate with meaning. If a modicum of speeding up or slowing down the speed of projection can achieve this, it does not matter much whether or not the choice is historically accurate. Choosing the projection speed for a silent film should not be equated to the subjective re-editing of a nitrate negative, or to altering a tinting scheme to make it more attractive for a modern viewer: the preference expressed for a given projection speed applies only to a single show, and can be modified at any time when the appropriate equipment is available.

In the language of film curatorship, historical evidence is like a dictionary that should be used as a tool, not as an intellectual straightjacket to be passively worn. Curators have the right and the duty to disobey when needed, as long as they are doing so for good reason. Maybe, one hundred years from now, Gottfried Huppertz' claim that *Metropolis* should be screened at 28 frames per second will seem perfectly acceptable; today, it just isn't. Because it was made when sound cinema was in full swing, *Keisatsukan* (Uchida Tomu, 1933) was believed to require a projection speed of 24 frames per second, which is at odds with the lower projection speeds documented in Japan during the silent period: 'authentic' or not, a speed of 18 frames per second makes the film's poignant atmospheres shine on the screen; 'sound' speed doesn't.

Each culture – through its emissaries and interpreters – should be allowed to apply the performing style it deems appropriate for its public constituency. Curators should also take full responsibility for their decisions on the subject, and stand by them in the name of the films they are showing. In this sense, projection speed can become an expression of creative freedom at its very best, similar to the right to execute a symphony as slowly or as fast as the conductor deems appropriate. Authenticity in film projection is an aesthetic principle and an aspirational goal, not a dogma.

Music

Sound accompaniment to silent films is regarded as a matter of course wherever silent cinema is shown. This wasn't always the case. Until the mid-1980s, silent films were regularly exhibited with no sound whatsoever in many archival and museum venues around the world, including the Cinémathèque française in Paris; according to witnesses from the period, long-time patrons of the institution were not at all happy when live music performances were gradually introduced as part of the shows. Their position found its most coherent expression at the Österreichisches Filmmuseum in Vienna, whose founders – Peter Konlechner and Peter Kubelka – firmly asserted their conviction that no aural distraction should interfere in the viewer's experience of silent cinema (this position was still held in 2017 by the Anthology Film Archives in New York).

Kubelka and Konlechner were not oblivious to the fact that films had originally been shown with various forms of live sound. Nevertheless, they adamantly rejected any attempt to artificially revive what in their opinion could never be recreated, the only certainty being the pure authenticity of the visual event (for similar reasons, they were also opposed to the reproduction of tinting and toning in modern prints). It is worth remembering that, for many decades, the sounds of silent films on television were often pre-recorded ragtime tunes; some theatrical venues of the mid-twentieth century fared only marginally better by playing phonograph records (a practice sometimes followed by film archives and museums around the 1960s), pedal organs, or other domestic instruments during projection. Nostalgia was the main expressive mode of cinematic revivals.

Kubelka's and Konlechner's philosophical stance was supported by the justified belief that the average music played in film theatres during the silent era was equally mediocre if not outright ugly, and by the more subjective claim that it is not possible to accurately reproduce live music performances of the early twentieth century. Both objections deserve to be taken very seriously, as they highlight the core objectives and ambiguities of film curatorship. When embracing the cause of authenticity in silent cinema, it must be reckoned that many performances of the period were nothing short of appalling, both in terms of projection quality and sound accompaniment. From this perspective, presenting a restored silent film with live music from the period is both an educated guess and an exercise in wishful thinking, influenced by the vagaries of modern taste. This is not a good enough reason not to try imagining live music for silent cinema at its best: there must have been great, uncelebrated musicians – quietly earning their living in second- or third-run film theatres – whose genius will never be known, as there is no tangible record of what they did. The same, after all, could be said about classical music concerts. At many points in history, vocal and instrumental works of the Baroque period were performed in public by incompetent people. Their past deeds are not deterring today's musicians and listeners from trying to do better with the same scores and 'authentic' instruments.

The real problem with the ideology of faithfulness in silent film music is that its alleged loyalty to actual facts applies to a very small portion of history, the one that left a published or phonographic footprint of its existence. These traces should definitely be preserved. This does not mean that they should also be regarded as evidence of the best possible – or, worse, the only legitimate – silent film music for public presentation. By embracing silence as the price to pay against mediocrity, Konlechner and Kubelka (both music connoisseurs) have addressed the question of why silent cinema is worth watching at all. Their answer was as blunt as unequivocal: it depends on where the priorities lie. If adherence to history is the main concern, one must be ready to embrace its consequences.

When the Globe Theatre in London was reconstructed in 1997, one of its rules was that audiences at the base of the stage ('the pit') would behave like their predecessors by observing the show as if in Shakespearean times – that is, standing up in front of the players. To ensure compliance with historical facts, the new theatre's management systematically wetted the floor before each performance. This compulsory but ill-fated method for achieving authenticity is a good point of comparison with film preservation as a pretence of an unattainable truth. Music for silent films performed exclusively as an imitation of history is the equivalent of spraying water on the floor of the Globe Theatre.

Silent film music in a theatrical context found a new audience in 1980, when two orchestral scores for Gance's *Napoléon*, respectively from Carl Davis and Carmine Coppola, celebrated the renaissance of a dormant art form. Musicologists and conductors of various artistic backgrounds are now showcasing silent cinema all over the world with the performance of music from the period; with new works inspired by the musical tradition of the early twentieth century; or, more frequently, with piano improvisation (other forms of sound accompaniment based on historical evidence, such as *benshi* and spoken commentaries, are generally limited to Japanese and early cinema). This kind of approach remains by far the preferred one in 'generalist' and specialized film festivals. Despite their large numbers and wide availability, music cue sheets (p. 199) are sparsely used in conjunction with silent films, either because they require considerable work in interpreting their instructions, or because they are drawn from relatively obscure musical sources.

Full piano or orchestral scores from the silent era are immune from such challenges, but they also entail a careful comparison between printed music and surviving projection prints, whose length rarely matches those of the originals. In quantitative terms, this repertoire is very limited; not much is left beyond recognized classics such as D.W. Griffith's *Broken Blossoms* and Sergei Eisenstein's *Bronenosets Potemkin* (*Battleship Potemkin*, 1925). They are also orchestral works of uneven quality, frequently based on the assemblage of tunes and arias from the classical or popular music repertoire. Thanks to these documents, modern audiences are able to see films more or less as they were exhibited in prestigious theatres of the silent era. In some cases, musical notations can assist in the restoration process of the films themselves; in others, strict compliance with original directions has the opposite effect of turning the magic of silent cinema into a lethargic, joyless, or painful experience, vindicating Kubelka's plea for silence.

Modern artists have drawn inspiration from these original scores in order to create new orchestral or chamber music for silent films. Their style, largely indebted to the expressive codes of the nineteenth century tradition, is sometimes a powerful complement to the film's emotional trajectory; when applied too literally, this method can also be formulaic and repetitive. To avoid such risk, a small but thriving community of piano accompanists elevated the art of improvisation to extraordinary heights by developing a true dialogue between their musical instruments and the projected image. A thorough understanding of the film's narrative and visual rhythm has given birth to some of the most enthralling live performances ever heard in modern times in front of the big screen; their unique ability to capture visual atmospheres and the innermost emotions of characters (the best pianists can do so for films they have never seen before) has contributed in no small measure to the revival of silent cinema as an art form. It is impossible to tell whether or not this exquisite artistry was frequent in actual music performances of the silent era.

The undeniable difficulty in reaching this special symbiosis explains why so many attempts at creating new forms of sound accompaniment for silent films have failed miserably: major personalities in rock, jazz, folk, ethnic, and avant-garde music have tried to do so, too often with dismal results; an even larger number of not so famous soloists and bands have similarly fallen in the trap of believing that originality alone can inject new creative energy into silent cinema. A discouraging effect of these mistakes is the widespread feeling that no good music for silent film can or should exist outside the conventions of melodic piano, organ, or orchestral performances. If pushed to extremes, this prejudice may suffocate all further attempts to give silent cinema a second life with contemporary audiences.

The truth of the matter is that no music genre is unsuitable for silent films, as long as the artist makes a genuine and humble effort to understand what silent cinema is, be alert to its expressive codes, and learn from the nuances within the mute flow of its images. A bad piece of silent film music is easily recognizable by its indifference to what is happening on the screen, and by the dominance of the performer over the projected image; in a great silent film score, the musician and the cinematic event become one and the same. Being audible but 'invisible' is a sure indication that the symbiosis has been achieved. Any talented rock band could create the most compelling music for silent cinema if its members aimed at merging with the film, rather than thinking of themselves as the centre of the show.

Giorgio Moroder's pioneering score for *Metropolis* has proven that post-Romantic music does not have monopoly over the enjoyment of silent cinema by new audiences. Widely maligned at the time of its original release, Moroder's 'disco' version triggered in the mid-1980s the rediscovery of a film hitherto revered as a cultural relic. It wasn't 'authentic' music at all, but it reconnected *Metropolis* with modern viewers, sixty years after the film's premiere (Moroder never called it a 'restoration'). There is no reason why this should not happen with other silent films. Murnau's *Sunrise* is preserved with the recorded Movietone soundtrack of a live orchestral performance conducted by Hugo Riesenfeld at the Roxy Theatre in New York. This version is, by all means, entirely faithful to one event in history (1927), but the film was seen as a silent in many other theatres, with the live performance of different music scores. It is not a 'sound' picture. There is room for other music interpretations of this beautiful love story. It should preferably be good music. It should also make *Sunrise* find new audiences. When it comes to listening, the 'authenticity' of a silent film is measured by how deeply it resonates with its public. Music is only a tool for making it emerge in a cinema auditorium: at festivals, special events, or in dedicated museum settings.

Festivals

The first known exhibition of silent cinema in 'festival' form took place on 24 April 1909 in Fort Lee, New Jersey, when eight short films by D.W. Griffith were screened in a special presentation of productions made in that area. As a modern phenomenon, silent film festivals are the offspring of retrospective film series presented by cultural associations, where silent cinema occupied a prominent place by default (the London Film Society was born in 1925). Film collectors, too, had begun 'festivals' of their own silent film holdings; they continued doing so through the end of the twentieth century and beyond. Six years after its inception, the Mostra Internazionale d'Arte Cinematografica in Venice held in 1938 its first 'archival' monograph, a historical survey of French cinema (1892–1933). No curator was mentioned, but there is evidence of a direct involvement by Henri Langlois in its preparation (Langlois' name would be explicitly credited only in 1953, in relation to another series on French silent cinema).

In the late 1950s, Davide Turconi began his collaboration with the Venice Film Festival. He curated an archival programme of Mack Sennett comedies in 1961; others followed in the next two decades. By 1968, on the occasion of a tribute to Jean Renoir's early career (1924–39), Turconi became persuaded that a special section within the 'generalist' film festival's schedule was too narrow a space for archival exhibitions. However small, their audience was enthusiastic about silent films. It was eager to see more. Turconi had also heard about the Museum of Modern Art's Circulating Film Library and the 16mm prints available for purchase from the Library of Congress. He had friends at the Cineteca Nazionale in Rome. A big budget wasn't required for a dedicated event focusing on silent cinema; Turconi had enough curatorial experience to make it happen on a shoestring.

He did so in 1970, in the seaside resort of Grado, a few miles south-west of Venice. It was a short-lived experiment, three years in all, but the Incontri Cinematografici di Grado was by all means a full-fledged silent film festival, with a formal schedule and a programme leaflet. In all likelihood, this was the earliest attempt to showcase the history of silent cinema in a structured public event that took place for more than one day outside a film archive. Regardless of its negligible echo at the time, its symbolic significance was bound to have major repercussions for the future of film festivals focused on the rediscovery of the silent cinematic heritage.

The programmes of the Incontri Cinematografici di Grado had not been promoted by a collecting institution; they were conceived and presented by people outside film archives and academia. Nevertheless, many of the silent films exhibited on those occasions had been loaned by institutional entities, which provided their archival prints either because they were equipped to do so through dedicated channels of distribution (MoMA), by virtue of their statutory obligations (Library of Congress), or because these archives trusted the festival's curators enough to open their doors to bona fide researchers. The Grado festival also exhibited prints from private collectors; by doing so, it inadvertently highlighted the presence of two competing approaches to film preservation.

Film museums and archives did not initiate archival film festivals. They did not oppose them, either, but observed their growth with a somewhat cautious attitude, as these events were implicitly challenging the authority of collecting institutions as the only places where film history could be properly learned and interpreted. Without knowing it, they were also enabling audiences to compare the work of different organizations and to assess the strengths and weaknesses of their collections. Archive and museum curators could no longer claim to be the exclusive ambassadors of film history; other people were demonstrating their ability to take on their role. They were not professional scholars, as cinema didn't yet have a meaningful place in academia; they were nonetheless eager to learn,

they had the research tools necessary to do so, and they wanted to be taken seriously.

In the 1970s, these independent researchers represented an insignificant minority of the film community. Their effort was barely noticed by the local media, and largely ignored outside the circle of an association of Italian film historians – arguably the first of its kind in the world – established in 1964 (the Grado festival was discontinued after its third instalment in 1972). It took a decade for its seeds to germinate not far from there, with Le Giornate del Cinema Muto (Pordenone Silent Film Festival), in 1982. Why non-archival curated retrospectives of silent film flourished in Italy before anywhere else can be explained by a propitious alignment of circumstances. The early years of cinema were, by a long stretch, the least known to the general public at the time when the festival came into existence. Scholarly literature on the subject was relatively scarce; the festival's team had chosen Turconi as their mentor in what was quite appropriately perceived as a venture into a *terra incognita*.

Much as they would have preferred to be the protagonists of this enterprise, film archives did not feel threatened by it, as the titles to be screened at the Giornate did not play any significant role in their regular exhibition activities, and would not steal any thunder from the programmes of their respective venues. Most of these films were in the public domain; if they weren't, copyright owners were either unaware of the event, or couldn't care less about it, given that there was no foreseeable prospect of earning any profit by resurrecting these works from oblivion.

Within two decades from Pordenone's inaugural season, film festivals exclusively dedicated to silent cinema sprang up everywhere in the world. Many of them are now defunct: the remarkable Rencontres Cinématographiques d'Avignon in the late 1980s, organized by Christian Belaygue; its more glamorous avatar, CinéMémoire, in Paris (1991–7);

Musik und Stummfilm in Frankfurt (only in 1988); the Jornada Brasileira do Cinema Silencioso in São Paulo, Brazil (2007–12). Others were resilient enough to cultivate a faithful audience and achieve a broader reputation in the field: the San Francisco Silent Film Festival (born in 1992), the Silent Cinema Days in Istanbul (2014) and Bristol Silents (2000, currently called Slapstick Festival), to name a few, had been part of this small but burgeoning constellation. Silent cinema also features prominently in other festivals of film preservation under the aegis of film archives and museums (To Save and Project at MoMA, Il Cinema Ritrovato in Bologna, Toute la mémoire du monde at the Cinémathèque française, UCLA's Festival of Preservation in Los Angeles, the Lumière Film Festival in Lyon).

In the wake of the rising popularity of film classics, archives could also find renewed attention from 'generalist' film festivals; they did it by launching high-profile film restorations at the Berlin International Film Festival (in its 'retrospective' section, which featured more than one reconstructed version of *Metropolis*) and the Festival de Cannes (where the 2011 version of *A Trip to the Moon* received its premiere). Film museums and archives were demanding, quite legitimately, the kind of public exposure they couldn't obtain in archival film festivals. These institutions had been showing silent films for decades, but it was only by turning them into 'special events' that their work began to be celebrated worldwide.

Spectators

A cinema audience is a collective body of people watching films and, when possible, feeling engaged with what they see. Some of these people are spectators: they want to enjoy the show like everybody else, but also interrogate themselves and the film about its style, technique, and subject matter: how a given sequence is staged, what it intends to achieve, why it was done that way. Scholars and critics try to explain the nature of these choices in intelligible and meaningful terms. Curators take another step further by selecting and exhibiting films, in order to persuade audience members that being spectators is a good and useful thing. Curators do not necessarily write about cinema; they express their opinions primarily through the works they have chosen to share with others. They are not artists, but use aesthetic tools to facilitate and promote a dialogue between the creators and their public. The curator's job is, in aspirational terms, a service to society.

Film archives, museums, and festivals are now teeming with exhibition projects where silent cinema is the main focus of attention. By joining forces through their respective knowledge, these cultural agents act as envoys of film history and as mentors to those who wish to know more about it. When they succeed, they also make way for tomorrow by encouraging their audiences to discover the beauty and intricacies of curatorship. There is a mistaken belief that selecting film titles by director, country, or theme for a festival, and writing programme notes about them, is primarily what is required to be a curator, but that is not enough. Choosing the films to be exhibited, and commenting upon them, is both the beginning and the very end of a far more complex itinerary. It is necessary, of course, to know the history of cinema; being able to convey in persuasive terms the logic of the selection is also a must. Both require time, patience, and personal investment.

If this were all that is needed, there would be millions of film curators around the world, which is not the case (unless the definition of 'curator' is forcibly extended to all those who select, assemble, and show films on a personal basis). In fact, it is quite the contrary: one of the most difficult tasks for existing curators is to help their institutions in seeking their own successors. The main obstacles they face are connected to the qualities that are normally associated with film expertise – that is, the number and variety of films viewed, and the scholarly intelligence connected to them. This is the reason why the elders are so circumspect when asked to interview aspiring curators who exude passion for cinema and can quote any line from a film dialogue on demand, or when reading the curricula of academic writers. Indispensable as they may be, enthusiasm, erudition, and initiative are not sufficient to make a good film curator.

Edith Kramer, one of the most inspiring voices in the world community of film curators, effectively summed up the issue by acknowledging that her main professional ambition was to be a good spectator. She never wrote a book or a major essay on cinema, but knows it more intimately than many of her colleagues. No doubt, she has seen many films. Their number, however, is not a measure of her wisdom. Over her long career, Kramer learned which questions to ask herself, both in the course of the show and afterwards. Spectators are not magically born by sitting in front of a screen; this title is earned through a disciplined exercise of empathy and detachment, participation and vigilance, in the awareness that there is no contradiction

between feeling totally immersed in a film and being inquisitive about it, without prejudice but also without distraction.

An underrated aspect of curatorial work is the patient, relentless caring for the conditions of spectatorship, and being alert to what can improve, modify (Fig. 213), or compromise it altogether. This involves two kinds of action, performed concurrently. One is the imaginary conversation with the film and, by reflection, with its makers (what is the reason for this shot; why this lighting, composition, camera movement). The other is a dialogue with the medium itself: here, now, on this screen, in the print being shown, with this projection equipment. In this film theatre. With this audience.

There is a third, fundamental variable in the equation of film curatorship. What has been described so far is the arena in which the spectator engages with the cinema event and extracts aesthetic pleasure and meaning from its performance. When the spectator is the same person who has chosen a specific film, selected one print instead of another, and shaped the environment where the projection event is about to be performed, film curatorship begins to exist as a cultural practice. In making these decisions, curators are addressing their audiences, groups of individuals whose opinions and expectations about the film being screened are not known.

In a commercial theatre or at home, spectators interact with cinema with no intermediaries, like people who are preparing their own evening meal. There is nothing wrong with that: a curator does this too every day, but with another goal in mind. When the curator is present, spectators are no longer alone at the table. Someone has invited them to see one or more films rarely shown on the big screen, like a special recipe experimented for the occasion. Its particular texture may become a topic of conversation, in which case the curator

Fig. 213 *By Might of His Right* (Sidney Drew, 1915). 35mm polyester positive with resized frame from a digital intermediate, 2011. Source: George Eastman Museum.

will be happy to explain the choices made in that particular context, comparing them with alternative film ingredients and maybe with other cinematic banquets (Fig. 210 shows Peter Kubelka elaborating on the affinities between cinema and food in one of his legendary public performances). If the guests have politely refrained from finishing their course, the curator will thank them anyway for the visit, and start devising a more appealing menu for the next show. Among other things, good curators never impose their own judgement upon their patrons. They do not require them to declare their liking of a newly discovered or preserved silent film as a mere act of courtesy if the copy is painful to look at, or poorly presented. Audiences can and should exercise their right to civil disobedience by declining to see films duplicated and exhibited in ways they find unacceptable, and by making their position known to the community.

Spectators are offered this prerogative at film festivals, archival or museum exhibitions, and elsewhere: by making use of it in the collective space of a film theatre, they help film curatorship evolve with its audience. The combination of being a guest and a host at the same time – a spectator and a presenter – is what the curatorial synthesis is about, and why it is so difficult to achieve. It is not about knowing as many films as possible, or about making a spectacle out of it. Regardless of their personal charisma, those who have mastered this blend of dedication and modesty are aware that film curatorship is essentially an ongoing pledge of unselfishness. When applied to the exhibition of silent cinema, some extra chores are inevitable; others are optional; but the meals have to be rewarding, and no curator should take pride in satisfying the appetite of audiences who would eat whatever is on the plate without at least responding to the taste of a new offering, or at least sharing their impressions with the kitchen crew: archivists, projectionists, scholars, technicians, curators.

Cinema thrives with spectators, and wanes with consumers. Silent cinema is no exception, as spectators are an integral part of its life as a performing event. Being co-protagonists of the show should be both a pleasure and a political opportunity: spectators do not acquiesce to a drama shown at the speed of a slapstick (or vice versa), do not automatically cheer at its accompaniment just because there is live music on stage; they ask questions about print format and source, and would not mind knowing the truth about *A Trip to the Moon*, unglamorous or fragmented as it may be. The rights and duties of spectatorship – participation, opinion, freedom of choice, dissident action when necessary – were very important to one of France's greatest film critics, Serge Daney. A few months before his death, in a film interview with philosopher and journalist Régis Debray for the documentary *Serge Daney: itinéraire d'un ciné-fils* (Pierre-André Boutang and Dominique Rabourdin, 1992), he made a passing comment of enduring resonance. 'As long as cinema gives me this,' Daney said about Kenji Mizoguchi's camera movements, 'I am a citizen of the world, even of a world that is no more, of history.' Film curatorship is a fitting paraphrase of Daney's statement: silent or sound, with or without interpreters, cinema can make us good citizens.

Bibliographic Resources and Research Tools

Note: Bibliographic references within each section are given in chronological order of publication. All websites were last accessed on 8 June 2018.

Preface (pp. xxxi–xxxiii)

Dagrada, Elena (ed.), *International Bibliography on Early Cinema* (s.l.: Domitor, 1985).

Flaig, Paul and Katherine Groo (eds.), *New Silent Cinema* (New York and London: Routledge, 2016).

Internet Resources

Domitor – International Association for the Study of Early Cinema: www.domitor.org

Introduction (pp. 1–5)

Reference Works on Pre-Cinema and Film Beginnings

Deslandes, Jacques and Jacques Richard, *Histoire comparée du cinéma. Vol. 1: 1826–1896* (Paris: Casterman, 1966).

Hecht, Hermann (Ann Hecht, ed.), *Pre-Cinema History. An Encyclopaedia and Annotated Bibliography of the Moving Image Before 1896* (London: Bowker-Saur/BFI Publishing, 1993).

Rossell, Deac, 'A Chronology of Cinema, 1889–1896', special issue of *Film History* vol. 7 no. 2 (Summer 1995).

Mannoni, Laurent, Donata Pesenti Campagnoni, and David Robinson, *Light and Movement: Incunabula of the Motion Picture* (Pordenone, Paris, and Turin: Le Giornate del Cinema Muto/Cinémathèque française – Musée du Cinéma/Museo Nazionale del Cinema, 1995).

Mannoni, Laurent, *Le Grand art de la lumière et de l'ombre. Archéologie du cinéma* (Paris: Nathan, 1994); English translation, *The Great Art of Light and Shadow: Archaeology of the Cinema* (Exeter: University of Exeter Press, 2000).

Herbert, Stephen (ed.), *A History of Pre-Cinema* (London and New York: Routledge, 2000, 3 vols.).

Robinson, David, Stephen Herbert, and Richard Crangle (eds.), *Encyclopaedia of the Magic Lantern* (Leicester: The Magic Lantern Society, 2001).

Vivié, Jean, *Prélude au cinema: de la préhistoire à l'invention* (Paris: l'Harmattan, 2006).

Films

A Movie Trip Through Filmland (Paul M. Felton, US 1921, c. 32′)

Der Film im Film (Friedrich Porges, Germany 1925, c. 130′).

Thirty Years of Motion Pictures (Otto Nelson and Terry Ramsaye, National Cash Register Company/ National Board of Review of Motion Pictures, US 1927, c. 180′).

The Romance of Celluloid (Metro-Goldwyn-Mayer, US 1937, 11′).

Another Romance of Celluloid (Herman Hoffman, US 1938, 11′).

Was geschah wirklich zwischen den Bildern? (*Film Before Film*, Werner Nekes, Werner Nekes Filmproduktion, West Germany, 1985, 83′).

Overviews and Reference Works on Silent Cinema

Franklin, Joe and William K. Everson (uncredited), *Classics of the Silent Screen: A Pictorial Treasury* (New York: Bramhall House, 1959).

Ceram, C.W. [pseud. of Kurt Wilhelm Marek], *Eine Archäologie des Kinos* (Darmstadt: Deutsche Buch-Gemeinschaft, 1965); English translation, *Archaeology of the Cinema* (New York: Harcourt, Brace & World, 1965).

O'Leary Liam, *The Silent Cinema* (London: Studio Vista; New York: E.P. Dutton, 1965; reprint, 1968; 2nd edition, 1970).

Pratt, George C., *Spellbound in Darkness* (Greenwich, CT: New York Graphic Society, 1973).

Spehr, Paul C., *The Movies Begin. Making Movies in New Jersey, 1887–1920* (Newark, NJ: The Newark Museum/ Morgan & Morgan, 1977).

Güttinger, Fritz, *Kein Tag ohne Kino. Schriftsteller über den Stummfilm* (Frankfurt am Main: Deutsches Filmmuseum, 1984).

Güttinger, Fritz, *Der Stummfilm im Zitat der Zeit* (Frankfurt am Main: Deutsches Filmmuseum, 1984).

Salt, Barry, 'What We Can Learn from the First Twenty Years of Cinema', *Iris* vol. 2 no. 1 (1984), pp. 83–90.

Burch, Noël, *Life to Those Shadows* (Berkeley: University of California Press, 1990).

Elsaesser, Thomas (ed.), *Early Cinema: Space, Frame, Narrative* (London: BFI Publishing, 1990).

Cosandey, Roland, André Gaudreault, and Tom Gunning (eds.), *Une Invention du diable? Cinéma des premiers temps et religion/An Invention of the Devil? Religion and Early Cinema* (Lausanne: Éditions Payot, 1992).

'The Philosophy of Film History', special issue of *Film History* vol. 6 no. 1 (Spring 1994).

Abel, Richard (ed.), *Silent Film* (New Brunswick, NJ: Rutgers University Press, 1996).

Rossell, Deac, *Living Pictures. The Origins of the Movies* (Albany: State University of New York, 1998).

Bottomore, Stephen, 'Introduction: The Cambrian Cinema', *Film History* vol. 10 no. 1 (1998), pp. 3–7.

Popple, Simon, '"Cinema Wasn't Invented, It Growed": Technological Film Historiography Before 1913', in John Fullerton (ed.), *Celebrating 1895: The Centenary of Cinema* (Sydney: John Libbey, 1998), pp. 19–26.

Grieveson, Lee and Peter Kramer (eds.), *The Silent Cinema Reader* (London: Routledge, 2003).

Herbert, Stephen (ed.), *A History of Early Film* (London and New York: Routledge, 2003).

Popple, Simon and Joe Kember, *Early Cinema: From Factory Gate to Dream Factory* (New York: Wallflower, 2004).

Kobel, Peter, *Silent Movies: The Birth of Film and the Triumph of Movie Culture* (New York: Little, Brown & Co., 2007).

Robb, Brian J., *Silent Cinema* (Harpenden: Oldcastle Books, 2007).

Abel, Richard (ed.), *Encyclopedia of Early Cinema* (London and New York: Routledge, 2010, 2nd edition).

Gaudreault, André, Nicolas Dulac, and Santiago Hidalgo (eds.), *A Companion to Early Cinema* (Malden, MA: Wiley-Blackwell, 2012).

Abel, Richard (ed.), *Early Cinema. Critical Concepts in Media and Cultural Studies* (London and New York: Routledge, 2014, 4 vols.).

Withall, Keith, *Studying Early and Silent Cinema* (New York: Columbia University Press; Leighton Buzzard: Auteur, 2014).

Napper, Lawrence, *Silent Cinema: Before the Pictures Got Small* (London and New York: Wallflower Press, 2017).

Interdisciplinary Studies

Kaes, Anton, *Kino-Debatte. Texte zum Verhältnis von Literatur und Film, 1909–1929* (Tübingen and Munich: Niemeyer-Deutscher Taschenbuch-Verlag, 1978).

Allen, Robert C., *Vaudeville and Film, 1895–1915: A Study in Media Interaction* (New York: Arno Press, 1980).

Abramson, Albert, *The History of Television, 1880 to 1941* (Jefferson, NC, and London: McFarland, 1987).

Toulet, Emmanuelle, 'Cinema at the Universal Exposition, Paris, 1900', *Persistence of Vision* no. 9 (1991), pp. 10–36.

Franklin, Peter, 'Movies as Opera (Behind the Great Divide)', in Jeremy Tambling (ed.), *A Night at the Opera* (London: John Libbey, 1994), pp. 77–110.

Tsivian, Yuri, 'Russia, 1913: Cinema in the Cultural Landscape', *Griffithiana* vol. 17 no. 50 (May 1994), pp. 125–47.

Kirby, Lynne, *Parallel Tracks: The Railroad and Silent Cinema* (Durham, NC: Duke University Press; Exeter: University of Exeter Press, 1997).

Rossell, Deac, 'Double Think: The Cinema and Magic Lantern Culture', in John Fullerton (ed.), *Celebrating 1895: The Centenary of Cinema* (Sydney: John Libbey, 1998), pp. 27–36.

Dupré la Tour, Claire, André Gaudreault, and Roberta Pearson (eds.), *Le Cinéma au tournant du siècle/Cinema at the Turn of the Century* (Quebec and Lausanne: Éditions Nota Bene/Éditions Payot, 1999).

Quaresima, Leonardo and Laura Vichi (eds.), *The Tenth Muse: Cinema and the Other Arts* (Udine: Forum, 2001).

Allen, Robert C., '"A Decided Sensation": Cinema, Vaudeville, and Burlesque', in Patricia McDonnell (ed.), *On the Edge of Your Seat: Popular Theater and Film in Early Twentieth-Century American Art* (New Haven, CT: Yale University Press, 2002), pp. 61–89.

Lack, Roland-François, 'First Encounters: French Literature and the Cinematograph', *Film History* vol. 20 no. 3 (2008), pp. 133–43.

Abel, Richard and Amy Rodgers, 'Early Motion Pictures and Popular Print Culture', in Christine Bold (ed.), *The Oxford History of Popular Print Culture. Vol. 6: US Popular Print Culture, 1860–1920* (Oxford: Oxford University Press, 2012), pp. 191–209.

Griffiths, Alison, *Carceral Fantasies: Cinema and Prisons in Early Twentieth-Century America* (New York: Columbia University Press, 2016).

Shepherd, David J. (ed.), *The Silents of Jesus in the Cinema (1897–1927)* (New York and London: Routledge, 2016).

Johnson, Martin L., 'The Theater or the Schoolhouse? The Social Center, the Model Picture Show, and the Logic of Counterattractions', *Film History* vol. 29 no. 4 (2017), pp. 1–31.

Preusser, Heinz-Peter (ed.), *Späte Stummfilm. Ästetische Innovation im Kino, 1924–1930* (Marburg: Schüren Verlag [Schriftenreihe zur Textualität des Films, Bd. 9], 2017).

Curtis, Scott, Philippe Gauthier, Tom Gunning, and Joshua Yumibe (eds.), *The Image in Early Cinema. Form and Material* (Bloomington: Indiana University Press, 2018).

Dahlquist, Marina, Doron Galili, Jan Olsson, and Valentine Robert, *Corporeality in Early Cinema. Viscera, Skin, and Physical Form* (Bloomington: Indiana University Press, 2018).

Scholarly Journals

1895 – Revue de l'Association Française de Recherche sur l'Histoire du Cinéma (Print ISSN 0769-0959; online ISSN 1960-6176).

Early Popular Visual Culture (Print ISSN 1746-0654; online ISSN 1746-0662).

Film History (ISSN 0892-2160).

Griffithiana, 1978–2004 (ISSN 0393–3857).

Immagine – Note di storia del cinema (ISSN 1128-7101).

The Magic Lantern Gazette, 1989–2015 (ISSN 1059-1249).

Moving Image. Journal of the Association of Moving Image Archivists (ISSN 1542-4235).

The Silent Film Quarterly (ISBN 13-2966-6763).

Vivomatografías. Revista de estudios sobre precine y cine silente en Latinoamérica (ISSN 2469-0767).

Regional and National Cinemas

Overviews

Cosandey, Roland and André Gaudreault (eds.), *Cinéma sans frontières/Images Across Borders* (Lausanne: Éditions Payot, 1995).

Abel, Richard, Giorgio Bertellini, and Rob King (eds.), *Early Cinema and the 'National'* (New Barnet, Herts.: John Libbey, 2008).

Continental and Regional Cinemas

Africa

Convents, Guido, *Préhistoire du cinéma en Afrique, 1897–1918. À la recherche des images oubliées* (Brussels: OCIC, 1986).

Speciale, Alessandra (ed.), *La nascita del cinema in Africa* (Turin: Lindau, 1998).

Goerg, Odile, *Fantômas sous les tropiques: aller au cinéma en Afrique coloniale* (Paris: Vendémiaire, 2015).

Reynolds, Glenn, *Colonial Cinema in Africa. Origins, Images, Audiences* (Jefferson, NC: McFarland, 2015).

Asia

Deocampo, Nick (ed.), *Early Cinema in Asia* (Bloomington: Indiana University Press, 2017).

Central and South America

Hennebelle, Guy and Alfonso Gumucio-Dagron (eds.), *Les Cinémas de l'Amérique latine* (Paris: L'Herminier/CinémAction, 1981).

Paranaguá, Paulo Antonio, *O cinema na América Latina. Longe de deus e perto de Hollywood* (Porto Alegre: L&PM Editores, 1985).

Schumann, Peter B., *Historia del cine latinoamericano* (Buenos Aires: Editorial Legasa, 1986).

García Mesa, Héctor (ed.), *Cine latinoamericano,
1896–1930* (Caracas: Fundación del nuevo cine latinoamericano, 1992).

López, Ana M., 'Early Cinema and Modernity in Latin
America', *Cinema Journal* vol. 40 no. 1 (2000), pp. 48–78.

Cortés, María Lourdes, *La pantalla rota. Cien años de cine
en Centroamérica* (Mexico: Taurus, 2005).

de los Reyes, Aurelio and David Wood (eds.), *Cine mudo
latinoamericano: inicios, nación, vanguardias y transición* (Mexico: UNAM, 2015).

Cuarterolo, Andrea and Rielle Navitski, 'Bibliografía sobre
precine y cine silente latinoamericano', *Vivomatografías*
vol. 3 no. 3 (December 2017), pp. 248–415.

National Cinemas

Argentina

*Historia de los primeros años del cine en la Argentina,
1895–1910* (Buenos Aires: Fundación Cinemateca
Argentina, 1996).

Finkielman, Jorge, *The Film Industry in Argentina. An
Illustrated Cultural History (1896–1940)* (Boston, MA:
McFarland & Company, 2003).

Maranghello, César, *Breve historia del cine argentino*
(Barcelona: Laertes, 2005).

Cuarterolo, Andrea, *De la foto al fotograma. Relaciones
entre cine y fotografía en la Argentina, 1840–1933*
(Montevideo: CdF Ediciones, 2013).

Armenia

Zakoian, Garegin, *Armianskoe nemoe kino* (Yerevan:
Izdatelstvo AN Armianskoi CCR, 1976).

Australia

Pike, Andrew and Ross Cooper, *Australian Film, 1900–1977*
(Melbourne: Oxford University Press, 1980).

Adams, Brian and Graham Shirley, *Australian Cinema:
The First Eighty Years* (Sydney: Angus & Robertson/
Currency Press, 1983).

Bertrand, Ina and William D. Routt, 'The Big Bad Combine:
Some Aspects of National Aspirations and International
Constraints in the Australian Cinema, 1896–1929', in
Albert Moran and Tom O'Regan (eds.), *The Australian
Screen* (Ringwood: Penguin, 1989), pp. 3–27.

Long, Chris, 'Australia's First Films', *Cinema Papers* no. 91,
January 1993 (Part 1), pp. 36–43; no. 92, April 1993
(Part 2), pp. 36–43, 62–3; no. 93, May 1993 (Part 3), pp.
34–41, 60–1; no. 94, August 1993 (Part 4), pp. 34–9,
62–3; no. 95, October 1993 (Part 5), pp. 38–43, 59–61;
no. 96, December 1993 (Part 6), pp. 32–7, 59–61 (with
Pat Loughren); nos. 97–8, April 1994 (Part 7), pp. 34–41,
64–66; no. 99, June 1994 (Part 8), pp. 60–5, 84–5 (with
Pat Loughren); no. 100, August 1994 (Part 9), pp. 60–7,
82–3 (with Clive Sowry); no. 101, October 1994 (Part
10), pp. 56–61, 82–3; no. 102, December 1994 (Part 11),
pp. 52–7, 80–2 (with Clive Sowry); no. 103, March 1995
(Part 12), pp. 40–3, 56–7 (with Clive Sowry); no. 104,
June 1995 (Part 13), pp. 40–3, 55 (with Clive Sowry); no.
105, August 1995 (Part 14), pp. 36–9, 57–8 (with Clive
Sowry); no. 106, October 1995 (Part 15), pp. 38–41, 54–5;
no. 107, December 1995 (Part 16), pp. 34–7, 56–7; no.
108, February 1996 (Part 17), pp. 34–7, 54–5; no. 109,
April 1996 (Part 18), pp. 34–7, 54–5 ('History: Morals
and the Mutoscope', with Bob Klepner); no. 110, June
1996 (Part 19), pp. 42–5, 61 ('History: Australian Cinema,
1894–1904'); no. 112, October 1996, pp. 36–9 ('Australian
Film History: Three New Projects. Early Queensland and
Tasmanian "Narrative" Films', with Wendy Rogers).

Austro-Hungarian Empire and Austria

Fritz, Walter, *Kino in Österreich: Der Stummfilm,
1896–1930* (Vienna: Österreichischer Bundesverlag,
1981).

Kosanović, Dejan, *Kinematografske delatnosti u Puli,
1896–1918* (Belgrade, Pula: Institut za Film/Festival
Jugoslavenskog Igranog Filma, 1988).

Schwartz, Werner M., *Kino und Kinos in Wien: eine
Entwicklungsgeschichte bis 1934* (Vienna: Turia & Kant,
1992).

Büttner, Elisabeth and Christian Dewald, *Das tägliche
Brennen. Eine Geschichte des österreichische Films
von den Anfängen bis 1945* (Salzburg and Vienna:
Residenz-Verlag, 2002).

Belarus

Avdeev, Igor and Larisa Zaitseva, *Vse belorusskie filmy.
Vol. 1: Igrovoe kino, 1926–1970* (Minsk: Belaruskaia
navuka, 1996).

Belgium

Convents, Guido, *Van Kinetoscoop tot Café-Ciné. De eerste jaren van de film in België* (Leuven: Universitaire Pers Leuven, 2000).

Mosley, Philip, *Split Screen: Belgian Cinema and Cultural Identity* (Albany: State University of New York Press, 2001).

Bolivia

Mesa Gisbert, Carlos D. (ed.), *Cine boliviano del realizador al critico* (La Paz: Editorial Gisbert, 1979).

Gumocio Dagron, Alfonso, *Historia del cine boliviano* (Mexico: Filmoteca de la UNAM, 1983).

Susz, Pedro, *La campaña del Chaco: el ocaso del cine silente boliviano* (La Paz: Universidad Mayor de San Andrés, 1990).

Brazil

De Paula Araujo, Vicente, *A bela época do cinema brasileiro* (San Pablo: Editora Perspectiva, 1976).

Galvão, Maria Rita, 'Le Muet', in Paulo Antonio Paraganuá (ed.), *Le Cinéma brésilien* (Paris: Centre Georges Pompidou, 1987), pp. 51–66.

Noronha, Jurandyr, *No tempo da manivela* (Rio de Janeiro: Ebal/Kinart/Embrafilme, 1987).

Ramos, Ferrão and Luis Felipe (eds.), *Enciclopédia do cinema brasiliero* (São Paulo: Editora Senac, 2000).

Trusz, Alice Dubina, *Entre lanternas mágicas e cinematógrafos: as origens do espetáculo cinematográfico em Porto Alegre. 1861–1908* (São Paulo: Terceiro Nome/Ecofalante, 2010).

Paiva, Samuel and Sheila Schvarzman (eds.), *Viagem ao cinema silencioso do Brasil* (Rio de Janeiro: Beco do Azougue Editorial, 2011).

Canada

Morris, Peter, *Embattled Shadows: A History of Canadian Cinema, 1895–1939* (Montreal and Kingston: McGill-Queen's University Press, 1978; reprint edition, 2008).

Graham, Gerald G., *Canadian Film Technology, 1896–1986* (Newark, London, and Toronto: University of Delaware Press/Associated University Presses, 1989).

Gaudreault, André, Germain Lacasse, and Jean-Pierre Sirois-Trahan, *Au pays des ennemis du cinéma … pour une nouvelle histoire des débuts du cinéma au Québec* (Quebec: Nuit Blanche, 1996).

Moore, Paul S., *Now Playing: Early Moviegoing and the Regulation of Fun* (Albany: State University of New York Press, 2008).

Chile

Jara Donoso, Eliana, *Cine mudo chileno* (Santiago: Ceneca, 1994).

Iturriaga, Jorge, *La masificación del cine en Chile, 1907–1932. La conflictiva construcción de una cultura plebeya* (Santiago: LOM, 2015).

Colombia

Martínez Prado, Hernando, *Historia del cine colombiano* (Bogotá: Libreria y Editorial America Latina, 1978).

Salcedo Silva, Hernando, *Crónicas del cine colombiano, 1897–1950* (Bogotá: Carlos Valencia Editores, 1981).

Franco Díez, Germán, *Mirando solo a la tierra. Cine y sociedad espectadora en Medellín, 1900–1930* (Bogotá: Pontificia Universidad Javeriana, 2013).

Concha Henao, Álvaro, *Historia Social del Cine en Colombia, Tomo 1, 1897–1929* (Bogotá: Publicaciones Black Maria, 2014).

Rico Agudelo, Angie, *Las travesías del cine y los espectáculos públicos. Colombia en la transición del siglo XIX al XX* (Bogotá: Cinemateca Distrital, 2016).

Costa Rica

Marranghello, Daniel, *El cine en Costa Rica, 1903–1920* (San José, Costa Rica: Colección Cultura Cinematografica, 1988).

Cortés, María Lourdes, *La pantalla rota. Cien años de cine en Centroamérica* (Mexico: Taurus, 2005).

China

Leyda, Jay, *Dianying. Electric Shadows. An Account of Films and the Film Audience in China* (Cambridge, MA, and London: MIT Press, 1972).

Suyuan, Li and Hu Jubin, *Chinese Silent Film History* (Beijing: China Film Press, 1997).

Jubin, Hu, 'Yingxi (Shadow Play): The Initial Chinese Conception about Film', *Screening the Past* no. 11 (November 2000): http://www.screeningthepast. com/2014/12/yingxi-shadow-play-the-initial-chinese-conception-about-film/.

Zhang, Yingjin, *Chinese National Cinema* (New York: Routledge, 2004).

Zeng, Zhang, *An Amorous History of the Silent Screen: Shanghai Cinema, 1896–1937* (Chicago: University of Chicago Press, 2005).

Xuelei, Huang, *Shanghai Filmmaking: Crossing Borders, Connecting to the Globe, 1922–1938* (Leiden: Brill, 2014).

Cuba

Rodriguez González, Raúl, Maria Eulalia Douglas, and Héctor Garcìa Mesa, 'Le Cinéma muet', in Paulo Antonio Paranaguá (ed.), *Le Cinéma cubain* (Paris: Centre Georges Pompidou, 1990), pp. 49–62.

Rodríguez González, Raúl, *El cine silente en Cuba* (Havana: Letras Cubanas, 1992).

Douglas, Maria Eulalia, *La tienda negra. El cine en Cuba (1897–1990)* (Havana: Cinemateca de Cuba, 1997).

Fornet, Ambrosio, 'Del silente al sonoro: la prehistoria del cine en Cuba', *Archivos de la Filmoteca* [Valencia] no. 59 (June 2008), pp. 17–33.

Agramonte, Arturo and Luciano Castillo. *Cronología del cine cubano (1897–1936)* (Havana: Ediciones ICAIC, 2011).

Denmark

Engberg, Marguerite, *Dansk Stumfilm* (Copenhagen: Rhodos, 1977).

Mottram, Ron, *The Danish Cinema, 1896–1917* (Ann Arbor: University of Michigan Press, 1982).

Tybjerg, Casper, *An Art of Silence and Light: The Development of the Danish Drama to 1920* (Copenhagen: Department of Film and Media Studies, University of Copenhagen, 1996).

Thorsen, Isak, *Nordisk Films Kompagni 1906–1924: The Rise and Fall of the Polar Bear* (New Barnet, Herts.: John Libbey, 2017, KINtop Series 5).

Ecuador

'El cine mudo en Ecuador', in Héctor García Mesa (ed.), *Cine latinoamericano, 1896–1930* (Caracas: Fundación del nuevo cine latinoamericano, 1992), pp. 169–76.

Granda, Wilma, *El cine silente en Ecuador, 1895–1935* (Quito: Casa de la Cultura Ecuatoriana/Cinemateca Nacional/UNESCO, 1995).

Finland

Uusitalo, Kari, *Eläviksi syntyneet kuvat. Suomalaisen elokuvan mykät vuodet, 1896–1930* (Helsinki: Kustannusosakeyhtiö Otava, 1972).

Hirn, Sven, *Kuvat kulkevat. Kuvallisten esitysten perinne ja elävien kuvien 12 ensimmäistä vuotta Suomessa* (Helsinki: Suomen elokuvasäätiö, 1981).

Hirn, Sven, *Kuvat elävät. Elokuvatoimintaa Suomessa 1908–1918* (Helsinki: VAPK-Kustannus/Suomen elokuva-arkisto, 1991).

France

Demenÿ, Georges, *Les Origines du cinématographe* (Paris: H. Paulin, n.d. [1909]).

Kress, Émile, *Bibliothèque générale de cinématographie, Conférences sur la cinématographie organisées par le Syndicat des auteurs et gens de lettres. Première conférence, Historique du Cinématographe* (Paris: Comptoir d'édition de 'Cinéma-Revue', n.d. [1912]).

Coissac, Guillaume-Michel, 'Le Cinéma. Son passé, son présent, son avenir', in *Annuaire général de la Cinématographie française et étrangère* (Paris: Éditions de Ciné-Journal, 1917), pp. 457–507.

Rosen, J., *L'Histoire d'une industrie. Le cinématographe: son passé, son avenir et ses applications* (Paris: Société d'Éditions Techniques, n.d. [c. 191?]).

Turpain, Albert, *Conférences scientifiques. Cinquième fascicule: Le Cinématographe. Histoire de son invention, son développement, son avenir* (Paris: Gauthier-Villars, 1924).

Coissac, Guillaume-Michel, *Histoire du cinématographe de ses origines à nos jours* (Paris: Éditions du Cinéopse/Gauthier-Villars, 1925).

Le Cinéma des origines à nos jours (Paris: Aux Éditions du Cygne, 1932).

Abel, Richard, *French Cinema: The First Wave, 1915–1929* (Princeton, NJ: Princeton University Press, 1984).

Guibbert, Pierre (ed.), *Les Premiers ans du cinéma français* (Perpignan: Institut Jean Vigo, 1985).

Kermabon, Jacques (ed.), *Pathé, premier empire du cinéma* (Paris: Centre Georges Pompidou, 1994).

Abel, Richard, *The Ciné Goes to Town: French Cinema, 1896–1914* (Berkeley: University of California Press, 1993; updated and expanded edition, 1998).

Salmon, Stéphanie, *Pathé. À la conquête du cinema* (Paris: Tallandier, 2014).

Georgia

Amiredzhibi, Natia, *Na zare gruzinskogo kino* (Tbilisi: Khelovneba, 1978).

Germany

Narath, Albert, *Oskar Meßter. Der Begründer der deutschen Kino- und Filmindustrie* (Berlin: Stiftung Deutsche Kinemathek, 1966).

Dahlke, Günther and Günter Karl (eds.), *Deutsche Spielfilme von den Anfängen bis 1933* (Berlin/DDR: Henschel Verlag, 1988).

Cherchi Usai, Paolo and Lorenzo Codelli (eds.), *Before Caligari. German Cinema, 1895–1920* (Pordenone: Le Giornate del Cinema Muto, 1990).

Heide Schlüpmann, *Unheimlichkeit des Blicks: das Drama des frühen deutschen Kinos* (Basle: Stroemfeld/Roter Stern, 1990); English translation, *The Uncanny Gaze: The Drama of Early German Cinema* (Urbana: University of Illinois Press, 2010).

Jacobsen, Wolfgang, Anton Kaes, and Hans Helmut Prinzler (eds.), *Geschichte des Deutschen Films* (Stuttgart: Metzler, 1993).

Müller, Corinna, *Frühe Deutsche Kinematographie. Formale, wirtschaftliche und kulturelle Entwicklungen* (Stuttgart: Metzler, 1994).

Elsaesser, Thomas, Michael Wedel, and Martin Loiperdinger (eds.), *A Second Life: German Cinema's First Decades* (Amsterdam: Amsterdam University Press, 1996; German edition, Berlin: Vorwerk, 2000).

Bock, Hans-Michael (ed.), *Recherche. Film: Quellen und Methoden der Filmforschung* (Munich: edition text+kritik, 1997).

Gandert, Gero (ed.), *Der Film der Weimarer Republik 1929. Ein Handbuch der zeitgenössischen Kritik. Herausgegeben im Auftrag der Stiftung Deutsche Kinemathek* (Berlin and New York: Walter de Gruyter Verlag, 1997).

Putz, Petra, *Waterloo in Geiselgasteig. Die Geschichte des Münchner Filmkonzerns Emelka (1919–1933) im Antagonismus zwischen Bayern und dem Reich. Mit einer Konzern-Filmographie von Uli Jung* (Trier: Wissenschaftlicher Verlag, 1997).

Schöning, Jörg (ed.), *Triviale Tropen. Exotische Reise- und Abenteuerfilme aus Deutschland 1919–1939* (Munich: edition text+kritik, 1997).

Müller, Corinna and Harro Segeberg (eds.), *Die Modellierung des Kinofilms: zur Geschichte des Kinoprogramms zwischen Kurzfilm und Langfilm 1905/06–1918* (Munich: Fink, 1998, Mediengeschichte des Films, Vol. 2).

Koebner, Thomas (ed.), *Diesseits der 'Dämonischen Leinwand'. Neue Perspektiven auf das späte Weimarer Kino* (Munich: edition text+kritik, 2003).

Mühl-Benninghaus, Wolfgang, *Vom Augusterlebnis zur UFA-Gründung. Der deutsche Film im Ersten Weltkrieg* (Berlin: Avinus Verlag, 2004).

Great Britain

Low, Rachael, *The History of the British Film* (London: George Allen & Unwin, 1948 [Vol. 1: 1896–1906, in collaboration with Roger Manvell], 1949 [Vol. 2: 1906–14], 1950 [Vol. 3: 1914–18], 1971 [Vol. 4: 1918–29]).

Brown, Richard and Barry Anthony, *The History of the British Mutoscope and Biograph Company* (Trowbridge, Wilts.: Flicks Books, 1995).

Herbert, Stephen and Luke McKernan (eds.), *Who's Who of Victorian Cinema* (London: BFI Publishing, 1996).

Sopocy, Martin, *James Williamson. Studies and Documents of a Pioneer of the Film Narrative* (London: Associated University Presses, 1998).

Burton, Alan and Laraine Porter (eds.), *Scene Stealing: Sources for British Cinema Before 1930* (Trowbridge, Wilts.: Flicks Books, 2003).

Grieveson, Lee and Colin MacCabe (eds.), *Empire in Film* (London: BFI Publishing/Palgrave, 2011).

Barnes, John, *The Beginnings of the Cinema in England, 1894–1901* (Exeter: University of Exeter Press, 2015, 5 vols.).

Greece

Démopoulos, Michel, *Le Cinéma grec* (Paris: Centre
Georges Pompidou, 1995).

Guatemala

'Guatemala: café, capitalismo dependiente y cine silente',
in Héctor-García Mesa (ed.), *Cine latinoamericano,
1896–1930* (Caracas: Fundación del nuevo cine latinoamericano, 1992), pp. 177–88.

Hungarian countries in Austria-Hungary (to 1918) and Hungary (from 1918)

Jordáky, Lajos, *Az erdélyi némafilmgyártás története,
1903–1930* (Bucharest: Kriterion, 1980).

Balogh, Gyöngyi and Zágoni Bálint, *A kolozsvári
filmgyártás képes története 1913-tól 1920-ig* (Kolozsvár
and Budapest: Filmtett Egyesúlet/Magyar Nemzeti
Filmarchívum, 2009).

India

Chabria, Suresh (ed.), *Light of Asia. Indian Silent Cinema,
1912–1934* (Pordenone and New Delhi: Le Giornate del
Cinema Muto/Wiley Eastern Ltd., 1994), pp. 72–235;
revised edition (New Delhi: Niyogi Books, 2013).

Rajadhyaksha, Ashish and Paul Willemen, *Encyclopaedia
of Indian Cinema* (London and New Delhi: BFI
Publishing/Oxford University Press, 1999).

Fletcher, Tony, *The Salvation Army and the Cinematograph,
1897–1929: A Religious Tapestry in Britain and India*
(London: Local History Publications, 2015).

Mahadevan, Sudhir, *A Very Old Machine. The Many
Origins of the Cinema in India* (Albany: State
University of New York Press, 2015).

Dass, Manishita, *Outside the Lettered City:
Cinema, Modernity, and the Public Sphere in
Late Colonial India* (Oxford: Oxford University
Press, 2015).

Iran (Persia)

Ali Issari, Mohammad, *Cinema in Iran, 1900–1979*
(Metuchen, NJ, and London: Scarecrow Press, 1989).

Mottahedeh, Negar, 'Collection and Recollection: On
Studying the Early History of Motion Pictures in Iran',
Early Popular Visual Culture vol. 6 no. 2 (July 2008),
pp. 103–20.

Naficy, Hamid, *A Social History of Iranian Cinema. Vol. 1:
The Artisanal Era, 1897–1941* (Durham, NC: Duke
University Press, 2011).

Ireland and Irish Free State

Flynn, Arthur, *The Story of Irish Film* (Dublin: Currach
Press, 2005).

Condon, Denis, *Early Irish Cinema, 1895–1921*
(Newbridge, Co. Kildare: Irish Academic Press,
2008).

Italy

Bernardini, Aldo, *Cinema muto italiano, 1896–1914* (Bari:
Laterza, 1980–2, 3 vols.).

Brunetta, Gian Piero, *Guida alla storia del cinema italiano,
1905–2003* (Turin: Einaudi, 2003).

Alovisio, Silvio and Alberto Barbera (eds.), *Cabiria &
Cabiria* (Milan: Il Castoro, 2006).

Canosa, Michele, Giulia Carluccio, and Federica Villa
(eds.), *Cinema muto italiano: tecnica e tecnologia.
Volume 1: Discorsi, precetti, documenti; Volume
2: Brevetti, macchine, mestieri* (Rome: Carocci,
2006).

Bertellini, Giorgio (ed.), *Italian Silent Cinema: A Reader*
(New Barnet, Herts.: John Libbey, 2013).

Quaresima, Leonardo, *Storia del cinema italiano. Vol. 4,
1924–1933* (Venice: Marsilio, 2014).

Japan

Tanaka, Junichiro, *Nihon eiga hattatsu shi* [A History
of the Development of Japanese Cinema], vols. 1–2
(Tokyo: Chuo koronsha, 1975–6).

Imamura, Shohei, Tadao Sato, Kaneto Shindo,
Shunsuke Tsurumi, and Yoji Yamada (eds.), *Nihon
eiga no tanjo* [The Birth of Japanese Film], Vol. 1 of
Koza nihon eiga [Japanese Film] (Tokyo: Iwanami
shoten, 1985).

Imamura, Shohei, Tadao Sato, Kaneto Shindo, Shunsuke
Tsurumi, and Yoji Yamada (eds.), *Musei eiga no kansei*
[The Perfection of Silent Film], Vol. 2 of *Koza nihon
eiga* [Japanese Film] (Tokyo: Iwanami shoten, 1986).

Iwamoto, Kenji (ed.), *Nihon eiga to modanizumu 1920–1930* [The Japanese Cinema and Modernism, 1920–1930] (Tokyo: Libroport, 1991).

Komatsu, Hiroshi, 'Some Characteristics of Japanese Cinema Before World War I', in Arthur Noletti and David Desser (eds.), *Reframing Japanese Cinema: Authorship, Genre, History* (Bloomington: Indiana University Press, 1992), pp. 229–58.

Yoshida, Yoshishige, Masao Yamaguchi, and Naoyuki Kinoshita (eds.), *Eiga denrai: shinematografu to Meiji no Nihon* [The Introduction of Film: The Cinematograph and Meiji Japan] (Tokyo: Iwanami shoten, 1995).

Bernardi, Joanne, *Writing in Light: The Silent Scenario and the Japanese Pure Film Movement* (Detroit, MI: Wayne State University Press, 2001).

Gerow, Aaron A., *Visions of Japanese Modernity: Articulations of Cinema, Nation, and Spectatorship, 1896–1925* (Berkeley: University of California Press, 2010).

Nornes, Markus, and Aaron A. Gerow, *Nihon eiga kenkyū e no gaidobukku* (Tokyo: Yumani shobo, 2016); English translation, *Research Guide to Japanese Film Studies* (Ann Arbor: Center for Japanese Studies, University of Michigan, 2009; Kindle edition, 2016).

Internet Resources

NHK Archives Meisakusen Minokashi Natsukashi (online database of Japanese films from the 1920s; films available on streaming): https://www.nhk.or.jp/archives/search/year/

Liechtenstein

Ling, Annette, 'Das Kino im Wirtshaus "Rössle" in Schann', *Jahrbuch des Historischen Vereins für das Fürstentum Liechtenstein* no. 103 (2004), pp. 139–89.

Mexico

de los Reyes, Aurelio, *Los orígenes del cine en México, 1896–1900* (Mexico: FCE/Secretaría de Educación Pública, 1973).

de los Reyes, Aurelio, *Vivir de sueños. El cine mudo en México de 1896 a 1920* (Mexico, DF: Universidad Nacional Autónoma de México, 1979).

de los Reyes, Aurelio. *Cine y sociedad en México, 1896–1920. Vol. 1: Vivir de sueños* (Mexico: UNAM/Cineteca Nacional, 1981).

'El cine en México (1896–1930)', in Héctor García Mesa (ed.), *Cine latinoamericano, 1896–1930* (Caracas: Fundación del nuevo cine latinoamericano, 1992), pp. 189–278.

de Los Reyes, Aurelio, *Cine y sociedad en México, 1896–1930* (Mexico, DF: Universidad Nacional Autónoma de México, 1993).

de los Reyes, Aurelio, *Cine y sociedad en México, 1920–1924. Vol. 2: Bajo el cielo de México* (Mexico: Universidad Nacional Autónoma de México, 1993).

Miquel, Ángel. *En tiempos de revolución. El cine en la ciudad de México (1910–1916)* (Mexico: Universidad Nacional Autónoma de México, 2013).

de los Reyes, Aurelio, *Cine y sociedad en México, 1896–1930. Vol 3: Sucedió en Jalisco o los Cristeros* (Mexico: Universidad Nacional Autónoma de México, 2014).

'Mexican Silent Cinema', monograph issue of *Film History* vol. 29 no. 1 (2017).

Netherlands

Dibbets, Karel and Frank van der Maden (eds.), *Geschiedenis van de Nederlandse Film en Bioscoop tot 1940* (Weesp: Het Wereldvenster, 1986).

New Zealand/Aotearoa

Dennis, Jonathan, 'A Time Line', in Jonathan Dennis and Jan Bieringa (eds.), *Film in Aotearoa New Zealand* (Wellington: Victoria University Press, 1992), pp. 183–219.

Ottoman Empire and Turkey

Basutçu, Mehmet (ed.), *Le Cinéma turc* (Paris: Centre Georges Pompidou, 1996).

'The Middle East and North Africa', special issue of *Early Popular Visual Culture* vol. 6 no. 2 (July 2008).

Peru

Carbone, Giancarlo, *El cine en el Perú, 1897–1950: testimonios* (Lima: Universidad de Lima, 1992).

Bedoya, Ricardo, *100 años de cine en el Perú: una historia critica* (Lima: Universidad de Lima/Instituto de Cooperación Iberoamericana, 1995).

Bedoya, Ricardo, *El cine silente en Perú* (Lima: Universidad de Lima, 2009).

Núñez Gorriti, Violeta, *El cine en Lima 1897–1929* (Lima: Concejo Nacional de Cinematografía, 2010).

Philippines

Quirino, Joe, *History of the Philippine Cinema* (Manila: Phoenix Publishing House, 1983).

Deocampo, Nick, *Cine: Spanish Influences on Early Cinema in the Philippines* (Manila: Cinema Values Reorientation Program, National Commission for Culture and the Arts, 2003).

Musser, Charles, 'Nationalism, Contradiction, and Identity: Or, A Reconsideration of Early Cinema in the Philippines', in Nick Deocampo (ed.), *Early Cinema in Asia* (Bloomington: Indiana University Press, 2017), pp. 71–109.

Poland

Hendrykowska, Małgorzata, *Sladami tamtych cieni. Film w kulturze polskiej przelomu stuleci 1895–1914* (Poznán: Oficyna Wydawnicza, 1993).

Skaff, Sheila, *The Law of the Looking Glass: Cinema in Poland, 1896–1939* (Athens: Ohio University Press, 2008).

Portugal

Ribeiro, M. Félix, *Filmes, figuras e factos da história do cinema português, 1896–1949* (Lisbon: Cinemateca Portuguesa, 1983).

Romania

Cantacuzino, Ion I., *Uzina de basme. Scrieri despre cinema* (Bucharest: Maiko, 2004).

Russia and Soviet Union; *see also* Armenia, Belarus, Georgia, Ukraine

Likhachiov, Boris, *Kino v Rossii (1896–1926): materialy k istorii russkogo kino. Part 1: 1896–1913* (Leningrad: Academia, 1927).

Eikhenbaum, Boris (ed.), *Poetika kino* (Moscow and Leningrad: Kinopechat, 1927; 2nd edition, Berkeley: Berkeley Slavic Specialties, 1984; 3rd edition, with extended commentaries, *Poetika kino. Perechityvaia 'Poetiku kino'*, St Petersburg: RIII, 2001).

Likhachiov, Boris, 'Materialy k istorii kino v Rossii (1896–1926)', in *Iz istorii kino: materialy i dokumenty* [Moscow: Izdatelstvo AN SSSR] no. 3 (1960), pp. 37–103.

Leyda, Jay, *Kino. A History of Russian and Soviet Film* (London: George Allen & Unwin, 1960; 3rd edition, Princeton, NJ: Princeton University Press, 1983).

Ginzburg, Semion, *Kinematografiia dorevoliutsionnoi Rossii* (Moscow: Iskusstvo, 1963; 2nd edition, Moscow: Agraf, 2007).

Abul-Kasymova, Khanzara, Semion Ginzburg, Iosif Dolinskii, Sergei Drobashenko, Georgii Zhurov, Mark Zak, Iurii Kalashnikov, Ivar Kosenkranius, Samir Rizaev, Semion Freilikh, Yurii Khaniutin, and Kora Tsereteli (eds.), *Istoriia sovetskogo kino, 1917–1967* [4 vols.]. *Vol. 1: 1917–1931* (Moscow: Iskusstvo, 1969).

Selezniova, Tamara, *Kinomysl 1920-kh godov* (Leningrad: Iskusstvo, 1972).

Chernyshov, Andrei, *Russkaia dooktiabrskaia zhurnalistika* (Moscow: Izdatelstvo MGU, 1987).

Tsivian, Yuri, with Paolo Cherchi Usai, Lorenzo Codelli, Carlo Montanaro, and David Robinson, *Silent Witnesses. Russian Cinema, 1896–1919* (Pordenone and London: Biblioteca dell'Immagine/BFI Publishing, 1989).

Tsivian, Yuri, *Istoricheskaia retsepsiia kino: kinematograf v Rossii, 1896–1930* (Riga: Zinatne, 1991); abridged and revised English translation, *Early Cinema in Russia and Its Cultural Reception* (London and New York: Routledge, 1994).

'Russian and Soviet Cinema: Continuity and Change', special issue of *Historical Journal of Film, Radio and Television* vol. 11 no. 2 (1991).

Youngblood, Denise J., *Movies for the Masses: Popular Cinema and Soviet Society in the 1920s* (Cambridge, MA: Cambridge University Press, 1992).

Taylor, Richard and Ian Christie (eds.), *The Film Factory: Russian and Soviet Cinema in Documents, 1896–1939* (Cambridge, MA: Harvard University Press, 1988; reprint, London: Routledge, 1994).

Youngblood, Denise J., *The Magic Mirror: Moviemaking in Russia, 1908–1918* (Madison: University of Wisconsin Press, 1999).

Batalin, Viktor, *Kinokhronika v Rossii, 1896–1916 gg. Opis' kinosjomok, khraniaschikhsia v RGAKFD* (Moscow: Olma-Press/Astrel, 2002).

Deriabin, Aleksandr (ed.), *Letopis' rossiiskogo kino, 1863–1929* (Moscow: Materik/NII kinoiskusstva, 2004).

Deriabin, Aleksandr (ed.), *Letopis' rossiiskogo kino, 1930–1945* (Moscow: Materik/NII kinoiskusstva, 2007).

Korotkii, Viktor, *Operatory i rezhissiory russkogo igrovogo kino, 1897–1921: biofilmograficheskii spravochnik* (Moscow: s.n., 2009).

Spain

González López, Palmira, *Els anys daurats del cinema clàssic a Barcelona, 1906–1923* (Barcelona: Publicacions de l'Institut del Teatre de la Diputació de Barcelona/ Edicions 62, 1987).

Cine mudo español. Un primer acercamiento de investigación (s.l. [Madrid]: Universidad Complutense, 1991).

Martinez, Josefina, *Los primeros veinticinco años de cine en Madrid, 1896–1920* (Madrid: Filmoteca Española, 1992).

Letamendi, Jon and Jean-Claude Seguin, *Los orígenes del cine en Cataluña* (Barcelona: Generalitat de Catalunya/Institut Català de les Indústries Culturals, 2004).

Sweden

Robin Hood [pseud. of Bengt Idestam-Almquist], *När filmen kom till Sverige – Charles Magnusson och Svenska Bio* (Stockholm: P.A. Norstedt & Söners förlag, 1959).

Robin Hood [pseud. of Bengt Idestam-Almquist], *Filmstaden Göteborg: Hasselblads – Georg af Klercker – en bortglömd epok* (Gothenburg: Göteborgs stads jubileumsnämnd 350 år, 1971).

Werner, Gösta, *Den svenska filmens historia* (Stockholm: P.A. Nörstedt & Söners förlag, 1978).

Florin, Bo, *Den nationella stilen: studier i den svenska filmens guldålder* (Stockholm: Aura förlag, 1997).

Björkin, Mats, *Amerikanism, bolsjevism och korta kjolar: filmen och dess publik i Sverige under 1920-talet* (Stockholm: Aura förlag, 1998).

Söderbergh Widding, Astrid, *Stumfilm i brytningstid* (Stockholm: Aura förlag, 1998).

Fullerton, John and Jan Olsson (eds.), *Nordic Explorations: Film Before 1930* (Sydney: John Libbey, 1999).

Thailand

Sukwong, Dome, *Prawat phaphayon thai* (Bangkok: Ongkan kha kho'ng khurusapha, 1990).

Barné, Scot, 'Early Thai Cinema and Filmmaking: 1897–1922', *Film History* vol. 11 no. 3 (1999), pp. 308–18.

Turkey *see* Ottoman Empire and Turkey

Ukraine

Mislavskii, Vladimir, *Faktograficheskaia istoriia kino v Ukraine. 1896–1930* (Kharkiv: Torsing plus, 2013, 2 vols.).

United States

Jacobs, Lewis, *The Rise of the American Film: A Critical History* (New York: Harcourt & Brace, 1939; reprint, New York: Teachers College Press, 1978).

Brownlow, Kevin, *The Parade's Gone By …* (New York: Alfred A. Knopf, 1968).

Balio, Tino, *The American Film Industry* (Madison: University of Wisconsin Press, 1976; second edition, 1985).

Everson, William K., *The American Silent Film* (New York: Oxford University Press, 1978).

Brownlow, Kevin, *The War, the West, and the Wilderness* (New York: Knopf, 1979).

May, Lary, *Screening Out the Past: The Birth of Mass Culture and the Motion Picture Industry* (New York and Oxford: Oxford University Press, 1980).

Bordwell, David, Janet Staiger, and Kristin Thompson, *The Classical Hollywood Cinema: Film Style & Mode of Production to 1960* (New York: Columbia University Press, 1985).

Bowser, Eileen, *The Transformation of Cinema: 1908–1915* (New York: Scribner's, 1990).

Koszarski, Richard, *An Evening's Entertainment: The Age of the Silent Feature Picture, 1915–1928* (New York: Scribner's, 1990).

Musser, Charles, *The Emergence of Cinema: The American Screen to 1907* (New York: Scribner's, 1990).

Brownlow, Kevin, *Behind the Mask of Innocence. Sex, Violence, Prejudice, Crime: Films of Social Conscience in the Silent Era* (New York: Knopf, 1991).

Bernardi, Daniel, *The Birth of Whiteness: Race and the Emergence of U.S. Cinema* (New Brunswick, NJ: Rutgers University Press, 1996).

Keil, Charlie, *Early American Cinema in Transition: Story, Style, and Filmmaking, 1907–1913* (Madison: University of Wisconsin Press, 2001).

Gaudreault, André (ed.), *American Cinema, 1890–1909: Themes and Variations* (New Brunswick, NJ: Rutgers University Press, 2009).

Keil, Charlie and Ben Singer (eds.), *American Cinema of the 1910s: Themes and Variations* (New Brunswick, NJ: Rutgers University Press, 2009).

Fischer, Lucy (ed.), *American Cinema of the 1920s: Themes and Variations* (New Brunswick, NJ: Rutgers University Press, 2009).

Hallett, Hilary, *Go West, Young Women! The Rise of Early Hollywood* (Berkeley: University of California Press, 2013).

Lucia, Cynthia, Roy Grundmann, and Art Simon (eds.), *The Wiley-Blackwell History of American Film. Vol. 1: American Film to 1928* (Chichester, W. Sussex: Blackwell, 2013).

Bridges, Melody and Cheryl Robson, *Silent Women: Pioneers of Cinema* (Twickenham: Supernova Books, 2016).

Horak, Laura, *Girls Will Be Boys: Cross-Dressed Women, Lesbians, and American Cinema* (New Brunswick, NJ: Rutgers University Press, 2016).

Vernet, Marc, *Ainsi naquit Hollywood. Avant l'âge d'or, les ambitions de la Triangle et les premiers studios* (Paris: Armand Colin, 2018).

Uruguay

Hintz, Eugenio and Graciela Dacosta, *Historia y filmografía del cine uruguayo* (Montevideo: Ediciones de la Plaza, 1988).

Zapiola, Guillermo, 'El cine mudo en Uruguay', in Héctor García Mesa and Teresa Toledo (eds.), *Cine latinoamericano (1986–1930). Fundación del Nuevo Cine Latinoamericano* (Caracas: Consejo Nacional de la Cultura, Fondocine, Fundacine UC, 1992), pp. 319–32.

Torello, Georgina, *La conquista del espacio. Ficciones del cine silente uruguayo, 1915–1932* (Montevideo: Yaugurú, 2017).

Venezuela

Hernández, Tulio (ed.), *Panorama histórico del cine en Venezuela, 1896–1993* (Caracas: Fundación Cinemateca Nacional, 1997).

Caropreso Ponce, Luis, *Breve historia del cine nacional, 1909–1964* (Caracas: Consejo Nacional de Cultura [CONAC]/ Cinemateca Nacional de Venezuela, n.d. [1993]).

Chapter 1 – PIXELS (pp. 6–20)

Solomon, Matthew, *Fantastic Voyages of the Cinematic Imagination. Georges Méliès's* Trip to the Moon (Albany: State University of New York Press, 2011).

Cherchi Usai, Paolo, 'Early Films in the Age of Content; or, "Cinema of Attractions" Pursued by Digital Means', in André Gaudreault, Nicolas Dulac, and Santiago Hidalgo (eds.), *A Companion to Early Cinema* (Malden, MA: Wiley-Blackwell, 2012), pp. 527–49.

Facsimiles (pp. 7–8)

Rodowick, David, *The Virtual Life of Film* (Cambridge, MA, and London: Harvard University Press, 2007).

Marketplace (pp. 9–10)

Loiperdinger, Martin (ed.), *Celluloid Goes Digital. Historical-Critical Editions of Films on DVD and the Internet. Proceedings of the First International Trier Conference on Film and New Media, October 2002* (Trier: Wissenschaftlicher Verlag Trier, 2003).

Crisp, Virginia and Gabriel Menotti Gonring, *Besides the Screen: Moving Images Through Distribution, Promotion and Curation* (Basingstoke, Hants., and New York: Palgrave, 2015).

Mazzanti, Nicola; European Commission, Directorate-General for the Information Society and Media;

Peacefulfish; IPR; Red Cat Technologies, *Challenges of the Digital Era for Film Heritage Institutions* (Luxembourg: Publications Office, 2011; Executive Summary, 2012): http://ec.europa.eu/digital-agenda/sites/digital-agenda/files/final_report_en.pdf.

Aura (pp. 10–11)

Benjamin, Walter, 'Das Kunstwerk im Zeitalter seiner technischen Reproduzierbarkeit', first published in translation by Pierre Klossowski as 'L'Œuvre d'art à l'époque de sa reproduction mécanisée', *Zeitschrift für Sozialforschung* vol. 5 no. 1 (Paris: Alcan, 1936), pp. 40–66; English translation, *The Work of Art in the Age of Mechanical Reproduction* (London: Penguin, 2008).

Hansen, Miriam Bratu, *Cinema and Experience: Siegfried Kracauer, Walter Benjamin, and Theodor W. Adorno* (Berkeley: University of California Press, 2012).

Migrations (pp. 11–13)

Kokaram, Anil, *Motion Picture Restoration. Digital Algorithms for Artefact Suppression in Degraded Motion Picture Film and Video* (London: Springer-Verlag, 1998).

Project FIRST: Film Conservation and Restoration Strategies. State of the Art Reports (Brussels: European Commission/Information Society, 2003; CD-Rom).

Science and Technology Council of the Academy of Motion Picture Arts and Sciences, *The Digital Dilemma* (Los Angeles: AMPAS, 2007; 2nd printing, 2008).

Ethics (pp. 13–14)

International Federation of Film Archives, *Code of Ethics* (Brussels: FIAF, 1998; 3rd edition, 2008).

Placebo (pp. 14–16)

Fossati, Giovanna, *From Grain to Pixel* (Amsterdam: Amsterdam University Press, 2009; revised edition, 2018).

Bordwell, David, *Pandora's Digital Box: Films, Files, and the Future of Movies* (Madison, WI: The Irvington Way Institute Press, 2012; eBook: http://www.davidbordwell.net/books/pandora.php).

Content (pp. 16–18)

Thompson, Kristin, 'The Celestial Multiplex', in www.davidbordwell.net, 27 March 2007; reproduced in Paolo Cherchi Usai, David Francis, Alexander Horwath, and Michael Loebenstein, *Film Curatorship: Archives, Museums, and the Digital Marketplace* (Vienna: Synema – Gesellschaft für Film und Medien/Österreichisches Filmmuseum, 2008), pp. 216–21.

Cherchi Usai, Paolo, 'Archival Cinema', in Rob Stone, Paul Cooke, Stephanie Dennison, and Alex Marlow-Mann (eds.), *The Routledge Companion to World Cinema* (London and New York: Routledge, 2018), pp. 426–35.

Performance (pp. 18–19)

Loiperdinger, Martin (ed.), *Early Cinema Today: The Art of Programming and Live Performance* (New Barnet, Herts.: John Libbey, 2012).

Blawat, Meinolf, Jean Bolot, and Christophe Diot, 'Storing Movies in DNA', *Innovation in Motion* (Summer 2015), pp. 38–42.

Digital(e) – L'argentique à l'heure du numérique (Marseille: Éditions commune/l'Abominable/Film flamme, 2015).

Films

What Do Those Old Films Mean? (Noël Burch, Channel 4 TV, UK 1985, six episodes of 26' each).

Side by Side (Christopher Kenneally, US 2012, 99').

Cinema Futures (Michael Palm, Österreichisches Filmmuseum, Austria/India/Norway/US 2016, 126').

Chapter 2 – CELLULOID (pp. 21–42)

Vitoux, Georges, *La Photographie du mouvement: chrono-photographie, kinétoscope, cinématographe* (Paris: Chamuel, 1896).

Jenkins, Charles Francis, *Picture Ribbons: An Exposition of the Methods and Apparatus Employed in the Manufacture of the Picture Ribbons Used in Projecting Lanterns to Give the Appearance of Objects in Motion* (Washington, DC: [Press of H.L. McQueen], 1897).

Gastine, Louis, *La Chronophotographie sur plaque fixe et sur pellicule mobile* (Paris: Gauthier-Villars, 1897).

Trutat, Eugène, *La Photographie animée* (Paris: Gauthier-Villars, 1899).

Vollmer, Henry, *Lehrbuch der Photographie: mit besonderer Berücksichtigung der Filmphotographie und einem Anhang über Bildmässige Photographie* (Leipzig: Verlag von Aktiengesellschaft Fritzsche, 1905).

Hepworth, Cecil M., *Animated Photography: The ABC of the Cinematograph: A Simple and Thorough Guide to the Projection of Living Photographs, With Notes on the Production of Cinematograph Negatives* (London: Hazell, Watson, & Viney, 1897; 2nd edition, 1900; Hector Maclean, co-author).

Frippet, E., *La Pratique de la photographie instantanée par les appareils à main, avec méthode sur les agrandisse-ments et les projections et notes sur le cinématographe* (Paris: J. Fritsch, 1899).

Talbot, Frederick Arthur Ambrose, *Moving Pictures. How They Are Made and Worked* (London: Heinemann, 1912; Philadelphia, PA: J.B. Lippincott & Co., 1914).

Welsh, Robert E., *A-B-C of Motion Pictures* (New York and London: Harper & Brothers, 1916).

Jones, Bernard E., *The Cinematograph Book, a Complete Practical Guide to the Taking and Projecting of Cinematograph Pictures* (London: Cassell, 1915; 2nd edition, 1921).

Mariani, Vittorio, *Guida pratica della cinematografia* (Milan: Ulrico Hoepli, 1915; reprint, 1916; 2nd edition, 1923).

Faure, Jacques, *L'Entretien et l'exploitation du cinéma. Comment on tourne, comment on fabrique, comment on exploite un film* (Paris: Éditions de 'Sciences et Voyages', n.d. [c.1925]).

Brayer, Elizabeth, *George Eastman: A Biography* (Rochester, NY: University of Rochester Press, 1996).

Braun, Marta, 'Chronophotography', in Nancy M. Mathews (ed.), *Moving Pictures: American Art and Early Film, 1880–1910* (Manchester, VT: Hudson Hills, 2005), pp. 95–9.

Spehr, Paul, *The Man Who Made Movies: W.K.L. Dickson* (New Barnet, Herts.: John Libbey, 2008).

Emulsion (pp. 26–27)

del Amo García, Alfonso, *Inspección técnica de materiales en el archivo de una filmoteca* (Madrid: Filmoteca Española, 1996).

Fernández Colourado, Luis, Rosa Cardona Arau, Jennifer Gallego Christensen, and Encarnación Rus Aguilar, *Los soportes de la cinematografía 1*;

Fernando Catalina and Alfonso del Amo García, *Los soportes de la cinematografía 2* (Madrid: Filmoteca Española, both published in 1999. Vol. 2 is in Spanish and English).

Shanebrook, Robert L., *Making Kodak Film* (Rochester, NY: Robert L. Shanebrook, 2016; 2nd edition).

Base (pp. 27–30)

Films

Secrets of a World Industry – The Making of Cinematograph Film (Walturdaw Company, UK 1922, 478 ft, 8').

Highlights and Shadows (James Sibley Watson Jr, US 1938, 55').

Formats (pp. 30–32)

Belton, John, 'The Origins of 35mm Film as a Standard', *SMPTE Journal* vol. 99 no. 8 (August 1990), pp. 652–61.

Göllner, Peter, *Ernemann Cameras: Die Geschichte des Dresdener Photo-Kino-Werks* (Hückelhoven: Wittig Fachbuchverlag, 1995).

Spehr, Paul C., 'Unaltered to Date: Developing 35mm Film', in John Fullerton and Astrid

Söderbergh-Widding (eds.), *Moving Images: From Edison to the Webcam* (Sydney: John Libbey, 2000).

Spira, Siegfried Franz (Fred), *The History of Photography as Seen Through the Spira Collection* (New York: Aperture, 2001).

Meusy, Jean-Jacques, 'Un Astronome dans le monde du showbiz: Henry Chrétien, père du Cinémascope', *Cinegrafie* vol. XV no. 16 (2003), pp. 226–43.

Mebold, Anke, Martina Roepke, and Dan Streible, 'Nontheatrical film', monograph issue of *Film History* vol. 19 no. 4 (2007), pp. 344–52.

Frames (pp. 32–34)

Hovet, Ted, 'The Persistence of the Rectangle', *Film History* vol. 29 no. 3 (Fall 2017), pp. 136–68.

Perforations (pp. 35–37)

Standards Adopted by the Society of Motion Picture Engineers (Washington, DC: Society of Motion Picture Engineers, 1917).

Edges (pp. 38–40)

Löbel, Léopold, 'Machines à brosser et à signer', in *La Technique cinématographique* (Paris: Dunod et Pinat, 1912), pp. 204–6; 2nd edition, revised and expanded (Paris: Dunod, 1922), pp. 209–11.

Splices (pp. 40–42)

Godefroy, Thomas, 'Quand l'amateur s'y colle. (Modes d') emploi de la presse à coller dans le cinéma amateur entre 1910 et 1930', *Journal of Film Preservation* no. 98 (April 2018), pp. 33–9.

Chapter 3 – CHROMA (pp. 43–61)

Coe, Brian, 'The Development of Colour Cinematography', in Roger Manvell (ed.), *The International Encyclopedia of Film* (New York: Crown, n.d. [1972]), pp. 29–32.

Nowotny, Robert A., *The Way of All Flesh Tones: A History of Color Motion Picture Processes, 1895–1929* (New York and London: Garland, 1983).

Ledig, Elfriede and Gerhard Ullmann, 'Rot wie Feuer, Leidenschaft, Genie, Wahnsinn. Zu einigen Aspekten der Farbe im Stummfilm', in Elfriede Ledig (ed.), *Der Stummfilm. Konstruktion und Rekonstruktion* (Munich: Schaudig, Bauer, Ledig, 1988), pp. 89-116.

Hertogs, Daan and Nico de Klerk (eds.), *Disorderly Order. Colours in Silent Film* (Amsterdam: Stichting Nederlands Filmmuseum, 1996).

Yumibe, Joshua, *Moving Color: Early Film, Mass Culture, Modernism* (New Brunswick, NJ: Rutgers University Press, 2012).

Brown, Simon, Sarah Street, and Liz Watkins (eds.), *Color and the Moving Image: History, Theory, Aesthetics, Archive* (New York: Routledge, 2012).

Fletcher, Alicia and Joshua Yumibe, 'From Nitrate to Digital Archive: The Davide Turconi Project', *The Moving Image* vol. 13 no. 1 (2013), pp. 1–32.

Morrissey, Priska and Céline Ruivo (eds.), *Le Cinéma en couleurs. Usages et procédés avant la fin des années 1950.* Special issue of *1895* no. 71 (Winter 2013).

Gunning, Tom, Joshua Yumibe, Giovanna Fossati, and Jonathon Rosen, *Fantasia of Color in Early Cinema* (Amsterdam: Eye Filmmuseum/Amsterdam University Press, 2015).

Flueckiger, Barbara, 'A Digital Humanities Approach to Film Colors', *The Moving Image* vol. 17 no. 2 (Fall 2017), pp. 71–94.

Internet Resources

The Davide Turconi/Josef Joye Collection of 35mm nitrate frames at the George Eastman Museum, Rochester NY: http://www.cinetecadelfriuli.org/progettoturconi/database.html

The Edith Schlemmer Collection of 35mm nitrate frames at the Österreichisches Filmmuseum, Vienna: https://www.filmmuseum.at/jart/prj3/filmmuseum/main.jart?j-j-url=/en/collections/special_collections/schlemmer_frame_collection&ss1=y

Timeline of Historical Film Colors, http://zauberklang.ch/filmcolors/

Hand-colouring (pp. 44–46)

Brown, Harold G., *An Account of the Hand and Stencil Colouring Processes* (London, document mimeographed by the author and distributed at the FIAF Berlin Congress, 1967), published in Italian as 'Tecniche di colourazione a mano e a pochoir', *Griffithiana* vol. 10 nos. 26–7 (September 1986), pp. 72–3.

Malthête, Jacques, 'Les Bandes cinématographiques en couleurs artificielles. Un example: les films de Georges Méliès coloriés à la main', *1895* no. 2 (April 1987), pp. 3–10.

Coupry, Claude, Françoise Froment, and Jacques Malthête, 'La Microspectrométrie Raman dans l'analyse des premiers films en couleurs', *CoRé* no. 16 (February 2006), pp. 29–33.

Bottomore, Stephen, 'The Early Film Colorists Speak', *Film History* vol. 28 no. 4 (2016), pp. 159–81.

Stencil (pp. 46–48)

Ruot, Marcel and Louis Didiée, 'The Pathé Kinematograph Colour Process', *The Photographic Journal*, new series, vol. 65 no. 3 (March 1925), pp. 121–6.

Marette, Jacques, 'Les Procédés de coloriage mécanique des films', *Bulletin de l'Association Française des Ingénieurs et Techniciens du Cinéma* vol. 7 (1950), pp. 3–8; reproduced in *Journal of Film Preservation* vol. 22 no. 47 (October 1993), pp. 54–9.

Tinting (pp. 48–51)

Tinting and Toning of Eastman Motion Picture Film (Rochester, NY: Eastman Kodak Company, 1916, 1918 [2nd edn.], 1922 [3rd edn.], 1924 [4th edn.], 1927 [5th edn.]).

Didiée, Louis, 'Opérations postérieures au développement des positifs'; 'Film à support teinté Pathé', in *Le Film vierge Pathé. Manuel de développement et de tirage* (Paris: Établissements Pathé-Cinéma, 1926), pp. 123–38, 139–41.

AGFA Kine-Handbuch, IV, Film-Muster-Tabellen; English version, *Kine Handbook*; Spanish version, *Manual de cinematografía AGFA* (s.l. [Wolfen],. n.d. [*c.* 1929]).

New Color Moods for the Screen (Rochester, NY: Eastman Kodak Company, n.d. [*c.* 1930]).

Crabtree, John I. and Charles E. Ives, 'Tinting and Toning Motion Picture Film', in Hal Hall (ed.), *Cinematographic Annual*, Vol. 2 (Hollywood, CA: The American Society of Cinematographers, 1931), pp. 576–90.

Toning (pp. 51–52)

Löbel, Léopold, 'Les Nouveaux procédés de virage par mordançage', *Bulletin de la Société Française de Photographie* vol. 63, 3rd series, vol. VIII no. 3 (March 1921), pp. 78–80.

Crabtree, John I. and Charles E. Ives, 'Dye Toning With Single Solution', *Abridged Scientific Publications from the Kodak Research Laboratories*, Vol. 12 (1928), pp. 249–53.

Nickolaus, John M., 'Toning Positive Film by Machine Methods', *Journal of the Society of Motion Picture Engineers* vol. 38 (July 1936), p. 67.

Ruedel, Ulrich, 'Visual Appearance of Silent Era Toning: Silver-Iodide-Based Mordant Colours in the Agfa Kine-Handbuch and the Joseph Joye Collection', *Journal of Film Preservation* no. 98 (April 2018), pp. 61–7.

Fossati, Giovanna, Victoria Jackson, Bregt Lameris, Elif Rongen-Kaynakçi, Sarah Street, and Joshua Yumibe, *The Colour Fantastic. Chromatic Worlds of Silent Cinema* (Amsterdam: Amsterdam University Press, 2018).

Synthesis (pp. 52–54)

Mees, Charles Edward Kenneth, 'The Processes of Color Photography. III. Color Cinematography', *The Journal of Chemical Education* vol. 6 no. 1 (January 1929), pp. 44–51.

'The Brewster Colour Process', *The Photographic Journal*, Royal Photographic Society of Great Britain, vol. 75 (new series, vol. 59), August 1935; reproduced in Roderick T. Ryan, *A Study of the Technology of Color Motion Picture Processes Developed in the United*

States. Doctoral thesis presented September 1966 at the University of Southern California (published Ann Arbor, MI: University Microfilms International, 1979), p. 150.

'Kodacolor Finishing Stations', in Hal Hall (ed.), *Cinematographic Annual*, Vol. 2 (Hollywood, CA: The American Society of Cinematographers, 1931), p. 591.

Kinemacolor (pp. 54–56)

Anon., *Kinemacolor and Some American Criticisms* (London: The Natural Color Kinematograph Co., 1910).

Anon., *Handbook* (London: The Natural Color Kinematograph Co., 1910).

Bennett, Colin N., *On Operating Kinemacolor* (London: The Kinematograph and Lantern Weekly, n.d. [1910]).

Joy, Henry W., *Book of Instructions for Operators of Kinemacolor Appliances* (London: The Natural Color Kinemagraph Co., 1910).

Bennett, Colin N., 'Filter Absorptions for Two-Colour', *British Journal of Photography* [Supplement on Colour Photography] (7 July 1911), p. 45.

Bennett, Colin N., *The Handbook of Kinematography* (London: The Kinematograph Weekly, 1911).

Smith, George Albert, 'The Kinemacolor Process', *The Moving Picture News* vol. 5 (9 March 1912), pp. 12–17.

Urban, Charles, 'Kinemacolor Press Appreciations: British, Continental and American' [collection of articles, n.d., at the Science Museum Library, London].

Catalogue of Kinemacolor Film Subjects. Animated Scenes in Their Actual Colors (London: The Natural Color Kinematograph Co., 1913).

Kindem, Gorham, 'The Demise of Kinemacolor: Technological, Legal, Economic and Aesthetic Problems in Early Color History', *Cinema Journal* vol. 20 no. 2 (Spring 1981), pp. 3–14.

Chronochrome (pp. 56–57)

Le Film colorié Gaumont (Paris: L. Gaumont, 1912).

Filmparlants (Talking Pictures) and Chronochrome Gaumont (Flushing, Long Island, NY: Gaumont Company, 1913).

Baudry de Saunier, Louis, 'La Cinématographie en couleurs naturelles', *L'Illustration* (Paris) no. 4010 (10 January 1920), pp. 27–30.

Établissements Gaumont, 1895–1929 (Paris: Imprimerie Gauthier-Villars, n.d. [1935]).

Cherchi Usai, Paolo, 'Le Miracle du Chronochrome', *Cinémathèque* (Paris) no. 3 (Spring/Summer 1993), pp. 83–91.

Corcy, Marie-Sophie, Jacques Malthête, Laurent Mannoni, Jean-Jacques Meusy (eds.), *Les Premières années de la société L. Gaumont et Cie* (Paris: Association Française de Recherche sur l'Histoire du Cinéma/Bibliothèque du Film/Gaumont, 1999).

Pranchère, Victor, 'La Sortie du laboratoire ou les stratégies d'exploitation du procédé trichrome de cinématographie en couleurs de la Société des Établissements Gaumont (1913–1921)', *1895* no. 71 (Winter 2013), pp. 61–80.

Handschiegl (pp. 57–59)

Van Doren Kelley, William, 'Imbibition Coloring of Motion Picture Films', *Transactions of the Society of Motion Picture Engineers* vol. 10 no. 28 (October 1926), pp. 238–41.

Van Doren Kelley, William, 'The Handschiegl and Pathéchrome Color Processes', *Journal of the Society of Motion Picture Engineers* vol. 17 no. 2 (August 1931), pp. 229–34.

Jarman, Derek, *Chroma* (Woodstock, NY: The Overlook Press, 1994).

Technicolor (pp. 59–61)

Haines, Richard W., *Technicolor Movies: The History of Dye Transfer Printing* (Jefferson, NC: McFarland, 1993).

Kalmus, Herbert T., with Eleanore King Kalmus, *Mr. Technicolor* (Absecon, NJ: MagicImage Filmbooks, 1993).

Layton, James and David Pierce, *The Dawn of Technicolor, 1915–1935* (Rochester, NY: George Eastman House, 2015).

Internet Resources

The Technicolor Papers at George Eastman Museum: http://technicolor.eastman.org/technicolor-online-research-archive

Chapter 4 –MACHINES (pp. 62–91)

Coissac, Guillaume-Michel, *La Théorie et la pratique des projections* (Paris: Maison de la Bonne Presse, n.d. [1906]).

Ducom, Jacques, *Le Cinématographe scientifique et industriel. Traité pratique de cinématographie* (Paris: Librairie des Sciences et de l'Industrie/L. Geisler, 1911).

Löbel, Léopold, *La Technique cinématographique* (Paris: Dunod et Pinat, 1912; 2nd edition, revised and expanded, Paris: Dunod, 1922; 3rd edition, revised and expanded, Paris: Dunod, 1927).

Hulfish, David S., *Motion-Picture Work: A General Treatise on Picture Taking, Picture Making, Photo-Plays, and Theater Management and Operation* (Chicago, IL: American Technical Society, 1911; reprints, 1913, 1915, and 1918); also reprinted as *Cyclopedia of Motion-Picture Work* (Chicago, IL: American Technical Society, 1914, 2 vols.).

Thun, Rudolf, *Der Film in der Technik* (Berlin: VDI-Verlag, 1924).

Richardson, Frank H., 'What Happened in the Beginning', *Transactions of the Society of Motion Picture Engineers* vol. 9 no. 22 (September 1925), pp. 63–114.

Hilfsbuch für den Kameramann (Halle [Saale]: W. Knapp, 1926).

Vivié, Jean, *Traité general de technique du cinema. Tome 1: Historique et développement de la technique cinématographique* (Paris: Bureau de Presses et d'Informations, 1946).

Fielding, Raymond (ed.), *A Technological History of Motion Pictures and Television: An Anthology from the Pages of the Journal of the Society of Motion Picture and Television Engineers* (Berkeley: University of California Press, 1967; reprint, 1984).

Coe, Brian, *The History of Movie Photography* (London: Ash & Grant, 1981).

Robinson, Jack Fay, *Bell & Howell Company. A 75-Year History* (Chicago, IL: Bell & Howell Company, 1982).

Ehrenberg, John M. and Laurence J. Roberts, 'Seventy-Five Years of Motion-Picture Standards: Contributions of the Bell & Howell Co.', *SMPTE Journal* vol. 92 no. 10 (October 1983), pp. 1058–65.

Salt, Barry, *Film Style and Technology: History and Analysis* (London: Starword, 1983; 3rd edition, 2009).

Enticknap, Leo, *Moving Image Technology: From Zoetrope to Digital* (New York: Wallflower Press, 2005).

Turquety, Benoît, *Inventer le cinéma: épistemologie, problèmes, machines* (Lausanne: Éditions l'Âge d'Homme, 2014).

Cleveland, David and Brian Pritchard, *How Films Were Made and Shown. Some Aspects of the Technical Side of Motion Picture Film, 1895–2015* (Manningtree, Essex: David Cleveland, 2015).

Fossati, Giovanna and Annie van den Oever, *Exposing the Film Apparatus: The Film Archive as a Research Laboratory* (Amsterdam: Amsterdam University Press, 2016).

Mannoni, Laurent (ed.), *La Machine cinéma. De Méliès à la 3D* (Paris: La Cinémathèque française/Lienart, 2016).

Journals

Revue scientifique et technique de l'industrie cinématographique et des industries qui s'y rattachent (Paris), 1912–14.

Transactions of the Society of Motion Picture Engineers (1916–29).

Die Kinotechnik (1919–43).

The American Cinematographer, 1920–present.

Science, technique et industrie photographiques (1921–3), later renamed *Science et industrie photographiques* (1924–68).

Die Filmtechnik (1925–43).

Internet Resources

Cinémathèque française, Paris:
    http://www.cinematheque.fr/fr/catalogues/appareils/
George Eastman Museum, Rochester, NY:
    http://collections.eastman.org/collections/20333/
    technology/objects
Industrie- und Filmmuseum, Wolfen:
    http://www.ifm-wolfen.de/de/
Kent Museum of the Moving Image, Deal:
    https://www.kentmomi.org
Musée des arts et métiers, Paris:
    http://www.arts-et-metiers.net/musee/
    recherche-sur-les-collections
Museo Nazionale del Cinema – Fondazione Maria
    Adriana Prolo, Turin, Italy:
    http://www.museocinema.it/collezioni
Národní technické muzeum (National Technical
    Museum): Prague
    http://www.ntm.cz/en/en-expozice/fotograficky-
    atelier
National Science and Media Museum, Bradford:
    http://collection.sciencemuseum.org.uk/search/
    objects/images/categories/Cinematograph
The Projected Picture Trust:
    www.ppttrust.org
Stiftung Deutsche Kinemathek, Berlin:
    https://www.deutsche-kinemathek.de/en
Technès – International Research Partnership on Cinema
    Technology:
    www.technes.org

Processing (pp. 68–72)

Didiée, Louis, *Le Film vierge Pathé. Manuel de développe-
    ment et de tirage* (Paris: Établissements Pathé-Cinéma,
    1926).
*AGFA Kine-Handbuch, I. Allgemeiner Teil; II. Negativ-Film;
    III, Positiv-Film; IV, Film- Muster-Tabellen*; English
    version, *Kine Handbook*; Spanish version, *Manual de cine-
    matografía AGFA* (s.l. [Wolfen], n.d. [c. 1929], 3 vols.).
Malthête, Jacques and Stéphanie Salmon (eds.), *Recherches
    et innovations dans l'industrie du cinéma: les cahiers des
    ingénieurs Pathé, 1906–1927* (Paris: Fondation Jérôme
    Seydoux-Pathé, 2017).

Projectors (pp. 77–81)

Le Fraper, Charles, *Les Projections animées. Manuel
    pratique à l'usage des directeurs de cinéma, des
    opérateurs et de toutes les personnes qui s'intéressent
    à la cinématographie* (Paris: Éditions du Courrier
    Cinématographique, n.d. [1913]).
Richardson, Frank Herbert, *Motion Picture Handbook. A
    Guide for Managers and Operators of Motion Picture
    Theatres* (New York: The Moving Picture World, 1910;
    2nd edition, 1912; 3rd edition, 1916; 4th edition,
    *Richardson's Handbook of Projection for Theatre
    Managers and Motion Picture Projectionists*, New York:
    Chalmers Publishing Company, 1922; 5th edition,
    1927, 2 vols.).
Rousset, Henri, *Pour le photographe et le cinéma; recettes,
    procédés, formules, tours de mains et 'trucs' divers pour
    la photo et le cinématographe, pour l'amateur et le
    professionnel* (Paris: Dunod, 1927).
Cameron, James R., *Motion Picture Projection*
    (Manhattan Beach, NY: Cameron Publishing
    Company, 1928).
Joachim, Hermann, *Die Kinematographische Projektion*,
    part of a series by Guido Seeber and F. Paul Liesegang
    (eds.), *Handbuch der Praktischen Kinematographie.
    Band III: Die Vorführung des Films. 1. Teil* (Halle
    [Saale]: Wilhelm Knapp, 1928).

Journals

The American Projectionist (American Projection Society,
    1923–31).

Films

[Ein neuer Apparat zur Verhütung von Kinobränden]
    (Germany, 1912, 3′).

Shutters (pp. 81–83)

Marbe, Karl, *Theorie des Kinematographischen
    Projektionen* (Leipzig: Johann Ambrosius Barth, 1910).

Lanterns (pp. 83–86)

Rousseau, A., *Notes pratiques d'électricité à l'usage des
    projectionnistes* (Paris: Charles-Mendel, n.d. [190–?]).

Cameron, James R., *Electricity for the Motion Picture Operator* (New York: Technical Book Co., 1922).

Magdsick, H. Herbert and Carl E. Egeler, *Motion Picture Projection With Mazda Lamps: A Practical Discussion of the Principles of Mazda Lamp Projection and Their Application* (Cleveland, OH: Engineering Dept., National Lamp Works of General Electric Co., 1922).

Reels (pp. 86–88)

Soar, Matthew, 'The Beginnings and Ends of Film: Leader Standardization in the United States and Canada (1930–1999)', *The Moving Image* vol. 16 no. 2 (2016), pp. 21–44.

Tools (pp. 88–91)

Re, Guglielmo, *Il cinematografo* (Milan: Ulrico Hoepli, 1907).

Price List of Everything Required for the Bioscope Business from the Theatre to the Films (London: The 'Walturdaw' Company, 1908).

Wolf-Czapek, Karl Wilhelm, *Die Kinematographie. Wesen, Entstehung und Ziele des lebenden Bildes* (Dresden: Union Deutsche Verlagsgesellschaft, 1908).

Liesegang, F. Paul, *Handbuch der praktischen Kinematographie* (Leipzig: Edition Liesegang's Verlag, 1908).

Lehmann, Hans, *Die Kinematographie. Ihre Grundlagen und ihre Anwendungen* (Leipzig: Teubner, 1911).

Jones, Bernard E., *How to Make and Operate Moving Pictures* (New York and London: Funk & Wagnalls, 1916).

Schrott, Paul, *Leitfaden für Kinooperateure und Kinobesitzer* (Vienna and Leipzig: Waldheim Eberle/ Otto Klemm, 1919).

Films

Sprockets and Splices (Paramount, 1923, 1,836 ft., 22′).

Chapter 5 – PEOPLE (pp. 92–121)

Internet Resources

Who's Who of Victorian Cinema:
http://www.victorian-cinema.net

Women Film Pioneers Project:
https://wfpp.cdrs.columbia.edu

Amateurs (pp. 93–96)

Talbot, Frederick A., *Practical Cinematography and Its Applications* (Philadelphia, PA, and London: J.B. Lippincott/Heinemann, 1913).

Frenk, Willy, *Der Kino-Amateur* (Berlin: Verlag Guido Hackebeil, 1926).

Schmidt, Hans, *Kino-Taschenbuch für Amateure und Fachleute* (Berlin: Union Deutsche Verlagsgesellschaft, 1926).

Frerk, Friedrich W., *Der Kino-Amateur: ein Lehr- und Nachschlagebuch* (Berlin: G. Hackebeil, n.d. [*c.* 1926]).

Cameron, James R., *Amateur Movie Craft* (New York: Cameron Publishing Company, 1928).

Herrnkind, Otto Paul, *Die Schmalfilm Kinematographie. Ein Leitfaden für Fachleute und Amateure* (Vienna and Leipzig: A. Hartleben's Verlag, 1929).

Auer, Michel, *Histoire de la camera ciné amateur* (Paris: Éditions de l'Amateur, 1979).

Zimmerman, Patricia R., *Reel Families: A Social History of Amateur Film* (Bloomington: Indiana University Press, 1995).

Kattelle, Alan, *Home Movies. A History of the American Industry, 1897–1979* (Nashua, NH: Transition Publishing, 2000).

Stone, Melinda and Dan Streible, 'Small Gauge and Amateur Film', special issue of *Film History* vol. 15 no. 2 (2003).

Wade, John, *Lights, Camera, Action! An Illustrated History of the Amateur Movie Camera* (Atglen, PA: Schiffer Publishing, 2014).

Abel, Richard, 'The "Much Vexed Problem" of Nontheatrical Distribution in the Late 1910s', *The Moving Image* vol. 16 no. 2 (Fall 2016), pp. 91–107.

Internet Resources

Toy Film Museum, Kyoto:
    http://toyfilm-museum.jp/

Entrepreneurs (pp. 96–98)

Seabury, William M., *The Public and the Motion Picture Industry* (New York: Macmillan, 1926).

Kennedy, Joseph P. (ed.), *The Story of the Films, As Told by Leaders of the Industry to the Students of the Graduate School of Business Administration, George F. Baker Foundation, Harvard University* (Chicago and New York: A.W. Shaw Company, 1927).

Friedman, Lester D., *Hollywood's Image of the Jew* (New York: Frederick Ungar, 1982).

Gabler, Neal, *An Empire of Their Own: How the Jews Invented Hollywood* (New York: Random House, 1998).

Bowser, Pearl, Jane Gaines, and Charles Musser, *Oscar Micheaux & His Circle: African-American Filmmaking and Race Cinema of the Silent Era* (Bloomington: Indiana University Press, 2001).

Melnick, Ross, *American Showman: Samuel 'Roxy' Rothafel and the Birth of the Entertainment Industry* (New York: Columbia University Press, 2014).

Krefft, Vanda, *The Man Who Made the Movies: The Meteoric Rise and Tragic Fall of William Fox* (New York: HarperCollins, 2017).

Financers (pp. 98–100)

Huettig, Mae D., *Economic Control of the Motion Picture Industry: A Study in Industrial Organization* (Philadelphia, PA: University of Philadelphia Press, 1944).

Jobes, Gertrude, *Motion Picture Empire* (Hamden, CT: Archon, 1966).

Writers (pp. 100–102)

Sargent, Epes W., *The Technique of the Photoplay* (New York: The Moving Picture World, 1912; 2nd edition, 1913; 3rd edition, 1916).

Ball, Eustace Hale, *The Art of the Photoplay* (New York: Veritas Publishing Company, 1913).

Phillips, Henry A., *The Photodrama; The Philosophy of Its Principles, the Nature of Its Plot, Its Dramatic Construction and Technique, Illumined by Copious Examples, Together With a Complete Photoplay and a Glossary, Making the Work a Practical Treatise* (Larchmont, NY: The Stanhope-Dodge Publishing Company, 1914).

Gordon, William Lewis, *How to Write Moving Picture Plays* (Cincinnati: Atlas Publishing Company, 1915).

Ball, Eustace Hale, *Photoplay Scenarios. How to Write and Sell Them* (New York: Hearst's International Library Company, 1915).

Freeburg, Victor Oscar, *The Art of Photoplay Making* (New York: Macmillan, 1918).

Palmer, Frederick, *Palmer Handbook of Scenario Construction* (Los Angeles: Palmer Photoplay Corporation, 1920).

Patterson, Frances Taylor, *Cinema Craftsmanship. A Book for Playwrights* (New York: Harcourt, Brace and Howe, 1920).

Wright, William L., *Photoplay Writing* (New York: Falk Publishing Co., 1922).

Nihon shinario taikei, Vol. 1 (edited by the Shinario Sakka Kyokai. Tokyo: Eijinsha, 1973).

Azlant, Edward, 'Screenwriting for the Early Silent Film: Forgotten Pioneers, 1897–1911', *Film History* vol. 9 no. 3 (1997), pp. 228–56.

Raynauld, Isabelle, 'Original Screenplays, Collections, and Writing Practices in France Between 1896 and 1918', *Film History* vol. 9 no. 3 (1997), pp. 257–68.

Alovisio, Silvio, *Voci del silenzio. La sceneggiatura nel cinema muto italiano* (Milan: Il Castoro, 2007).

Production (pp. 102–104)

Jasset, Victorin, 'Études sur la mise en scène en cinématographie', *Ciné-Journal* nos. 165–8 and 170 (21 October–26 November 1911); reprinted in Marcel Lapierre (ed.), *Anthologie du cinéma* (Paris: La Nouvelle édition, 1946), pp. 82–98.

Rathbun, John B., *Motion Picture Making and Exhibiting* (Los Angeles: Holmes, 1914).

Croy, Homer, *How Motion Pictures Are Made* (New York: Harper, 1918).

Gregory, Carl L. (ed.), *A Condensed Course in Motion Picture Photography* (New York: New York Institute of Photography, 1920; 2nd edition, *Motion Picture Photography*, 1927).

Boughey, Davidson, *The Film Industry* (London and New York: Pitman & Sons, 1921).

Lescarboura, Austin C., *Behind the Motion-Picture Screen* (New York: Scientific American Publishing Company/Munn & Company, 1919; 2nd edition, 1922).

Milne, Peter, *Motion Picture Directing* (New York: Falk Publishing Company, 1922).

Hughes, Laurence (ed.), *The Truth about the Movies – By the Stars* (Hollywood, CA: Hollywood Publishers, Inc., 1924).

McKay, Herbert C., *The Handbook of Motion Picture Photography* (New York: Falk Publishing Company, 1927).

Seeber, Guido, *Der praktische Kameramann. 1 – Band: Arbeits-Gerät und Arbeits-Stätten des Kameramannes* (Berlin: Verlag der 'Lichtbildbühne', 1927; facsimile edition, Frankfurt am Main: Deutsches Filmmuseum, 1980).

Gregory, Carl L., *Motion Picture Photography* (New York: Falk Publishing Company, 1927).

Blakeston, Oswell, *Through a Yellow Glass* (London: Pool, 1928).

Patterson, Frances Taylor, *Scenario and Screen* (New York: Harcourt, Brace and Company, 1928).

Bell, Monta, 'The Director: His Problems and Qualifications', *Theatre Arts Monthly* vol. 13 no. 9 (September 1929), pp. 645–9.

Koszarski, Richard (ed.), *Hollywood Directors, 1914–1940* (London, Oxford, and New York: Oxford University Press, 1976).

Pinchon, Jean-François (ed.), *Rob.[ert] Mallet-Stevens: architecture, mobilier, décoration* (Paris: Action Artistique de Paris/Sers, 1986); English translation, *Rob. Mallet-Stevens: Architecture, Furniture, Interior Design* (Cambridge, MA: MIT Press, 1990).

Kevin Brownlow, 'Ben Carré', *Griffithiana* vol. 11 nos. 32–3 (September 1988), pp. 20–32.

Curtis, James, *William Cameron Menzies: The Shape of Things to Come* (New York: Pantheon Books, 2015).

Acting (pp. 104–106)

Agnew, Frances [pseud. of Frances May Scheuing], *Motion Picture Acting. How to Prepare for Photoplaying; What Qualifications Are Necessary; How to Secure an Engagement. Salaries Paid to Photoplayers* (New York: Reliance Newspaper Syndicate, 1913).

Blaché [Guy-Blaché], Alice, 'Woman's Place in Photoplay Production', *The Moving Picture World* vol. 21 no. 2 (11 July 1914), p. 195.

Marsh, Mae, *Screen Acting* (New York and Los Angeles: Frederick A. Stokes/Photostar Publishing Company, 1921).

Klumph, Inez and Helen, *Screen Acting* (New York: Falk Publishing Company, 1922).

Jones, Charles R., *Breaking into the Movies* (New York: The Unicorn Press, 1927).

Pudovkin, Vsevolod Illarionovich, *Aktior v filme* (Leningrad: Gosudarstvennaia akademiia iskusstvoznaniia, 1934); English translation, *Film Acting* (London: George Newnes, 1935).

Gunning, Tom, 'The Cinema of Attractions: Early Film, Its Spectator and the Avant-Garde', *Wide Angle* vol. 8 nos. 3–4 (1986), pp. 63–70.

deCordova, Richard, *Picture Personalities: The Emergence of the Star System in America* (Urbana: University of Illinois Press, 1990).

Pearson, Roberta, *Eloquent Gestures: The Transformation of Performance Style in the Griffith Biograph Films* (Berkeley: University of California Press, 1992).

Mayer, David, 'Which Legacy of the Theatre? Acting in Silent Film: Some Questions and Some Problems', in Alan Lovell and Peter Krämer (eds.), *Screen Acting* (London and New York: Routledge, 1999), pp. 10–30.

Basinger, Jeanine, *Silent Stars* (New York: Knopf, 1999).

Bull, Sofia and Astrid Söderbergh Widding (eds.), *Not So Silent: Women in Cinema Before Sound* (Stockholm: Acta Universitatis Stockholmiensis, 2010).

Bean, Jennifer M. (ed.), *Flickers of Desire: Movie Stars of the 1910s* (New Brunswick, NJ: Rutgers University Press, 2011).

Richard, Jacques (ed.), *Dictionnaire des acteurs du cinéma muet en France* (Paris: Fallois, 2011).

Väliaho, Pasi, *Mapping the Moving Image: Gesture, Thought and Cinema circa 1900* (Amsterdam: Amsterdam University Press, 2011).

Loiperdinger, Martin and Uli Jung (eds.), *Importing Asta Nielsen: The International Film Star in the Making, 1910–1914* (New Barnet, Herts.: John Libbey, 2013).

Duckett, Victoria, *Seeing Sarah Bernhardt: Performance and Silent Film* (Urbana: University of Illinois Press, 2015).

Förster, Annette, *Women in Silent Cinema. Histories of Fame and Fate* (Amsterdam: Amsterdam University Press, 2017).

O'Rourke, Chris, *Acting for the Silent Screen: Film Actors and Aspiration between the Wars* (London: I.B. Tauris, 2017).

Makeup (pp. 106–108)

Kress, Émile, 'Le Maquillage', *Conférences sur la cinématographie* (Paris: Charles-Mendel, 1912), Vol. I, pp. 161–4.

Bernique, Jean, *Motion Picture Acting for Professionals and Amateurs* (s.l. [Chicago]: Producers Service Company, 1916).

'Urge Need for Good Publicity Stills', *The American Cinematographer* vol. 4 no. 12 (March 1924), pp. 9, 16–18.

Archer, Fred R. and Elmer Fryer, 'Still Photography in Motion Picture Work', *Transactions of the Society of Motion Picture Engineers* vol. 12 no. 33 (April 1928), pp. 167–72.

Brown, George Barr, 'The Still Camera in Motion Pictures', *The International Photographer* vol. 1 no. 11 (December 1929), pp. 20, 27, 43.

Workers (pp. 112–113)

Kress, Émile, 'Comment on installe et administre un cinéma', *Conférences sur la cinématographie* (Paris: Charles-Mendel, 1912), Vol. II, pp. 7–37.

Franklin, Harold B., *Motion Picture Theater Management* (New York: George H. Doran Company, 1927).

Projectionists (pp. 113–115)

Richardson, Frank H., *Operators' Hand Book: A Book of Practical Hints and Instruction for the Owner and Operator* (s.l. [Chicago]: F.H. Richardson, *c.* 1907).

Jenkins, Charles Francis, *Handbook for Motion Picture and Stereopticon Operators* (Washington, DC: The Knega Company, n.d. [*c.* 1908]).

The Modern Bioscope Operator (London: Ganes, 1910).

Cameron, James R., *Motion Picture Projection. An Elementary Text-Book* (New York: Theatre Supply Co., 1921).

O'Conor Sloane, Thomas, *Motion Picture Projection* (New York: Falk Publishing Company, 1922).

Cameron, James R. (ed.), *A Home Study Course in Professional Motion Picture Operating and Projection* (New York: New York Institute of Photography, 1929).

Barnard, Timothy, 'The "Machine Operator": Deus ex Machina of the Storefront Cinema', *Framework* vol. 43 no. 1 (Spring 2002), pp. 40–75.

Musicians (pp. 115–116)

Rapée, Ernö, *Cinema Music as a Profession* (Torquay, Devon: Educational Section, Screen Music Society, 1925).

Riesenfeld, Hugo, 'Music and Motion Pictures', *Annals of the American Academy of Political and Social Science*, vol. 128 (November 1926), pp. 58–62.

Marks, Martin, 'The First American Film Scores', *Harvard Library Bulletin* vol. 2 no. 4 (1991), pp. 78–100.

Carli, Philip C., 'Musicology and the Presentation of Silent Film', *Film History* vol. 7 no. 3 (Autumn 1995), pp. 298–321.

Audiences (pp. 116–120)

Gorkij, Maksim, 'Beglye zametki. Sinematograf Lyum'era' ([Fleeting Notes. The Lumière Cinematograph]), *Nizhegorodskii listok*, 4 July 1896; English translation in Ian Christie and Richard Taylor (eds.), *The Film Factory* (Cambridge, MA: Harvard University Press, 1988), pp. 25–6.

Claudy, Carl H., 'The Degradation of the Motion Picture', *Photo-Era* vol. 21 no. 4 (October 1908), pp. 161–5.

Ginestous, Étienne, 'Les Cinématophtalmies (troubles oculaires par cinema)', *Gazette hebdomadaire des sciences médicales* no. 23 (6 June 1909), pp. 266–9.

Romains, Jules, 'La Foule au cinématographe', in *Les Puissances de Paris* (Paris: Eugène Figuière 1911); English translation in Richard Abel, *French Film Theory and Criticism. A History/Anthology, 1907–1929* (Princeton, NJ: Princeton University Press, 1988), p. 53.

Steer, Valentia, *The Romance of the Cinema. A Short Record of the Development of the Most Popular Form of Entertainment* (London: C. Arthur Pearson, 1913).

Altenloh, Emilie, *Zur Soziologie des Kinos* (Jena: Verlag Eugen Diedrichs, 1914); English translation, 'A Sociology of the Cinema: The Audience', *Screen* vol. 42 no. 3 (Autumn 2001), pp. 249–93; reprinted in Philip Simpson, Andrew Utterson, and Karen J. Shepherdson (eds.), *Film Theory: Critical Concepts in Media and Cultural Studies*, Vol. III (London and New York: Routledge, 2003), pp. 9–55.

Serao, Matilde, 'Parla una spettatrice', *L'arte muta* [Naples] vol. 1 no. 1 (15 June 1916), pp. 31–2; English translation, 'A Spectatrix Is Speaking to You', in Antonia Lant, *The Red Velvet Seat: Women's Writing on the First Fifty Years of Cinema* (New York: Verso, 2006), pp. 97–9.

Münsterberg, Hugo, *The Photoplay: A Psychological Study* (New York: Appleton & Co., 1916).

Mitchell, Alice M., *Children and Movies* (Chicago, IL: University of Chicago Press, 1929).

Seabury, William M., *Motion Picture Problems. The Cinema and the League of Nations* (New York: The Avondale Press, 1929).

Mayne, Judith, 'Immigrants and Spectators', *Wide Angle* vol. 5 no. 2 (1982), pp. 32–41.

Crafton, Donald (ed.), 'Early Cinema Audiences', special issue of *Iris* no. 11 (Summer 1990).

Hansen, Miriam, *Babel and Babylon: Spectatorship in American Silent Film* (Cambridge, MA: Harvard University Press, 1991).

Staiger, Janet, *Interpreting Films: Studies in the Historical Reception of American Cinema* (Princeton, NJ: Princeton University Press, 1992).

Waller, Gregory A., 'Another Audience: Black Moviegoing, 1907–1916', *Cinema Journal* vol. 31 no. 2 (Winter 1992), pp. 3–25.

Lefebvre, Thierry, 'Une "Maladie" au tournant du siècle: la "cinématophtalmie"', *Revue d'Histoire de la Pharmacie* vol. 40 no. 297 (April–June 1993), pp. 225–30.

Tsivian, Yuri, 'Russia, 1913: Cinema in the Cultural Landscape', *Griffithiana* vol. 17 no. 50 (May 1994), pp. 125–47.

Belton, John (ed.), 'Audiences and Fans', special issue of *Film History* vol. 6 no. 4 (Winter 1994).

Waller, Gregory A., *Main Street Amusements: Movies and Commercial Entertainment in a Southern City, 1896–1930* (Washington, DC: Smithsonian Institution Press, 1995).

Fuller-Seeley, Kathryn, *At the Picture Show: Small-Town Audiences and the Creation of Movie Fan Culture* (Washington, DC: Smithsonian Institution Press, 1996).

Bachmann, Gregg, 'Still in the Dark: Silent Film Audiences', *Film History* vol. 9 no. 1 (1997), pp. 23–48.

Hiley, Nicholas, '"At the Picture Palace": The British Cinema Audience, 1895–1920', in John Fullerton (ed.), *Celebrating 1895: The Centenary of Cinema* (Sydney: John Libbey, 1998), pp. 96–103.

Stokes, Melvyn and Richard Maltby (eds.), *American Movie Audiences: From the Turn of the Century to the Early Sound Era* (London: BFI Publishing, 1999), pp. 46–63.

Stamp, Shelley, *Movie-Struck Girls: Women and Motion Picture Culture After the Nickelodeon* (Princeton, NJ: Princeton University Press, 2000).

Keil, Charlie and Shelley Stamps (eds.), *American Cinema's Transitional Era: Audiences, Institutions, Practices* (Berkeley: University of California Press, 2004).

Stewart, Jacqueline Najuma, *Migrating to the Movies: Cinema and Black Urban Modernity* (Berkeley: University of California Press, 2005).

Abel, Richard, *Americanizing the Movies and 'Movie-Mad' Audiences, 1910–1914* (Berkeley: University of California Press, 2006).

Lant, Antonia (ed.), *The Red Velvet Seat: Women's Writing on the First Fifty Years of Cinema* (New York: Verso, 2006).

Musser, Charles, 'A Cinema of Contemplation, a Cinema of Discernment: Spectatorship, Intertextuality and Attractions in the 1890s', in Wanda Strauven (ed.), *The Cinema of Attractions Reloaded* (Amsterdam: Amsterdam University Press, 2006), pp. 159–79.

Maltby, Richard, Melvyn Stokes, and Robert C. Allen (eds.), *Going to the Movies: Hollywood and the Social Experience of Cinema* (Exeter: Exeter University Press, 2007).

McKernan, Luke, 'A Fury for Seeing: Cinema, Audience and Leisure in London in 1913', *Early Popular Visual Culture* vol. 6 no. 8 (2008), pp. 271–80.

de la Bretèque, François Amy, Michel Cadé, Angel Quintana Moraja, and Jordi Pons (eds.), *Les Cinemas périphériques dans la période des premiers temps* (Perpignan/Girona: Presses Universitaires de Perpignan – Institut Jean Vigo/Museu del Cinema, 2010).

Braun, Marta, *Beyond the Screen: Institutions, Networks and Publics of Early Cinema* (New Barnet, Herts.: John Libbey, 2012).

Hennefeld, Maggie, 'Women's Hats and Silent Film Spectatorship: Between Ostrich Plume and Moving Image', *Film History* vol. 28 no. 3 (2016), pp. 24–53.

Interpreters (pp. 120–121)

Abel, Richard (ed.), *French Film Theory and Criticism. A History/Anthology, 1907–1929* (Princeton, NJ: Princeton University Press, 1988).

Anděl, Jaroslav and Petr Szczepanik (eds.), *Cinema All the Time: An Anthology of Czech Film Theory and Criticism, 1908–1939* (Prague/Ann Arbor, MI: National Film Archive/Michigan Slavic Publications, 2008).

Banda, Daniel and José Moure, *Le Cinéma: naissance d'un art. Premiers écrits, 1895–1920* (Paris: Flammarion, 2008).

Abel, Richard, *Menus for Movieland: Newspapers and the Emergence of American Film Culture, 1913–1916* (Berkeley: University of California Press, 2015).

Kaes, Anton, Nicholas Baer, and Michael Cowan (eds.), *The Promise of Cinema: German Film Theory, 1907–1933* (Berkeley: University of California Press, 2016).

Chapter 6 – BUILDINGS (pp. 122–145)

AGFA Kine-Handbuch, I. Allgemeiner Teil; English translation, *Kine Handbook*; Spanish version, *Manual de cinematografía AGFA* (s.l. [Wolfen], n.d. [*c.* 1929]).

Leggio, Angeletta, 'A History of Australia's Kodak Manufacturing Plant', *Topics in Photographic Preservation* vol. 12 (2009), pp. 67–73.

Studios (pp. 124–127)

Jacobson, Brian R., *Studios Before the System: Architecture, Technology, and the Emergence of Cinematic Space* (New York: Columbia University Press, 2015).

Lighting (pp. 127–129)

Lomas, H.M., *Picture Play Photography* (London: Ganes, 1914).

Nasaw, David, 'It Begins With the Lights: Electrification and the Rise of Public Entertainment', in Patricia McDonnell and Robert Allen (eds.), *On the Edge of Your Seat: Popular Theatre and Film in Early Twentieth-Century American Art* (New Haven, CT: Yale University Press, 2002), pp. 45–63.

Theatres (pp. 131–134)

Jason, Alexander (ed.), *Handbuch der Filmwirtschaft. Europäische Statistiken und Verzeichnisse seit 1926. Band II: Film-Europa* (Berlin: Verlag für Presse, Wirtschaft und Politik, 1930).

Hall, Ben M., *The Best Remaining Seats* (New York: Bramhall House, 1961).

Atwell, David, *Cathedrals of the Movies. A History of British Cinemas and Their Audiences* (London: The Architectural Press, 1980).

Valerio, Joseph M., and Daniel Friedman, *Movie Palaces: Renaissance and Reuse* (New York: Educational Facilities Laboratories Division, Academy for Educational Development, 1982).

Melnick, Ross and Andreas Fuchs, *Cinema Treasures. A New Look at Classic Movie Theatres* (St Paul, MN: MBI Publishing, 2004).

Meusy, Jean-Jacques (ed.), *Cinémas de France (1894–1918): une histoire en images* (Paris: Arcadia, 2009).

Mahadevan, Sudhir, 'Traveling Showmen, Makeshift Cinemas: The *Bioscopewallah* and Early Cinema History in India', *BioScope: South Asian Screen Studies* vol. 1 no. 1 (2010), pp. 27–47.

Paul, William, *When Movies Were Theater. Architecture, Exhibition, and the Evolution of American Film* (New York: Columbia University Press, 2016).

Thissen, Judith, 'Multifunctional Halls and the Place of Cinema in the European Countryside, 1920–1970', *Cinémas* vol. 27 nos. 2–3 (2017), pp. 91–111.

Periodicals

Marquee – Journal of the Theatre Historical Society of America (ISSN 0025-3928).

Internet Resources

The London Project: The Birth of the Film Business in London, 1894–1914: http://londonfilm.bbk.ac.uk/

Auditoriums (pp. 134–139)

Meloy, Arthur S., *Theatres and Picture Houses* (New York: Architects' Supply & Publishing Company, 1916).

Screens (pp. 139–142)

Paul, William, 'Uncanny Theater: The Twin Inheritances of the Movies', *Paradoxa: Studies in World Literary Genres* vol. 3 nos. 3–4 (1997), pp. 321–47.

Booths (pp. 142–145)

Donnadieu, Adolphe-Louis, *La Photographie animée: ses origines, son exploitation, ses dangers* (Paris and Lyon: Charles-Mendel/E. Vitte, 1897).

Huret, Jules (ed.), *In Memoriam. La catastrophe du bazar de la Charité (4 mai 1897). Historique du bazar de la Charité, La Catastrophe, Les victimes, Les sauveteurs, Les blessés, Les funérailles, Détails rétrospectifs, Les responsabilités, Liste officielle des récompenses, etc., Liste complète des souscripteurs du 'Figaro'* (Paris: F. Juven, n.d. [1897]).

Baldizzone, José (ed.), 'L'Incendie du Bazar de la Charité', *Archives* [Perpignan] no. 12 (March 1988), pp. 1–16.

Fletcher, Tony, *Regulating the Cinematograph in London 1897–1906* (London: Local History Publications, 2017).

Chapter 7 – WORKS (pp. 146–170)

Genres (pp. 149–152)

Ancient History

Michelakis, Pantelis and Maria Wyke, *The Ancient World in Silent Cinema* (Cambridge: Cambridge University Press, 2013).

Animation

Lutz, Edwin G., *Animated Cartoons. How They Are Made, Their Origin and Development* (New York: Scribner's, 1925).

Crafton, Donald, *Before Mickey: The Animated Film, 1898–1928* (Chicago, IL: University of Chicago Press, 1993).

Merritt, Russell and J.B. Kaufman, *Walt in Wonderland: The Silent Films of Walt Disney* (Baltimore, MD: Johns Hopkins University Press, 2001).

Robinson, David, Victor Bocharov, and Birgit Beumers, *Alexander Shiryaev: Master of Movement* (Pordenone: Le Giornate del Cinema Muto, 2009).

Crafton, Donald, *Emile Cohl, Caricature, and Film* (Princeton, NJ: Princeton University Press, 2014).

Bendazzi, Giannalberto, *Animation: A World History* (Boca Raton, FL: CRC Press/Taylor & Francis, 2016).

Avant-Garde

Schleugl, Hans and Ernst Schmidt (eds.), *Eine Subgeschichte des Films: Lexicon des Avantgarde-, Experimental- und Undergroundfilms* (Frankfurt am Main: Suhrkamp, 1974, 2 vols.).

Horak, Jan-Christopher, *Lovers of Cinema: The First American Film Avant-Garde, 1919–1945* (Madison: University of Wisconsin Press, 1995).

Comedy

Kerr, Walter, *The Silent Clowns* (New York: Knopf, 1975; reprint, New York: Da Capo Press, 1990).

Bernardini, Aldo (ed., in collaboration with Vittorio Martinelli), 'I comici del muto italiano', *Griffithiana* vol. 8 nos. 24–5 (October 1985), pp. 63–134; vol. 9 nos. 26–7 (September 1986), pp. 99–101.

Burton, Alan and Laraine Porter (eds.), *Pimple, Pranks & Pratfalls: British Film Comedy Before 1930* (Trowbridge, Wilts.: Flicks Books, 2000).

King, Rob, *The Fun Factory: The Keystone Film Company and the Emergence of Mass Culture* (Berkeley: University of California Press, 2009).

Le Roy, Éric (ed.), 'Aux sources du burlesque cinématographique: les comiques français des premier temps', special issue of 1895 no. 61 (2010).

Hennefeld, Maggie, *Specters of Slapstick & Silent Film Comediennes* (New York: Columbia University Press, 2018).

Wagner, Kristen Anderson, *Comic Venus: Women and Comedy in American Silent Film* (Wayne, MI: Wayne State University Press, 2018).

Horror

Rhodes, Gary D., *The Birth of the American Horror Film* (Edinburgh: Edinburgh University Press, 2018).

Literature

Tsivian, Yuri, 'The Invisible Novelty: Film Adaptations in the 1910s', in Robert Stam and Alessandra Raengo (eds.), *A Companion to Literature and Film* (Malden, MA: Blackwell, 2004), pp. 92–111.

Non-Fiction

Fielding, Raymond, *The American Newsreel, 1911–1967* (Norman: University of Oklahoma Press, 1967).

Levy, David, 'Re-Constituted Newsreels, Re-Enactments and the American Narrative Film', in Roger Holman and André Gaudreault (eds.), *Cinema 1900–1906: An Analytical Study* (Brussels: FIAF, 1982), Vol. 1, pp. 243–58.

Convents, Guido, 'Documentaries and Propaganda Before 1914: A View on Early Cinema and Colonial History', *Framework* no. 35 (1988), pp. 104–13.

Hertogs, Daan and Nico de Klerk, *Nonfiction in the Teens* (Amsterdam: Stichting Nederlands Filmmuseum, 1994).

Smither, Roger and Wolfgang Klaue (eds.), *Newsreels in Film Archives: A Survey Based on the FIAF Newsreel Symposium* (Trowbridge, Wilts.: Flicks Books, 1996).

Hertogs, Dan and Nico de Klerk (eds.), *Uncharted Territory: Essays on Early Nonfiction Film* (Amsterdam: Stichting Nederlands Filmmuseum, 1997).

Toulmin, Vanessa, Simon Popple, and Patrick Russell (eds.), *The Lost World of Mitchell & Kenyon: Edwardian Britain on Film* (London: BFI Publishing, 2004).

Peterson, Jennifer L., *Education in the School of Dreams: Travelogues and Early Nonfiction Film* (Durham, NC: Duke University Press, 2013).

Ruppin, Dafna (ed.), *The Komedi Bioscoop: Early Cinema in Colonial Indonesia* (New Barnet, Herts.: John Libbey, 2016).

Science

Lefebvre, Thierry, 'The Scientia Production (1911–1914): Scientific Popularization Through Pictures', *Griffithiana* vol. 16 no. 47 (1993), pp. 137–55.

Tosi, Virgilio, *Cinema Before Cinema: The Origins of Scientific Cinematography* (London: British Universities Film & Video Council, 2005).

Gaycken, Oliver, *Devices of Curiosity: Early Cinema & Popular Science* (Oxford and New York: Oxford University Press, 2015).

Curtis, Scott, *The Shape of Spectatorship: Art, Science, and Early Cinema in Germany* (New York: Columbia University Press, 2015).

Serials

Balshofer, Fred J. and Arthur C. Miller, *One Reel a Week* (Berkeley: University of California Press, 1967).

Dahlquist, Marian (ed.), *Exporting Perilous Pauline: Pearl White and the Serial Film Craze* (Champaign: University of Illinois Press, 2013).

Sports

Streible, Dan, *Fight Pictures: A History of Boxing and Early Cinema* (Berkeley: University of California Press, 2008).

Stereoscopy

Weiberg, Mark, 'Functional Colors: The Varied Applications of Complementary Hues', *Film History* vol. 29 no. 2 (2017), pp. 9–107.

Strongmen

Farassino, Alberto and Tatti Sanguineti (eds.), *Gli uomini forti* (Milan: Mazzotta, 1983).

Dall'Asta, Monica, *Un cinéma musclé. Le surhomme dans le cinéma italien, 1913–1926* (Crisnée: Éditions Yellow Now, 1992).

Reich, Jacqueline, *The Maciste Films of Italian Silent Cinema* (Bloomington: Indiana University Press, 2015).

Theatre

Gifford, Dennis, *Books and Plays in Films, 1896–1915* (London and New York: Mansell, 1991).

Brewster, Ben and Lea Jacobs, *Theatre to Cinema. Stage Pictorialism and the Early Feature Film* (Oxford and New York: Oxford University Press, 1997).

Mayer, David, *Stagestruck Filmmaker: D.W. Griffith and the American Theatre* (Iowa City: University of Iowa Press, 2009).

War

De Lange, J.H., *The Anglo-Boer War 1899–1902 on Film* (Pretoria: Department of National Education, State Archives and Heraldic Services, 1991).

DeBauche, Leslie Midkiff, *Reel Patriotism: The Movies and World War I* (Madison: University of Wisconsin Press, 1997).

Western

Langman, Larry, *A Guide to Silent Westerns* (New York: Greenwood Press, 1992).

Simmon, Scott, *The Invention of the Western Film: A Cultural History of the Genre's First Half-Century* (Cambridge and New York: Cambridge University Press, 2003).

Smith, Andrew Brodie, *Shooting Cowboys and Indians: Silent Western Films, American Culture, and the Birth of Hollywood* (Boulder: University of Colorado Press, 2003).

Tricks (pp. 153–156)

Méliès, Georges, 'Les Vues cinématographiques', in *Annuaire général et international de la photographie* (Paris: Plon, 1907), pp. 362–92; abridged English translation in Richard Abel, *French Film Theory and Criticism, 1907–1929* (Princeton, NJ: Princeton University Press, 1988), pp. 35–47.

Babin, Gustave, 'Les Coulisses du cinématographe', 'Les Coulisses du cinématographe II', 'Le Théâtre cinématographique', *L'Illustration* (Paris) vol. 66 no. 3396 (28 March 1908), pp. 211–15; no. 3397 (4 April 1908), pp. 238–42; no. 3427 (31 October 1908), pp. 286–7.

Barnouw, Eric, *The Magician and the Cinema* (New York and Oxford: Oxford University Press, 1981).

Malthête, Jacques, 'Le Collage magique chez Edison et Méliès avant 1901', *CinémAction* no. 102 (January–March 2002), pp. 96–109.

Intertitles (pp. 157–161)

Raffaelli, Sergio, *La lingua filmata. Didascalie e dialoghi nel cinema italiano* (Florence: Le Lettere, 1992).

Pitassio, Francesco and Leonardo Quaresima (eds.), *Scrittura e immagine: la didascalia nel cinema muto/ Writing and Image: Titles in Silent Cinema* (Udine: Forum, 1998).

Dupré la Tour, Claire (ed.), *Intertitle and Film. History, Theory, Restoration/Intertitre et film. Historie, théorie, restauration* [Proceedings of the Cinémathèque française International Conference, Paris, March 1999], *Iris* (2000), pp. 31–2.

Dupré la Tour, Claire, *Bibliographie chronologique sur l'intertitre/Chronologische Bibliographie des Zwischentitels.*

'Zwischentitel'. *Medienwissenschaft/Hamburg: Berichte und Papiere*, no. 145, 2012, pp. 3–20.

O'Sullivan, Carol and Jean-François Cornu (eds.), *The Translation of Films, 1900–1950* (Oxford: Oxford University Press/The British Academy, 2019).

Commerce (pp. 163–165)

Thompson, Kristin, *Exporting Entertainment: America in the World Film Market, 1907–1934* (London: BFI Publishing, 1985).

Koszarski, Richard (ed.), 'Exhibition', special issue of *Film History* vol. 6 no. 2 (Summer 1994).

Abel, Richard, *The Red Rooster Scare. Making Cinema American, 1900–1910* (Berkeley: University of California Press, 1999).

Rossell, Deac, 'A Slippery Job: Traveling Exhibitors in Early Cinema', in Simon Popple and Vanessa Toulmin (eds.), *Visual Delights: Essays on the Popular and Projected Image in the 19th Century* (Trowbridge, Wilts.: Flicks Books, 2000), pp. 50–60.

Quinn, Michael, 'Distribution, the Transient Audience, and the Transition to the Feature Film, *Cinema Journal* vol. 40 no. 2 (2001), pp. 35–56.

Alvarez, Max J., 'The Origins of the Film Exchange', *Film History* vol. 17 no. 4 (2005), pp. 431–65.

Lewis, Leslie Anne, 'The Corrick Collection: A Case Study in Asia-Pacific Itinerant Film Exhibition (1901–1914)', *National Film and Sound Archive Journal* vol. 2 no. 2 (2007), pp. 1–12.

Frykholm, Joel, *George Kleine & American Cinema: The Movie Business and Film Culture in the Silent Era* (London: BFI Publishing/Palgrave, 2015).

Lacasse, Germain, '*Dream World*': parcours et discours d'un duo d'exploitants français aux USA, 1899–1910* (Quebec: Germain Lacasse, 2017).

Copyright (pp. 165–167)

Maugras, Émile and Maurice Guégan, *Le Cinématographe devant le droit* (Paris: V. Giard & E. Brière, 1908).

Pouillet, Eugène, Georges Maillard, and Charles Claro, *Traité théorique et pratique de la propriété littéraire et artistique et du droit de représentation* (Paris: Marchal et Billard, 1908, 3rd edition).

Cohn, Georg, *Kinematographenrecht* (Berlin: Decker's Verlag, 1909).

Apollinaire, Guillaume [under the pseudonym Pascal Hédegat], 'Le Cinéma à la Nationale', *L'Intransigeant* (1 March 1910), pp. 1–2.

Potu, Émile, *La Protection internationale des oeuvres cinématographiques d'après la Convention de Berne, revisée à Berlin en 1908* (Paris: Gauthier-Villars, 1912).

May, Bruno, *Das Recht des Kinematographen* (Berlin: Falk, 1912).

Marchais, Jean, *Du cinématographe dans ses rapports avec le droit d'auteur* (Paris: V. Giard et E. Brière, 1912).

Frohlich, Louis D. and Charles Schwartz, *The Law of Motion Pictures, Including the Law of the Theatre* (New York: Baker, Voorhis & Co., 1917).

Tiranty, Umberto, *La cinematografia e la legge* (Milan, Turin, and Rome: Fratelli Bocca, 1921).

Lapie, Pierre-Olivier, 'Un problème de propriété intellectuelle en droit comparé. La determination de l'auteur d'une oeuvre cinématographique', *Bulletin de la Société de Legislation Comparée* vol. 56 (1927), pp. 123–31.

Devillez, Hubert, *L'Oeuvre cinématographique et la propriété artistique* (Paris: Les Presses Universitaires de France, 1928).

Satanowsky, Isidro, *La obra cinematográfica frente al derecho* (Buenos Aires: Ediar, 1948–55, 5 vols.).

Kamina, Pascal, 'History of Film Protection in Europe', in *Film Copyright in the European Union* (Cambridge: Cambridge University Press, 2002; 2nd edition, 2016), pp. 7–50.

Paper Prints (p. 166)

Niver, Kemp R., *Motion Pictures from the Library of Congress Paper Print Collection, 1894–1912* (Berkeley: University of California Press, 1967).

Loughney, Patrick, *A Descriptive Analysis of the Library of Congress Paper Print Collection and Related Copyright Materials* (Ann Arbor: UMI, 1988).

Grimm, Charles 'Buckey', 'A Paper Print Pre-History', *Film History* vol. 11 no. 2 (1999), pp. 204–16.

Censorship (pp. 167–170)

Oberholtzer, Ellis Paxson, *The Morals of the Movie* (Philadelphia, PA: Penn Publishing Company, 1922).

'The Motion Picture in Its Economic and Social Aspects', special issue of *Annals of the American Academy of Political and Social Science* vol. 128 (November 1926).

Hunnings, Neville March, *Film Censors and the Law* (London: Allen and Unwin, 1967).

Masato, Hase, 'The Origins of Censorship: Police and Motion Pictures in the Taishō Period', *Review of Japanese Culture and Society* no. 10 (1988), pp. 14–23.

Olsson, Jan, 'Magnified Discourse: Screenplays and Censorship in Swedish Cinema of the 1910s', in John Fullerton (ed.), *Celebrating 1895: The Centenary of Cinema* (Sydney: John Libbey, 1998), pp. 239–52.

Makino, Mamoru, *The History of Japanese Film Censorship* (Tokyo: Pandora, 2003).

Grieveson, Lee, *Policing Cinema: Movies and Censorship in Early Twentieth-Century America* (Berkeley: University of California Press, 2004).

Yangirov, Rashit M., 'Censorship and Film Distribution in Russia, 1908–1914', in Frank Kessler and Nanna Verhoeff (eds.), *Networks of Entertainment* (Eastleigh, Hants.: John Libbey, 2007), pp. 77–84.

Sikminji-sidae-ui-Youngwha-Gumyeol, 1910–1934 [Film Censorship during the Japanese Colonization, 1910–1934] (Seoul: Korean Film Archive, 2009).

Chapter 8 – SHOW (pp. 171–187)

Meusy, Jean-Jacques, 'Palaces and Holes in the Wall: Conditions of Exhibition in Paris on the Eve of World War I', *Velvet Light Trap* vol. 37 (Spring 1996), pp. 81–98.

Garncarz, Josef, *Maßlose Unterhaltung* (Frankfurt: Stroemfeld Verlag, 2010).

Meusy, Jean-Jacques, *Écrans français de l'entre-deux-guerres. Vol. I: L'Apogée de 'l'art muet'* (Paris: Association Française de Recherche sur l'Histoire du Cinéma, 2017).

Tickets (pp. 172–173)

Seabury, William M., 'Admission Prices', in *The Public and the Motion Picture Industry* (New York: Macmillan, 1926), pp. 111–31.

Programmes (pp. 177–179)

Toulmin, Vanessa, 'The Importance of the Programme in Early Film Presentation', *KINtop* no. 11 (2002), pp. 19–33.

Movement (pp. 179–181; see also pp. 314–316)

Irie, Yoshiro, 'Silent Japanese Films: What Was the Right Speed?', *Journal of Film Preservation* no. 65 (December 2002), pp. 36–41.

Undercranking (pp. 184–185)

Aleinikov, Moisei and Iosif Ermoliev, *Prakticheskoe rukovodstvo po kinematografi* (Moscow: Aleinikov/Ermoliev, Moskovskoe izdatelstvo, 1916).

Model, Ben, '"Undercranking": The Magic behind the Slapstick', *Journal of Film Preservation* no. 93 (October 2015), pp. 21–5.

Ambiance (pp. 186–187)

Townsend, Lewis M. and Lloyd A. Jones, 'The Use of Color for the Embellishment of the Motion Picture Program', *Transactions of the Society of Motion Picture Engineers* vol. 9 no. 21 (August 1925), pp. 38–66.

Chapter 9 – ACOUSTICS (pp. 188–205)

Anderson, Gillian B., *Film Music Bibliography I* (Hollywood, CA: Society for the Preservation of Film Music, 1995).

Eyman, Scott, *The Speed of Sound: Hollywood and the Talkie Revolution, 1926–1930* (New York: Simon & Schuster, 1997).

Abel, Richard, and Rick Altman (eds.), *The Sounds of Early Cinema* (Bloomington: Indiana University Press, 2001).

Altman, Rick, *Silent Film Sound* (New York: Columbia University Press, 2004).

Fuchs, Maria, *Stummfilmmusik: Theorie und Praxis im 'Allgemeinen Handbuch der Film-Musik', 1927* (Marburg; Schüren Verlag [Marburger Schriften zur Medienforschung, Bd. 68], 2016).

Voices (pp. 190–191)

Coissac, Guillaume-Michel, *Manuel pratique du conférencier-projectionniste* (Paris: Maison de la Bonne Presse, 1908).

van Beusekom, Ansje, 'The Rise and Fall of the Lecturer as Entertainer in the Netherlands', *Iris* no. 22 (1996), pp. 131–44.

Gunning, Tom, 'The Scene of Speaking: Two Decades of Discovering the Film Lecturer', *Iris* no. 27 (Spring 1999), pp. 67–79.

Pisano, Giusy and Valérie Pozner (eds.), *Le Muet a la parole. Cinéma et performances à l'aube du XXe siècle* (Paris: Association Française de Recherche sur l'Histoire du Cinéma, 2005).

Boillat, Alain, *Du bonimenteur à la voix-over. Voix-attraction et voix-narration au cinéma* (Lausanne: Éditions Antipodes, 2007).

Benshi (pp. 191–193)

Komatsu, Hiroshi and Frances Loden, 'Mastering the Mute Image: The Role of the Benshi in Japanese Cinema', *Iris* no. 22 (1997), pp. 33–52.

Friends of Silent Films Association/Matsuda Film Productions, *The Benshi. Japanese Silent Film Narrators* (Tokyo: Urban Connections, 2001).

Noises (pp. 193–195)

Bottomore, Stephen, 'An International Survey of Sound Effects in Early Cinema', *Film History* vol. 11 no. 4 (1999), pp. 485–98.

Automata (pp. 195–196)

Bowers, Q. David, *Encyclopedia of Automatic Musical Instruments* (Vestal, NY: Vestal Press, 1972).

Das Mechanische Musikinstrument enhält Die Drehorgel, special issue on mechanical instruments for film theatres, vol. 11 no. 41 (April 1987).

Scores (pp. 196–199)

Ahern, Eugene A., *What and How to Play for Pictures* (Twinfalls, ID: Newsprint, 1913).

Zamecnik, John S. (ed.), *Sam Fox Moving Picture Music* (Cleveland, OH: Sam Fox, 1913 [vols. 1 and 2]; 1914 [vol. 3]).

Becce, Giuseppe, *Kinobibliothek* (Berlin: Schlesingersche Buch- und Musikhandlung Robert Lienau, 1919 ff.).

Lang, Edith and George West, *Musical Accompaniment of Moving Pictures* (Boston, MA: Boston Music, 1920; reprint, New York: Arno Press, 1970).

Benyon, George W., *Musical Presentation of Motion Pictures* (New York: G. Schirmer, 1921).

Buckley, P. Kevin, *The Orchestral and Cinema Organist* (London: Hawkes, 1923).

Rapée, Erno, *Motion Picture Moods for Pianists and Organists: A Rapid-Reference Collection of Selected Pieces* (New York: G. Schirmer, 1924; reprint, New York: Arno Press, 1970).

Rapée, Erno, *Encyclopedia of Music for Pictures* (New York: Belwin, 1925; reprint, New York: Arno Press, 1970).

Erdmann, Hans and Giuseppe Becce, *Allgemeines Handbuch der Film-Musik I & II* (Berlin and Leipzig: Schlesingersche Buch- und Musikhandlung Robert Lienau, 1927).

Hofmann, Charles, *Sounds for Silents* (New York: Drama Book Specialists, 1970).

Berg, Charles M., *An Investigation of the Motives for and Realization of Music to Accompany the American Silent Film, 1896–1927* (New York: Arno Press, 1976).

Anderson, Gillian B. (ed.), *Music for Silent Films, 1894–1929. A Guide* (Washington, DC: Library of Congress, 1988).

Recordings (pp. 200–205)

Olsson, Jan, *Från filmjud till ljudfilm* (Stockholm: Proprius förlag, 1986) [including an audiotape recording of seventeen phonograph discs for silent films in the period 1903 to 1914].

Barnier, Martin, 'Le Cinéphone et l'Idéal-Sonore, deux appareils sonores Gaumont des années 1920–1930', *1895* no. 24 (June 1998), pp. 37–53.

'Global Experiments in Early Synchronous Sound', special Domitor issue of *Film History* vol. 11 no. 4 (1999).

O'Brien, Charles, *Technology and Film Style in France and the United States* (Bloomington: Indiana University Press, 2005).

O'Brien, Charles, 'Sound-on-disc Cinema and Electrification prior to WWI: Britain, France, Germany, and the United States', in Richard Abel, Giorgio Bertellini and Rob King (eds.), *Early Cinema and the 'National'* (Eastleigh, Hants.: John Libbey, 2008), pp. 40–9.

Loiperdinger, Martin, 'German Tonbilder of the 1900s', in Klaus Kreimeier and Annemone Ligensa (eds.), *Film 1900: Technology, Perception, Culture* (New Barnet, Herts.: John Libbey, 2009), pp. 187–200.

Chapter 10 – COLLECTIONS (pp. 206–222)

National Film Archive Catalogue. Part I, Silent News Films, 1895–1933 (London: British Film Institute, 1965); *Part II, Silent Non-Fiction Films, 1895–1934* (1960); *Part III, Silent Fiction Films, 1895–1930* (1966).

National Film Archive Catalogue, Volume 1: Non-Fiction Films (London: British Film Institute, 1980).

Horwitz, Rita and Harriet Harrison (eds.), *The George Kleine Collection of Early Motion Pictures in the Library of Congress: A Catalog* (Washington, DC: Library of Congress, 1980).

Magliozzi, Ronald S. (ed.), *Treasures from the Film Archives: A Catalog of Short Silent Fiction Films Held by FIAF Archives* (Metuchen, NJ, and London: Scarecrow Press, 1988).

Restaurations et tirages de la Cinémathèque française, vols. 1–4 (Paris: La Cinémathèque française, 1986–9).

Fons de nitrats de la Filmoteca. Volum I – Films de ficció (Barcelona: Ambit Serveis Editorials, 2001).

Selected Internet Databases of Silent Film Holdings

International Federation of Film Archives (FIAF): Treasures from the Film Archives Database
www.fiafnet.org

France

Archives françaises du film:
www.cnc-aff.fr

Gaumont Pathé Archives:
www.gaumontpathearchives.com

Germany

Filmportal.de:
http://www.filmportal.de/movies

Great Britain

British Film Institute National Archive:
http://collections-search.bfi.org.uk/web

National Library of Scotland – Moving Image Archive:
https://movingimage.nls.uk/search

Sweden

Svenska Filminstitutet – Svensk Filmdatabas:
www.svenskfilmdatabas.se

United States

Academy Film Archive:
http://www.oscars.org/film-archive/collections

Berkeley Art Museum/Pacific Film Archive:
http://oskicat.berkeley.edu/

George Eastman Museum:
http://collections.eastman.org

Library of Congress:
https://www.loc.gov/

Museum of Modern Art:
https://www.moma.org/collection/

UCLA Film and Television Archive:
   http://cinema.library.ucla.edu/vwebv/searchBasic

Destruction (pp. 208–209)

Hollis, A.P., 'The Film Prayer', instructional leaflet (Fargo,
   ND: Visual Instruction Service of the State, 1920),
   reproduced in Paolo Cherchi Usai, *Silent Cinema. An
   Introduction* (London: BFI Publishing, 2000), p. 206.

Spiridovskii, Nikolai, *Gibel' filmy. Porcha filmy i mery
   preduprezdeniia* (Moscow and Leningrad: Kinopechat,
   1927).

Pierce, David, 'The Legion of the Condemned: Why
   American Silent Films Perished', *Film History* vol. 9 no.
   1 (1997), pp. 5–22.

Smither, Roger (ed.), *This Film Is Dangerous: An
   Anthology in Celebration of Nitrate Film* (Brussels:
   FIAF, 2000).

Hall, Phil, *In Search of Lost Films* (Albany, NY: BearManor
   Media, 2016).

Decay (pp. 209–211)

Films

Lyrical Nitrate (Peter Delpeut, Netherlands 2002, 50′)

Decasia (Bill Morrison, US 2002, 70′)

Disposal (pp. 211–215)

Gordon, Paul L. (ed.), *The Book of Film Care* (Rochester,
   NY: Eastman Kodak Company, 1983).

Rescue (pp. 215–216)

Dickson, William Kennedy Laurie, *History of the
   Kinetograph, Kinetoscope and Kinetophonograph*
   (New York: Albert Bunn, 1895; reprint, New York and
   London: Museum of Modern Art/Thames & Hudson,
   2001).

Matuszewski, Bolesław, *Une Nouvelle source de l'histoire,
   création d'un dépôt de cinématographie historique* and
   *La Photographie animée, ce qu'elle est, ce qu'elle doit
   être* (Paris: Noizette, 1898), reprinted in Zbigniew

Czeczot-Gawrak (ed.), *Bolesław Matuszewski i jego
   pionierska mysl filmowa* (Warsaw: Filmoteka Polska,
   1980), translated as 'A New Source of History', *Film
   History* vol. 7 no. 3 (Autumn 1995), pp. 322–24; *A
   New Source of History/Animated Photography. What It
   Is, What It Should Be* (Warsaw: Filmoteka Narodowa,
   1999).

Matuszewski, Bolesław, *Écrits cinématographiques* (Paris:
   Association française de recherché sur l'histoire du
   cinéma/Cinémathèque française, 2006).

Pierce, David, *The Survival of American Silent Films: 1912–
   1929* (Washington, DC: Library of Congress, 2013).

James Card

Reynolds, Herbert, '"What Can You Do for Us, Barney?"
   Four Decades of Film Collecting: An Interview With
   James Card', *Image* vol. 20 no. 2 (June 1977), pp.
   13–31.

Card, James, *Seductive Cinema. The Art of Silent Film*
   (New York: Knopf, 1994).

Will Day

Day, Wilfred E.L., *The Will Day Historical Collection of
   Cinematograph & Moving Picture Equipment* (London:
   Harris & Gillow, 1930).

Aubert, Michelle, Laurent Mannoni, and David
   Robinson (eds.), *The Will Day Historical Collection of
   Cinematograph & Moving Picture Equipment* (special
   issue of *1895*, October 1997).

Jean Desmet

Blom, Ivo, *Jean Desmet and the Early Dutch Film Trade*
   (Amsterdam: Amsterdam University Press, 2003).

Josef Joye

Cosandey, Roland, *Welcome Home, Joye! Film um 1910:
   aus der Sammlung Joseph Joye* (Basle: Stroemfeld
   Verlag, 1993 [*KINtop* Schriften 1]).

Yumibe, Joshua, 'From Switzerland to Italy and All
   around the World: The Josef Joye and Davide Turconi
   Collections', in Richard Abel, Giorgio Bertellini, and
   Rob King (eds.), *Early Cinema and the 'National'*
   (Bloomington and New Barnet, Herts.: Indiana
   University Press/John Libbey, 2008), pp. 321–31.

Kawakita Kashiko

Kawakita, Kashiko, *Kawakita Kashiko – Eiga hitosuji ni* (Tokyo: Nihon Tosho Center, 1997).

Komiya Tomijiro

The National Film Center [Masatoshi Ohba, Yoriaki Sazaki, Noriyuki Suzuki (eds.)], *Cinema: Lost and Found – From the Collection of Komiya Tomijiro* (Tokyo: National Museum of Modern Art, 1991).

Paramesh Krishnan (P.K.) Nair

Nair, P.K., *Yesterday's Films for Tomorrow* (Mumbai: Film Heritage Foundation, 2017).

Films

Celluloid Man (Shivendra Singh Dungarpur, Dungarpur Films, India 2012, 164′).

Shelters (pp. 216–218)

Scaife Gott, Benjamin, *The Film in National Life* (London: Allen and Unwin, 1932).

Institutions (pp. 218–221)

Borde, Raymond, *Les Cinémathèques* (Paris: L'Âge d'Homme, 1983).

Francis, David, 'Définition et fonction des archives cinématographiques', in Emmanuelle Toulet (ed.), *CinéMémoire* (Paris: Centre National de la Cinématographie/Ministère de la Culture et de la Communication, 1991), pp. 29–33.

Slide, Anthony, *Nitrate Won't Wait. A History of Film Preservation in the United States* (Jefferson, NC, and London: McFarland, 1992).

Houston, Penelope, *Keepers of the Frame: The Film Archives* (London: BFI Publishing, 1994).

Borde, Raymond and Freddy Buache, *La Crise des cinémathèques ... et du monde* (Lausanne: L'Âge d'Homme, 1997).

Bottomore, Stephen, 'Film Museums: A Bibliography', *Film History* vol. 18 no. 3 (2006), pp. 327–49.

Griffiths, Alison, *Shivers Down Your Spine: Cinema, Museums, and the Immersive View* (New York: Columbia University Press, 2008).

Le Roy, Éric, *Cinémathèques et archives du film* (Paris: Armand Colin, 2013).

Dupin, Christophe, 'First Tango in Paris: The Origins of FIAF, 1936–1938', *Journal of Film Preservation* no. 88 (April 2013), pp. 43–58.

Binder, Michael, *A Light Affliction: A History of Film Preservation and Restoration* (s.l.: Lulu Press, 2015).

Ishihara, Kae, *History of Film Archiving in Japan* (Tokyo: Bigaku Shuppan, 2018; Museum Library Archives Series, no. 2).

Trnka, Jan, *The Czech Film Archive 1943–1993. Institutional Development and Problems of Practice* (Prague: National Film Archive, 2018).

Iris Barry

Barry, Iris, *Let's Go to the Movies* (New York and London: Payson & Clarke/Chatto & Windus, 1926; facsimile edition, New York: Arno Press/The New York Times, 1972).

Abbott, John E. and Iris Barry, 'An Outline of a Project for Founding the Film Library of the Museum of Modern Art', 17 April 1935, reproduced in Film History vol. 7 no. 3 (Autumn 1995), p. 325.

Barry, Iris, 'Why Wait for Posterity?' *Hollywood Quarterly* vol. 1 no. 2 (January 1946), pp. 131–7.

Wasson, Haidee, *Museum Movies: The Museum of Modern Art and the Birth of Art Cinema* (Berkeley and Los Angeles: University of California Press, 2005).

Sitton, Robert, *Lady in the Dark: Iris Barry and the Art of Film* (New York: Columbia University Press, 2014).

Frank Hensel

Aurich, Rolf, 'Cinéaste, Collector, National Socialist: Frank Hensel and the Reichsfilmarchiv', *Journal of Film Preservation* no. 64 (April 2002), pp. 16–21.

Henri Langlois

Langlois, Henri and Maria Adriana Prolo, *Le Dragon et l'alouette: correspondance 1948–1979*, edited by Sergio Toffetti (Turin: Museo Nazionale del Cinema, 1992).

Myrent, Glenn and Georges P. Langlois, *Henri Langlois, premier citoyen du cinéma* (Paris: Denoël, 1986); English translation, *Henri Langlois, First Citizen of Cinema* (New York: Twayne, 1995).

Roud, Richard, *A Passion for Films* (Baltimore, MD: Johns Hopkins University Press, 1999).

Films

Citizen Langlois (Edgardo Cozarinsky, Cinémathèque française/Canal+/Institut National de l'Audiovisuel (INA), France 1994, 69′).

Jacques Ledoux

Head, Anne (ed.), *A True Love for Cinema* (The Hague: Universitaire Pers Rotterdam, 1988).

Nasta, Dominique (ed.), 'Jacques Ledoux, L'éclaireur', special issue of *Revue belge du cinéma* no. 40 (November 1995).

Ernest Lindgren

Lindgren, Ernest, 'The Work of the National Film Library', *Journal of the British Kinematograph Society* vol. 8 no. 1 (January–March 1945), pp. 13–22.

Lindgren, Ernest, 'The Importance of Film Archives', *Penguin Film Review* no. 5 (1948), pp. 47–52.

Butler, Ivan, '*To Encourage the Art of the Film*': *The Story of the British Film Institute* (London: Robert Hale, 1971).

Dupin, Christophe, 'The Origins and Early Development of the National Film Library: 1929–1936', *Journal of Media Practice* vol. 7 no. 3 (2007), pp. 199–217.

Cinémathèque française

Olmeta, Patrick, *La Cinémathèque française de 1936 à nos jours* (Paris: CNRS, 2000).

Barbin, Pierre, 'Contribution à une histoire de la Cinémathèque française', *Commentaire* vol. 101 (Spring 2003), pp. 155–66.

Mannoni, Laurent, *Histoire de la Cinémathèque française* (Paris: Gallimard, 2006).

Cineteca Italiana

Casetti, Francesco (ed.), *La Cineteca Italiana. Una storia milanese* (Milan: Il Castoro, 2005).

Collectors (pp. 221–222)

Kula, Sam, *Appraising Moving Images: Assessing the Archival and Monetary Value of Film and Video Records* (Lanham, MD, and Oxford: Scarecrow Press, 2003).

Bartok, Dennis and Jeff Joseph, *A Thousand Cuts: The Bizarre Underground World of Collectors and Dealers Who Saved the Movies* (Jackson: University Press of Mississippi, 2016).

Internet Resources

Nitrateville:

https://www.nitrateville.com

Films

Saving Brinton (Tommy Haines and Andrew Sherburne, Bocce Balls Films/Northland Films, US 2017, 90′).

Chapter 11 – Evidence (pp. 223–240)

Internet Resources

The Bioscope:

http://thebioscope.net (2007–12)

Le grimh:

www.grimh.org

Internet Archive:

www.archive.org

Media History Digital Library:

http://mediahistoryproject.org

Stories (pp. 225–226)

Bergsten, Bebe (ed.), *Biograph Bulletins, 1896–1908* (Los Angeles: Locare Research Group, 1971).

Bowser, Eileen (ed.), *Biograph Bulletins, 1908–1912* (New York: Octagon Books, n.d. [1973]).

Herbert, Stephen, Colin Harding, Simon Popple (eds.), *Victorian Film Catalogues. A Facsimile Collection* (London: The Projection Box, 1996).

Jenkins, Reese V. (ed.), *The Thomas A. Edison Papers: A Guide to Motion Picture Catalogues by American Producers and Distributors, 1894–1908* (Frederick, MD: University Publications of America, 1985 [six reels of 35mm microfilm]).

Wlaschin, Ken and Stephen Bottomore, 'Moving Picture Fiction of the Silent Era, 1985–1928', *Film History* vol. 20 no. 2 (2008), pp. 217–60.

Periodicals (pp. 226–228)

Internet Resources
Domitor Film Journals Project:
  https://domitor.org/journals

Yearbooks
The Bioscope Annual and Diary for 1909 (London: The Bioscope Press, 1909).

The Bioscope Annual and Trades Directory (London: Ganes, 1910–15).

Kinematograph Year Book (London: Kinematograph Publications, 1914–71).

Motion Picture Studio Directory and Trade Annual (New York and Chicago: Motion Picture News, 1915–21).

Annuaire général de la cinématographie française et étrangère (Paris: Éditions de Ciné-Journal, 1917–18).

The Film Daily Yearbook of Motion Pictures (New York: Wid's Film and Film Folk): *Wid's Yearbook* (1918–21); *Film Year Book* (1922–6); *Film Daily* (1927); *Film Daily Yearbook* (1928–9).

Le Tout-cinéma. Annuaire général illustré du monde cinématographique (Paris: Filma, 1921–35).

Pascal, Jean (ed.), *Annuaire général de la cinématographie et des industries qui s'y rattachent* (Paris: Cinémagazine/Publications Jean Pascal, 1922–30).

Wolffsohn, Karl (ed.), *Jahrbuch der Filmindustrie* (Berlin: Verlag der 'Lichtbildbühne', 1923–33).

Selected Periodicals of the Silent Film Era

Argentina
Excelsior (1914–32)
La Película (1916–48)
Imparcial Film (1918–48)
Cine Universal (1919–21)
Revista del Exhibidor (1926–66)

Australia
Australian Variety (1913–16), later renamed *Australian Variety and Show World* (1916–20), *Everyone's Variety: with which is incorporated Australian Variety and Show World* (1920–7), *Everyone's* (1927), and *Everyone's: The Motion Picture Authority* (1927?–37)
The Film Weekly (1926–73)
The Regent Magazine: A Weekly Journal Dedicated to the Art of Moving Pictures (1928–35)

Austro-Hungarian Empire and Austria
Das Kino-Journal (1908–38)
Kinematographische Rundschau (1909–16)
Kinematografski vjesnik (1916) [Croatia]
Der Kinobesitzer (1917–19)
Paimann's Filmlisten (1916–65)
Neue Kino-Rundschau (1917–21)
Der Filmbote (1918–26)
Die Kinowoche (1919–22)
Die Filmwelt (1919–25)
Österreichische Film-Zeitung (1927–38)

Belgium
La Cinématographie et les industries connexes, supplement mensuel de la Comète belge (1907–1911), later renamed *La Comète Cinéma* (1911–14)
La Revue belge du cinéma (1911–14; 1919–40)
Le Cinéma belge (1918–31)
Cinema en Toneelwereld (1919–20), later renamed *Weekblad Cinema* (1920–40)
Ciné Revue (1921–5)
Le Cinéma international (1921–35)
Bulletin de la fédération belge cinématographique (1923–32)
Film-revue (1923–36)
Bulletin de l'Association cinématographique de Belgique (1924–32)

Bosnia-Herzegovina *see* Kingdom of Serbs, Croats, and Slovenes

Brazil
A Scena Muda (1921–55)
Cinearte (1926–42)
O Fan (1928–30)

Bulgaria

Nasheto kino Нашето кино (1924–36)

Kino Кино (1927–36)

Kinopregled/Kinematographicheski pregled Кинопреглед/ Кинематографически преглед (1920–3)

Kinozvezda – Kinostar Кинозвезда (1920–9)

Kinovestnik Киновестник (1924–5), merged with *Kinozvezda* in 1925

Kinoek – Kinopeal Киноек (1925–7)

Canada

La Revue du Ouimetoscope (1906–9)

Le Panorama (1919–21)

The Canadian Moving Picture Digest (1919–57)

Le Film (1921–62)

Cinéma (1921–4)

Le Studio (1924)

Le Bon Cinéma (1927–9)

L'Écran (1927)

La Revue de Manon (1925–30)

Chile

Cinema (1913–14)

Chile Cinematográfico (1915–?)

Cine Gaceta (1915–?)

La semana cinematográfica (1918–20)

Ecran (1930–69)

China

Yingxi zazhi 影戲雜誌 (1921–2)

Yinxing 银星 (1926–8)

Yingxi huabao 影戏画报 (1927–8)

Dianying yuebao 電影月報 [Cinema Monthly] (1928–9)

Colombia

Cinematógrafo (1908–?)

El Olympia (1913–?)

Croatia see Kingdom of Serbs, Croats, and Slovenes

Cuba

Cuba cinematográfica (1912–14)

Czech countries in Austria-Hungary (to October 1918) and Czechoslovakia (from 28 October 1918)

Český kinematograf (1911–12)

Kinematografický věstník (1914–19)

Zprávy (1917–20), later renamed *Zpravodaj. Spolku českých majitelů kinematografů* (1921–2) and *Zpravodaj. Zemského svazu kinematografů v Čechách* (1922–30)

Československý film (1918–21)

Filmschau (1919–20), later renamed *Internationale Filmschau* (1920–34)

Die Lichtspielbühne (1920–33)

Český filmový zpravodaj (1921–42)

Film (1921–38)

Český filmový svět (1922–8)

Denmark

Teatret (1901–31)

Nordisk Biograf Tidende (1909–11)

Masken (1910–24)

Biografteaterbladet (1911–13)

Filmen (1912–19), later renamed *Kinobladet* (1919–26), then *Biograf-Bladet* (1927–73)

Palads-Teatrets Filmnyheder (1919–28)

Finland

Bio (1910)

Biograafi (1915); Swedish edition: *Biograftidning*, both merged into *Bio* (1915–16)

Filmiaitta (1921–32); also in Swedish, as *Filmrevyn* (1921–7)

Elokuva (1927–32)

France

Ciné-Journal (1908–37)

Ciné pour tous (1919–23)

Cinéa (1921–3)

Cinéa-Ciné pour tous (1923–30)

Cinéa-Ciné pour tous réunis (1930–2)

Le Cinéopse (1919–67)

Le Courrier cinématographique (1911–14; 1917–36)

Phono-ciné-gazette (1905–9)

Germany

Erste Internationale Filmzeitung (1907–20)

Bild und Film (1912–15?)

Der Film (1916–43)

Filmkurier (1919–44)

Der Kinematograph (1907–35)

Lichtbild-Bühne (1908–39)

Great Britain

The Bioscope (1908–32)

The Era (1838–1939)

The Optical Magic Lantern Journal (1889), later renamed *The Optical Lantern and Cinematograph Journal* (1904), *The Kinematograph and Lantern Weekly* (1907), and *The Kinematograph Weekly* (1919–59)

The Cinema: News and Property Gazette (1912–57)

Pictures and the Picturegoer (1914–20), later renamed *Picturegoer* (1921–60)

Greece

Kinematographos Κινηματογράφος (1923–4?)

Kinematographike bibliotheke Κινηματογραφική βιβλιοθήκη (1923–4?)

Kinematographikos aster Κινηματογραφικός αστήρ (1924–70)

Hungarian countries in Austria-Hungary (to 1918) and Hungary (from 1918)

Mozgófénykép híradó (1908–20)

Mozivilág (1912–?)

A mozgószínház (1913–?)

Mozi (1913–?)

Mozifutár (1918–?)

Mozihét (1918–22)

Az új film (1919–?)

Filmjáték (1925–?)

Magyar Filmkurir (1927–?)

Filmkultúra (1928–38)

India

Bijoli (1920–?; in Bengali)

Mojmajah/*Mouji* [*Moj*] *Majah* (1924–50?; in Gujarati)

Photoplay (1926–?; in English)

Movie Mirror (1927–?; in English)

Kinema/*Cinema* (1927–40?; in English)

Shabistan (1929–?; in Urdu)

Chitrapat (1929–?; in Gujarati)

Dipali (1929–55; in Bengali and English)

Italy

Rivista fono-cinematografica (1907–9), later renamed *La cine-fono e la rivista fono-cinematografica* (1909–28)

La cinematografia italiana (1908–26)

Lux (1908–11?)

La vita cinematografica (1910–33)

Film (1914–28)

La rivista cinematografica (1920–43)

L' eco del cinema (1923–43)

Il corriere cinematografico (1924–40)

Turconi, Davide and Camillo Bassotto, *Il cinema nelle riviste italiane dalle origini ad oggi* (Venice: Edizioni Mostracinema, n.d. [1972]); revised and updated edition: Riccardo Redi (ed.), *Cinema scritto. Il catalogo delle riviste italiane del cinema, 1907–1944* (Rome: Associazione Italiana per le Ricerche di Storia del Cinema, 1992).

Japan

Katsudo shashin kai 活動写真界 (1909–11)

Film Record フィルム•レコード (1913)

Kinema Record キネマ•レコード (1913–17)

Kinema junpo キネマ旬報 (1919–present)

Katsudo shashin zasshi 活動寫眞雑誌 (1915–20?)

Katsudo no sekai 活動之世界 (1916–23)

Katsudo gaho 活動畫報 (1917–23)

Katsudo hyoron 活動評論 (1918–19)

Katsudo kurabu 活動倶楽部 (1918–27)

Reprint and Facsimile Editions

Mamoru, Makino (ed.), *Nihon eiga shoki shiryo shusei* [A Collection of Research Material from the Early Days of Japanese Film]. Facsimile editions: *Katsudo shashin zasshi*, June–December 1915 [vols. 1–2]; *Katsudo no sekai*, January–December 1916 [vols. 3–5]; *Katsudo gaho*, January–December 1917 [vols. 6–9]; *Katsudo kurabu* (originally *Katsudo hyoron*), December 1918–December 1920 [vols. 10–14] (Tokyo: Sanichi shobo, 1990–1).

Iwamoto, Kenji and Makino Mamoru (eds.), *Fukkokuban: Kinema junpo* (Tokyo: Yushodo, 1994–6, 19 vols.).

Kingdom of Serbs, Croats, and Slovenes/ Kingdom of Yugoslavia see also Austro-Hungarian Empire

Kinofon (1921–3) [Croatia]

Comedia – Časopis za pozorište, muziku i film (1923–7) [Serbia]

Filmska revija (1925–6) [Bosnia-Herzegovina]

Filmske novine (1926–7) [Serbia]

Filmska revija, stručni filmski list (1926–33) [Croatia]

Kino i film (1926?–33?) [Croatia]

Narodna filmska umjetnost (1926?–33?) [Croatia]

Filmska revija (1927–41) [Croatia]

Kulisa (1927–35; 1937–9) [Croatia]

Mexico

Cine-Mundial (1920–?)

Magazine Fílmico (1926–9)

Mundo Cinematográfico (1930–4)

Netherlands

De Bioscoop-Courant (1912–19)

De Kinematograaf (1913–19), later renamed *De Film* (1919–20)

Tooneel en Bioscoop (1915–25?)

De Lichtstraal (1916–21)

De Film-Wereld (1918–20)

Kunst en Amusement (1920–7?)

(Het Weekblad) Cinema en Theater (1921–44)

Nieuw Weekblad voor de Cinematografie (1922–64)

Het Lichtbeeld (1923–33)

New Zealand

The New Zealand Theatre & Motion Picture (1920–30)

Norway

Norsk Kinematograf-Tidende (1915–17), later renamed *Film og Kino* (1917–22)

Helt og skurk (1918–20)

Filmen og vi (1919–30)

Poland

Kino-Teatr i Sport (1914–?)

Kino (1919–20)

Kinematograf Polski (1919–21)

Przegląd Teatralny i Kinematograficzny (1921–2)

Ekran i Scena (1923–32)

Tygodnik Filmowy i Teatralny (1925–6)

Comoedia (1926–7)

Kino-Teatr (1926–8)

Kino dla Wszystkich (1926–34)

Portugal

Cine-revista (1917–24)

Porto cinematográfico (1919–24)

Jornal dos cinemas (1923)

Invicta cine: semanário ilustrado de cinematografia (1923–33)

Cine: revista mensal de arte cinematográfica (1928–31)

Cinéfilo (1928–39)

Imagem: tribuna livre do cinema (1928)

Romania

Revista pentru fotografie, stereoscopie, proiecțiuni cine-matografice și foto (1904)

Viața cinematografică în România, Bulgaria, Serbia, Grecia, Turcia și Egipt (1914)

Filmul (1923–5)

Cinema (1924–48)

Clipa cinematografică (1925–8)

Viața cinematografică (1927)

Filmul meu (1927–30)

Russia and Soviet Union

Sine-fono Сине-фоно (1907–18)

Kine-zhurnal Кине-журнал (1910–17)

Vestnik kinematografii Вестник кинематографии (1910–17)

Kinoteatr i zhizn' Кино-театр и жизнь (1913)

Pegas Пегас (1915–17)

Proektor Проэктор (1915–18)

Ekran kino-gazety Экран кино-газеты (1925, as a supplement to *Kino* [Moscow]), renamed *Sovetskii ekran* Советский экран (1925–9), *Kino i zhizn'* Кино и жизнь (1929–30), *Proletarskoe kino* Пролетарское кино (1931–2), *Sovetskoe kino* Советское кино (1933–5), and *Iskusstvo kino* Искусство кино (1936–present)

Serbia *see* Kingdom of Serbs, Croats, and Slovenes

Slovenia *see* Kingdom of Serbs, Croats, and Slovenes

Spain

Artistico-Cinematografico (1907–8)

Arte y Cinematografía (1910–36)

El cine (1911–29; 1931–2)

El mundo cinematográfico (1915–27)

Cine-Mundial (1916–48; Spanish edition of *The Moving Picture World*)

Cinema [Madrid] (1918–26?)

Tras la Pantalla (1920–2)

Cinema-Variedades (1920–7)

Popular Film (1926–36)

Sweden

Filmbladet (1915–25)

Biografen (1913–15)

Filmen (1918–20)

Filmjournalen (1919–53)

Filmnyheter (1920–9)

Switzerland

Kinema (1913–19)

Schweizer Cinéma Suisse (1919–37)

Revue suisse du cinéma (1919–29)

Ciné. Revue d'art cinématographique (1926–9)

Close Up (1927–33)

United States

The New York Clipper (1853–1923)

The New York Dramatic Mirror (1879–1922)

Views and Film Index (1906–8), later renamed *The Film Index* (1908–11)

Show World (1908–9)

Nickelodeon (1909–11), later renamed *Motography* (1911–18), *Exhibitors' Herald and Motography* (1918–19), and *Exhibitors' Herald* (1919–27)

Moving Picture News (1908–13)

The Moving Picture World (1907–27)

Motion Picture News (1908–30)

D'Agostino, Annette, *An Index to Short and Feature Film Reviews in the* Moving Picture World: *The Early Years 1907–1915* (Westport, CT, and London: Greenwood Publishing Group, 1995).

D'Agostino, Annette, *Filmmakers in the* Moving Picture World: *An Index of Articles, 1907–1927* (Jefferson, NC: McFarland, 1997).

Variety Film Reviews: Vol. 1: 1907–1920; Vol. 2, 1921–1925; Vol. 3: 1926–1929; Vol. 16: Index to Titles (New York: Garland Press, 1983).

The New York Times Film Reviews, 1913–1968 (New York: The New York Times/Arno Press, 1970).

Uruguay

Semanal Film (1920–2)

Cinema y Teatros (1920–1)

Cine Revista (1922–3)

Montevideo Film (1923)

Uruguay Cinema (1927–8)

Yugoslavia *see* Kingdom of Serbs, Croats, and Slovenes

Comic Strips and Caricatures (p. 228)

Bottomore, Stephen, *I Want to See This Annie Mattygraph. A Cartoon History of the Coming of the Movies* (Pordenone: Le Giornate del Cinema Muto, 1995).

Commentaries (pp. 229–230)

Urban, Charles, *The Cinematograph in Science, Education, and Matters of State* (London: Charles Urban Trading Company, 1907).

Grau, Robert, *The Theatre of Science. A Volume of Progress and Achievement in the Motion Picture Industry* [or Motion Picture Art, as it appears on the cover] (New York, London, and Paris: Broadway Publishing Company, 1914; reprint, New York: B. Blom, 1969).

Lindsay, Vachel, *The Art of the Moving Picture* (New York: Macmillan, 1915; revised edition, 1922; reprint, New York: Modern Library, 2000).

Dench, Ernest A., *Making the Movies* (New York: Macmillan, 1915).

The Cinema. Its Present Position and Future Possibilities (London: Williams and Norgate, 1917).

Dench, Ernest A., *Motion Picture Education* (Cincinnati, OH: The Standard Publishing Company, 1917).

Wagner, Rob [pseud. of Robert Leicester], *Film Folk. 'Close-Ups' of the Men, Women and Children Who Make the 'Movies'* (New York: The Century Company, 1918).

Young, Donald, *Motion Pictures. A Study in Social Legislation* (Philadelphia, PA: Westbrook Publishing Company, 1922).

Van Zile, Edward Sims, *That Marvel – The Movie. A Glance at Its Reckless Past, Its Promising Present, and Its Significant Future* (New York and London: G.P. Putnam's Sons/The Knickerbocker Press, 1923).

Bloem, Walter S. [Julius], *The Soul of the Moving Picture* (New York: E.P. Dutton, 1924).

Reboul, Eugène, *Le Cinéma scolaire et éducateur* (Paris: Les Presses Universitaires de France, 1926).

Delpeuch, André, *Le Cinéma* (Paris: Librairie Octave Doin, 1927).

Fletcher, John Gould, *The Crisis of the Film* (Seattle: University of Washington Book Store, 1929).

Memoirs (p. 230)

Arvidson, Linda, *When the Movies Were Young* (New York: E.P. Dutton, 1925).

Ghione, Emilio, 'Memorie e confessioni', *Cinemalia*, March–December 1928; reprinted in Ghione, *Scritti sul cinematografo* (Ancona: Cattedrale, 2011).

Mesguich, Félix, *Tours de manivelle. Souvenirs d'un chasseur d'images* (Paris: Grasset, 1933).

Messter, Oskar, *Mein Weg mit dem Film* (Berlin and Schöneberg: M. Hesse, 1936).

Méliès, Georges, *La Vie et l'Œuvre d'un des plus anciens pionniers de la Cinématographie Mondiale, Georges Méliès, créateur du spectacle Cinématographiquees mémoires* [ms, 1936]; facsimile reproduction in the first 500 copies of Maurice Bessy and Giuseppe Maria Lo Duca, *Georges Méliès, mage* (Paris: Prisma, 1945).

Gardin, Vladimir, *Vospominaniia*. Vol. 1 (Moscow: Goskinoizdat, 1949); Vol. 2 (Moscow: Goskinoizdat, 1952).

Hepworth, Cecil M., *Came the Dawn. Memoirs of a Film Pioneer* (London: Phoenix House, 1951).

Vidor, King, *A Tree Is a Tree* (New York: Harcourt, Brace, 1952).

Fescourt, Henri, *La Foi et les montagnes, ou le 7ème art au passé* (Paris: Publications Photo-Cinéma Paul Montel, 1959).

Wagenknecht, Edward, *The Movies in the Age of Innocence* (Norman: University of Oklahoma Press, 1962).

Balshofer, Fred and Arthur C. Miller, *One Reel a Week* (Berkeley and Los Angeles: University of California Press, 1967).

Gish, Lillian, *The Movies, Mr. Griffith and Me* (Englewood Cliffs, NJ: Associated University Presses, 1969).

Brown, Karl, *Adventures With D.W. Griffith* (New York: Farrar, Straus & Giroux, 1973).

Guy, Alice, *Autobiographie d'une pionnière du cinéma* (Paris: Denoël/Gonthier, 1976).

Iwasaki, Akira, *Eiga ga wakakatta toki: Meiji, Taisho, Showa no kioku* [When Film Was Young: My Memories of Meiji, Taisho, and Showa] (Tokyo: Heibonsha, 1980).

Iwamoto, Kenji and Tomonori Saiki (eds.), *Kikigaki: kinema no seishun* [Interviews: Japanese Cinema in Its Youth] (Tokyo: Libroport, 1988), pp. 77–100.

Pathé, Charles, *Écrits autobiographiques* (Paris: l'Harmattan, 2006).

Ephemera (p. 230–233)

Songs (p. 231)

Wlaschin, Ken, *The Silent Cinema in Song, 1896–1929. An Illustrated History and Catalog of Songs Inspired by the Movies and Stars, With a List of Recordings* (Jefferson, NC: McFarland, 2009).

Publicity Stills (pp. 231–232)

Martin, Shirley V., 'The Still Camera. A Maker of Still Photography Tells the Value of Good Stills in Selling a Motion Picture to the Public', *The American Cinematographer* vol. 2 no. 20 (1 November 1921), pp. 6–7.

Kobal, John, *Film and Entertainment, Including the Private Collection of John Kobal* (London: Christie's South Kensington, 1992).

Kobel, Peter, *Silent Movies: The Birth of Film and the Triumph of Movie Culture* (New York: Little, Brown and Company, 2007).

Shields, David S., *Still: American Silent Motion Picture Photography* (Chicago, IL: University of Chicago Press, 2013).

Posters (p. 231)

Capitaine, Jean-Louis, *Invitation au cinématographe. Les affiches des origins, 1895–1914* (Paris: Maeght, 1993).

Baburina, Nina I., *The Silent Film Poster, 1908–1934* (Moscow: Art-Rodnik, 2011).

Della Torre, Roberto, *Invito al cinema. Le origini del manifesto cinematografico italiano, 1895–1930* (Milan: EDUCatt, 2014).

Histories (pp. 233–234)

Hopwood, Henry V., *Living Pictures: Their History, Photo-Production and Practical Working, With a Digest of British Patents and Annotated Bibliography* (London: Optician & Photographic Trades Review, 1899).

Konwiczka, Hans, *Kinematograph* (Leipzig: H. Beyer, 1911).

Forch, Carl, *Der Kinematograph und das sich bewegende Bild. Geschichte und technische Entwicklung der Kinematographie bis zur Gegenwart* (Vienna and Lipsia: A. Hartleben's Verlag, 1913).

Lubschez, Ben Jehudah, *The Story of the Motion Picture 65 B.C. to 1920 A.D.* (New York: Reeland, 1920).

Ramsaye, Terry, *A Million and One Nights: A History of Motion Picture Through 1925* (New York: Simon & Schuster, 1926; reprint, Touchstone/Simon & Schuster, 1986).

Hampton, Benjamin B., *A History of the Movies* (New York: Covici-Friede, 1931).

Bardèche, Maurice and Robert Brasillach, *Histoire du cinéma* (Paris: Denoël et Steele, 1935); English translation by Iris Barry, *The History of Motion Pictures* (New York: W.W. Norton/Museum of Modern Art, 1938).

Sadoul, Georges, *Histoire générale du cinéma. Vol. 1: L'Invention du cinema, 1832–1897; Vol. 2: Les Pionniers du cinema (de Méliès à Pathé), 1897–1909; Vol. 3: Le Cinéma devient un art, 1909–1920; Vol. 4, L'Art muet, 1919–1929* (Paris: Denoël, 1946–75).

Toeplitz, Jerzy, *Historia sztuki filmowej* (Warsaw: Filmowa Agenca Wydawnicza, 1955); German translation, *Geschichte des Films* (Munich: Rogner & Bernhard, 1973).

Paolella, Roberto, *Storia del cinema muto* (Naples: Giannini, 1956).

Deslandes, Jacques and Jacques Richard, *Histoire comparée du cinéma. Vol. 2: 1897–1906* (Paris: Casterman, 1968).

Mitry, Jean, *Histoire du cinéma: art et industrie. Vol. 1: 1895–1914; Vol. 2: 1915–1925; Vol. 3: 1923–1930* (Paris: Éditions Universitaires, 1967–73).

Inventories (pp. 234–236)

Mitry, Jean (ed.), *Filmographie universelle* (Paris: IDHEC, 1963–73; Service des Archives du film du CNC, 1979–88, 35 vols.).

Goble, Alan (ed.), *The International Film Index, 1895–1990* (London: Bowker-Saur, 1991).

Filmographies (pp. 236–238)

Nowell-Smith, Geoffrey, 'Filmography', *Screen* vol. 32 no. 4 (Winter 1991), pp. 452–5.

The 1978 Brighton FIAF Conference on Early Cinema (pp. 236–237)

Bowser, Eileen, 'The Brighton Project: An Introduction', *Quarterly Review of Film Studies* vol. 4 no. 4 (Fall 1979), pp. 509–38.

Holman, Roger and André Gaudreault (eds.), *Cinema 1900–1906: An Analytical Study* (Brussels: FIAF, 1982, 2 vols.).

'The Brighton FIAF Conference (1978): Ten Years After', *Historical Journal of Film, Radio and Television* vol. 11 no. 3 (1991), pp. 279–91.

National Filmographies

Argentina

La epoca muda del cine argentino (Buenos Aires: Centro de Envestigacion de la Historia del Cine Argentino, 1958, 2nd edition).

'Filmografia. Películas nacionales estrenadas entre 1896 y 1910 en las ciudades de Buenos Aires y Mar del Plata', in *Historia de los primeros años del cine en la Argentina, 1895–1910* (Buenos Aires: Fundación Cinemateca Argentina, 1996), pp. 113–23.

Mafud, Lucio. *La imagen ausente. El cine mudo argentino en publicaciones gráficas. Catálogo. El cine de ficción, 1914–1923* (Buenos Aires: Teseo, 2016).

Australia

Pike, Andrew and Ross Cooper, *Australian Film, 1900–1977: A Guide to Feature Film Production* (Melbourne: Oxford University Press/Australian Film Institute, 1980).

Austro-Hungarian Empire and Austria

Fritz, Walter, *Die Österreichischen Spielfilme der Stummfilmzeit, 1907–1930* (Vienna: Österreichisches Filmarchiv/Osterreichische Gesellschaft für Filmwissenschaft, 1967).

Thaller, Anton, *Österreichische Filmografie. Spielfilme 1906–1918* (Vienna: Filmarchiv Austria, 2010).

Belgium

Thys, Marianne (ed.), *Belgian Cinema: Filmography of Belgian Movies, 1896–1996* (Brussels: Ludion, 1996).

Brazil

Bernadet, Jean-Claude, *Filmografia do cinema brasileiro: 1900–1935* (São Paulo: Secretaria da Cultura de São Paulo, 1979).

Noronha, Jurandyr, *Dicionário de cinema brasileiro. De 1896 a 1936. Do Nascimento ao sonoro* (Rio de Janeiro: EMC, 2008).

Bulgaria

Kardzhilov, Peter, *Bulgarian Feature Films. An Annotated Illustrated Filmography, Vol. 1 (1915–1948)* (Sofia: Bulgarska Nacionalna Filmoteka/Peter Beron State Publishing House, 1987).

Canada

Turner, D. John, *Canadian Feature Film Index/Index des films canadiens de long métrage, 1913–1985* (Ottawa: National Film, Television and Sound Archives/ Archives nationales du film, de la télévision et de l'enregistrement sonore, 1987).

Morris, Peter and Larry Kardish (ed.), *Canadian Feature Films, 1913–1969: Part 1, 1913–1940* (Ottawa: Canadian Film Institute, 1970).

Chile
Internet Resources

Cine Chile. Enciclopedia del cine chileno: http://www.cinechile.cl/

China

Jihua, Cheng, Li Shaobai, Xing Zuwen, 'Chinese Cinema: Catalogue of Films, 1905–1937', *Griffithiana* vol. 18 no. 54 (October 1995), pp. 4–77.

Toroptsev, Sergei Arkadevich, *Ocherk istorii kitaiskogo kino, 1896–1966* (Moscow: Nauka, 1979).

Colombia

'Indice de peliculas y casas productoras', in Hernando Martínez Prado, *Historia del cine colombiano* (Bogotá: Libreria y Editorial America Latina, 1978).

Largometrajes colombianos en cine y video, 1915–2004 (Bogotá: Fundación Patrimonio Fílmico Colombiano, 2005).

Documentales colombianos 1915–1950 (Bogotá: Fundación Patrimonio Fílmico Colombiano, 2007).

Central America

'Filmografía centroamericana (1896–2004)', in María Lourdes Cortes (ed.), *La pantalla rota. Cien años de cine en Centroamerica* (México: Taurus, 2005).

Costa Rica *see* Central America

Cuba

Douglas, María Eulalia, *Catálogo del cine cubano 1897–1960* (Havana: Ediciones ICAIC, 2008).

Czech countries in Austria-Hungary (to October 1918) and Czechoslovakia (from 28 October 1918)

Cesky hraný film I, 1898–1930 (Prague: Národní filmový archiv, 1995).

Kolar, Jan S. and Myrtil Frida, Ceskoslovensky Nemy Film 1898–1930 (Prague: Ceskoslovensky Film, 1957).

Denmark

Engberg, Marguerite, Registrant over danske film, 1896–1930, Vol. 1: 1896–1909; Vol. 2: 1910–1912; Vol. 3: 1913–1914; Vol. 4: 1915–1917; Vol. 5: 1918–1930 (Copenhagen: Institut for Filmvidenskab, 1977–82).

Internet Resources

Det Danske Filminstitut – Filmdatabasen: http://www.dfi.dk/FaktaOmFilm.aspx

El Salvador see Central America

Finland

Suomen Kansallisfilmografia. Vol. I: 1907–1933 (Helsinki: Suomen elokuva-arkisto, 1996).

France

Frazer, John, Artificially Arranged Scenes: The Films of Georges Méliès (Boston, MA: G.K. Hall, 1979).

Malthête-Méliès, Madeleine, Anne-Marie Quévrain, and Jacques Malthête, Essai de reconstitution du catalogue français de la Star-Film (Bois d'Arcy: Centre National de la Cinématographie, 1981).

Chirat, Raymond, Catalogue des films français de long métrage: films de fiction, 1919–1929 (Toulouse: Cinémathèque de Toulouse, 1984).

Gaumont: 90 ans de cinéma (Paris: Ramsay/La Cinémathèque française, 1986).

Tharrats, Juan Gabriel, Los 500 films de Segundo de Chomón (Zaragoza: Prensas Universitarias, 1988).

'Société Française des Films et Cinématographes Éclair (1907–1919): A Checklist', Griffithiana vol. 15 nos. 44–5 (May–September 1992), pp. 28–88.

Bernard, Youen, Les Petites maisons de production cinématographique française de 1906 à 1914 [filmographies of Le Lion, Lux, Radios, Théophile Pathé, and Film des auteurs. Doctoral thesis presented at the University of Paris III, 1994].

Bousquet, Henri, Catalogue Pathé des années 1896 à 1914 (Bures-sur-Yvette: Éditions Henri Bousquet, 1996 [1896–1906], 1993 [1907–9], 1994 [1910–11], 1995 [1912–14], 1999 [1915–18], 2001 [1919–22], 2004 [1923–7]); online edition: http://filmographie.fondation-jeromeseydoux-pathe.com.

Loné, Éric, 'La Production Lux (1906–1913)', 1895 no. 16 (June 1994), pp. 59–76.

Chirat, Raymond (with the collaboration of Éric Le Roy), Catalogue des films français de fiction de 1908 à 1918 (Paris: Cinémathèque française, 1995).

Malthête-Méliès, Madeleine, Analyse descriptive des films de Georges Méliès rassemblés entre 1981 et 1996 par la Cinémathèque Méliès (Paris: Les Amis de Georges Méliès, 1996).

Aubert, Michelle, and Jean-Claude Seguin (eds.), La Production cinématographique des frères Lumière (Paris: Éditions Mémoires de cinéma/Bibliothèque du Film [BIFI]/Centre National de la Cinématographie/Premier siècle du cinéma, 1996; book plus CD-Rom).

Germany

Lamprecht, Gerhard, Deutsche Stummfilme, 1903–1931 (Berlin: Stiftung Deutsche Kinematek, 1967–70, 10 vols.).

Birett, Herbert, Verzeichnis in Deutschland gelaufener Filme. Entscheidungen der Filmzensur 1911–1920, Berlin/Hamburg/Munich/Stuttgart (Munich: Saur, 1980).

Bock, Hans-Michael (ed.), CineGraph – Lexikon zum deutschsprachigen Film (Munich: edition text+kritik, 1984 ff.).

Birett, Herbert, Das Filmangebot in Deutschland, 1895–1911 (Munich: Filmbuchverlag Winterberg, 1991).

Great Britain

Gifford, Denis, The British Film Catalogue. Vol. 1: Fiction Film, 1895–1994; Vol. 2: Non-Fiction Film, 1888–1994 (London and Chicago: Fitzroy Dearborn, 2001).

Gifford, Denis, British Animated Films, 1895–1985. A Filmography (Jefferson, NC: McFarland, 1987).

Guatemala *see* Central America

Hungarian countries in Austria-Hungary (to 1918) and Hungary (from 1918)

Kovács, Ferenc (ed.), *Magyar filmográfia, 1901–1961* (Budapest: Magyar Filmtudományi Intézet és Filmarchivum, 1963).

India

Rangoonwalla, Firoze, *Indian Filmography: Silent and Hindi Films, 1897–1969* (Bombay: J. Udeshi, 1970).

Dharamsey, Virchand, 'Filmography: Indian Silent Cinema, 1912–1934', in Suresh Chabria (ed.), *Light of Asia. Indian Silent Cinema, 1912–1934* (Pordenone and New Delhi: Le Giornate del Cinema Muto/Wiley Eastern Ltd, 1994), pp. 72–235; revised and expanded edition (New Delhi: Niyogi Books, 2013), pp. 127–319.

Ireland and Irish Free State

Rockett, Kevin (ed.), *The Irish Filmography: Fiction Films, 1896–1996* (Dublin: Red Mountain Press, 1996).

Italy

Elenco delle Pellicole Cinematografiche approvate dal Ministero dell'Interno (monthly bulletin of released films, issued by the Italian government from 1913 to 1925).

Bernardini, Aldo (ed.), *Archivio del cinema italiano. Vol. I: Il cinema muto, 1905–1931* (Rome: Edizioni Anica, 1991).

Martinelli, Vittorio, *Il cinema muto italiano* (Rome: Nuova ERI/Edizioni RAI/Centro Sperimentale di Cinematografia, 1996 [1905–9; 1910], 1995 [1911, Part I], 1996 [1911, Part II]; special issues of *Bianco & Nero*, vol. 55, nos. 1–2, 1994 [1912, Part I]; vol. 55, nos. 3–4, 1994 [1912, Part II]; vol. 54, nos. 1–2, 1993 [1913, Part I]; vol. 54, nos. 3–4, 1993 [1913, Part II]; vol. 53, nos. 1–2 and 3–4, 1992 [1914]; vol. 52, nos. 1–2 and 3–4, 1991 [1915]; vol. 51, nos. 1–2 and 3–4, 1990 [1916]; vol. 50, nos. 3–4, 1989 [1917]; vol. 50, nos. 1–2, 1989 [1918]; vol. 41, nos. 1–3, 1980 [1919]; vol. 41, nos. 4–6, 1980 [1920]; vol. 42, nos. 1–3, 1981 [1921–2]; vol. 42, nos. 4–6, 1981 [1923–31]).

Bernardini, Aldo (ed.), *Cinema italiano delle origini. Gli ambulanti* (Gemona: La Cineteca del Friuli, 2001).

Bernardini, Aldo (ed.), *Cinema muto italiano. I film 'dal vero', 1895–1914* (Gemona: La Cineteca del Friuli, 2002).

Bernardini, Aldo (ed.), *Cinema delle origini in Italia. I film 'dal vero' di produzione estera, 1895–1907* (Gemona: La Cineteca del Friuli, 2008).

Japan

Nihon eiga sakuhin jiten senzenhen (1896–1945/8) [Complete Dictionary of Japanese Films from 1896 to August 1945]. (Tokyo: Kagaku shoin, 1996, 5 vols., including a filmography of foreign films released in Japan).

Internet Resources

JMDB Japan Movie Database:
www.jmdb.ne.jp
National Diet Library:
http://www.ndl.go.jp/en/index.html

Latvia

Redovičs, Agris, *Latvijas kino, 1920–1940. Iepazīšanās* (Riga: Rīgas Kino muzejs, 1990).

Mexico

Dávalos Orozco, Federico and Esperanza Vázquez Bernal, *Filmografía general del cine mexicano, 1906–1931* (Puebla: Universidad Autónoma de Puebla, 1985).

de Los Reyes, Aurelio, *Filmografía del cine mudo en México. Vol. 1: 1896–1920* (Mexico, DF: Filmoteca de la Universidad Nacional Autónoma de México, 1986); *Vol. 2: 1920–1924* (1994); *Vol. 3, 1924–1931* (2000).

Leal, Juan Felipe and Carlos Arturo Flores, *Anales del cine en México, 1895–1908* (Mexico: Ediciones y Gráficas Eón/Voyeur, 2003–16, 20 vols.).

Amador, María Luisa and Jorge Ayala Blanco, *Cartelera cinematográfica 1912–1919; 1920–1929* (Mexico: Centro Universitario de Estudios Cinematográficos de la UNAM, 2009, 2 vols.).

Netherlands

Donaldson, Geoffrey, *Of Joy and Sorrow: A Filmography of Dutch Silent Fiction* (Amsterdam: Stichting Nederlands Filmmuseum, 1997).

New Zealand/Aotearoa

Aotearoa and the Sentimental Strine. Making Films in Australia and New Zealand in the Silent Period (Wellington: Moa Films, 1993).

Norway

Bech, Leif-Erik (ed.), *Norsk Filmografi, 1908–1979* (Oslo: Norsk kino-og Filmfond/Norsk Filminstitutt, 1980).

Hanche, Øivind (ed.), *Register over Norske Langfilmer 1908–1.4.1990* (Oslo: Norsk Filminstitutt, 1990).

Ottoman Empire and Turkey

Özgüc, Agah (ed.), *Türk Filmleri Sözlügü, 1914–1972* (Istanbul: Cahit Poyraz, 1963).

Palestine

Tryster, Hillel (ed.), *Israel Before Israel: Silent Cinema in the Holy Land* (Jerusalem: Steven Spielberg Jewish Film Archive of the Avraham Harman Institute of Contemporary Jewry, Hebrew University of Jerusalem, 1995).

Panama *see* Central America

Peru

Bedoya, Ricardo, *Un cine reencontrado. Diccionario ilustrado de las películas peruanas* (Lima: Universidad de Lima, 1997).

Poland

Bochenska, Jadswiga, and others (eds., compiled by Jerzy Toeplitz), *Historia Filmu Polskiego. Vol. 1: 1895–1921* [with a filmography of silent fiction films produced between 1911 and 1929] (Warsaw: Wydawnictwa Artystyczne i Filmowe, 1966).

Portugal

de Matos-Cruz, José, *Prontuario do cinema portugues, 1896–1989* (Lisbon: Cinemateca Portuguesa, 1989).

de Matos-Cruz, José, *O cais do olhar. O cinema portugues de longa metragem e a ficçao muda* (Lisbon: Cinemateca Portuguesa, 1999).

Romania

Cantacuzino, Ion I. and Bujor T. Rîpeanu (eds.), *Producţia cinematografică din România, 1897–1970. Filmografie adnotată; Vol. I/1: Cinematograful mut (1897–1930). Filmul de nonficţiune; Vol. II/1: Cinematograful mut (1897–1930). Filmul de ficţiune* (Bucharest: Arhiva Naţională de Filme, 1970).

Russia and Soviet Union

Vishnevskii, Veniamin, *Khudozhestvennye filmy dorevoliutsionnoi Rossii. Filmograficheskoe opisanie: filmy do 1917 goda* (Moscow: Goskinoizdat, 1945).

Macheret, Aleksandr, Lev Parfionov, Odissei Iakubovich, and Mark Zak (eds.), *Sovetskie khudozhestvennye filmy: Annotirovannyi katalog. Vol. 1: Nemye filmy, 1918–1935* (Moscow: Iskusstvo, 1961).

Vishnevskii, Veniamin, *Dokumentalnye filmy dorevoliutsionnoi Rossii 1907–1916* (Moscow: Muzei kino, 1996).

Spain

González Lopez, Palmira and Joaquín T. Cánovas Belchi, *Catálogo del cinema español. Vol. F2: Peliculas de ficción, 1921–1930* (Madrid: Filmoteca Española, 1993).

Ruiz Álvarez, Luis Enrique, *El cine muto español en sus películas* (Bilbao: Ediciones Mensajero, 2004).

Bello, José Antonio, *Cine mudo español, 1896–1920* (Barcelona: Laertes, 2010).

Sweden

Svensk filmografi (Stockholm: Svenska Filminstitutet, 1986 [Vol. 1: 1897–1919], 1982 [Vol. 2: 1920–9], 1979 [Vol. 3: 1930–9]).

Internet Resources

Swedish Film Database: http://www.sfi.se/en-GB/Swedish-film-database/

Switzerland

Buache, Freddy and Jacques Rial, *Les Débuts du cinématographe à Genève et à Lausanne* (Lausanne: Cinémathèque suisse, 1964).

Dumont, Hervé, *Histoire du cinéma suisse: films de fiction 1896–1965* (Lausanne: Cinémathèque suisse, 1987).

Pithon, Rémy (ed.), *Cinéma suisse muet. Lumières et ombres* (Lausanne: Éditions Antipode/Cinémathèque suisse, 2002).

Zimmermann, Yvonne, Pierre-Emmanuel Jaques, Anita Gertiser, *Schaufenster Schweiz. Dokumentarische Gebrauchsfilme 1896–1964* (Zurich: Limmat Verlag, 2011).

Turkey *see* Ottoman Empire and Turkey

United States

Savada, Elias (ed.), *The American Film Institute Catalog of Motion Pictures Produced in the United States. Vol. A: Film Beginnings, 1893–1910. A Work in Progress* (Metuchen, NJ, and London: Scarecrow Press, 1995); *Vol. F1: Feature Films, 1911–1920* (Berkeley: University of California Press, 1988); *Vol. F2: Feature Films, 1921–1930* (New York: R.R. Bowker, 1971). Note: the *Film Beginnings* volume includes foreign films distributed in the United States.

Lauritzen, Einar, and Gunnar Lundquist, *American Film Index, 1908–1915. Motion Pictures, July 1908–December 1915; American Film Index, 1916–1920. Motion Pictures, January 1916–December 1920* (Stockholm: Film Index, 1976–84).

Karel Čáslavský, 'American Comedy Series: Filmographies, 1914–1930', *Griffithiana* vol. 17 nos. 51–2 (October 1994), pp. 9–168.

Spehr, Paul C., *American Film Personnel and Company Credits, 1908–1920: Filmographies Recorded by Authoritative Organizational and Personal Names from Lauritzen and Lundquist* (Jefferson, NC, and London: McFarland, 1996).

Catalog of Copyright Entries: Motion Pictures. Vol. 1: 1894–1912; Vol. 2: 1912–1939 (Washington, DC: Library of Congress, Copyright Office, 1951–3).

Internet Resources

AFI Catalog:
https://catalog.afi.com/Catalog/Showcase
Early Cinema History Online (ECHO):
echo.commarts.wisc.edu

Uruguay

Hintz, Eugenio and Graciela Dacosta, 'Filmografia de largometrajes', in *Historia y filmografia del cine uruguayo* (Montevideo: Ediciones de la Plaza, 1988), pp. 63–84.

Venezuela

Tirado, Ricardo, *Memoria y notas del cine venezolano 1897–1959* (s.l. [Caracas]: Fundación Neumann, n.d.).

Chapter 12 – DUPLICATES (pp. 241–258)

Reilly, James M., Peter Z. Adelstein, and Douglas W. Nishimura, *Preservation of Safety Film* (Rochester, NY: Image Permanence Institute, 1991).

Reilly, James M., Peter Z. Adelstein, Douglas W. Nishimura, and Catherine Erbland, *New Approaches to Safety Film Preservation* (Rochester, NY: Image Permanence Institute, 1994).

Bigourdan, Jean-Louis and James M. Reilly, *Environment and Enclosures in Film Preservation* (Rochester, NY: Image Permanence Institute, 1997).

Dekkers, Midas, *De vergankelijkheid* (Amsterdam and Antwerp: Contact, 1997); English translation, *The Way of All Flesh* (London: Harvill Press, 2001).

Budgets (pp. 244–245)

Gracy, Karen F., *Film Preservation: Competing Definitions of Value, Use, and Practice* (Chicago, IL: Society of American Archivists, 2007).

Frick, Caroline, *Saving Cinema: The Politics of Preservation* (New York: Oxford University Press, 2010).

Jones, Janna, *The Past Is a Moving Picture* (Gainesville: University Press of Florida, 2012).

Dagna, Stella, *Perché restaurare i film?* (Pisa: ETS, 2014).

Generations (pp. 245–247)

Malthête, Jacques, 'Un nitrate composite en couleurs: le *Voyage dans la Lune* de Georges Méliès, reconstitué en 1929', *1895* no. 71 (Winter 2013), pp. 163–81.

Dawson City Collection (p. 246)

Kula, Sam, 'There's Film in Them Thar Hills!', *American Film* vol. 4 no. 8 (July–August 1979), pp. 14–18.

Weschler, Lawrence, 'The Discovery, and Remarkable Recovery, of the King Tut's Tomb of Silent-Era Cinema', *Vanity Fair* (14 September 2016): http://www.vanityfair.com/hollywood/2016/09/the-discovery-and-recovery-of-the-king-tuts-tomb-of-silent-era-cinema.

Films

Dawson City: Frozen Time (Bill Morrison, Hypnotic
Pictures/Picture Palace Pictures/Arte France/La
Lucarne, US 2016, 120′).

Prints (pp. 253–255)

Sargent, Ralph N., *Preserving the Moving Image*
(Washington, DC: Corporation for Public Broadcasting/
National Endowment for the Arts, 1974).

Guide de la conservation des films (Paris:
Commission Supérieure Technique de l'Image et
du Son, 1995).

Surowiec, Catherine A. (ed.), *The Lumiere Project: The
European Film Archives at the Crossroads* (Lisbon:
Associação Projecto Lumiere, 1996).

McGreevey, Tom and Joanne L. Yeck, *Our Film Heritage*
(New Brunswick, NJ, and London: Rutgers University
Press, 1997).

Meyer, Mark-Paul and Paul Read, *Restoration of Motion
Picture Film* (Newton, MA: Butterworth-Heinemann,
2000).

The Film Preservation Guide (San Francisco, CA: National
Film Preservation Foundation, 2004).

Enticknap, Leo, *Film Restoration* (Basingstoke, Hants., and
New York: Palgrave, 2013).

Marie, Michel and André Habib (eds.), *L'Avenir de la
mémoire. Patrimoine, restauration et réemploi cinématographiques* (Villeneuve d'Ascq: Presses Universitaires
du Septentrion, 2013).

Cioccolo, Anthony, *Moving Image and Sound Collections
for Archivists* (Chicago, IL: Society of American
Archivists, 2017).

Journals

Journal of Film Preservation (ISSN 1609-2694).

Dyes (pp. 255–258)

Currò, Daniela and Ulrich Ruedel, 'The Restoration
of Color', in Sarah Street, Simon Brown, and Liz
Watkins (eds.), *Color and the Moving Image* (London
and New York: Routledge [AFI Film Reader Series;
Edward Braningan and Charles Woolf, eds.], 2012).

Film, Video, and Digital-Born Works on Film Preservation

Forgotten Treasure (Sammy Lee, Loew's Incorporated/
Metro-Goldwyn-Mayer, US 1943, 10′).

The Work of a Film Archive (Orly Yadin, Flashback
Television Ltd, UK 1992, 27′ 13″).

Sauver les films. Une mémoire pour demain (Jacques
Mény, Sodaperaga/Centre National de la
Cinématographie/Ministère de la Culture et de la
Communication, France 1991, 33′).

À la recherche des films perdus (Jacques Mény, Oneline
Productions/La Sept/ARTE, France 1996, 75′).

La Mémoire retrouvée (Jacques Mény, Oneline
Productions/La Sept/ARTE, France 1996, 63′).

The Race to Save 100 Years (Scott Benson, Warner Bros./
Turner Entertainment, US 1997, 55′ 57″).

Keepers of the Frame (Mark McLaughlin, WinStar
Cinema/Mount Pilot Productions, US 1999, 70′).

These Amazing Shadows (Paul Mariano and Kurt Norton,
Gravitas Docufilms, US 2011, 88′).

Chapter 13 – LACUNAE (pp. 259–276)

Principles (pp. 261–263)

Bowser, Eileen, 'Some Principles of Film Restoration',
Griffithiana vol. 11 nos. 38–9 (October 1990),
pp. 170–3.

Hybrids (pp. 265–267)

Flueckiger, Barbara, Franziska Heller, Claudy Op
den Kamp, and David Pfluger, '"Digital Desmet":
Translating Early Applied Colors', *The Moving Image*
vol. 16 no. 1 (Spring 2016), pp. 106–24.

Translations (pp. 267–270)

Price, Nicholas Stanley, M. Kirby Talley Jr, and
Alessandra Melucco Vaccaro (eds.), *Historical and
Philosophical Issues in the Conservation of Cultural
Heritage* (Los Angeles, CA: Getty Conservation
Institute, 1996).

Dupré la Tour, Claire, 'La Restauration des intertitres: pratiques et enjeux', *CinémAction* no. 97 (2000), pp. 178–85.

Fictions (pp. 271–274)

'*Le Voyage dans la Lune*: Open Forum', *Journal of Film Preservation* vol. 87 (October 2012), pp. 7–22.

Brandi, Cesare, *Teoria del restauro* (Rome: Edizioni di Storia e Letteratura, 1963; reprint, Turin: Einaudi, 1977); English translation, *Theory of Restoration* (Florence: Nardini Editore/Istituto Centrale per il Restauro e la Conservazione del Patrimonio Archivistico e Librario, 2005).

Bonnard, Martin, 'Méliès's *Voyage* Restoration: or, The Risk of Being Stuck in the Digital Reconstruction', *The Moving Image* vol. 16 no. 1 (Spring 2016), pp. 139–47.

de Pastre, Béatrice and Laurent Véray, 'Faut-il manipuler les images du passé pour les transmettre?', *Journal of Film Preservation* no. 95 (October 2016), pp. 37–43.

Terminology (pp. 274–276)

Ledig, Elfriede (ed.), *Der Stummfilm: Konstruktion und Rekonstruktion* (Munich: Schaudig, 1988 [*Diskurs Film. Münchner Beitrage zur Filmphilologie*, no. 2]).

Cosandey, Roland, 'L'Édition des films restaurés', in 'Les Archives du cinéma et de la télévision', special issue of *CinémAction* no. 97 (2000), pp. 199–205.

Chapter 14 – TRACES (pp. 277–301)

Internet Resources

The Giornate Database: Silent Films Exhibited at the Pordenone Silent Film Festival Since 1982: www.cinetecadelfriuli.org/gcm/ed_precedenti/screenings_db.html

Repositories (pp. 279–283)

Hiller, John, 'Film History for the Public: The First National Movie Machine Collection', *Film History* vol. 11 no. 3 (1999), pp. 371–86.

Horak, Jan-Christopher, 'The Universal Studios Archives and Collections Department', *Historical Journal of Film, Radio and Television* vol. 19, no. 3 (August 1999), pp. 405–6.

Provenance (pp. 283–285)

Adams, Frederick B., *The Uses of Provenance* (Berkeley: School of Librarianship, University of California, 1969).

Abukhanfusa, Kerstin and Jan Sydbeck (eds.), *The Principle of Provenance: Report from the First Stockholm Conference on Archival Theory and the Principle of Provenance, 2–3 September 1993* (Stockholm: Swedish National Archives, 1994).

Uhl, Bodo, 'The Significance of the Principle of Provenance for Archival Science and Historical Research', *Archivalische Zeitschrift* vol. 84 no. 1 (2001), pp. 91–122.

Feigenbaum, Gail and Inge Reist (eds.), *Provenance: An Alternate History of Art* (Los Angeles, CA: Getty Research Institute, 2013).

Douglas, Jennifer, 'Origins: Evolving Ideas about the Principle of Provenance', in Terry Eastwood and Heather MacNeil (eds.), *Currents of Archival Thinking* (s.l.: Praeger Publishers, 2016, 2nd edition), pp. 23–43.

Bernardi, Joanne, Paolo Cherchi Usai, Tami Williams and Joshua Yumibe (eds.), *Provenance and Early Cinema* (in preparation; Bloomington: Indiana University Press, 2020).

Senses (pp. 286–289)

Farge, Arlette, *Le Goût de l'archive* (Paris: Seuil, 1989); English translation, *The Allure of the Archives* (New Haven, CT: Yale University Press, 2013).

Practice (pp. 289–291)

Nuffer, Eberhard, *Filmschnitt und Schneidetisch. Eine Zeitreise durch die Klassische Montagetechnologie* (Potsdam: Polzer Media Group GmbH, 2003, 7th edition).

Cuts (pp. 293–295)

Bottomore, Stephen, 'Shots in the Dark: The Real Origins of Film Editing', *Sight & Sound* vol. 57 no. 3 (Summer 1988), pp. 200–4.

Identification (pp. 295–299)

Brown, Harold, *Physical Characteristics of Early Films as Aids to Identification* (Brussels: FIAF, 1990).

Richard, Suzanne, 'Pathé, marque de fabrique: vers une nouvelle method pour la datation des copies anciennes', *1895* no. 10 (1991), pp. 13–27.

Lenk, Sabine, 'Insight and Axioms: Harold G. Brown and the Identification of Early Films', *The Moving Image* vol. 16 no. 1 (Spring 2016), pp. 35–56.

Blot-Wellens, Camille, 'Vie(s) de Jésus. Essai d'identification et de compréhension', *Journal of Film Preservation* no. 97 (October 2017), pp. 17–24.

Chapter 15 – CURATORSHIP (pp. 302–323)

Edmondson, Ray, 'Is Film Archiving a Profession?' *Film History* vol. 7 no. 3 (Autumn 1995), pp. 245–55.

Cherchi Usai, Paolo, David Francis, Alexander Horwath, and Michael Loebenstein, *Film Curatorship: Archives, Museums, and the Digital Marketplace* (Vienna: Synema – Gesellschaft für Film und Medien/Österreichisches Filmmuseum, 2008).

Thompson, John M.A., *Manual of Curatorship* (London: Routledge, 2012, 2nd edition).

Bovier, François and Adeena Mey (eds.), *Exhibiting the Moving Image: History Revisited* (Zurich and Dijon: JRP Ringier/Les presses du réel, 2015).

Williams, Tami (ed.), 'Early Cinema and the Archives', monograph issue of *The Moving Image* vol. 16 no. 1 (Spring 2016).

Lameris, Bregt L., *Film Museum Practice and Film Historiography. The Case of the Nederlands Filmmuseum, 1946-2000* (Amsterdam: University of Amsterdam Press, 2017).

Edmondson, Ray, 'Is Film Archiving a Profession Yet? A Reflection – Twenty Years On', *Synoptique* vol. 6 no. 1 (2017), pp. 14–22: http://synoptique.hybrid.concordia.ca/index.php/main/article/view/167/210.

Cherchi Usai, Paolo, 'Archival Cinema', in Rob Stone, Paul Cooke, Stephanie Dennison, and Alex Marlow-Mann (eds.), *The Routledge Companion to World Cinema* (London and New York: Routledge, 2018), pp. 426–35.

Accountability (pp. 303–304)

Cherchi Usai, Paolo, Jon Wengström, and Elaine Burrows, 'Suggested Template for a Collection Policy', *Journal of Film Preservation* no. 91 (October 2014), pp. 9–11.

Edmondson, Ray, *Audiovisual Archiving. Philosophy and Principles* (Paris: UNESCO, 2016, 3rd edition).

De Klerk, Nico, *Showing and Telling: Film Heritage Institutes and Their Performance of Public Accountability* (Wilmington, DE: Vernon Press, 2017).

Selection (pp. 304–305)

Bowser, Eileen and John Kuiper, *A Handbook for Film Archives* (Brussels: FIAF, 1980; New York and London: Garland, 1991).

Magliozzi, Ronald S., 'Film Archiving as a Profession: An Interview With Eileen Bowser', *The Moving Image* vol. 3 no. 1 (2003), pp. 132–46.

Orphans (pp. 306–307)

Kofler, Birgit, *Legal Questions Facing Audiovisual Archives* (Paris: UNESCO, 1991).

Kramer, Edith, 'Should a FIAF Archive Ask for Copyright Clearance Before Showing a Film?', *Journal of Film Preservation* vol. 22 no. 47 (October 1993), pp. 51–2.

Henry, Michael, 'Copyright, Neighbouring Rights and Film Archives', *Journal of Film Preservation* vol. 23 no. 49 (October 1994), pp. 2–9.

Strible, Dan, 'The Role of Orphan Films in the 21st Century Archive', *Cinema Journal* vol. 46 no. 3 (Spring 2007), pp. 124–8.

Technology (pp. 310–312)

Christie, Ian, 'Toys, Instruments, Machines: Why the Hardware Matters', in James Lyons and John Plunkett (eds.), *Multimedia Histories. From the Magic Lantern to the Internet* (Exeter: University of Exeter Press, 2007), pp. 3–17.

Parth, Kerstin, Oliver Hanley, and Thomas Ballhausen (eds.), *Works in Progress. Digital Film Restoration Within Archives* (Vienna: Synema – Gesellschaft für Film und Medien, 2013).

Hidalgo, Santiago (ed.), *Technology and Film Scholarship: Experience, Study, Theory* (Amsterdam: Amsterdam University Press, 2017).

Events (pp. 312–314)

Film Mutilation and How to Prevent It (Rochester, NY: Eastman Kodak Company, 1924).

Cherchi Usai, Paolo, 'Preserving Films outside the Vaults: A Report on Projection, Shipping and Temporary Storage Facilities', *Journal of Film Preservation* no. 64 (April 2002), pp. 9–15.

Cherchi Usai, Paolo, Spencer Christiano, Catherine A. Surowiec, and Timothy J. Wagner (eds.), *The Art of Film Projection* (Rochester, NY: George Eastman Museum, 2019).

Speed (pp. 314–316; see also pp. 179–181)

Brownlow, Kevin, 'Silent Films: What Was the Right Speed?', *Sight & Sound* vol. 49 no. 3 (March 1980), pp. 164–7; reproduced in *Classic Images* no. 108 (June 1984), pp. 52–5.

Card, James, 'Silent-Film Speed', *Image* vol. 4 no. 7 (October 1955), pp. 55–6; reproduced in Marshall Deutelbaum (ed.), *'Image' on the Art and Evolution of Film* (New York and Rochester: Dover Publications Inc./George Eastman House, 1979), pp. 145–6.

Music (pp. 316–319)

Anderson, Gillian B., 'The Presentation of Silent Films, or Music as Anaesthesia', *The Journal of Musicology* no. 5 (1987), pp. 257–95.

Tieber, Claus and Anna Katharina Windisch, *The Sounds of Silent Films: New Perspectives on History, Theory and Practice* (Basingstoke, Hants.: Palgrave, 2014).

Festivals (pp. 319–321)

Marlow-Mann, Alex (ed.), *Archival Film Festivals* (St Andrews: St Andrews Film Studies, 2013).

Internet Resources

British Silent Film Festival:
www.britishsilentfilmfestival.com

Le Giornate del Cinema Muto (Pordenone Silent Film Festival):
http://www.cinetecadelfriuli.org/gcm/

San Francisco Silent Film Festival:
www.silentfilm.org

Silent Cinema Society:
www.silentcinemasociety.org

Silent Era:
www.silentera.com

Slapstick Festival (formerly Bristol Silents):
www.slapstick.org.uk

Spectators (pp. 321–323)

Delage, Christian (ed.), *Serge Daney. Itinéraire d'un ciné-fils* (Paris: Éditions Jean-Michel Place, 1999).

Horwath, Alexander, 'The Market vs. the Museum', *Journal of Film Preservation* no. 70 (November 2005), pp. 5–9.

Cherchi Usai, Paolo, 'The Lindgren Manifesto: The Film Curator of the Future', *Journal of Film Preservation* no. 84 (April 2011), p. 4; revised version in Scott MacKenzie (ed.), *Film Manifestos and Global Cinema Cultures* (Berkeley, Los Angeles, and London: University of California Press, 2014), pp. 558–9.

Appendix 1 Film Measurement Tables

35mm		Projection speed (frames per second)					16mm	
		16	18	20	22	24		
metres	feet	running time					metres	feet
0,3	1	1"	1"	1"	1"	1"	0,1	0,4
0,7	2	2"	2"	2"	2"	1"	0,3	1,0
1,0	3	3"	3"	2"	2"	2"	0,4	1,3
1,2	4	4"	4"	3"	3"	3"	0,5	1,6
1,5	5	5"	4"	4"	4"	3"	0,6	2,0
1,8	6	6"	5"	5"	4"	4"	0,7	2,4
2,0	7	7"	6"	6"	5"	5"	0,8	2,7
2,3	8	8"	7"	6"	6"	5"	0,9	3,0
2,7	9	9"	8"	7"	7"	5"	1,0	3,3
3,0	10	10"	9"	8"	7"	7"	1,2	4,0
3,3	11	11"	10"	9"	8"	7"	1,3	4,4
3,8	12	12"	11"	10"	9"	8"	1,5	5,0
4,0	13	13"	12"	10"	9"	9"	1,6	5,3
4,3	14	14"	13"	11"	10"	9"	1,7	5,6
4,6	15	15"	13"	12"	11"	10"	1,8	6,0
5,0	16	16"	14"	13"	12"	11"	2,0	6,5
5,1	17	17"	15"	14"	12"	11"	2,0	6,6
5,3	18	18"	16"	14"	13"	12"	2,1	7,0
5,8	19	19"	17"	15"	14"	13"	2,3	7,6
6,0	20	20"	18"	16"	14"	13"	2,4	7,8
6,1	20	20"	18"	16"	15"	13"	2,4	8,0
6,4	21	21"	19"	17"	15"	14"	2,6	8,4
6,7	22	22"	20"	18"	16"	15"	2,7	8,8
7,0	23	23"	21"	18"	17"	15"	2,7	9,0
7,3	24	24"	22"	19"	17"	16"	2,9	9,6
7,6	25	25"	22"	20"	18"	17"	3,0	9,9
7,6	25	25"	22"	20"	18"	17"	3,1	10
8,0	26	26"	23"	21"	19"	18"	3,3	11

35mm		Projection speed (frames per second)					16mm	
metres	feet	16	18	20	22	24	metres	feet
			running time					
8,2	27	27"	24"	22"	20"	18"	3,3	11
8,5	28	28"	25"	22"	20"	19"	3,4	11
8,8	29	29"	26"	23"	21"	19"	3,5	12
9,0	30	30"	27"	24"	22"	20"	3,6	12
10,0	33	33"	30"	26"	24"	22"	**4,0**	13
10,7	35	35"	31"	28"	25"	23"	4,3	14
12,2	40	40"	36"	32"	29"	26"	4,9	16
12,5	41	41"	36"	32"	30"	27"	**5,0**	16
13,7	45	45"	41"	36"	32"	30"	5,5	18
15,0	49	49"	44"	39"	36"	32"	6,0	20
15,2	**50**	50"	45"	40"	36"	33"	6,1	**20**
16,8	55	55"	50"	44"	40"	36"	6,7	22
18,3	60	1'00"	54"	48"	43"	40"	7,3	24
19,8	65	1'05"	59"	52"	47"	43"	7,9	26
20,0	66	1'05"	59"	53"	48"	44"	8,0	26
21,3	70	1'10"	1'03"	56"	50"	46"	8,5	28
22,9	75	1'15"	1'08"	1'00"	54"	50"	9,2	30
24,4	80	1'20"	1'12"	1'04"	58"	53"	9,8	32
25,0	82	1'21"	1'13"	1'05"	1'00"	55"	**10,0**	33
25,9	85	1'25"	1'17"	1'08"	1'01"	56"	10,4	34
27,4	90	1'30"	1'21"	1'12"	1'05"	59"	11,0	36
28,9	95	1'35"	1'25"	1'16"	1'08"	1'03"	11,6	38
30,0	98	1'37"	1'27"	1'18"	1'11"	1'05"	11,9	39
30,5	**100**	1'40"	1'29"	1'19"	1'12"	1'07"	12,2	40
35,0	116	1'55"	1'43"	1'32"	1'24"	1'17"	14,1	46
38,1	125	2'05"	1'51"	1'39"	1'30"	1'24"	15,2	**50**
40,0	131	2'10"	1'56"	1'44"	1'35"	1'27"	16,0	52
45,0	147	2'26"	2'11"	1'57"	1'46"	1'38"	17,9	59
45,7	150	2'30"	2'15"	2'00"	1'48"	1'40"	18,3	60
50,0	164	2'43"	2'25"	2'11"	1'59"	1'49"	**20,0**	66
53,3	175	2'55"	2'37"	2'20"	2'06"	1'56"	21,3	70
55,0	180	2'59"	2'40"	2'25"	2'11"	2'00"	21,9	72
60,0	197	3'16"	2'54"	2'38"	2'23"	2'11"	24,0	79
61,0	**200**	3'20"	2'58"	2'40"	2'25"	2'13"	24,4	80
62,5	205	3'25"	3'02"	2'44"	2'29"	2'17"	**25,0**	82

35mm		\multicolumn{5}{c}{Projection speed (frames per second)}					16mm	
metres	feet	16	18	20	22	24	metres	feet
		\multicolumn{5}{c}{running time}					
65,0	216	3'35"	3'12"	2'53"	2'37"	2'24"	26,3	86
68,6	225	3'45"	3'22"	3'00"	2'42"	2'29"	27,4	90
70,0	230	3'49"	3'24"	3'04"	2'47"	2'33"	28,0	92
75,0	246	4'05"	3'38"	3'16"'	2'59"	2'44"	30,0	98
76,2	**250**	4'10"	3'41"	3'19"	3'01"	2'47"	30,5	**100**
80,0	262	4'21"	3'52"	3'29"	3'10"	2'54"	31,9	105
82,3	270	4'30"	4'00"	3'35"	3'16"	3'00"	32,9	108
83,8	275	4'34"	4'08"	3'40"	3'18"	3'02"	33,5	110
85,0	286	4'45"	4'13"	3'48"	3'28"	3'10"	34,9	114
90,0	295	4'54"	4'22"	3'55"	3'35"	3'16"	36,9	118
91,4	**300**	5'00"	4'27"	3'59"	3'38"	3'20"	37,0	120
95,0	316	5'15"	4'40"	4'12"	3'50"	3'30"	38,5	126
100,0	328	5'27"	4'51"	4'22"	3'59"	3'38"	40,0	131
106,7	350	5'49"	5'15"	4'40"	4'12"	3'51"	42,7	140
121,9	**400**	6'40"	5'56"	5'19"	4'51"	4'27"	48,8	160
125,0	410	6'50"	6'04"	5'24"	4'58"	4'35"	**50,0**	164
137,2	450	7'29"	6'45"	6'00"	5'24"	4'57"	55,0	180
150,0	492	8'11"	7'16"	6'33"	5'57"	5'28"	60,0	197
152,4	**500**	8'19"	7'23"	6'39"	6'03"	5'33"	61,0	200
167,6	550	9'09"	8'15"	7'20"	6'36"	6'03"	67,0	220
182,9	**600**	10'	9'00"	8'00"	7'12"	6'36"	77,2	253
198,1	650	11'	9'45"	8'40"	7'48"	7"09"	79,2	260
200,0	656	11'	9'50"	8'44"	7'57"	7'17"	80,0	262
213,3	**700**	12'	10'	9'20"	8'24"	7'42"	85,3	280
228,6	750	12'	11'	10'	9'00"	8'15"	91,4	300
243,8	**800**	13'	12'	11'	9'36"	8'48"	97,5	320
250,0	820	14'	12'	11'	9'56"	9'06"	99,9	328
250,1	820	14'	12'	11'	10'	9'09"	**100,0**	328
259,1	850	14'	13'	11'	10'	9'21"	103,6	340
266,7	875	15'	13'	12'	11'	10'	106,7	350
274,3	**900**	15'	13'	12'	11'	10'	109,7	360
281,9	925	15'	14'	12'	11'	10'	112,8	370
289,6	950	16'	14'	13'	11'	11'	115,8	380
297,2	975	17'	14'	13'	12'	11'	118,9	390
300,0	984	17'	15'	13'	12'	11'	120,0	394

Projection speed (frames per second)								
35mm		16	18	20	22	24	16mm	
metres	feet	running time					metres	feet
304,8	**1000**	17'	15'	13'	12'	11'	121,9	400
350,0	1148	19'	17'	15'	14'	13'	140,0	459
381,1	1250	21'	19'	16'	15'	14'	152,4	**500**
400,0	1312	22'	19'	17'	16'	15'	160,0	525
450,0	1476	25'	22'	20'	18'	16'	179,9	590
457,2	1500	25'	22'	20'	18'	16'	182,9	600
500,0	1640	27'	24'	22'	20'	18'	199,9	656
500,1	1641	27'	24'	22'	20'	18'	**200**,0	656
533,4	1750	29'	26'	23'	21'	19'	213,4	700
548,6	1800	30'	27'	24'	22'	20'	219,4	720
579,1	1900	32'	28'	25'	23'	21'	231,6	760
600,0	1969	33'	29'	26'	24'	22'	240,1	788
609,6	**2000**	33'	30'	27'	24'	22'	243,8	800
625,0	2051	34'	30'	27'	25'	23'	250,0	820
685,8	2250	37'	33'	30'	27'	25'	274,3	900
700,0	2297	38'	34'	31'	28'	26'	280,0	919
750,0	2461	41'	36'	34'	30'	27'	300,0	984
762,2	2500	42'	37'	33'	30'	28'	304,8	**1000**
800,0	2625	44'	39'	35'	32'	29'	320,0	1050
900,0	2953	49'	44'	39'	36'	33'	360,0	1181
914,4	**3000**	50'	44'	40'	36'	33'	365,8	1200
990,6	3250	54'	48'	43'	39'	36'	396,2	1300
1000,0	3281	55'	49'	44'	40'	36'	400,0	1312
1066,7	3500	58'	52'	47'	42'	39'	426,7	1400
1142,9	3750	62'	56'	50'	45'	42'	457,2	1500
1219,2	**4000**	67'	59'	53'	48'	44'	487,7	1600
1250,0	4101	68'	61'	55'	50'	46'	**500**,0	1640
1295,3	4250	71'	63'	57'	51'	47'	518,1	1700
1371,5	4500	75'	67'	60'	54'	50'	548,6	1800
1447,7	4750	79'	70'	63'	57'	52'	579,1	1900
1500,0	4922	82'	73'	66'	60'	55'	600,0	1969
1524,0	**5000**	83'	74'	67'	61'	56'	609,6	**2000**
1600,1	5250	87'	78'	70'	63'	58'	640.0	2100
1676,3	5500	91'	82'	73'	66'	61'	670,5	2200
1752,5	5750	96'	85'	77'	70'	64'	701.0	2300

35mm		Projection speed (frames per second)					16mm	
metres	feet	16	18	20	22	24	metres	feet
				running time				
1828,8	**6000**	100'	89'	80'	73'	67'	731,5	2400
1904,9	6250	104'	93'	83'	76'	69'	762,0	2500
1981,1	6500	108'	96'	87'	79'	72'	792,4	2600
2000,0	6562	109'	97'	87'	80'	73'	800,0	2625
2057,3	6750	112'	100'	90'	82'	75'	822,9	2700
2133,6	**7000**	117'	104'	93'	85'	78'	853,4	2800
2209,7	7250	120'	108'	96'	88'	80'	883,9	2900
2285,9	7500	125'	111'	100'	91'	83'	914,4	**3000**
2362,1	7750	129'	115'	103'	93'	86'	944,8	3100
2438,4	**8000**	133'	118'	107'	97'	89'	975,4	3200
2500,0	8203	137'	121'	109'	99'	91'	**1000**,0	3281
2590,7	8500	142'	126'	113'	103'	94'	1036,3	3400
2743,2	**9000**	150'	133'	120'	109'	100'	1097,3	3600
2895,5	9500	161'	141'	126'	115'	105'	1158,2	3800
3000,0	9843	164'	146'	131'	119'	109'	1200,0	3937
3048,0	**10000**	167'	148'	133'	121'	111'	1219,2	**4000**

Note: Running times above ten minutes are rounded to the minute.

Running times are also calculated with the following table (valid only for lengths expressed in metres):

Frames per second	35mm	16mm
24	27.36	10.97
22	25.08	10.03
20	22.80	9.12
18	20.52	8.21
16	18.24	7.29

For example, in order to determine the screening time of a 16mm print of 219.4 metres at 24 frames per second, the equation is the following:

$$219.4 \text{ (metres)} : 10.97 = 20 \text{ minutes}$$

A third method (also for prints measured in metres) works for all projection speeds (including sub-decimals): multiply the length by 52 (for 35mm prints) or by 130 (for 16mm); divide the result by the desired projection speed, then by 60, thus obtaining the running time in minutes. At present, various websites feature conversion charts for film: see, for instance, https://www.kodak.com/US/en/motion/tools/film_calculator/default.htm

Appendix 2 Eastman Kodak Edge Codes on Motion Picture Film Stock, 1913–28

In 1913, the Eastman Kodak Company began printing inscriptions on the margins of the raw film stock manufactured at its plant in Rochester, New York. For a brief period, the inscription consisted only of the word 'Eastman' in stencilled block letters, between perforations, repeated along the length of the film; in the summer of 1914, Kodak inaugurated a coded system consisting of geometric symbols appearing two or three frames away from the word 'Eastman' (until early 1916) or near the word 'Kodak' (from early 1916 onwards). The same method was followed, with different edge codes, for motion picture film stock manufactured in Great Britain (from 1917) and Canada (from 1925). Kodak edge codes remained in use after 1928, with the same sequences of symbols recurring every twenty years on all 35mm and 16mm film elements.

In the early period of application of this method, film stock manufactured in the first six months of the year reproduced the edge codes immediately after the word 'Kodak'; in the film stock made in the second half of the year, the edge codes were printed about 10mm after the company's corporate name. In 1927, Kodak acquired Pathé's film manufacturing plant in France. From that year, the word 'Pathé' is still printed along the margins of the film stock, with the occasional appearance of Kodak's edge code for Great Britain.

It is important to note that Kodak edge codes indicate the year of manufacture of the film stock, which does not necessarily correspond to the year when the film was exposed, processed, or released. The edge code for a given year can therefore appear on film productions made at a later time (generally the following year). Edge codes were printed on the film stock by means of a photographic process similar to that used by Pathé (see Appendix 3 and p. 39) and other production companies. They are seen as black characters or symbols on a clear background in the film stock upon which they were originally applied. The codes can therefore appear on film elements of a later generation, where they show as clear characters or symbols on a dark background. In the next printing stage, the same codes appear again in black on a clear background, as in the original (only slightly blurred or faded), and so on after each printing generation. For this reason, edge codes for a given year may be reproduced in film elements made at a much later date: two or more edge codes are sometimes found on the same film element.

The above rules do not necessarily apply to 'reversal' film stock (p. 27). In this case, clear characters or symbols are often seen on the black margins of reversal film stock; occasionally, the edge codes are in black on a clear background.

Year	United States (Rochester)	Great Britain (Harrow)	Canada
1913 to summer 1914	ʁ ʌ s ᴛ ᴍ ʌ λ		
summer 1914 to late 1915	▬ E A S T M A N		
early 1916	•• E A S T M A N		
1916	●		
1917	■	▾	
1918	▲	L	
1919	● ●	▬	
1920	■ ■	▾ ▾	
1921	▲ ▲	L L	
1922	● ■	▬ ▬	
1923	● ▲	▾ L	
1924	▲ ■	▬ L	
1925	■ ●	▾ ▬	● L
1926	▲ ●	▬ ▾	● ▬
1927	■ ▲	L ▬	● ▾
1928	● ● ●	L ▾	L ●

Source: Harold Brown, *Physical Characteristics of Early Films as Aids to Identification*
(Brussels: FIAF, 1990), p. 17.

Appendix 3 Identification of Pathé Films by Their Edge Inscriptions

Beginning in April 1905, the French company Pathé Frères distributed projection prints with inscriptions printed on both margins of the film stock, between the perforations (see Plates 36, 38, and 39). From 1905 to late 1912, these inscriptions were in large capital letters; from the end of 1912 onwards, the font was smaller and thinner. In the chart below, boxes divided by a dotted line indicate a different wording on each margin of the print. In release prints made between 1921 and 1927, inscriptions are followed by four digits: the first two indicate the year of printing. The chart does not include edge inscriptions in Pathé's 35mm prints on diacetate stock for non-theatrical distribution.

1899 to April 1905	[no inscription along the margins]
April to December 1905	PATHE FRERES PARIS 1905
1906 to April 1907	PATHE FRERES PARIS
May to December 1907	PATHE FRERES 14 RUE FAVART PARIS
1908	PATHE FRERES 14 RUE FAVART PARIS EXHIBITION INTERDITE EN FRANCE ET EN SUISSE
1909 to 1911	PATHE FRERES 14 RUE FAVART PARIS EXHIBITION INTERDITE EN FRANCE EN SUISSE EN BELGIQUE [or ET EN BELGIQUE]
late 1911 to late 1912	PATHE FRERES 14 RUE FAVART PARIS EXHIBITION INTERDITE EN FRANCE EN SUISSE EN BELGIQUE ET EN ITALIE
c. 1912 (US only)	PROPERTY OF PATHE FRERES NEW YORK LEASED FOR USE ONLY ON MACHINES LICENSED BY MOTION PICTURE PATENTS CO NY
late 1912 to 1913	[same text as late 1911 to late 1912, smaller type, italics]
1913	[same text as late 1911 to late 1912, smaller type, print]
end 1913 to 1914	[same text as late 1911 to late 1912, taller and narrower print]

1914	PATHE FRERES PARIS [in taller, narrower print] or [no inscription along the margins]
1921	PATHE CINEMA FRANCE 16.. or 17.. [or] PATHE CINEMA PARIS 16.. or 17..
1922	[same text] 18.. or 19.., 20.., 21..
1923	[same text] 22.. or 23.., 24.., 25..
1924	[same text] 26.. or 27..
1925	[same text] 28.. or 29..
1926	[same text] 30.. or 31..
1927	[same text] 32.. or 33.., 34.., 35.., 36..

Sources: Gerhard Lamprecht, unpublished manuscript, *c.* 1965; George Eastman Museum; Harold Brown, *Physical Characteristics of Early Films as Aids to Identification* (Brussels: FIAF, 1990), p. 16.

Index

Note: Numbers followed by 'p' refers to plate numbers.